DATE DUE

FEB 16 2017		
JUL 13 2017		
		PRINTED IN U.S.A.

THE YALE-HOOVER SERIES ON AUTHORITARIAN REGIMES

SCORCHED EARTH

STALIN'S REIGN OF TERROR

JÖRG BABEROWSKI
Translated by Steven Gilbert,
Ivo Komljen, and
Samantha Jeanne Taber

Hoover Institution
Stanford University
Stanford, California

Yale UNIVERSITY PRESS
New Haven and London

Yale University Press books may be purchased in quantity for educational, business,
or promotional use. For information, please e-mail sales.press@yale.edu (U.S. office) or
sales@yaleup.co.uk (U.K. office).

Set in Sabon type by Newgen North America.
Printed in the United States of America.

Library of Congress Control Number: 2015959904
ISBN 978-0-300-13698-2 (cloth: alk. paper)

A catalogue record for this book is available from the British Library.

This paper meets the requirements of ANSI/NISO Z39.48–1992 (Permanence of Paper).

10 9 8 7 6 5 4 3 2 1

Contents

Preface

"It should be customary, it should be called culture," observes the German writer Martin Walser, "that someone who makes a claim also refutes what he claims."[1] Novelists are freed from this constraint because they are allowed simply to write down whatever their freely chosen narrative perspective yields. Historians weighing in on an issue, however, must present something that is also recognizable as scholarship. At least this is what readers expect when they look for truths in history books that promise to answer unsolved questions. Historians know, when they resolve to write a book, that they will be identified as advocates of certain theses and opinions and will thus be required to repeat what is already known. Apparently, there are also certain historians who have the tendency to cling to opinions and elevate them to the rank of eternal truths, merely because they wrote them down at some point in time. Having to be right is tedious. Having to be always right with the same opinion is even more tedious. Thus, I was glad when I was unexpectedly given the opportunity to say something new and discard some of my old ideas.

Six years ago, when I was asked whether I could rework my 2003 book *Der rote Terror* (The Red Terror) for an English translation, I did not know what I would be getting myself into. In my mind it was all quite simple: I would read through the text and then add in anything noteworthy that had been discussed on the topic since 2003. But the more I read, the greater my disappointment. Reading my own book was agonizing. Its sentences, its turns of phrase no longer appealed to me, and I could not imagine that my readers thought otherwise. My own book no longer suited me. Everything I had read and said and written about Stalin and Stalinism since then stood in odd contrast to all the strong opinions that had given the book its structure. Although I was unwilling to dispense with an identifiable text, under no circumstances did I want to repeat what I had said in 2003. So much of what I had said (and what had seemed right seven years ago) now appeared to be complete nonsense. The new book needed to be clearer. It needed to be more elegant. And to this end I would have to refute what I had previously written. Within a matter of weeks I was no longer working on the old book but on a new one instead.

Since 2003 I have spent several years explaining to myself how it was possible for so many millions of people in the Soviet Union under Stalin to have been killed, displaced, imprisoned in camps, or allowed to starve to death. Back then, in 2003, I still believed that the theses of the sociologist Zygmunt Bauman could provide an answer. The pursuit of certainty, the overcoming of ambivalence, and the obsession with order in the modern "gardening state," wrote Bauman, had led to the monstrous exterminatory excesses of the twentieth century. It was a nice idea for sure, but one that still remained an unverified claim.

The more I read about violence under Stalin, however, the clearer it became that my earlier interpretations of events needed to be revised. Stalin was—the documents I have read since then leave no room for doubt—the author and director of the mass murder of millions. The communist experiment of the New Man gave Stalin and those in power the justification they needed to murder enemies and outcasts. It did not, however, prescribe mass murder. Stalin and his companions did not speak of the brave new world when they discussed what to do with the supposed enemies of this new order. They talked instead about techniques of violence. Only in a state of emergency did it become possible for a psychopath like Stalin to let his malevolence and criminal energy reign free. The dream of communist salvation was drowned in the blood of millions because the violence became detached from the original motives, and eventually was subject to the purposes of the dictator alone. In the end all that mattered was the recognition of total power, of Stalin's total power, as master over life and death. Had it not been for the atmosphere of paranoia and mistrust, the despot would never have been able to force his will on others or make his world the one that everyone had to live in.

I tried to imagine what the world of Stalin and his companions consisted of, and the more I read, the clearer it became to me that ideas do not kill. Violence, on the other hand, is contagious, and for anyone who experiences it, it cannot be ignored—regardless of the motives with which a person enters a violent situation. Violence cannot be understood in terms of its origin, only in terms of its dynamic. Violence changes people. It turns the world on its head, and it destroys the trust that people need in order to be able to live together in a civil society. But it is also the lifeblood of the unscrupulous, those who feel authorized to do the things that others only dare imagine. If we try looking at the world through the eyes of Stalin, things that we would never have expected of ourselves become normality. This alone is what this book speaks of.

Why write a book at all? Are there not other ways to challenge life? Anyone who writes knows that ultimately only a few people will actually read what the author would have liked to impart anyway. People who write engage in a soliloquy, and as a writer one discovers more about oneself than about the subject matter being described. The violence came to haunt me in my sleep. It preyed on my mind so severely that there were days when I wished I was writing a different book. And yet, writing about life in the midst of violence also imbued me with a feeling of deep gratitude. There was no country in which class antagonisms could have been worse or the privileges of the ruling caste greater, no country in which people could have lived in greater fear than in Stalin's Soviet Union. I on the other hand never had to experience the things that Stalin's victims had to endure. "The lesson taught by this type of experience, when put into words," wrote Arthur Koestler in his memoirs, "always appears under the dowdy guise of perennial commonplaces: that man is a reality, mankind an abstraction; that men cannot be treated as units in operations of political arithmetic because they behave like the symbols for zero and the infinite, which dislocate all mathematical operations; that the end justifies the means only within very narrow limits; that ethics is not a function of social utility, and charity not a petty-bourgeois sentiment but the gravitational force which keeps civilization in its orbit."[2] And one might add that it is good fortune to live under a legal order where different people are treated as equals and where the freedom of one individual is reconciled with the freedom of the other. Anyone who has lived in a society corroded by mistrust and violence, even for just a short time, understands immediately that this is a civilizational achievement that protects us from each other. We should be grateful for it, every day.

Without the help of friends and colleagues, I would have failed at this endeavor of creating a new book from an old one. I thank Ulrich Herbert and Jörn Leonhard for the wonderful time I was allowed to spend at the Freiburg Institute for Advanced Studies (FRIAS) in spring 2010, where I was able to contemplate what I was reading and could write down whatever appealed to me. I am indebted to Paul Gregory for inviting me to a two-week workshop in 2008 at Stanford University and for providing me with access to the archives of the Hoover Institution. He was also the one who suggested writing a new book about the Stalinist terror. Paul read the first draft of the new manuscript and recommended it for an English translation. Shiva Baberowski, Adil Dalbai, Laura Elias, Sandra Grether, Laetitia Lenel, and Felix Schnell read the final version, made suggestions for improvements, and led me to ideas that would not have occurred to me on my own. Philine Apenburg and Dolly Rodriguez worked on the English version and corrected all the mistakes I made. Without their help I would have written a worse book. Anastasia Surkov helped me get the notes into a legible order, and Benedikt Vogeler intervened whenever the computer yet again wanted to decide on its own which book needed to be written. Above all, though, I thank the translators, Steven Gilbert, Ivo Komljen, and Samantha Jeanne Taber, who took on the difficult task of producing an English rendition of this history of violence. Without them, this translation would never have become a reality. I thank them and all my assistants and colleagues for the esprit, for the pleasant mood, and for the joy I experience when I encounter them. But there is also a life outside of academia. Without love it would be meaningless. Thank you, Shiva, for being there!

Without Andrei Doronin I would have never reached my goal in the Moscow archives. More importantly, though, he helped me see Russia through his eyes, and for this I am infinitely grateful. But nothing counts more than the friendship that has connected us for nearly twenty years. It deserves to be cherished through thick and thin. This book is therefore dedicated to him, to my friend, in gratitude.

SCORCHED EARTH

1 What Was Stalinism?

IN THE SECOND volume of *The Gulag Archipelago*, Alexander Solzhenitsyn relates an episode that took place in 1937, the year of the Great Terror:

A district Party conference was under way in Moscow Province. It was presided over by a new secretary of the District Party Committee, replacing one recently arrested. At the conclusion of the conference, a tribute to Comrade Stalin was called for. Of course, everyone stood up (just as everyone had leaped to his feet during the conference at every mention of his name). The small hall echoed with "stormy applause, rising to an ovation." For three minutes, four minutes, five minutes, the "stormy applause, rising to an ovation," continued. But palms were getting sore and raised arms were already aching. And the older people were panting from exhaustion. It was becoming insufferably silly even to those who really adored Stalin. However, who would dare be the *first* to stop? The secretary of the District Party Committee could have done it. He was standing on the platform, and it was he who had just called for the ovation. But he was a newcomer. He had taken the place of a man who'd been arrested. He was afraid! After all, NKVD men were standing in the hall applauding and watching to see *who* quit first! And in that obscure, small hall, unknown to the Leader, the applause went on—six, seven, eight minutes! They were done for! Their goose was cooked! They couldn't stop now until they collapsed with heart attacks! At the rear of the hall, which was crowded, they could of course cheat a bit, clap less frequently, less vigorously, not so eagerly—but up there with the presidium where everyone could see them? The director of the local paper factory, an independent and strong-minded man, stood with the presidium. Aware of all the falsity and all the impossibility of the situation, he still kept on applauding! Nine minutes! Ten! In anguish he watched the secretary of the District Party Committee, but the latter dared not stop. Insanity! To the last man! With make-believe enthusiasm in their faces, looking at each other with faint hope, the district leaders were just going to go on and on applauding until they fell and were carried out of the hall on stretchers! And even then those who were left would not falter . . . Then, after eleven minutes, the director of the paper factory assumed a businesslike expression and sat down in his seat. And, oh, a miracle took place! Where had the universal, uninhibited, indescribable enthusiasm gone? To a man, everyone else stopped dead and sat down. They had been saved! The squirrel had been smart enough to jump off his revolving wheel. . . . That, however, was how they discovered who the independent people were. And that was how they went about eliminating them. That same night the factory director was arrested. They easily pasted ten years on him on the pretext of something quite different. But after he had signed Form 206, the final document of the interrogation, his interrogator reminded him: "Don't ever be the first to stop applauding!"[1]

For hundreds of thousands of people in the Soviet Union of 1937, what Alexander Solzhenitsyn described was a reality. It was a collective madhouse, one in which all sense of normality had been lost and all social ties had been severed. Anyone at any time could fall victim to state-organized terror—perhaps by belonging to a stigmatized social or ethnic group, by being denounced, by mere chance, or simply because the dictator enjoyed putting people to death and watching them live in fear and dread. In the state of emergency that existed in the Soviet Union of this time everything that had once been purely imaginable became possible. Terror became boundless, and violence became detached from its original causes. For both the rulers and the ruled, violence became normality. In the state of emergency imposed by the dictator all social systems, which, under peaceful conditions, had protected people from violence and arbitrary prosecution were now gone.

For the communists who dreamed of the dawning of a new age, violence was an indispensable instrument for disciplining and reeducating the uncivilized peasant masses. For many of the victims, however, it spelled the end of everything. It destroyed all predictability, legal certainty, and trust—in short, everything necessary for life in a civil society. Bolshevism was a "religion of hatred, of envy, of enmity among people," wrote peasants from the Kalinin area (formerly Tver) in 1930, decrying their experiences with the armed organs of the Soviet state.[2] But what they said openly was experienced by millions as a silent daily reality. Stalin's Soviet Union was a place where people could be stigmatized, terrorized, or killed arbitrarily, all at the caprice of the regime's henchmen. Stalinism's manic destructiveness knew no bounds, and in the end even the party was no longer a safe refuge. It too disintegrated into an arena of bloody terror during the purges of the 1930s and was eventually destroyed. And it was Stalin himself who relentlessly drove this destruction forward. Why? Because for him it held the promise of total power.

Even after the Great Terror had ended, peace did not return to Soviet society. While the Second World War wore on, the regime was occupied with another bloody war, directed against its purported enemies within. These enemies included war-weary soldiers, deserters, refugees, and national minorities suspected of cooperating with the Germans— all of whom were punished violently. After everything Stalin and his aides had inflicted on the people, they were amply justified in being suspicious. Terror was cultivated as a style of leadership, simply because those in power could not imagine a world in which obedience was enforced without the threat and use of violence.

During the war the terror extended beyond the borders of the Soviet empire. Its ravages, however, were not confined to those neighboring countries occupied by the Red Army. Even within the Soviet Union, violence came to celebrate unexpected triumphs. The regime sent soldiers and forced laborers returning from German captivity to concentration camps, resumed the war against its peasants and ethnic minorities, and ultimately destroyed all hope that the end of the war might mean an end to the violence. "We were all like rabbits," wrote screenwriter Valerii Frid, "who recognized the right of the boa constrictor to swallow us."[3] Millions became emotional cripples, as they were forced to adapt to an order based on fear and mistrust. The social order of Stalinism was one of permanent violence. Only those who mastered its rules and survival techniques could survive in it, and only after Stalin's death in March 1953 was it possible for the despot's successors to end the game of violence.

This book focuses on the violent excesses of Stalinism and the culture that made them possible. This is not a history of the Soviet Union[4] but of Stalinism, and as such it can afford to omit much that would be essential to a general history of the country. Communism as an ideology is also a side issue, because although Stalinist terror was founded in the name of communist ideas and beliefs, this was not its motivation. Many twentieth-century rulers considered themselves communists without seeing their commitment to communism as a license to commit mass murder. Some terrorist regimes also declared their commitment to communism, but—contrary to what Stéphane Courtois recently suggested in the preface to *The Black Book of Communism*—not all communist regimes were terroristic.[5] Stalin's regime was marked by the omnipresence of terror, but how is this terror to be understood? Those in power suffused the societies of the multiethnic Soviet empire with violence, but what was the source? And what sort of havoc did this violence wreak? This book seeks to provide answers to these questions.[6]

Stalinism's acts of violence were not the product of texts or ideas. They developed in historical spaces that made their epidemic spread possible. This is why communist regimes are not all the same. And yet all previous attempts to determine the essence of Stalinism have neglected the social and cultural conditions in which these violent excesses assumed their particular form. Hannah Arendt and Carl J. Friedrich, the chief proponents of the theory of totalitarianism, at least made the observation that the fascist and communist dictatorships of the twentieth century differed from all other forms of authoritarian and autocratic rule. "Totalitarian dictatorship is a recent development. There had never been anything quite like it in the past," wrote Friedrich in his book on the dictatorship of a new type, which appeared right after Stalin's death.[7] Friedrich was a contemporary of the dictatorships he was attempting to describe, and his book appeared before de-Stalinization in the Soviet Union had begun, preventing him from being able to say how this particular totalitarian dictatorship would end. This is why, as he wrote in the foreword to the German edition, there was no reason to believe "that anything fundamental had changed in the Soviet Union or in the totalitarian system."[8] We now know better of course, but this does not refute Friedrich's analysis of totalitarian dictatorship.

For Friedrich, totalitarian dictatorships were not "static structures with fixed contours." Instead, they were "subject to continuous development," and their emergence was neither inevitable nor did they necessarily remain the same forever."[9] "It is to be presumed," wrote Friedrich, "that if a communist dictatorship were to be established in England or France, many institutions of the liberal era would persist long thereafter."[10] But this insight contradicts everything Friedrich said elsewhere about the reality of the Stalinist dictatorship. Like Arendt, Friedrich spoke of the total state, total control, and subjugation, and in doing so he confirmed the exact public image that the fascist and communist dictatorships had created for themselves in their propaganda.[11]

Among the many objections to the concept of totalitarian dictatorship, the most notable is that it almost completely obliterated the differences between communist and fascist dictatorships. This charge, however, is not entirely persuasive, as Friedrich was not writing about the goals of power but about its practices.[12] At the same time, there have been some legitimate criticisms of the theory of totalitarianism. For one, it confused the aspirations of modern dictatorships with their actual practices. It also allowed itself to be deceived by the self-portrayals of power, conveying a static image of rule and presenting society as nothing more than a passive victim of the total state. In the historiography of National Socialism there have been discussions of chaos within the administration, a weak dictator, and niches within society that were not subjugated by the National Socialist state. For historians taking this perspective, even the popular approval experienced by the National Socialists did not prove that the regime exerted total control over the masses.[13]

In the 1970s and 1980s totalitarianism theory also came under fire in the historiography of the Soviet Union. Although the Bolsheviks had tirelessly claimed and projected the omnipotence of their state, this was only an unfulfilled aspiration, not a reality. This was the main objection to the notion of a total Soviet state. The Stalinist state was never able to attain total control over the societies of its empire. It was also difficult to speak of any sort of conversion of its subjects to the Bolshevik ideology, at least not beyond the limits of larger cities. Not even Nazi Germany—which, unlike the Soviet Union, was a modern industrial nation—could claim total control of its society. Thus, the critics argued, the notion of the total state should be discarded.[14] Historians should focus instead on the social conditions under which the Stalinist order was able to develop.

The so-called "revisionists" wanted to make sense of what they too called Stalinism and began looking at society "from below." What did this mean? It meant looking at what was happening in society, in the villages, in the factories, and in the cells of the party, to discover that the state's claims to absolute control had foundered on reality. What might be called Stalinism was actually a societal process that was never, at any point in time, actually run by the Bolsheviks. The Stalinist system had not been a creation of Stalin's will or the Bolshevik program, they argued. It had instead grown out of the ambitions of social climbers and profiteers, out of the envy and discontent of denouncers, and out of the struggle for power between different interest groups, organizations, and rival party committees. Accordingly, Stalinism had not only come "from below" but had also been supported "from below." And in this way the revisionists discovered a Soviet Union that was no longer totalitarian.

Of course no one will deny that the regime failed to exert control over the numerous societies of the empire and their ways of life and that it lacked the necessary number of communists, secret police officers, and justice officials to control the population. Nor will anyone question that violence was born out of local constraints or that the regional party leaders used violence in anticipatory obedience and were "working towards the Führer."[15] After all, for a great number of people, Stalin's revolution had meant a chance to rise in social rank, gain power, and taste prosperity. These beneficiaries of the revolution were naturally tied to the regime and its goals. There were also fellow travelers and sincere communists who did many things on their own initiative that the political leadership had never demanded of them. Nikita Khrushchev, Leonid Brezhnev, Alexei Kosygin, and others who rose through the party ranks during the 1930s were not merely products of the dictatorship of social engineering. They were also its pillars.[16]

Nevertheless, this perspective conveys an image of the Stalinist dictatorship that is blurred beyond recognition. Some revisionists disputed the very existence of a central strategy for the systematic transformation and terrorization of the Soviet Union. To them, Stalin and his aides were, if anything, merely driven by events, capable only of reaction, not decisive action. But can we really believe that the murder of millions was simply an undirected process in which those under Soviet rule voluntarily terrorized themselves? Did the mass killings, the expulsion of ethnic groups, and the system of forced labor camps really come "from below"? Should we really believe that collectivization, cultural revolution, and all the horrors of the Great Terror arose from social conflicts or simply from the initiatives of overly zealous Communists? Would you not also have to inquire into the preconditions and individual possibilities of action that enable people to inflict violence on others? Revisionist historical accounts of Stalinism have found no satisfactory answer to these questions. Above all, they have had nothing significant to say about the violence itself and its perpetrators. In their interpretation, everything could have come to pass just as it did, even if Stalin and his aides had never existed.

Indeed, Soviet institutions were primitive and the dictator was absent from local decision-making processes. This does not, however, exclude the possibility of terror being subject to central control. How else can we explain the fact that even the mass terror of 1937 could be ended, seemingly without difficulty, with a simple order from Stalin?[17] The will of the political leadership to use violence for political ends is key to understanding a situation that transformed people into vicious wolves. This context is also crucial for investigating the ideological justifications that allowed both perpetrators and their victims to endow the violence with meaning, to rationalize it, and thus to endure its everyday madness.

Although the regime claimed to exercise total power in each and every corner of the multiethnic empire, this was a hollow claim—one that could not be enforced. The Bolsheviks held unwaveringly to their assertion of power, even when the opposite was being proven on a daily basis.[18] In this project of turning the world on its head and cleansing the empire of its enemies, both public and private spheres were reordered and organized according to principles of repression. The pursuit of enemies, the enforcement of blind obedience and conformity, the mobilization of consent and resentments, and the spread of fear and panic—all this became part of the political culture that can be termed Stalinist.

Most workers and peasants were not communists, nor were they New Men, nor even loyal subjects. This is why, even as the new order dawned, the Bolsheviks were not able to transform them into switch points of power or to make them voluntarily internalize what it meant to be New Men. Expressions of praise for the new order—whether expressed in public or in private, in diaries or in letters—were not produced under freely chosen circumstances. They were produced under the circumstances of systematically distorted communication. Those who spoke in public knew what they could say and what they had to say. Those who wrote also often did so out of fear or in an attempt at making sense of a world gone mad. At some point, the Bolshevik system had effectively become the only space of communication for Soviet citizens. They continued living within the system and on the terms of the system simply because they had no other choice. The new power holders forced themselves deeply into the lives of their subjects and forced them to decide for or against Soviet power, by parading all the possibilities of the revolutionary state before them: propaganda, public celebrations, marches, cultural revolutionary reeducation campaigns, and also the threat of terror and violence. Even in those regions where the desire for total control had remained an impossible claim—even here the new masters could not be ignored. By the 1930s, even in remote mountain regions and villages and in the borderlands of the empire, a life without communism had become unthinkable. The violent events that occurred here can only be understood when we consider the Bolshevik claim of transforming every distant corner of the multiethnic empire and making it into a Bolshevik world.

The essence of Bolshevik power lay in the regime's ability to force its subjects, even in the farthest reaches of the empire, to respond to its challenges. The Soviet order became part of a world experienced by millions. Some historians have taken this to mean that people became Soviet subjects by refining or modifying themselves. They were not simply forced to find their way within the new order and its systems of control—they voluntarily internalized and embraced its premises. From this perspective, the assertions that people announced to one another in public were to be understood as truths of life. Can we truly believe, though, that the Soviet system actually gave people a choice? Why were people tortured? Why were the 1930s blackened by millions being terrorized, locked away in camps, and severed from all information? If the empire's subjects were truly so consumed with refining and recasting themselves into a new Soviet people, then why were even loyal party members not exempt from the bloodshed? Any interpretation that ignores the dictatorship and its twisted worldview can offer no answers. An alternative explanation is that Soviet subjects were not switch points, but rather multipliers of power. They reacted to the demands they were confronted with, and ultimately they had no choice but to accept the dictatorship and its lies. Totalitarian government, wrote Hannah Arendt, "bases itself on loneliness, on the experience of not belonging to the world at all, which is among the most radical and desperate experiences of man."[19]

"I was a Communist," confessed Arthur Koestler, who had traveled to the Soviet Union in 1932, "but I found life in Russia terribly depressing . . . The drab streets, the unrelieved shabbiness and poverty, the grim pomposity of everything said and written, the all-pervading atmosphere of a reformatory school. The feeling of being cut off from the rest of the world. The boredom of newspapers, which contained nothing critical or controversial, no crime, no sensation, no gossip, sex, scandal, human interest. The constant exhortations, the stereotyped uniformity and, the eternal portrait of Big Brother following you everywhere with his eyes. The over-whelming bleakness of an industrialized Neanderthal."[20] It was precisely this atmosphere that made it possible for a small number of determined violent criminals to transform the Soviet Union into a madhouse and to modify social relationships to such a degree that nothing remained the same.

In the words of Orlando Figes, the Soviet Union under Stalin became a land of "whisperers."[21] And yet the subjects were not the only ones who were transformed. The regime was subject to change as well. Its confrontation with the empire's adversities prompted it to modify its ruling practices, and indeed, the intensity of the violence seemed to increase in proportion to the level of resistance as perceived by the Bolsheviks. It was only after it became impossible to ignore the contradictions between life in the "industrialized Neanderthal," on the one hand, and the totalitarian claims of total power, on the other, that an impasse was reached, which in the minds of the Bolsheviks could only be resolved by violent means. The grandiosity of the Bolshevik vision stood in stark contrast to the awkwardness with which their premodern system of government attempted to realize this vision. It made for a setting in which the regime could only ensure the obedience of its functionaries by threatening them with violence. It also provided the conditions under which the lust for power of a single individual was able to unfold with all its lethal effects. The Bolshevik order became a despotic order. The daily lives of its functionaries and their subordinates were structured by the arbitrariness of the dictator, and from there it proceeded to spread into all areas of life. Although this interpretation of the Soviet Union under Stalin had always been conceivable, it could only be verified once historians gained access to the archives.

In the early 1990s, what had lain buried for decades was dragged out of the darkness: stenographic protocols of Central Committee meetings, correspondence between the central party apparatus and provincial committees, administrative documents and records, and the papers of Stalin, Molotov, Kaganovich, and other political leaders. These documents allowed new insight into life within the inner circle of power and revealed a Soviet Union that had hitherto been unknown to us.[22] Most importantly, though, they confirmed what had previously been in question—that Stalin and his most loyal followers not only enabled the violent excesses of the 1930s but also systematically initiated them. Stalin and his cohorts forced their vassals in the provinces to execute their will in the most radical manner possible. Stalin also ordered the arrest and murder of the kulaks and sanctioned the deportation of more than two million peasants to camps and special settlements in Siberia. Little was left to chance, not even the transport of peasants taken captive. Without directives from the Politburo and from Stalin, the violent excesses against the Soviet peasantry could never have taken place.[23]

The same applies to the Great Terror of 1937 and 1938. It too bore Stalin's signature and was kept in motion thanks to his decrees. In July 1937 the dictator sent telegrams to party leaders in the provinces, specifying in detail who was to be shot and who was to be deported. Throughout the years of mass terror, the head of the NKVD, Nikolai Yezhov, regularly submitted lists of people marked for death, which were then signed by Stalin. Over forty thousand people were sent to their deaths by means of this "album procedure" alone.[24] Nowhere did subordinate officials dare perform executions without the dictator's prior consent. Any plans to increase body counts required his permission, but since Stalin took such initiatives as symbols of loyalty he generally agreed to them. Even in the camps of Dalstroy in Magadan the Chekists waited for permission from the Kremlin before they began murdering prisoners.[25]

The stenographic protocols of the Central Committee also provide insight into how leading Bolsheviks spoke and behaved among themselves. They suggest that the party leaders were ruthless executioners who confessed their bloody deeds freely and showed no reservations in sending their victims to gruesome fates. In the inner circle of power they spoke of annihilating their enemies no differently than they did in public—with the decided difference that the official legitimization for the murder campaigns carried no meaning inside the despot's court. For Stalin and his friends, violence was a natural course of action. A discussion of reasons or purposes was thus unnecessary.[26]

Throughout the years of the Soviet dictatorship the oppressed, the excluded, the stigmatized, and the tortured remained silent because all attempts at speaking out against the horrors of the Stalinist terror were suppressed. For a long time historians thus had to settle for the regime's self-representation or the recollections of emigrants and dissidents to make their interpretations of the past. The victims, who had no forum in the state-controlled press, were only given a voice when records from the secret police and judicial authorities became available. What these documents revealed is that collectivization had more closely resembled a civil war than mere submission, that the peasants had indeed resisted, and that for most people in Stalin's Soviet Union life had largely been an experience of enduring poverty.[27] In short, the Soviet state was neither strong nor absolute, but "Stalinism from below" did not exist either. Instead, we must imagine a state that was weak and whose representatives found it useful to stage scenes of permanent chaos and violence. This was, after all, their only means of reminding their subjects of their claims to power.

The British-Polish sociologist Zygmunt Bauman categorized the annihilative violence of twentieth-century totalitarian dictatorships as a phenomenon of modernity. In this interpretation, the Stalinist version of socialism deemed itself the only true culmination of modernity. Its goals were to overcome disorder—the hallmark of a fragmented and poorly organized society—and to remove all ambiguities. Nothing would be left to chance anymore, and all actions would be subordinate to a larger plan for the reshaping of mankind. In a figurative sense, the Bolsheviks were like a gardener who tore out weeds, transformed wild landscapes into symmetrically arranged parks, and removed everything that did not belong in the garden. The socialist human park was to consist of modern Europeans, New Men who had freed themselves from the spiritual and cultural orders of the past and who celebrated the feasts of their new rulers, wore their clothes, and spoke their language.

The kingdom of heaven on earth would accommodate only one kind of human being, only one language. The establishment of this new world required that the "backward" multiethnic empire be transformed into a realm of social and cultural homogeneity. In keeping with Baumann, one would have to concede that the Russian communists were indeed eager students of the Age of Reason. What had been neglected by nature would be accomplished by the human hand. Everything seemed possible, and thus it was necessary to dispose of the "waste" that accrued as a by-product of their "landscaping."[28]

It is possible to live with differences when one accepts that the worldview held by the other can accommodate a world that is just as reasonable as one's own—even when it deviates from one's own vision of life. But when the very possibility that the other could also be right is called into question, then all hope of accord must be abandoned. For the Bolsheviks there was only one interpretation of the world, namely their own. In order to understand the essence of Bolshevism, wrote Arthur Koestler, it was necessary to understand that the party and its leaders were not expressing preexisting truths, but that the truth emanated from the leaders themselves. This meant that anyone who disagreed was a traitor.[29] Experience can never compete with utopia, as utopias suspend the past, present, and future, and exist in a world of mythical time. They can only accommodate changes that are approved of by their interpreters, and this is why life in a utopia is a constant negation of everyday experience. It is also why deviant thought must be criminalized and why everything that contradicts the blueprint of the new order must be stigmatized.

The will for transformation had already existed in the late tsarist empire. But unlike the tsarist bureaucrats, the Bolsheviks imagined far more than simply transforming, ordering, and controlling the societies of the empire. For them the project belonged to a narrative of salvation, a teleology of deliverance. Accordingly, socialism was not simply an order in which its subjects were to be obedient. It was a blueprint for a society that sought to exist without enemies, despite permanently being in the process of producing them. There was no room for dissent or resistance, and if the Bolshevik project were to succeed they needed to be crushed at their first signs. Furthermore, because the Bolsheviks were convinced that their enemies were representatives of hostile social and ethnic collectives, any person suspected of belonging to one of these adversarial groups could become a victim of violence as well. It was the Bolshevik predisposition to resort to violent measures that gave their quest for clarity a remarkable radicalism. Had the notion of history as a battlefield not existed, the Bolsheviks would have invented it, for in their eyes it reflected their struggle perfectly.

The Bolshevik claim of penetrating and transforming the societies of the empire could never be fully realized. In fact, it could only very rarely be enforced. First of all, this was because the social model promoted by the Bolsheviks encountered resistance. Secondly, competing interpretations of reality prevented them from gaining access to the hearts and minds of their subjects. And finally, in many places violence was the only way that the communists could make themselves heard at all. Only with great difficulty could the culture of hegemony be pressed into the consciousness of the subjects. In many areas the power holders remained voiceless, despite the official propaganda suggesting that they and the people spoke a common language. The wall separating the leaders from the people was invisible but high. As they saw it, this wall could only be surmounted by subjugating the menacing "dark masses" of peasants and workers to a brutal dictatorship of discipline and re-education. This is why the Stalinist terror was, more than anything, a response to the inability of the power holders to enforce their claims. And so it came to pass that even the functionaries in the provinces, when they were unable to enforce the Bolsheviks' claims to power and remove their enemies, also became victims of the violence. Stalinism was only possible under circumstances where the dismal reality made a mockery of the exaggerated expectations.

But does this adequately explain the extent of the violence? Bauman's description of the project of modernity does not apply to the ruling practices of the Soviet Union under Stalin. The societies of the multiethnic empire were no more modern than the techniques the regime employed to achieve its aims. The most that could qualify as modern were its notions of a rigid order. Even if Bauman's claims were valid—the claim, for example, that the destructive excesses of modern dictatorships were "legitimate children of the modern spirit" and not just simple barbarism—they do not explain how ideas became acts of murder.[30] Governments elsewhere also dreamed of a clear social order, but these dreams were not necessarily associated with the slaughter of millions. And how can we explain the fact that it was not simply "human waste" that was eliminated but Communists, military officers, state officials, and members of the Politburo too? Apparently, anyone could become a victim of Stalinist terror, and in the end it did not matter where they were from, what they were accused of, or which social group they belonged to. "Ambivalence, I think, is the chief characteristic of my nation," wrote the poet Joseph Brodsky in his recollections of Petersburg. "There isn't a Russian executioner who isn't scared of turning victim one day, nor is there the sorriest victim who would not acknowledge (if only to himself) a mental ability to become an executioner."[31]

There is no causal relationship between modernity and the monstrous violence fomented by the National Socialists and communists in the first half of the twentieth century. Modernity is not the source of totalitarian, annihilative terror. The modern world is governed by legal systems and rules that are guaranteed by the authorities and upheld by participatory procedures. Individuals condition themselves for life in society. They adapt themselves without the state forcing them to do so, and in this way they and others know what is permitted and what is prohibited. In a society governed by categories, rules, and discipline, neither the state nor the citizens have the license to arbitrarily enforce their will on others. The practices of self-adjustment are mechanisms for limiting the development of delusional notions about what is feasible. All citizens living in the modern world know that they are not merely slaves, but also masters of the unambiguous orders to which they must submit. The rules are established jointly, and the citizens know that they can also prevent others from disobeying them. Citizens exercise self-restraint on a daily basis and thus prohibit themselves from forcing their will to change on others or taking someone else's life for their own amusement. Above all, though, modern people can retreat into spaces free from surveillance. They can be alone with in private and can slip into different roles where they are free from the pressures of public discipline. This is the intrinsic achievement of the modern state. It increases the density of communication between people, allows for participation, creates rules that everyone is prepared to acknowledge, subjects its citizens to a form of discipline that they consider an expression of their own will, but still allows people to escape from the pressures of the community. This is neither conceivable nor enforceable in a premodern society. It is also why it was so easy for the totalitarian state to mobilize the authoritarian conceptions of premodern societies for its destructive ends.[32]

It seems to be no coincidence that the most gruesome and violent excesses of the twentieth century did not celebrate their greatest triumphs in modern civil societies but in premodern spaces, far removed from the state, where opposition to the hubris of the modern interventionist state was minimal. It was in the areas with the fewest visible signs of modern statehood, where life was structured by war, that the greatest, most violent excesses occurred. Whenever the hybris of modernity came up against the norms and rules of civil society it failed. The modern quest for clarity was only able to truly unfold its lethal effects in those premodern spaces where the delusional notions of fanatical ideologues knew no limits. These were the actual sites of modern mass terror. "It's hard to believe," wrote the Muscovite student Nina Lugovskaia in her diary in late December 1934, "that in the twentieth century there is a corner of Europe where medieval barbarians have taken up residence, where savage concepts are accompanied so strangely by science, art and culture." Bauman's sociology of nonambiguity, where premodern society is a peaceable idyll, cannot account for this.[33]

Stalinist terror was not without causes, but it took on its truly monstrous momentum under circumstances that were not modern. The Soviet Union had no bureaucracy, no civil society, no rule of law, and no institutional framework to stand in the way of the violent orgy of the Bolshevik rulers. From 1914 onwards the empire was in constant turmoil. The First World War, the Civil War, and the violent subjugation of remote and ungoverned spaces by the Bolsheviks had thrown the multiethnic empire into a permanent state of emergency. The Soviet Union was a nation at war, and under the conditions of war who was there to prevent the Bolsheviks from carrying out their violent will? The Stalinist reign of violence was characterized by the attempt to create a new world out of the raw materials of the old, and in the process all sense of proportion was lost.

The Soviet Union of the 1930s was not governed by bureaucracies and regulations but by patrons and clients. At the top was the dictator, who drew his power from the loyalty of his vassals in the provinces. It is worth remembering that the subjects of the multiethnic empire had no common language and only limited means of communication.

The regime attempted to overcome these obstacles by personifying its total claims and enlisting reliable people in the provinces to carry out its project of social engineering.[34] Stalin, however, was mistrustful of everyone, except those he knew very well. Stalin's vassals were no exception, and to make sure that they executed his will he played them off against each another, placed them under surveillance, or expressed provocative suspicions about their loyalty. It was only possible to disprove suspicions and prove one's loyalty by bringing the despot more victims. Under these circumstances it was essential that the leading Bolsheviks remain loyal to each other, that betrayal be punished, and that good conduct be rewarded. This atmosphere of mistrust, suspicion, and fear provided fertile ground for spreading rumors, "uncovering" conspiracies, and committing acts of violence. Here, survival required unconditional submission to the dictator, as well as the ability to anticipate his every desire.

Stalin's model of control was similar to that of the Mafia. It involved the creation of permanent psychological stress. It was also based on the internal fashioning of Stalin's followers who, like the dictator, had grown up in a world of violence and considered violence a fully reasonable means of conducting politics. Almost all Bolshevik perpetrators had suffered and committed violence themselves in the prerevolutionary underground or during the Civil War, before entering the inner circle of power.[35] Their immediate physical relationship with violence had prepared them for the ruthless murder of their opponents and enemies. It had also helped them internalize the rules of Stalin's court and endure the psychological pressure he imposed on those around him. Even in hindsight, Vyacheslav Molotov and Lazar Kaganovich, who had once been among Stalin's most faithful and brutal followers, made no efforts to distance themselves from their earlier crimes but instead openly confessed to them. Only once did Kaganovich fear that his crimes might cost him his life. Upon his defeat in the power struggle of 1957 he begged Nikita Khrushchev to spare his life. Although torture and death would have been certain penalties for having opposed Stalin, "Iron Lazar" got off with a mild punishment. Khrushchev had him removed from the Politburo in 1957 and then sent him to work as director of an asbestos factory in the Urals. The past soon returned to haunt him when a factory employee confronted him about his crimes under Stalin, calling him a murderer and a criminal with the blood of his victims on his hands. "Not a single centimeter of your skin is clean," Kaganovich's accuser told him. "Everything is full of blood." "Iron Lazar," however, had no regrets and responded by saying, "That's how it had to be" (*Tak nado bylo*).[36]

In all probability, the Stalinist functionaries were not even capable of imagining a world without violence. In a world where Bolshevik fantasies were supposed to become reality, acts of violence escalated into orgies of violence and acquired apocalyptic proportions. Simply pointing to the ideological orientation of the power holders and their use of utopian social engineering does nothing to further the understanding of Stalinism.

Stalin gave Stalinism more than his name. Without him it would never have existed, just as without Hitler the national socialist system would have been inconceivable. When the Bolshevik project of societal reorganization degenerated into mass terror this was not least due to the fact that the dictator himself had a passion for violence. "Nor should we neglect the obvious point," wrote the British author Martin Amis, "that Stalin did it because Stalin liked it. He couldn't help himself."[37] Without Stalin's criminal energy, his malevolence, and his archaic notions of friendship, loyalty, and betrayal, the murderous excesses of the 1930s would hardly have been possible. His way of life was one of excesses. Every murderous action was performed in full knowledge that it would please the despot in the Kremlin. More than fifteen years after the opening of the central archives in Moscow no doubts remain about the authorship of the terror. Stalin signed orders for the terror with which the regime sent millions to their doom. Moreover, he expected the perpetrators to seek his permission before killing anyone whose death he had not explicitly ordered. Stalin drove his followers onward in pursuit of alleged enemies and demanded their utmost exertion in this task. Neither friends nor relatives were safe. The key to explaining the excessive violence is the dictator himself. As Oleg Khlevniuk wrote in his book on Stalin and his inner circle, terror was the simplest and most efficient method of disciplining society and maintaining an atmosphere of fear and dread.[38] It was also how the dictator was able to justify his acts of violence—by pointing to their efficacy. Part of the logic of the Stalinist terror was that it transgressed all boundaries because the despot in the Kremlin simply could not refrain from being a violent perpetrator. Only with the death of the dictator did the terror machine finally come to a halt, so that the death of the despot marked the end of Stalinism.

Those living in peace like to believe that the violence others have to endure is only a temporary disturbance. People look for noble motives, for necessity, and for immutability, in an attempt at overcoming their confusion at what seems like senseless torturing and killing. Victims too try to give their sufferings a meaning that will allow them to preserve their sanity. Those who have suffered injury, imprisonment, and pain, and who have witnessed the violent deaths of friends and relatives, are unable to bear the notion that there was no reason for any of it. Violence should have causes that are comprehensible, people insist.[39] The perpetrators of violence take the same approach when they try to rationalize their actions to themselves and those around them. They attempt to justify their decisions in such a way that both victims and observers will understand that they could not have acted otherwise. Whenever they are called to account for their crimes they plead superior orders or point to the deadly consequences of disobedience. This was the explanation that Nikita Khrushchev and Anastas Mikoyan gave after Stalin's death, regarding their roles in the violent excesses of the 1930s. Others—because they were never held accountable for their crimes—attempted to endow the terror with meaning by speaking of noble motives, the conquest of backwardness, or defense against foreign threats. Even decades after Stalin's death, Molotov justified the violence of the 1930s by tying it to the victory in the Second World War and insisting that it had been a necessary means of protecting the Soviet Union against its enemies.[40]

But were the justifications of 1975 also the motives of 1937? This is hard to believe. Why then the murder of old men and children? Why the destruction of the Communist Party? Why did the executioners of the NKVD have to die once their bloody work had been completed? And why, in the end, were even Politburo members killed? Even if Stalin and his helpers had been convinced that they were surrounded by enemies from within and without, how did this justify the murder and deportation of millions? The answer is that the dictator's official justifications were simply a means of diverting attention from his true motives. People can have many different reasons for doing the same thing. The connection between actions and motives is not mandatory.

"In the meantime," wrote Imre Kertész,

we have experienced empires ruled by ideologies that in practice revealed themselves as mere word games, whereby this very characteristic was what made them suitable as an effective instrument of terror. We have experienced that both murderers and victims were well aware of the emptiness, the meaninglessness of such ideological orders in equal measure: and it was precisely this awareness that gave the atrocities committed in the name of such ideologies their particular, incomparable disgracefulness and perverted the societies in the grip of such ideologies down to their roots. Murderous salvos, the bare fist, "the murderous stroke of the cane" with the accompanying roar of a truly murderous folly have proven to be the most pleasurable feeling of power. Corrosive to reason, the murdering created an orgiastic feeling of exuberance, which opens up truly apocalyptic perspectives to man and his future.[41]

That is what this book is about.

2 Imperial Spaces of Violence

The Bolshevik attempt at refashioning the Soviet Union according to their vision involved a continuation of the tsarist project of registering, homogenizing, and subjugating the populations of the empire. Ever since Peter I (1682–1725) had opened Russia to the West, political rule of the tsarist empire had been in the service of an ambitious project of modernization. Nothing was to remain the same, and in their way, the Bolsheviks felt committed to this legacy. Although the dream had different meanings at different times, the Russian elite had always dreamed of Europeanizing their country. Despite changes in what "Europeanization" meant, the method of measuring progress remained the same. Progress was not about making the best of what this heterogeneous country had to offer. It was about making it resemble Europe—Europe as it existed in the minds of the elite. In this regard, Russian life failed miserably to conform to its rulers' conceptions. Peter I had wanted to turn his subjects into Englishmen and Germans rather than making Russians out of them. As the French philosopher Jean-Jacques Rousseau wrote in his *Social Contract*, "He prevented his subjects from ever becoming what they might have been by persuading them that they were what they are not."[1]

Russia's Westernization, which began in the final third of the eighteenth century and culminated in the Great Reforms of Alexander II (1855–81), was a product of the absolutist state. The state lacked many of the preconditions required for this project but sought to create them by decree. Apart from the landowners, there was no one in the rural parts of the empire to represent the interests of the autocracy. The tsarist state claimed absolute power over its subjects, but in practice this claim could only rarely be asserted. The only solution to this dilemma was for the people to assume the tasks that the state was incapable of fulfilling. Under Tsarina Catherine II (1762–96) the empire was divided into provinces, and the populations were registered, hierarchically ordered, and organized into corporate estates. Merchants and noblemen were expected to do everything that the state authorities could not, meaning that Russia's absolutism was based on preconditions that it could not guarantee. Corporations of nobility, merchant organizations, and artisan guilds were children of the absolutist state. They failed to develop independently, and only rarely did their interests coincide with those of the state.[2] They also lacked the necessary regional roots, traditions, and cohesion to justify autonomy and claims to power in the distant reaches of the empire. Power and esteem were reserved for those who could bask in the reflected glory of the autocrat, and this was the basis of most of the nobility's self-conception as well. The ambitious and educated were drawn to the tsar's court, close to the inner circle of power, where they could enjoy the privileges that dull provincial life could not offer. But the developments that were taking place in seclusion, beyond the capital, were unlikely to please the tsarist state. Elected estate officials were uneducated and corrupt, ill-suited for the demanding legal and administrative tasks required of them.[3] Russia's rulers had great plans for the country, but they lacked the instruments necessary for fulfilling these ambitions. They were also beginning to discover just how backward their country really was.

The autocracy had been a European power since the mid-eighteenth century, and it saw the overcoming of backwardness as its raison d'être. Russia's reformers believed that great tasks awaited them and strove to bridge the gap between their claims and their possibilities. They became modernizers and educators who exploited the autocrat's claim to total power to achieve their own goals. "Enlightened bureaucrats" was the name later given to the European-educated men serving in the ministries of Nicholas I and Alexander II. They were bound together by their common professional training, a downright fanatical devotion to the service, and the firm belief that Europe's present would become Russia's future. It was the elite's desire for European conditions—not economic pressure or social protests—that created the atmosphere in which the Great Reforms of Alexander II became possible.[4] The abolition of serfdom, the separation of the administrative and judicial branches, the eventual introduction of compulsory military service, and the establishment of self-administration at the municipal level during the 1860s and 1870s—none of these developments stemmed from the needs or traditions of the subjects. They were the products of a thought experiment that attached little meaning to the people's wishes. Given the voicelessness and powerlessness of the society of the propertied and educated (obshchestvo) it could be no other way. Symbolic capital was concentrated around the tsar, where education, organizational, and communication skills had a chance to effect change. No one could have prevented the enlightened officials from carrying out their ambitious plans of transforming state and society: all they needed to do was enlist the autocrat to their cause.

Russia's rulers were conquerors, and they had devoted their lives to the subjugation of the empire. This attitude was clear from the kind of symbolism the rulers selected for their public displays of power. The ruling house was not a "Russian" dynasty but a "European" one. Never once did the public ceremonial productions of Alexander III (1881–94) or Nicholas II (1894–17) reflect the needs of the people. Instead they sought to project the spirit of the bureaucratic and nation-states of Europe.[5] In this way, the self-conception of the monarchy and the yearnings for modernization of the enlightened officials could not have been better suited to each other. What may have been achievable in some European countries encountered its limits in Russia. The autocratic concept of *mission civilisatrice,* that is, the homogenizing and civilizing of diverse modes of life, could not be reconciled with the heterogeneity of the empire because it already took preconditions for granted that still had to be fulfilled. For most of Russia's subjects, modernization meant coercion, as voluntary submission to the proposals of the elite, who rarely had anything to offer them, was unlikely. Why should the peasants want to wear the uniform of the autocratic state, pay its taxes, or abide by its laws when it offered them nothing in exchange? Externally imposed discipline was rarely transformed into voluntarily self-imposed discipline. Peasants and workers were expected to follow the rules and conventions of a society of which they could never become a part, and ultimately they became neither Russians nor citizens. As the tsarist project of modernization advanced into the fringes of the empire, encountering the nomads of Central Asia and the inhabitants of the Caucasus, it became quite clear that the cultural divisions this project was supposed to overcome were not small. In striving to unite the empire the modernizers produced differences and disjointedness instead. Modern disciplinary techniques were not successful in Russia, and the elites were well aware of this.[6]

The internal colonialism of the tsarist state did more to generate cultural differences than it did to erase them. In seeking to turn its peasants into Russians and Europeans it made strangers of them and was never able to successfully convert them. People are generally only willing to alter their personal circumstances when this does not lead to cultural self-abandonment and only when they do not have to betray their own in order to become someone else. "When someone feels," wrote the Arab essayist, Amin Maalouf, "that his language is despised, his religion ridiculed and his culture disparaged, he is likely to react by flaunting the signs of his difference. When someone feels he has a place in the country where he has chosen to live, then he will behave in quite another manner."[7] Tsarist modernization, however, had come in the form of an internal colonialism that demanded much of the lower classes and offered them little in return. State-building reforms produced no improvements in the daily lives of most people and seemed to offer little more than tax collectors, policemen, military conscription, bizarre laws, and judges. The project of state building thus remained in a rudimentary form.

Elites and peasants rarely came together in their voicelessness. Indeed, the enlightened bureaucrats had fulfilled a heartfelt wish when they freed the serfs from their feudal bondage in 1861. Still, an unbridgeable cultural divide separated peasants and elites, and efforts to overcome it often had the opposite effect. Tsarist officials considered agrarian reform a benevolent deed, performed by the state for good of the people. For most peasants, however, it only produced hardships that the peasants were unwilling to accept. How were they to understand that the land they had tilled for centuries—on which their huts

had stood and their cattle had grazed—would now have to be purchased from the lords?[8] Peasants failed to understand the concept of
aristocratic property rights, and state officials took this to indicate that
they had no conception of justice. But without a common conception
of rights and duties, how could they have taught the peasants that they
were wrong and the landowners were right? When the enlightened bureaucrats suspended the administrative functions of the landlords, they
lost the intermediaries who had given the state a voice in the village.
The elites now had no choice but to come to terms with their new relationship with the peasants. They bound them to the land, curtailed
their mobility, and coerced them into doing what the landowners were
no longer capable of. Given the absence of the state in the village, there
was simply no alternative.[9]

Every civilizing effort of the state was met with resistance. While the
state authorities spoke of duties they offered nothing in return. The law
was the most visible expression of a cultural imperialism that showed
complete disregard for the traditions of its subjects. It was not Russian
but was an imitation of something from abroad, and its implementation
in Russia was correspondingly difficult. It had an ahistorical status: it
was neither derived from Russian traditions and myths nor generated
via consensus. This meant that it could be arbitrarily imposed but not
enforced. Anything the tsar's bureaucrats prescribed or wrote into law
could be freely replaced and manipulated, as it had nothing to do with
justice as the people understood it.[10]

In a world whose inhabitants knew little of modern life—who lived
in a world without hospitals, schools, police, or judges—the village
community performed the tasks that the state was unable to carry out.
Peasants were not part of society, and they rarely came into contact
with the tsarist state bureaucracy. Instead, they should be seen as members of small, local societies based on the presence and participation of
their members, where conflicts were settled face to face. In an unpredictable world it was crucial that everyone observe the norms that lent
stability to village life. The social cosmos of the Russian village was
thus governed by rigid social discipline, which punished deviant behavior with beatings and degradation. Offenses that villagers might commit outside of the village, however, were overlooked. Behavior that was
prohibited without exception inside the village was justifiable when
directed against outsiders. Outsiders, after all, are not part of the weave

that integrates one's own social group, and in a world where much is unpredictable, mistrust of strangers is fully justified. Killing an outsider was a far less serious offence than causing even the accidental death of a community member. Within this context, something was right if it increased the community's chances of survival. Therefore, the theories of virtue preached by the state elite had no universal validity for the peasants.[11]

Contrary to what Slavophiles and romantic Social Revolutionaries liked to believe, rural life was neither peaceable nor marked by solidarity. Drunkenness, avarice, and violence were rampant. Men beat their wives and children, outsiders were isolated or cast out of the community, and holidays were filled with drunken brawls that had potentially deadly outcomes. The behaviors and attitudes that defined village life stood in sharp contrast to the norms and legal conceptions drafted by the autocratic state. For the peasants, the state's concept of ownership was fully foreign, because in their understanding, only those working the land were entitled to own it. If God had created the land to be plowed, then why should it be a crime to chop wood in the landlord's forest or make use of land that was not being used by others? In this sense, it was the officials rather than the peasants who defied laws and conventions, for they were the ones who punished what was acceptable according to village law.[12] State laws that violated local conventions and traditions were simply ignored. Precisely because the central authorities insisted that their laws be enforced, they lost the respect needed to establish a social consensus.

The liberal philosophy held that only an order based on law could ensure the freedom of the individual. A law-based order was intended to reconcile the freedom of one group with the freedom of another group and to offer different people equal treatment before the law. Socialists and liberals alike understood freedom as emancipation from economic enslavement and deliverance from desolation and despair. When they spoke of the freedom of the individual, they envisioned societies and their citizens. Peasants, meanwhile, took freedom to mean the power to withhold obedience from society and its rules. Their freedom (*volia*) had no place for the state and rejected elitist notions of order. Unbridled drunkenness, the looting of noble estates, the expulsion of landowners, or the murder of state officials were all expressions of freedom, according to the peasant conception of it. In October 1905, when the tsar's manifesto granting civil liberties was publicly announced in the villages, the peasants chiefly understood this as a free pass to start seizing land, expelling landowners, and withdrawing their allegiance from state authorities.[13] When the state wanted to make itself heard in the village, it had no choice but to suspend the law and intervene in village life with a force that was not provided for by the law. Anytime the state lacked decisiveness, its claims were forgotten or ignored. The state's only hope of asserting itself was to generate trust by its presence and to give free rein to local governors, viceroys, and land captains. Outside of Saint Petersburg, even on the eve of the First World War the tsarist empire was still a country that was governed by procedures based on personal ties rather than by bureaucracies and regulations, and this is likely the very reason that the empire lasted so long.[14] Historians who base their interpretations of the past on legislation, constitutions, and parliamentary debates discover how the elites thought about the people, but they gain no insight into the encounters between rulers and their subjects. In this case the encounter was a cultural misunderstanding, and it cumulated in two bloody confrontations: the Revolution of 1905 and the Revolution of 1917.

This confrontation took place not only in the village but also in the city. Starting in the final third of the nineteenth century, several hundred thousand peasants began streaming into the major cities and industrial settlements of the tsarist empire in search of work. Industrialization and migration are synonymous. Wherever large cities and industrial complexes emerge, wherever new perspectives are offered, people migrate from the countryside to the city. In this regard Russia was no exception. Within a matter of a few years, some Russian cities had become so overrun by peasant masses that they were unrecognizable. Moscow, Saint Petersburg, Odessa, Baku, Tiflis, and other major cities became peasant metropolises, administered but not controlled by the propertied and educated. Some cities only came into existence in the course of industrialization, initially consisting of small bands of subaltern state officials and merchants, before succumbing to the peasant masses. Rather than the city conquering the village, the village had conquered the city and had given it a Russian face.[15]

The state authorities were not prepared for this onslaught. The integration of the peasant into the urban space was not easy. The working-class neighborhoods of industrial towns could offer next to nothing in the way of schools, hospitals, doctors, or police. Four decades later,

Nikita Khrushchev would still look back in horror at his youth in the industrial district of the Donbass where workers, far from the over-sight of any sort of armed authorities, had killed Jews and foreign-ers. "I saw a gendarme for the first time," he recalled, "when I was around twenty-four years old. There were no gendarmes at the mines. We had one policeman, the Cossack Klintsov, who would meet the miners and get drunk with them. Apart from him there was not a single policeman under the old regime."[16] As it was, the peasant migrants remained among themselves. The factories and their surroundings became state-free spaces in which state law had no meaning. Within these immigrant communities village culture was kept alive with all the traditional cycles of life, customs, rituals, holidays, and conflicts. Urban society would only come into contact with this culture when workers protested. Strikes were violent eruptions, in which the peasant migrants demanded justice as they understood it—that is, as freedom from orders and rules that clashed with their expectations. Long-term improvements in living conditions, political reforms, and civil liberties, meanwhile, were of no interest to workers eking out a daily existence. Anyone who had left his village on good terms could always return, meaning that workers had invested little in their surroundings and had few reservations about destroying them.[17]

Most migrants did not become city people. They did not become part of society and its order, and they remained largely at the mercy of their employers. Working-class districts were islands of peasant culture within the city, and accordingly they were not governed by state law but by village common law. Russia's workers were village people, held together by regional ties, and members of ethnic or religious groups. Arrival in the city did not mean assimilation to the working class there. This had both advantages and disadvantages for the autocratic state. Although the state was unable to reach the workers, it did not need to fear them as a political force. Instead, the autocratic state was able to play them off against the state's liberal and middle-class critics. Despite the violence of worker protests, they were usually confined to factories and local districts, and they generally collapsed as soon as the demands for higher wages and better living and working conditions had been satisfied.

All the same, entrepreneurs, intellectuals, and liberals still had reason to fear popular violence. In the revolutionary year of 1905, when the government and the oppositional liberals met to discuss the country's political course, Prime Minister Witte issued a warning that would turn out to be a self-fulfilling prophecy twelve years later. The liberal movement, Witte promised, could be easily destroyed by promising every peasant twenty-five desyatins of land. The landowners, and by extension liberal Russia, would then be "swept away" by the peasants as if they had never existed.[18] "Such as we are," wrote the Russian cultural philosopher Mikhail Gershenzon in 1909, "we not only cannot dream of merging with the people, but we must fear them more than all the government's executions, and we must bless this government which alone, with its bayonets and prisons, still protects us from the people's wrath."[19]

Russia did not provide fertile ground for the flourishing of liberalism. The revolutionaries understood this, and they knew they needed a means of overcoming their isolation from the workers and peasants, whom they claimed to represent. Social Revolutionaries and Social Democrats alike had inherited the traditions of the nineteenth-century Russian intelligentsia that had worshiped the people as a concept yet knew little about them. In their cultural and political isolation they placed their hopes on lofty utopias, whose only claims to truth were that the power holders were opposed to them. Ideas became icons, and Marxism became a revelation that was immune to objections—if only because it had not yet become necessary to put these ultimate truths into practice. "Our intelligentsia is rich in knowledge from books and poor in knowledge about the Russian reality," wrote Maxim Gorky. "The body lies on the ground, but the head is high up in the sky—as is well known, everything appears better from a distance than from up close."[20] The conventions of the radical intelligentsia were imitations of literary ideals, staged in theatrical poses: Lenin trying to fill the role of the ascetic and joyless Rakhmetov, the hero of Nikolai Chernyshevsky's *What Is to Be Done?*; Leon Trotsky busy reliving the French Revolution; and Social Revolutionary terrorists styling themselves as martyrs and romantic peasant leaders and envisioning a reality that the workers and peasants did not see.[21] Most revolutionaries were, after all, separated by their background and life experiences from the workers and peasants in whose name they spoke. This, of course, made for a very fragile relationship between workers and revolutionaries, and whenever joint protests were unsuccessful, friendship could quickly turn into enmity—particularly when the revolutionaries publicly ridiculed the tsar or religion. In any case, if any sort of revolution was to succeed, agitators and workers needed to find a common language. Intellectuals needed to remove themselves from their isolation and adapt habits and speech that would appeal to peasants and illiterates. Revolutionaries who had come from below and had a visceral understanding of poverty and violence did not need to tailor their behavior. They despised elections and constitutional orders and had never expected anything from them anyway. They were satisfied with giving a voice to the people's anger by providing it with a target. Such was the world of the young, violent Bolshevik revolutionaries who made up the provincial committees. They gave a public voice to what had been the reality for millions, and their hatred of the old order knew no limits. As long as the tsarist state was able to maintain control, their radicalism and extremism remained without consequences. But when the empire sank into misery and violence, everything changed. This is exactly what happened in the summer of 1914 when the tsarist government committed itself to a war that it could not win.

The First World War was the gravedigger of the old order and the midwife of the new. The tsarist reformers had spent more than fifty years trying to establish the state in the empire's provinces and turn its peasants into citizens. The autocracy had been able to survive the violent outbreaks of the 1905 Revolution by granting the liberal elites a parliament and a constitution and by continuing to enforce its authority in the cities and villages. The fragility of this order, however, became apparent when it was harshly tested by war. What had taken decades to create collapsed within a matter of months. In August 1914 no one could have imagined that ten years would pass before the war would end for most of the empire's population. The war was a violent orgy of apocalyptic proportions in which millions died. Under these conditions, programs, constitutions, and elections no longer seemed relevant. The war spawned men of violence who knew how to enlist chaos and anarchy to their cause. "He who accepts the class struggle cannot fail to accept civil wars, which in every class of society are the natural, and under certain conditions inevitable, continuation, development, and intensification of the class struggle." Thus wrote Lenin in September 1916, after the war had already destroyed all bulwarks of civilization. "To repudiate civil war, or to forget about it, is to fall into extreme opportunism and renounce the socialist revolution."[22] To Lenin, wars were abstractions and people mere numbers. They were all simply parts of that great game of violence where the reward was power. Just as the Bolsheviks needed the war because it suited their purposes as well as their nature, they also needed the defeat so that their planned upheaval could succeed.

Russia's armies were poorly equipped, and their soldiers were insufficiently trained. In the battles of attrition of the First World War, they were unable to withstand the superior German forces. Battles could only be won by those who possessed modern weaponry and supply lines to get rifles to their soldiers. Compared to the rest of the participants in this war, tsarist Russia was exceptionally badly off. Looking back after the revolution, General Aleksei Brusilov remembered the folly with which Russia had entered the war. No one had made preparations, and even within the first year of the war it had become clear to the generals that wars of such magnitude could only be endured by mobilizing "the entire people" in the struggle of life and death.[23] The war had brought crises, supply bottlenecks, and famines that were already strangling the metropolitan cities of the empire by 1915. In late 1916 violent strikes and hunger uprisings began to erupt in the cities, but the state authorities had no means of responding to them. In the end they even lost control over the undisciplined peasant soldiers in the city garrisons who were waiting to be sent to the front. At the same time, in Russia too a modern dictatorship of resource mobilization was developing in the course of the First World War. Its goal was to subjugate the interests of the population to those of the war. It sought to improve the production and distribution of armaments, and it put the administration at the service of the front. This command state, however, was not built on a Russian model but was instead a failed copy of the German war economy. And despite its best efforts, the tsarist war machine was never really able to cope with the millionfold deaths of its people or the destruction of its land.

The war revealed the extreme weakness of the foundation upon which the tsarist elites had based their rule. In sending its armies to the front, the existing order had deprived itself of its last means of local enforcement, and without armed and loyal soldiers in the cities, the elites had no protection against the people and their rage.[24] After the outbreak of the war nothing was the same as before. Where war was fought on Russian soil, nothing remained unscathed. Legions of soldiers were transported from the hinterland to the front, and millions of peasants were suddenly thrown into an alien world with no opportunity to adjust to the shocking realization that there was a world beyond their home villages. The war also opened up new spaces of communication and possibilities of movement. Under the circumstances of mass death, however, the peasants' experience was not just that of being part of a greater whole. More than that, they experienced the empire as a space of extreme violence—one in which survival meant knowing how to use a rifle. The societies of the multiethnic empire became societies of mistrust and violence, where the unarmed and unprotected could no longer rely on the state to protect them from the ravages of war. The world was coming apart at the seams. This was not simply the experience of the peasants in uniform, who had little idea of what to make of the war they had been sent to fight. For the civilian population, too, the war was a senseless theater of dread, featuring performances by squalid and undisciplined soldiers, foreign occupiers, deserters, and refugees.[25]

Russia was a land on the run. The exodus began during the second year of the war, when tsarist generals began cleansing the border regions of "unreliable" population groups suspected of collaborating with the enemy. The General Staff of the tsarist military dreamed of ordered and ethnically homogeneous zones that would be inhabited by Russians and Slavs and cleansed of Jews, Germans, and Gypsies. As they saw it, loyalty to the tsarist state was chiefly a matter of ethnic affiliation. Jews, Muslims, and Germans could not possibly be on their side, and by 1915, throughout the cities of the empire, the hunt for saboteurs and spies suspected of working for the enemy had begun.[26]

In withdrawing from Galicia in 1915, the tsarist army destroyed not only the infrastructure of the territory it left behind but also the living spaces of its inhabitants. Crops, cattle, and even bells from the village churches were destroyed. Ukrainian peasants were forced to join the retreating army and settle in villages where colonists of German descent had lived before the war. Galicia was ravaged by the terror regiment of Governor Bobrinsky, who had set about transforming the region into "Russian soil," by ordering the deportation of Ukrainian nationalists, Eastern Catholic bishops, and Germans to Siberia. Thousands of Jews fled to escape the fate of deportation, and those who stayed behind were taken "hostage." In early May 1915, all Jews living in Kaunas and

Courland were expelled for their alleged betrayal of the Russian army, and by summer, more than 200,000 Jews had left the region. When the issue was raised at the Council of Ministers, Foreign Minister Sazonov responded without hesitation: "They are traitors, and we are a Christian government." Jewish spies had supposedly infiltrated all levels of the administration and needed to "be annihilated." The Germans of Galicia could expect no mercy either, as Chief of Staff Yanushkevich, who pursued ethnic cleansing with particular zeal, had this human "waste" expelled from Galicia as well.[27]

Russia's cities were overwhelmed by the flood of soldiers and refugees. 750,000 Latvians alone had left their homes and fled to the interior of the tsarist empire. The administration could neither control nor channel the stream of refugees. Streets were clogged with masses of homeless people, bringing both military operations and the railway system to a standstill. By summer 1915, the governor of Volhynia saw no other option than to deploy Cossacks to combat the uncontrollable masses. According to the minister of agriculture, Krivoshein, Russia's future was bleak. It was a land of hundreds of thousands of starving people, all rags and tears, wiping out fields, clearing forests, and spreading panic like a swarm of locusts.

Wherever living conditions became unbearable, conflicts erupted between refugees, soldiers, and local residents. Jewish refugees suffered the most at the hands of frustrated peasant soldiers who routinely carried out armed attacks. In the Caucasus, bloody skirmishes ensued between Muslims and Armenian soldiers, who were fighting against the army of the Turkish sultan while wearing the uniform of the tsar. In larger cities, bloody conflicts broke out between Armenian refugees and Muslim peasants. Whenever the conditions deteriorated, the state authorities attempted to deport the refugees, which meant that conflicts were not resolved but simply displaced.

In some areas, the influx of refugees had a significant impact on the ethnic composition of the population. In August 1915 more than 250,000 Armenians, trying to escape the Turkish army, fled across the border into the largely Turkish Caucasus region of the tsarist empire. In early 1916 the small town of Yerevan was colonized by some 105,000 Armenian refugees; before 1915 it had contained a mere 30,000 (mostly Muslim) inhabitants. The tsarist government supported this population transfer since it considered the Christian Armenians allies in the struggle against the Ottoman Empire. But these population shifts also sowed discord and violence that, in the end, the tsarist state could no longer control. This was not least due to the fact that it left the task of managing the refugees up to the national committees of Latvians, Lithuanians, Armenians, and Poles. Rather than promoting peace, these committees served as further instruments of national mobilization,[28] and for them, refugees represented chaos and anarchy. Dreaded by the tsarist elites, the refugee was a synonym for cholera, typhus, and criminality. Male workers and soldiers in the large cities were known for their violent tendencies, and the prospect of uncontrolled mass migration elicited fear and panic among the educated and propertied.[29]

During the war, most of the empire's inhabitants were confronted with the very size and heterogeneity of the empire by way of their encounters with soldiers and refugees. The expulsions, the sermons of hate preached by the nationalists, and the competition for scarce goods also built up enormous tensions between different ethnic and religious groups. The conditions of war and misery allowed hatred, jealousy, and violence to thrive. Once the old order and its instruments of power had been destroyed by war and revolution, all the institutional and mental checks that might have prevented people from injuring and murdering one another were gone. Thus the First World War was also the midwife of aggressive nationalism, ethnic cleansing, and pogroms in Russia. Embodying the disorder and anarchy so feared by the tsar's generals and ministers, refugees and marauding soldiers became the visual representation of the erosion of the old order. And since refugees and marauders were neither workers nor peasants, neither nobility nor civilians, but were instead nomadic vagrants without any sort of ties, they were feared by the socialists too, who spoke of social classes but found themselves surrounded by human vagrancy.

REVOLUTIONS

The 1917 Revolution was a revolt of embittered people, brutalized by the war. Along with the old order, it drove the spirit of European civilization out of the land. In February 1917, when state authority collapsed, all the civilian checks and balances that even tsarist Russia had provided collapsed along with it. Governors, judicial authorities, organs of local self-administration, the parliament, and the constitution

were all washed away in the victory of the revolution. Russian liberalism's designs for reform were forever lost in a flood of peasant violence. In this sense the 1917 Revolution was an upheaval in keeping
with the peasant and worker conception of freedom. Liberals who had
once argued for the freedom of the people soon came to fear their
rage. Peasants and soldiers, who had once been nothing more than
subjugated persons, were now occupying public spaces and staging
spectacles of anarchic freedom in both the countryside and city. Publicly executed acts of violence humiliated the elites and inverted the
apartheid of the tsarist order. What took place in the 1917 Revolution
might be described as a symbolic turning upside down of the world.
The carnival of the people revealed to the elites that the cultural codes
of old were no longer valid and that there was not a thing the liberals
in the provisional government could do about it. No one understood
the hopelessness of the situation better than Vladimir Nabokov (father
of the prominent writer). Before the revolution he had belonged to the
central committee of the liberal Constitutional Democratic Party, and
in early 1917 he watched his world and that of his family collapse. He
no longer saw peasants in need of liberation and emancipation but
was instead indignant as he watched the "jaded and bestial faces" of
the peasant soldiers roaming the streets of Petrograd, boasting of their
unrestrained power.[30]

In some places, such as in the coal and steel regions of the Donbass,
workers exacted bloody revenge on factory managers, engineers, and
representatives of the state they blamed for their misery. Armed workers patrolled the streets, strung up policemen of the old regime, and
murdered thieves and hooligans.[31] By spring 1917, they had also taken
control of the local factories and mines so that the former masters were
forced to submit to the will of the workers and perform rituals of public humiliation. Managers and engineers who refused to obey this rule
could expect to be punished cruelly by the workers' own justice (*samo-
sud*). The streets were ruled by the tyranny of the people. Criminals
pilfered and looted, and there was absolutely nothing to contain the
exuberance of the violence. In Orenburg, a circus performance was
interrupted when soldiers spotted members of the old elite in the front
rows. They were unceremoniously driven out by the rioting soldiers,
who then continued on to the municipal police station, where they
stoned two policemen to death and then dragged their naked corpses

through the streets. Excesses in other cities generally followed the same pattern. Pogroms usually began with the looting of wine dealerships, after which the drunken soldiers would raid shops and homes and lynch passersby they deemed enemies. In this atmosphere of violence, everything was possible and everything was permissible. In spring 1917 the anarchist and brigand Nestor Makhno was released from the Petrograd prison by the provisional government and returned to his hometown in the Donbass. Upon arrival, Makhno proceeded to the local police department to search its records for the names of those who had betrayed him to the tsarist secret police ten years earlier. After tracking down one of his betrayers, he dragged him from his house and shot him in the street. Makhno's other betrayer, a priest, ended up decapitated. But this sort of violence no longer really surprised anyone anymore.[32] What had been punishable by law only a few months before was now normalcy. Violence had the final say, and no one except the violent perpetrators themselves were in a position to end it.

By spring 1917 the tsar's army had more or less fallen apart. State authority was now little more than an empty claim that the liberal ministers of the provisional government could declare but not enforce. No one understood this better than Lenin. As the Bolshevik leader declared after his return from exile, power lay in the streets. It was only a matter of seizing it. But who was to discipline the armed and brutal mass of soldiers? Who was to direct their rifle barrels at a target? Undisciplined soldiers in the cities were a security risk. They ignored their officers' orders and decided for themselves which directives they would follow. Officers were killed, humiliated, and degraded. Their epaulettes were ripped from their uniforms, and they were forced to submit to the orders of the soldiers' committees. Soldiers symbolically occupied the places of power in the garrisons and front line cities under their control. The educated and propertied were terrorized. This rage was an expression of the peasant soldiers' desire for a world without a state, landowners, taxes, or compulsory military service. Russia would henceforth belong to the peasants alone and be governed according to their fashion.[33]

In the summer of 1917 revolutionary violence found its way into the villages as well, as deserters and workers who had left the cities began storming the estates of the former elite. In places where peasants successfully expelled the landlords, the land was divided equally among the insurgents. The pastures and forests, meanwhile, were handed over to the land communes. Never before in Russia had there been such a large number of people bearing arms and exercising violence, who were not wearing the uniform or carrying the banner of the state. The revolution allowed the lower classes to loot estates and expel landlords. It also enabled workers to advance from their ghettoes into the city centers, conquer the public spaces, and force their rules upon what was left of society. From the perspective of the elite, this meant total disregard for the law. For the lower classes, however, the rule of law had only now been established.[34] This attitude was evident in the rhetoric of the workers and peasants, who portrayed the "bourgeoisie" as anyone who wore a suit or did not perform manual labor. The democracy that the soldiers, peasants, and workers spoke of was based on the exclusion of all non–working folk. Property owners were naturally excluded, as were the intellectuals who had been trying to educate the people with whom they had nothing in common. In 1917, throughout Russia workers' councils cropped up, espousing the notion that democracy was a system in which the working classes ruled over the propertied.[35] To the peasants, the state machinery was nothing more than a large village assembly that needed to be ruled by a "landlord." Even after the revolution peasants remained "monarchists," but their monarchism was based on village conceptions of justice.

The provisional government took no measures to restore state authority and was thus unable to avert the continuous decay of state power. Rather than delaying the collapse, it certified it by signing it into law. As late as summer 1917 the liberals and moderate socialists in the government still believed in their laws and constitutions, even after they had long since been annulled by reality. They insisted that only a constituent assembly could give them the authority to distribute land to the farmers, hand places of production over to workers, or negotiate peace with the Central Powers. In the summer of 1917 Fyodor Kokoshkin, a member of the Constitutional Democrats, was still insisting on restructuring the empire according to economic rather than ethnic principles because he considered it imperative that Russia remain a unified multiethnic empire. Although the peripheries of the empire had developed quite independently of Russia, the liberals still insisted that the future for the entire empire should be decided in a central parliament rather than at the regional level. The liberals and moderate socialists, too, continued to speak of constitutions and laws, even after all matters of import had long since been settled by the revolution in the streets.[36]

This was the hour of the Bolsheviks. At a time when no one else wanted it, they were prepared to seize power. How was it possible, though—not just for the Bolsheviks to seize power in October 1917 but also for them to retain it? Konstantin Teploukhov, who had served as a tax official in the state administration before the revolution, first became aware of the revolutionaries in April 1917, after Lenin's return to Russia. He wrote in his diary that members of a "new party" had arrived in Petrograd by train but made no further mention about who the Bolsheviks were or what they were up to.[37] Why did workers and soldiers follow a party whose leader was largely unknown in Russia and whose program promised a socialism that no one needed? Lenin and his supporters despised the Russia of "icons and cockroaches" (Trotsky) as well as what the ministers of the tsar had done. But they fancied themselves men of power and bearers of a new civilization, who were unwilling to settle for simply forcing obedience. Unlike the liberals and moderate socialists, however, they did not fear the people's rage but instead lent it a voice. The people's limitless violence was vindicated, and the constitutional experiment of the liberals was relegated to the "ash heap of history" (Trotsky) before it could even be tried out. When Lenin demanded in April 1917 that all power be transferred to the workers' councils, that workers assume control of the places of production, and that the demands of the peasants be satisfied, he played the violence of the streets against the lawfulness of the moderate parties in government.

Lenin and his radical followers found words for the discontent and the hatred that the lower classes felt for the old order and its elites. Anyone living in desperation and misery could understand their slogans, as the Bolshevik vocabulary was not taken from the dictionary of scholarly Marxism but from the handbook of violence. Lenin understood very well that the anger of the people was the key to achieving his goals. He and the other leading Bolsheviks spoke of cleansing the Russian soil of vermin and waste, or of ridding it of insects and bugs. They suggested that members of the tsarist elite be forced to wear yellow signs to mark them as the refuse of society. They legitimized the peasants' rage, and within a matter of weeks they were able to destroy what the tsarist bureaucracy had worked several decades to create.[38]

Amid war and economic precariousness the discontent of urban residents with the governing liberals and moderate socialists continued to grow. While the leaders spoke of freedom and socialism, the people saw nothing but poverty and arbitrariness. With chaos and anarchy as its midwives, the Bolshevik revolution promised to effect overnight what the previous government had only offered as a vague and distant prospect. But the self-proclaimed avant-garde of the proletariat did not win the people's respect by means of radical shibboleths alone. In the provinces, the new masters presented themselves, optically even, as advocates of unrestrained violence. They represented a cult of machismo and murdering, and the primitivism and viciousness of their language were designed to establish them as men of action. In contrast to the intellectualism of the moderate socialists, these revolutionaries wore heavy boots and leather jackets and exuded an aura of masculinity and determination. Georgy Pyatakov, who led the Bolshevik Party organization in Ukraine between 1917 and 1919, only ever appeared in public wearing a "long sheepskin," a rakish fur cap, and a revolver in his belt. One English journalist described Pyatakov as looking like one of the bandits out of a story by Shevchenko. Stalin, Voroshilov, Kaganovich, and all the other second-in-line Bolsheviks, who were more familiar with revolvers than with Marxism, presented themselves in much the same way.[39]

The Bolsheviks cultivated a style of violence that remained alien to the liberals and the educated. Although the latter had long sought to educate and enlighten the people, they had never been able to understand them. The power of the Bolsheviks, in contrast, rested on their firm belief in the power of the rifle. And that is why they triumphed over their socialist adversaries, even in places like the Donbass where workers and peasants were less interested in joining them and considered them "Jews" and "bourgeois." Under the conditions of war, power could only be exercised by those who were able to harness and direct the revolutionary storm with violence. In Voronezh the altercations between revolutionary groups lasted several months, and in the end the Bolsheviks prevailed, not because they had the most attractive political program, but because they were definitive about applying force. While their adversaries were busy looking for legislative solutions to their problems, the Bolsheviks were busy taking the streets. Resistance groups that did not resort to superior means of violence were no match for the Bolshevik terror.[40] Revolutionary Russia thus became the fulfillment of Carl Schmitt's dictum that in a state of emergency sovereignty rests in the hands of those who decide.[41]

The violent Bolshevik overthrow put an abrupt end to the democratic experiments of the liberals and socialists. The legitimacy of Bolshevik power was not to be found in a parliament but on the streets. Rather than trying to contain the outbursts of popular freedom (*narodnaia volia*), they legitimated them and in doing so secured their own victory. The new regime disbanded the tsarist judiciary and police. It issued decrees on peace and on land use, and it sanctioned the illegal seizure of land by the peasants. It offered the ethnic minorities of the empire the prospect of national self-determination. By December 1917 the regime had abolished private ownership of land and buildings. It declared that cities with more than ten thousand residents would no longer have any privately owned apartments at all, and in February 1918 the Bolsheviks began removing wealthy families from their homes and moving in unemployed proletarians and soldiers in their place. The city councils of all the major cities appointed "Housing Committees," which registered landlords and homeowners and then had them removed from their property.[42] The new era offered many new opportunities for workers and peasants, but for the old elite it meant the end of everything that had made life worth living.

The Bolsheviks were destroyers, and this was the source of their success. For the writer Zinaida Gippius, the months following the Bolshevik seizure of power were an unending nightmare. "We have already lived for so long," she wrote, "in the stream of official words—'crush,' 'smother,' 'annihilate,' 'grind to a pulp,' 'exterminate,' 'drown in blood,' 'drive into the grave' etc.—that the daily repetition of scurrilous curse words no longer makes an impression on us." Such raw violence was only possible because those who might have resisted it had become so famished and weakened by this time that all will to resist was gone.[43] Until summer 1918, the major cities where the Bolsheviks had seized power were actually ruled by lynch mobs. Aleksei Tatishchev, who had worked in the Ministry of Agriculture before the revolution, recalled that no one dared go into the streets of Petrograd in the evening, as the streets and empty squares were ruled by thieves. Random shootings, lootings, and attacks on all those tainted with the blemish of the "bour-geois" were daily occurrences in the early years of the Soviet rule. A visitor from Switzerland described the revolutionary guards in the district of Kherson as "drunk and armed to the teeth," busy looting stores and stealing food. In some regions pogroms broke out. In September 1917, in the small southern Russian town of Bakhmut, a mob raided liquor stores and then killed the Jews in the town. On December 17 violence broke out in Orenburg, after soldiers and workers had raided the municipal wine and liquor reserves and stolen several thousand liters of alcohol. For days the drunken mob rioted in the streets, setting houses on fire and causing some two hundred deaths. In the large Caucasian cities of Tiflis, Baku, and Yerevan, the revolution was largely a bloody interethnic conflict, which depended on either killing or deporting the enemy group. In Central Asia, bloody clashes between Russian and Ukrainian settlers and Muslim nomads ensued, after the power vacuum created by the revolution had been exploited to establish a system of authority based on ethnicity.[44] In the empire's remote spaces, ruthless violent perpetrators could injure and kill with impunity. The practice of unrestrained violence destroyed and changed the lives of everyone involved because no one could escape the forces of this war that had crossed all boundaries. Excess became a way of life.

The revolution unleashed no small amount of senseless violence. In light of this, wrote Maxim Gorky, he wanted to hear nothing more about the intelligentsia's supposed love of the people: "I say frankly that those who speak grandiloquently of their love for the people have always aroused me in a feeling of distrust and suspicion. I ask myself, I ask them: Do they really love those peasants who, swilling vodka until they become savage, kick their pregnant wives in the stomach? Those peasants who waste several thousand poods of grain making 'moon-shine,' and leave those who love them to perish from hunger? ... Those peasants who even bury each other alive, who stage bloody mob trials in the streets, who look down with glee when a man is beaten to death or drowned in the river?" The people did not need to be loved; they needed to be enlightened. They needed to be taught how to be more "human." "I do not," Gorky concluded, "love the people."[45]

Even during the Revolution of 1905 the radical intelligentsia of Social Revolutionaries, anarchists, and Bolsheviks had engaged psychopaths, criminals, and thieves to carry out muggings, raids, and assassinations against representatives of the tsarist state. The struggle demanded men of action, not lofty theoreticians, and this call for men of action had the effect of turning violence into an end in itself. Soon, violence was the only thing that united the extremist intelligentsia and the popular rage. The Russian revolution was an earthquake, wrote the historian and liberal politician Pavel Miliukov, an earthquake in which Russia's thin veneer of civilization was destroyed:

> For, in spite of the ultra-modern content of the programs, labels, and slogans of this revolution, its inner reality has disclosed the intimate and indissoluble bonds which tie it to the whole of Russia's past. The Russian Revolution is like some mighty geological eruption which playfully throws off the thin crust of latter-day civilizations and violently hauls to the surface those remnants of long-hidden and long-gone epochs of terrestrial history which dimly recall the past. . . . Lenin and Trotsky, in the eyes of such students, are leading a movement much closer to those of Bolotnikov, Razin and Pugachev—that is, to the seventeenth and eighteenth centuries—than to the latest fashions of European anarcho-syndicalism.[46]

Ultimately, though, the Bolsheviks knew better than anyone that, without popular consent, the foundations of their rule were shaky at best. Although they feared the people no less than their tsarist predecessors, they had fewer scruples about using excessive violence to quell opposition. The Bolsheviks were weak, and this is why they resorted so frequently to violence—with neither pause nor reservation. This strategy, however, could only succeed under the conditions of war, and for that reason the Bolsheviks made war into a way of life. Had the Civil War not occurred, the Bolsheviks would have needed to declare a war in order to justify their practices. The Civil War was a conflict that required complete annihilation of the enemy. For Lenin and Trotsky, the military defeat of the Whites and the peasants was not enough. And they were not alone with this view. When it came to unscrupulousness, to the propensity for violence, and to the willingness to match the rhetoric of annihilation with action, the Bolsheviks far outmatched all other participants in the Civil War. Their victory was a victory of annihilation, and it left behind scorched earth and devastation, both material and psychological. The Bolsheviks prevailed, not because they offered the most attractive political program but because they were the most violent. And in the end, the starving weakened population apathetically abandoned itself to their madness. Only someone who views the revolution and the Civil War as a conflict about how to achieve the best possible world will struggle to understand why the Bolsheviks were victorious.

CIVIL WARS

In the chaotic spaces of violence the counterrevolution was also given the opportunity to arm itself for war. In summer 1918 the military resistance of the old elite, headed by the tsarist generals, Kornilov and Alekseyev, gathered in the south of Russia. A government in exile under the leadership of Socialist Revolutionaries and moderate socialists was founded in Samara, on the Volga. In the industrial cities, famished and discontented workers, disappointed by the promises of the revolution, began to strike for better living conditions. Ultimately the Bolsheviks triumphed, but their victory was a fragile one, and it rested more on the weakness of their opponents than on their own strength. The soldiers of the Red Army were poorly trained, and supplies were lacking. Even in the first year of the Civil War the forcibly recruited peasants deserted in large numbers whenever the opportunity arose.[47] And since the new power holders were requisitioning grain in the villages to feed the cities and the army they could no longer depend on the loyalty of those left in the countryside either. Barely a year into the Civil War, peasant unrest had broken out in several regions, at times seeming to call the Red Army's effort into question altogether. Had it not been for the political incompetence of the White generals and had several former tsarist officers not defected to the Bolsheviks, it is doubtful whether the Red Army would have survived even the first few months of the war.

Although the Whites were militarily superior to the Reds they failed to exploit this advantage. The Civil War was not so much about fighting battles as it was about depleting the enemy's resources. The warfare was mobile, and since there was no front, success meant preventing the civilian population from aiding the opponent. This could be achieved by terrorizing the civilians and spreading fear and dread among them; in this arena the Bolsheviks were clearly superior. The counterrevolutionary camp was also plagued by chronic internal disunity and a lack of clear ideas. Not even its generals could agree on a common strategy, and their military prowess ultimately came to naught. The Whites had nothing to offer the peasants and ethnic minorities of the empire either. Their commitment to a "unified and indivisible Russia" and the restoration of prerevolutionary property ownership did nothing to help their cause among the peasants, and without peasant support, neither a military nor a moral victory against the Reds was possible. The counterrevolution was not directed against the Bolsheviks alone. The Whites also had to contend with the peasant bands of the partisan leader, Makhno, and with the Bashkir regiments of Ahmet-Zaki Validov, who had defected to the Bolsheviks in the second year of the war. But military reasons alone did not doom the Whites. From the very beginning they had been crippled by the mistrust of the peasants, who feared that a White victory would restore the rule of the landlords.[48]

While the Civil War was producing nothing but violence, misery, and death the Bolsheviks were promising paradise on earth. In his 1917 brochure, *State and Revolution,* Lenin himself had predicted the impending dawn of the classless society. While he spun fantasies about the dictatorship of the proletariat and the withering away of the state apparatus and the rule of law, he made no mention of how such programs were to be implemented. The economy would be organized on the "example of the post office," and once the communists had crushed all opposition the state apparatus would be restricted to essential repressive functions. "The whole of society" was to "become a single office and a single factory, with equality of labor and equality of pay." Lenin was convinced that under communism, "any person in mastery of the four rules of arithmetic and able to issue the appropriate receipts" would be able to participate in the public administration. The classless society would not need an apparatus of repression. It would also not need law or a judiciary because there would no longer be any reason to punish deviant behavior. The law, after all, was nothing more than a reflection of power relations, and it too would become obsolete once the causes of social inequality had been eradicated. For Lenin, the law was merely an instrument of state repression, manipulated at will by those in power to crush their enemies. The possibility that the law might also have a protective function did not factor into Lenin's equation.[49]

In all probability, neither Lenin nor his followers believed that the promises of *State and Revolution* or any of Bolshevism's other doctrinal scriptures were truly plausible. Death and decay were, after all, the opposites of abundance and prosperity. And yet, their thoughts and actions were informed by the belief in the limitlessness of possibilities and the controllability of circumstances. This justified their violent acts and gave them meaning. To them, violent acts were like surgical procedures, intended to heal a diseased system. Although this may appear absurd to a present-day individual, to Lenin and his followers these were acts of higher insight. They were rational because they fulfilled self-formulated premises.

The new power holders saw the world differently than many of their contemporaries. To them, economic crises, discontent, and criticism were the work of enemies; and without these enemies none of these things would exist. The task of the revolution was to expose the enemy and rid the world of him forever. Those in power could justify every act of violence by invoking the "laws" of History, on whose behalf they claimed to be acting. The Civil War had provided them with an opportunity to differentiate between friend and foe, prosecute a life-and-death struggle between imagined classes, and also stage this struggle as the decisive battle between the forces of light and darkness. The Civil War was the dress rehearsal for Stalinism. It was an experimental ground upon which the Bolsheviks could both realize their delusions of a socially "purified" world and also deploy men of violence. It was Stalinism before the fact.[50]

The counterrevolutionary violence, meanwhile, was hardly less cruel. In spring 1918, the German occupiers helped the old elites in Ukraine regain control of the land. In the industrial settlements of the Donbass, the officers of Hetman Skoropadsky took revenge on rebellious peasants who had expelled factory directors, managers, and engineers one year earlier. More than eight thousand workers were killed by counterrevolutionary forces in the settlement of Shakhty alone (either shot or beaten to death). In spring 1919, when White soldiers under the leadership of General Denikin marched into the region, they too showed no mercy to the communists and rebellious workers; they had several hundred of them either shot or lynched to deter future uprisings.

A similar fate befell the peasants who had expropriated land during the revolution. Under the supervision of German soldiers, White officers subjected rebellious peasants to the customary prerevolutionary practice of whipping. An eyewitness recalled how peasants near Samara were terrorized by White officers, who had returned in May 1919 in their uniforms, demanding their land and property back.

The peasants were driven before the staff and told that they would need to return all the property they had taken from the estate immediately. The peasants would not have been able to do that, not by any stretch of the imagination: a lot of water had flowed down the mountain in two years. Then they began to arrest them, condemn them, shoot them, torture them. . . . After a few days the entire estate had been burned to the ground. As retaliation, the staff gave orders to raze the entire village, and within three hours all that remained of a once flourishing village with 10,000 inhabitants were two, three houses and thousands of orphans.[51]

In the second half of 1919, as the Volunteer Army withdrew into southern Russia, its soldiers began massacring the Jews living there. Before it was all over several tens of thousands of Jews had lost their lives. The peasant bands, led by Nestor Makhno and Ataman Symon Petliura (which opposed both the Reds and the Whites) also took to murdering the Jews, simply because such pogroms promised easy victories and rich bounty. The White terror was fragmented, and its intensity and purpose depended on the person in command. Apart from their shared hatred of the Communists, there was little to unify the leaders of the White movement. There was neither a White government nor a White political program, and none of the numerous White leaders were able to muster the necessary authority to subject the warlords and Cossack atamans in Siberia, Ciscaucasia, and Ukraine to any sort of central control. In this sense, what can be referred to as the White terror was really just a great anarchic pogrom—one that did not even have the pretense of serving higher aims.[52] Although there was much to fight against, there was rarely anything to fight for.

The Red terror preceded the White terror. Although it purported to be a matter of self-defense it was not. The Bolshevik violence was not just directed against actual enemies either. It also targeted the social groups that the Bolsheviks had deemed lepers. This included the nobility, landowners, officers, priests, Cossacks, and kulaks. For the Bolsheviks, it was irrelevant how the actual members of these groups viewed themselves and whether or not they supported the revolution. Ultimately the enemy existed in the minds of the Bolsheviks alone, and this is why the terror was able to grow to such excessive and monstrous proportions. The Bolsheviks represented a new style of justice that held law and civil liberty in contempt and that made its appearances in the revolutionary tribunals instead. The tribunals provided the Bolsheviks with a forum where they could expound on their worldview and on their notions of values, and also where the friends and enemies of the people were identified. The tribunals were stages, and both the accusers and the accused were actors in a play in which the actual questions of crime and punishment had no relevance.[53] It was not about serving justice or enforcing the law. It was about stigmatizing the enemy.

Still, the vengeful justice of the revolutionary tribunals did not always serve Bolshevik purposes. The power holders found naked terror to be a better method of combating their purported enemies, and in December 1917 the Cheka was founded for this purpose. Grigory Zinoviev, the Petrograd party leader and member of the ruling circle, explained in a September 1918 interview in the newspaper *Severnaia Kommuna* (The Northern Commune) how the terror was to play out: "In order to overcome our enemies, we need our own socialist militarism. Of the one hundred million people living in Russia, we must take 90 million with us. As for the rest, we have nothing to say to them, they must be annihilated." Shortly thereafter, in November 1918, Martin Latsis, one of the deputies of Cheka leader Felix Dzerzhinsky, published an article in the journal *Krasny Terror* (The Red Terror), in which he explained what the future could be expected to bring: "We are not waging war against individual persons. We are exterminating the bourgeoisie as a class. During the investigation, do not look for evidence that the accused acted in deed or word against Soviet power. The first questions that you ought to put are: To what class does he belong? What is his origin? What is his education or profession? And it is these questions that ought to determine the fate of the accused. In this lies the significance and essence of the Red Terror."[54]

Latsis spoke the language of the Bolshevik terrorists. At the same time he anticipated the Stalinist creed that it must be the task of the revolution to exterminate enemies like weeds and rid the social body of vermin. For the Russian revolutionaries, human happiness became tied to the physical annihilation of human beings, and this is where the totalitarian desire to reorder the world through murderous violence was born. In this sense, the Bolsheviks were the first to incorporate state-organized mass murder into the practice of modern politics. It was first applied during the Russian Civil War. Although people may have been inflicting violence on one another since time immemorial, now it was no longer confined to the theater of war but had instead become an instrument of state intervention.

The terror began immediately after the October overthrow. In November 1917 the Constitutional Democrats were outlawed, and in early January 1918 Red Guard sailors attacked and brutally murdered the prominent liberal politicians Andrei Shingarev and Fedor Kokoshkin, while they lay in their hospital beds. Within months the Bolsheviks had widened the scope of their terror to include striking workers and rebellious peasants. All resisters were arrested and shot. Not even the Socialist Revolutionary people's commissar of justice, Isaac Steinberg, understood what purpose the terror was supposed to be serving. "Why do we bother with the Commissariat of Justice at all?" he asked. "Let's call it frankly the 'Commissariat of Social Extermination' and be done with it." Lenin did not appreciate such criticism. His revolution served the cause of annihilation, and "social extermination" was thus the sole task of the People's Commissariat of Justice.[55]

It was not until the late summer of 1918, however, after Socialist Revolutionaries had attempted to assassinate Lenin and Moisei Uritsky, head of the Cheka in Petrograd, that the terror began to reach truly monstrous proportions. Although the assassins had come from the ranks of the Socialist Revolutionaries, the Cheka sought revenge in September 1918 by killing members of the former elite. Every time resistance flared up, innocent people were taken hostage and shot. In the same month the government ordered the Cheka to set up concentration camps (*kontslager*) where "class enemies" and "members of White Guard organizations" would be detained.[56] Such was the mindset of people who were fighting a war not against individuals but against abstract collectivities. The class did not belong to the individual; the individual belonged to his class. Above all stood the will to power. The Bolsheviks knew that their power rested on their ability to spread fear and dread, and this meant making sure that everyone knew they could be arrested or killed at any time. Under the circumstances of fear and dread, all safeguards and relationships of trust that enable people to live with each other in society were ripped apart. The state of emergency was elevated to a governing principle, and in the process power was totalized.

In September 1918 in Moscow, twenty-five former tsarist ministers and higher officials were shot along with 765 so-called "White

Guards." The list with the names of the victims was signed by Lenin himself. In Kursk, a Duma delegate, the local marshal of the nobility, all former police officers, and all employees of the local government were executed by the Cheka. Soon thereafter the regime extended its murder campaign to other cities.[57] After the withdrawal of White forces from southern Russia and the Urals in the second half of 1919, the Bolshevik commissars began with the systematic persecution of "former people" there as well. White Army officers, nobility, and members of the middle classes were registered and shot. Thousands lost their lives in the Cheka's summary shootings in the cities of Odessa, Kiev, Rostov-on-Don, on the Crimean peninsula, and in the Urals. On the Crimean peninsula the Civil War drew to a close in a drama of apocalyptic proportions. In early summer 1920 more than 200,000 people gathered there during the retreat of the collapsing White army, hoping to find refuge from the advancing Bolsheviks. Not everyone was able to escape across the Black Sea, however, and some 50,000 refugees who stayed behind were murdered by the victors. Sevastopol would be remembered by the survivors as the "city of the hanged." According to Mikhail Frunze, Trotsky's successor as war commissar, the services that the Cheka performed here were indispensable. The Chekist Yefim Yevdokimov, whose unit killed 12,000 people within a few days, was nominated by Frunze to receive a decoration.[58]

The political leadership in Moscow made certain that there were no doubts about the authorship of the terror. The Bolsheviks admitted their actions openly. They celebrated their killings in the Communist press and published the names of their victims. When it came to the annihilation of enemies, Lenin demanded top performance from his henchmen in the Cheka. In August 1918, as civil unrest mounted in the province of Nizhny Novgorod, Lenin sent the chairman of the local executive committee a telegram that contained detailed instructions for dealing with the discontent. The chairman was to establish a dictatorship, "introduce mass terror," and have "hundreds of prostitutes shot and deported." Those in possession of weapons needed to be killed outright, and "Mensheviks and unreliable elements" were to be removed from the region as well. The local Cheka acted without delay, immediately killing forty officers, state officials, and priests, and taking an additional seven hundred "former people" hostage. Lenin had no reservations about using terror to solve military problems either. In order to ward off the White General Yudenich's advance on Petrograd, he said, it would be necessary to place ten thousand "bourgeois" in front of the workers' machine guns and have several hundred of them shot. In summer 1918, as Turkish troops were advancing toward Baku, Lenin ordered the local Bolsheviks to burn the city to the ground as a preventative measure, in case the enemy tried to take the city. The fate of the civilian population was not discussed. To Lenin it was likely of little concern.[59]

Lenin was a malevolent armchair criminal, to whom human tragedy, suffering, and misery were of no consequence. He was not, however, a cynic whose only interest lay in maintaining power. On the contrary, he had a vision of how things should be and was willing to fight to have this vision realized. As Lenin saw it, the Bolsheviks were on a crusade. They were warriors of faith on a holy mission, and they would enforce the will of History without mercy or pity. Nobody represented their violent style in such an uncompromising manner as Felix Dzerzhinsky, a Polish nobleman who had spent many years in tsarist prisons before becoming director of the Cheka. The "Iron Felix" saw himself as a "proletarian Jacobin" in the service of the revolution. The German Expressionist Arthur Holitscher, who traveled to Russia in 1920, planning to experience the exhilaration of communism, described the "Iron Felix" as someone who could accomplish "the appalling yet unavoidably necessary," and knew how to dispose of "human waste."[60] Dzerzhinsky had no scruples when it came to killing people in the name of the revolution. On a single day in January 1920 he sent more than sixty people to their deaths with the single stroke of a pen, by signing a list with the names and "sentences" of some seventy-seven supposed "counterrevolutionaries." Soon thereafter, in September 1920 he sent a telegram to Oryol, ordering the execution of thirty-one hostages held by the local Cheka.[61] If someone were to have called him an unscrupulous murderer, it is likely that he would not have even understood.

Of course a regime claiming to be carrying out the will of the people could not dispense with helpers and enforcers. The government could not be expected to manage the task of identifying and annihilating enemies all on its own. This was a task of universal concern, and only when this was recognized would the revolution truly become embedded in the consciousness of the subjects. "We must," demanded Nikolai Bukharin, "now all become agents of the Cheka."[62] All good

Communists needed to perform the honorable service of denouncing their neighbors. It was the Bolshevik experience of isolation, of being encircled by hostile forces, and of standing perpetually on the brink of disaster that lent plausibility to the delusions of persecution and spy mania in the first place. In the space of violence created by the Civil War, people only encountered each other under conditions framed by violence. All those required to move within this space of violence had no choice but to respond to it. Without the experience of the Civil War there would have been no Stalinism.

The Red terror combined obsessions and delusions with the lust for violence, and the Chekists were the embodiment of this synthesis, brutalized sailors and soldiers with a limitless hatred for people who wore glasses, read books, believed in liberalism, and were well nourished. Drawing from the ranks of criminals, hooligans, and the mentally ill, the Cheka and its auxiliary forces consisted of people who were incapable of conceiving of a world that was not a perpetual spectacle of violence. By early 1918 at the latest the Bolsheviks had already begun to show what sort of brutality they were capable of. In Yevpatoria, a small town near the Black Sea, the Bolshevik party secretary collected a list of all former tsarist army officers and members of the "bourgeoisie." The list was then handed over to the sailors stationed in Yevpatoria, who drowned their victims in the ocean and cut off their ears, noses, and genitalia. Elsewhere, orchestras provided the soldiers of the revolution with musical accompaniment while they murdered their victims. In Kharkov, the Cheka chairman, Sayenko, not only selected the victims himself but also made a point of torturing and shooting them personally. He also had the habit of numbing himself with alcohol and cocaine before satisfying his murderous desires. Everywhere, violence was becoming an end in itself, detached from the purposes it was supposed to be serving. The conceivable had become the feasible, and no one who killed or tortured had any reason to fear punishment. Victims were scalded in boiling water, skinned, impaled, burned, and buried alive. They were driven naked into the streets in the middle of winter and doused with water until they became frozen pillars of ice. In Pensa, the chairman of the Cheka, who happened to be mentally ill, had his victims sewn into bags before they were thrown into ice holes.[63] In Kamensk, a settlement east of Lugansk, Red Guards who had captured White officers hacked them to pieces with their sabers. As one foreign observer recalled, the faces of the abused officers were transformed into a "mass of bloody flesh."[64] While workers and Bolsheviks found common ground in the violence, no one ever reached agreement on what the actual purpose of this feast of cruelty was supposed to be.

The Red victory took place under circumstances that provided the Bolsheviks with a constant supply of new enemies. By early 1918, nothing remained of the factory committees that had been expressions of worker control. Bankruptcies, spiraling inflation, and the deadlock in production had turned worker control of the factories into a blunt sword. Where nothing was produced, nothing could be controlled either. The Bolshevik government countered the economic catastrophe by placing factories in the hands of the state and centralizing the regulation of trade. Lenin and his followers were apparently convinced that the people could only be taken care of and that the land could only be controlled if all goods were centrally distributed. Free trade was prohibited, and the chain of vital supplies to the cities was interrupted. Meanwhile, the promise of central delivery went unfulfilled, as the peasants refused to yield their surplus grain to the requisitioning commandos that had been dispatched to the villages. There was no escaping the misery.[65]

Wherever the suffering became unbearable, workers and peasants turned their backs on the city and fled to the villages. From spring 1918 onwards, tens of thousands abandoned the metropolises and industrial cities of central Russia and returned to their home villages. In 1918 alone, Petrograd lost 850,000 people, more than half the city's population. Moscow forfeited 40 percent of its population during the Civil War. Those without village ties and thus with no other choice stayed behind in the city, where theft and black market dealings were the only means of avoiding starvation. Discipline in the workplace deteriorated too, as workers were primarily occupied with ensuring their own survival. Some factories were dismantled completely by thieving workers, who took what they considered to be rightfully theirs. "In Samara," recalled a member of an American aid organization,

> the conscripts of the Red Army conceived the idea that as soon as their barracks became uninhabitable they would be demobilized and sent home. They, thereupon, systematically and thoroughly wrecked every structure in which they were successively quartered. During the bleak

days of war communism, fuel was as scarce as food and half frozen people searched for unoccupied or unguarded buildings from which to get wood. Floors, doors, even roof-beams disappeared miraculously, and soon the houses collapsed, completely wrecked. . . . Emaciation, deformity from hunger, filth and disease were, of course, everywhere.

In many places production came to a standstill and the settlements became desolate. "In the factories," recalled one worker from the region, "stray dogs looked for shelter from bad weather. Wolves lived below the roofs. The ovens were cold, there was no fuel. Garbage, piles of bricks and rusted iron collected in front of the factory gates." The grain requisitions and the prohibition on free trade were thus virtually suicidal for the Bolsheviks and placed their control of the country in serious jeopardy. Had it not been for the "sack people"—peasants who procured wares from the villages and then sold them in the cities—the city dwellers would have starved.[66]

Unbearable living conditions bred discontent and protest, especially among the urban working classes. In some cities the outlawed Mensheviks had even been able to regain the majority in the local soviets. The Bolsheviks responded to this threat with violence. They had the newspapers of the oppositional socialists banned and dissolved the soviets in which the majority situation had changed to their disadvantage. Though the regime was able to suppress its political opponents, it could not silence the workers' protests in the same manner. In March 1919 ten thousand workers at the Putilov factories in Petrograd went on strike. Their ringleaders were no longer open to compromise. They called for an end, not only to the dictatorship, but also to the system of "serfdom" under which the workers had allegedly been subjugated. As the situation spiraled out of control, Lenin, accompanied by the Petrograd party chief Grigory Zinoviev, began visiting the factories personally. It was Lenin's first time speaking to the workers he was accustomed to only reading about in books. His speech, however, was drowned out by howls of protest. In the end, armored cars and armed Cheka units were dispatched to the working-class districts. Two hundred strike leaders were shot without trial, and hundreds of workers were arrested. In Astrakhan, where similar protests had broken out, striking workers were massacred. Sergei Kirov, the military commissar in charge, ordered his troops to pacify the city and crush the protests, and ultimately more than three thousand workers were either shot or drowned in the Volga by the soldiery.[67]

The Bolsheviks could have resolved this crisis by restoring the free market. They could have reversed the state appropriation of trade and industry. They could have ended the violent grain requisitions. They could also have broken with the system of war communism and tried to produce loyalty that was of a voluntary nature. But those in power would have none of it. Instead, they resorted to coercion and terror to solve the problems they had created. They demanded that insubordinate workers be coerced into behaving in a manner that was fitting for good proletarians. It was, after all, in the name of the proletariat that the Bolsheviks had seized power, and it was in the name of the proletariat that they were trying to deliver humanity from its suffering. This modern working-class messiah, however, had not yet shaken his "Russian" flaws. The proletariat was not only hungry; it was unruly and uneducated too. To Lenin and Trotsky, Russian workers were backward, barbaric creatures, tainted by village culture. They required iron discipline if they were to be liberated from this village backwardness and become modern, class-conscious proletarians. That was why workers who had not yet grasped their true historical identity needed to be, not just represented, but also educated and trained.

As the Civil War drew to a close, the radical Bolsheviks were given the chance to combine their concept of socialism in the barracks with other, more pragmatic considerations. Vast numbers of soldiers would be returning home from the revolution, but nobody knew what was to become of them. Trotsky recommended militarizing the workforce and tying the workers to their places of production. The thought was that military-style command would result in maximum output. As military leader of the revolution, Trotsky dreamed of army regiments that would be organized into production units, an idea that had already been tried unsuccessfully in the early 1800s by the tsarist war minister, Arakcheyev. The workers were supposed to be the soldiers of socialism, who would provide for themselves and win battles on the production front. In this vision, civil institutions no longer had any right to exist but would instead be subordinated to the War Commissariat, which would deploy workers' armies and subjugate them to central control. Workers who deserted the production front would be deported to punishment battalions or concentration camps. Trotsky's radicalism did not, however, remained unopposed. It was of particular concern to the trade union functionaries among the Bolsheviks, who feared that a militarization of labor might resurrect the spirit of slavery, which the workers' revolution was supposed to have abolished. Trotsky's response to this criticism was to call it "the most pathetic and miserable liberal prejudice." The slave economy had been productive in its time, and under Russian conditions, it had been indispensable.[68]

In the end, Trotsky's visions were destroyed by the very circumstances under which they were supposed to be realized. It was indeed possible to transform army regiments into labor units that harvested lumber and built roads—the demobilized soldiers had little else available to them—but when it came to turning nonmilitary workers and peasants into slaves the project failed. And here, as was so often the case, violence had the final say. In early 1920 Trotsky gave orders to impose martial law on all railroads and to bring every railroad worker in violation of workplace disciplinary regulations before a revolutionary tribunal. Between February and July 1920 alone 3,666 railroad workers and employees were condemned by these tribunals.

In the industrial cities of Russia the prisons were filling with workers. In the workplace too the Red terror now reigned. Chekists monitored production in the factories and arrested anyone refusing to bow to the directives of the regime. In summer 1920 and February 1921, when workers again went on strike and the sailors of Fort Kronstadt revolted at the gates of Petrograd, the regime showed no restraint in the use of crushing force. It deployed the military and had thousands of workers deported to concentration camps. In summer 1920 the Cheka had the leadership elite of the Mensheviks arrested, and their party ceased to exist. There was no reason for the soldiers at Fort Kronstadt to expect leniency either. In March 1921 Lenin ordered the storming of the fort, and soon thereafter more than two thousand sailors were shot without trial under the authority of the Petrograd party chief, Zinoviev. Insurgents who survived the massacre were hauled off to a concentration camp on the Solovetsky Islands.[69]

The future of the Bolshevik order would be decided in the countryside, for no one could triumph in this power struggle without the resources of the land. Control of the village meant access to recruits and provisions. From the very beginning, the Bolsheviks had used violence to force peasants into their armies and relieve them of their grain, which was needed for the cities. The Bolsheviks were in desperate need of allies, though, and without peasant collaboration and support they could not hope to succeed. They also believed that their world of social conflicts and rich-versus-poor antagonisms figured in the Russian village as well. This led them to the idea of pitting the poorer peasants against their richer neighbors. The problem, however, was that the social categories the Bolsheviks used to order their environment did not apply to the village. Here, patriarchal bonds were stronger than any divisions created by social disparities. Wealthy peasants were not just feared, but they were protectors and mediators too, and they represented the village in the outside world. Kulaks were indeed more powerful than poor peasants, but they did not simply oppress the poor with this power. Peasants were interconnected in a multitude of ways, as this had been crucial to their survival. The problem with joining the Bolshevik class struggle was that it sought to destroy the very thing that was necessary for survival in the eyes of the village dwellers. In the world of the peasants, the class struggle simply made no sense, and accordingly only a minute number of peasants heeded the Bolshevik call to rise up against the kulaks. Committees of Poor Peasants were enlisted to help the Bolsheviks in staging class struggle in the village. Often, though, they had to be staffed by imported agricultural workers or city dwellers, who had nothing to lose by opposing the village community. As is usual in wartime, this was the hour of the adventurer and the soldier of fortune—those who were prepared to do the things that others merely dreamed of. Some committees were thus nothing more than bands of robbers who preyed on peasant villages and terrorized their residents.[70]

The Bolshevik state was weak. It required campaigns to make its presence in the village noticed at all. When the state needed to break resistance and extort obedience, it resorted once again to the well-proven instrument of terror. Cheka units and worker brigades raided villages and forced peasants to hand over their surplus grain. The requisitioning, which began in winter 1918, was pursued with particular zeal in the central Volga region, especially in the Saratov, Samara and Pensa provinces. Following the victory over the Whites in 1919 the requisitioning campaigns also extended into the Black Earth Region. Nowhere did the raids follow any sort of predictable pattern. The requisition brigades took whatever they could from the peasants. Sometimes this meant not just their entire harvest of grain, but their seeds as well. As a peasant from the Yekaterinburg province wrote to his son in the summer of 1920, "Life really is in complete disarray, the people are being tormented by the damned Communists." Almost all the peasants here tried to escape hunger by fleeing to the city of Kazan, only to be "mugged" by the Communists on the streets. The brigades spread fear and dread wherever they went. Peasants were whipped, and their children and wives were taken hostage, in an effort to squeeze every last reserve out of the villages. Lenin himself issued detailed instructions on how local party leaders were to deal with unruly peasants. In August 1918 his advice was to have "at least hundred notorious kulaks, wealthy bloodsuckers hanged" in public, "within a radius of one hundred versts." This is how Soviet power was to show the peasants that it was well versed in cruel punishment.[71]

The peasants had nothing to lose, and wherever hunger had not yet broken their resistance, they fought the terror. In spring 1919 in Ukraine and in the provinces of Samara, Pensa, and Simbirsk, peasants and Cossacks revolted against Bolshevik rule. Between 1918 and 1920 more than twenty thousand Bolshevik activists and functionaries died at the hands of the rebels. The peasants repaid their enemies brutally, as they felt compelled to demonstrate that village punishment could be just as cruel. Communists were ambushed and bestially killed: they were crucified, buried alive, or torn to pieces. In Ukraine and in the central Volga Region requisition brigades no longer dared enter the villages without armed escorts. It would be autumn 1920, though, before the rebellions would develop into peasant wars. In the steppes of southern Ukraine, de facto authority rested in the hands of peasant leaders and warlords like Nestor Makhno. At the pinnacle of their military success, Makhno's bands could count more than fifteen thousand gunmen. Hundreds of small peasant armies also sprang up in the provinces of Voronezh, Saratov, Samara, Simbirsk, and Pensa, driving fear into the hearts of the Communists there. In the province of Tambov the rebellion led by the outlaw Alexander Antonov became a conflagration that spread into the steppe region to the north of the Caucasus mountains and into western Siberia, where at one point more than sixty thousand peasants were bearing arms.

Without deserters and defectors from the Red Army, however, the military successes of the peasant armies would have been impossible. They supplied the insurgents with both weapons and military knowledge. The peasants operated under cover of the villages, and they could go from being peasants to soldiers and then back to peasants again whenever they pleased. They were also intimately familiar with the terrain, while the enemy troops were still trying to find their bearings. When the rebellions began, many Communist functionaries fled the villages in panic. In the Tambov region some local officials even defected to the peasants. Most importantly, however, once a peasant had joined a rebel band, he had little choice but to continue fighting. Surrender would have meant death at the hands of the Communists, and desertion would have meant death at the hands of his own people. Soldiers have a home country that they can retreat to, whereas partisans have nowhere to go. The peasants engaged in war thus had no choice but to continue fighting. Under such desperate circumstances the Red commanders' attempts at retaking the villages were destined to fail.[72]

Neither Reds nor Whites could boast of any victories in the war with the peasants. The peasant revolt was based on the village conception of freedom—that is, free access to land and freedom from the state and its officials. In this scheme the Bolsheviks represented the counterrevolution too. "Long live the Bolsheviks! Death to the Communists," "Long live Soviet power! Down with the Bolsheviks and the Jews!"—such slogans could now be heard. Many peasants were firmly convinced that communism and Bolshevism were opposites, for one was associated with divine promises and the other was associated with the bitter reality of repression.[73]

Still, the work of the rebels was not confined to wreaking vengeance on their tormentors or killing them in gruesome ways. It also involved the destruction of bridges, railroads, and telegraph poles linking the villages to the outside world. If the outsiders were to be defeated, the infrastructure upon which their power rested needed to be destroyed as well. The peasants had understood this immediately, and accordingly, the places of power—police stations, courthouses, party offices, and even schools where the regime promulgated its teachings—were set on fire. The architectural symbols of the state were reduced to dust and rubble, and the visible representations of the state as an institution vanished. By early 1921, in many regions of the empire, state power had broken down completely. For the peasants, this generally sufficed, as their wars were largely confined to their local living spaces. None of their leaders would have ever considered pursuing the Bolsheviks onto their own territory or trying to drive them out of their capital. They would have lacked the necessary means for such measures anyway. The peasants were interested in the village alone, and it was in the name of the village that they exercised their violence. As soon as the state authorities had been expelled and the liberties the peasants had formerly enjoyed had been restored, they lost all interest in continuing the war.

Although the Bolsheviks had numerous opponents, they ultimately prevailed because none of these opponents were able to form a united front against them. And yet it was not until after the final victory of the Reds over the Whites in the winter of 1920–21 that the regime mustered enough strength to quash the peasant rebellions. In June 1921 the Central Executive Committee of the RSFSR issued a decree that officially declared terror against the peasantry legal. People who refused to give their names to the security authorities or who were suspected of harboring "bandits" or hiding property were to be shot on the spot.[74] In order to force the peasant rebels to surrender, the Red commissars had entire villages taken hostage. In the Tambov province, by early summer 1921, over fifty thousand peasants had been sent to concentration camps. For every Communist killed, dozens of peasants were shot as retribution. The Bolsheviks even deployed airplanes and gas bombs against the insurgent peasants to "smoke them out" of the swamps into which they had fled.[75]

Terror was not reserved for the peasantry alone. In January 1919 as the Red Army advanced further south, the local party committee first raised the issue of what was to become of the Cossacks in southern Russia who had cooperated with the Whites or resisted the Reds. Nine days later, the organizational bureau of the Central Committee in Moscow delivered an answer. In a briefing issued to all subordinate organs, the party leadership determined that the only viable option would be a "merciless struggle" against the hostile Cossacks until their "complete annihilation" had been achieved. Cossacks who had served the tsar as guardians of the old order had a bad reputation among the revolutionaries anyway, as they were suspected of being allies of the counterrevolution. Most Cossacks, however, wanted no state at all, neither a Red nor a White one. By late February 1918, the Bolsheviks had already devastated the area of the Don Cossacks with systematic terror. They had killed their officers, confiscated their grain, and driven their cattle away, before burning their settlements to the ground. It was only after the bloody clashes with insurgent Cossack units in February 1919, however, that the Bolsheviks initiated the liquidation program. Thousands of Cossack insurgents were rounded up and summarily shot or taken hostage. In February 1919 alone more than eight thousand Cossacks were sentenced to death by the revolutionary tribunal of the Eighth Army. In April Lenin gave orders to depopulate the villages of the Don Cossacks. The residents were to be deported, and the land was to be colonized by peasants from the provinces of central Russia. Only the advance of the White army prevented the Bolsheviks from executing these plans immediately. Instead it would be 1920 before the Bolsheviks would complete this project of expelling some 300,000 Cossacks from their homeland and having them carted off to the coal mines of the Donbass or nearby concentration camps.[76]

For those in power, the Civil War was also an opportunity to deal a final death blow to religion and its representatives. The clerics of all religious denominations were subjected to merciless terror. Churches were closed, and monasteries were burnt to the ground. The number of clerics who actually died in this orgy of violence remains unknown. In some regions the crusade against religion was not limited to Christian churches and their priests but included the stigmatization of ethnic minorities as well. Particular targets were the Orthodox Jews and Muslims, whose religions were also considered expressions of hopeless backwardness. In spring 1918, when the Bolsheviks temporarily seized power in the industrial city of Baku on the Caspian Sea, the Muslims there became the chief target of Bolshevik aggression and became victims of a dreadful massacre. In central Asia and in the northern Caucasus, bloody battles ensued between representatives of the Bolshevik state and the Muslim nomads who had no place in the new order. As long as the violence could be legitimized as a struggle against "backward" conventions and customs the Bolsheviks did nothing to prevent the Red Army's pogroms against the Jews either.[77]

What occurred here was nothing but a "purge"—a project of ridding society of its "waste" and "weeds." The question of what had originally triggered the violence, however, soon became irrelevant. The Bolsheviks had set a process in motion, but soon they could no longer control it. It took on a life of its own, one that existed independently of the reasons used to justify its application. It existed within the imperial spaces of violence where peasant leaders, warlords, commissars, White generals, robber bands, and clan leaders ruled supreme and where violence always had the final say. Here, the Bolsheviks were unable to exercise the power they had claimed. And this lack of power was the source for the constantly recurring violence, since the powerless can only choose between surrender and attack.

Revolution and civil war opened up floodgates, and violence poured forth into the empire like an inexorable stream. War provided unscrupulous violent perpetrators with the chance to do the things that others merely spoke of, and amid the excesses of civil war the conceivable becomes the feasible. Violent criminals could act out their fantasies as at no time before. This is what Stalin and his friends had in mind eight years later, when they decided to initiate a war against their own population and once again transform the Soviet Union into a space of violence. Their model of rule was the state of emergency.

The Civil War produced more than just a synthesis of delusions and excessive violence. It also produced the Stalinist functionary. To Lenin, Bukharin, Zinoviev, Trotsky, and their intellectual appendages, violence and terror were mere abstractions, surgical operations performed on the social body. Their war was a clash between imagined collectivities, and it is likely that Lenin had no conception of the primal and bloody violence that his terror engendered. For Stalin and his companions, though, the war represented a chance to fulfill dreams of a lifetime: to injure and kill with impunity. The years of revolution and civil war may well have been the happiest of their lives, when battles were waged and people were killed. Violence was the lifeblood of the Stalinist functionary, a man whose career had been forged in the bloody battles of the Civil War. To him, fame and honor were to be found in the form of rich plunder, devastated landscapes, and enemies annihilated. This functionary usually came from a humble background, from one of the working-class neighborhoods or villages of the empire. He had spent many years of his life underground, in tsarist prisons, or in exile. But the Civil War had been his hour of glory. This is when the regime began enlisting the help of executioners, violent perpetrators, and terrorists who not only spoke of annihilating their enemies but were also prepared to do it. Stalin, Kaganovich, Voroshilov, Mikoyan, Ordzhonikidze, Kirov, and Yezhov were all embodiments of the political style, the language, and the violent habitus of the Stalinist functionary. And Stalin, that "wonderful Georgian" as Lenin had once called him, was their idol. He combined all the characteristics that, in their world, mattered: simplicity, determination, and a propensity for violence.[78]

Civil war and terror did not just wreak havoc and psychological devastation. Russia lost its intellectual and political elite as well. Those who survived the excesses fled to seek their fortunes elsewhere. Berlin, Prague, and Paris became new homes to old Russia.[79] The new Russia meanwhile became a land of terror. Peasants and workers were beaten down, and the elites of the now defunct tsarist empire were persecuted. Priests were murdered, Cossacks were deported, and ultimately no one was safe from the violence. During the 1930s Stalin's reign of violence elevated mass murder to a basic principle of state action, but it was born out of a culture of war and was itself a civil war being fought with different means.[80]

3   Pyrrhic Victories

THE BOLSHEVIKS PREVAILED. They broke the military resistance of the Whites, crushed the unrest and strikes of the peasants, and even restored the multiethnic empire, which, in the early months of revolution, had largely fallen apart. In spring 1921, when the Red Army marched into Georgia, the Civil War was officially over. For the Bolsheviks, however, military victory was not the end but rather the beginning of a mission, not simply to shake the world but to transform it. Although weapons may have decided the war in favor of the revolutionaries they had not settled the question of power. The Bolsheviks were rulers of a devastated realm. They could control it with military force, but exercising power over its population was another matter.

War and terror left their marks of destruction. In winter 1921–22 hunger invaded the Russian villages. In the provinces of the central Volga Region hundreds of thousands of peasants died. Members of American aid organizations, visiting the region at that time, spoke of peasants lying in their huts, apathetically waiting for death. In their despair, some of the starving had butchered rats, mice, and dogs, or even killed and eaten their own children. Typhus and cholera finished off what little had not yet been destroyed by hunger. In 1920 more than two million people in central Russia were suffering from typhus. Cholera and syphilis ravaged the cities. In the second half of 1921 several million peasants abandoned their villages in hopes of escaping their misery. Nomad-like, with neither destination nor homeland, these refugees wandered from place to place. One eyewitness, corresponding with an American aid organization trying to alleviate the hunger, reported, "There is no possibility of stopping this enormous wave of starving peasants flooding into the cities to die." And some villages did simply die out: "Not a living soul could be seen in the street, which seemed to have given up its function and now merely divided the rows of silent huts." In the Samara province, famished peasants roamed the streets like packs of wolves, feeding on leaves and shrubs or even on the entrails of perished animals. People murdered each other in the quest to stay alive, but some also killed themselves. Three decades later, looking back on his time in the Donbass at the end of the Civil War, the Cossack Nikolai Borodin recalled how peasants had died "like autumn flies," and how cats and dogs had vanished from the streets, having been eaten by starving people. In the workers' settlement of Shakhty, an old woman was reportedly selling human meat at the bazaar, and in Kamensk people were arrested and tried for cannibalism. A British eyewitness working for the Nansen Aid Committee reported to the *Times* that he had seen abandoned villages in the Saratov and Samara provinces, where the streets were paved with corpses being devoured by dogs. In some areas up to a hundred people died each day. American aid workers witnessed dreadful images in the orphanages there:

> The children, their bodies deformed by starvation, covered with vermin-infested rags, huddled together on the floor like blind kittens, the sick, the starving, and the dead indiscriminately. The buildings invariably lacked even the crudest sanitary equipment, and the rooms in which these helpless creatures were confined gave off the stench of a long neglected latrine. To such places came boys and girls whose parents had died or had deserted them, ghastly caricatures of childhood, with faces emaciated and yellow, swollen and blue, with eyes burning with the terrible sparkle of hunger, with angular shoulders and arms like flails."[1]

In its wake, the Civil War left more than seven million orphans, who could be provided with neither adequate nutrition nor medical care. In the Volga province of Simbirsk, bands of children eked out miserable existences in the forests, living on grass. One American observer, encountering some of these little beggars at a train station, suffered a shock upon seeing their bloated bellies. Many orphans set out for the larger cities of central Russia by train or on foot in search of the bare means of survival. More than 70 percent of the street children arriving in Moscow in 1923 had been born in a village in the central Volga Region.[2] They dwelled in slums at the outskirts of the metropolises, living on the trash they found in the streets, or getting what little they could to eat by stealing and robbing.

By the end of the Civil War, Russia's cities, which were now depopulated and deserted, had become little more than shadows of their former selves. For their inhabitants, existence had been reduced to a primitive struggle for survival. Even the buildings and streets in many of these cities had been reduced to dust and rubble. In some regions of the Urals and the Caucasus, burnt-out homes were the only reminders that people had once lived there. In many places state authority had collapsed altogether, and violence and criminality reigned supreme. In the Caucasus, in Siberia, and in eastern Ukraine, refugees, deserters, and peasant rebels formed criminal bands that left the state authorities no peace. Especially at the edges of the empire and in the cities devastated during the civil war, the world had been turned upside down. Even ten years after the revolution, residents of the Caspian city of Baku still lived in constant fear of roaming bands of outlaws. By day the city belonged to the militia (the civil police), and by night it belonged to robbers from nearby villages.[3]

The violence of war left its marks of devastation in the minds and souls of the people. In the midst of the daily struggle for survival, people began to doubt whether man was indeed friend to his fellow man and whether it was circumstances alone that led him to malevolence. By this time hardly anyone considered it remarkable that people were killing and being killed. It was also not surprising that, wherever state instruments of enforcement were absent, the law of the fist reigned supreme. The war was an enabling space for violent criminals. Every violent, criminal action that normal circumstances would have prevented was now possible. More than seven years of killing and maiming had prepared both perpetrators and victims for violence. The aggressiveness and brutality of the Bolsheviks grew out of the experience that power could only be asserted by those prepared to meet opposition with force. Their thuggish rhetoric was a sign of reckless determination. The Bolshevik state was weak, and that is why it resorted to threats of violence in an attempt to win obedience and loyalty. Instead, though, this unpredictable economy of violence had the effect of potentiating mistrust. From the very beginning the Soviet project was based on creating fear in those who were supposed to obey, standing in blatant contrast to the Bolshevik claim of creating a world where power was based on self-discipline and voluntary obedience.

Without institutions or individuals to carry the mandate of the revolution into the villages, without a system that could provide the people with security and subsistence, the Bolsheviks would have been forced to remain warriors. Practices and circumstances that might have been tolerated in times of war, simply because there was no alternative, could not succeed in times of peace. The multiethnic empire required an administrative and economic system that made it possible to live in the Soviet Union without being a Communist. By the end of the Civil War Lenin at least had grasped this. At the Tenth Party Congress in early March 1921 he gave a signal for retreat in the form of the proposed New Economic Policy (NEP), a magic formula that was intended to pull the regime out of its self-inflicted crisis.

Lenin's about-face was an attempt at stabilizing the political order, restoring the exchange and production mechanisms of the free market, and negotiating peace with the peasants and the nations at the empire's periphery. The Bolsheviks withdrew from the lives of their subjects and surrendered themselves to a pragmatism that allowed space for people's own designs. It was precisely this withdrawal that gave those in power the breathing space required to provide socialism with a state system. Some historians believe that this policy change was more than just a simple attempt at establishing a functioning state. Stalinism was not the inevitable consequence of the Bolshevik October coup, they argue, and the New Economic Policy was indeed an alternative that might have even won a majority in the Bolshevik Party. So runs the argument of those who see the New Economic Policy as more than just a tactical retreat. But one could just as easily argue that the Bolsheviks never for a minute abandoned their goal of establishing a dictatorship run by their party. The debate over the right path to socialism, as it had unfolded in the party during the 1920s, was not a dispute over the sense or nonsense of the dictatorship of the proletariat that the Bolsheviks were always talking about. Instead, it was a debate over how this dictatorship and its social safeguards were to be established.

There was never any dissent among the party leadership regarding the purpose of the revolution. Economic regeneration was not followed by pluralization or democratization of the political system. Instead, the 1920s saw opposition disappear from political life completely. The regime also disempowered the soviets as representatives of the working people and made them into executive organs of the state, the Council of People's Commissars. The press, schools, and universities were brought into line, and without exception free speech was suppressed. Even now the regime punished resistance and criticism with ruthless persecution—with mass shootings, show trials, and deportations. In summer 1922, prominent members of the Socialist Revolutionary Party were arrested, tried, and sentenced in a spectacular show trial. The tribunal handed down sentences of death or multiple years in prison to this "party of White terror and bandit assaults," as Felix Dzerzhinsky, former head of the Cheka and current head of the State Police Directorate (GPU), phrased it.[4] In that same year, Lenin ordered the arrest and deportation of intellectuals who were unwilling to bow to the regime. More than one hundred intellectuals, including the philosopher Nikolai Berdyaev and the historian Alexander Kiesewetter, were expelled from the country, while hundreds of others were hauled off to Siberia or to other remote regions of the empire. Several prominent Mensheviks and spokesmen of the Ukrainian national movement vanished from political life along with them. On August 29, 1922, Grigory Zinoviev, speaking before the Petrograd Soviet, declared that the Bolshevik leadership would continue to punish anyone refusing to submit to its will: "Five years have cost us enough blood, we want to leave civil war behind us. But anyone sowing even the smallest seed of civil war, be it in scientific or poetic form, will encounter armed resistance. We have resorted to humane measures, to banishing these people abroad. If, however, they continue their underground work against us, if they begin destroying the restored economic front, if they declare a civil war against us, we will not merely resort to humane measures—we will draw the sword."[5]

In 1924 the sharpness of this sword was felt by Georgian peasants who had begun revolting against the Bolshevik regime. In what was referred to as a pacification campaign, tens of thousands of peasants were dragged before a dreadful punishment tribunal and either gunned down by the Chekists or shipped off to concentration camps. Go-goberidze, the deputy chairman of the Georgian Council of People's Commissars, was growing steadily more alarmed and wrote a letter to Vissarion Lominadze, who was the chairman of the party's Transcaucasian Regional Committee at the time and also a close confidant of Stalin. In his letter, Gogoberidze complained that innocent people were being shot indiscriminately. What he failed to understand, however, is that this was exactly the point. The terror was intended to be indiscriminate. It was intended to engender an atmosphere of fear and dread, as this, the power holders understood, would prevent resistance from forming. This method of governance, however, had drawbacks, one of them being that it did not win the state one single loyal subject. As Gogoberidze summed it up, the problem faced by the power holders was that there "simply is no Soviet power in the villages."[6] Unable to establish a state in the village, the power holders could only make their appearance in the form of recurring violence.

And yet the relief people felt as the war came to an end must have outweighed everything else. For the first time, the Bolshevik power holders could turn to collaborators for help in stabilizing the economy and anchoring the new state in the provinces of the empire. New circumstances could only arise if New Men created new institutions. And so the power holders embarked on a project of weaving the empire together with a web of institutions. They initiated literacy and secularization campaigns as a means of mobilizing their subjects, and they sought to reform marriage and family law, to establish institutes for proletarian education, and to revolutionize art, literature, and architecture.

A revolutionary state demanded a revolutionary elite. The new institutions would be staffed by New Men—men who had freed themselves from the traditions of the past and were bound together by the habitus of revolution. But the Bolshevik regime was ill-prepared for the lofty tasks it set itself. Its power was limited, and beyond the metropolises of the empire, it barely existed at all. The party leaders felt the indifference and hostility surrounding them and thus had no choice but to isolate themselves from the outside world. The party became a fortress, a space that was governed by its own laws, and in this isolation everything was possible, because all that mattered was the will of the leader. The wishes and needs of the subjects on the outside were irrelevant.

And this is the reason that the end of the Civil War did not mark the end of the dictatorship. The era of the New Economic Policy, which began in 1921, was instead the incubation period of Stalinism.

ECONOMIC REFORMS

The New Economic Policy began with the Tenth Party Congress in spring 1921. In light of the peasant unrest, worker strikes, and the sailors' uprising at Kronstadt, Lenin at least was forced to concede that failure to make some changes could result in a total loss of power. The majority of Bolshevik leaders affirmed this assessment. Lenin had not lost sight of his goal of overcoming the "anarchy" of the market, but he now realized that there was indeed a correlation between the purchasing power of the peasantry and the prospects for industrial development. The state had been relieving peasants of the fruits of their labor for some time now. In return, the state had been giving them nothing, and so their response had been to stop producing anything at all. In this economy of robbery, where the state was the robber and the peasants were the tributaries, there were both criminals and victims but neither taxpayers nor buyers. Peasants who owned nothing could not be expected to purchase anything either. Lenin understood that predictability was a precondition for economic success and that even a command economy required some degree of security. Arbitrary grain procurements were thus suspended and replaced by a tax in kind, which was determined in advance and was supposed to provide peasants with some kind of legal security. It was important to establish exchange relationships between the city and countryside and to encourage peasants to buy goods and sell grain. Lenin and his disciples of pragmatism also hoped to overcome the supply crisis in the cities by allowing peasants to retain their surpluses, to buy and sell their goods freely, and to hire wage workers. State-owned enterprises were given permission to lease their factories to private individuals and place matters of finance, logistics, and entrepreneurship in private hands. July 1921 even saw the restoration of free trade for craftspeople and small industrial enterprises.

But even such minor reforms required governmental safeguards to prevent temporary concessions from turning into economic upheavals. Although free trade was now allowed, a restoration of property rights would have been far too radical. The regime's alternative was to establish centrally directed production cooperatives, which were supposed to organize the exchange of products between city and countryside. All businesses with more than twenty employees remained under state ownership. Although the Supreme Economic Council was initially authorized to direct commercial enterprise, this power was later rescinded due to its unwieldiness and inefficiency. Despite this, a true de-bureaucratization of the economic structures never took place. Instead, different enterprises within the same branch of industry were consolidated into so-called trusts, which remained under state ownership but were allowed to operate and plan at their own discretion (*khozrashet*).

Successes were apparent within months of these reforms. Peasants producing surpluses brought them to market, and by 1923, market relations between city and country had been restored. This transformation was due in large part to the so-called Nepmen, small traders who had monopolized trade with the peasants before the revolution and still had access to all the necessary contacts and channels of distribution that others did not have. The large-scale sale of industrial goods only achieved a breakthrough after the trusts were allowed to establish their own trade syndicates and start selling their products in state-owned shops. In 1923, however, the prices for industrial and agricultural products fell out of balance, and as industrial goods became more and more expensive peasants stopped buying them. This loss of revenue for the trusts was then transferred to workers in the major cities in the form of wage cuts and layoffs. In many urban regions strikes and unrest flared up once again, while discontent in the countryside continued to grow as well. In 1924, after a period of drought had resulted in a poor harvest, the peasants became unable to provide the deliveries and taxes the power holders demanded of them. For the power holders this was irrelevant, and they still continued to seize whatever they could without mercy. Even Felix Dzerzhinsky, head of the secret police, expressed concern, questioning whether a pauperization of the peasantry was really in the regime's best interest. The peasants sensed that the workers were privileged and that they were disadvantaged. City dwellers seemed to live better lives and carry a far smaller share of the work burden. This made for an extremely dangerous situation, as the alliance between workers and peasants was based on the principle of equality, and a violation of this principle could be catastrophic for the state.

By this time, some Bolsheviks saw no other option than to combat the economic crisis by way of state planning and to carry the class struggle into the village in order to eliminate enemies of the new order. The term "kulak terror" first surfaced in secret police reports from 1925, and from this point on, all economic questions were questions of power—power that could be secured with violence. Trotsky had hoped to use planning to regulate the anarchy of the market and promote state-organized industrialization. In neither 1924 nor 1925, however, did his proposals find approval in the Politburo. According to the credo espoused by Stalin and the majority that now supported him, industry's first task was to lower production costs and reduce the prices of industrial goods by rationalizing production.[7]

By autumn 1925 it had become universally apparent that the market could not be controlled. The artificially maintained discrepancy between low prices for agriculture and high prices for industry made it impossible for peasants to sell their products. What they produced they now consumed or held onto, and the delivery wagons of the state buyers remained empty. Privileging the peasants had not increased the influence of the state but had instead reduced it. This is how most of the party leadership saw it at any rate. It was a dilemma that could have been resolved in a number of ways—by allowing more open market forces, for example, or perhaps by offering peasants incentives to resume grain sales—but not even the moderate Bolsheviks were open to such discussions. For the party leadership, a dictatorship that bowed to the caprices of the peasants and their manner of business was simply unthinkable. At the Fourteenth Party Congress in December 1925 the State Planning Committee (Gosplan) was tasked with preparing development targets for the future central economy. Then in December 1927 at the Fifteenth Party Congress a new course in economic policy was announced: the Five Year Plan for the National Economy of the Soviet Union. It laid plans for the industrialization of the country and recommended that agriculture be placed under state control. This was the first time that the "collectivization of agricultural production" was spoken of as such, but it gave expression to an attitude that had already been prevalent within the party leadership for some time. Furthermore, it demonstrated the kind of economic approach in which the leading Bolsheviks had placed their faith.[8]

1925 ushered in a new period also for industry. The Supreme Economic Council reclaimed its supremacy over industry, and by summer 1927 the state trusts had lost their autonomous steering functions. All branches of Soviet industry were subordinated to the departments of the Economic Council. The functionaries in the State Planning Committee were not merely discussing the possibility of a planned economy but were instead already discussing how to maximize it. Naturally, this scheme would have no place for the economic independence of agriculture, and in 1928 what was left of this independence came to an end as collectivization was initiated.

Indeed, what took place between 1928 and 1932 was not merely the result of economic deliberations. Outside of the major cities the Bolsheviks had no power to speak of. They were not masters of the situation but were instead men under the pressure of circumstances, prisoners of necessity, acting only in response to their constraints. In their isolation, they abandoned themselves to fantastic ideas and developed a paranoid belief that they were under siege, a mentality that left deep marks on their style of governance. Their only hope of escaping this isolation was for the village become part of a larger whole and for the peasants to surrender themselves to the new order and become New Men. The Bolsheviks were, however, no closer to this objective then they had been in 1921—in fact they were even further from it.

THE STATE IN THE VILLAGE

In early 1921, when Lenin and his closest comrades in arms resolved to abandon their war against the peasantry, they were essentially robbing themselves of power. Just as before, the Communists were still faced with the dilemma that their dictatorship lacked the necessary institutional preconditions. When the requisitioning commandos and Cheka brigades withdrew from the villages, the state's claim to power disappeared along with them. It would have been of little consolation to the Bolsheviks that just as little remained of the old elites, the estate owners, land captains, magistrates, and police. The thin veneer of "civilization" had been blasted off during the years of Civil War, and the Bolsheviks too had experienced the forces that unbridled violence in remote places could unleash. To most of them, the world of the peasantry was one of barbarism. This was a people that was incapable of diagnosing and healing its own afflictions, and it was thus imperative that the peasantry not only be subjugated but also controlled. The path to a peaceful seizure of power was a rocky one, and ultimately the Bolsheviks failed to reach their goal, because the things that meant nothing to the authorities meant everything to the peasants. The wishes of the peasantry had been granted. They had finally been given a taste of that long yearned-for freedom, and the yoke of the state was finally gone. What took place in the early 1920s marked the conclusion of a people's revolution that the Civil War had merely interrupted. The village had been returned to the peasants and freed from the state, and it now enjoyed a degree of sovereignty that it had never before possessed.

Peasant life was primitive, filthy, and short, and there was nothing the state authorities could offer that would make their farewell to a way of life they had known for centuries any less painful. In a world afflicted by poverty, famine, and bad harvests, it was reasonable to be apprehensive about changes whose effects no one could predict. In this cosmos there was no room for outsiders or strangers, and the only people who could be trusted were one's own kind. The experiences of the Civil War had confirmed the peasant judgment of outsiders—that all they brought was calamity. In the face of the violence visited upon the peasants by the outside world, the only path of escape was inner withdrawal. The traditional village order became a refuge of safety and stability. These were the preconditions that fed into the conservative habitus and rigid internal social discipline that bring life into balance whenever order is threatened.[9] In this way the traditional village authorities also increased in power and influence within the village, further hindering the Bolshevik project of establishing state authority there.

It was not just the established structures and systems of power that were destroyed in the Civil War. The war also wiped out what frail infrastructure and communication had previously connected the village to the outside world. The transportation of goods and people sank to prewar levels. The Russian railways, for example, had half the passengers in 1922 than they had had in 1913. In many regions it was only the "sack people"—traveling merchants who supplied the cities with the bare necessities—that kept communication between city and countryside from being dissolved altogether. The merchant became a traveler on foot.

Depopulation and devastation were not the only factors preventing the power holders from wielding influence and exercising control.
Much of the empire was simply inaccessible, with people living beyond
the reach of the world that the Communists deemed habitable. Even in
the province of Tver to the north of Moscow some peasants still lived
in complete isolation. Although the Moscow-Leningrad express train
ran through the region, most of the villages had no roads to connect
them with the railway line. At the periphery of the empire, in the Urals,
Siberia, Central Asia, and the Caucasus, the only chance that peasants
would have any contact at all with the outside world was if they lived
near a major railway axis or if they had the misfortune of being visited
by hostile tribes, robber bands, or soldiers passing through. For the
state and its officials, the mountain regions of the Caucasus remained
downright unreachable. In the Caucasus republics of Georgia, Armenia,
and Azerbaijan roads were few and far between, and some regions had
no connections with administrative centers at all. As one prominent
member of the Transcaucasian Regional Party Committee remarked
indignantly in late 1923, many village residents had only even became
aware of Soviet power by "coincidence," from "passersby."[10]

Under these conditions, village and state only encountered each other
in the mode of presence. And since there were neither radios nor newspapers to impart the intentions of the government the voice of power
remained silent in the village. What was proclaimed in Bolshevik newspapers was of little relevance to the empire's peasants anyway. As a correspondent working for the *Krestianskaia Gazeta* (Peasant Newspaper,
established in 1923) reported to his superiors during his trip through
the villages of central Russia, there was next to no one there who actually read the newspaper. Instead, peasants drew their information from
local priests or traveling "sack people." The village was held in sway by
rumors, which spread far more rapidly than any newspaper headline.
Peasants from one village in central Russia were convinced that a special tax would be levied on any peasant with a newspaper subscription.
England, it was also reported, had apparently declared war on Russia,
and villagers were in danger of being drafted. Others believed that the
French had elected Nicholas II to be their tsar. "Soon peasants under
the leadership of prominent people will rise up against Soviet power,"
villagers from the Tula province claimed, "and then the Communists

will be wiped out." To be sure, the peasants had a conception of high politics, but one that made sense in their scheme of the world.[11]

Most of Russia's peasants did not read. They saw and heard very little of the Soviet achievements that the Bolsheviks proclaimed. Although the government had been opening schools and promoting literacy since the mid-1920s, this endeavor apparently had only limited success. According to official data the results were very impressive. In their internal correspondence, however, leading Bolsheviks spoke openly about the failure of these campaigns, which ultimately reached only a small number of peasants. The peasants' conservative mentality and distrust of new ideas were not the only limiting factors in this Bolshevik project of enlightenment. There was also a shortage of potential authority figures. With the disappearance of the clergy the state not only lost its eyes and ears in villages, it lost a crucial means of influencing the peasantry as well. The literacy promotion project was also plagued by a lack of textbooks and teachers. In many places the teachers were barely better educated than their pupils.[12]

The Soviet state schools were hindered by the same problems as the literacy programs. When peasants even attended them at all, it was only the rare exception that the messages the regime intended actually caught on. The peasants did learn how they needed to speak when coming in contact with state officials, but all that demonstrated was their ability to mechanically repeat what they had been taught. Nowhere was there any question of an adoption of the hegemonic culture. Lenin considered this a mere technological problem. To him, Russian misery was due to nothing more than a lack of technological capabilities. The electrification of Russia that he dreamed of—"Communism is electrification plus Soviet power"—would be one vehicle for bringing progress to the village. Electric light would not only immerse the village huts in a bright glow, it would brighten the dim wits of the peasantry as well. People whose evenings were illuminated by bright light would begin to read books and their alcoholism would become a thing of the past. This is what Lenin believed at any rate. Unfortunately, though, electrification did not turn drunkards into readers, and when it came down to the choice between the book and the bottle, vodka usually came out on top.

The peasantry had no conception of state law either. In most regions, the long arm of state justice appeared only sporadically. In the mid-1920s there were no more than 250 policemen stationed in the province of Tver. A single militiaman was responsible for an area of 150–200 square kilometers (roughly 60–80 square miles), and in some cases he had to perform his duties on foot. The eyes of the law were uneducated, poorly paid, and corrupt. They commanded no respect and wielded no authority whatsoever when they identified themselves to the peasants as agents of state power. Only in rare cases did state law correspond to peasant notions of law. More importantly, though, the peasants knew no more about the law than the militiamen who were meant to enforce it. Those representing state law did nothing to help its poor reputation, as they themselves were generally weak, lacking in authority, and inclined to abuse the law as a source of personal enrichment. In the worst cases the law entered the village in the form of the armed revolutionary, who threatened the peasants with violence and confirmed their belief that justice belonged to those who could enforce their will without being contradicted. The only way for villagers to oppose this was to refuse to submit. In February 1925 Felix Dzerzhinsky, head of the Soviet secret police (GPU), informed the Politburo that there had been an upsurge in assaults against state officials and worker and peasant correspondents reporting from villages in the rural parts of the empire. Representatives attempting to intervene in village life had been beaten, and some had even been killed. According to a GPU report from September 1926, it was "hooligans" and "bandits" who had been responsible for these attacks on Soviet functionaries. "Anti-Soviet elements," meanwhile, had apparently exploited the attacks to weaken state authority in the village.[13]

Into the late 1920s a deep cultural chasm still separated the city from the village. Peasants believed in magic and miracles. They called on higher powers to free them from evil spirits and sought advice from "medicine men," faith healers, and fortune tellers. Alcohol and violence ruled supreme. The patterns of daily life were determined by religious rituals and church holidays. And since the official Orthodox Church had disintegrated in the turmoil of the revolution the peasants now selected their own clerics. The Bolsheviks attempted to combat tradition and belief by pointing out that they were unscientific. But their propaganda, which arrived in the form of traveling cinemas and display boards, was unsuccessful. The peasants looked to religion for answers that would confirm the meaning of life not redefine it.[14]

The village assembly, which was dominated by the well-respected and influential members of the community, determined which forms of economic activity, celebration, and dispute were acceptable. The Bolsheviks, however, saw the peasant community as class society in a nutshell, where wealthy kulaks oppressed landless workers and poor peasants. This interpretation came from a distorted understanding of the peasant worldview. Most Bolsheviks believed that conflicts were the result of asymmetrical power relations and social divisions. For the peasants, however, the supposed antagonism between rich and poor made no sense whatsoever. When peasants came into conflict over land or influence these were disputes between families or clans, and the primary goal was to prevent damage to one's reputation within the power fabric of the village. The peasant community was, after all, held together by a system of rules and norms that was based on the family and its need to secure its subsistence. The kulaks were not simply the masters of the village, but they were also its protectors. In times of misery and poverty their power and influence among the other peasants actually increased. But the Bolshevik leaders were blind to this. They simply could not imagine that they would face the opposition of the entire peasantry. One GPU report from September 1926 speaks of "the hooligan nuisance." In many cases this was "overtly political in character" and appeared "in the persecution of Soviet power in the village in the form of kulak terror and the employment of fascist pogrom methods in the struggle against the organizations of political enlightenment in the village."[15] The Chekists speaking here left no doubt that such refractoriness would require an armed response from the Soviet state.

After the expropriation of the estates, the land was handed over to the peasants. The rights to the land had been established by the Agrarian Codex of 1922, but the details of its distribution were left up to the village community of male farm owners. The amount of land awarded depended on the number of family members. Who got which plot of land was determined by chance. Families with plenty of children had better chances of successfully securing their subsistence than families who had none. Wealth and influence depended on the number of children, marital status, or death of a family member. Bad harvests, the death of livestock, or unforeseen fatalities could drive a well-respected family to ruin. Conversely, less well-off peasants were able to improve their status in the village by means of cleverly arranged marriages, a large number of children, and hard work. Under these circumstances, marriage became a strategic alliance that was negotiated between patriarchs. Married couples also generally understood that their union was an arrangement for the purpose of securing subsistence and demanded that both partners fit themselves into the life cycle of the village. While the Bolshevik conceptions of marriage and spouse selection were based on the principle of free choice, this was a luxury that was not open to most impoverished peasants. Although the state had not missed any opportunities to remind villagers that it would not relinquish its claims to power, the Communists required multipliers to represent them in the villages and enforce their will. This was the task of the village soviets and the members of the communist youth organization (Komsomol) who were represented in them. The village soviet served as a deputy for state authority: it enforced laws, collected taxes, oversaw the administration of justice, and also the construction of roads. The village soviets did not take their orders from the village assemblies but from distant state authorities in Moscow. While the chairmen of the soviets rarely consulted the village assemblies they knew that authority was on their side and thus tended to affect autocratic poses. This, however, only served to undermine their reputation in the village even further. In some places they behaved as petty despots who harassed and tyrannized the peasantry and decided for themselves who could become a member of the soviet and who could not.

Most soviet functionaries were overextended, incompetent, and incapable of understanding the intentions of the Communists in the nearest provincial capital.[16] They confused the tasks of party cells with those of the soviets, provided their relatives with sinecures in the local administration, and embezzled tax money. And since many soviet functionaries themselves could neither read nor write they failed to understand the purpose of directives coming from Moscow and never bothered to make sure that they were implemented. The peasants consequently ignored the village soviets and left matters of importance to be discussed in the village assembly, the *shkod,* instead.

Although the state did manage to force its way into the village, establishing authority there was another matter. Since 1926 the regime had been using soviet elections as a means of mobilizing support and transforming peasants into loyal subjects. The elections were not intended to familiarize the peasants with parliamentary procedures or systems of representation. Instead they were measures intended to help mobilize the people and mark out enemies. Elections rested on the principles of inclusion and exclusion to an equal degree, and they served to provoke conflicts by pitting poor peasants against kulaks and clergy. The elections usually began with the public stigmatization of class enemies, which included kulaks, clerics, and those who had held office during the time of the tsar. These offenders were named, their names were entered into lists identifying them as enemies, and they were stripped of their voting rights. In many regions, however, the soviets fell apart once the brigades of the Communist Youth and party activists had left the village. Nowhere was the powerlessness of the Communists more apparent than in the village. If the party could not somehow establish its presence permanently, its campaigns would remain ineffective. This is what made the staging of a permanent state of emergency necessary, as it was the Bolsheviks' only hope of establishing their claims to power in the hearts and souls of their subjects. And so the Bolsheviks repeated their campaigns, year after year, usually on the occasion of new holidays, which the regime started introducing during the early 1920s.[17]

While the soviets had been of little help, the party leadership could not expect much more from the village Communists—the supposed eyes and ears of the regime. Only a handful of villages even had a Communist Party cell at all, and where such cells did exist they tended to be composed of demobilized Red Army soldiers, workers, and petty white-collar workers who had ended up in the provinces. The peasants did not trust the strangers who had entered their lives uninvited and begun telling them how they were supposed to work, celebrate, and believe. To the peasants, the Communist functionaries were generally nothing more than representatives of an alien authority that demanded taxes and spoke an incomprehensible language. The Communists were members of a foreign world. Had they not arrived as agents of a power whose punitive measures could arouse fear and dread, they would probably simply have been laughed at.

Although the New Economic Policy brought political stability it also veered the Bolshevik leadership away from its ultimate goals. With the NEP the village returned to being a space in which state authority carried little weight. The Bolsheviks were forced to acknowledge that the peasant way of life and the socialist program of civilization were mutually exclusive. Peasants had no conception of socialist forms of labor or the lifestyle of "modern" man as propagated by the Bolsheviks. Furthermore, they were not interested in hearing about the class struggle. The Bolshevik mission of carrying power into every corner of the empire had come to a screeching halt at the village gates.

DICTATORSHIP WITHOUT THE PROLETARIAT

Upon his release from a Moscow prison in January 1922, the prominent Menshevik Fyodor Dan could not believe his eyes. What he saw on the streets of the capital reminded him of the final years before the outbreak of the First World War. He saw portly parvenus shamelessly flaunting their wealth, blind to the misery that reigned throughout Russia. Shop windows were filled with candies, fruits, and luxury goods of all sorts. Moscow's theaters and concert halls were resplendent once again, and audience members were wearing fur and diamonds. Merchants who would have been persecuted as "speculators" two years before were now parading their riches openly through the public spaces. People on the streets were once again addressing each other as *barin* (Sir). This was not how he had imagined the beginnings of socialism. Some members of the Bolshevik Party also harbored a disdain for the New Economic Policy and the inequality it had engendered that was scarcely less severe. For the young Communist Alexander Barmin the pain that his party's retreat had caused him was physical. For him and his like-minded comrades, he wrote, the new economic course was a betrayal of the revolution and was even grounds for leaving the party.

The regime, however, had little choice. Peasants were granted privileges so that they would export their surplus grain, and the state needed these surpluses. Without them the state had no source of hard currency and no means of driving the industrialization of the country forward. There was simply no alternative to the privatization of trade. Lenin and the leading Bolsheviks believed that free trade would eventually disappear in its competition with the state cooperatives. Such predictions, however, were far divorced from reality because in the end it was mainly the Nepmen, traveling merchants and traders, who supplied both the cities and villages with all the consumer goods they needed. In the end even the state enterprises began turning to private merchants to sell their products on the free market. The Bolshevik leadership began to panic. It sensed the state's dwindling influence on the economy and it feared that even the peasant grain surpluses might be lost. Beginning in 1926 the regime's old strategies of repression returned. The regime began harassing Nepmen with additional taxes and dues, as well as stigmatizing other merchants and traders as "socially alien elements" and driving them into illegality. Finally, in 1928, the regime announced the "liquidation of the Nepmen."[18]

The New Economic Policy was intended to rebuild the economy and increase industrial performance. The problem, though, was that it contradicted the ideological promises of the party as well as the egalitarian notions of justice shared by most industrial workers. To make matters worse, the regime had committed the trusts to a system of economic accountability (*khozrashet*). This, along with the principle of single command (*edinonachalie*), the rationalization of production, and the introduction of Taylorist work methods in the factories, changed the very rhythm of life in the major cities of the empire. The triumphant advance of "capitalism" returned foreign machines and engineers to the factories and also reestablished the rule of managers over workers. The "Americanization" of industry, as the rationalization of production came to be called, meant that unprofitable companies were closed down, workers were laid off, and some employees received significantly lower wages than others. Moreover, it helped poison the relationship between workers and Communists, which in any case was already under strain.

In 1923, as economic recovery proceeded, thousands of demobilized soldiers, peasants, and workers who had fled to the villages during the Civil War began flooding back into the cities. They lived in decrepit tenements, barracks at city outskirts, wooden sheds, or mud huts. Workers living in misery were unable to muster much understanding for the Bolshevik program of rationalization. Although production rates were increasing and costs were falling, this did nothing to raise the standard of living. More importantly, unemployment was on the rise. In June 1929 the state employment service in the city of Nizhny Novgorod alone registered more than sixteen thousand unemployed persons. While the revolution had promised wealth and affluence, all privileges and benefits seemed to be reserved for the middle-class specialists and foreign experts, whom the New Economic Policy had reintegrated into industrial planning. These specialists lived in comfortable houses, shopped in special stores, and received bonuses. In the Donbass, even engineers and managers who had colluded with the Whites during the Civil War were reintegrated into the industrialization program. It was not uncommon for workers to encounter their former bosses, whose overbearing arrogance and self-importance were still fresh in the minds of many. In light of this state of affairs it is hardly surprising that the majority of workers rejected the new course. A revolution that had invoked the will of the workers must by now have seemed like an utter betrayal. "It's like in the bourgeois countries (*kak v burzhuaznykh stranakh*) here now, where there are many unemployed," a worker from Balashov (Saratov province) wrote in 1927 in a letter to the newspaper *Batrak* (Village Laborer). "The worker goes to the employment bureau and leaves again with nothing. He then occupies himself with thievery, for which they have no understanding there." While the Communists spoke of a dictatorship of the proletariat, in reality the industrial cities of the Soviet Union were ruled by a dictatorship of managers and Communists. And so from 1921 onward not a single year passed without strikes and violent outbursts of discontent. Workers struck for higher wages, but more than that they demanded equality, justice, and dignity, as they had been promised by the Revolution of 1917.[19]

During this period the relationship between workers and Communists changed as well. Communist leaders began surrounding themselves with all the trappings of power. They masqueraded as proletarian commanders, leaders of worker brigades, and representatives of the authoritarian state, but in the eyes of the workers they were nothing more than accomplices of the middle-class specialists and advocates of capitalist methods of production. They spoke of cost reduction, of the Americanization of industry, of Taylorism and Fordism, but the needs and concerns of the workers seemed to play no role for them. The workers' control that the revolution had promised had by this time been replaced by the rule of managers and engineers. Workers no longer expected the Communist Party's unions and factory cells to represent their interests, and in many places their anger was also directed against the Communist functionaries and petty despots who subjugated the proletariat in its own name and bound them to the dictates of the middle-class specialists.

Workers sometimes seized on the Bolshevik rhetoric of enmity and turned it against the power holders themselves. Their list of class enemies not only included specialists, but also those Communists who seemed to have entered an alliance with the *burzhui* (bourgeois) of the old regime. The Donbass miners not only saw an alliance between Communists and managers, they also distinguished "true" Communists, who were on the side of the workers, from Jewish exploiters, who merely disguised themselves as Communists in order to carry out their evil work unhindered. In one Donbass settlement a rumor began that Trotsky the Jew was about to seize power and have himself declared tsar. "The Jews have taken power into their hands and want to seat their own Jewish tsar," it was told. At least that is what a GPU report from 1925 relayed.[20] In the 1930s, when Stalin gave the signal to begin pursuing enemies and spies, he could exploit these absurd conspiracy scenarios without causing any shock.

For the party leadership in Moscow, the New Economic Policy was merely a temporary compromise, and this applied to its role in industry as well. From the very beginning the question of how to deal with specialists was a point of contention within the party executive. On one side were the more moderate and pragmatically oriented members of the party. On the other side were those who took more radical positions. Radical positions were more predominant within the party base, particularly in the Donbass and in Baku, where worker insubordination went beyond the usual measure. In these regions the local Communists would sometimes participate in strikes simply to avoid losing all legitimacy in the eyes of those they were supposed to be representing. By the mid-1920s the regime had already staged several show trials in the Donbass, in which engineers and managers had been accused of sabotaging production and purposely causing accidents. In 1926 more than half of all technical specialists and engineers there were facing charges. The situation in Baku was similar. Accidents and explosions were becoming more frequent in the oil fields in the city's outer districts because workers were unfamiliar with modern, imported technology. There was no doubt in the minds of local Communists, however, that these accidents were the fault of the class enemy, and here too, dozens of specialists were put on trial.[21] In this way, workers and Communists found a common language; the former exacted revenge and acted on their resentments, and the latter indulged their obsessions. It would seem that the basic structural principle of Stalinism was already in place: society had become contaminated with hate and violence.

THE NATIONALIZATION OF THE EMPIRE

Russia was a multiethnic empire, but this was something the Bolsheviks first began to recognize as they extended their rule into its periphery. The Bolshevik Party had originally been a conglomerate of Russians and Russified Jews, city people who had little in common with the empire's peasant populations. The Muslims of the Caucasus, the Tatars and Bashkirs, the nomads of central Asia, and the small ethnic groupings of Siberia were initially of little interest to the revolutionaries. And yet, the Bolshevik victory was not confined to the cities of European Russia but involved a reconquest of the Asiatic periphery of the empire as well. Upon the restoration of the tsarist multiethnic empire, socialism became an imperial project, and the power holders were forced to reconcile the idea of socialism with the heterogeneity of languages, religions, and cultures that the empire contained. Some of the "leftist" intellectuals in the Bolshevik Party initially expressed reservations about a nationalization of the socialist project, but Lenin saw further than the radical internationalists in his party. To him, the right to national self-determination was more than just a façade for placating the non-Russian elites. "We have Bashkirs, Kirghiz and a number of other peoples," Lenin told the delegates at the Eighth Party Congress, "and to these we cannot deny recognition. We cannot deny it to a single one of the peoples living within the boundaries of the former Russian Empire."[22]

In spring 1919, at the peak of the Civil War, the national question became an existential, political one. Finland, Poland, Ukraine, and the provinces of Transcaucasia had left the empire and declared their independence. White forces meanwhile controlled the greater part of the Asiatic periphery. Under these circumstances, an insistence on pitting the class struggle against the nation meant confusing wish with reality. Lenin for one yielded to the bitter insight that in some parts of the empire national identification trumped all others. When some of his opponents expressed doubt about the sense and purpose of nationalization Lenin's answer was that "one would have to be insane to continue the policy of Tsar Nicholas."[23] In the end, Lenin again managed to overcome all opposition and have his way in the national question as well. This was not least due to his support from Bolshevik functionaries in the periphery. During the Civil War, the party had ceased to be a political home for Russians and Jews exclusively and had instead become a multiethnic organization. This changed the relationship between the Communists and the peoples they purported to rule. It was no coincidence that Lenin entrusted Stalin, a Georgian, with the post of People's Commissar of Nationalities Affairs. This decision had symbolic significance, demonstrating that the party leadership no longer considered the reshaping of the multiethnic empire the task of the Russian center alone. It was a project that all peoples of the empire were to partake in.

"Taking root" (*korenizatsiia*) was the term that the Bolsheviks used for their concept of indigenizing and nationalizing governance (a decision that had been reached at the Twelfth Party Congress in spring 1923). The political organization of the empire was to be based on ethnicity, and the Soviet Union was to be divided into republics, autonomous republics, autonomous regions, and districts. National minorities were granted cultural autonomy and minority rights, not only in the Russian Soviet Republic, but in all national republics established on Soviet territory. From this point on the natives of many regions would be governed, sentenced, and educated by natives—in national soviets, national courts, and national schools.

The concept of indigenization was more than just a pragmatic solution or a means of communicating the socialist project to the cultures at the periphery. It also grew out of the conviction held by leading Bolsheviks that Russians needed to atone for their former primacy and chauvinism. Before 1917 the Russian peasants had scarcely been any closer to the ruling elites than the villagers in other regions of the empire. Now, though, they belonged to a nation of oppressors. This meant that Russians living outside of the Slavic core republics were not only saddled with the stigma of peasantry but were also forced to bear the burden of belonging to a chauvinist great power. This strategy of "positive discrimination" placed a heavy burden on Soviet nationality policy and meant that the Russian cultural nation was forced to constitute itself negatively as a federation of oppressors. Whenever Russians came into conflict with others, regarding a matter such as preferential treatment on the job, they invoked the dictatorship of the proletariat in whose name the Bolsheviks had allegedly seized power. Thus, Russians were proletarians, and non-Russians were, above all, non-Russians.[24]

The system of nationalization and affirmative action celebrated great triumphs in all those parts of the empire where the culture of "backwardness" prevailed and where the lives of past centuries still seemed to exist. Ukrainian and Georgian peasants, Kazakh and Turkmen nomads all needed to overcome their backwardness and become proletarians so that socialism could reach them too. To the leading Communists at least, nations were vessels in which the progression from capitalism to socialism took place. And so it came to pass on the peripheries of the empire that modernization and nationalization became inextricably linked. At the Tenth Party Congress in March 1921, Stalin declared that it would be a crime to "go against history," that the development of national cultures was a "duty for the Communists." The homogenization of ethnic maps was thus unavoidable.[25] Although Stalin spoke of socialist content in national forms the truth was that the Bolsheviks ascribed not only social but also ethnic identities to their subjects. They categorized and organized the population hierarchically and endowed both classes and nations with distinctive properties.[26]

The party and state administration were indigenized, ethnic minorities were privileged over Russians, and native languages were privileged over the Russian language. This, however, made the power holders in Moscow dependent on translators, and these people tended to favor the autonomy of their home regions over the establishment of socialism. In some areas, *korenizatsiia* actually generated the very nationalism it was supposed to be helping to overcome. In the multiethnic metropolises of the empire, ethnic conflicts gained in intensity because the Bolsheviks had endowed certain ethnic groups with privileges and established hierarchies among the different groups. As a result, all the national traditions that socialism was supposed to be replacing were signed into law. Socialist in form, nationalist in content is perhaps a better description of this reality. The indigenization of the empire also raised the justifiable question of whether the nation still had any use for communism at all. It ceded cultural hegemony to the "former people," which included "bourgeois" elites in Ukraine and Belorussia, and to tribal leaders, clan chiefs, and Islamic clerics in the Caucasus and central Asia. Furthermore, everyone knew that the national Communists were far more loyal to their nations than to the socialist blueprint for the future. Attractive countermodels of national emancipation were also appearing in the Soviet Union's neighbors, Iran, Turkey, Poland, and Finland. By the late 1920s pressure on the central government in Moscow was therefore mounting. The leaders began to fear for the attractiveness of their project of reordering society and also for their own power. And so the Bolsheviks eventually fell into conflict with the very spirits they themselves had conjured up: the national Communists who dreamed more of national self-determination than of socialism, the workers who wanted no part in a working class that included outsiders, and the representatives of those traditions that had constituted the nation in the first place.[27]

THE RISE OF STALIN

The Bolsheviks were now faced with the task of integrating a multitude of "backward" peoples and unruly peasants into the empire. Furthermore, this would have to occur without expecting too much help from the institutions that the revolution had so proudly proclaimed. The soviets contained neither "class-conscious" proletarians nor reliable and skilled laborers. For this reason as well the government of the Soviet state—the Council of People's Commissars—was not appointed by the soviets, but by the party leadership. The Communists could not even bring the ministries, which from 1917 on were called People's Commissariats, fully under their control. Although the People's Commissariats purported to be the executive branch of the proletarian dictatorship, this claim was a far cry from the reality, and as late as the mid-1920s they were still heavily dependent on the expertise of tsarist officials.[28] Although many of those employed in the ministries had been critics of the old autocracy and its methods of governing, this did not automatically translate into friendship and alliance with the Bolsheviks. The Bolsheviks, after all, had difficulty accepting anyone not completely devoted to the new cause, and they knew that a dictatorship of the proletariat without Bolshevik cadres would amount to nothing. They would have preferred to not have to depend on "bourgeois specialists" and leftist intellectuals who came from outside the Communist Party, but since this seemed unavoidable, the next best solution was for the party to monitor potentially unreliable public officials.

Such controlling measures were necessary if the will of the Bolshevik revolution was to be executed at all, and the party alone could see to it. The party, which was simultaneously an instrument of control and intervention, enabled the political leadership to break resistance and neutralize the latent opposition of old elites who were still in the Soviet state administration. It also offered the power holders a means of weaving together the disparate parts of the multiethnic empire. Decentralization and indigenization of the administration had robbed the regime of many of the instruments of rule that it needed if it was going to be taken seriously by the inhabitants of the empire's periphery. But just as the tsar had served as a symbol for uniting old Russia, the party too had a symbolic presence throughout the empire that allowed it to convey some sense of unity.

In the official state imagery the leading Bolsheviks presented their party as an order of the chosen, a sworn community of the resolute. These self-projections, however, merely served to conceal the brittleness of power and the weakness of the Bolshevik state. Just as the old autocracy had staged fantastical dreams of omnipotence in order to disguise its weakness, the Communists too presented a façade that was intended to disguise something else.[29] Only when we consider this weakness does it become clear why debates within the party's inner circle of power ultimately led to the dictatorship of a lone individual. Ultimately, the struggle for power unfolded on unsafe grounds and in isolation. Intraparty conflicts could be exploited by enemies of Soviet power, meaning that, potentially, every difference of opinion could be used to bring the Bolshevik rule down. This was a very real fear, and it haunted the intraparty debates that still took place during the 1920s. What would have been tolerated elsewhere as a simple exchange of views was perceived by Stalin and his supporters within the party as an existential threat. In February 1926 Stalin warned Politburo members against carrying the dispute between the leaders into the open: "What has been written down will be read in the provinces, and I must say that this is dangerous and incorrect." As early as autumn 1925 Mikhail Kalinin, the nominal head of state of the Soviet Union, had warned against making stenographic transcripts of Politburo meetings available to those outside the core party leadership. If people outside the inner circle were to read them they would reveal weakness and disunity: "If we conducted discussions only in the Politburo, without stenograms, without announcements, we could allow ourselves more leeway. But this discussion is tied into an extraparty milieu and in a significant degree has weakened Soviet power."[30]

What were these debates about? Influence and power might be one answer. At the heart of this struggle for influence and power, though, were differing notions of how the socialist dictatorship was to be established in the Soviet Union. The dispute over the right course had begun as early as 1923, when Grigory Zinoviev, head of the Communist International and the party organization in Petrograd, along with his alter ego, Lev Kamenev, entered into an alliance against the organizer and grand strategist of the revolution, Leon Trotsky. Zinoviev, Kamenev, and the still marginal general secretary of the party, Joseph Stalin, joined together and set about systematically discrediting the charismatic leader of the revolution. After Lenin's death in January 1924, the struggle for power broke out into the open. Trotsky's behavior, in this altercation with his adversaries, was far from surprising. Rather than addressing his rivals he simply ignored them, because to him they were simple-minded, talentless, and inept. Trotsky did not even seize the opportunity to present himself at the revolutionary leader's coffin and proclaim himself Lenin's successor. When Lenin died, he was at the Black Sea coast, recovering from a mysterious illness.[31] And so, Stalin held the eulogy in Trotsky's place, giving the crowd a first taste of his talent for presenting opinions as creeds.

Lenin's funeral was not the only thing Trotsky missed. His absence and inaction, when it came to defending his own position against his rivals, was conspicuous. He relied instead on his charisma and cachet as a leader of both the revolution and the Civil War. In all probability, Trotsky could not have dreamed that these mediocre figures surrounding him were even capable of engineering his downfall. He left the dull, day-to-day business of politics to his opponents and contented himself with demonstrating his intellectual brilliance and rhetorical agility. Lenin's final political "testament" contains a warning against Stalin, who Lenin considered to be both a brute and a danger to the Bolshevik Party. Trotsky also failed to capitalize on this, and in doing so squandered all chances of succeeding Lenin as leader of the revolution.

The initial quarrel between Stalin and Trotsky had to do with their disagreement over the right strategy for steering the socialist project to success. Trotsky saw no other option than to promote the "permanent revolution." Socialism could only really succeed in the Soviet Union if it prevailed on a global scale as well, which was why the revolution needed to be carried beyond the borders of the Soviet Union. At the same time, though, the concept of permanent revolution was the admission of an orthodox Marxist that the Bolshevik seizure of power had been premature. For all intents and purposes, a socialist revolution should not have taken place in a backward agricultural country like Russia that lacked the necessary social and economic preconditions. Trotsky's solution to this contradiction was that the Bolshevik revolution would only survive if the advanced nations of western Europe took it as a signal and if workers in Germany, England, and France also allowed themselves to be swept up in the tide of revolution and resolved to overthrow their "bourgeois" governments. After being carried into the developed capitalist world, the revolution would flourish and would then return to Russia, in a great movement of solidarity, and complete itself there as well. In May 1926, when British workers declared a general strike, Trotsky mistook this as a sign of the impending socialist overthrow in Europe and demanded of the Politburo to do everything in their power to help bring the British government down.[32]

In the realm of domestic policy too Trotsky and his supporters promoted a different approach from that of Stalin and Nikolai Bukharin, the party's theoretician. The group surrounding Trotsky—most notably Yevgeni Preobrazhensky, economic theoretician and head of the People's Commissariat of Finance, and Georgy Pyatakov, deputy chairman of the Supreme Council for the National Economy—argued for a rapid expansion of heavy industry and a repeal of the New Economic Policy, which in their eyes privileged agricultural backwardness at the expense of industrial development. Peasants, they said, should instead be bound to the land and forced to deliver their grain to the state, just as during the Civil War. Trotsky's followers believed that the industrialization of the Soviet Union could only be achieved by excluding peasants from consumption and by exporting grain.[33] In their vision of the new society, there was no place for the Russian peasant or his needs. Instead there would only be class-conscious proletarians and civilized Europeans, living in vast industrial landscapes. This dream, however, could only be realized if the industrial states of Europe supported the emerging Soviet state in its economic modernization.

Trotsky's arguments were bolstered by the fact that in many ways they were supported by the writings of Lenin. They also seemed to reflect an attitude that was predominant among many leading Bolsheviks of the time. Lenin and Trotsky both believed that a revolution that overlooked Germany, the fatherland of the organized workers' movement, was a faulty construction. Zinoviev and Kamenev held similar views regarding the Bolshevik strategy but refrained from showing this openly, as the removal of Trotsky from the inner circle of power was apparently of greater concern to them. This constellation of relations and circumstances presented Stalin—who was still not really taken seriously—with an opportunity to play his various rivals off against each other and simultaneously elevate himself to become Trotsky's true adversary. As Stalin pointed out to the Central Committee, the long-awaited revolution in Europe had still failed to materialize, the economies of the capitalist West had stabilized, and its democratic states seemed to have recovered, for the time being at least. Accordingly, there seemed to be no alternative to "socialism in one country," as Stalin termed his strategy of confining the revolution to the Soviet Union. If permanent revolution were to fail, the October Revolution would lose all legitimacy too. It would be pure folly to make the survival of the Russian revolution dependent on expectations that, for the foreseeable future, would remain unfulfilled. Otherwise, even the revolution in the Soviet Union would have to be given up. But who, in all seriousness, would aspire to such self-demolition? Stalin promoted a strategy for establishing the Soviet economy and building up the state. His foreign policy designs included peacekeeping and cooperation with socialist parties abroad. His strategy also committed the Communists to cooperating with Social Democratic and "bourgeois" parties in order to create the necessary preconditions for a future socialist revolution.

In the struggle for power Trotsky came out the loser. Stalin had him removed from his post as war commissar, and his supporters expelled from the Central Committee. In 1926 the political careers of Zinoviev and Kamenev also came to an end when they not only entered into an alliance against Stalin with their former arch nemesis, but adopted his arguments as well. The United Opposition made its final stand in 1927, when Great Britain terminated all diplomatic relations with the Soviet Union and war seemed to be imminent. That same year, the Chinese Kuomintang government of Chiang Kai-shek carried out a massacre against its communist allies, and in 1928 this scenario was repeated in Shanghai. Taken together, these circumstances might have seemed to support the opponents of the Popular Front strategy, but in this matter too Stalin prevailed. Zinoviev and Kamenev were expelled from the Politburo, and Nikolai Bukharin replaced Zinoviev as chairman of the Communist International. The posts of those expelled from the Politburo were filled by Mikhail Kalinin, Kliment Voroshilov, Vyacheslav Molotov, Valerian Kuybyshev, and Jan Rudzutak. Meanwhile, the Stalinists Grigory (Sergo) Ordzhonikidze, Lazar Kaganovich, Andrei Andreyev, Sergei Kirov, Vlas Chubar, Stanislav Kosior, and Anastas Mikoyan entered the Politburo. In 1927 Zinoviev, Kamenev, and Trotsky were even expelled from the party, and Trotsky, whom Stalin considered a particular threat, was banished to Kazakhstan in 1928 and expelled to Turkey soon thereafter.

In the late 1920s, Stalin turned on his former allies—Nikolai Bukharin, Alexei Rykov (head of government), and, Mikhail Tomsky (chairman of the Soviet labor unions). Bukharin, Rykov, and Tomsky promoted a continuation of the New Economic Policy and a moderate approach in dealing with the peasants. By this time, however, Stalin had already struck out a new path. As early as 1926 he and his entourage had determined that the NEP experiment needed to be ended and that Trotsky's program of industrialization and collectivization should be carried out. A conflict with Bukharin over the question of how to implement industrialization was thus unavoidable. Although Stalin edged toward the positions of Trotsky and Zinoviev in the process, he made no moves to rehabilitate them politically. Stalin had become a Trotskyite, who believed he could dispense with Trotsky the person. By 1929 the "Right Opposition," as Stalin now referred to his enemies within the party, had already been stripped of much of its power, and in 1930 Bukharin, Rykov, and Tomsky were banished from the inner circle of power once and for all. This time, though, Stalin was not able to dispose of his former companions in any manner he pleased, and unlike Trotsky and Zinoviev, they kept their seats in the Central Committee. This was in part due to their popularity (which the smug Trotsky did not enjoy) and in part due to Bukharin's willingness to perform public self-criticism and to submit to Stalin unconditionally.[34]

By 1929 nothing stood in the way of Stalin's autocratic rule. To be sure, he still needed to show consideration for his supporters and see that they submitted to his will, but the strife was over. The cult of personality that rose up around Stalin is a clear indication of this. Nothing made this new development more evident than the dictator's fiftieth birthday in 1929, where he was lauded as both a leader and a father.[35] From this moment on, criticism within the party leadership was gone. Stalin became the sole ruler, and within the space of a few years no one dared express doubts about anything Stalin had laid out as the general party line. In the event that any prominent Bolshevik should dare voice dissent in secret, the consequences could be severe. This is what happened in autumn 1930 when Sergei Syrtsov, head of the RSFSR, ventured to criticize the degree of violence being employed in collectivization: Syrtsov was humiliated and punished in public so that others could make no mistake about where dissent and criticism could lead.[36]

How was it then that Stalin of all people—who had never been a significant theoretician or eloquent orator within the circle of leading Bolsheviks—was ultimately able to triumph over all adversaries and become master of life and death? Who, during the years of the revolution and the Civil War—even among Stalin's closest confidants—would have imagined that he would emerge victorious from the power struggle after Lenin's death? In 1917 many did not even know his name.[37] Historians in the West were often surprised by this because they believed that even in the Soviet Union a dictatorship needed to legitimize itself by mobilizing the masses. Apparently they could only conceive of the revolutionary as a people's tribune in the midst of modern mass society—not as a far-removed despot, barricaded behind Kremlin walls. But the Soviet dictatorship was weak, and it possessed no means of mobilizing its subjects for its aims. It tried to invoke the people's will but was unable to make this will speak. If a dictatorship of this sort was to function, the ruler needed to be able to exercise power over his followers and his apparatus. This was especially the case for a dictatorship that could not rely on the will of the people, let alone invoke it. No one expected Stalin to hold fiery or demagogic speeches that would enthrall the masses. Stalin was instead a master of intrigue and games of power. He played his opponents off against each other. He had their apartments bugged and their mail opened. He always knew in advance what his adversaries might be plotting against him.[38] And, above all, he was adept at enlisting fellow travelers, careerists, and violent perpetrators to his cause, ensnaring them in crimes and then forcing them to surrender themselves to him fully. The party's institutional structure allowed him to eliminate his enemies one by one, and in doing so, Stalin could depend on the support of proletarians and peasants who had been able to rise in the party ranks. He could also rely on the national peripheries, where thousands of Communists had been recruited to the party since Lenin's death. At the Tenth Party Congress Lenin had convinced the delegates that faction building within the party needed to be forbidden, and whenever Stalin wanted his adversaries removed from the Politburo this was what he invoked. With great skill, he was able to shape his environment in such a way that by the end of the 1920s dissent was tantamount to treason. The canonization of ideology and the strict rituals of discipline made it possible to justify and rationalize any act of violence by invoking higher goals. Trotsky later recalled how Zinoviev had once alluded to the dangers that could result from Stalin's manipulations: "Do you think that Stalin hasn't discussed the question of our physical removal?"[39]

The organizational structure of the party changed in the 1920s. Before the outbreak of the Civil War, it was largely a conglomerate of like-minded comrades and friends, held together by the Central Committee in Moscow. Power was concentrated in the Council of People's Commissars rather than in the party leadership. Lenin was the head of the government, but not the head of the party—such a post had never existed. It was only during the Civil War, as the party accumulated new members and tasks, that its structure was modified to handle these new circumstances. 1919 saw the creation of a number of executive organs within the Central Committee. These included the Politburo, which was occupied by the most important Bolshevik revolutionaries, the Organizational Bureau, the Secretariat, and the Central Control Commission, which was home to the administration and disciplinary jurisdiction of the party. Although the Central Committee was still the official center of decision making, over time its actual power slowly evaporated—a change that was not least facilitated by Stalin himself. The Politburo, which was originally intended to manage the day-to-day business of governing, developed into the actual fulcrum of power. In 1924, after the founding of the Soviet Union, the Politburo replaced the government, because, unlike the Council of People's Commissars, it could directly intervene in the affairs of the non-Russian national republics. This shift in responsibilities was also evidenced by the fact that the ministers were now accountable to the Politburo and required to attend its meetings and brief its members. As the workload grew, however, the Politburo began to require an administrative apparatus of its own, and so the 1920s also saw an enlargement of the Organizational Bureau and the Secretariat, which prepared Politburo meetings and managed the party's staffing policy.[40]

Stalin was not just a member of the Politburo and the Organizational Bureau. In 1922 the Central Committee appointed him General Secretary as well. This post allowed him to fill the Secretariat and its subdivisions with his confidants and proceed with his covert work of expanding his power base. Lenin himself had laid the groundwork for this. Following his dispute with the "Workers' Opposition" and other critics within the party, Lenin had sought to tighten control by increasing the number of institutions. He had apparently been convinced that the despotism of the administration, "bureaucratism" as he called it, could be curbed by introducing new controlling authorities. And so the Secretariat and the Central Control Commission were born—to control and monitor within the party. Within these new institutions, it was Stalin who decided what needed to be done to preserve party discipline. He also had two compliant and devoted servants in the Secretariat—Vyacheslav Molotov and Valerian Kuybyshev—to do his bidding. Like Stalin, Molotov and Kuybyshev came from the second tier of the Bolshevik party. They were young and ambitious and did everything in their power to shield their protector from criticism and competition. Until the end of the Second World War, Molotov would remain the second man in both state and party and would also serve as Stalin's unofficial deputy. Beginning in 1923 Kuybyshev additionally served as chairman of the Central Control Commission, the party's supreme disciplinary authority. This is what allowed Stalin to gain total control over the party apparatus and even influence party jurisdiction. From this time on, anytime that a Communist was appointed to the post of party secretary, or was relocated, demoted, or promoted, the order required Stalin's signature.

The Secretariat served as a connection between the party's provincial committees and its central command. It also replicated itself by establishing subordinate branches at every level of administration. Secretaries of local party committees were now appointed by the Secretariat of the Central Committee and subordinated to its disciplinary authority. From this point on elections of party leaders were mere formalities. Provincial party secretaries were no longer dependent on their local supporters alone because they were now involved in clientele relationships with members of the Secretariat. And since Stalin reserved influential positions for those closest to him and his entourage, within the space of a few years the party structure had changed drastically. Stalin sought to dispatch trustworthy individuals to the provinces to serve in the local party committees. Of course he could not personally vet every single functionary he had appointed, but he had two methods of managing this difficulty. The first was to have his functionaries reassigned to Moscow for a while, so that they would become part of his entourage before being sent back to the provinces. The other was to simply buy their loyalty with privileges and promotions. Whoever obeyed and fulfilled Stalin's expectations was richly rewarded. Stalin protected his followers in the provinces from critics and detractors and enabled them and their friends to govern without opposition. As a result, he could trust the party secretaries to cast their votes according to his expectations at party congresses and plenary sessions of the Central Committee.[41] For Trotsky and Zinoviev this sort of political maneuvering was boring as it failed to satisfy their vanity and thirst for glory. Stalin on the other hand enjoyed working in the party Secretariat as it gave him all the necessary opportunities to realize his goals.

Even as early as the beginning of 1923, Stalin had been attuned to Lenin's criticism of the bureaucratization of the party and had used it to reorganize the executive bodies. At the Twelfth Party Congress in April 1923 he pushed through an enlargement of the Central Committee and the Central Control Commission, from twenty-seven to forty and from five to fifty members respectively. According to the official explanation it was essential that the executive committees be refreshed, rejuvenated, and proletarianized. Only then would it be possible to curtail the creeping bureaucratization of the party. One year later, at the Thirteenth Party Congress, the executive organs were enlarged once again. The Central Committee grew to include fifty-three members and thirty-four candidates, while the Central Control Commission now had 151 members. By this time Stalin had started summoning members of both the Central Committee and the Central Control Commission to hold joint sessions, despite the fact that this was expressly forbidden by party by-laws. The composition of the Politburo remained unchanged for the time being, but Stalin was busy devising means of isolating his opponents in the supreme executive body without having to challenge them directly. Stalin enlarged the Central Committee and the party congresses, installed his people in the provincial party committees, and gradually robbed the remaining Politburo members of the support they would have needed to oppose him.[42]

The Soviet Union was not governed by bureaucracies and offices, but by individuals and their networks. It was run by people who performed assignments in exchange for privileges. These political apparatuses were not subject to the rule of law but to the regime of personal allegiance, which committed patrons and their followers to unconditional loyalty. Anatoly Lunacharsky, the People's Commissar of Education, Yakov Sverdlov, the secretary of the All-Russian Central Executive Committee, and Lenin himself provided their closest friends and relatives with posts and privileges in the administration and the party. The wives of leading Communists found work in the Women's departments of the party or in the People's Commissariat of Education. Marital alliances were forged, and promises of loyalty were made between Bolshevik families. In the provinces in particular, where local Communists could trust almost no one but their relatives and friends, this style of rule was uncontested. Here, Communists established ties based on family and friendship, set boundaries between their dominions and the outside world, and did their best to keep strangers from acquiring any power. At the empire's Asiatic periphery, in the Caucasus and in Central Asia, the party was ruled by clans and powerful families. A system of "relationships" (blat), nepotism, and benefits reigned supreme. Even if the party center had attempted to commit the provincial apparatuses to abstract laws and regulations it is unlikely that it would have succeeded. The party was simply unable to sufficiently compensate the local functionaries, and thus its leadership had no choice but to leave the governance of the provinces in the hands of local Communists.[43]

Before the revolution the Bolshevik Party had just over 10,000 members. Following the revolution its number grew dramatically—allegedly reaching around 400,000 by the end of 1917—as everyone who had previously been excluded from power could now participate. This included members of the revolutionary underground, young men, workers and peasants, the uneducated, ethnic minorities—Jews in particular—and women. Amid the turmoil of the Civil War, the composition of local party committees changed further. Death, flight, military drafts, and the constantly changing location of action threw the party into a state of permanent unrest. In the second half of 1919 the party acquired thousands of new members, mainly young men hardened through the war, who soon eclipsed the older generation of Bolsheviks and brought a violent military habitus to the party. In 1922, when the Civil War ended, the party still counted some twelve thousand old guard Bolsheviks among its ranks, who had once fought underground for the revolutionary cause. Now, however, they were facing increasing competition from those who had joined during the early Civil War years. These old fighters were replaced by careerists. In December 1921 the party leadership had declared that only those who had belonged to the party before 1917 could become local party secretaries, but this simply served to show just how precarious the position of the old Bolshevik generation had become.[44]

In late 1923 the inner circle of leadership began toying with the idea of increasing the number of workers within the party as a means of breaking the power of those petty despots Lenin had denounced. For Stalin and his followers, a proletarianization of the party promised to positively change the make-up of the party since they expected more from the workers and peasants than the intelligentsia and its revolutionary romanticism had to offer. After Lenin's death in 1924 Stalin gave the recruitment program a new name intended to lend it further credence. It was renamed the Lenin Enrollment (*Leninskii prizyv*), and between 1924 and 1925 it brought more than 500,000 production workers into the party fold. In 1926 the Secretariat expanded the recruitment effort to include peasants as well. The party also gained tens of thousands of non-Russian members, who had the task of bringing socialism to the languages and traditions of their nations at the edges of the empire.[45]

Stalin was not just the friend of the upwardly mobile proletarian, but he was also his representative. He and his followers had also come from below, where they had suffered poverty, experienced violence, and exercised it. They spoke a common language and shared the habitus of violent men ready for anything. By the mid-1920s these upwardly mobile proletarians were able to assert themselves within the party leadership as well. Stalin, who controlled the secretaries in the provinces, aided his friends and allies, helping them to ascend to the highest positions of power. What Stalin's friends had to say on questions of a political nature was initially of secondary importance. That was why the Georgian, Vissarion Lominadze, who belonged to Stalin's followers, spoke in Trotsky's favor during the intraparty conflicts—not because he shared his views, but because he believed it necessary that controversial discussion be allowed within the Central Committee. There were, however, no doubts regarding his loyalty to Stalin.[46]

Among the circle of uneducated social climbers, Stalin was able to command respect and renown early on. Nikita Khrushchev remembered the first time he met Stalin at the Fourteenth Party Congress in Moscow in 1925. He had expected a distinguished personality vested with all the insignia of power. Instead the general secretary faced him in proletarian plainness, with a modest demeanor and a democratic attitude. Stalin's language was simple and crude and free from any sort of intellectual brilliance. This made it easy for uneducated working-class Communists to behave freely and openly in his presence. Trotsky found it unbearable to be surrounded by people with modest intellectual gifts and made no secret of his feelings of disdain for them. Stalin on the other hand presented himself as a man of the people. Khrushchev was impressed not only by the Georgian's "democratic" plainness, but also by his bricks-and-mortar approach to work. Stalin attended to every detail of administrative work, and no banality of daily business was beneath him. While he was deified in public, Stalin always stooped to an earthly level in private. Anastas Mikoyan recalled how, in 1923, Stalin lived in a very small apartment in the Kremlin compound with only very "simple" furnishings. He abstained from luxuries of any kind while on holiday, and he invited his friends and followers to eat and drink with him and to spend their vacations with him at his summer dacha in Sochi. Stalin's closest confidants, such as Ordzhonikidze and Mikoyan, old friends from the Caucasus, not only attended Stalin's nightly gatherings but were invited to spend the night at his house as well. On such occasions Mikoyan assumed the role of *tamada* (master of ceremonies) and proposed the dinnertime toasts, as was the custom in Stalin's homeland.[47]

Stalin's companions—Ordzhonikidze, Mikoyan, Voroshilov, and Kaganovich, to name only the most important of them—were simple men, followers of the proletarian cult of masculinity. The vocabulary of violence informed their speech, and they had no reservations about translating their language into action. An example of a minor yet telling episode may illustrate the kind of style the Stalinists brought to the party's executive bodies. During a June 1929 Politburo meeting Bukharin and Voroshilov began arguing about how the Comintern in China should respond to the Kuomintang massacre of Communists. When Bukharin accused War Commissar Voroshilov of advocating support for the Chinese nationalists in the Kuomintang despite their slaughter of Communists, Voroshilov responded by calling him a "liar" and a "scoundrel" who "ought to get a punch in the snout." That was how the war commissar saw fit to conclude a discussion that he considered inadmissible. Stalin's friend Ordzhonikidze did not shy away from physical violence either. At a summer 1922 meeting with Georgian Communists in Tiflis, where Georgia's future status within the Soviet federation was being discussed, one of the attending Communists complained that Ordzhonikidze's style was too dictatorial and that he was really nothing more than "Stalin's ass." Ordzhonikidze's response was to knock over the table and punch the critic in the face. Stalin and his followers had no scruples about using violence, because they came from a world where physical violence was an expression of male power. Stalin himself had a passion for it, and he appreciated other men of violence. He once told Kamenev that his "greatest pleasure" was "to choose one's victim, make one's plans, exact proper revenge, and then go to bed." Indeed, anyone who wanted to enter into the inner circle of power needed to be able to cope with the exertions that the Stalinist style of work demanded. But this alone was not enough. Stalin could only tolerate having people in his presence whose hands did not shake.[48]

Stalin's followers had difficulties with the complexities and subtleties of socialist ideology. To them, socialism essentially boiled down to the industrialization and militarization of the Soviet Union, along with the annihilation of enemies that would have hindered these projects. Their world was populated by enemies and structured by conspiracies. Trotsky, Bukharin, Zinoviev, Pyatakov, and Radek—the party's theoreticians—despised the general secretary and his entourage of dull-minded simpletons. The small flock of upwardly mobile peasants who sat at Stalin's side in the Central Committee and the Politburo was referred to by Trotsky as the "Savage Division." Everyone knew that the "Savage Division" had been a unit of largely Muslim soldiers from the Caucuses, who had served in the tsar's army during the First World War. Apart from demonstrating intellectual Bolshevism's disdain for the simple people, Trotsky's characterization also showed the disdain that

Russian and Jewish intellectuals had for the Asiatic peoples of the empire and their representatives in the party.[49] When it came to a struggle for leadership within the party it is hardly surprising that the national Communists from the periphery sided with Stalin.

"We as members of the Central Committee vote for Stalin, because he is one of us," proclaimed Jan Rudzutak, a member of the Politburo, speaking in 1933 of his relationship with the dictator. To his followers and his supporters, Stalin was more than just the first among equals. He was also their teacher and, as Kaganovich referred to him in the beginning of the 1930s, their "father." Fathers could raise, instruct, and command their children, and like a father Stalin intervened in the private lives of his protégés. He advised Mikoyan's children and chastised Kaganovich into parting with his full beard. And no one really took offense at this. Mikoyan, Ordzhonikidze, Kaganovich, and Voroshilov were helpless dilettantes. They knew that they were in over their heads, and they had their speeches and projects revised by Stalin before they dared to present them in public. In 1926 Stalin invited Mikoyan to join the Politburo and take over as People's Commissar of Foreign Trade, but Mikoyan turned him down: "I immediately spoke out against my candidacy, stating that I was unfit for such a role." Stalin usually responded to such modesty with assurances that practical experience and intimacy with "reality" would make up for the candidate's lack of formal training. Stalin himself possessed no higher education, and according to Lenin, was an uncouth "Asian." In the company of his protégés, however, Stalin came across as a man of education, allowing him to gradually assume the role of a supreme fatherfigure.[50]

But what produced a situation in which critics within the party were not only forced to accept defeat, but also had to cower in public, before meekly accepting their death sentences? Behavior that initially appears fully irrational only becomes intelligible when we consider the isolation the Bolsheviks found themselves in. They saw themselves as the members of a chosen order, as the defenders of a fortress that was under enemy assault. And this fortress would only withstand attack if those defending it desisted from internal bickering and presented a united front to the outside world. The individual party member was subordinate to the collective and its rules, because he knew full well that every mistake had the potential to aid the enemy, who was lying in wait to raze the Bolshevik fortress. In 1921 Lenin himself had forced through a prohibition against the formation of factions within the party, to be punishable by expulsion. At that time the party leadership had begun staging public rituals as displays of their unity. Leading Bolsheviks confirmed their mutual loyalty and friendship and presented the party as an association of the strong-willed. Strangely enough, it was Trotsky of all people—a man whose introverted individualism eluded all disciplinary efforts—who gave voice to the collectivist disciplinary program at the Thirteenth Party Congress in May 1924: "Comrades, none of us wishes or is able to be right against his party. The party in the last analysis is always right, because the party is the sole historical instrument given to the proletariat for the solution of its basic problems . . . I know that one cannot be right against the party. It is only possible to be right with the party and through the party for history has not created other ways for the realization of what is right."[51]

What took place was nothing less than an act of social disciplining, in which deviation from the norm was punished with exclusion from the community. From this point on it was not enough for party members to bow before the resolutions of the Politburo. They also began to speak a prescribed language, and as soon as they came under suspicion of having violated a "general line" they expressed their great regret publicly and performed self-criticism. In one regard, the series of doctrines that had to be recited and repeated throughout the 1920s was aimed at disciplining the upwardly mobile peasantry, who had risen in the party but had not yet developed the appropriate habitus or behavioral codex. For this purpose Stalin assumed the role of the high priest and made certain that these rituals did not fail in their purpose. His time as a pupil at the Orthodox theological seminary had prepared him well.

Immediately after Lenin's death the party leadership began naming factories, schools, streets, and squares after the revolutionary leader. Petrograd, the cradle of the revolution, was renamed Leningrad, and Lenin's body was embalmed and put on display in a mausoleum on the Red Square in Moscow.[52] Lenin was elevated to the level of a revolutionary saint, and his writings were canonized and sacralized. They could be cited but no longer criticized. Anyone seeking to make himself heard within the party needed to present a case that made reference to the works of Lenin. And it was Stalin, general secretary and manipulator extraordinaire, who ultimately presided over what could be discussed and how it could be discussed. Those in the party leadership began to speak of Leninism as a canon of dogmas, to which every party member was required to submit unconditionally. In November 1929 Vladimir Zatonsky, who belonged to the old generation of Bolsheviks and was serving as secretary of the Central Committee of the Ukrainian Communist Party, published an article in the journal *Letopisi Revoliutsii* (Annals of the Revolution), suggesting that Lenin had once discussed a possible merger with the Left Socialist Revolutionaries. Without delay, he was met with Stalin's rebuke. How dare he spread such stories? When Zatonsky insisted that Lenin had indeed considered such a merger possible, Stalin's answer was that no one but himself had the right to interpret Lenin's actions: "It seems to me that your explanation (your answer to my note) is wholly unsatisfactory. It is unthinkable to conceive of this, and it is absolutely inadmissible to presume that Lenin ever spent even a second on the pursuit of merging the Bolshevik Party with the Left Socialist Revolutionaries, or even permitted 'toying' with such an idea. It seems to me that you should unambiguously declare in the press that you were mistaken about the established points in your article in 'Letopisi Revoliutsii.'"[53]

Anyone who spoke out against Stalin or his supporters was in violation of the commandment of unity. Furthermore, he made himself guilty of treason against Leninism and its ruling doctrines, which by this time had been elevated to the rank of divine laws. During the 1920s party congresses and plenary sessions of the Central Committee, the occasional verbal duel was still present. Although this would suggest that some differences of opinion still existed, the language was always the same. Speakers exchanged quotations from the works of Lenin and substantiated their claims by invoking dicta of the deceased leader. Their concerns were always dressed in a standardized rhetoric that was reminiscent of scholastic disputes from the Middle Ages. And since no one called the canonized rules into question, because no one—apart from a few exceptions—wanted to destroy the party's monolithic façade, those defeated in the power struggle were forced to show remorse and confess their sins publicly. And a sin was anything that violated the dominant general party line—as personified by Stalin himself. Those who had fallen out of favor were required to express public remorse in rituals of self-criticism and promise to be better in the future—serving as a warning for those who had not yet fallen out of favor. These were the causes of the degrading and grotesque charade of criticism and self-criticism, which, by the 1930s, had penetrated into every level of party organization. Self-criticism was a ritual of subjugation for the offender. It served to reveal enemies and to publically degrade "traitors" and prepare them in advance for their physical annihilation. The leading Bolsheviks were all complicit in the establishment of a spiritual prison that held all party members captive. This meant that when the system's bizarre rules came to be directed against them, they did not have the option of simply suspending them. When Mikhail Tomsky, a former trade union director and Stalin supporter, fell out of favor with Stalin in the early 1930s he could invoke neither the right to free speech nor the right to criticize Stalin. In 1926 he himself had participated in the public degradation of Trotsky and had denied Trotsky any right to criticize the general party line or to behave in a manner that was "prohibited" within the Bolshevik Party. In 1927 Tomsky had jokingly declared in *Pravda* that "under the dictatorship of the proletariat, two, three or four parties may exist, but on the single condition that one of them is in power and the others in prison." Such a fate would also befall Tomsky in 1937, when Stalin decided to have him arrested and executed, along with Rykov and Bukharin.[54]

Since no one could speak except in the prescribed language and since no one could act without the prescribed rituals of insincere friendship, the leading Bolsheviks all mistrusted each other. Wherever oaths and avowals were mandatory, suspicion reigned supreme. The rehearsed manner of speech betrayed critics and deviants as liars, who were simply feigning loyalty so as not to be excluded from the inner circle of power. Paranoia flourishes wherever it becomes impossible to tell conviction from pretense, and herein lies the root of the grotesque delusions of espionage and paranoia, which Stalin and his aides seized on during the 1930s to carry out a war against their own people.

4　Subjugation

STALINISM WAS a dictatorship of subjugation. It was a war against its own people that respected no boundaries. But its violence did not arise from ideas. It arose from situations and their possibilities. People who enjoy inflicting violence on others have always existed, and when circumstances permit them to justify death and injury to those around them as unavoidable evils they are provided with a clear advantage. It was the atmosphere of total arbitrariness and uncertainty ruling the Soviet Union at this time that allowed Stalin to live out his fantasies of total power and sate his lust for violence. The Bolsheviks had begun a crusade against old Russia, and in doing so floodgates had been opened, from which violence could pour unabated. The constant presence and threat of violence altered peoples' moral frame of reference, and for both victims and perpetrators a life informed by violence became the norm. In the chaos created by the campaigns of the Cultural Revolution, by the collectivization of agriculture, and by the rapid industrialization every violent act could be justified by invoking higher purposes and ideals. At some point, however, even Stalin no longer required a justification for his actions. Violence simply became a matter of course. Once a certain line is crossed, the motives that initially set a process in motion no longer matter. And this is when the professional perpetrators of violence come into their hour of glory. They invoke the state of emergency and use it to justify every atrocity that peaceful conditions would have precluded. The Cultural Revolution campaigns and the struggle against the peasantry produced a chaos that allowed the regime to unfold a madness that eventually knew no limits. Social orders can be established to prevent people from inflicting violence on one another—to limit the use of violence. Such limits, however, would have found little favor among Stalin and his associates. For them the state of emergency was a golden opportunity. It was a chance to give violence free reign. The fact that the dream of the New Man would be drowned in blood did not matter.

NEW MEN

The Bolsheviks were isolated. Outside of the larger cities their only means of exercising power was with disciplinary violence. Their only means of forcing themselves into the consciousnesses of their subjects was by conducting periodic campaigns. A continuous political operation based on cruelty and disciplinary measures may generate fear, but it will not engender an order in which people voluntarily behave as the ruler imagines. A state that seeks to be strong and subjugate its enemies must establish strict discipline among its subjects. It must train them. It must standardize their behavior. This was how Stalin and his supporters saw it at any rate. The Cultural Revolution was supposed to achieve this social homogenization, to do away with old Russia, and to transform its peasants into Communists. But the despotic state was weak and knew little about its own territory and people, and thus it attempted to compensate for this crippling blindness by resorting, again and again, to the tried and true instruments of sporadic terror and random violence. "As a result," writes the American anthropologist James Scott, "its interventions were often crude and self-defeating."[1]

The Bolshevik Cultural Revolution sought to create a new kind of human being—one who no longer harbored any affection for the traditional life. This was someone who had committed himself fully to the new order, cast off all familial and religious ties, and surrendered every last bit of individuality. This was a human being who had defeated the enemy within himself and committed himself to cauterizing out everything foreign that remained. After undergoing a certain process of self-actualization this person would become a New Man. The New Man forgot. The New Man came from nowhere. In his text *Literature and Revolution*, Trotsky outlined how this man was to be conditioned:

> Man at last will begin to harmonize himself in earnest. He will make it his business to achieve beauty by giving the movement of his own limbs the utmost precision, purposefulness and economy in his work, his walk, and his play. He will try to master first the semi-conscious and then the subconscious processes in his own organism, such as breathing, the circulation of the blood, digestion, reproduction, and, within necessary limits, he will try to subordinate them to the control of reason and will. Even purely physiologic life will become subject to collective experiments. The human species, the coagulated Homo sapiens, will once more enter into a state of radical transformation, and, in his own hands, will become an object of the most complicated methods of artificial selection and psycho-physical training. This is entirely in accord with evolution. Man first drove the dark elements out of industry and ideology, by displacing the barbarian routine by scientific technique, and religion by science. Afterwards he drove the unconscious out of politics, by overthrowing monarchy and class with democracy and rationalist parliamentarianism and then with the clear and open Soviet dictatorship. The blind elements have settled most heavily in economic relations, but man is driving them out from there also, by means of the Socialist organization of economic life. This makes it possible to reconstruct fundamentally the traditional family life . . . Man will make it his purpose to master his own feelings, to raise his instincts to the heights of consciousness, to make them transparent, to extend the wires of his will into hidden recesses, and thereby to raise himself to a new plane, to create a higher social biological type, or, if you please, a superman . . . Man will become immeasurably stronger, wiser and subtler; his body will become more harmonized, his movements more rhythmic, his voice more musical. The forms of life will become dynamically dramatic. The average human type will rise to the heights of an Aristotle, a Goethe, or a Marx. And above this ridge new peaks will rise.[2]

For the Bolsheviks, what they referred to as the proletariat was a higher state of consciousness, an attitude toward life that the "barbarian" man of old was not capable of. Becoming a proletarian meant rejecting the past and gaining new knowledge and insight about oneself and the world. Being the son or daughter of a worker was not enough. Only with this consideration in mind does it become possible to understand how the Bolsheviks were able to speak of cultivating

New Men, grown in the laboratory of the revolution. The tenets of dogmatic Marxism were no less relevant to this way of thinking than the romanticist anticapitalism of the avant-garde and Expressionism. In these visions workers and members of the underclass were projections of the ideal intellectual, rebels who would restore the lost unity of mankind by ripping away the masks that capitalism used to represent a false world.

Trotsky's 1923 commentary on the New Men did not arise from the Marxist rhetoric of progress, but was instead an expression of the cult of feasibility. This belief, that anything was possible, was necessary if the ambitious tasks that the Bolsheviks had set themselves were to be taken seriously. Anyone wishing to catapult a backward, agrarian multiethnic empire into modernity within a matter of years needed to either believe in the infinite possibilities of the human will or abandon the idea of revolution altogether. This is also why the visions of the avant-garde and the Bolshevik will for change were able to merge for a time after the revolution. Shortly after the revolution, the Bolsheviks came to discover that theater was an ideal venue for revolutionary expression and education. It had the power to move the human soul, even to the point of inducing states of religious entrancement. Enlightenment and spiritual inspiration were the common goals uniting the Bolsheviks and the avant-garde. Even before the revolution, artists and scientists had believed in the power of architecture, science, and theater to synchronize Russia with the European West. In their theory, theater was a tool for exposing banal reality as an empty mirage. It had the task of uncovering the strengths and emotions within people and subjugating their speech to the rhythm and gestus of their bodies. The aesthetic notions of the avant-garde, the desire of the intellectuals to become one with the people, and the Bolshevik fantasies of enlightenment and spiritual inspiration all came together in the mass spectacles of 1920. This was when the theater director Nikolai Evreinov had *The Storming of the Winter Palace* performed under the open skies of Petrograd and in doing so transformed the city into a stage with several thousand actors and a crowd of some 100,000 spectators. The early Soviet experiments in theater and film sought to create emotions and control movements and effects, not just to train the actors, but also to manipulate the audience and make them receptive to the project of the New Man.[3]

The doctrines of Marxism and the experiments of the avant-garde were not the Bolsheviks' only sources of ideas. Representatives of the natural sciences also helped in figuring out how a "superhuman" might be created. The chemist Vladimir Vernadsky agitated for the establishment of a central academy in which intellectuals would work on the scientific remodeling of man. And among the leading circle of Bolsheviks no one was held in higher esteem than the physiologist Ivan Pavlov, who shared Trotsky's belief that human history was a process in which consciousness was continuously working to silence the animalistic needs of the body. It was within man's power to discipline and train himself, and the Bolsheviks knew that it was their destiny, acting in the name of History, to ensure that this project of self-disciplining be carried out. In 1929 the geneticist Alexander Serebrovsky even established a link between the Bolshevik regime and cultivation of the New Man. The question of "selection in human society," he wrote, could "undoubtedly only be answered in socialism." And it could only occur "after the final destruction of the family, the transition to socialist education, and the separation of love and procreation." The reason, Serebrovsky wrote, was that, in biological terms, love was nothing more than "the sum of unconditioned and conditioned reflexes."[4]

If people were truly free and if they were capable of recognizing themselves as both the first and final authorities, then it followed that they could also be shaped and altered at will. The problem, though, was that Russia's people were not free. They had not yet recognized what the Bolsheviks had already discovered for them, and it was thus the task of the Bolsheviks to educate the people, to enlighten them, and also to discipline them. Only with their help would the people understand how to exploit their newly acquired freedom. Maxim Gorky, writer of the proletarian revolution and despiser of rural Russia, had been dreaming of reeducating the man of old long before the revolution. He shared Lenin's belief that peasants and workers were a malleable mass that could be shaped by the hands of enlightened educators. But how, they both asked, could communism be built with a "mass of human material" that had been "tainted by slavery, serfdom and capitalism" for centuries? Their answer, which left no room for ambiguity, was that if barbarians were to become New Men then their environment needed to be turned into a disciplinary machine. Suddenly there was no longer any contradiction between the "Americanization" of production and the project of liberating workers from the burdens of the past. Instead, wherever workers became cogs in the mighty machine of communism, New Men also emerged.[5]

These disciplinary practices were not supposed to be limited to the standardization and mechanization of production processes either. The New Man was also a fighter. He struggled to strengthen his body and was prepared to surmount all obstacles that nature laid in his path. Back during the revolution and Civil War, military experts had devised methods of disciplining the bodies of Red soldiers and training them to reach peak performance. The ideal Red soldier, however, was to be more than just a fighter, devoted to the revolutionary cause out of conviction. He was supposed to enter battle with a contempt for death, with toughness, agility, strength, and persistence—features that characterize both men and victors. The tsarist soldier, meanwhile, had none of these qualities, and that of course was why he had been defeated.

For the Bolshevik leaders violence was more than just a means to an end. The cult of violence and killing was instead an integral part of the Bolshevik worldview. In this conception of the world violent perpetrators were indeed the New Men. When the German Social Democrat Karl Kautsky criticized the Bolshevik reliance on violence, he was met with bitter contempt. According to Trotsky, this prominent Marxist theoretician was a mere man of the quill, lacking any sort of solidity of will. The Bolsheviks, on the other hand, were men of action. For them, the very purpose of the warrior was to kill and be killed, and this was the cruel logic of the class struggle that the new power holders embraced and surrendered themselves to unconditionally. They had no doubts that they would emerge as the victors from any battlefield, and so they also knew that they must not let the destructiveness and escalatory dynamic of violence deter them. The Red Army, which was much better versed in offense than in defense, did not fail to teach its new recruits the craft of killing. Their training was supposed to teach them to identify enemies and annihilate them in the life-and-death struggle. The Bolshevik cult of killing taught soldiers to systematically remove all inhibitions and prepare themselves to obliterate all enemies—both internal and external. The concept of the state's monopoly on violence holds that the state reserves the right to use force in order to deter others from exercising violence and that it limits its combat activities to those necessary for incapacitating the enemy. In a sense, the Bolsheviks appropriated this concept and perverted it. They transgressed boundaries and failed to consider the consequences that the uninhibited discharge of weapons would bring. But as long as the Bolshevik cult of violence was tied up with the demand for social disciplining, there was no way of escaping this dilemma.[6]

The New Man was not just at war with internal and external enemies. To him, life itself was a war—a war against backwardness and barbarism. Only when these were overcome would it be possible for him to free himself from the old way of things. Only a healthy body could summon the strength needed to pass the necessary tests, and only a healthy body could free itself from depravity. Sickly bodies, on the other hand, were unable to hear the signals transmitted by the conscious mind, and this was why the New Man needed to discipline his body. That was why he needed to transform it into a standardized machine that had no will of its own and belonged instead to the collective. In 1920, when Trotsky called for the militarization of labor, he was combining the pragmatic notion of forced labor with utopian visions of a perfect social order. Militarized labor held out the promise of disciplining workers and training them to become New Men. According to Mikhail Frunze, Trotsky's successor as war commissar, the actual task of the Soviet Army was to shape "human material." This, he said, was far more important than the development of modern weaponry. After all, once the iron will of toughened proletarians had prevailed, defeat would become a thing of the past.

The Bolshevik cult of the body also found visual expression, appearing in the form of posters that displayed the athletic bodies of the New Men. These bodies could also be encountered on regime-sponsored holidays, as well-toned athletes marched through Moscow's Red Square past the party leadership. Bodies that would fulfill the tasks expected of New Men required care, and the Bolshevik ideologues and their allies in science and in the military were hard at work on this problem. Insufficient physical exercise and poor personal hygiene, the consumption of alcohol and sexual debauchery, fasting on religious holidays —these all took their toll on the body and damaged the social collective. The New Man in contrast succumbed to none of these vices. He took care of his own body, because ultimately this was for the sake of the greater good. It was not just belief and prayer that needed to be removed from the catalog of every day practices but the bodily rituals associated with religion too. The flagellant processions of the Shia Muslims, the ritual baths of Orthodox Jews, and the fasting of Christians—none of these practices had a place in the new social order. In the Bolshevik crusade against religion it was not just the souls of their subjects that were at stake, but their bodies as well.

But the workers the Bolsheviks encountered were not the workers that existed in their grand visions. Nikolai Semashko, people's commissar of health and a close companion of Lenin's, even came to the dismal conclusion that there was nothing in the Soviet Union that could convince him that this would be the birthplace of the New Man. In his 1926 text, *Ways of Soviet Physical Culture,* he expressed his downright disgust for Russian life. During his exile in Europe Semashko had encountered a culture where people aired their beds, washed their bodies with soap, and laundered their clothing. In Russia, however, none of these things seemed to happen. According to another contemporary propaganda pamphlet, Russia's workers were engaged in the impossible task of "building a new society without having become New Men themselves." They were not yet "cleansed of the dirt of the old world" but were instead "up to their knees in dirt."[7] The regime tried mobile agitation units, educational campaigns, and theater productions in the villages, all in an attempt at teaching the people about the socialist program of hygiene. The regime's educational plays encouraged the peasantry to bid farewell to the ways of old and embrace the new way of life (*novyi byt).* Dirty pots and lice-ridden clothes were symbolically put on trial and sentenced to lifelong isolation if found "guilty." People were supposed to recognize that a life lived in dirt and squalor both ruined their health and shortened their lives.[8]

But there was more to the New Man than just his physical existence. The New Man was also a reader, and he surrounded himself with books—books that had received the party's seal of approval, of course. If the forces of the free market were allowed to determine what people read, the minds of the subjects of the Soviet multiethnic empire would quickly degenerate. Of this the Bolshevik leaders were sure. But in the hands of the dictatorship the book could also be an educational tool, and the regime sought to impose reading regulations as a means of improving the habits and customs of the peasantry. As Stalin formulated it during the early 1930s, writers were to be the "engineers of the human soul." Writers and booksellers had the task of developing

Soviet culture. They were not simply there to entertain their readers or appeal to their aesthetic sensibilities but to turn them into New Men. The project of introducing previously illiterate peasants to books was not just about teaching them the letters of the alphabet. For peasants who had no idea why they should become part of an unfamiliar system, books were an important means of teaching them the language and formulas needed for conceptualizing the visible world. The books promoted by the regime introduced the peasantry to the Manichean worldview of the Bolsheviks and taught them about the new way of life. The language, which was simple and formulaic, was intended to help these strangers to the new order orient themselves within it. The Soviet book also mirrored the aesthetic style of the Stalinist party elite, as expressed in what came to be referred to as Socialist Realism. It combined the educational needs of those in power with the receptive capabilities of simple readers. People not only learned the language the books were written in, they also grew accustomed to the style and militant content of the writing, which told tales of conspirators, enemies, and heroic conquerors.[9]

In the Red multiethnic empire, it was essential that the subjects from different cultures and language areas have a common canon of texts and styles to unite them. This, the power holders hoped, would enable them to not only claim power but also assert it. The book as an educational tool was not supposed to be read silently and introspectively but aloud. Readers did not always understand what was being explained or described on the pages they read out to themselves, but this was not terribly important. Membership in Soviet society meant working on oneself to become a "cultivated" person, and the book symbolized the habitus of the New Man, who did not merely read texts, but "studied" them. "Sidi spokoino, utchi knigu!" (Sit still and study the book!) was a common expression of the time.[10] The book was also the status symbol of the Stalinist functionary, who rose from below and used his collection of books to demonstrate how far he had come. Although it is unlikely that Nikita Khrushchev, Kliment Voroshilov, or Lazar Kaganovich had read many books themselves, they promoted reading as the recreational activity of choice for the cultivated man. Those who read and demonstrated this skill in public were eligible for membership in the society of the cultivated, and in this sense, Soviet education through books was not intended to develop differentiated literary tastes but was instead a means of homogenizing cultural practices. In a world dominated by people with humble origins, who had equally humble senses of literary aesthetics, it is hard to imagine how it could have been otherwise. Nevertheless, Soviet society made the book an object of high regard, and this influenced the recreational habits of many people. It was not just the representation of a cultivated person. It facilitated social distinction and advancement as well.[11]

In the early years of the Soviet Union collectors of books and readers of novels were despised. Books were not supposed to be read for entertainment but for social education. According to the *Great Soviet Encyclopedia* of 1927, a book was supposed to be treated as an object of scientific interest and nothing more. Romance novels, thrillers, and comics had no place in the new society. They did nothing to educate the people and only corrupted their morals. Most importantly, though, reading was not intended to create individualists but members of collectives—people who read books together, repeated what they heard, and recognized themselves as members of an ideological community where everyone shared the same views. The reader was not supposed to be a consumer. He was supposed to read in order to become a useful member of society. There was even a particular genre of books that explained why one should read, how one should read, and how this would help one to become a cultivated person. Ultimately, the Bolshevik obsession with transforming peasants into readers only remains elusive when it is looked at as nothing more than an effort to consolidate the dictatorship. On the contrary, it was also the by-product of the Bolsheviks' attempts at solidifying the Soviet state and homogenizing the multiethnic peasant empire.[12]

If the power holders were to achieve their dreams they needed eliminate all competing literary offerings and their interpreters. New traditions could only be established if old traditions were forgotten. As far back as November 1917 the People's Commissariat of Education had ordered the Russia-wide confiscation of all private book collections that contained more than five hundred books. In September 1919 Lenin instructed the Cheka to seize and destroy all privately owned books with suspicious content. During the Civil War millions of books were stolen, consigned abroad, sold on the black market, or burned.[13] The New Economic Policy of 1921 to 1927 lifted the ban on the free sale of books and made it legal to establish private publishing houses and bookstores. The power holders assumed readers would still prefer the books offered by the state, but as it turned out state-sponsored literature could not compete with the offerings of the free market. This was especially problematic in the national border regions, where the published literature bore little resemblance to the cultural standards established by the Bolsheviks. The free book trade became a threat, and the Bolshevik educators began to fear that they would lose their readers in the free literary market. In the end, the Cultural Revolution was more than just a crusade against the old elites and their interpretations of the world. It was an attempt to remove all books and printed materials that offered competing interpretations.[14]

Of course there was nothing to stop the regime from hindering the publication of books it considered dangerous. Beginning in 1929, after the publishing and distribution of books had been nationalized, only books that had received a seal of approval from the supreme censorship authority could be published. The cultural legacy of the tsarist empire and its libraries, however, presented a problem. What was to be done with all the old libraries filled with stories of a world that the peasants and their children were supposed to forget? The Bolshevik solution was to either destroy those books or to make them inaccessible. From the late 1920s onwards, libraries throughout the Soviet Union were plundered and their contents were incinerated. In 1935 Stalin ordered that all libraries establish so-called special sections, in which dangerous literature was to be stored and closed off from the public.[15] Throughout the Stalinist period, as the number of imaginary enemies grew, the number of books that required quarantine in these special sections increased accordingly. The cultural legacy of the tsarist empire sank into oblivion, and the writers who had emigrated or had otherwise been deemed politically suspect were declared unpersons. All books penned by Mensheviks and other out-of-favor revolutionaries were eventually consigned to the vaults of oblivion as well.

The New Men spoke the language of revolution. They celebrated its feasts, and they shared the customs of the revolutionaries. For a multiethnic peasant empire to become a socialist society its subjects needed to recognize that they were not simply members of village communities but of something much larger. The standardization of rituals and customs was thus a crucial part of the state-building process. Once a practice becomes a habit it becomes internalized in such a way that it can no longer be banished from life. The Bolsheviks grasped this early on and did everything possible to encourage the peasants and workers of the multiethnic empire to become acquainted with all the symbols and practices of the new order. During the early 1920s the regime began introducing new rituals into family life in the hopes that this would help tie people to the socialist state. Not only were there "Red weddings" and "Red funerals," the regime even invented a replacement for Christian baptisms. In a ritual that the power holders referred to as "Octobering," parents had the opportunity to give their children a communist baptism and pledge their allegiance to the Bolshevik order. There were also new names for children born under the star of the new order. In this realm there were few limits to the imagination. Names such as Bebelina and Marx, Engelina and Robespierre, appeared. Composite names such as Melor (Marx-Engels-Lenin-October Revolution) and Revmir (revolution and peace) were particularly popular. Some people even named their children Traktorina, Textil, Okean, or Militsiya, in a demonstration of which world they wanted to belong to. Those who failed to grasp the purpose of this practice but did not want to be left out chose names with a foreign, mysterious ring like Markisa, Embryo, or Vinaigrette.[16]

The Nisovtsevs, a married couple of Leningrad functionaries, who had named their daughter Marxena, provided an excellent example of how the New Men were supposed to live. They despised "bourgeois" virtues and familial ties, and they combined their selfless devotion to the party with a lifestyle that drew no distinction between public and private spheres. Their sons and daughters were not children but comrades. Yelena Bonner, who would later become the wife of Andrei Sakharov, grew up under similar conditions. Her memories of growing up in a Red household during the 1920s were of a family life marked by coldness and desolation. It was rare that her parents caught so much as a glimpse of her and her siblings as they left the house while the children were still asleep, and "often returned after we were asleep. "Although the Bonners belonged to the privileged elite of Soviet functionaries they had neither the leisure for Sunday dinners nor any sense of the beautiful things in life. As Bonner later described it, her mother was "indifferent" toward her children because "in their milieu being a 'crazy mother' must have been considered nonsense." It was only the maidservants from the Russian villages that taught the children of

Communist functionaries what a world structured by religious practices and habits was like.[17]

The Bolsheviks realized that their only hope of reaching the hearts
and minds of their subjects was in appealing to their feelings and al-
tering their habits. In the daily lives of workers and peasants, however, there was no place for the Bolsheviks. Anytime the people could
be found enjoying themselves, the Bolsheviks were conspicuously absent. At Easter, Pentecost, and Christmas; during the Islamic month of
Ramadan and the Shia month of mourning (*Muharram*); during the
Jewish Passover—on all these occasions that the people held sacred
the Bolsheviks had nothing to contribute. Festivals and holidays meanwhile endowed life with a fixed rhythm. Apart from establishing a link
between the peasants and their departed ancestors, the holiday served
as a fixed point in the village calendar. It determined the cycle of life,
and it structured people's sense of time into a past, present, and future.
What this meant of course was that any revolutionary with dreams
of remaking man and his habits needed to gain control of the holiday calendar. Holidays were also problematic in that the peasants used
them as occasions to binge on alcohol, commit all sorts of excesses,
and make a mockery of the state order. In the early 1930s, as several
hundred thousand peasants, fleeing hunger and violence, arrived in the
cities, they brought their village customs and habits with them. Soon
even the cities were polluted by the customs of the village, and the
Bolsheviks quickly realized that if they did not intervene their project
of civilization would have to be abandoned altogether. And so they
did intervene by creating a new holiday calendar for the people. International Women's Day, May Day, the Day of the Revolution, sporting
events, and socialist harvest celebrations all became part of the new
Red calendar. Since they were specifically intended to eclipse the old
customs they were held on the same days as the old village holidays.

In the major cities, this project of remaking the holiday calendar
seemed to be bearing fruit. This was, of course, due in large part to
the facts that production was suspended on socialist holidays and that
participation in the holiday marches and parades was compulsory. Of
course, not everyone marching past the podiums where the Bolshevik
leaders stood looming above the people shared the worldview of their
new masters. Nevertheless, after years of being called onto the streets,
people did slowly become used to the rituals and holidays of the new

system, and they slowly forgot the meaning and purpose of the old festivals. This purging of minds could not be achieved everywhere, though.
In the villages, where most traditions were handed down orally, those
who came promoting the new social order were largely ignored, and
here the old festivals and customs survived much longer than in the
cities. For many years to come Bolshevik festivals would remain urban
phenomena, confined to the European part of the Soviet Union. Even
here, though, the old holidays persisted, and although the new ones
were observed, they were often depoliticized and altered through appropriation. Otherwise, it is unlikely that would have caught on among
the people at all.[18]

New Men lived in new cities. From the very beginning, the Bolsheviks
knew that they needed to restyle the cities of the empire in a way that
would allow them to direct the movements and practices of their residents. The inner cities were becoming desolate. Old Moscow, with its
intricate maze of alleys, back streets, and unlit spaces, belonged to the
Muscovites. What happened here eluded the control of state authority,
and so the reshaping of cities was a question of power as well. As the
Bolshevik planners went to work, the symbols of the old regime vanished from the cityscape and imperial monuments were replaced with
communist ones. Billboards were also replaced with propaganda posters, which were nearly impossible to ignore. The public sphere became
a political space, which served to broadcast the state-sponsored visions
of the new life. It consisted of squares and broad streets that no longer
invited people to linger. It created spaces where the Bolsheviks and the
people encountered each other on terms determined by the authorities.
Shops, insurance companies, banks, department stores, and cafés soon
disappeared from the city centers and with them did the vitality of
city life. The boulevards, once stages for urban self-expression, became
desolate, empty spaces. Flâneurs and people taking a walk were soon
gone, and with them the joie de vivre of the urban residents. Cities like
St. Petersburg became dead, museum-like landscapes. Anyone who has
ever been to a Soviet square knows the gaping void left behind by the
disappearance of markets and shops. The emptiness created distance,
and encounters on the streets and in the squares became a thing of
the past. All that remained were vacant Soviet parade grounds and
the architecture of intimidation, which was there to remind the subjects of the regime's power. Soviet architecture was an architecture of

subjugation. It "nationalized" public spaces, and it sought to discipline its people through control and surveillance.[19]

The "culture and recreation parks" that the regime began opening in Moscow and other major cities in the late 1920s were part of an attempt at bringing even the leisure activities of Soviet subjects under central direction and control. The peasant immigrants arriving in the major cities needed to be supervised and trained, not just at work and during the Soviet holidays, but in their free time as well. This was the intention at least. But not every attempt at reeducation led to an increase in power for the regime. The Bolsheviks could abolish contact zones. They could force people to communicate with each other in heavily monitored public spaces, and they could force them to adopt a standardized rhetoric. But all the talk that took place in public—in clubs and in party cells, at factory assemblies and during holiday parades—was little more than a stylistic exercise in Bolshevik jargon. From this point on, the regime only heard what was communicated to them in the new language. The only possibility for the power holders to find out anything else about the needs of the people was through the reports of the secret police, which had the task of exposing the truth hidden behind the mask of propaganda. Soviet subjects were forced to live a lie that was orchestrated from above, and whenever the power holders called on them to speak in public they had no choice but to be untruthful. The Bolsheviks could alter the conditions of communication at their discretion. They could monopolize the media, and they could make certain that whichever rules of speech were in effect at the current moment were adhered to. With these methods, however, those instituting them only served to undermine their cause. They could assert their power in the public spaces—the world of the lie—and they could force the people to sing the praises of a life that did not exist, but the private realm was ruled by ridicule and alcohol.[20]

Corners of the private realm that were not in the public eye made the power holders nervous. And so, from the very beginning, they did their best to bring the living spaces of their subjects under state control as well. Even residential apartments became part of the socialist collective and the property of the state. In the first years after the Civil War, communal apartments began to appear in major cities throughout the Soviet Union. They had initially been nothing more than makeshift solutions, as the Bolsheviks did not know what else to do with the large apartments they had appropriated from those they had deemed bourgeois. Lavish four- or five-bedroom apartments were transformed into crowded living quarters that were shared by several working-class families. The *kommunalka* was a Soviet Union in miniature, an everyday representation of the new social order. It was a place of destructiveness, in which complete strangers were forced to share toilets, baths, and kitchens, and to acquiesce whenever new tenants were brought in. The communal apartments also fostered lifelong friendships, particularly in the years following the end of the Stalinist terror, but the conditions of violence, scarcity, and mistrust that dominated the early decades of the Soviet Union primarily served to promote fear and hate. "They all lived in communal apartments," Joseph Brodsky wrote even about the late Stalinist period, "four or more people in one room, often with three generations all together, sleeping in shifts, drinking like sharks, brawling with each other or with neighbors in the communal kitchen or in a morning line before the communal john, beating their women with a moribund determination."[21]

In late 1927, as the pressure of peasants flooding into the large cities mounted, the regime began evicting more and more people from their apartments. From this point on nobody was permitted to occupy a living space larger than eight square meters (86 square feet). The chairmen of the housing committees were responsible for notifying the rayon soviets when living quarters became vacant. In addition to keeping tabs on their tenants' every move, they also scanned their buildings for illegal residents and people without residence permits and denounced them to the authorities. The chairmen of the housing committees were an extension of the arm of the Stalinist terror apparatus, and when necessary, they were generally not shy about giving their tenants a taste of what this apparatus was capable of. In April 1929 the government issued a decree instructing all local soviets to register all former landlords and expel them from their apartments. The chairmen of the housing committees were tasked with delivering the message to the outlaws and distributing the newly vacant living spaces to workers. In Leningrad alone, in the course of the early 1930s, thousands of so-called "socially alien elements" were removed from their homes. The communal apartments became realms ruled by fear and mistrust, where the slightest provocation could lead to denunciation and expulsion. The regime also introduced the ruling principle of collective joint liability, meaning that the guilt of one apartment resident could result in punishment for the others. In the years of the Great Terror this principle helped the madness of denunciations and persecutions spiral out of control so that eventually the violence could no longer be contained at all. Residents of the *kommunalka* were required to elect a "representative" and a "people's judge" who had the tasks of maintaining order within their apartments and seeing to it that their tenants were subjected to an iron discipline. Vandalism, unfavorable remarks about the state, and inappropriate social behavior were to be reported to the authorities, and offenders were to be removed from the premises. Out of fear of being punished themselves, the representatives did what the regime demanded of them. Although not every denunciation necessarily led to the loss of freedom or life, the system of arbitrariness bred fear and mistrust and spawned hate and violence. This made for a system in which it was wise to be wary of strangers and to reserve one's trust for only the closest of friends and relatives.[22]

Nowhere was the struggle for souls more vicious than in the Soviet Orient, in the Caucasus and in central Asia. This was a space free of proletarians, and thus the New Man was the product of a Cultural Revolutionary test tube. Here, the New Man was someone whose language, clothing, and habits identified him as (the Bolshevik version of) a European. In the Bolshevik mind, Europeans wore proletarian clothing, suits, and peaked caps. They listened to European music and used the Latin alphabet. Anyone wanting to become a European needed to cast off the dark rituals of the past and renounce both religion and tradition. This started with the Latinization of the written language. The project of "modernization," as it was first conceived in the Islamic periphery, in Azerbaijan, included the prescription that all Turkic-speaking and Islamic peoples of the Soviet Union begin using the Latin alphabet. Unlike Arabic, the Latin script had letters and syllables that corresponded to distinct sounds, promising to facilitate the promotion of literacy in parts of the empire where illiteracy tended to be the rule. In Tatarstan and in the Crimea, however, compulsory Latinization had the effect of turning tens of thousands of previously literate individuals into illiterates. Although more prudent language reformers within the party raised some objections, the responsible party committees in Baku and Moscow largely ignored them. But the Latin alphabet was not just a means of promoting literacy. It was also intended to separate Muslims from their religious traditions and "educate them in the struggle against ignorance" and "religious stupefaction." It was supposed, as the journal of the Soviet of Nationalities phrased it, to "bring them closer to the great cause of socialist construction." Ultimately this was the true point of the project and the source of its revolutionary strength. It made mullahs into illiterates, it made the book of the Prophet unreadable, and it made the subjects forget.[23]

The Islamic societies at the periphery of the Soviet empire had no proletariat and none of the conflicts that made sense in the Bolshevik understanding of the world. Without proletarians to fill the roll of the New Men, who would? The Communist leaders in the Islamic republics had a clear answer: These premodern feudalistic societies did not have working classes, but they did have women to fill the role of the oppressed. Here, the revolutionary struggle, it was determined, would mean freeing women from the bondage of the past and creating a society that would allow them to enjoy all the freedoms that the proletarians and Communists in the European part of the Soviet Union were entitled to. It meant delivering this part of the world from darkness and smashing the systems that kept women shackled like slaves. In these societies at the Asiatic edges of the Soviet Union it was the women who raised the children, preserved the memories of the ancestral traditions, and passed on the pronouncements of the religious authorities as truth. Thus, the liberation of women was the key to the transformation of this part of the empire. To win the souls of the women was to win the whole of Islamic society.

In 1927 the central government in Moscow abolished Sharia law in civil suits, annulled the traditional Islamic marriage contracts, and outlawed polygamy and the marriage of minors. From now on, anyone who kidnapped a woman or inflicted violence on her could reckon with retribution from the state. But the real dispute between the Bolsheviks and the Islamic world ignited over the veiling of women. To Communists—both in Moscow and in the peripheries of the empire— the veil symbolized the enslavement of women and their isolation from social life. The Bolsheviks had no doubt that the hated Oriental order would disintegrate if its symbols were destroyed, and ultimately the struggle for women's equality was a symbolic dispute. Only when we consider the symbolic potency of this war is it possible to comprehend the zeal with which members of Komsomol brigades burst into the Islamic villages for soviet elections, demanding that peasants present their wives in public and strip them of the veils, the *parandzha* or *chador*. In the course of 1927 and 1928, tens of thousands of women were unveiled in this manner. Many also became delegates in the village and city soviets. For the revolutionaries this represented a mission accomplished. Not only were women "liberated," but they had even become equal members of society. Women who took the power holders up on their offer of emancipation became revolutionaries. To ensure that everyone was made aware of what these liberated individuals were capable of, activists from the cities saw to it that it was women who denounced enemies marked for exclusion from village communities— mullahs, kulaks, and clan leaders. As Samed Agamali-Ogly, chairman of the Executive Committee of the Supreme Soviet in Azerbaijan, explained it in late December 1927, women were already on the side of the oppressed, so they behaved "more honestly toward the cause than men." Further, he explained, "due to this honesty," women enjoyed "the respect and attention of the population."[24]

But these Cultural Revolutionary campaigns in central Asia and in the Caucasus were not just stories of liberation. Not surprisingly, they met with resistance and also sowed the seeds of violence. Women who had cast off their veils or joined the party were often assaulted physically. In Uzbekistan, in a matter of two years (spring 1927 to spring 1929), nearly four hundred women were killed. Throughout the Islamic parts of the empire women were disfigured, raped, pilloried, or banished from the community. This orgy of violence lasted until 1930, but the Bolshevik state also responded with force. Security organs in all the Islamic republics intensified their repression. Flying courts martial appeared in the villages, and men who had killed, disfigured, or raped women were executed. Show trials, which were meant to serve as didactic plays, were staged as a reminder that the revolutionary state, too, was well versed in the language of punishment and that those defying its demands had no reason to expect any mercy. The women who were killed, meanwhile, became martyrs. They had not been murdered but had fallen in battle.

The violence that the local societies inflicted on outsiders and city people was not the only reason that the Bolshevik project of emancipation ultimately fell apart. Resistance often came from the women themselves. Despite the promises of the revolutionaries, an unveiled women had neither perspectives nor hope, either inside or outside the village. The relationship between men and women was, indeed, a relationship of oppressor and oppressed. But this was not all. Men and women also depended on each other. They also worked together and were united in this way. The program of unveiling and emancipation may have been intended to free the women, but it also "dishonored" them and exposed them to sexual violence. For these reasons even the Communists in the village tended to disapprove. A policy that would have subjected their own wives and daughters to public ridicule simply could not win their support. The Cultural Revolution in the Soviet Orient criminalized customs and conventions, and it launched a direct attack on the very notions of national-cultural autonomy that the Bolsheviks had so enthusiastically supported only a few years earlier. A nation's backwardness, which had once been considered an asset, was now seen as a flaw. The result was that the resistance of "backward peoples" acquired a national hue. Customs whose sense and purpose had previously not been given much consideration in their daily practice now obtained a new meaning. They became reflexive, because from this point on Muslims no longer had the choice of only half-heartedly performing the rituals and traditions they had grown up with. Now their only choices were to either embrace them or abandon them altogether. The wearing of a veil or the observance of a religious ritual became acts of national resistance. Of course this link did not remain a secret to the directors of the Cultural Revolution—either at the periphery or at the center. Stalin and his entourage also understood that once the national minorities began resisting and once their elites began invoking their national traditions to justify resistance then the concept of national autonomy had been turned on its head. Not only classes, but nations too could commit treason and become enemies.[25]

ENEMIES

Bolshevism was a secularized religion, a religion that could tolerate no others. Wherever bells rang and muezzins called down from the minarets, wherever priests and deacons expounded holy texts or performed sacred rituals—here, the Bolsheviks were confronted again and again with their own impotence and inability to free the minds of their subjects from the spiritual clutter of the past. Hence they persecuted religion and its representatives with a degree of revulsion and hatred that is otherwise difficult to comprehend. These were two separate worlds, and the possibility of reconciliation did not exist. For the Communists, the religious frame of mind always represented an ideological concealment of actual circumstances. For them, there was only one correct interpretation of the world. Their interpretation.

Old Russia had been characterized by many intertwinings between church and state. After 1917, however, church schools were dissolved and subordinated to the People's Commissariat of Education. Church courts were abrogated, and marriage and divorce were subjected to the laws of the state. Religion became a private matter. Even Orthodox clerics initially supported some of the Bolshevik reforms as they saw them as freeing the church from the tutelage of and domination by the state. Some clerics were sympathetic toward the revolution. But the illusion that church and revolution could achieve peaceful coexistence did not last long. For the Bolsheviks, a simple separation of church and state was not enough. Instead, the subjects of the empire were expected to renounce their faith and publicly reject the religious traditions they had observed all their lives.

Back during the Civil War the new power holders had already demonstrated their position regarding the church. Not only did they deprive Orthodox clerics of their voting rights and stigmatize them as enemies of the people, but they also had them killed. Wherever the Red terror raged, priests and nuns were among its first victims. The famine of 1922 was an occasion to confiscate church property, melt down church bells, destroy relics, and steal religious icons. This was all performed under the cynical pretense of needing to liquidate the church's wealth in order to help the hungry. Ultimately, though, Lenin's intention was to discredit the church and its dignitaries as agents of capitalism, parasites who enriched themselves at the expense of the starving. In the regime's war against religion, neither peasants nor workers were spared. In March 1922, Chekists arrived in the industrial city of Shuya in Ivanovo-Voznesensk Oblast, where they confiscated church property and threw holy objects onto the streets. When workers began rioting in protest the regime used machine guns to quell the angry crowds and had their ringleaders executed. According to the secretary of the local party committee a conspiracy had been afoot. The resistance, he was certain, was not simply due to the workers' genuine rage at the desecration of something they held dear. It had instead been sparked by "monarchist popes and Social Revolutionaries."[26] For Lenin, there was only one solution. In March 1922 he issued a directive, stating that "one dozen representatives of the local clergy," needed to be arrested and executed, along with "the local petty bourgeoisie and the local bourgeoisie." This directive applied to Moscow and to all other centers of religion in the country as well. It was essential, Lenin wrote, to act quickly and decisively, before news of the violence could find its way into the foreign press and spark protest abroad. The peasants, meanwhile, were nothing to worry about. Who could really expect much resistance from people who were starving to death? In that same month, in a letter to Molotov, Lenin spoke with brutal openness about his views regarding the use of violence against the church:

> I think that here our enemy is committing an enormous strategic mistake in trying to drag us into a decisive battle at a time when it is particularly hopeless and particularly disadvantageous for him. On the contrary, for us this moment is not only exceptionally favorable but generally the only moment when we can, with ninety-nine out of a hundred chances of total success, smash the enemy and secure for ourselves an indispensable position for many decades to come. It is precisely now and only now, when in the starving regions people are eating human flesh, and hundreds if not thousands of corpses are littering the roads, that we can (and therefore must) carry out the confiscation of church valuables with the most savage and merciless energy, not stopping [short of] crushing any resistance.[27]

In spring 1922 major cities throughout Soviet Russia became the scene of a series of show trials against Orthodox bishops and priests. Members of the Politburo determined the penalty in advance and also decided whether clemency would be an option. Generally, however, these trials culminated in death for the accused. Among the victims was the prominent Bishop Veniamin of Petrograd, who was put on trial in early July 1922 for supposed counterrevolutionary activities and then, along with several other high-ranking members of the clergy, condemned to death. In an act intended to demonstrate that the regime was serious in its determination to break religious resistance, even Veniamin was denied clemency. By 1923 more than eight thousand Orthodox clerics had been killed, and the number that disappeared into camps and prisons remains unknown. This terror was directed against

Jewish and Christian clerics alike. In their dealings with the leaders of Islam the Bolsheviks initially practiced some restraint, because without at least a transient alliance with the native elites the Bolsheviks had little hope of making any inroads into this part of the empire at all. By the late 1920s, however, the local Islamic clerics were no longer safe from the terror either.[28]

With the introduction of the New Economic Policy, the state's terroristic raids against the church were temporarily suspended. In June 1923 the Politburo even approved the release of the imprisoned Patriarch Tikhon, once he had publicly renounced his "anti-Soviet" activities of the past and promised to be a loyal supporter of Soviet power in the future. While the Orthodox Church was allowed to exist, the Bolsheviks embarked on an effort to make it into a church that they could control and saw to it that only friends of the regime were allowed to enjoy its positions of power. A certain movement of "reformers," who referred to their institution as the "Living Church" (*Zhivaia Tserkov'*), also sprang up. The Living Church professed loyalty to Soviet power and a commitment to the democratization of church hierarchies. With support from the GPU, the Living Church was able to occupy several dioceses with their bishops, but as the church of collaboration, its success with local congregations was limited, and its clerics were usually rejected. Attempts at establishing state-sanctioned Jewish and Islamic worship institutions fared no better as they were generally met with indifference from the faithful. The Christian "reform churches," while initially enjoying some success, ultimately crumbled too, because of their inability to mobilize supporters, and once they were no longer of any use to the secret service they sank into oblivion.[29]

In the early 1920s the use of raw violence was scaled back, and the Bolsheviks attempted to change the people by way of educational campaigns instead. Popular brochures, theater productions, antireligious agitation, and fictional show trials (*agitsud*) were all educational instruments that the Bolsheviks used to carry their message to the people. Activists from the League of the Godless (*Soiuz Bezbozhnikov*) believed that simply through demonstrating the new way of life, its attractiveness would soon be self-evident. Anyone who looked close enough and recognized all the advantages that real life had to offer would no longer need to cling to the old ways of religion and superstition. And why should anyone resist something that appeared so reasonable? Once people understood what the new way of life was about, they would embrace it and become New Men. These New Men would no longer respond to the messages of handed-down traditions because they would no longer understand them. Bolshevik cultural hegemony was the ultimate goal, but on the path to achieving this goal the authorities needed to assert themselves against a good deal of competition.

The power holders encountered their limits as they attempted to smash the influence of religion in peasant society. The new way of life remained something reserved for Communists and educated city dwellers, and in the rural regions of the empire there were few incentives for giving up a way of life that had existed for centuries. Even for peasants who had migrated to the cities, the new way of life promoted by the Bolsheviks held little appeal. When the world as they knew it had already fallen apart around them, what reason could they have had for giving up the one thing that offered them a bit of security and comfort? Why would they have preferred a way of life that was foreign and unknown to one that had accompanied them and their fathers for as long as they could remember? Even within the party no one had any good answers to these questions. The 1920s and early 1930s also saw a change in the leadership structure of the Communist Party, as thousands of peasant functionaries assumed leading positions. Their attitude toward the Cultural Revolution was ambivalent, as they had already made the discovery that reeducation campaigns could only hope to be successful if they were combined with at least the promise of improving the peasants' daily lives. To the Cultural Revolutionaries, however, religion was a grave threat. It was little more than a carefully orchestrated spectacle with the sole purpose of clouding human consciousness. They saw in its hierarchy a reflection of the Communist Party, although it was really only the Protestant and Catholic churches that had a hierarchy like this. In Orthodox Christianity and in Islam, on the other hand, the number of theologians and trained priests was small. These were religions that could go on existing even without clerics, as everyone possessed the knowledge necessary for practicing religious rituals. The piety of the people in any case had no space for the state-sanctioned church.[30]

The regime was unsuccessful in expunging the old religions from the Soviet Union. But why did this failure lead to terror? The reason is that the Bolsheviks saw all their disappointments and setbacks as being due to more than just the simple inadequacy of their disciplinary techniques. Instead, these failures bore the handwriting of malevolent enemies. Anyone who tried to prevent the triumph of a way of life that was both inevitable and downright reasonable demonstrated that he had sided with the enemy. Mischief and crises were the work of the enemy. And since the Bolsheviks did not trust their functionaries and mediators of power in the provinces, they clung unswervingly to this interpretation of events. Ultimately, the paranoid search for enemies and the intensification of repression were attempts at compensating for the weakness of the Bolshevik state. The Cultural Revolution was more than just an attempt at reeducating and disciplining the people and destroying the old Russia of "cockroaches and icons." It was a project that combined the dreams of a new world, held by idealistic young Communists and enthusiasts, with the claims to total power and the violent fantasies of Stalin and his entourage. For this latter group there was no dream of creating a New Man. Instead there were only dreams of subjugation and control. And the state of emergency gave them the opportunity to do what they felt was necessary.

The Cultural Revolution, as it began in 1927, was not an episode, but was instead the defining feature of Stalinism. To Stalin and his associates, it was not just about erasing and reconfiguring popular memory but was also about disposing of enemies. The Communist "engineers of the soul" (Stalin) could only do their work if those who had previously enjoyed interpretive predominance disappeared from the fulcrums of power. The enemy resided in the collective, and Stalin and his followers could only conceive of the enemy as an agent of a larger social or ethnic group. Just as the friend was a proletarian, the enemy belonged to the societies of "former people" (*byvshie liudy*), landlords, capitalists, and kulaks.[31] For those who belonged to one of these communities of the stigmatized, the hope of escaping this identity was nonexistent. Those who wanted to survive the violence had to either hide or disguise themselves, so as not to fall into the clutches of the regime's henchmen.

In summer 1928, throughout the Soviet Union, the regime's attack on religion intensified once again. *Pravda,* in December 1928, declared that the time of peaceful coexistence was over. From this point on, violence was to have the final say, and it would triumph over religion. For the propagandists at the League of the Godless, now no holds were barred. Religious associations were placed under state supervision, churches were closed, and the performance of religious rituals became a punishable offense. For a time the regime even introduced the uninterrupted work week and abolished the Sunday sabbath. At the same time, there was a surge in Cultural Revolutionary agitation for Soviet holidays. On the days of traditional holidays fights often broke out between believers and Communists, as the Communists attempted to conquer the public spaces, interrupt processions, and occupy churches. During the collectivization of agriculture, churches and mosques throughout the country were closed, religious icons were "shot," and bells melted down. The "beautiful corners" were now reserved for portraits of Lenin and Stalin for peasants to gaze at and admire.

The Cultural Revolution also sounded the death knell for the clergy. They were stigmatized as "socially alien elements" and registered in lists that marked them as outlaws. Tens of thousands of priests, mullahs, monks, and shamans were stripped of all freedoms and sent to their deaths. The precise number of clergy who were murdered and deported remains unknown, but in all probability, in the course of the late 1920s and 1930s, some eighty thousand clerics of various confessions ended up dead. Those with competing interpretations of the world were banished from the world. Murder was the regime's method of trying to silence religion. And indeed, the Bolsheviks did destroy all the religious symbols they could get their hands on. They defiled holy sites, and they even succeeded in banishing religion from public life in the major cities of the Soviet Union. But the popular religion, the religion that was practiced in the villages, was much more difficult to eradicate. For all their brutal measures the Bolsheviks could not silence it.[32]

But the Cultural Revolution was not just a crusade against religion and its representatives. It was also a struggle against the old elites and "former people," who in the 1917 Revolution had been stripped of all prestige. It was not just their comfortable bourgeois positions that were threatened, but their physical existence as well. Between 1928 and 1931 a wave of violence swept the country's institutions, and several thousand members of the old elite were expelled from the ministries, soviets, schools, and universities of the Soviet Union. Subjects who lost their voting rights lost their jobs, their entitlement to food rations, and their homes as well. In some areas, even teachers were driven out of the villages simply because their fathers had been clerics. And, indeed, the children of "former people" generally fared no better than their parents. They were socially stigmatized, barred from higher education, and made into outcasts.

Two of the most important tasks in Stalinist society were to expose and to select enemies. Before this selection could begin, however, both city and village soviets needed to register and catalog all people without voting rights (*lishentsy*). The secret police kept comprehensive lists containing the names of those who had belonged to prerevolutionary parties, along with the names of former tsarist officials, priests, landowners, and nobility. Once a person's name was on a list there was no longer any protection against arrest. People seeking to make a plausible case that their voting rights had been unjustly revoked had the burden of proof to show that they were not enemies. Outcasts had the right to file complaints against such discrimination, and people whose identities were in doubt could apply for the restoration of rights with the soviets and appropriate party organs. Between 1928 and 1934 several thousand *lishentsy* were actually rehabilitated in this manner. Anyone seeking rehabilitation, however, needed to prove that they had never belonged to the ranks of kulaks or the former elite, because by this time there was no debating the fact that the nobility and kulaks were enemies of the Soviet order. Once a person was accused of being an enemy the only recourse was to argue that the accusation in this particular case was baseless. Working on the enemy was an insidious game of identity, in which the victims confirmed the worldview of the perpetrators. By this time no one dared to say what everyone knew—namely, that the enemy only existed in the imagination—and so the delusions of the power holders were signed into law. Working on the enemy was a daily plebiscite.[33]

And so the number of enemies grew beyond measure. After the violent excesses and expulsions following the collectivization of agriculture in the early 1930s, several million people had already been branded class enemies. Tens of thousands of dispossessed and disenfranchised individuals sought refuge in the cities and on the construction sites of the first Five Year Plan. Many of them were kulaks and merchants who had not only lost their possessions but also their passports and civil rights. These people lived in constant fear of being discovered and arrested. They lodged illegally in their apartments and claimed rights and benefits they were not entitled to. They were made into criminals, and they lived in constant fear of detention and expulsion—fates that were certain to befall them should they ever be discovered in a GPU raid. Individuals who had been uprooted, stigmatized, and outlawed were a constant threat. They had no place in societal life and thus had every reason to defy the regime and its representatives. When they were discovered, the hidden enemy became a visible and nameable enemy. In unmasking them, the power holders demonstrated again and again that lurking enemies did indeed exist, and in doing so endowed their terror with meaning and legitimized their use of violence.

People who were in danger of becoming social outcasts and wanted to avoid this sorry fate needed to make sacrifices and invent new identities for themselves. And they had good reason to do so, for outside of the new social order the chances of survival were slim. The writer Konstantin Simonov, whose mother was the Countess Obolenskaya, spoke of the heavy burden that his aristocratic background placed on his shoulders. He did his best to distance himself from it and reinvent himself as a proletarian by learning a manual trade and disavowing his relatives. The new elite were richly rewarded for their self-adjustment. They received official residences, cars, chauffeurs, and servants, who came from the peasant world that the Bolsheviks so deeply despised. Some careerists were even prepared to betray their own families out of ambition and self-loathing. This was the fate that befell the father of the poet Alexander Tvardovsky, who had been banished into the Urals as a kulak and then traveled to Smolensk in 1931 to ask his son for help. Not only did the son refuse to help his father, but he even denounced him to the police, who then arrested him and returned him to his exile. As the party boss of the Western Region, Ivan Rumiantsev, had told Tvardovsky, he needed to make a choice between family and revolution. And in the end the poet chose revolution. Had he chosen to aid his father this would have meant the end of his literary career and his physical existence as well.[34]

Those seeking to become Communists needed to successfully submit to a series of conformity rituals that the party leadership had devised as a means of disciplining the elite. Communists, it was understood, struggled against deviations. They silenced their inner doubts, and they were prepared—of their own free will—to submit to every general line. Those who knew how to read the signs of the times understood that there was no hope of escaping the mounting pressure. There was, however, the option of submitting to it and letting oneself be carried away. Workers, scientists, and intellectuals, who possessed skills the regime was interested in could compensate for their social stigma by demonstrating dedication to the regime. Such loopholes, however, were only open to a small number of people.

"Sons are not responsible for their fathers." This was what Stalin told a group of party functionaries and harvester drivers who were gathered at the Kremlin in December 1935, in the presence of a young peasant whose father had been deported as a kulak. This statement was immediately seized upon by the press, which presented it as a directive of the dictator. Ultimately, though, it was an empty promise, intended only for propaganda purposes. In truth, children of people who had been branded enemies were themselves stigmatized and discriminated against for many years after their parents' "crimes." It was impossible to avoid the shame and public humiliation of having come from the wrong kind of background, and no affirmations of loyalty to socialism could ever really cleanse a person of this stain. The proletariat was a community of heirs, which refused entry to those who had been born the sons and daughters of the enemy. Socialism of the Stalinist variety was a dictatorship of parents over their children. At the age of eleven, Antonina Golovina, whose father had been branded a kulak, was reviled at school as the "kulak daughter." Even her teacher told her she was nothing more than "kulak filth," who "certainly deserved to be deported." "I hope," said the same teacher, "that you're all exterminated here!"[35]

Once a person had been classified as a kulak or a class enemy, the possibility of simply living on as though nothing had happened did not exist. Many of those who met with this fate tried to go into hiding and then resurface with a new identity. Some tried to become part of the new order by struggling to overcome their own flaws. Sometimes both things happened simultaneously, as was the case with young Stepan Podlubny, whose father had been banished as a kulak. He managed to go into hiding in Moscow, where he lived a life of conformity, but he also kept a diary in which he poured out the sorrows of his soul. He saw no escape from his plight, and for this he suffered deeply. Podlubny did his best to become an exemplary Komsomol member. He internalized the propaganda of the regime, and he struggled to find meaning in its rhetoric of enmity. He despised the drinking habits and raw violence of the young workers around him, and ultimately he reinvented himself as a "New Man," who read books and abstained from alcohol. In many ways his story was typical for similarly stigmatized children and young people who could not bear the prospect of social exclusion. For thousands of young people who found themselves in this position, projects of self-conquest became their means of attempting to find a place in the new society.

By this time it had become impossible for the stigmatized to ignore the new order. All spaces of retreat were gone, and alternative ways of life no longer existed. But no one can live a lie forever and maintain sanity. Some people led lives pretending to be someone else and in the end they truly believed that they were that someone. One intelligence officer, who came from an aristocratic family, spent so many years concealing his background that, for him, dissimulation eventually became second nature. At some point the fictitious life story even became more real for him than reality. "I began to feel like the person I was pretending to be," the officer recalled. Apart from the psychological damage of having to live a lie, the danger of being caught was also considerable. This is what happened to Podlubny. When the authorities discovered that he had concealed this true identity he was required to write informers' reports for the secret police. His October 1, 1932 diary entry reads, "Damn, I am so upset that I have gotten myself involved with this GPU. They are completely spoiling my mood, robbing me of a part of my life. When I come out of there, it's as though I'm drunk, so exhausted that I could fall asleep on the spot. I come out of there sick, and all this within 25 minutes. And what if they were to keep me there for an entire day? It would surely drive someone insane. Terrible. Pain, heart cramps. Scattered thoughts race through the mind. On the first day there I was truly in despair." Podlubny's service to the regime did not help him overcome the dilemma of his existence either, and in the years of the Great Terror he was arrested and imprisoned in a camp anyway.[36]

Without the entanglement of tens of thousands of helpers in the system of informing and surveillance, what happened in the Soviet Union at the beginning of the 1930s would not have been possible. Some people voluntarily participated in the witch hunts, hoping that this would improve their personal circumstances or serve their political goals. Young Communists and Komsomol members and also many workers were simply interested in anything that involved terrorizing the old elites and stripping them of all power. These people were happy to fulfill Stalin's request that they pursue and expose enemies. Students and Komsomol members took to the schools and universities, where they denounced "bourgeois" professors as "socially alien elements." Communist lecturers, meanwhile, chased the partyless intelligentsia out of their lecture halls. The Nepmen, those small traders who had attained a modest degree of wealth, were frequent victims of the system of denunciations. Old regime officials who still worked in the ministries began losing their jobs and sometimes their freedom as well. Starting in 1929, after a review conducted by the People's Commissariat of Workers' and Peasants' Inspection, 164,000 employees were removed from their posts in the state administration. At the beginning of 1928, in Irkutsk alone, Cultural Revolutionaries ousted more than eight hundred administrative officials, who were then replaced by Communists and industrial workers who were incompetent but reliable.

In the academies and universities, respected scholars were replaced by ideological zealots. In the factories, upwardly mobile proletarians replaced the "bourgeois" engineers who had been expelled and arrested. By the beginning of the second Five Year Plan, more than half of all factory directors came from working-class backgrounds. Universities and schools were governed by quota systems, and in their admissions processes the children of workers received preferential treatment. It was these upwardly mobile proletarians (*vydvizhentsy*) who gave the Stalinist system its unmistakable face. Nikita Khrushchev, Leonid Brezhnev, Alexei Kosygin, and Andrei Gromyko all came from extremely humble backgrounds, and without the Cultural Revolution their lives would have taken very different paths. Everything they owned and had achieved was thanks to Stalin, and they expressed their gratitude by offering him their unconditional obedience and loyalty. The upwardly mobile proletarian was thus both an accomplice and a perpetrator.[37]

Without denunciations the witch hunts would not have been possible. The Stalinist subject was vigilant. He was a denouncer, and his loyalty to the regime trumped all ties to family and friends. For Bolshevik enthusiasts, denunciation was a way of life. Denouncers were memorialized and honored in song. This cult of the denouncer began in late 1932 at a time when the Bolsheviks were becoming increasingly dependent on mobilizing support in the villages. In September 1932 a group of peasants in the village of Gerasimovka in the Urals killed an eleven-year-old boy who, one year earlier, had denounced his father to the GPU as a grain speculator. The boy's father had been hauled off to a concentration camp in the northern Urals and then most likely murdered by the GPU in winter 1932 during a mass shooting of prisoners. The name of the murdered denouncer was Pavlik Morozov, and the local Communists used his death as an occasion to take bloody revenge on the rest of his family. Morozov's grandfather, grandmother, an uncle, and a cousin were all taken hostage and locked up in the local prison. In November 1932 Communists, GPU men, and Komsomol members from the neighboring city arrived in Gerasimovka to stage a show trial against the detainees. Village residents were instructed to gather in front of specially prepared propaganda posters, where they were then required to demand that the delinquents be shot. Within a few hours the show trial was over, and all of the accused, including Pavlik Morozov's grandparents, were condemned to death and shot by the GPU's henchmen.

But Pavlik Morozov was no Bolshevik. He was an eleven-year-old peasant boy, and his reasons for denouncing his father were that the man had turned his back on the village and abandoned his family to poverty and misery. The actual circumstances of the event, however, did not prevent the regime from using Morozov's death to establish a heroic cult around him. Even directly after the boy's murder, Vasily Arkhipov, deputy chairman of the Central Bureau of the Young Pioneers, used the occasion to make an announcement in the *Pionerskaia Pravda* that Pavlik Morozov was to be "a shining example for all children of the Soviet Union." By December 1932, the Komsomol Central Committee had begun discussing how Morozov's "heroic deed" could be exploited by the regime, and as usual Stalin was the source of the proposal. Pavel Postyshev, secretary of the Central Committee, speaking in Stalin's name, began attacking the youth organization, claiming that it lacked the necessary determination in matters of the ideological education of Soviet youth. Pavlik Morozov, however, the young denouncer, could now become a role model for everyone. In the years of the Great Terror Pavlik Morozov was even elevated to the rank of a great socialist martyr. As part of a massive propaganda campaign he became the person that all Soviet youth were supposed to strive to emulate. Hundreds of books and brochures told of his heroic deed, and schools, villages, ships, and libraries were named after him. There were Pavlik Morozov museums, Morozov sports trophies, numerous Morozov statues, and even the Cultural Palace of the Young Pioneers bore his name. As late as 1991, Moscow's city center still featured a memorial portraying the young denouncer in bronze.[38]

More than just a proletarian luminary, the New Man was also a denouncer. In reality, though, it was only on rare occasions that a denouncer acted out of true loyalty to the regime. Most denunciations were acts of retribution for private matters of wounded honor, avarice, or envy. In many cases, those who spied on their neighbors and denounced them to the authorities were themselves people with damaged biographies, people who themselves had been victimized by the regime. They denounced others either because they had been forced to do so or because they belonged to the ranks of the stigmatized and in denouncing others they hoped to prove their devotion to the regime. Most importantly, though, the denunciation was a weapon, and the subjects of the Soviet Union used it to combat the enemies of their daily lives. It gave people access to the punitive arm of the state, which they could then use for their own private purposes. Those who wrote letters to Stalin and his paladins did it in hopes of accomplishing all the things that could not be achieved by way of regular complaints. Denunciations not only struck fear and dread into the hearts of the general population, but into those of the party functionaries as well. The Stalinist functionaries understood that denunciation was a powerful tool and that it could lead to the loss of position and influence. By the late 1930s a denunciation was frequently the equivalent of a death sentence. Although the functionaries worshiped the concept of the denouncer, this person rarely served their interests or the interests of the system. Instead, the denouncer contributed to the destruction of both. In this respect, however, the denouncer demonstrated that he was indeed a docile student of Stalin's, someone who took pleasure in seeing the functionaries of the Soviet state writhe in fear.[39] In January 1930, peasants from the Orel area petitioned Stalin with a complaint regarding a peasant who had apparently tormented the village residents before becoming a member of the Executive Committee of the All-Union Soviet:

> Dear Comrade Stalin, all the newspapers of our [Soviet] Union are filled to overflowing with articles about the fight against kulaks and kulak

henchmen. We in the provinces fight using the slogan you unfurled and we fight not because we are afraid but because we are conscientious. Permit us to ask you and put before you our proletarian question. Are you fighting against kulaks and their henchmen in the center itself, in the very apparatus of Soviet power? You have no small number of them there. Take, for example, the Presidium of VTsIK [the All-Union Central Executive Committee of the Soviets], where there's not just a kulak but an arch-kulak. This is Stepan Nikolaevich Izvekov from Orel, known all over the Orel District (*uezd*) as Styopa Izvekov. How he got there and how he made his way into VTsIK is very mysterious and strange . . . Who exactly is this Styopka? A prosperous arch-kulak from Orel Province (*guberniia*) and District, Pokrov Volost, Ovsiannikov Village, who in the old tsarist times served in the army and after coming back from there served as a gendarme under Captain of the Provincial Investigation Department Schulz, infamous throughout the Orel area for reprisals against workers and peasants, especially during the memorable days of 1905 . . . Comrade Stalin, there's no place for him there. Where there's a place for him is Solovki [the Solovetsky Islands, located in the White Sea at the entrance to Onega Bay, the site of the Northern Special Purpose Forced Labor Camps (SLON), founded in 1922] or with his forefathers, given his old dirty tricks and the position he used to hold.

Although Stalin did not reply to the peasants' letter, it was followed by an order to purge the Executive Committee and the People's Commissariat of Agriculture of class enemies.[40]

The spirit of the new age was also evident in the regime's show trials. These were forums for publicly naming the enemies of the people and presenting the regime's version of events. Show trials were stages on which dramas between the forces of good and evil were played out. In the end, though, the malevolent enemy was always defeated. These melodramas acquainted the public with the self-conception of the party elite and their style of dealings. But the creeds and language of Bolshevism were not the only things presented here. Show trials also gave spectators and listeners an understanding of the mental and physical properties of the enemy, all the while making reference to the rules that structured the Bolshevik power universe.

In May 1928 the regime presented the people with a show trial of a new sort. Several Russian and German engineers from the Shakhty region in the Donbass were brought before a Moscow court to stand trial. Stalin had already anticipated the court's findings when he spoke to a plenum of the Central Committee the previous April. According to him, the accused were traitors, who had been paid by foreign countries to sabotage the economic recovery of the Soviet Union. Stalin explained: "The facts show that the Shakhty affair was an economic counter-revolution, plotted by a section of the bourgeois experts, former coal-owners. The facts show, further, that these experts were banded together in a secret group and were receiving money for sabotage purposes from former owners now living abroad and from counter-revolutionary anti-Soviet capitalist organizations in the West. The facts show, lastly, that this group of bourgeois experts operated and wrought destruction to our industry on orders from capitalist organizations in the West." As in other cases when Stalin desired violence, his arguments were clothed in the garments of a conspiracy theory. He also offered up rhetorical questions: "Could certain bourgeois experts, former mine owners, have organized the Shakhty affair here without the financial and moral support of international capital, without the prospect of international capital helping them to overthrow the Soviet regime? No, they could not have done so, of course."[41]

The verdict was clear and there was a lesson to be learned before the court had even convened. The state prosecutor accused the specialists of sabotage and conspiracy against the socialist order, and in July 1928 eleven of the fifty-three defendants were condemned to death—on the basis of extorted confessions. Soon thereafter, similar show trials were held in other industrial cities throughout the empire. Each successful show trial seemed to provide further evidence for the existence of an intricate web of conspiracies and also attested to the vigilance of proletarian justice, which was ever-prepared to catch and choke off every threat to the existing order that might arise. This proletarian watchfulness was expressed symbolically by the workers' representatives who sat next to the judges during these trials and by their presence represented the punitive dictatorship of the proletariat.

The accused expressed their great penitence, outdoing each other in absurd self-incriminations and ritualized admissions of guilt, which appeared particularly untrustworthy to foreign observers. But this penitence helped little. This Stalinist script did not include provisions for the remorseful sinner's reentry into society. The condemned carried the stigma of enemies of the people, and in this way helped provide the regime with scapegoats for its failed industrialization policies. The dramaturgy of the show trial demanded that the accused confess their guilt in public and that they act out the roles assigned to them, under the direction of the prosecutor. In their publicly recited confessions the enemies of the people were expected to document their malignancy before the world. Andrei Vyshinsky, Stalin's unscrupulous state prosecutor who presided over the Shakhty trial, merely had to repeat what the defendants had said and use it against them. Defendants who combined their penitence with a plea for reentry into society were insulted by Vyshinsky as a "pack of Judases," undeserving of leniency. Not even the defenders of the accused deviated from the script. Not only did they make no attempt to shake the credibility of the prosecution, but they even sided with the prosecutor.

The Shakhty trial taught its spectators some valuable lessons. First, crises were due to enemies, and second, loyalty to the regime was more important than loyalty to friends or family. Brothers denounced each other as saboteurs in court, and the son of one defendant announced in the newspaper *Krasny Shakhter* (Red Miner) that he would drop the tainted name of his father and henceforth be called Shakhtin. Even the language the regime used in speaking of the accused was an expression of the new style, which knew penitence and punishment but not forgiveness. Pests, vermin, bacteria, and human waste were the terms used when speaking of the enemy. This applied in the courtroom, in the press, and even at public gatherings. Never again would there be any doubt that a society seeking to become healthy must free itself of its enemies. To the Bolsheviks society was a bodily organism that could become infected by bacteria. To cure it, it was simply necessary to cut out the infected ulcers and remove the bacteria. The rhetoric of violence and the language of bacteria and vermin dehumanized the enemy and helped create a distance between those doing the killing and those being killed. Physical annihilation was preceded by the dehumanization of victims.

It is possible to argue that the outlook presented here had no effect on the regime's subjects—that it failed to reach them or that it simply did not interest them. But the GPU's elaborate staging of the trial precluded the possibility of disinterest. The power holders' chief objective was to create a public mood that would translate into a mighty choir of accusers in the courtroom. The secret police distributed admission tickets, and after each act the audience was replaced, making it possible for tens of thousands to witness the events in the courtroom. But the impact of the Shakhty trial was much greater than the mere numbers of courtroom viewers would suggest. The reason was that it was simply impossible for anyone to ignore what was taking place in the courtroom. Newspapers spoke of little else, and newsreels in the cinemas showed images of the accused. Schools, factories, and workers' clubs held mandatory "discussions" of the trial, which were of course mediated by the appropriate Communist functionaries. Ultimately, the stage on which this spectacle took place thus extended far beyond the confines of the courtroom.

What did the viewers of the Shakhty trial propaganda film get to see? They saw a self-confident prosecutor who defended the cause of the state and its workers, insulted the accused, and drew lessons from what had happened. They also saw the accused, looking like miserable sinners, standing before the judges with bowed heads and faces showing that they were bitterly penitent. Whenever the accused came into view subtitles were superimposed, informing the viewers that this was scum they were looking at. The Shakhty trial was a visual representation of the dualistic friend-enemy world that existed in the minds of the Bolsheviks—an understanding of the world the viewers were supposed to adopt as well. Enemies were everywhere, and even when they hid themselves and operated in secrecy they could not be forgotten. Ultimately, victory over the hidden enemies was only possible if all citizens recognized their duties of vigilance and denunciation. This was the real point of these spectacles: to make sure that the people heard this message loud and clear.[42] Show trials were the core of the Stalinist Cultural Revolution. They ordered the public sphere according to principles of repression and subjugated society to the rituals of accusation, penitence, and punishment.

What took place in the Soviet Union during the 1930s and 1940s—the murder and deportation of several million people—was not limited to annihilation of the class enemy. The state-sponsored terror of these decades spared no one—neither workers nor peasants. Even friends of the regime, if they did not continuously work to refine themselves, lived in constant danger of suddenly being transformed into enemies. Only those who were prepared to give up everything, to overcome all inner resistance, and to relinquish their former selves could reach the heights of the New Man. The Soviet Union, however, was an empire of backwardness. It had plenty of workers, peasants, and nomads, but not very many New Men. The power holders were aware of this fact, and it was a constant reminder that their power ended with the borders of the major cities. Furthermore, it served as a reminder that their version of socialism was largely a product of their imaginations. There was indeed a dictatorship of the proletariat, but there were very few proletarians who were prepared to voluntarily submit to its demands. It was an order that offered little other than poverty and violence, so that the incentives to join it were few. There was not a single place in the empire where the regime was able to secure its presence without resorting to the use of exemplary punitive violence. Thus, what had begun as a Cultural Revolution and a struggle for souls soon became a war, directed against the peasantry of the empire. This war began in 1929, when the regime embarked on the project of the forced collectivization of agriculture, and it continued, with varying degrees of intensity, into the late 1940s.

WAR AGAINST THE PEASANTRY

The war began with a grain procurement crisis. The cities were threatened by a lack of food, and the power holders were becoming keenly aware that their grand plans of remaking society could not be reconciled with the possibilities available to them. Stalin and his associates had grand visions, but their means of intervention were primitive. This contradiction could not be resolved, and what was initially intended as an enormous reconfiguration and homogenization of the empire turned into an improvised orgy of violence. The regime was able to exercise violence indiscriminately since there was no civil society functioning as a firewall that would have prevented it from doing so. Still, the regime used the grain procurement crisis to justify its interventions and to motivate violence. The result was a bloodbath of apocalyptic proportions. It began when the peasants could no longer sell their grain for high enough prices. Additionally, they had little interest in spending the proceeds on the industrial goods being offered, so they started withholding their grain. To Stalin and his supporters in the leadership this constituted a crisis because it jeopardized the cities' food supply but also made it impossible to export grain abroad. Furthermore, it was an axiom of Stalinist economic policy that the ambitious industrialization targets of the first Five Year Plan could only be achieved if agricultural resources were exploited. The problem, though, was that the peasants' reasons for resisting were good, and there was little chance of convincing them otherwise. Violence seemed to be the only solution, and in 1928 the brutal procurement methods used during the Civil War were resurrected. Persuasion held little promise of working, and apart from sporadic raids, the regime had no other means of asserting itself.

In January of that year Stalin himself traveled to western Siberia to oversee the seizure of grain by the local procurement organs there and to tell the local functionaries about the organization of agriculture according to his preferences. Many peasants still remembered the dreadful years of the Civil War, when armed bands had arrived in their villages to rob them, and thus they were suspicious when armed procurement brigades once again appeared. Although there were some refractory Communists and judges who still opposed the use of violence against the peasants, Stalin warned the local party secretaries against catering to such folk and instructed the GPU to arrest them. Furthermore, the grain needed to be delivered in the quantities demanded, and if this did not happen those responsible were liable to be punished. "Grain procurements are the fortress that we must capture at any cost," Stalin told the regional committee of the western Siberian party organization. "And we will certainly capture it if we carry out the work in a Bolshevik manner, with Bolshevik pressure." All the other regions of the Soviet Union had already fulfilled their tasks. Only Siberia was still lagging shamefully behind, and this was because it was "terribly backward" and because its Communists lacked initiative. Everyone knew that Stalin was talking nonsense, but this was not of primary importance. Stalin's functionaries were haunted by the fear of falling into disfavor and losing their positions and freedom, so they did what Stalin demanded of them. The procurement brigades robbed the peasants of everything they had and shipped the confiscated grain out of the villages. Under Stalin's watchful eye, class enemies in the villages were exposed, and peasants who refused to hand over what was demanded of them were punished. Almost immediately after Stalin's departure from Siberia, violent assaults in the Altai region began. Requisitioning commandos held peasants at gunpoint, demanding their grain, and those who refused to obey were tortured and beaten or abused in mock executions. This violence, however, was a mere dress

rehearsal for the collectivization of agriculture that would begin a few
months later.

In January 1928 Stalin returned to Moscow triumphantly with several wagons of grain in tow. This was his ocular proof that the new
order had prevailed.[43] During the Civil War Stalin had shown that he
had no scruples when it came to using violence to crush resistance, and
there was no reason to expect that violence would not be his ultima
ratio in this case as well. The "Ural-Siberian method," as he referred to
his procedure of grain procurement, was intended to destroy the market economy, engender fear, and force peasants to hand over the hard-
earned fruits of their labors. "We must employ all necessary measures,"
Anastas Mikoyan declared to the Central Committee in April 1928,
"so that we don't face another grain procurement crisis." This, he explained, would require "even more extreme measures." He also added
that the leadership would not be shy about applying such "extreme
measures" should "adversity demand it."[44]

The Stalinist state reverted to the looting economy of the Civil War,
and with its strategy of violence it held the peasantry hostage. During
the Civil War there had still been peasant armies to contend with. Now,
ten years later, the Bolsheviks had a monopoly on violence and could
crush resistance in the village with greater ease. In the question of how
to manage the empire's agricultural regions, however, serious economic
considerations played no role. Why else would Stalin and his cronies
have ordered the plundering and confinement of the peasants in collective farms and then have had several hundred thousand people either
killed, deported, or left to starve? Collectivization plunged the Soviet
Union into the throes of chaos and anarchy. It drove the agricultural
system to ruin, unleashed a devastating famine in the countryside, and
even threatened to lead to mass hunger in the cities. Despite this, Stalin
and his associates held unwaveringly to their strategy of violence.

Collectivization was a war that could only end with the subjugation and enslavement of the peasantry. Despite serious difficulties in
the provinces Moscow was bombarded with reports of success. In early
1929 Boris Sheboldaev and Andrei Andreyev, party bosses in the lower
Volga region and in the northern Caucasus, sent reports claiming that
peasants in their regions were joining kolkhozy by the thousands. In
October they reported that almost 20 percent of all farms had been
nationalized. By November 1929 the targets that the regime had set the

previous April were no longer good enough. The regime's initial goal had been to expropriate only 9.6 percent of all farms by 1933, but now, it was decided, 1930 was to be the year of total collectivization. In December the Politburo established a commission headed by the People's Commissar of Agriculture, Yakov Yakovlev, which had the sole task of preparing the country for a war against the peasantry. By the end of 1930 all peasants in the grain-producing regions of the Soviet Union were supposed to have joined the kolkhozy, and by the end of 1931 all remaining regions were to have followed suit. Although words of reservation were expressed here and there, they fell on deaf ears. By this time only the enthusiasts and extremists found a voice, and they demonstrated their devotion to the leader by demonstrating their willingness to overstep all boundaries. Mendel Khataevich, party boss of the Central Volga regional committee, told his staff that although the official target was to nationalize 50 percent of farms by May 1930, this target would not only be "fulfilled, but overfulfilled."[45]

The great hunt for grain, cattle, and slaves began in 1930. Stalin and his cronies set the Soviet Union on a path of no return and transformed the collectivization of agriculture into a bloody crusade against the peasantry, in which millions became victims of starvation, deportation, or liquidation. Collectivization was the last act in a drama that had begun in 1917. It was the last forceful attempt to abolish all that remained of old Russia and crush every last vestige of resistance with violence. The kolkhoz was the instrument with which this subjugation was to be achieved. It robbed the peasants of everything they had worked for, made them slaves to the regime, and reintroduced the system of serfdom that had been abolished by the tsar.

But the peasants resisted the GPU units and workers' brigades bitterly, and the dictatorship was only really able to assert itself once this resistance had been broken. Peasants in the grain-producing regions of the Soviet Union left their harvested grain to rot and slaughtered their animals to prevent them from being appropriated by the Communists. In autumn 1931 "entire herds" of stray horses, which had been abandoned by their peasant masters, could be spotted roaming the outskirts of Kharkov. According to one Ukrainian GPU report, the kolkhozy "refused to take in the horses, because they would not have been able to feed them." In one village near Kharkov, in a single night,

thirty pigs were slaughtered in anticipation of the arrival of the procurement brigades.[46]

The resistance was not just passive. Armed revolts broke out across
the Soviet Union, reminding the Communists that their grip on power
was far from certain. Communists and peasants alike remembered the
Civil War and all its excesses and brutality. "If only some organizer
would show up," the secret police overheard a peasant from a village
in Ukraine saying, "then the entire village would stand up to Soviet
power like one man."[47] And it did come to violent clashes between
peasants and Communists in Ukraine, in the northern Caucasus, and in
the central and lower Volga regions. Kolkhozy were set on fire, administrative buildings were destroyed, and members of the Komsomol and
procurement brigades were lynched. In some regions, peasants even
formed small bands that attacked GPU units and outposts of state authority. Never again, however, did the resistance reach the intensity of
the Civil War years. Circumstances were now on the side of the Communist authorities. What the peasants could do, though, was spread
rumors. They dispatched runners to pass information between villages,
and rumors began to spread that the rule of the godless was coming
to an end. Some peasants also began to believe that the Antichrist had
appeared and that the end of the world was near. Others expected the
British, the Poles, or the Germans to attack the Soviet Union and liberate them from their oppressors. Such news spread just as quickly in the
Caucasus as they did in Ukraine, and this became a source of insecurity
for the power holders. It made them feel that they were at the mercy of
circumstances, and peasants suspected of spreading rumors were soon
arrested.[48]

Despite their efforts the peasants could not bring the state to its knees.
Only in the mountains of the Caucasus, in Azerbaijan, and in Georgia
did peasants possess weapons they could use against the Bolsheviks. In
spring 1930, for example, a group of peasants armed with guns and can-
nons conquered the city of Quba in Azerbaijan and killed all its functionaries. In most regions of the Soviet Union, however, the rebel bands
had nothing more than shotguns, daggers, and knives to carry into
battle against GPU units and Red Army battalions. Russia's peasants
had been disarmed in the 1920s, and in 1930 their chances of equip-
ping themselves with rifles and cannon were no better. In some regions

of the empire the violence of rebel bands grew to such extremes that it became detached from its original motives, and the partisans became robbers who plundered and destroyed what remained of the kolkhozy following the great raids. The kulaks who had fled their villages found themselves in an impossible predicament. They could neither surrender nor return to the villages they had been expelled from, and their only chances of survival were as robbers. In late autumn 1929 several peasants descended on a village in the lower Volga region and assaulted the head of the kolkhoz along with two members of the village soviet. They threatened the remaining Communists with bloody retribution and then smashed all the windows in the huts and kicked down their doors before departing. "The pogrom lasted several hours," reported the GPU. The whole village had been stricken with panic, and some peasants had even fled. By the next day, however, the assailants had been arrested. This kind of violent resistance encountered limits that could not be overcome. The Bolshevik adversaries were determined to do anything necessary to crush it, and they possessed both the violent means and the informational advantages to do so. In the end the peasants had no escape.[49]

For a short time it seemed as though the power holders were backing down and giving in. In March 1930 Stalin published an article in *Pravda,* claiming that party leaders in the provinces had been "dizzy with success," and that this was the reason for their violent excesses against the peasantry, which were really supposed to be prohibited. When the peasants got wind of this they understood it as a sign of weakness, and in the spring and early summer of 1930 the resistance to collectivization intensified. Stalin instantly recognized that his power was at stake. He realized that he could not afford any concessions after all and that he needed, instead, to continue governing his country by using violence. Stalin and his associates had decided to pursue an economy of robbery, and although the peasants were resisting it fiercely, they had no choice but to finish the war they had started. In spring 1930 the despot dispatched Lazar Kaganovich to Ukraine and the northern Caucasus to accelerate the campaign of forcing peasants into the kolkhozy. News of Kaganovich's planned arrival soon reached the peasants, and rumors began to spread through the villages that "the Antichrist from the center" would be arriving to hold a tribunal. Kaganovich kept his promise. He forced peasants to hand over their last grain reserves and promised bloody punishment for insubordination.[50] Molotov, who later arrived in Kharkov, was unambiguous in speaking to the Ukrainian party leadership: "There is only one conclusion: No mercy toward the class enemy. Wherever he sticks out his head, we will smash his skull. This is how the Bolshevik must respond to the class enemy's attempts at offering resistance." Furthermore, he told those present, every Communist "must now become an agent of the GPU."[51]

In summer and autumn 1930 the terror reached a new pitch. Peasants were shot and driven out of their villages. Thousands fled across the borders into neighboring countries to escape the massacres. In the central Volga region, in Ukraine, and in the Caucasus, Red Army units employed artillery and poison gas in their war against rebellious peasants. In the Caucasus alone more than ten thousand people lost their lives in the massacres of 1930.[52] The peasants had lost. They knew that they had lost, and they knew that their only remaining options were to flee or to submit. For Stalin and his entourage, the battle for the village meant breaking peasant resistance forever and establishing the Bolshevik monopoly on violence for good.

From the very beginning, the Bolsheviks recruited poor peasants, criminals, and deadbeats living at the edges of villages and equipped them with weapons and sentry posts. They dispatched them to spread fear and dread within the villages and offered them possessions of the outlawed and murdered in return. But resistance could only be broken if agitators and ringleaders were hunted down and eliminated. The authorities also needed to become a permanent presence in the lives of the peasantry. Subjugation could only succeed if all suspected enemies of the new order disappeared from the villages. In 1928 Stalin and his aides were apparently still convinced that "wealthy" peasants were responsible for the resistance, but one year later any villager who offered resistance could be declared a kulak. What was to be done with these offenders? The answers that the leaders gave in July 1928 were different from those given in autumn 1929. "It is clear to everyone," explained Boris Sheboldaev, party boss of the Lower Volga region, speaking before the Central Committee in July 1928, "that one has to fight the kulak, who at this very moment is sabotaging the procurement of grain."[53] But it remained unclear what this fight should entail. Some Communists even considered it possible to exclude kulaks from the kolkhozy but allow them to remain in the villages. By 1929, however, all such traces of moderation had vanished. Under the banner of the war against the peasantry, Stalin and his friends forced the Central Committee to accept an uncompromising strategy of violence. On November 15, 1929, Molotov told a plenary session of the Central Committee, "We cannot overlook the fact that the kolkhozy are not even fulfilling the most elementary duties towards the Soviet state. Is it not the case that the kolkhozy are failing to fulfill their grain procurement quotas? Is this not a direct act of sabotage against the policies of Soviet power? Are these facts not a demonstration of how the kulaks, who have seized the kolkhozy for themselves, are exploiting their influence to pit the kolkhozy against the Soviet state? And therefore we must drive the kulaks out of the kolkhozy." Molotov already knew that the expulsion of peasants would become part of the collectivization program. "The kulak not only harms the kolkhozy by open struggle, but sometimes also in the administrative organs of the kolkhozy that he penetrates. Therefore, all measures resulting from this approach toward the kulak as a malevolent and not yet crushed enemy will be right and necessary. Without such an approach to kulakdom we will not master the challenge of collectivization."[54]

Then, in late December 1929, at a conference of Marxist agronomists, Stalin publicly announced that the time had come to "liquidate" the kulaks as a class, and with this the floodgates burst open. On January 15, 1930, the Politburo established a commission headed by Molotov to discuss the practical implementation of the elimination program. In addition to Molotov, the commission contained party leaders and GPU bosses from the most important republics and regions. It took no more than a week for the commission to decide the fate of several hundred thousand people, and by January 30 the Politburo had resolved that all peasants registered as kulaks were to be expelled from their villages and either sent to concentration camps or deported.

The perpetrators in the service of Stalin and Molotov were issued licenses that authorized them to exercise unrestrained violence against anyone they wished. At a gathering of party secretaries from the provinces in February 1930, Molotov announced his ideas for the struggle against the kulaks. Kulaks who offered resistance would be drowned like cats in the rivers, and their families would be dissolved.

"We will welcome all useful proposals coming from the provinces (*na mestakh*)," he told them, leaving no doubt "that we may also have to shoot." Those who were spared would be deported to work in Siberia. Anyone seeking a position of prestige within Stalin's inner circle needed to quote from the dictionary of the violent perpetrator. In September 1935 Nikolai Yezhov, secretary of the Central Committee, for example, offered the proposal, "The kulak must be deported; he is nothing more than a swine. Deport him."[55]

The rhetoric the regime used to justify its misdeeds spoke of cold calculation but also of pure and simple hatred. The hatred was for the "wretched, stubborn reality," as Maxim Gorky, the wordsmith of Communism, had described the peasant world. This was a world, he wrote, that should be torn out at the roots "from the memory of the human soul" and made to disappear forever. Stalin and his associates hardly held this world in higher esteem. For them, it was a mirror in which they saw their own past. It was a reflection of everything they had suffered and believed they had finally freed themselves from. The merciless destructiveness with which Stalin's henchmen attacked rural life was in no small measure due to a certain measure of self-hatred. As they sought to destroy village life they sought to destroy the very world they themselves had come from. Nothing is more vexing than to be suddenly faced in the mirror with one's own deepest humiliation. And that is why the Communists spoke of "making soap of kulaks" or "shooting the kulak scum." One Communist wanted to have the kulaks "wiped off the face of the earth," while another, who had seized fugitive peasants hiding in a Ukrainian forest, did not see humans but rather "kulak whelps."[56]

The revolution lent legitimacy to spaces of violence where law no longer applied. These were zones where no inhibitions were required. Violent perpetrators could act with ruthlessness (and did so), not merely because they despised peasants and wanted to rid the world of them, but also because there was no danger of legal retribution. What some did for reasons of hatred or delusion, others did for reasons of greed, and still others did it simply because they enjoyed violence. In many cases, the brigade leaders and plenipotentiaries who robbed and terrorized the peasantry in the service of the regime were nothing more than criminal entrepreneurs of violence. Looting was their way of life, and the possibility of giving up these practices of stealing and plundering was out of the question. The cruelty they visited upon others knew no limits. The marauding commandos set peasant huts ablaze, smashed out windows, and destroyed bread ovens in order to ruin the peasants' means of livelihood. They shaved the heads of their victims or made them carry humiliating signs. They forced their victims to sit on burning stoves, or they drove them into the cold and then doused them in ice water. They spat in their faces, plucked out their beards hair by hair, or forced them to do push-ups in the village square. In some places, brass bands accompanied the henchmen as they relieved the peasants of their grain and screened kulaks for deportation. In spring 1930 brigades in Kherson had apparently driven both poor and wealthy peasants naked in the streets and beat them, and had organized drinking-bouts in the houses of the arrested. "They shot over their heads, forced them to dig their own graves, and the women to undress themselves." This was a report coming from the GPU, and as the regional boss Levytsky complained, the brigades had been assembled "in haste," which was why they had contained so many "class-alien elements" and "criminals."[57] According to a report by the Ukrainian GPU from December 1931 the looting and pillaging by the brigades had caused "outrage." Peasants everywhere had been beaten and abused, and many had even "fled" their villages in panic and hidden in the fields to avoid falling victim to the brigades.[58]

In Ukraine and in the Caucasus there were mock executions and mass rapes. In one Ukrainian village near Uman the chairman of the village soviet ordered peasants to stand against a wall and then yelled at them, "Everyone must join the collective; if you refuse, we will shoot you, we will bury you alive."[59] On February 19, 1930, Red Army soldiers advanced into the village of Chai-Abas, near Ganja in Azerbaijan, where they carried out a dreadful massacre. An official fact-finding commission was dispatched to the region the following year to compile a report on the ghastly events:

> During the seizure of the eight bandits who were hiding in said village, around 30 people, i.e. all residents of the village, were shot by a detachment of the 4th Infantry Regiment in a bestial manner on 19 February 1930. The houses and other buildings were burned down, and property was destroyed. Among those shot were 14 children, nine of whom were between the ages of two and six. Beyond this, four infants, clinging to the corpses of the mothers, were left behind and died of hunger and

cold. An inspection of the place of the shootings found the remains of a pyre with five corpses on it, including three children. One of the corpses was almost completely burnt, and only the head still remained.[60]

Few people found the courage to voice their outrage over the inhumane treatment of the peasantry. In March 1930 Mikhail Kalinin, the nominal head of state of the Soviet Union, received a letter from Leningrad workers, complaining about the terror their friends and relatives back in their native villages had to endure. Never in their wildest dreams had they imagined that the "worker and peasant power" would one day inflict such violence on their own "fathers and brothers." "You kill, arrest, and take everything we have earned with our calloused hands," the petitioners complained.[61] At times even ardent supporters of the regime could no longer bear what was being done to the peasants. In April 1933 the writer Mikhail Sholokhov sent a letter to Stalin, seeking to draw his attention to the violent excesses in the villages of the Don Cossacks. Old people, children, and women had all been thrown out of their homes and left to starve in the cold. Peasants seeking to aid the unfortunate had been threatened with violence. The nights had been filled with the screams of children lying on the bare ground, clothed only in rags. Peasants had been beaten, stripped down to their underwear, and driven into the cold. In one instance mock executions had been performed, after which the peasants had been abandoned naked on the ice-cold steppe. Never would he forget the things he had witnessed in the villages. "How can one mock people this way?" Stalin received the letter and responded in his own fashion. What was happening in the villages was actually a "silent war against Soviet power," Stalin explained. In fact, it was a "war of starvation" that the peasants were waging against the cities.[62]

The perpetrators made a point of demonstrating that the peasants they encountered were worth less than the cattle being confiscated. Between February 1 and March 15, 1930, the GPU arrested more than 25,000 peasants, in Ukraine alone, who had resisted collectivization. 656 people were shot on the spot, 3,673 were sent to concentration camps, and 5,580 were exiled to Siberia. There was no room for compassion because what was being carried out was a "historically necessary act," as Lev Kopelev later recalled his own role in collectivization. This was a situation in which the usual prohibition against murder did not apply. Circumstances allowed violent perpetrators to act without fear of punishment. And what this meant is that the years of collectivization were years of glory for psychopaths and sadists who could torture and murder with impunity. For such people, the reference to historical necessity was nothing more than a cynical license to kill. Perpetrators acting out of conviction spoke of historical necessity to ease their own consciences, while psychopaths spoke of it so that everyone around them would understand that the most gruesome excesses of collectivization really were unavoidable. In both cases, however, the disinhibition of the perpetrators was preceded by the dehumanization of the victims. In the Bolshevik orbit so many boundaries had already been transgressed that it was possible to pass the final barriers without too much difficulty. When the moral coordinates are shifted and killing and torture become permissible, it follows that even the most gruesome of actions are not only conceivable but also possible.[63]

In the course of collectivization more than two million peasants were robbed of their possessions and deported to Siberia and central Asia. Over 30,000 people were condemned to death by troikas (three-person special tribunals—*troiki*) and shot. This terror did not end with the conclusion of collectivization, though, and in fact it never ceased. Those who refused to work or were accused of damaging machinery or kolkhoz inventory were punished with detention and banishment. And ever since the farms had become state property, the peasants were no longer allowed to enjoy the fruits of their efforts either. In August 1932 the government passed a law on the "Protection of Socialist Property," making the theft of kolkhoz property an offense that was punishable by death or deportation to a concentration camp. Within a matter of days Stalin wrote a letter to Kaganovich, complaining that the law had not yet produced any visible results. Any party secretary found guilty of trying to "put off this matter" needed to be punished. And Judges and public prosecutors caught showing leniency toward thieves needed to be "pilloried." Moreover, sentences were to be announced in a public, "visible place" in order to deter peasants from stealing kolkhoz property.[64]

Between 1932 and 1933 more than sixteen thousand peasants were condemned to death on the basis of this barbaric law. Several tens of thousands were sent to camps for stealing tomatoes or ears of grain. When this did not work and peasants still resisted, the regime confiscated the inventories of entire kolkhozy and had all the residents deported. In October 1932 the Politburo prohibited the sale of goods and grain in the Ukrainian countryside because the kolkhozy there had not met their plan targets.[65] At the same time, Molotov arrived in Kharkov to commit the Ukrainian party leadership to the Stalinist course. "We are using industrial goods as an incentive," wrote Molotov from Kharkov, "and the withdrawal of a part of the industrial goods as a means of repression toward the kolkhoz peasants and independent farmers in particular." Kaganovich, too, who appeared in Rostov-on-Don in November 1932, demanded the impossible from both Communists and peasants. The party organizations in the village were "not up to scratch," he told the local party leadership in Rostov. "And to be a bad Communist is worse than being no Communist at all." Bad Communists, after all, aided the kulaks. "What is to be done?" asked Kaganovich. "One has to publicly accuse three to five villages, prohibit them from trading, purge them and hold a number of show trials, and then report this in the press." Before any decisions could be made in Rostov, however, Kaganovich called Stalin. Shortly thereafter the dictator ordered the deportation of two thousand families from the Kuban for the "malevolent manner" in which they had allegedly concealed their grain from the authorities. According to Pavel Postyshev, who was both a Politburo member and second secretary of the Communist Party of Ukraine, this kind of terror was first and foremost a "weapon." It was also a "method of reeducation" with which the regime taught peasants what socialism and the kolkhozy expected of them.[66]

Why did the Communists offer no resistance? Why was there no insubordination? The reason is that the functionaries in the provinces feared the wrath of the despot just as much as the peasants did. In December 1932 Stalin warned the chairman of the Transcaucasian regional party committee, Lavrenty Beria, that "repressive measures" would be necessary if he failed to organize a "fundamental turnaround in procurement in general and the procurement of tobacco in Abkhazia within the next ten days."[67] He also wrote to Robert Eikhe, the party boss in western Siberia, demanding that he order the directors of the collective farms in his region to "immediately organize honest and Bolshevik grain procurements with timely plan fulfillment, if they don't want to be cruelly punished."[68] He warned Ivan Kabakov, party boss in the Urals, that being a Communist was no protection against repression: "Explain to the directors [of the sovkhozy (state farms)] that their party membership cards will not save them from arrest, that the enemy with a party membership deserves a greater punishment than the enemy without one."[69] Words were followed by actions. In December 1932, near Kharkov, 144 Communists were expelled from the party and shot for failing to meet their grain-requisitioning targets. At a Politburo meeting of the Ukrainian Communist Party, Vsevolod Balitsky, regional head of the GPU, announced that between November 15 and December 15, 1932, 11,000 people had been arrested in the villages in his region. This included 435 party functionaries, 2,260 kolkhoz employees, 409 kolkhoz heads, 441 bookkeepers, and 107 chairmen of village soviets. While 108 of them had already been shot, another 100 of them were still awaiting their deaths. Kaganovich, who participated in the Kharkov talks, confided in his work diary that a decision had been reached to have 50 expelled party functionaries imprisoned in concentration camps. Their families would also be deported, and show trials in the villages would be organized. Any party secretaries who failed to "bring about a turnaround in the next two to three days" would also have to "reckon with a similar fate."[70]

Collectivization was more than just a series of brutal acts of violence. It also precipitated a famine that, between 1932 and 1933, claimed between three and seven million lives. Hardest hit were Ukraine, the northern Caucasus, the central and lower Volga regions, and Kazakhstan. Collectivization destroyed agriculture, triggered mass exoduses, left the rural regions of the country desolate, and ultimately produced exactly the opposite of what Stalin had intended. The collectivization of agriculture did absolutely nothing to generate investment capital for industrialization. On the contrary, it turned out to be a heavy burden on the state treasury, as starving peasants and desolate stretches of land were costly and could no longer contribute anything to supply the cities. Quite simply, the collectivization of agriculture was both a human and an economic catastrophe.[71]

Of course Stalin and his aides heard what was happening in the villages. They knew that people were starving and going insane. They received dossiers and detailed reports from the provinces. In September 1932 a high-ranking central government functionary traveled to the famine areas of Kazakhstan and compiled a shocking report on what he saw, which was read by both Stalin and Molotov:

We ourselves witnessed how the starving population, people swollen from hunger, nibbled like rats and mice on a piece of cheese; how six Kazakhs, among them two women, cruelly beat each other because of a tiny piece of flatbread; how people weakened by hunger collected and ate garbage from the waste-water pits near the canteens and rotten scraps from the fishmongers. There is talk of starving people taking decaying corpses from the graveyards and eating them. Dreadful scenes occur at the train stations: begging has gained strong currency, people swollen from hunger stagger about, and there are cases where the corpses of the dead are scavenged. The mass of kolkhoz peasants has fled and roves about in the steppe, close to the railway lines, and there were attempts by individual groups to escape abroad. Some regions have become devoid of people.[72]

Day after day the leaders received new horrific reports detailing the masses of people dying in broad daylight. The dead lay scattered around train stations, on the streets, and in hospitals. Refugees meanwhile were spreading typhus and cholera, and in many regions the dead were no longer even registered but only buried as quickly as possible in an attempt at containing the epidemics. In some places, in the remote steppe regions of the lower Volga in particular, the bloated corpses of the starved were left to rot under the open skies. There was no one left to bury them. In one collective farm called "Savet Ilicha" (Lenin's Legacy), where everyone was starving, the children in the kindergarten received a mere 100 grams of bread substitute per child per day. "The children are losing their strength and their viability," reported the political department of the machine tractor station, "and before their death they are sent home to their parents."[73]

Molotov and Kaganovich saw the misery and hunger for themselves when they traveled to Ukraine and the northern Caucasus in summer and winter 1932 to oversee the execution of Stalin's orders. Molotov reported his impressions to the Politburo and made no secret of the fact that famine had broken out in this "rich grain-producing region." In the northern Caucasus Kaganovich too was confronted with unpleasant truths. According to his travel log, GPU agents had informed him that the famine in the villages was not only killing peasants but that "activists" were dying as well.[74] The members of the Politburo, however, were apparently unmoved. In March 1933 Stalin, Molotov, and Kaganovich received a report from the Central Committee apparatus on the famine in Ukraine. "Cases of cannibalism" had been uncovered. In one village a peasant had "devoured" her husband's corpse, and in the village of Ruda, a nine-year-old boy had gone mad from hunger and had killed and eaten his four-year-old sister. In the end, hunger came to haunt the workers in the cities of Uman and Zhytomyr too. Molotov read the report but was apparently only interested in the famine as it was affecting workers in the cities. This was what he underlined in black ink at any rate. The fate of the starving peasants was apparently of no consequence to him. He marked the report with bold letters, "Into the archive," and that was the end of it.

Stalin was a malevolent and pitiless man of violence. The news he received from the provinces left him untouched. In March 1933 he was approached by Turar Ryskulov, Kazakh Communist leader and deputy head of the RSFSR, who briefed him on the outcome of collectivization in Kazakhstan. Ryskulov took pains to demonstrate that Kazakhstan's drastic reduction of livestock was due to "malicious butchering . . . by the beys [members of the local upper classes]." He could not, however, avoid pointing out that it was the violent settlement and resettlement of the nomads and the confiscation of their livestock that had caused them to resist in the first place. The nomads now had nothing. They were homeless, exposed to the elements, and had neither cattle nor shelter. Using them for farm work was not a possibility. A number of rayons had experienced uprisings, in which famished peasants had attacked Chekists and requisitioning commandos. Trains meanwhile had been raided and looted. As usual Stalin read this report attentively and underlined several passages, demonstrating his interest.[75] Once again, however, he apparently did not feel compelled to issue any directives to curb this madness. For Stalin, there was no reason to end the terror against the peasantry, and pity was a sign of sentimentality. In late 1932, when the party boss of the Kharkov regional committee sought to draw Stalin's attention to the mass fatalities in Ukraine, the dictator's response was dismissive: "They tell us, Comrade Terekhov, that you're a good orator, but it transpires that you're a good storyteller. Fabricating such a fairytale about famine! Thought you'd scare us but it won't work. Wouldn't it be better for you to leave the post of [Area Committee and] Ukrainian CC Secretary and join the Writers' Union: you'll concoct fables, and idiots will read them." Terekhov was relieved of his post two weeks later.[76]

Stalin only saw those realities that were of his own making. Nikita
Khrushchev recalled how, after the Second World War, he had alerted
the dictator that starving peasants in Ukraine had gone mad and become cannibals. "You're being soft-bellied!" Stalin had rebuked him.
"They're deceiving you. They're counting on being able to appeal to
your sentimentality when they report things like that. They're trying to
force you to give them all your reserves."[77]

The regime kept silent about the famine. The Soviet press reported
on famines in Poland and Czechoslovakia, but there was not one single
word about hunger in the Soviet Union. Outside of the Soviet Union, at
least, Stalin did have to pay a price for his cynical indifference. Those
watching from abroad could not fail to notice the fact that while hundreds of thousands of its own people were in the throes of starvation the Soviet Union was still selling grain abroad. Hitler's Germany
launched a relief campaign to support the German colonists in Stalin's
Soviet Union who were starving. American, British, and German diplomats traveled the areas afflicted by the famine and documented the
dreadful scenes they witnessed. The Soviet Union's reputation as the
stronghold of socialism was at stake, and Stalin knew it. In February
1933, when Stalin heard that American journalists were providing the
New York Times with reports on the famine, his instructions to Molotov and Kaganovich were unambiguous: "Molotov! Kaganovich! Do
you know who allowed the American correspondents in Moscow to
travel to the Kuban? They cobbled together hideousness about the situation in the Kuban. We have to put an end to this and prohibit these
gentlemen from traveling around the USSR. There are already enough
spies in the USSR."[78]

To ensure that no one found out what was going on, the regime imposed an information blackout. In the Republic of Volga Germans the
civil registry offices were still permitted to register those who had died,
but the cause of death could no longer be given on the death certificates. By spring 1933 at the latest, the provincial party secretaries had
comprehended that discussion of the famine was off limits. Although
the regime could not force foreigners to submit to its speech rules, it
could restrict their radius of activity. In the aftermath of the excesses of
collectivization, the government closed the consulates of the most important European states in Ukraine, limited the free movement of diplomats, and prohibited journalists from traveling to the Soviet Union

without registering in advance and being accompanied by a state agent during their stay.

And yet hundreds of thousands managed to flee the villages, escape the hunger and violence, and go into hiding in the cities and major construction sites of the country. Since the end of the First World War there had not been an exodus of such proportions. The regime tried in vain to slow the peasant migration, and in the end it resorted to violence in this matter also. In December 1932 internal passports—which had been abolished in 1907 by the tsar's last prime minister, Pyotr Stolypin—were reintroduced at Stalin's behest. Kolkhoz peasants, who were denied passports, were bound to the soil and could not leave their villages without permission from the authorities. In some areas, in the central Volga region and Ukraine in particular, GPU units sealed off villages from the outside world and patrolled train stations to prevent peasants from leaving. Tens of thousands were seized at the border and returned to the areas of famine. Those living in cities without the necessary permits or "useful" state-sanctioned jobs were arrested and deported. This was not how the Bolsheviks had imagined socialism. Things had not turned out at all as they had planned. And yet they seemed to know exactly what needed to be done: the "senseless" and "superfluous" migration from the village to the city simply needed to be stopped. This, at least, was the solution offered by Avel Enukidze, secretary of the Central Executive Committee and a confidant of Stalin. Removing "parasitic elements" and "social garbage" from the cities, he explained, was the only viable course of action.[79]

For Stalin the state of emergency he had imposed on the Soviet Union was a chance to give violence free rein and solve the country's social problems on his own terms. In January 1933 the deputy leader of the GPU, Genrikh Yagoda, acting on Stalin's behalf, devised a grandiose plan for the expulsion of "parasites" and "social garbage" from major cities. Two million people were to be arrested, deported, and hauled off to Siberia, which Yagoda referred to as the "garbage zone." And indeed, beggars, orphans, vagrants, gypsies (*tsygany*), and peasants without residence permits were picked up in cities throughout the Soviet Union and deported. In 1933, in Moscow alone more than 300,000 people were registered as "socially alien elements" and then expelled. The people departing from the cities had neither passports, nor food cards, nor anything else but the clothes they were wearing. In July 1933

Yagoda received a report from Israel Pliner, the deputy leader of the Gulag administration, who briefed him on the deportation of gypsies from Moscow. In only eleven days Pliner had overseen the arrest of more than ten thousand gypsies, all of whom had arrived in Siberia on trains. "The loading and dispatching of the trains," he reported, had "proceeded without incident (*spokoino*)."[80]

DEATH ZONES

What was to become of the hundreds of thousands of people who had been deported from the villages and the cities? The answer that Stalin and his assistants in the GPU gave was unambiguous. The peasants were to become slaves, ready to be deployed for any forced labor project, at any place and at any time. By 1929 Stalin had approved the expansion of the concentration camp complex and tasked the GPU with deploying prisoners to clear forests and build dams and canals. In July of that same year, the government issued a law declaring that all persons serving prison sentences of more than three years were to be handed over to the GPU and sent to labor camps. The deportation of several million people provided the secret police with unforeseen possibilities for expanding the concentration camp system into a gigantic economic enterprise. Collectivization marked the birth of the Gulag and the end of all experiments at reeducating people through labor. From now on, the only thing that mattered was that slaves be hunted down and sacrificed to the economically senseless megalomania of despotism. In early 1934 the head of the NKVD, Yagoda, announced that he needed twenty-thousand prisoners who were "fit for work" and could help build the Moscow-Volga Canal. He gave the Ukrainian bureaus the task of coming up with the necessary manpower, and a colossal manhunt was set in motion. The number of prisoners who starved, froze to death, or were shot on the construction sites of this monstrous project remains unknown. But the White Sea Canal alone, which was completed in summer 1933, likely claimed the lives of upwards of twenty-five thousand prisoners. Upon its completion Stalin took a boat ride to appraise the work and determined that it was too "narrow and shallow" and that it had been "a senseless undertaking" after all. All those thousands of slave laborers who had worked to complete it had died for something that was "of no use to anyone."[81]

The people who were taken from their homes, deported, and thrown into camps experienced a kind of violence that had absolutely no sense to it and followed absolutely no predictable patterns. Anyone could be stigmatized, and anyone could be arrested and stripped of all rights—at any given time. When they entered the "Gulag Archipelago," perpetrators and victims alike understood that they were entering into a different world. As the camp gates closed behind them, they ceased to be citizens of a state where the rule of law played even a nominal role. Inside the camps people were stripped of all dignity and returned to a mode of existence in which all that mattered was survival. People were nothing more than the objects of an absolute power that was free to do with them as it pleased. "You can forget all the rights you have had up to now," were the words that the first commandant on the Solovetsky Islands used to welcome new arrivals.[82] In this sense, the Stalinist concentration camp was a representation of the total power of the totalitarian state. Those who disappeared into the Gulag departed from the realm of laws and entered into the realm of absolute power. "The camp was a laboratory of violence," writes Wolfgang Sofsky in his anatomy of the National Socialist camps. "Absolute power in action liberates a perpetrator from all inhibitions; cruelty becomes unhinged. Virtually anything can be ventured, repeated, intensified, or halted, without reference to norms and goals."[83]

But the representation of dread was not intended for the prisoners alone. It was a message for the free and for the survivors as well. One should not forget, writes Jan-Philipp Reemtsma, about "the satisfaction that the inherently powerless can get from exercising negative power," from elevating themselves above the lowest of the low, in order to still retain a sense of superiority despite their powerlessness. There is nothing quite as uplifting as the feeling that the master of today might become the prisoner of tomorrow. There is also nothing quite as terrifying. Those living in fear of an unknown place but knowing they could be brought there at any moment will do everything possible to avoid meeting this fate. They will denounce, and they will obey. And this was essentially the point of it all for Stalin and his assistants.[84] And yet they were at pains to prevent those in the West from discovering the existence of a system that inside the Soviet Union was a secret to no one. Beyond its borders, Stalin's revolution was supposed to be seen as an act of liberation, not as the enslavement of masses of starving peasants. When an investigative commission from Great Britain came to the

Soviet Union in the early 1930s, Leningrad's party boss Sergei Kirov had camp inmates and special settlers driven into the forests of Karelia. The clueless Englishmen saw only workers and peasants who had been brought there for the purpose of showing the foreigners how fortunate their lives were. The actual prisoners only returned once the members of the commission had departed.[85]

The gigantic camp compounds spread throughout the Asiatic regions of the Soviet Union like ulcers. The GPU was no longer merely the punitive arm of the Soviet State. It was now master of an economic empire that procured, employed, and exploited slaves. But this exploitation did not remain limited to the camps. In early 1930 the Politburo had decided to shoot or imprison only the "most malevolent" kulaks and have the others deported to "remote northern regions."[86] These "special settlers" did not live behind the barbed wired fences of the camps, but they still belonged to the GPU's slave army of forced laborers. Between 1930 and 1931, 1,803,392 peasants—men, women, and children—were given the status of "special settlers" and were hauled off to the inhospitable regions of the far north, the Urals, or Kazakhstan. In spring 1930 alone, 150,000 peasant families from all regions of the Soviet Union were deported per order of Stalin. 70,000 were sent to the Northern Territory (Severnyi Krai), 50,000 to Siberia, 25,000 to the Urals, and 25,000 to Kazakhstan. But neither the Chekists nor the authorities in the destinations were prepared for this mass exodus. In late January 1930 the party boss of the Northern Territory, Sergei Bergavinov, complained in a letter to Molotov about the GPU's fantastical plans. Deporting more than 300,000 people into his jurisdiction in the course of only a few weeks was out of the question, he wrote. There were neither houses nor barracks to accommodate the new arrivals, and meeting the GPU's requirements, he explained to the Politburo, would mean taking in up to 20,000 people per day. Although Bergavinov protested, it was not out of pity. He needed people who could chop wood in the inhospitable areas of his jurisdiction, and the "special settlers" represented a cheap source of labor. Should his workforce starve or freeze to death before the plans could be completed, his career would be in jeopardy. Stalin, however, found such criticisms baseless, and on February 17, 1930 he informed Bergavinov that he would indeed be receiving 50,000 families—around 250,000 people—by mid-April. And so the calamity commenced.

February 1930 saw the arrival of the first families in the Northern Territory. There were 1,760 people per train, forty to each freight car. On their long journey from Ukraine into the far north they were given nothing to eat and almost nothing to drink. Without winter clothing or any sort of provisions, many peasants died of starvation, exhaustion, or disease before even reaching their destination. Although Stalin and his followers in the Politburo received unvarnished reports about what was taking place they took no action to prevent the mass deaths. By early April 1930, 204,927 banished individuals had arrived in the Northern Territory. Only a fraction of them, however, were capable of performing the difficult forest labor they were intended for. Upon arrival in the north, prisoners were brought to transit camps where the able-bodied were separated from the rest. The able-bodied were then brought to the inner areas of the region where they were forced to build the huts they would live in. Those left behind did their best to survive in hastily dug holes in the ground, in abandoned monasteries, or in decrepit transit prisons. They were crowded together under appalling hygienic conditions, and within the first weeks of the prisoners' arrival epidemics of measles, scarlet fever, and typhus had broken out. In the town of Kotlas alone thirty children died each day.

The occurrences in the region were no secret to the political leadership. Mikhail Kalinin, chairman of the Presidium of the Central Executive Committee of the Soviet Union, received letters and petitions from banished individuals, detailing the horrors of their daily existences. A letter from Ukrainian women reported that prisoners were being housed in unheated churches and that children were dying like flies. Within the last six weeks, they wrote, more than three thousand children had been buried in the Vologda cemetery. The prisoners' barracks in the woods were heavily crowded, with over 150 people being forced to share a single unit. All food they had brought with them had been confiscated by the authorities in Vologda, and they had nothing left to eat but breadcrumbs. "Mikhail Ivanovich, save us from such poverty and starvation. . . . They sent us here to our ruin and what kind of kulaks are we?" The "brutality" was hard to bear, wrote the anonymous sender of another letter. "It is a pity to look at these people who lie about on the bunks with despair in their eyes or loaf among the barracks with nothing to do and only wishing to eat something . . . All the barracks are filled with cries and the wailing of children . . . To

leave these people in this situation for a long time—this is brutality . . .
A person cannot remain a person in such conditions."

Although the economy of forced labor claimed the freedom and lives
of millions, it gave the power holders little of the returns they had
hoped for. The regime had to organize the transportation of prisoners,
and it had to finance the construction of labor camps. It had to provide
for the children, the elderly, and the women who had not starved or
frozen to death, and it had to compensate several thousands of guards
and Chekists who had been hired to watch over the slaves. Beyond
that, security forces had to invest significant energy and resources in
hunting down escapees and returning them to the camps. Dekulakization was a human catastrophe anyway, but it was also devoid of every trace of economic logic. Furthermore, the Stalinist leadership pursued this crime with full knowledge of its human costs. Between 1932
and 1934 more than 280,000 "special settlers" perished. Many of the
banished—21,000 in the Northern Territory alone—did not even live
to see the end of 1930.[87] Only in spring 1933 did Stalin give the order
to end the deportation of kulaks.

Collectivization did not make proletarians out of peasants. If anything, it degraded them to second-class subjects, who were bound to
the soil and could be plundered at will. The regime eliminated priests
and kulaks, it terrorized the countryside, and it subjugated the village
to its violence. And despite all these efforts no New Men were created.
This system of apartheid—expressed in the system of kolkhozy, camps,
and special settlements—seems to have promoted little other than the
obedience of frightened peasants, for whom the Bolsheviks were nothing more than violent perpetrators and devils in human form.

COMMAND ECONOMY

A society that sought to be socialist needed to be industrialized. Of
this the Bolsheviks were certain. Their revolution would only succeed
if they were able to complete the modernization of the backward multiethnic empire and transform the Soviet Union into an industrialized
great power. Stalin's revolution from above was an attempt at wiping
out every last trace of old Russia and transforming it into a country
that—in a matter of years—would be in a position to accomplish feats
that would dwarf those of Europe. For Stalin, the backwardness of

the Soviet Union was a source of shame. Russia had been beaten and humiliated time and time again in the past, and even now the West was centuries ahead. More importantly, though, the dictator believed he had found the solution to this problem. As he explained it, "One feature of the history of old Russia was the continual beatings she suffered because of her backwardness. She was beaten by the Mongol khans. She was beaten by the Turkish beys. She was beaten by the Swedish feudal lords. She was beaten by the Polish and Lithuanian gentry. She was beaten by the British and French capitalists. She was beaten by the Japanese barons. All beat her—because of her backwardness." The Soviet Union simply needed to overcome its backwardness. In other words, everything that Europe had achieved over the course of centuries, the Soviet Union would have to accomplish overnight. "We must make good this distance in ten years," Stalin continued. "Either we do it, or we shall go under."[88]

Stalin and his minions were prepared to do anything necessary to achieve this goal. Their problem, though, was that they were trying to create something new using the means of the past. Their expectations were exaggerated, their plans were grandiose, and all they had at their disposal to achieve them were the means of despotism. Industrialization and the Cultural Revolution were tightly intertwined. Wherever industrial landscapes were established, economic activity could be planned and controlled, the "anarchy" of the market could be overcome, and workers could be civilized. Moreover, the centralized economy employed heroic people, who had iron wills and could surmount every obstacle. They had freed themselves from the chains of the past and had become one with the grand collective of New Men. Industrialization was thus the key to ridding Russia of its backwardness forever. A landscape that had previously been one of nothing more than pathetic peasant settlements would soon be host to great cities. The wilderness would be transformed into industrial parks, and peasants would become proletarians.

Stalin's target was for the Soviet Union to have caught up with and surpassed the industrial nations of the West by the end of the 1930s. New technologies would be introduced, and capital-intensive branches of industry that could employ state-of-the art Western technology would be expanded. The backward regions of the country would be industrialized, and within a matter of years the Soviet Union would have achieved economic independence and military supremacy. No effort would be spared in conjuring great industrial complexes into being in any part of the empire—but most particularly in the Urals and in Siberia. Tractor works, tank factories, dams, and power stations were proof that the possibilities for transformation were limitless. In the early 1930s a gigantic industrial complex in Magnitogorsk was created in the midst of the wilderness. Steelworks and factories were soon followed by barracks settlements and a dam. This is how the party leadership demonstrated that it was indeed capable of moving mountains at the world's end, and Magnitogorsk became a symbol of Stalinist omnipotence and megalomania. The message could hardly have been clearer: even backward nations could achieve what the industrial nations of Europe had accomplished long ago. Within a matter of years, foreign specialists, engineers, architects, and technicians, Komsomol members and Communists, workers and slaves had implemented something that no one had considered possible. Unfortunately, however, it came at a very high price—one that was paid for in human lives, poverty, and misery.[89]

Soviet industrialization followed the logic of an economy of power. Political will trumped economic rationality, and almost no concern was paid to which consumption goods the people actually needed. It was an economy of robbery. It ravaged man and nature alike and gave them nothing in return but gigantic dams, hydroelectric power stations, and industrial complexes that produced steel, tanks, and railroad tracks. Workers and prisoners dug for gold, cleared forests, and mined for coal, and they did it all in the service of a higher purpose. But ultimately Soviet industry was also a representation of power, a demonstration of strength. It was proof that the Bolsheviks were indeed capable of achieving military might. It showed that they could create cities and industrial complexes out of thin air and that they were not just importers of modern technology but also masters of it. And perhaps most importantly, these industrial accomplishments were living proof that there was no obstacle large enough to stand in the way of the New Man.

Soviet man was a man of action. He stormed impregnable fortresses and set new records in production. Production records, however, were only possible when workers renounced consumption and subordinated their own needs to the needs of the economy of power. For the Bolsheviks, economic success was measured in tons of steel produced. The standard of living enjoyed by those producing the steel, meanwhile, was of little interest. Neither Magnitogorsk nor any other places of Stalinist megalomania provided workers with adequate streets, schools, hospitals, food or anything else necessary for a reasonable standard of living. Had it not been for the forced laborers and slave workers, the power holders would never have realized their ambitious prestige projects. The people were subjugated and exploited for the glory of the socialist state, and in this sense, Stalinism was a form of internal colonialism that enslaved and exploited its own subjects in the service of higher goals. The Bolsheviks spoke of human happiness and presented the country's supposedly great prosperity as a state-given gift, but in the end their economic style produced nothing but misery. Ultimately, it undermined their revolution as well, making for a harsh contrast between the rosy tales of social utopia and the unhappy realities of daily life.

The plan loomed above everything else. Factories and construction sites would run like grand clockworks, performing each and every task the planners had devised for them. Nothing would be left to chance. Workers would become cogs in a great machine and would carry out their prescribed functions with mechanical efficiency. But what use are the grandest of ideas if they are contradicted by reality on a daily basis? The Soviet economy was a command economy, but it was not a planned economy. In fact it had the effect of making all planning disappear. Every ministry, every branch of industry, and every enterprise was now focused exclusively on meeting the short-term targets set by the People's Commissariats and on competing with one another for scarce resources. Bitter disputes over raw materials and investments also broke out between ministers, when the steel industry, for example, wanted access to the same resources that the railroads did. These conflicts were not limited to steel but occurred in every branch of industry. Industrial complexes, both in the center and in the provinces, were islands of production. The sole focus of their managers was to advance their own enterprises and fulfill their plan targets. People's Commissars advocated for "their" enterprises, at the expense of all others. Factories and industrial complexes became small feudal dominions, each with its own system of procurement and supply. Each was a small self-contained economy, which answered to a People's Commissariat but had no connection with any of the other enterprises in the region. The needs of the provinces, which the industries were supposed to be serving, faded into obscurity. For Stalin, though, this form of economic organization also had its advantages, as it allowed him to play the People's Commissariats off against each other and punish disloyalty. In this regard, economic policy was just one more of Stalin's many methods for increasing his personal power. As long as the people's commissars and their satraps were busy fulfilling their plan targets and denouncing each other as failures, he could remain master of all decisions and dispose of anyone he considered a traitor.

For the party leadership, planning meant setting and surpassing targets. Rational planning, however, did not really figure in. Instead, factory directors, managers, and workers were officers and soldiers who won battles on the production front. Engineers were commanders and generals who faced down the enemy without fear. Bolshevik commanders who succeeded in implementing the latest technology on their production fronts were proof of the superiority of the Soviet system, for they showed that the Bolsheviks could indeed move mountains and storm fortresses. "It is sometimes asked," Stalin declared at the beginning of the 1930s, "whether it is not possible to slow down the tempo somewhat, to put a check on the movement. No, comrades, it is not possible! The tempo must not be reduced! On the contrary, we must increase it as much as is within our powers and possibilities. . . . To slacken the tempo would mean falling behind. And those who fall behind get beaten."[90] Failures and weaklings simply had no place in the leadership of the Communist economy, where no feat was too great and where nothing was impossible. But what if the impossible did occur? What if plans were not fulfilled? What if managers buckled under the pressure of their assignments? In these cases Stalin and his people's commissars would initiate a hunt for saboteurs and spies.

By the early 1930s economically informed debates had become a thing of the past. The utopian demands of the political leadership had to be met at all costs, even if this meant stretching industry far beyond its limits. Shock worker campaigns and bouts of socialist emulation, which took place between factories, staff, and brigades, did nothing to help the economy. Furthermore, workers were untrained and inexperienced, ultimately machinery and material were overburdened, and goods of only the poorest quality were produced. It was not unusual for dams, power stations, houses, and factories to have to be torn down immediately after their completion due to faulty construction—despite having been completed on time. The goods produced by the clothing and food industries were of a quality that defied all description. To Stalin and his followers, these shortcomings were not due to incompetence and poor planning but to acts of sabotage committed by the enemy. Sergo Ordzhonikidze, who had become director of the People's Commissariat of Heavy Industry in 1923, had managers and directors who failed to meet their plan targets removed from their posts, demoted, or arrested. Excuses and justifications were of little interest to the choleric people's commissar, who declared to a gathering of managers in autumn 1934, "We will not listen to those people who say our materials have not been delivered, because we say that a good manager, a good shop director, a good master technician knows how to organize things and produce the required results." He continued, "Our equipment, our plants are ready to serve the Soviet Union, ready to produce massive tons of metals. What is preventing them? Poor work."[91] In September 1931 the people's commissar of transport and communication, Moisei Rukhimovich, dared to suggest that perhaps the provisions for industry were inadequate or that perhaps the investments were insufficient. Stalin was furious at the suggestion and wrote in a letter to Kaganovich:

> Although decrees of the Central Committee have great significance they cannot save the day. Why? Because as long as a pack of narcissistic and self-satisfied bureaucrats such as Rukhimovich are sitting in the Commissariat of Transport, avoiding fulfilling the decrees of the Central Committee and sowing seeds of skepticism, the decrees of the Central Committee will be put off until doomsday. To save the railroads, it is necessary to drive out this pack. Should you need my help in this matter, then let me know. If you can manage without my help, then exterminate this pack before it's too late. New people, who believe in our cause and can successfully replace the bureaucrats, can always be found within our party if they are properly sought out.[92]

In other economic questions too, Stalin's solutions were all of a terroristic nature. In August 1930, when the cities began to suffer money shortages, he ordered Molotov to "thoroughly cleanse" the State Bank and the People's Commissariat of Finance and then have "two, three dozen scum from these apparatuses shot, including ten cashiers of all types." In the same letter he demanded that "vermin in the meat industry" be shot and that this be reported in the press. Stalin also had plans for the eminent Russian economists Nikolai Kondratiev and Vladimir

Groman. "Kondratiev, Groman, and a few other scoundrels," he wrote
to Molotov on August 6, 1930, "must be shot." A few weeks later Stalin announced that the State Bank and the People's Commissariat of Finance should henceforth be staffed with "people from the GPU," who
would introduce some "control via bitch-slapping."[93]

This terroristic style of command destroyed production processes, en-
tangled directors and managers in murderous conflicts with competing
enterprises, and isolated the country's industrial complexes from each
other. The system rewarded managers and Communists who devoted
themselves unquestioningly to the regime's goals and were prepared to
abandon all reason and judgment in obedience to their leaders. Red
managers, engineers, and shock workers, who set production records
and exposed enemies, were given medals, accolades, and awards. Some
even received automobiles, luxury goods, and comfortable state apartments or were allowed to shop in special stores that offered items most
peasants and workers were never so much as allowed to lay eyes on.
Parallel to its repression and violence, industrialization opened up a
world of possibilities for thousands hoping to improve their position
in life. Among them were the proletarian engineers, products of the numerous workers' training schools, along with the young working-class
Communists, whose chief ability lay in chanting the current slogans of
the regime. Without the enthusiasm of the Komsomol members and
young laborers, who worked themselves into the ground building met-
ros, dams, and hydroelectric power plants, the mobilization of thousands of others would not have been possible. The New Man wanted
a better life, and he yearned for prosperity, advancement, and career
opportunities. Engineers, meanwhile, dreamed of the modernization
and mechanization of their country. There were also Komsomol members, seeking adventure and an escape from the life of their fathers and
grandfathers. Workers wanted a chance to use their power and social
capital against the managers and bourgeois specialists poised above
them. And even those Communists who truly believed in the declarations of their political leaders now hoped to witness the fulfillment of a
lifetime dream: the establishment of the dictatorship of the proletariat
that the revolution had promised.[94]

Apart from modernizing the economy and infrastructure, the Bolshevik project of industrialization was also meant to transform the
social map of the Soviet Union. The old elites were to be stripped of

all power, and the peasants were to be transformed into workers. Magnitogorsk and other sites of Stalinist industrialization not only tamed the wilderness but also helped create New Men. Here, peasants shared experiences and participated in heroic battles to achieve production goals—and in the process really did become New Men. The Magnitogorsk dam, which was built in record time, was a faulty construction and had to be demolished. But that was beside the point. "The dam of Magnitogorsk," wrote one propagandist, "was a school where people learned to respect Bolshevik wonders."[95] Reeducation could be achieved through labor, and no waste of resources could be large enough to prevent bringing this project to a successful completion. As the revolutionaries imagined it, people who knew nothing but the new life would learn to despise the life of their forefathers and would soon have no more reason to resist the dictatorship. Once obedience could be achieved without coercion then the power of the few would be able to rest on the voluntary approval of the many.

But the New Man did not come from the test tube; he came from the village. Life in the city did not protect him against hunger and privation either. In 1932, even in Moscow, workers received only 52 percent of the wages they had earned in 1928. Often, the shock workers and even the engineers lived lives that were no better than those of the peasants working as slaves on the construction sites. A machinist from Voronezh, who had distinguished herself through particular zeal, wrote to her sister about being accepted into the ranks of the shock workers. "What privileges they give us for this shock work, I don't know. It seems none at all."[96] Poverty and misery were everywhere, and for most laborers, achieving the status of shock worker was a poor consolation. "In the three years I have been living in Moscow," the peasant son Stepan Podlubny confided to his diary in May 1933, "I can't remember ever having felt full to the brim. I always ran around hungry. In the first year of my life [sic] I ate just enough so that I didn't die from hunger. I would find frozen crusts of bread on the street. I blew off the snow and the dirt and ate them."[97]

The cities and major building sites of Communism were places of ambivalence. They were crossroads of languages and cultures. At the beginning of collectivization, hundreds of thousands of peasants from all parts of the empire had fled their native villages, trying to escape the approaching terror commandos. Throughout the Soviet Union people had gone into hiding in the barracks settlements of the major construction sites, but generally no one stayed for long. There were always other construction sites where new work could always be found. Millions were on the move, and nobody could control where these industrial nomads came from or where they were going. The Soviet Union, wrote Stalin's acolyte Ordzhonikidze, had become a gigantic "nomad camp" that could no longer be controlled. And this was a serious problem: How could cities be built overnight and how could a model socialist society be established when almost no one was prepared to put down roots? The proletariat disappeared into the maelstrom of the peasant masses, and when they did settle in the cities they generally formed their own insular communities on the outskirts, far removed from the reach of the power holders. As late as the mid-1930s, even Moscow's city center was only poorly connected to its outer districts, where there were neither hospitals nor schools and where even the armed branch of the state only rarely dared to venture.[98]

In light of such bleakness and scarcity, it seemed unlikely that the peasants on the city outskirts would voluntarily transform themselves into what the revolution imagined of them. Everything that the Cultural Revolution had sought to banish from the cities had now returned: rampant alcoholism, village mentality and customs, and violence as a means of resolving conflicts. As Stepan Podlubny noted in his diary in April 1933, even Moscow had few visible traces of the promised new world. His quarter was home to "boys and girls from the most backward of milieus," uncultured peasants, and "shit-faced fellows" who brawled and boozed rather than becoming New Men. And when there were no incentives to change their lives, how could these peasant-workers have been expected to do so? In the world of propaganda, workers lived in abundance and thanked their leader for their fortunate and joyful existences. In truth, however, workers lived in squalid conditions, and their lives stood in complete contradiction to the propaganda of the brave new world. In spring 1938, when Podlubny visited his father in Yaroslavl, he also surveyed the city's working-class districts near the auto factory:

> The auto-works look revolting from the outside. The long, low-ceilinged, barrack-like buildings, blackened by soot, built in army-style line and column and with round roofs—nose to tail they stand there, huddled

together like pigs that have been wallowing in the dirt. The wooden barracks at the city outskirts behind the works are a horrible sight: low ceilings, small windows, black and dirty. They are built in rows with streets of impenetrable filth in between them, which serve as a dumping ground for garbage and are also where the reeking communal latrines can be found. The view from the barrack windows is one of misery and filth. The people are sullen, I did not see a single cheery face.

A few days later in Moscow, Podlubny noted, some people had been trampled to death at a fabric sale in the central department store by the Petrovka, as there was nowhere else in the city to buy clothes.[99]

The onslaught of people fleeing the villages did not change the face of the cities alone. Factories and building sites too were conquered by the peasants and their way of work. In the early years of the first Five Year Plan, enormous fluctuations of the workforce caused significant problems. Peasants came and went, and the only means of preventing them from turning their backs on a place of employment was violence. Unskilled workers who failed to blend into the urban rhythm of life and work caused disruptions in the production process. Idleness, alcoholism, and the wanton destruction of tools and machinery continued, but they were still the least of the problems the peasants brought with them. Ultimately, the regime determined, draconian punishment was the only answer. All across the Soviet Union, factory directors and engineers were arrested and shot as "saboteurs," "spies," and "vermin." Every accident, every failure, every delay was now the fault of some enemy. And enemies were everywhere, robbing and cheating workers on behalf of foreign governments. Stalin and his assistants were well aware of the lower-classes' hatred toward the educated and bespectacled, toward people with soft hands, white shirts, and starched collars. They were also aware that this hatred had great potential, and they had no reservations about exploiting it to maximize their own power. To have missed this opportunity would have been contrary to their nature.[100]

Nevertheless, unruly peasants could expect no better treatment from the Bolsheviks than they were receiving from the factory directors and engineers. The Stalinist dictatorship not only attempted to discipline and subjugate its workers but also entered their lives with punitive force. Anyone caught destroying machinery or violating workplace discipline could expect the worst. Factories became barracks in which workers were trained and punished like soldiers. In summer 1932, when workers near Ivanovo rose up in protest at their wretched living conditions and the terror they had to endure, the GPU showed no mercy. The ringleaders of the strike were arrested and sentenced to eight years in concentration camps, while the others involved were deported to Siberia.[101] In summer 1940 the regime passed a law stating that workers caught being late, idle, or drunk could be sentenced to forced labor and camp detention. Between June and September 1940 alone, 906,824 culprits were convicted on the basis of this law. 755,440 had been guilty of idleness, 131,718 had missed work without authorization, and 2,949 had failed to report the disciplinary violations of their fellow workers. The people's courts did not even shy away from sentencing minors in violation of workplace regulations to forced labor. In Moscow, even university professors who arrived late for work were punished. By June 1941, when war broke out, Soviet courts had condemned more than three million people on the basis of these workplace disciplinary laws, which in most cases resulted in prison sentences ranging from two to four months.[102]

The regime bound workers to the factories and peasants to the collective farms. And it despised proletarians who lived like peasants. To the Bolsheviks, laborers were nothing more than raw material from which New Men were to be sculpted. In October 1934 Stalin received word that a Soviet sailor, on shore leave in Danzig, had refused to return to his ship. To Stalin, Soviet subjects were slaves, and this was thus an act of treason. Although the traitor had escaped, Stalin wanted the "family members of the sailor arrested" as retribution.[103] Strong disdain was not the least of the reasons for the remorselessness with which Stalin and his assistants terrorized their own people. In winter 1942, after having been released from prison, the Polish officer Gustav Herling was walking through the city of Sverdlovsk when he came upon a group of soldiers who were sitting on the pavement. The men were hunched over, breaking the ice with hammers, and as they worked a decorated Soviet general stood above them, stamping on their backs.[104] This little episode is more telling of the relationship between the Bolsheviks and their subjects than any scholarly treatise ever written on Stalinism.

5 Dictatorship of Dread

POWER AND VIOLENCE

Stalin's slave state destroyed and uprooted millions in a series of violent interventions that showed regard for neither human lives nor dignity. Kolkhoz peasants were bound to the land, while draconian disciplinary laws tied workers to the factories. In the special settlements and concentration camps of the Soviet Union several million prisoners eked out their pitiful existences. By the early 1930s, however, this misery was nowhere to be found in the Soviet Union's outward presentation of itself. Education and information were monopolized and ideologized by the regime. It moralized the economy, and the relationship between rulers and their subjects was transformed into an enormous theatrical production that merely served to convey the rules and language of obedience. The Bolshevik public sphere left few possibilities for eluding the regime's prescribed rituals and rules of language. Should there be any criticism at all, it needed to be presented using the prescribed rhetoric. Furthermore, the world needed to be separated into categories of friends and enemies, right orders and wrong ones, or else the criticism had no hope of achieving anything at all. Worse still, the critic ran the risk of being accused of playing into the hands of enemies. Every single day millions of people were forced to decide between taking part or resigning themselves to the unavoidable. "Today they herded us out to march around the streets," wrote Nina Lugovskaya in her diary on the holiday celebrating the revolution in November 1932, "which made me absolutely furious and aggravated my feeling of helplessness even more. Walking over the cold, gray ground in the damp, dull light of an autumn day, stamping my frozen feet during the breaks, and cursing Soviet power to myself, with all its lying and bragging to foreigners and all the rest." While Lugovskaya may have been able to confess such thoughts in her diary, these were thoughts that needed to be hidden from even her most immediate surroundings.[1]

From this point on the party could only be portrayed as the redeemer of the people. Every good deed had to be praised as an act of Bolshevik creativity and as one of the leader's many great feats. The workers, in whose name the revolutionaries had once spoken, were now expected to keep silent—except to express their gratitude to the party for their wonderful lives. By the onset of collectivization at the latest, the Bolshevik interpretations of reality had diverged significantly from the experiences of most people. But what the Soviet subjects actually experienced played no role in the world of socialism as the Bolsheviks presented it. No one was allowed to speak of their poverty or humiliation because there simply were no unhappy people in the Bolshevik state. The press, which was tightly controlled by those in power, described a reality that was unfamiliar to most Soviet subjects, and the result was that people became accustomed to living in a public world of lies and a private world of truth. The regime had no other choice. The lie gave meaning to the poverty and misery that characterized most people's lives, and it helped train young, upwardly mobile Communists who needed to learn how the new world was to be seen and comprehended. Both the cult of Stalin and the daily rituals of denying reality were designed to graft the new order into the minds of subjects. The moralization of the economy fulfilled the same purpose. It was claimed that the achievements of workers and peasants were really gifts from the party and its leader, Stalin. Workers, peasants, and scientists, meanwhile, did not work out of obligation but out of gratitude.

The concept of time also took on a new dimension. The future, present, and past became artificial products that contradicted all experience. From now on, the only future was the one that the party leadership had devised. Time itself was suspended. Everything that was happening and

had happened converged towards an unalterable future, and thus neither the past nor the present could change any longer. After the catas-
trophes of collectivization and the great famine, the utopia of the brave
new world became a rigid catalogue of provisions that determined
which experiences could be represented as reality and which could not.
The relentless invocation of a utopia that would never come to pass left
no other option than to deny everything that was actually happening.[2]

By the 1930s no one could simply ignore the Bolshevik claim to absolute power and withdraw into private life. Throughout the Soviet Union,
the population was confronted with the practice of public stigmatization, which served as a constant reminder of who could and could not
belong to the new order. The periodically recurring campaigns in preparation for elections to the Soviets helped serve this purpose. Elections
were rituals of acclamation that merely simulated integration, since vot-
ers were in no way entitled to decide how to vote or who to vote for. The
elections themselves were not terribly important. What mattered instead
was the public announcement of who was not allowed to vote, of who
did not belong. The regime's campaigns were intended to accustom the
people to the practice of unmasking enemies and then expelling them
from the community. The outcasts were the floating debris, the "social
garbage" of the socialist revolution. All the rage and embitterment aris-
ing from the excesses of the Bolsheviks could be redirected against these
social lepers. Outcasts could be evicted from their homes, banished from
villages and cities, and thrown into concentration camps. People who
might have felt guilty about denouncing their neighbors could comfort
themselves by remembering that what they had done was unavoidable.
Outcasts were fair game. They possessed no rights, and violence could
be inflicted on them with impunity. If nothing else, people living in poverty and misery, with no real power of their own, could at least destroy
the lives of others. It was a system that allowed even the lowest of the
low to drag themselves up above someone else.

During the 1930s more than four million people belonged to the
category of the *lishentsy* (people without voting rights), and with every
passing year this number of outcasts, that is enemies, grew. The socialist community included all those who were not outcasts, and one could
argue that belonging to the community of New Men meant having
the shared experience of excluding enemies. There was hardly a Soviet
citizen who could avoid these practices of daily stigmatization. Even

old friends unmasked one another as enemies and reported them to the authorities. The accused attempted to justify themselves, and in doing so confirmed that they were indeed enemies. Without intending to, they confirmed the delusions of the Bolshevik leaders for all the world to see. No one was safe in Stalin's dictatorship. Anybody could be declared an enemy, and anybody could become an outcast and be arrested. The chief feature of this dictatorship was that no one could ever be certain who could be trusted. Stalinism was a dictatorship that engendered fear and dread, destroyed the social fabric of relations between neighbors, and conditioned people for mechanical obedience. "We were all like rabbits," recalled the screenwriter Valeri Frid, "who recognized the right of the boa constrictor to swallow us."[3]

Life conformed to signals that came from a distance. People followed signals demanding that they submit to a code of behavior that held human beings in contempt. The daily staging of a dualistic world of good and evil and the public unmasking and dehumanization of outcasts left deep scars on the consciousnesses of Soviet citizens. They caused perception and speech to become two separate entities, and they sowed mistrust toward strangers and foreigners, but also toward co-workers, friends, and relatives. "People have completely ceased to confide in each other," wrote the author Mikhail Prishvin in his diary. The daily stigmatization of enemies—both verbally and visually—became the defining feature of Stalinist civilization. Tens of thousands became perpetrators, not because they were Communist enthusiasts, but out of fear of becoming victims themselves.[4]

Prishvin's diary offers the following description: "Our Russian people, like snow-covered trees, are so overburdened with the problems of survival, and want so much to talk to one another about it, that they simply lack the strength to hold out any more. But as soon as someone gives in, he is overheard by someone else—and disappears!"[5] Hannah Arendt spoke of the atomization of society, the powerlessness and isolation of individuals in the age of totalitarian dictatorships. Nobody could successfully oppose these dictatorships of a new type. People living in a state of emergency, permeated by fear, became unable to join forces against a determined clique of unscrupulous and violent perpetrators. This small but ruthless group was much better organized, and its members had no reservations about unleashing bloody force at the slightest provocation. Thus, an uprising was near impossible.

Stalin's power was based on the orchestration of a state of emergency. Only with a war against spies, traitors, and saboteurs was it possible for the dictator to prepare his followers for the great reckoning and the physical annihilation of enemies. This atmosphere of ubiquitous violence also taught the subjects that questions of power would be settled by arrests, wounds, and death. Ultimately, though, many people no longer defended themselves because in obeying they could hope for rewards, privileges, and positions of power. Those who offered resistance, meanwhile, risked death. No one knew better than Stalin that the power of the Bolshevik dictatorship rested on its proven ability to punish cruelly. After all, the fear of repression dwindles when the perpetrator appears reluctant, hesitates, or gives the impression that he might regret his vicious acts. The costs and benefits of resistance must thus be weighed against each other. No one is tempted to commit acts whose consequences are incalculable. When the oppressed fail to organize against those in power, it is not because they like the status quo but because they prefer it to the uncertainty of resistance. "The security of order in this sense," wrote the sociologist Heinrich Popitz, "can obviously also develop in a despotic system. It is perfectly reconcilable with oppression and exploitation." Only under circumstances of total arbitrariness and insecurity was it possible for a small group of determined power holders to force the majority of the people to submit to their logic of violence and to act as if they had lost all moral considerations. Without this atmosphere of fear and mistrust, it never would have been possible for these violent and unscrupulous perpetrators to manipulate the fear and aggression of so many people to their own advantage.[6]

But why did the regime not limit itself to the threat and selective application of violence? Was it not enough to simply force loyalty and obedience? Especially when organized resistance was, by this time, already a thing of the past. Why did Stalin and his assistants have more than a million people killed by quota, and why did they undermine the trust and security that are necessary for life in society? Why did they kill indiscriminately and seemingly without any plan, and why did they destroy the very institutions of the Soviet state? What did the dictator and his aids really expect from the unbridled and limitless violence they visited upon the Soviet Union?

Totalitarianism theory provided a simple and convincing answer to these questions. According to Hannah Arendt and Carl J. Friedrich,

Stalinist terror was an attempt at instilling fear and dread in the population. The ultimate goal was to create a state of permanent alarm that would dry up all sources of civil resistance. This could only be achieved, however, through a maximization of violence, because it lay in the nature of the total state to respect no boundaries. Then, in the 1980s the "revisionists" discovered a Stalinism that had come "from below" and tended to see the violent excesses as evidence that the political leadership had been unable to direct and control society. According to this interpretation, the terror was really an authorless event that had only been sustained by social conflicts of interest.[7] What are we to believe? That the suicidal campaigns arose from the destructive compulsions of the total state? Or that they were due to conflicts between interest groups? Neither of these interpretations is supported by the factual evidence. Stalin apparently had no trouble ordering the use of excessive violence against anyone he pleased. But he was also able to put an end to it just as easily. The terror came in waves. It gained in intensity whenever the dictator decided to give the violence free rein, and it died down again whenever he got tired of it. The violence was a product neither of the system nor of social conflicts. It was a product of Stalin. How else is it possible to explain the fact that mass terror as an instrument of political rule simply disappeared when the dictator himself died? Nothing in terms of social and political preconditions had changed. And why did Khrushchev, Molotov, Kaganovich, and Malenkov not continue the violence beyond March 1953 when they inherited the dictator's legacy? The answer is simple: they had finally recognized that there would be no winners at the end of this deadly game.[8]

Some historians have argued that ideas, motives, and intentions were to blame for the bloodbath under Stalin. According to this view, Stalin was a perpetrator out of conviction. He and his followers believed that a social utopia was possible and that they were justified in using any means possible to realize their ideological goals. The Stalinist leadership, they claimed, felt threatened militarily—by Poland, Japan, and Germany—and therefore decided to physically annihilate alleged spies and potential traitors. Molotov would still invoke this argument during an interview with the Soviet journalist Felix Chuev in the 1970s. The mass violence, he explained, had been unavoidable because it had been necessary to forever free the Soviet Union from its internal enemies and prepare it for the impending war. The mass killings of 1937 could not be traced back to the "arbitrariness of the leadership," he claimed. Instead, they were a "continuation of the revolution under difficult international circumstances."[9]

Japanese and German intelligence forces were indeed working to destabilize the Soviet Union. They were also trying to exploit ethnic tensions and social crises to their advantage. This is not pure invention. But why should we accept Molotov's claims that the fear of war had been the reason for the violence? Could he have known in 1933 what he knew in 1945? Why did Stalin and his followers kill children and old people, peasants and illiterates—people who knew just as little about foreign countries and their intelligence services as they did about the plans and intentions of the Stalinist leadership? Why was it necessary to murder tens of thousands of camp inmates in 1937? And why did Stalin order the execution of even his friends and relatives, along with the leadership of both the party and the army? Why did violence follow the principle of randomness, annihilating friend and foe alike and eventually eliminating even the very perpetrators who had set the mass murder in motion? Above all, though, why did the mass terror cease when war truly was imminent? An interpretation that invokes the leaders' fear of foreign threats provides no answers to these questions.[10] It confuses motives with justifications and insinuates that violent excesses can only be conceived of in terms of causal relationships between ideas and actions. In reality, however, violent perpetrators use such legitimizations to convince themselves that their violent acts are justified. The legitimizations provide them with a license to kill and can also serve as a justification in case they are ever held accountable for their deeds. People with the same motive can behave quite differently, and people can also do the same thing for different reasons.

The state of emergency is a paradise for sadists and some psychopaths, as it redefines the definition of normality and causes "normal" people to do things they otherwise would not. Stalin was such a psychopath. Forensic psychiatrists describe psychopathic criminals as people who show emotional indifference, lack of empathy, have a relationship with their environment that is based on manipulation, and are unable to feel compassion for other human beings—a description that probably also applies to Stalin. "Within their perceptual organization and their practical relationship patterns," writes the social psychologist Rolf Pohl, "other people rarely achieve a status beyond that of mere objects." Stalin's psychopathic framework fit well with dictatorship and war and also empowered other psychopaths and sadists to act on their vilest, innermost drives. Moreover, their paranoia even helped them to survive in these spaces of violence.

"When we read of the atrocities of the past," wrote Sigmund Freud in a letter to Albert Einstein in 1932, "it sometimes seems as though the idealistic motives served only as an excuse for destructive appetites."[11] The historical narrative, however, does not envision a place for violence with no purpose. People who are unfamiliar with violence and who themselves have never had to endure it are distraught when things that were once the stuff of nightmares become very real possibilities. People do not want violence to define their lives, so they turn to rationalization strategies and look for ideas and motives to give the violent excesses some meaning. Ultimately, though, this is nothing more than a means of coping with the bitter realization that violent excesses do not always have reasons but simply follow a dynamic of their own, one that they themselves create in the course of their execution.

Whatever motives the Stalinist perpetrators may once have had, the execution of violence rendered them meaningless. In the logic of despotic systems of power, violent acts compel subsequent actions, and for these subsequent actions reasons and legitimizations play absolutely no role. "Absolute power is self-based," writes Wolfgang Sofsky:

> not a means to an end, but an end in itself. Power that must legitimate itself is a weak mode of power. The conventional view of power is that it must always seek legitimization as a kind of shield. . . . Terror does not need to justify itself. Its basis is fear, an anxiety that it unceasingly generates. It is its own objective, self-contained. It proves itself by the act of its own exercise. . . . Absolute power does not obey the pattern of purposeful, result-oriented action. It is purposeless; not poiesis, but negative praxis. Ideology here is not just superfluous, but obstructive. It ties power to certain aims, degrading it to a mere instrument. Terror that allowed itself to be guided by aims and purposes would be calculable. It would no longer be terror. To take recourse in ideology is a false interpretation *post festum,* nourished by the mistaken belief that there always has to be an intellectual reason, that everything has some historical meaning.

It is not the motives behind the violence, but rather the enabling spaces in which the violence unfolds that are of primary importance. To put it in Erving Goffman's terms, this is not about people and their situations, but about situations and their people.[12]

The Stalinist state was weak. Its propensity for violence did not arise from its strength but from its weakness. Campaigns and violent exemplary punishments were its only methods of asserting its power, and it depended on the viceroys in the provinces to fulfill the tasks the dictator in faraway Moscow had assigned them. Stalinism, however, was a despotic regime that was unable to fulfill the demanding tasks it had set for itself, and so it resorted to the disproportionate use of arbitrary violence as a means for forcibly achieving everything that did not occur of itself. Considering the violent excesses of collectivization and the great famine, Stalin and his helpers had every reason to mistrust the people. Their own power was shaky. They could not even trust the intermediaries who were supposed to be enforcing their power in the empire's provinces. That is why Stalin led his followers into situations of struggle and placed extremely high demands on an already overwhelmed system of rule. Under these circumstances it was possible for the dictator to assert his violent style against all opposition and coerce people into obedience. Insecurity became a way of life, with spies, saboteurs, traitors, and "socially harmful elements" lurking around every corner. Everyone was a suspect. Those who were frightened and terrorized became perpetrators themselves to avoid becoming victims—a state of affairs that thrived in the state of emergency.[13] As the Soviet reformer Georgy Arbatov recalled it, the terror campaigns were designed to instill "the main code of behavior that subjects of a dictatorship have to follow: to be afraid of your own thoughts."[14]

In the self-representation of leading Bolsheviks, terror was a means of breaking resistance and punishing disloyalty. It was a "cleansing storm," designed to forever rid society of the "social waste" and "weeds" that the Cultural Revolution and collectivization had failed to stamp out completely. To those performing the violent acts, however, these intentions were meaningless. They used the context and its possibilities to give their violent tendencies free reign, as it pleased the dictator when their murderous accomplishments set new records. Mass terror altered the lives of perpetrators and victims in such a way that eventually no one responded to anything but violence. The meaning of punishment also changed, for when authority punishes arbitrarily and for no apparent reason, it loses its moral weight.[15] Something that can befall anyone at any given time loses its discriminating effect, which is why punishment in a despotic regime is only a matter of fate.

The year 1937 was not the beginning, but rather the peak of the terror. Taking the inner core of power as its starting point, it emanated in concentric circles into every strata of society, wreaking havoc. It was borne out of several different waves of repression and culminated in the killing frenzy of 1937 and 1938. This violent rampage included the physical eradication of the political leadership elite, which had loomed as a possibility throughout the early 1930s, before becoming a bloody reality in December 1934 after the murder of the Leningrad party boss, Kirov. It also included the party purges, beginning in spring 1937, and the murder of supposedly disloyal functionaries and office holders in the provinces. Between summer 1937 and autumn 1938 there were also the mass killings of kulaks, priests, members of the prerevolutionary elite, criminals, and camp inmates. And finally there was the arrest and execution of foreigners and members of ethnic minorities, along with the deportation of entire peoples.

THE SUBJUGATION OF THE PARTY ELITE

To Stalin and his henchmen, violence had always been an attractive course of action, and they resorted to it without any scruples. No one in the party leadership complained when peasants were deported or enemies of the regime were executed. There was no doubt whatsoever that the elite's power matched its ability to punish with exceptional cruelty and ruthlessness. The integration of the party, however, rested on the principle of ritualized discipline. From the late 1920s onwards, those who violated rules or criticized the general party line had to practice public self-criticism and repent their "sins"—a tradition that had never before existed in the Bolshevik party. "Such demands," Kamenev told the delegates at the Fifteenth Party Congress in 1927, "were never made in our party." And as late as 1930, Mikhail Tomsky too could openly proclaim that penitence was a religious term, but not a Bolshevik one. At that time, the defeated were reprimanded, degraded, expelled from the party or, as in Trotsky's case, deported—but they were not killed.[16]

For Stalin, the unconditional submission of critics and doubters was not enough. In his world, disloyalty was treason, punishable only by death. But only the state of emergency enabled him to assert his violent style within the inner circle of power as well. In the war against the peasantry, his adherents became hostages of a strategy of violence that they could no longer control. When the peasants revolted, putting the existence of the regime in jeopardy, Stalin was able to discredit all criticism directed against him as treason against the common cause. It was not just treason, though, but a mortal crime. Those who turned their backs on the party and its leader in its darkest hour could no longer be comrades. In his application for reentry to the party, Georgy Pyatakov, who had been expelled in 1927, claimed that a real Bolshevik would "readily cast out from his mind ideas in which he has believed for years." A true Bolshevik did not just part with old convictions but was also "ready to believe that black was white and white was black, if the party required it." Stalin needed to prepare his followers for this truth. He did this by entrapping them in situations that left them with no other choice than to agree to the punishment of "traitors." The violence crept on tiptoes into their daily lives, and ritualization gradually made it into a matter of course, so that soon its purpose was no longer even called into question.[17]

Stalin was a master of intrigue, and he knew how to conjure up threats to serve his own power interests. For him, all critics were enemies anyway, but in summer 1930 he ordered the GPU to stage a monstrous conspiracy that would allow him to officially and publicly discredit his adversaries as enemies of the regime. All across the Soviet Union, "bourgeois" specialists and experts from the ministries and planning authorities were arrested and exposed as saboteurs and spies. By August Stalin was ordering the executions of Kondratiev, Groman, and several other prominent economists. Their crimes were that they had spoken truths that were no longer allowed to be spoken.[18] In autumn 1930 the GPU staged a show trial against leading technicians and scientists who were accused of belonging to an "industrial party." The following year, former members of the Menshevik party were tried for collaborating with foreign powers and seeking to destroy the Soviet system via sabotage. They were condemned to death and paraded through the press as beasts in human form.

Stalin left nothing to chance. He gave GPU boss Vyacheslav Menzhinsky the task of establishing a link between enemies and his critics in the party leadership. Menzhinsky did as the dictator demanded and delivered the coerced confessions of the arrested. Among the accused were Stalin's political adversary Nikolai Bukharin, but also his follower Mikhail Kalinin and the prominent Red Army general Mikhail Tukhachevsky. Stalin confronted the accused and forced them to justify themselves. He then had their confessions circulated among the party leadership to generate an atmosphere of suspicion and mistrust. There could be no doubt, wrote Stalin in a letter to Sergo Ordzhonikidze, that Bukharin had sided with the enemies of the party and had been plotting a military coup to remove him and the rest of the leadership from power. Stalin's crude machinations fulfilled their purpose, and Bukharin was forced to respond to the dictator's absurd allegations. Stalin himself could not be a liar, so the accused had to confirm that dangerous conspiracies did indeed exist. They denied that they themselves had played any part in them, but simply in acknowledging their existence they had ensnared themselves in a cruel trap from which they could not escape. The suspicion had already been aroused, and now it was up to Stalin and his friends to decide whether or not they wanted to believe the suspects' affirmations of innocence. Kalinin had "sinned," Stalin agreed. This was beyond a doubt. But Stalin wanted to forgive him, so Kalinin was left with no choice but to become Stalin's grateful and devoted servant.[19] For Bukharin and the members of the so-called "Right Opposition," however, this was the beginning of an inexorable descent into the abyss.

In October 1930 Stalin was unexpectedly given the opportunity to put his words into action when he received a message from *Pravda*'s editor in chief Lev Mekhlis, who informed him of treason committed by Sergei Syrtsov, head of the government of the RSFSR, and Vissarion Lominadze, first secretary of the Trans-Caucasian Regional Committee. According to Mekhlis, Syrtsov and Lominadze had been complaining about the violent excesses during collectivization. Furthermore, while at a private gathering at the Institute of Red Professors they had spoken unfavorably about the Politburo's economic policies. Syrtsov had apparently prophesied that a peasant rebellion would cause the system to collapse like a house of cards and that the only way to avert this catastrophe would be to remove Stalin from power. Mekhlis had been notified of this by Reznikov, the party secretary of the literature department of the Red Professors. Reznikov, however, was apparently an agent provocateur in this case, acting on Stalin's orders, as the first report he delivered was immediately followed by a second one. In this second report he claimed not only that Syrtsov and Lominadze had divulged what had been discussed in the Politburo, but that they were also plotting to overthrow the general secretary as well. Stalin could hardly have asked for more.

Syrtsov and Lominadze had achieved their positions in the state and the party after making names for themselves during the 1920s as violent and ruthless Stalinists in Siberia and in the Caucasus. As early as June 1930, at the Tenth Party Congress of the Communist Party in Azerbaijan, Lominadze had recommended blood and terror as a means of suffocating peasant resistance to collectivization. "We must," he had told the delegates, "annihilate anyone who tries to raise their weapons against us, anyone who attempts an armed uprising, anyone who tries to lead anti-Soviet campaigns." He also went into detail about what this should entail: "For every murdered teacher, Communist, and Komsomol member, at least ten such scoundrels are to be sent to kingdom come."[20] If even the leader's closest confidants were traitors, then who could still be trusted? How threatening and perilous must the situation have become if even members of the inner circle of leadership were gathering in secret places to discuss the removal of the general secretary?

Stalin called them before the Politburo and confronted them with Reznikov's claims. He left no room for doubt about their "guilt," and neither Syrtsov nor Lominadze could defend themselves against the allegations In the meantime, Stalin had three additional participants in the discussion arrested and forced, under the threat of physical assault, to confirm that Syrtsov and Lominadze had not only criticized the party leadership but had also organized a resistance group. No one in the Politburo was willing to intervene on their behalf. In November 1930 Syrtsov and Lominadze were expelled from the Central Committee, and the remaining party secretaries were notified that criticism of the party leadership was a punishable offense. It was abundantly clear, Stalin announced, that the "rightists" Bukharin and Rykov were organizing against him and "cultivating a psychology of terrorism" to have him eliminated. Sooner than others, Bukharin had recognized what Stalin would be capable of if given free rein. On October 14 he wrote Stalin a letter, accusing him of planning the physical annihilation of his adversaries: "Koba. After our telephone conversation I immediately left work in a state of despair. Not because you had 'scared' me—you will not scare me and you will not intimidate me. But because those monstrous accusations that you threw at me are clear evidence of the existence of some sort of devilish, vile, and low *provocation,* that you believe, on which you are building your policy, and *that will lead to no good,* even if you were to destroy me physically as thoroughly as you are destroying me politically."[21]

Bukharin had no choice. All he could do was play along with Stalin's game of suspicion. The rules were simple. Anything that Stalin declared as truth had to be confirmed. All secrets, meanwhile, needed to be divulged and laid bare immediately. Anyone suspected of withholding information to try to deceive Stalin was in danger. Bukharin eventually resolved to submit himself to Stalin unconditionally, in the hopes of saving himself from prison and death. Only much later did he realize that the vengeful and mistrustful despot simply wanted him to confess to crimes he had never committed. Stalin had Bukharin wiretapped and thus knew that Bukharin's public proclamations of loyalty were insincere. Anna Larina, Bukharin's second wife, remembered how her husband had praised the violent excesses against the peasants in public, but had wept when he was confronted with their suffering on one of his journeys. "At the time of collectivization in 1930, when he was traveling through the Ukraine, he saw packs of children begging for alms at the little local stations, their stomachs swollen from hunger. Nikolai Ivanovich gave them all his money. When he got back to Moscow, he stopped by to see my father, told him about the trip, cried out, 'If more than ten years after the revolution one can see such things as this, what was the point of doing it?,' collapsed on the couch, and sobbed hysterically."

In summer 1928 Bukharin had told Kamenev that Stalin was a "power-crazed schemer without principles," that he "adjusted his politics according to whom he currently wanted to get rid of," and that he was surrounded by "spineless individuals" like the "stupefied stone-ass" Molotov.[22] These were words that Stalin never forgot. Bukharin was Stalin's living example of the mendacity of the enemy—someone who praised the dictator in public and denounced deviationists, but then presented another face in private. This was a cruel game in which Bukharin had nothing to gain, everything to lose, and could only hope to delay his own physical demise. Stalin meanwhile missed no opportunity to take Bukharin and his supporters down once and for all.

The noose gradually drew tighter as the dictator's preconceived conspiracies grew larger. Stalin's desire for stories of disloyalty and betrayal was insatiable. Month after month, he demanded new reports that would prove that his former adversaries were insincerely repentant and had indeed sided with the enemy. He ordered the deputy head of the GPU, Yagoda, to place all former Trotskyites and members of the opposition under surveillance, in the hopes that this would produce "evidence" of the treason that these "two-tongued" individuals were surely committing. Yagoda delivered what was expected of him and in late 1932 presented the dictator with the results of his surveillance. His agents, he wrote, had broken up a network of two hundred Trotskyites. Some had only recently been released from the camps and had been conspiring with other oppositionists against the party leadership. The conspiracy had been masterminded by Ivan Smirnov, a Trotskyite and former people's commissar of communications. Smirnov assured the Central Control Commission that he had broken all ties with the opposition and with Trotsky, but this of course was merely a defensive maneuver. Smirnov expressed his public contrition in an act that confirmed the conspiracy. He wanted, "at all costs," to reenter the party, but as Stalin knew with certainty, this was only in order to exploit the "discontent of the worker masses" and wait for the right moment to overthrow the leadership.

Yagoda's descriptions satisfied the fantasies of Stalin, who only wanted to hear what could be integrated into his understanding of the world. A handful of helpless Communists without any influence had now become an existential threat. Smirnov and his supporters were said to have met "for tea and for dinner" to discuss political matters in an intimate circle. It was beyond doubt that they had all acted on behalf of Trotsky, who was seeking to revive the opposition within the party and who could be expected to stop at nothing to "have Stalin removed." Smirnov, it was claimed, had traveled to Berlin in June 1931, and upon returning to the Soviet Union he had notified his friends that Trotsky had erred in "tactical matters." Apparently, the time had not yet been ripe for "active mass work." Stalin spoke through Yagoda, claiming that the sole purpose of Smirnov's journey to Berlin had been to receive instructions from Trotsky. Why else would he later say that he considered the outlaw Trotsky's estimates to have been a mistake? But what Smirnov actually said was of no consequence. Statements that did not correspond to Stalin's conceptions of grand conspiracy simply could not exist.[23] Smirnov was arrested, sentenced in 1933 to five years in prison, and then in 1936 shot. This was after being condemned to death in the first Moscow show trial, along several other members of the former opposition, including the Bolshevik economist and Stalin critic, Evgeny Preobrazhensky, and the Civil War hero Sergei Mrachkovsky.

In spring 1932 a paper of almost two hundred pages, penned by Martemian Riutin, former party leader of Dagestan and Central Committee delegate for collectivization, made its way through party circles. It described Stalin as an unscrupulous schemer and ruthless dictator who needed to be overthrown. Riutin had already been expelled from the party in September 1930, and in September 1932 he was arrested and sentenced to ten years' camp detention by the Collegium of the GPU. Twenty-four accomplices and confidants, who were supposedly members of a "counterrevolutionary" conspiracy, accompanied him to prison. Stalin's mistrust grew after his own wife, Nadezhda Alliluyeva, committed suicide in November and was found to have possessed a copy of the Riutin program. Soon thereafter, he received a letter from the old Bolshevik Maksimilian Savelev, who informed him that Nikolai Eismont and Vladimir Tolmachev, people's commissars of trade and transport of the RSFSR, were also plotting against him. Several prominent party members were said to have gathered in Eismont's apartment on the anniversary of the revolution, where they had discussed the famine in Ukraine and in the northern Caucasus and had blamed Stalin for the catastrophic state of the economy. There had also been talk of removing the general secretary from power.

Stalin did not hesitate. He instructed the GPU to interrogate Eismont and Tolmachev and arrest their friends. He then had the accused brought before the Central Control Commission, where they were again interrogated and forced to confirm their statements. Eismont named names and declared that one of the people he had discussed Stalin's removal with was Alexander Smirnov—the former people's commissar of agriculture and secretary of the Central Committee, as well as a close confidant of Lenin's.[24] Both the context and the web of interpersonal relationships seemed to support the conspiracy theory: Smirnov was friends with Mikhail Tomsky and also a member of the Central Committee. Moreover, he was a companion of Bukharin's and was affiliated with Alexei Rykov, who had been the Soviet Union's head of government until 1930. Stalin thus had every reason to be mistrustful of Smirnov, and he seized the moment to set an example before the eyes of the Politburo and the Central Committee and prepare his followers for the reckoning with Communists and cronies.

In November 1932, Stalin summoned Smirnov, Tomsky, and Rykov before the Politburo and confronted them with the allegation that they had known of the conspiracy and kept it a secret from the party. He himself remained in the background and left it up to his most trusted companions to hurl abuse at Smirnov and Tomsky and raise new accusations against them. Mikoyan was of the belief that one could hear and feel whether or not someone was telling the truth. Whenever Smirnov told the truth, he said, his words sounded convincing, but now he seemed to be lying. The rest of the Politburo apparently agreed. Why had Smirnov and Tomsky gone on holiday together, rather than staying to take part in a Central Committee meeting and discuss the Riutin affair? As if the joint holiday were not bad enough, they had gone hunting together and had even traveled in the same train carriage. What did they discuss in their time together? How could their conversation have failed to include the overthrow of Stalin or the Eismont conspiracy? Smirnov admitted to having met Eismont on one occasion, but he denied that there had ever being any talk of overthrowing Stalin. Tomsky lost his temper and told them he could not understand why the members of the Politburo were demanding that he humiliate himself before them. "Why are you lashing out at me, what use is it to you? Is it enough that the people have already spoken out against me."[25]

Stalin, of course, depended in no way whatsoever on public opinion. All that mattered to him was securing a small circle of followers and then disciplining them so that they would never again dare oppose him. For this purpose the despot needed opponents and enemies who could be brought down publicly—in order to show those who had not yet fallen from grace what could happen if they failed to obey. This is why Stalin said very little during these gatherings. He observed the others while they spoke and commented on their depictions of events. He always made one entrance at the beginning of the production to voice his suspicions. And then he appeared again at the end to tell the audience what lesson was to be learned from what had happened. Tomsky, however, failed to understand that he was a performer in a theatrical production directed by Stalin. He not only tried to prove his innocence but also sought to convince those present that the allegations made against him were absurd. Within this circle of vassals, however, the accused were supposed to confirm Stalin's version of reality, not to try to disprove it. For there to be any kind of meaningful resistance at this point it was too late. Stalin, by this time, had amassed far too much power. Criticizing him would have been unwise.

In January 1933 the dictator presided over a similar performance of this humiliation ritual in front of the Central Committee. This time Ian Rudzutak assumed the role of agent provocateur and accused Smirnov of having contrived counterrevolutionary plans against the leader: "In the conversations he said: scoundrels, rascals, vile knaves, where have they led our country?" Innocent people were apparently being shot for gleaning ears of grain from the fields, and Smirnov had blamed Stalin for this. According to the accusation Smirnov had asked, "Why can't a single person be found in our country who would be able to get rid of Stalin? A choice must be made: either Stalin or a peasant uprising."[26] Everyone present knew that these were words of truth, whether Smirnov had said them or not. But this no longer mattered. The task of the Central Committee was not to discover truth but to make an example out of the supposed traitor placed before them. Lies would be transformed into truth in the process. Smirnov and Bukharin understood what was demanded of them and obediently took their cues from the despot. They confirmed Stalin's conspiracy theories and demanded that the traitors be punished severely. The accusations as they applied to themselves, however, they denied. Smirnov condemned Eismont's "counterrevolutionary" speeches and insisted that no one could replace Stalin. Only a madman could demand his removal, he said. Such words could only come from the mouth of someone who was in league with the enemy, but he (Smirnov) had always "loved" Stalin and loved him still. In the hour of need, when threats were everywhere, the political leadership needed to be able to depend on the loyalty of party members, Smirnov continued. Furthermore, he knew that it was "abundantly clear" that every political action behind Stalin's back was an act against the party itself. It went on. Smirnov's situation was hopeless. No one believed a word he said. No matter what he did, no matter what he said—Stalin would always be able to use it against him.[27]

The accused were under suspicion, and they would remain so until Stalin decided what was to become of them. Everyone knew that there was no escape. All the others could demonstrate their devotion by reviling the accused and discrediting them as liars. Interjections came from the plenum that Smirnov, Tomsky, and Rykov were insincere and that they were concealing their true thoughts about Stalin and his leadership. Bukharin tried to counteract the suspicion directed against him by hysterically affirming that revolutionary vigilance was indispensable and that enemies who had wormed their way into the party would have to be punished "without the slightest mercy." Could he have sensed that he too would soon become a victim in this game? That Stalin would one day turn his demand for merciless punishment against him? Everyone knew what Stalin was capable of and that he had no reservations about translating his words into actions. But this was not the only reason that members of the Central Committee accepted their roles in Stalin's staged reality. In the end, those who had demanded punishment for doubters and deviationists and who had validated the absurdest of the conspiracy theories had no recourse when they themselves became victims. They could not suddenly suggest that it had all been a grotesque lie or that everything of which they had accused others did not apply to them.

In any case, what mattered to Stalin was that the accused perform a ritual of submission. In doing so they confirmed the rules whose validity they had once doubted and restored unity to the party's circle of leadership. What took place during the Central Committee sessions of the 1930s was nothing more than an attempt at subjugating the group to strict disciplinary control and punishing deviant behavior, achieved by the incessant repetition of rituals. Matvei Shkiriatov, who belonged to the Presidium of the Central Control Commission, spoke of conspiracies that had been plotted at "parties," in "taxis," and at secret gatherings, where former opposition members forged ties with one another and schemed against the leadership. The class enemy was everywhere, and his attacks were vicious. This meant that every thought, every joke, and every anecdote that cast doubt on the party's unity was a crime that warranted punishment. According to Shkiriatov, the party leadership expected members of the former opposition to reveal their ties to Stalin's critics in a "Bolshevik manner." At a Politburo meeting in November 1932, when Alexei Rykov, Lenin's successor as the head of government, tried to justify himself against accusations of disloyalty, Stalin's acolyte Ordzhonikidze told him to admit to his mistakes and surrender in public: "Speak openly so that the country can hear."[28]

The disciplinary effects of such rituals of violence had nothing to do with the values and content they purported to convey. After all, everyone involved knew that the allegations raised against Trotsky and Bukharin were absurd. But Stalin's power rested on his ability to coerce others into publicly accepting his accusations as incontrovertible truths. At a Politburo meeting in October 1938, he himself conceded that Trotsky and Bukharin had never been spies. But that was beside the point. The Stalinist principle of community building was based on public self-deprecation and raw verbal attacks. It mentally prepared Stalin's followers for the physical annihilation of potential enemies and kept them in a state of constant fear and dread. Survival in Stalin's environment required nerves of steel.[29]

"We're not shooting enough," complained Kaganovich at the plenum of the Central Committee in January 1933.[30] Not a single deviant from the party leadership had been killed. The murder of Leningrad's party boss, Sergei Kirov, however, gave Stalin an opportunity to let his lust for murder reign free. Kirov's death did not mark the birth of the terror, but it did change the atmosphere in which the party's inner circle operated. It was now overcast by the shadow of death. Before, only those outside the party could be killed, but now this basic principle was no longer valid. The Communists were at war with their own people, and mercy for those plotting to oust or kill the leader was thus out of the question. In the 1920s many deviations could still be atoned for with submission and penitence. Now, however, they were capital crimes. Victims were required to surrender before the Central Committee and participate in the legitimization of their own downfall—a procedure that everyone in the inner circle of leadership had agreed upon. When the engineers of this procedure later found their own heads on the block they could hardly refuse to submit to something they had demanded of so many others.[31]

On the afternoon of December 1, 1934, the Leningrad party boss Sergei Mironovich Kirov was assassinated. His assassin, Leonid Nikolaev, had approached him without arousing any suspicion, as he had been in possession of a party membership card when he had entered the Leningrad party headquarters at 1:30 P.M. He left the building at 2:30 P.M. and then returned at 4:30 P.M., at which time he made his way to the third floor and requested to be heard as a petitioner. No one took note of him. Moments later, Kirov and six bodyguards entered the building. When Kirov appeared in the corridor on the third floor Nikolaev pulled a revolver from his coat pocket and shot him in the head. The assassin then tried to take his own life too, but was tackled, bound, and removed from the premises by the NKVD guards.[32]

Nikolaev, who had only just turned thirty, came from a working-class family, and in 1932 he had started working as a locksmith in a number of Leningrad factories. From that time on he had been a card-carrying member of the party and had carried out several party administrative functions—as an industrial consultant in the Leningrad Area Committee, as a price controller in the People's Commissariat of Workers' and Peasants' Inspection, and most recently as an instructor at the Institute of Party History. The personnel file of the party portrays the young man as a slacker, a malcontent, and a schemer. He was supposedly chronically dissatisfied and never missed an opportunity to petition or complain to the authorities. After refusing to carry out an assignment in spring 1934, Nikolaev had been expelled from the party and lost his post at the Institute of Party History. Although his party membership was later restored, he was unable to return to his former place of employment and in his despair, he resumed his habit of petitioning. He appealed to the secretary of Leningrad's Municipal Party Committee, and in July 1934 he wrote to Kirov. In August, Stalin too received a letter, but all attempts at garnering attention were in vain, and his letters went unanswered. Immediately after his arrest, Nikolaev confessed that he had decided in early November to assassinate the head of the Leningrad party organization. His situation had become unbearable, he claimed, and with neither employment nor "moral support," he saw no solution other than to kill Kirov. There was nothing to suggest that someone else had instigated Nikolaev to commit the assassination.[33]

Molotov recalled how he and other Politburo members had been standing in Stalin's office when Filipp Medved, the head of the Leningrad NKVD, had phoned to deliver the news of Kirov's murder. Stalin called him a "moron" and hung up the phone.[34] Genrikh Yagoda, Stalin's people's commissar of internal affairs, arrived at the Kremlin that evening to take part in Politburo consultations and hear what Stalin had to say about the ongoing investigation in the Kirov case. That very evening, Stalin and his closest confidants from the Politburo boarded the night train to Leningrad. After arriving at the station, Stalin, Molotov, and Voroshilov proceeded to the municipal hospital to survey Kirov's corpse. Several hours passed before they arrived at the Smolny Institute, the headquarters of the Leningrad party organization, to form their own impression of the NKVD investigation. An employee of the local Komsomol leadership who was in the building at the time remembered Stalin's fearsome appearance. "It was in the main corridor. I saw a group of people approaching. I saw Stalin in the middle, in front of him Genrikh Yagoda with a revolver in his raised hand. He gave the order: 'Everyone with their face to the wall! Hands on the trouser seam!'"[35]

An NKVD officer recalled that Stalin interrogated the assassin himself. Nikolaev, however, had nothing of importance to tell the general secretary. He had been angered by his dismissal from the Institute of Party History and considered shooting Kirov to be his last resort. Such motives were not to Stalin's liking. He demanded to know who the assassin's accomplices were and who was paying him. Stalin also promised him that his life would be spared if he cooperated with the NKVD.[36]

The perpetrator's arrest set a manhunt for conspirators and class enemies immediately in motion. Before the Politburo in Moscow could even decide who was to blame for this bloody deed, Leningrad's secret police had already begun combing the city for former White Guards, who they assumed to be behind the assassination plot. The Chekists screened suspicious foreign nationals and searched for links between Nikolaev and members of the prerevolutionary elite who were registered in the files of the secret police. Yagoda encouraged his subordinates to track down foreigners and class enemies, and to force the assassin to reveal who had paid him. He questioned Fomin, the deputy leader of the Leningrad NKVD, about Nikolaev's clothing. He wanted to know whether it had been made in Russia or in a foreign country. Nikolai Bukharin spun tales of foreign intelligence services using Nikolaev to sow confusion and destabilize the Soviet order. Within days of Kirov's murder, 103 individuals from Poland, Finland, Romania, and Lithuania, who had been residing in the Soviet Union illegally, were arrested and shot without trial. On December 4 the TASS news agency reported that sixty-six "White Guards" had been condemned to death by a military tribunal.

But Stalin was already looking to the future. It was not just the "former people" who would pay for Kirov's death but his critics in the party leadership as well. Yagoda, representing the traditional school of thought, foolishly believed that only those without party membership cards could be traitors. Stalin, however, believed otherwise, and also had different ideas about how the murder of the Leningrad party boss should be dealt with. Furthermore, Stalin mistrusted Yagoda, and for these reasons he assigned Nikolai Yezhov, head of the Organizational Department (Orgraspred) of the Central Committee, to lead the investigation instead. Already during his tenure as Semipalatinsk party secretary and deputy people's commissar of agriculture, Yezhov had demonstrated his ability to act in accordance with the dictator's interests. Back in 1930 he had had more than seventy ministry employees arrested and charged with sabotage, an act that was difficult for Stalin not to take notice of. This was indeed an ambitious and unscrupulous functionary, and he seemed to be willing to do anything to win the dictator's favor. Soon, Stalin had taken Yezhov into his inner circle and had begun entrusting him with secret assignments. Yezhov for his part did not disappoint. He was able to anticipate Stalin's every wish and also demonstrated that he was capable of interpreting the necessary signs in a manner that his master found fitting.[37]

By the second day after Kirov's murder, Yezhov had begun searching for connections between Trotsky, Zinoviev, Kamenev, and the assassin. Stalin enlisted Yakov Agranov, Yagoda's deputy and adversary in the NKVD, along with Leonid Zakovsky, head of the Belorussian NKVD, to help Yezhov gather evidence. Zakovsky, who became head of the Leningrad secret police, subjected the assassin, his wife, and his colleagues to an interrogation that lasted for days and went through the nights. Stalin, who was kept informed about the investigation, was apparently dissatisfied with the statements, as Nikolaev and his wife had altered their confessions several times. Ultimately, though, they confessed to a great deal. They named accomplices and also confessed to belonging to a counterrevolutionary organization headed by Kamenev and Zinoviev. Nikolaev also claimed that he was "supposed to make the murder look like an act of a lone individual, in order to conceal the involvement of the Zinoviev group." Furthermore, he admitted that he knew the Latvian consul personally and that he had relations with a foreign power. By late December the papers were announcing that Nikolaev had not been a lone gunman but was indeed part of a large conspiracy masterminded by Trotsky, Zinoviev, and Kamenev. In the hopes that his life might be spared, Nikolaev confessed to every allegation leveled against him. In the end, however, Stalin did not keep his word in this case either, and on December 29, 1934, Nikolaev and thirteen of his alleged accomplices were condemned to death and executed. Even in the final minutes before the execution, Agranov, along with the state prosecutor, Andrei Vyshinsky, were still badgering the condemned to confess who had paid them.

The executions were directly followed by a Leningrad-wide NKVD dragnet. In January and February 1935 more than eleven thousand members of the tsarist elite were taken from their homes and deported and innocent people were shot as "hostages." On February 15 Stalin received a report from Zakovsky, informing him that more than ten thousand members of the old elite and aristocracy had been discovered alive and well, "polluting" the city of Leningrad. He had, thus, ordered the expulsion of some five thousand families from Leningrad and recommended that males among them be arrested and subjected to "operative work." The most "malevolent" prisoners would be sent to concentration camps, and the remainder would be sent into exile. Yezhov was also quick to report his successes: twenty-five hundred Zinoviev supporters had been tracked down and registered on his watch, and 283 of them had already been detained.[38]

For Stalin and the Politburo, executing the assassin and his alleged accomplices was not enough. The trials were also followed by the deaths—under mysterious circumstances—of a number of Leningrad NKVD officers. Other NKVD officers were transferred for disciplinary reasons, arrested, or shot. Medved, head of the Leningrad NKVD, was sent to a concentration camp for three years, and the last remaining Chekists who had been involved in the case were liquidated in 1937. After Stalin's death, rumors began to circulate that it was the secret police who had incited Nikolaev to murder Kirov. In December 1955 Mikoyan received a letter from the old Bolshevik Olga Shatunovskaya, informing him that Medved, when he was sent to a concentration camp, apparently seeking to relieve his conscience, had begun speaking about his past with other Communists in the camp. With Stalin still in the interrogation room, Nikolaev had supposedly pointed at Medved and the other intelligence officers present, exclaiming, "Comrade Stalin, they forced me to murder Kirov, they hounded me with it for four months, those scoundrels, they broke my will, so then I did it, and they placed the weapon in my hand." The Chekists had then reportedly struck Nikolaev on the head with their revolvers and dragged him out of the room. How did Shatunovskaya know this? According to her, she had heard it from a doctor in Kolyma who had been in the camp at the same time as Medved. Although there is reason to believe that Stalin was involved, there is no evidence that Nikolaev was acting on the dictator's orders. Stalin simply had no reason to distrust Kirov, who had in fact been one of his most trusted followers, a ruthless violent perpetrator, and an unscrupulous Stalinist. He had never once opposed Stalin and had enjoyed the leader's near total trust. And indeed, Kirov's closeness to Stalin made it all the easier for him to present the party boss's death as an attack against him, Stalin—and use it for his personal gain.[39]

The return of the terror came as a surprise. After everything that had happened since the end of collectivization, it seemed impossible that violence of such magnitude could be repeated. Just a short time before, in May 1933, Stalin had ordered an end to the deportations of peasants from the villages. Even the barbaric Law for the Protection of Socialist Property from August 1932 was seldom applied anymore. In August 1935 the regime announced amnesty for all kolkhoz farmers who had been sentenced to fewer than five years in camp detention, and in some areas peasants who had been unjustly convicted were even rehabilitated. Between 1933 and 1934 there had been attempts to curtail the punitive authority of the GPU and commit the judiciary to standards based on laws and regular procedures. Andrei Vyshinsky used his power as state prosecutor of the Soviet Union to restructure the judicial apparatus and expand the influence of professionally trained jurists, state attorneys, and judges to matters of jurisprudence and criminal prosecution. This was of particular concern to the state officials themselves, who were particularly interested in establishing a degree of legal certainty and order. And finally, in 1935, debates over the Stalin Constitution began, which was understood by many as an attempt at returning some degree of predictability to life and leaving chaos and violence in the past.[40]

Those within the party were also given a sense that the time of great reconciliation had arrived. At the Seventeenth Party Congress in January 1934—the "Congress of Victors"—the leadership took stock of past experiences. Bukharin, whom Stalin had removed from political leadership in 1929, was given an opportunity to speak, and even Zinoviev and Kamenev, the disgraced former members of the "Left Opposition," were allowed to address the delegates and declare their devotion. Pyatakov, once a close associate of Trotsky's, was readmitted into the Central Committee and allowed to become Ordzhonikidze's deputy in the People's Commissariat of Heavy Industry. Stalin, however, could not tolerate the peace. According to his logic, the traitors who were now groveling at his feet were merely waiting for an opportunity to overthrow him and take revenge for the humiliation they had suffered. Of this Stalin was sure. He simply could not imagine that those who had been humbled were not contemplating vengeance and retribution, as he himself would have done. The timing of Kirov's death was thus ideal for him, as it gave him the opportunity to reverse every step toward peace and reconciliation that had been made and return the country to a state of war.

The secret police regained the powers of which they had previously been deprived, and it was Vyshinsky who acted on Stalin's behalf to invalidate the very rules he himself had fought for. Within Stalin's inner circle Vyshinsky was very much the odd man out. He was articulate, intelligent, and educated—in contrast to the rest of the dull and primitive Politburo members. He and Stalin had shared a prison cell in Baku in 1903, and although Vyshinsky had sided with the Mensheviks during the revolution, Stalin trusted him and had him promoted. Vyshinsky's status as an "intellectual" and former Menshevik made him an outsider in the Bolshevik Party, but with Stalin's help he was able to become state prosecutor. He expressed his gratitude with doglike devotion and unconditional loyalty and demonstrated that he was prepared to do anything necessary to please his master.[41]

On 1 December 1934, Stalin issued a directive that permitted the NKVD to execute or deport people without trial. Anyone who came under suspicion could be detained in a camp for up to five years. Stalin himself penned a directive prohibiting legal counsel and appeals in criminal proceedings with a "terroristic" background. Proceedings before the military tribunal of the Supreme Court were to be concluded on the day of arraignment, and death sentences were to be carried out immediately. Soon thereafter, in April 1935, the death penalty was extended to apply to minors. From now on, anyone who had reached the age of twelve could be shot.[42]

On December 16, immediately after Kirov's murder, Stalin's former adversaries Zinoviev and Kamenev were arrested. After a secret trial in January 1935 they were each sentenced to ten years of detention. Before being sent to prison, however, Kamenev was forced to accept "moral" responsibility for Kirov's murder and deliver the talking points for Stalin's great reckoning. On December 24, one week after his arrest, he wrote a letter to Agranov, deputy leader of the NKVD, to "sincerely" confess and explain what had motivated him and Zinoviev to conspire against the party and its leader. As Kamenev explained it, their expulsion from the party leadership had led them to surrender, as they saw that the power struggle had been lost. Despite this, he had hoped that through submission he would one day be given the opportunity to influence Politburo policies again. Zinoviev and Pyatakov had similar opinions on the matter, and Kamenev went on to report that he and Zinoviev had met with the Trotskyites Yevdokimov, Bakaev, Pyatakov, and others in Kaluga, their initial place of exile, to discuss the reasons for their defeat. After Bukharin's falling-out with Stalin in 1928 he had hoped to return to power, and he had also met with Bukharin and Rykov to find out how the "rightists" judged Stalin. "This is all the work of Stalin," Bukharin had allegedly said when asked about collectivization. "We would not have allowed it." By winter 1928–29, Rykov reportedly considered himself to be nothing more than a head of government on call. "What kind of a chairman of the Council of People's Commissars am I even? I am kept in office for as long as they need me, and soon I'll be thrown out entirely." The "decisive moment" for him, Kamenev, and Zinoviev was when it became clear to them that Stalin would not allow them back into the inner circle of power. This had led him, Kamenev, to surrender in earnest at the Seventeenth Party Congress, while prompting the aggrieved Zinoviev to contact his former companions in Leningrad. Kamenev left unanswered the question of what this all meant, but he tried to shift all blame onto Zinoviev. In his eyes, he was the victim of a tragic friendship. "I did not terminate my personal relationship to him. This was my fatal mistake, my weakness, for which I must now pay dearly."

Unlike Bukharin, Kamenev sensed that his fate was sealed, for he knew Stalin, together with whom he had been in exile, better than any other Bolshevik. "Now that everything has already been decided and nothing can be changed," he said, his only wish was for the record to show that he knew nothing of a counterrevolutionary organization based in Leningrad. These justifications, however, meant nothing to Stalin. He knew that the conspiracies were all invented. He had commissioned Yezhov to stage them. But Kamenev had said what Stalin wanted to hear—that Stalin's former adversaries were upset, that they could not get over their loss of power, and that they were thus plotting an alliance with Stalin's enemies. And this was all that mattered.[43]

Stalin's orchestrations followed a logic that even his closest friends could not escape. Zinoviev had submitted to the point of self-humiliation. He had been aggrieved and defrauded of all his posts. Why wouldn't he seek retribution for this disgrace? What began with a suspicion grew into a monstrous conspiracy. Party organizations in Leningrad and other major cities were scrutinized for possible Zinoviev and Kamenev supporters. Rallying cries went up to unmask all Trotskyites and former deviationists, to expel them from the party, and to have them arrested. But Yezhov, the secretary of the Central Committee, was already one step ahead and was busy supplying the despot with exactly what he desired: new information about enemies and spies who had infiltrated the inner circle of power. Like tiles in a mosaic, Stalin pieced together all the details of a treacherous conspiracy. Trotsky's son Sedov was said to have met with former members of the "Left Opposition" abroad. Army leaders had been spying for foreign intelligence, and the Trotskyites were in collusion with the Gestapo.[44] Amid this atmosphere of suspicion and paranoia, everyone mistrusted everyone else, and soon Stalin's followers were concerned with nothing more than their own survival. Day after day, week after week, Stalin presented them with new evidence and confessions. Whether they were plausible or not, they had to be taken at face value. There was simply no other choice.

The paranoia quickly penetrated into the inner circle of power. In January and February 1935, 112 Kremlin administrative employees were arrested. It was not just guards and secretaries who fell victim to the paranoia, but cleaning staff and librarians too. According to the secret police they too had been plotting to trap and kill Stalin and the members of the Politburo. Fantastical as the story was, the only way for it to become plausible was for the culprits to confess to everything the secret police had invented for them. At a line-up in the NKVD headquarters, the arrested cleaning ladies accused each other of having made "counterrevolutionary" speeches. The leadership "drinks and eats well," one person had allegedly said. Stalin is "not a Russian," came from someone else. Another person had made the accusation that Stalin had "shot" his second wife. Others confessed to spying in Stalin's quarters after the death of his second wife, when he had moved into Bukharin's apartment. And after Kirov's death, when security measures in the Kremlin had been tightened, there had been talk of how much better it had been under the old order when "it had been easier to kill Comrade Stalin." On February 10, a librarian established the desired links, claiming that she had been hired by the commandant of the building, Piotr Oserov, without an initial hearing and without being asked to provide references. This had opened the doors for the prerevolutionary aristocracy to infiltrate the Kremlin library as employees under false names. The librarians Rayevskaya and Rosenfeld were in actual fact the daughters of Counts Urusov and Bebutov. To make matters worse they reportedly regretted Zinoviev's and Kamenev's exclusion from power. Additionally, Rosenfeld had worked for Czechoslovakian intelligence in the past.

And who was responsible for all these misdeeds? The librarian Sinelobova's answer left no room for ambiguity. Rayevskaya and Rosenfeld were friends with the Kremlin's head administrator, Avel Enukidze, and had also been to his dacha. Furthermore, Rosenfeld was married to Kamenev's brother, who blamed Stalin for Kirov's murder. Additional confessions, extracted under torture, followed in March 1935. They were all intended to prove that Lev Kamenev had incited the accused to kill Stalin. The deed was to be carried out by the mother, who worked in the Kremlin as a librarian: "Nina Alexandrovna Rosenfeld had been working in the Kremlin until recently, she had many acquaintances there, she had free access to the personal libraries of Politburo members (Molotov's library). I know that she tried to get appointed to Stalin's library. Under such circumstances she would have had the opportunity to directly carry out a terrorist attack." Soon thereafter,

Kamenev too was made to confess his involvement in this undertaking. "Counterrevolutionary conversations" had taken place between him and Zinoviev. They had also slandered Stalin, and it was quite possible that his brother had been prepared to act on his "terroristic intentions." And if Kamenev's sister-in-law worked in Molotov's library, what was to stop her from killing Stalin? With so much evidence it was impossible to claim that this whole complex chain of circumstances had simply been fabricated by the secret police. Stalin had many reasons to be mistrustful of his surroundings, but it remains a mystery whether he became a victim of his own paranoia or whether he was merely playing a cynical game with the lives of others. In any case, the interrogation protocols seemed to amuse him. In one of the protocols, where it was noted that the accused had initially been a cleaning lady before becoming a librarian, Stalin underlined the sentence and added the comment, "Ha ha, charwoman-librarian?"[45]

Yagoda apparently sensed that he might fall out of favor if he failed to widen the circle of conspirators. He thus began issuing orders to search for Trotskyites and supporters of Zinoviev and Kamenev in the provinces and to track down and arrest all "former people," nobility, and officials of the old regime. In summer 1935 Stalin determined the sentences for the arrested Kremlin employees. Nine were shot, including the deputy commandant of the Kremlin guard, and the remainder were sentenced to long terms in concentration camps.[46]

Then, Avel Enukidze, Stalin's friend and follower from Georgia and also director of the Kremlin administration, fell from grace. In March 1935 he was relieved of his post as secretary of the Central Executive Committee, and on June 6, 1935, he was called before the Central Committee plenum. Stalin entrusted Yezhov with the task of accusing his former friend and exposing him as a traitor. Yezhov obediently carried out Stalin's orders, accusing Enukidze of lacking vigilance, ignoring signals from the Kremlin commandant, and leaving the gates to the centers of power wide open for the enemy. For this he would need to be punished. Enukidze attempted to defend himself, but Stalin and the Politburo were not interested and insisted on Enukidze's submission. Some, who were unaware of Stalin's true intentions, recommended expelling Enukidze from the Central Committee. Others, Yagoda and Kaganovich in particular, called for his arrest. As always, however, Stalin remained silent until the end. When he finally did speak he proposed a mild punishment, as it was evidently difficult for him to abandon the friend with whom he had spent so many holidays. Enukidze would have to be expelled from the Central Committee and the party, but he would not be handed over to the NKVD. Although he had been duped by the "class enemy," he had not been part of an assassination plot.[47]

As a compatriot and a friend, Enukidze was one of Stalin's closest confidants. He lived next door to the dictator, and they spent their holidays together. He was part of his private life and therefore intimately acquainted with all his foul deeds and crimes. Stalin shared things with Enukidze that he told no one else. "I spent ten days in Tskaltubo. I took twenty baths. The water is marvelous." Soon thereafter, he extended an invitation to him. "Come to Sochi, take a couple of saltwater baths and rest your heart. Tell Kalinin I said he is committing a crime if he does not let you take at least a few weeks' vacation. You can come live at my dacha, where I have been sitting alone like an owl ever since Svetlana went back to Moscow."[48] At some point, however, Stalin realized that Enukidze, who had a tendency to talk too much and to confide in strangers, had become a liability. Enukidze had to vacate his Kremlin apartment and leave Moscow. He was appointed plenipotentiary of the Central Committee in Kislovodsk in the Caucasus, where he was put in charge of the state sanitarium. But here too he surrounded himself with friends and confidants from the Caucasus who were meant to help him regain his influence. "Enukidze is a stranger to us. It is peculiar that Sergo [Ordzhonikidze] and Orakhelashvili continue to maintain friendly relations with him," wrote Stalin in a letter to Kaganovich. He soon had Enukidze transferred to Kharkov, where he led a state-run shipping company, before deciding in February 1937 to have him arrested. Enukidze was shot before the year's end. The despot's message was unmistakable: if even his closest friends could be tossed into the bottomless pit, then no one was safe now.[49]

The atmosphere of suspicion and mistrust weighed like lead on the Stalinist entourage and its branches in the provinces. In summer and autumn 1935 Yagoda and Yezhov, who were vying with each other for the dictator's favor, began spreading new rumors and conspiracy theories. They sent Stalin anonymous letters from denouncers and exposed "counterrevolutionaries." In July of that year Chekists arrested a leading employee of the American Press Association, who confessed to leaking military secrets to the United States, along with "counterrevolutionary materials about Comrade Stalin." On November 1 Yagoda informed Stalin that the NKVD had foiled an assassination plot against him and the members of the Politburo, and that two laboratory assistants from the Institute of Electrical Technology had been arrested. They had reportedly confessed to having manufactured bombs in their apartments and had planned to go to Red Square on the anniversary of the revolution to throw grenades onto the podium and kill the leaders. In January 1936 Vyshinsky made a point of demonstrating that he too was capable of uncovering conspiracies. In a letter to Stalin, he claimed to have unearthed a counterrevolutionary terrorist group that intended to kill him (Vyshinsky), Stalin, and the Leningrad party leader, Andrei Zhdanov. By the next day Vyshinsky was reporting the arrest of several persons who had been expelled from the party in 1933 as Trotskyites. Interrogations had revealed that they had been planning to shoot Stalin on the 1935 anniversary of the revolution. In both cases, Vyshinsky recommended that the accused be brought before a military tribunal and shot. Stalin read these reports with great interest and left comments in the margins, suggesting that this kind of stories pleased him greatly.[50] Under different circumstances the stories invented by Stalin's followers would have been considered absurd. But the atmosphere of extreme paranoia, which penetrated everywhere and everything, made them possible and ultimately allowed Stalin to give his lust for murder free reign.

In August 1936, in Moscow, the first of three show trials of prominent members of the Communist Party began. Zinoviev, Kamenev, Ivan Smirnov, Grigory Yevdokimov, and other former oppositionists were among the main defendants. The accusation: they had been plotting an overthrow of the political leaders of the Soviet Union on behalf of Trotsky and the Gestapo. Moreover, they were expected to accept responsibility for Kirov's murder. Six months later, in February 1937, the Old Bolsheviks Georgy Pyatakov, Karl Radek, and Grigory Sokolnikov were put on trial, along with several leading economic experts. Here, the accusation was that they were saboteurs and spies, which allowed Stalin to shift the blame for his failed economic policies onto them. A year passed before Bukharin, Rykov, and the Uzbek national communists Faizulla Khodjaev and Akmal Ikramov, also came before the tribunal. The trial of Bukharin and Rykov, which began in March 1938, was undoubtedly the climax to a series of proceedings that presented the party, to the general public and to the outside world, as a hotbed of conspirators and traitors. Prior to being arrested in March 1937, the accused had all belonged to the Central Committee and had at one time been part of the dictator's inner circle of friends and accomplices.

The charges leveled against the accused could hardly have been more absurd. They were accused of wanting to kill Stalin and the members of the Politburo on behalf of Trotsky, the Gestapo, and Polish and British intelligence. Beyond having systematically sabotaged industrial production, the defendants were also said to have organized accidents and attacks on building sites, factories, and railroads. Moreover, they had been plotting on behalf of foreign intelligence to systematically break up the Soviet Union by "selling" the national republics at the empire's periphery to foreign powers.[51] Under these circumstances it was clear that there could be no mercy for the accused. Vyshinsky, who led the prosecution in these trials, demonstrated that he was indeed Stalin's docile pupil. In the Bukharin trial he demanded that the defendants receive the maximum penalty and also that the "damned otter-brood" be "trampled to death" and that the defendants be "shot like mad dogs." Under the leadership of "our beloved leader and teacher, the great Stalin," he said, the world would be cleansed of the "last remaining dirt and refuse of the past."[52]

Directly after the verdict was announced the accused were shot and their wives and children were declared outcasts, deported, or killed. A small number, including Radek, Sokolnikov, and Rakovsky, were initially kept alive, but this was also part of Stalin's calculations. They were reserved for a second show trial, as Stalin wanted to trick Bukharin and Rykov into believing that they might come out alive if they condemned each other in court. In the end, though, they were all sent to their deaths. Radek was killed in a concentration camp, and neither Rakovsky nor Sokolnikov lived to see the end of 1941 either.

What did Stalin and his followers hope to achieve with these crude theatrical productions? What was the point of portraying so many prominent Bolsheviks and former allies of Lenin as spies for foreign intelligence and contract killers hired by Trotsky? Why were the accused forced to humiliate themselves in public and confess to crimes they had never committed? What did Stalin hope to gain from so many confessions and admissions of guilt—from people he could simply have shot? The answer is clear. The show trials were Stalin's method of disciplining the party elite. They served to show potential rivals what could happen to those who even considered opposing him. Everyone in the Central Committee knew that the accused had never committed the crimes they confessed to. They knew that the confessions had only been extracted under torture, presided over by Yezhov. But no one doubted that Stalin was the director of this nightmare or that he alone decided over life and death. Moreover, they knew that all who hoped to avoid the same fate as the accused were well advised, in Stalin's presence, to unwaveringly affirm the plausibility of even the most absurd of conspiracies. That is why those within the inner circle of leadership chose to hurl abuse at the accused. It was how they proved their loyalty and trustworthiness and hoped to protect themselves from the same fate. The disciplining of the leader's closest followers through the creation of fear and dread was the prerequisite for the murder of millions and the establishment of a tyranny of blood.

Every theatrical production that the dictator presided over had to be presented as reality. His views had to become everyone else's views, as this was the only way of preventing the monolithic façade of unity from collapsing in on itself. What mattered was not what one believed but what one said. The rhetoric of vigilance and the raw attacks on the system's outcasts were the representational modes of Stalinist rule. Even beyond the center of power, however, Stalin's orchestrations of dread were supposed to be accepted as undeniable realities. The song of hate was sung everywhere—at party gatherings and at staff meetings, in schools and in universities. Everywhere, people lived in fear and called for traitors and spies to be shot without remorse. Writers too signed petitions, demanding that the accused be mercilessly exterminated. Even the loudspeakers that had been set up in the main streets of major cities resonated with the sounds of hate.[53] If even the Central Committee and the People's Commissariats were no longer safe from the enemy's mischief, then how could anyone still doubt his existence? The enemy could be anywhere, and that was why the Soviet and foreign public needed to know just what kind of threats the dictator was faced with on a daily basis.

Only with this in mind does it become possible to comprehend the zeal with which Stalin and his henchmen prepared their show trials. Stalin personally oversaw the preparations. He gave instructions on how the detainees were to be treated and how the hearings were to be held.

He rewrote the dramas' scripts several times and summoned those who had been tortured to his Kremlin office, where he confronted them with "witnesses" and their forcibly extracted confessions. Although Stalin was on vacation on the Abkhazian Black Sea coast in August 1936, when the first Moscow show trial took place, he was still in charge of the proceedings. Kaganovich, who chaired the Politburo sessions in Stalin's absence, informed his master that the defendants had accused Pyatakov of heading a "Ukrainian terrorist center." He also reported that "the role of the Gestapo" had been "uncovered in its entirety" and that there were ties to Rykov and Bukharin. Foreign ambassadors and correspondents had reportedly been shocked by the testimonies and confessions of the accused. "Should you wish to give directions in these points, we kindly ask you to notify us of them."[54]

Stalin had already issued all directives prior to his departure, but on August 19 he wrote to Kaganovich, informing him of a letter he had received from Karl Radek. The defendants in the case had sought to incriminate Radek, but Radek insisted that he was innocent. "Although the letter is not very convincing, I nevertheless propose postponing the question of Radek's arrest and giving him the opportunity of publishing an article against Trotsky in *Izvestia* with his signature." The article would of course need to be reviewed by him, Stalin, personally, prior to its publication. Three days later, the Politburo sent Stalin the verdict that was to be handed down against Zinoviev, Kamenev, and the remaining defendants. It was requested that Stalin provide further "directions." The verdict, replied Stalin, was "essentially correct" but needed to be reworked "stylistically." Trotsky and his son Sedov would need to be mentioned in both the verdict and the indictment, he said. Otherwise, the public might get the impression that the state prosecutor and the judges were not of one mind. Moreover, the clause that ruled out the possibility of an appeal would need to be removed. "These words are superfluous and give a bad impression. An appeal will of course be denied, but it is unwise to mention this in the verdict." Stalin was pleased with the denunciation articles penned by Radek and Pyatakov and wrote to Kaganovich the same day that he believed they had "turned out well." We must imagine Stalin as a happy person, someone who took pleasure in the anguish of his victims. According to Anna Larina, the wife of Bukharin, "Stalin combined relaxation with energetic efforts to escalate his tyranny. Or more precisely, he rested twice over, for tyranny is gratification for a sadist."[55]

The Moscow show trials were performed like a series of dialogues with preassigned roles. To some foreign observers, it seemed as though accusers and accused were engaged in a civilized conversation. The German writer Lion Feuchtwanger, who witnessed the dreadful spectacle, saw no reason, even in hindsight, to doubt the sincerity of the accusations. "It was more a discussion than an excruciatingly embarrassing trial." Feuchtwanger should have known better, but he lied because the dictator's praise was worth more to him than any love of the truth. "If it was a lie or prearranged," he wrote in his travel log, "then I do not know what truth is." In December 1936, however, when he visited the head of the Comintern, Georgi Dimitrov, at home, he was still curious as to why all of the defendants confessed to "everything" and why confessions had been the only evidence.[56]

The bland military judge Vasily Ulrikh presided over the trials but assumed only a supporting role in this production. Vyshinsky was the director. Krestinsky, the former Central Committee secretary and Soviet ambassador in Berlin, retracted the testimony he had given in the preliminary investigations for the Bukharin trial. But he was the exception. Other than him no one deviated from the assigned script. Those who refused to confess were confronted with forcibly obtained testimony from friends and work colleagues, or they were tortured by the Chekists until they gave the desired testimony themselves. This is what happened to Krestinsky, who was abused with particular cruelty. "Krestinsky was brought to our hospital station in an unconscious state," a hospital employee recalled. "He had been dreadfully beaten. His entire back was one big wound. He spent three days at the station in a very bad condition." Stalin himself had given the order to beat anyone who did not confess. "You are performing poorly, Genrikh Grigorievich," Stalin had threatened Yagoda, when he had failed to extract full confessions from Kamenev and Zinoviev in the preliminary investigations. "One must torture them so that they finally tell the truth and reveal all their ties." The Chekists threatened the detainees with beatings, sleep deprivation, and other forms of torture, but in addition to that they took the victims' relatives hostage and threatened to kill their wives and children too. The daughter of Ivan Smirnov was brought before him and then abused and raped before his eyes, before he finally broke down and gave the confession demanded of him.[57]

The accused had learned and practiced the rituals of submission during Central Committee plenary sessions throughout the 1930s. Now they carried them into the courtroom. After having devoted the better part of their lives to Stalin and the party, they were all prepared to render the despot some final services in the hopes that he would then spare their lives. Even before he was arrested and accused, Karl Radek had begun writing hysterical letters to the great leader. He was ready and willing to denounce Bukharin, Rykov, and all the leading generals of the Soviet Army as spies and terrorists. Pyatakov, before he was arrested, had offered Stalin his services as an executioner. He would personally shoot the condemned of the first Moscow show trial. He would even be willing to shoot his own wife to prove his loyalty. Bukharin too, the theoretician and "darling" of the party, lost his composure when he saw the end approaching. He knew he was under "investigation," and in his state of constant fear of being arrested he began writing letters to the despot. In one letter from September 24, 1936, he claimed that he was "mentally ill" and that it was impossible for him to "go on living." "Under these circumstances," he wrote, "life has become without perspective and meaningless." The psychological stress was becoming too much for him to bear. "This is surely a paradox: the more I devote myself to serving the party with all my heart, the worse my unfortunate predicament becomes, and now I no longer have the strength to fight against the attacks anymore." Despite everything, he still believed that he could change the dictator's mind: "I urgently beg of you to allow me to come and see you. . . . Only you can cure me (*vylechit'*). If my fate is of any concern to you . . . then meet with me"[58]

Although Stalin did not respond he did keep him alive. Bukharin was allowed to remain editor in chief of *Izvestia* and keep his Kremlin apartment. Although he had been linked to spies and Trotskyites in the press, the dictator even invited him to join him on the Lenin mausoleum on the occasion of the 1936 anniversary of the revolution. "By the end of November," however, remembered Bukharin's wife Anna Larina, "the nervous strain was so severe that he could not work at all. Confining himself to our apartment, he lurched back and forth like a caged beast. Every day he looked into *Izvestia* to see whether the paper listed another editor." Bukharin had no other choice but to engage in Stalin's cruel game. By late 1936 he had become a mere object in the hands of absolute power. He himself was powerless and at the mercy of the dictator's whim. Speaking at the Central Committee plenum in early December 1936, Bukharin denied all allegations of having conspired with Zinoviev, Pyatakov, or any other leading Bolsheviks to carry out terrorist attacks against the party leadership. He assured the Central Committee that he had not engaged with the "saboteurs" or "scum" at any point in time. But simply in protesting against his alleged role in these conspiracies Bukharin inadvertently acknowledged that these conspiracies did exist.[59]

Stalin delayed Bukharin's demise a bit longer, but only in order to demonstrate the supremacy of his own power. Then, in January 1937, he decided that the time had come to show what could happen if he decided to have a leading Bolshevik put to death. He summoned Bukharin before the Politburo, along with Karl Radek and Grigori Pyatakov, who had formerly been attached to Trotsky and had carried out important functions in the Soviet state apparatus. Until recently, Pyatakov had been serving as deputy to Sergo Ordzhonikidze, people's commissar of heavy industry. Stalin had them brought to his offices from prison to repeat the confessions they had made under torture. Radek did as he was told and denounced Bukharin as a terrorist and spy, saying that they had plotted together to kill Stalin. When forced to answer the dictator's questions, though, he trembled with fear. As Bukharin later told his wife, Anna Larina, Pyatakov had been reduced to a "skeleton with its teeth knocked out." Larina wrote that "great efforts must have been required to break Pyatakov. During his confrontation with Bukharin, Yezhov sat close by, a living reminder of what had been done to him."[60]

Bukharin sensed what was in store for him and pleaded for his life by appealing to the bond that he and Stalin had once shared. On February 20, 1937, immediately before the start of the infamous February–March plenum of the Central Committee, which was meant to decide his fate, Bukharin turned to Stalin once more. He emphatically declared that he had done a terrible wrong by opposing Stalin during the late 1920s. He had sinned against him because he had not "understood" the objective truth of the Stalinist standpoint. "However I am convinced that even then, if I had been in a place where you were in danger, I would have defended you with my entire body." He had atoned for his sins, and since then he had never again deviated from the party line. "Now I really love you dearly and with belated love (*Ia tebia seichas deistvitel'no goriacho liubliu zapozdaloi liubov'iu*)." Bukharin's self-degradation knew no limits. He now considered Stalin's mistrust to be a sign of "wisdom" and unmatched foresight. A new age would soon dawn, an even greater age, and Stalin was the embodiment of this new age. He himself was the very "world spirit" Hegel had once spoken of.[61]

Stalin could have ordered Yezhov to arrest and kill Bukharin, just as he had done with Zinoviev and many other Communists. In this particular case, however, the point was to break the will of the Central Committee, whose members were supposed to accept all the stories that no one else believed and confirm them as truth. The point was for Bukharin to sacrifice himself so that Stalin could demonstrate his omnipotence. When Bukharin and Rykov appeared at the Central Committee plenum in late February 1937 at which their case was to be discussed, no one apart from Uborevich and Akulov dared greet them. Everyone turned away from them, even Voroshilov and Kalinin, who had once entertained friendly relations with them. Bukharin, weakened and exhausted by a hunger strike, told his wife on the evening after the first session that he felt like an outcast and thus preferred to sit on the floor at the edge of the hall during the debates, rather than on the benches with the Central Committee. Even now, Stalin continued to lie. No one intended to expel him from the party, Stalin told Bukharin in confidence, but he would have to apologize to the plenum for the hunger strike, which was understood as an attempt to put him and the party under pressure. Bukharin, who by this time could barely stand up without help, did what Stalin demanded of him but continued to insist that he was neither a terrorist nor a traitor. He insisted that he had "really committed none of the crimes" that "false witnesses" had foisted on him. "I repeat, I have burdened myself with guilt, but with all the strength in my soul I protest against the accusations that I have committed treason against the homeland, engaged in wrecking activities, terror, and anything else, because any person endowed with such qualities would have become my mortal enemy. I am prepared to do anything, whatever you want, with such a person."

Stalin's henchmen Yezhov, Kaganovich, and Molotov drove the humiliated Bukharin into a corner and left him to be abused and mocked by those present. Bukharin collapsed. Only with great effort could he even respond anymore, and finally he abandoned all attempts at justifying himself. Meanwhile, a heckler exclaimed that it was "high time" for him to be "thrown into prison." Stalin had forced Kalinin to make an inflammatory speech, but as Anna Larina recalled, he was the only one who "arduously wrested every word from himself" and spoke with "inner pain." "The CC members were, according to N. I. [Bukharin], confused and troubled. M. I. Ulyanova [Lenin's sister], who had friendly ties to Bukharin, wiped her tears with a handkerchief."

Rykov, on the other hand, denied all allegations. "This gathering," he declared, "will be the last, the last party gathering in my life." This was "absolutely clear." Furthermore, he did not believe any of Stalin's assurances that his life would be spared if he confessed. Zinoviev, Pyatakov, and Radek, he said, had all confessed and incriminated him in the belief that it would ease their lot, and "in this they were mistaken." According to the stenographic protocol no one interrupted Rykov as he defied Stalin's stage directions, and the dictator himself was forced to intervene:

STALIN: There are people who make truthful statements, even though they are terrible statements, but they do it to completely cleanse themselves from the dirt that sticks to them. And there are people who don't make truthful statements, because they love the dirt that clings to them and don't want to part with it.

RYKOV: In such moments, under the circumstances in which I now find myself, you'll say whatever you need to get out of this dead end.

STALIN: Have you lost your mind? (*Vy golovu poteriali?*) What does one stand to gain from this?

RYKOV: What, what?

VOROSHILOV: What interest?

STALIN: What advantage does it bring us?

RYKOV: I'm saying that one can't simply automatically say something that isn't the case.

STALIN: Mrachkovsky, Shestov, Pyatakov—they wanted to free themselves at any cost from the dirt they had fallen into. People like that shouldn't be scolded like those who don't make truthful statements because they have gotten so used to the dirt that sticks to them.

RYKOV: That is true. It's completely clear to me now that they will treat me better if I confess, this is clear to me, and this whole series of torments will be ended, whatever the price, as long as it comes to an end.

Rykov refused to submit. He could not confess to what he "hadn't done." Although the temptation to lie in order to shorten the agony was great, in the end the outcome would be the same, whether he confessed or not. He was doomed to die, and these would be his final words. And for this very reason he failed to understand why it was necessary for the members of the Central Committee to mock him on his way to the gallows. "This is an odd thing (*dikaia veshch*)," he said.

Stalin left it to Yezhov to bring the members of the Central Committee into the right mood for the unavoidable. He himself remained silent as the reckoning with the deviationists began. Yezhov did as he had been instructed and held an insidious and malevolent speech in which he accused Bukharin and Rykov of having attempted to justify themselves and having refused to surrender. Furthermore, he said, they were guilty of having defended the "disgusting rabble of Trotskyite-Zinovievite scum" and of having attempted to raise doubts about the testimonies given during the show trials. "Bukharin built the whole thing on lies. He's lying, you see, at every turn, it is simply shameful to listen to." Nothing, however, was more reprehensible than his attempt at questioning the NKVD's "evidence" and the testimony of those who had been tortured. Never again should anyone dare cast doubt on the truths that had been proclaimed by Stalin and the organs. Surely, Yezhov said, no one would be so stupid as to declare during their interrogation, "I am a terrorist, a villain—all that is untrue, but shoot me for my pleasure."

In the end, Stalin could do with the culprits as he pleased. Rather than handing the decision on the fates of Bukharin and Rykov over to the Central Committee, he entrusted this matter to a special commission. This commission included all members of the Politburo, a number of prominent Central Committee members, including Nikolai Antipov, Iona Yakir, and Ian Gamarnik, and both the sister and the wife of Lenin—Mara Ulianova and Nadezhda Krupskaya. Stalin demanded that everyone suspected of sympathizing with the outcasts now submit to him. They were to stain themselves with blood and become accomplices. But not everyone who collaborated was kept alive. A short time later Yakir and Antipov were both arrested and shot, and Gamarnik committed suicide before Yezhov's henchmen could get to him.

Yezhov submitted a draft proposal to the commission. He recommended expelling Bukharin and Rykov from the party, trying them before a military tribunal, and having them shot. Stalin left it up to the members of the commission to decide the fate of the delinquents. Some supported Yezhov's recommendations, while others wanted to try them but spare their lives. Stalin recommended expelling Bukharin and Rykov from the party and handing them over to the NKVD. The following day, Stalin's proposition was the only one the Central Committee voted on. The dictator read out the proposal himself, and the members of the Central Committee had no other choice: Stalin's proposition, which at least held out the possibility that the accused might survive, was approved immediately. NKVD officers then arrived to remove Bukharin and Rykov. This marked the first time that the secret police had appeared at a Central Committee meeting to arrest expelled members.[62]

There was no escape from Stalin's orbit. The only option apart from becoming either a victim or a perpetrator was suicide. Mikhail Tomsky and Sergo Ordzhonikidze took their own lives prior to the February–March plenum, the former because he was unwilling to humiliate himself before the Central Committee and in court and the latter because he could not bear to accuse and betray friends. Besides, he feared that he would be killed anyway.

Anyone who raised doubts or expressed criticism was killed instantly. Stalin made sure of that, as that was his means of keeping the members of the Central Committee in a state of perpetual fear and dread. In June 1937 the prominent Old Bolshevik and Comintern functionary Iosip Piatnitsky held a courageous speech before the Central Committee plenum, calling the notion of Stalinist truth into question. He accused the NKVD of fabricating evidence and manipulating cases, and he demanded an inquiry. The session was interrupted, and Kaganovich, Molotov, and Voroshilov instructed Piatnitsky to retract his statements immediately. Otherwise, they warned, Stalin would have him killed— and what about his wife and children? Piatnitsky declined and declared that he was willing to give his own life for the sake of truth. When the Central Committee reconvened the next morning, Yezhov opened the session with a malevolent speech, in which he "unmasked" Piatnitsky as a spy who had been hired by foreign powers to infiltrate the Comintern. Like Bukharin, Piatnitsky also remained free for a number of weeks, but ultimately Stalin's henchmen arrested him in his apartment and brought him to the Lubyanka. For almost an entire year he remained in detention there, where he was tortured cruelly and then shot in July 1938. His name was on a list of 138 candidates for death, which Stalin had signed with the comment, "shoot all 138."[63] The Stalinist elite had learned its lesson. No one was allowed to contradict the dictator or call his truths into question.

Bukharin's agony lasted an entire year, before Stalin reached the decision in late 1937 to put him and Rykov on trial. As long as Bukharin and Rykov stayed alive the remaining members of the Central Committee and Politburo could expect Stalin to forgive them. But now the dictator could no longer afford such weakness. He assured Bukharin that he would be spared if he confessed to all the crimes he was accused of—just as he had promised Zinoviev and Kamenev, but in December 1937 the "darling of the party" sent the dictator a letter from prison in which he reiterated everything he had told the Central Committee plenum in February 1937. He denied all the allegations, but explained that he now understood that "great ideas" and "great interests" transcended individual needs. In light of the "universal-historical tasks" that rested on Stalin's shoulders he had to demand sacrifices. His own task would now be limited to representing the enemy who had tried in vain to resist the course of history. He, Bukharin, thus had no choice but to confess to the crimes of which he was being accused (whether they were true or not). Any other course of action, he wrote, would have created the impression that he was unwilling to surrender and bow to the will of the party.

But Bukharin had not yet given up hope that Stalin would spare him in the end. He suggested exile to the United States, under the supervision of a Chekist, where he could run a campaign for the popularization of the show trials and wage a war of annihilation against Trotsky. His wife could stay behind as a hostage in the Soviet Union for the time being. "But if there is the slightest doubt in your mind, then exile me to a camp in Pechora or Kolyma, even for 25 years. There I could set up the following: a university, a museum of local culture, technical stations, and so on, institutes, an art gallery, an ethnographic museum, a zoological and botanical museum, a camp newspaper and journal."[64] Galleries in the Gulag—this absurdity too belonged to a mentality that was no longer capable of distinguishing between reality and the regime's propaganda. In the end, Stalin's world had become the world of his victims, who rationalized what was inflicted upon them as a service to the party. Had they been forced to acknowledge that their impending death was due to nothing more than the dictator's whim or to simple coincidence they likely would have lost their minds.

Bukharin's end came in March 1938, after he and Rykov had been sentenced to death in the third Moscow show trial. As the condemned were being led into the cellar for their execution, the Chekists forced Bukharin to sit on a footstool and watch while his companions in suffering were shot. Then he was killed. While it remains unclear who devised this macabre incident, it is difficult to imagine that any Chekist would have dared stage such a drama had it not been ordered by Stalin himself. Forty years later, Molotov found only a laconic explanation for Bukharin's death: "Stalin too valued Bukharin highly. Yes he did! Bukharin was highly educated and cultivated. But what can you do?!"[65]

The atmosphere of suspicion spawned new conspiracy theories. They were engineered by zealous NKVD agents and denouncers in the knowledge that these new conspiracies would please the tyrant in the Kremlin. They too were working toward the leader. On August 23, 1936, the day that the verdict against Kamenev and Zinoviev was read out, Bukharin's first wife Nadezhda Lukina wrote a letter to Stalin. She claimed to have witnessed a conversation between Kamenev—the "vile monster"—and the Georgian Communist leader "Budu" Mdivani at Kirov's funeral in Red Square in December 1934. Kamenev had allegedly smiled at Mdivani with "blatant spitefulness," as though he wanted to express his joy over Kirov's death. As she could not see Mdivani's face, she was unable to say anything about his reaction. But why would Kamenev have smiled at Mdivani unless he saw him as an ally? She, Lukina, had witnessed this scene and could not bear to keep it a secret. "With one word: I simply couldn't keep myself from writing you."[66]

Stalin received thousands of letters, telegrams, and dossiers—all confirming the grand conspiracy that he himself was busy mapping out. Mdivani soon became a victim of this conspiracy too when Stalin ordered his arrest.[67] In the immediate aftermath of Kamenev's execution, Stalin wrote a letter to Kaganovich in which he described the physical annihilation of former oppositionists as a preventive measure. Kamenev was said to have contacted the French ambassador through his wife. "I believe that Kamenev also probed the English, German, and American ambassadors. This means that Kamenev was supposed to reveal the plans for the conspiracy and the murder of the leaders of the VKP [All-Union Communist Party] to these foreigners. This also means that Kamenev had already revealed these plans to them, for otherwise the foreigners would not have begun talking about the future Zinovievite-Trotskyite 'government' with him."[68]

Stalin's power is demonstrated by the fact that Kaganovich too found it necessary to advance this absurdity as truth. But even fifty years after these events, Kaganovich still saw no reason to disavow the conspiracy theories of the past. Stalin, he claimed, had been a "great strategist" who recognized the danger emanating from traitors within the party leadership and from "underground work and the conspiracies." "Perhaps they were not spies," Kaganovich conceded, "but they considered it possible to reach an agreement against the people."[69]

Whether or not Stalin believed the conspiracies that Yezhov and Vyshinsky staged for him remains a mystery. The evidence to suggest that he did so is scant. Speaking to the journalist Felix Chuev in 1973, Molotov at least conceded that the confessions elicited from Bukharin and others who had been tried were absurd. No one truly believed that they wanted to cede Ukraine and the Caucasus to foreign powers. The accused, he claimed, had devised such exaggerations to discredit Soviet power. "They confessed to certain things on purpose in order to show how preposterous the whole trial was."[70] Stalin frankly revealed on numerous occasions that he had had evidence fabricated and people framed for the sole purpose of getting rid of them. By 1937, however, he had already accumulated so much power that it was no longer necessary for him to justify his actions to his friends and followers. From this point on, the only person who could say anything different regarding the world of conspiracies was Stalin himself. He only heard what he wanted to hear, and, in a sense, the staged conspiracies became a reality from which he could no longer escape. But in any case, once the mass killings had begun, Stalin had reason to fear anyone and everyone in his vicinity as a potential assassin.

Whatever absurdities the dictator's cronies came up with, they knew that their own lives were on the line if they failed. After all, enemies needed to be countered with measures that matched the size of the supposed threat. Although Yagoda did his best to uncover new conspiracies and to supply Stalin with new information on enemies and traitors, he also made mistakes that aroused the dictator's suspicion.

In October 1935 he had ordered the arrest of Gai Dimitrievich Bshish-kian, a Red Army general and lecturer at the Air Force Academy. The accusation was that he had spoken ill of Stalin. But then something unheard-of had happened. En route to his place of detention the pris-oner had jumped out of the window of the railway car and vanished without a trace. Yagoda had been forced to notify Stalin of this failure but had assured him that he had taken all necessary measures. In addi-tion to instantly dispatching his deputy Frinovsky to the scene, he had mobilized all local Communists and kolkhoz farmers to recapture the escaped prisoner. The responsible guards had also been arrested.

But for Stalin, these were nothing but excuses, concealing the actual course of events. "The version of the escape through the window of the speeding train," he wrote to Yagoda, "is, in my opinion, improb-able. . . . It seems to me that Gai and his friends have their people in the Cheka. They organized his escape." Did that mean that even the NKVD could no longer be trusted? "One wonders what we need the Cheka for and for whom it even exists, when it is constantly forced to enlist the help of the Komsomol, the kolkhoz farmers, and the popula-tion at large for every inanity? . . . I think the secret police (*Chekistskaia chast'*) of the NKVD is suffering from a serious illness. We will soon concern ourselves with its cure."[71]

THE DESTRUCTION OF THE PARTY

Amid this atmosphere of violence, it did not take long until no one was able to protect themselves from persecution. The principle of gen-eral suspicion had become so deeply anchored in Stalinist despotism that it took a mere nod from the dictator to set the self-destruction of entire institutions in motion. But this atmosphere of paranoia had needed space to unfold. Little by little, step by step, Stalin had prepared his followers for the great reckoning. It began with the party purges of the early 1930s, which had initially served no other purpose than to rid the party of politically suspicious, passive, and inactive members. Such control procedures had been in place since 1921, but back then they had all been bloodless, resulting in expulsion from the party at worst. Back then, the thought of calling for the death of one of the expelled would have been inconceivable. It was only after Stalin and his accomplices had concluded that their vassals and intermediaries in the provinces had failed as instruments of central intervention that the purges became a lethal affair. But even then, Stalin and his cronies could still cite reasons that were considered plausible to the other Bolsheviks. According to the Stalinists, from the time of the first Five Year Plan onwards, the danger that enemies would take hold of the party had been increasing steadily. Between 1929 and 1933 more than 2 million people had joined the Communist Party, bringing it up to a membership of 3.5 million. The last vestiges of the professional revolutionaries, which still had existed in the early 1920s, were by this time long gone. By 1933, more than half of all factory party secretaries had joined the party after 1929.[72]

And how could all these young, inexperienced peasants, who had only just become party secretaries in the factories, be entrusted with overseeing crucial production processes? Who were these people anyway? And was being a worker enough to warrant the kind of trust that one was granted as a secretary? The purges of 1929 and 1933 were responses to this insecurity, intended to unmask and expel former oppositionists, unreliable peasants, and people who had concealed their social background from the party. These purges alerted the party leadership to the fact that their intermediaries had indeed been pursuing interests that only rarely matched the intentions of Stalin and his cronies. Beyond that, though, the purges provided them with a picture of the party's social and cultural profile and demonstrated that the possibilities of influencing and transforming it were limited.

The Stalinist revolution from above had a paradoxical consequence. It had aimed to erase Old Russia and create a society of New Men, but instead it had flushed more than a million uneducated workers and peasants into the party. Their presence not only gave the order of the chosen ones a proletarian image, but also altered its traditions and practices. Almost everything that these "new men" brought with them contradicted the programs of emancipation that the professional revolutionaries had once dreamed of. The party had become a place of political illiterates and ignoramuses, who were only interested in the party membership card and badge to protect them from prosecution, allow them to possess weapons, and provide them with privileges and access to scarce material resources. And since membership in the party was equivalent to a title of honor, it was also attractive to those who had been stigmatized. In the years of forced collectivization, tens of thousands of kulaks from the Caucasus, and also beys, clan leaders, and mullahs from central Asia had fled the villages and sought refuge in the larger cities or major construction sites. Some acquired forged papers, took on new identities, or sought refuge in the party. In the Caucasus and in central Asia the Bolshevik project was on shaky footing at best, making it highly dependent on the help of the traditional elites there. This meant that the party in these places had quickly been taken over by influential families, who got to decide who was allowed into the party and who was not. The actual purpose of the socialist program of enlightenment and mobilization eluded most party members, both in the Russian heartland and in the Asiatic periphery.

The purges revealed new truths. They confirmed the leadership's fear that the Communists in the provinces could not be trusted. By this time it had come to light that the local functionaries, fearing for their influence in the villages, had often condemned forced collectivization and sided with the peasantry. When the purge commission questioned a party member in the area of Smolensk about the intent and purpose of the collectivization campaigns, he said, "The kolkhozy are penal battalions where they stick people for self-criticism." Few Communists even realized that there was supposed to be a connection between membership in the party and allegiance to its goals. Party members in the factories protested against shock worker campaigns, workplace regulations, and strict workplace discipline. Many Communists participated in religious feasts, attended church sermons, had their children baptized, and drank alcohol—not just during the Easter holidays but on the anniversary of the October Revolution as well. According to the purge commission, up to 30 percent of the workforce in some Smolensk factories was "constantly drunk."[73]

Few Communists had a clear notion of what the party expected of its members. In Baku, the industrial center near the Caspian Sea, not even the agitators who were responsible for teaching party members the ABCs of Communism knew much of anything about Marxist ideology. One agitator was reported to have read out the textbook syllable by syllable, suggesting that he was both illiterate and only slightly more knowledgeable about the history of the party than the workers he was supposed to be lecturing. This was the impression of the indignant inspectors from the Central Committee, at least, who were forced to witness this spectacle. At times the responses that members of the Central

Control Commission received to their answers were of supreme hilarity. Communists from Baku were of the belief that the "rightist deviation" referred to a "great engineer." Elsewhere, party members told the purge commission that communism would be achieved in 1942, as this was the year in which party membership cards were due to expire.

Not surprisingly, the party leadership discovered that the secretaries and chairmen of the soviets and collective farms were not much better than the rank-and-file Communists. According to the verdict of the Central Control Commission, these "leaders" were uneducated, corrupt, and heavy-handed. In many regions the party was in the hands of influential families, groups of friends, or insiders' networks, whose members fought tooth and nail to keep outsiders out. Such Communists belonged to neither the "rightist" nor the "leftist" deviation. They were not even aware of the aims of their own party.[74] The party was not just filled with political illiterates—it was also being led by them.

More than 18 percent of all Communists lost their party membership in the purge of 1933. Others turned their backs on the party before they could be expelled. In some regions the purges extended into the year 1935, but rather than solving the myriad problems the purges merely made them visible. To the party leadership, it was quite clear that its most important instrument of intervention in the provinces was unreliable: it had been subverted by political ignoramuses, Trotskyites, former oppositionists, and kulaks. Furthermore, industrialization and collectivization truly had wrought such misery and chaos on the Soviet empire that it was not difficult for Stalin and his aides to make many of their conspiracy theories plausible. If even the party was not safe from the clutches of the enemy, then what place of safety still remained? The party leadership's answer could not have been clearer. The enemy was everywhere and needed to be removed from the party at any cost. And in this way, the purges, which had started as simple inquiries, soon became hysterical manhunts that knew neither limits nor reason.

In early 1935 Stalin ordered the local party committees to start inspecting all membership cards that had been issued since the purges. Stalin suspected the local party secretaries of attempting to deceive him, providing false information, and harboring enemies from persecution. Now, though, they could demonstrate their loyalty by finding the former oppositionists, saboteurs, and spies hiding in their districts and expelling them from the party. The campaign turned up a number of forged party cards, and the Politburo's suspicions were once again confirmed. Not only had party cards been forged, but they could also be purchased on the open market or borrowed for a fee. Some committees even had "dead souls" on file, and in Uzbekistan party memberships were being handed out as bonuses to female kolkhoz farmers.[75]

In late December 1935 Yezhov provided the Central Committee with a progress report, announcing that 33 percent of all Communists expelled from the party since July 1935 had been "spies," "White Guards," or "Trotskyites." That was more than forty-three thousand party members who had belonged to one of these categories. Yezhov knew what the dictator wanted to hear, which is why he made the purges political and exaggerated the dangers faced by the party. "Many, deeply malevolent enemies" had been exposed, he reported, in all organizations of the party. Lavrenty Beria, the first secretary of the Transcaucasian regional party committee, was also eager to inform Stalin that, in the Caucasus republics, more than a thousand "enemies" had been arrested by the NKVD.[76]

Stalin drew far-reaching conclusions from the purge commission reports he received. In 1936 he gave the order to confiscate all party membership cards and replace them with new ones—after thorough inspection of the applicants, of course. More importantly, though, everything that was being "discovered" in the provinces served to confirm Stalin's assumption that the provincial leaders were indeed sabotaging the directives from the center. After all, it did not escape him that local party secretaries were protecting their friends and clients from losing their privileges. Furthermore, they seemed to be going to great lengths to have friends who had been expelled from the party rehabilitated.[77]

The Stalinist system of rule was a personalized dictatorship. Local potentates and their patrons in the center were connected in a relationship of mutual dependence. Stalin needed his intermediaries in the provinces and would have been powerless without them. This mediation, however, came at a price, as these vassals, on whom Stalin so heavily depended, reserved the best positions in the party and state administration for their friends and clients. The Soviet provinces were small feudal empires ruled by the leaders' vassals and their clients. What this meant is that the political apparatus was being run by people whose loyalty was to the patrons they served, not to the laws and directives of the Soviet state. In one regard, this kind of system was actually commensurate with Stalin's style of rule, as he too reserved his trust for people who he knew personally and who had proven their unconditional loyalty to him. For those with ambitious aims, however, such patron-client forms of governance were far from ideal. Once the provincial vassals realized that they would be held accountable for blunders and failures in their districts, they simply restricted the flow of information to Moscow—they did not want to risk losing their own provincial power bases. Patrons and clients kept their mutual agreements under wraps and did their best to protect local functionaries and economic leaders from the punitive arm of the dictator.[78] In the end, increasing pressure from the center only resulted in greater deception and feigned loyalty.

In the official representation, the local party secretaries were Stalin's loyal servants. They stopped at nothing to fulfill the wishes of the Central Committee—and this without delay. Their language and rituals demonstrated that they understood what Stalin expected of them—that they hunt down and liquidate all enemies, even those who were their friends—but this façade merely served to conceal irreconcilable conflicts of interest. One side demanded grain deliveries and the fulfillment of production plans, while the other side did its best to subtly skirt these requirements. There was no nonviolent solution to this conflict. The provincial potentates understood that the dictator demanded violence and that they had no choice but to acquiesce. The best they could do was to try to direct it against rivals or people who did not belong to their own group.

Everywhere party secretaries and their clients were bound together in systems of mutual dependence and obligation. In Smolensk, the loyal group surrounding Ivan Rumiantsev, the party boss of the Western Region, was granted special privileges and invited to exuberant drinking bouts. At the end of June 1937, after Rumiantsev's arrest, the now deposed party boss was denounced by one of his own people. In a letter to Kaganovich, the denouncer repented his own "sins" against the party and divulged details of the pleasures Rumiantsev and his friends had indulged in. On weekends and during the numerous holidays, Rumiantsev used to gather his followers in a country retreat near Smolensk, where they were treated to "cognac, champagne, vodka, and the finest foods." Together with their wives and mistresses, comrades convened here to gamble and drink the night away. "The home of rest turned into a home of drunken orgies," the denouncer reported. Party secretaries and functionaries reportedly drank to Rumiantsev's health during these gatherings and praised him as their "leader." Moreover, Rumiantsev and his deputy, Akim Shilman, had shielded friends and relatives from repression. Rumiantsev's group had also exploited the party purges to wipe out their own adversaries. They had also helped their friends who had fallen out of favor by providing them with posts and official appointments in remote areas of the province.[79] "The exchange of the party documents," the denouncer wrote to Kaganovich, "was carried out in an even simpler manner, it became a banality. I remember how some kind of meeting between the secretaries of the Area Committees was convened. Shilman gave the order to issue party cards and memberships to all Area Committee secretaries. Within one week all documents had been filled out, and then they were delivered to the secretaries after the meeting."[80]

It was thus of crucial importance for the provincial party leaders that the agreements between patrons and clients for their mutual protection be adhered to. Stalin, meanwhile, needed informers and denouncers who would betray secrets, expose liars, and help override these mechanisms of self-protection. For this endeavor to succeed, Stalin needed to end his dependence on the monopoly of information held by local powers. Local leaders in the provinces saw this as an existential threat that needed to be resisted at all costs. When local functionaries began supplying the Politburo with news from the provinces in hopes of gaining esteem at the dictator's court, the local elites saw this as a clear violation of the internally established rules of the game and responded swiftly and violently. They had these informers relieved of their posts, exposed as enemies of the people, and arrested by the NKVD. In order to prevent the Politburo in Moscow from becoming suspicious, these dramas were passed off as part of the struggle against spies and saboteurs that Stalin and his cronies believed they were waging.

In July 1937 Stalin dispatched *Pravda* correspondents to the provinces to have them brief him on how the extermination of enemies was preceding. A journalist by the name of Kozlov, reporting from Ivanovo, claimed that while Nossov and other leading functionaries had exposed enemies, they were protecting their own people from persecution. "But if all the attention is concentrated on this alone," he wrote, "then they are only trying to divert the fire from someone else." Earlier that year, Solodovnikov, secretary of the regional party committee in Ivanovo, had allegedly committed suicide after his interrogation by the NKVD. "On the day of the suicide the deputy head of the NKVD, Kharakhonov, had a conversation with Comrade Nossov to the effect that Solodovnikov should be arrested. Nossov did not agree. And Solodovnikov shot himself that very same day." Who, other than Nossov, could have warned Solodovnikov? The betrayal was clear, and a betrayal of this kind was something Stalin could not forgive.[81]

The relentless hunt for spies and saboteurs that began in the second half of 1936 was only possible because of the predicament that local party secretaries found themselves in. If they wanted to avoid arousing suspicion they needed to participate in the systematic persecution of enemies. Specialists and economic experts everywhere were unmasked as enemies and handed over to the NKVD by local leaders, seeking to show Stalin that they possessed the necessary zeal. The party boss of Western Siberia, Robert Eikhe, even personally oversaw the arrest and execution of functionaries and state officials he deemed to be "wreckers." For the leadership in Moscow, however, such instances of unauthorized terror went too far.

At the end of 1936 the Central Committee declared it impermissible to arrest and condemn functionaries in show trials for petty offenses. It was the Sverdlovsk party committee that Stalin had in mind when making this decree. On February 13, 1937, moments before the opening of the Central Committee plenum, party secretaries in the republics and regions had received a telegram from the dictator, warning them against taking arbitrary action. He claimed to have discovered that party secretaries had "gladly" been giving the NKVD permission to arrest factory directors, engineers, and technicians in order to protect themselves from accusations. Such arbitrary action, however, was prohibited. "The CC reminds you that neither the Secretary of the Provincial Committee nor the Regional Committee, nor the Secretary of the CC, let alone other regional party or soviet leaders in the regions, have the right to give their approval for such arrests." Only the Central Committee—that is, Stalin himself—had the authority to approve such measures.[82]

The purges brought Stalin into a conflict of interests with his vassals in the provinces. The hunt for Trotskyites, spies, and saboteurs meant that his vassals in the provinces stood to lose the clients upon which their rule was based. In response, they did everything possible to prevent the destruction of their apparatuses. Since local NKVD leaders were also part of these local power relations, the Moscow leadership could no longer rely on them either. In the Ural region, the local party leadership and the NKVD had agreed to cooperate with each other. They withheld inconvenient truths from Moscow and remained silent about their failure to meet plan targets.[83] Gradually Stalin became aware of what was taking place. Although there was a terror at work in the provinces it was not in accord with the intentions of the center. Although it matched Stalin's own violent style, it did not match his interests.

The local potentates seemed to be fairly confident of their power, because as late as the mid-1930s they were still presenting themselves as almighty rulers of their provinces. They not only imitated Stalin's violent style of rule but also copied his cult of personality. Cities, factories, and collective farms bore their names. They had themselves immortalized in portraits and poems, and they surrounded themselves with servile sycophants who praised them in song. In the area of Smolensk, 134 collective farms were required to bear the name of the local party boss, Rumiantsev, who portrayed himself as the Stalin of the Western Region. He hosted "pompadour-salons," where he indulged in lavish feasts with his mistresses. The box in Smolensk's newly constructed theater was also connected to his office via an underground tunnel. Moderation, however, was evidently not one of his virtues. Week after week, he invited his friends and followers, women and mistresses to the retreat of the Municipal Party Committee. According to the testimony of one of his associates, his daughter shared "very salacious anecdotes" with the guests. In the early morning hours, the men would take the women to bed. Rumiantsev's journeys through the villages resembled processions, in which he drove along in an open car, surrounded by his followers, tossing kopek coins at famished peasants. On the occasion of his fiftieth birthday he was also not too modest to refrain from holding an obscenely expensive banquet. But beyond exhibiting the qualities of a megalomaniacal windbag, Rumiantsev also committed some errors that were truly unforgivable. In 1936, when speaking to the party organization about the new constitution, the attending Chekists were quick to note that Rumiantsev had only praised the constitution, not the "Stalinist constitution." On another occasion, Rumiantsev was accused of quoting from one of Stalin's speeches but without including the great leader's most important sentence—namely, that "the enemy's handwriting" could be seen in the provinces.[84]

Rumiantsev, however, was not the only one to strike Stalinist poses during these years. Lavrenty Beria, the first secretary of the Transcaucasian party organization, had himself celebrated as the father of Azerbaijan's crude oil industry. The party heads of the other Soviet republics, too, fostered personality cults that sometimes reached grotesque proportions. Levon Mirzoyan, the party boss of Kazakhstan and one of Stalin's closest confidants in the Caucasus, had the highest peak of the Pamir mountain range named after him. He surrounded himself with Armenian and Turkish Communists from his hometown of Baku, who praised their leader in song and fought successfully to defend the local power apparatus from central encroachment.[85]

In summary, Stalin had every reason to mistrust the vassals in the provinces. The Politburo considered opposition to central directives an act of both resistance and sabotage. Ultimately, though, Stalin had his way. From now on, any time that even the slightest suspicion was aroused, enemies would be hunted down and mercilessly eliminated. Stalin's vassals would now have to surrender their clients and friends to him, and they would not be allowed to show any mercy in executing his terror orders. Furthermore, they needed to prove that they were prepared to do so at any time. Terror was the Stalinist functionary's baptism by fire. To fail meant to lose the dictator's trust and ultimately one's own life.

The spy mania reached a first climax in summer 1936 during the show trial of Zinoviev and Kamenev. The provincial potentates could no longer withstand the pressure from the center. It began with the subjugation of the NKVD. In Stalin's mind the NKVD had failed in its task of uncovering "spies" and "saboteurs" in the provincial party and state organizations. The reason, it seemed, was that the bosses of the provincial NKVD branches were in bed with the local party leaders. The Chekists, too, seemed to be at the beck and call of the local leadership, which naturally put their loyalty in question. Kirov's murder and its aftermath had been a case in point. Although Stalin had demanded bloody retaliation within the party, the NKVD had hesitated to comply. When Yagoda, head of the NKVD, had voiced his reservations about the conspiracy scenarios being churned out by the Central Committee, Stalin's response had been, "Watch it, or we will punch you in the snout."[86] Yagoda's downfall had begun directly after the conclusion of the first Moscow show trial in August 1936. In September

Stalin sent the members of the Politburo a telegram from his holiday home in Sochi, demanding that Yagoda be dismissed for his failure to unmask the Trotskyite enemies who had supposedly infiltrated the party. Yagoda, he claimed, was out of his league and "four years behind schedule" in this matter. And incidentally, all "party workers and the majority of regional representatives of the NKVD" were of the same opinion.[87]

Nikolai Yezhov was appointed to succeed Yagoda as head of the NKVD. As director of the party purges and organizer of conspiracies and show trials, Yezhov had proven himself a loyal servant to the dictator. He was a brutal and unscrupulous criminal, whose violent energy and ambition were coupled with a slavish devotion to his lord and master. Nevertheless, within the state apparatus, his appointment was initially taken as a sign of détente. Although Stalin ordered him to "devote nine-tenths of his time to the NKVD," the new NKVD boss retained his position as secretary of the Central Committee. Accordingly, Yezhov's appointment was seen by many as an attempt to place the secret police under stricter control by subordinating it to the Central Committee. Even Bukharin considered the small-of-stature and inconspicuous functionary to be an "honest man devoted to the party," who would turn professional Chekists into loyal servants of the apparatus. In reality, however, Yezhov transformed the NKVD into an instrument of terror, used in the unceasing execution of Stalin's murderous plans. Immediately after his appointment, Yezhov restaffed the People's Commissariat and installed his people from the Central Committee apparatus in key positions. All of Yagoda's confidants were relieved of their posts and subsequently, in the early summer of 1937, arrested and shot. In the provinces too, Yezhov replaced Yagoda's people with his own associates. Yezhov's people would carry out the dictator's orders without opposition. Furthermore, they would not allow local party secretaries to determine who should be arrested and who should be spared.[88]

What Stalin desired, Yezhov could offer: conspiracy scenarios and reports detailing all the alleged spies and saboteurs who were subverting the party and state apparatus. As early as autumn 1936, a merciless manhunt for enemies and "wreckers" was underway in people's commissariats and enterprises throughout the Soviet Union. In February of the following year the Central Committee was summoned to Moscow for a plenary session to discuss the fates of Bukharin and Rykov, as well as the state of the party. By this time the foundations for the great orgy of violence to come had already been laid, and although the members of the Central Committee suspected nothing, Stalin had convened this meeting in order to prepare the party and its elite for self-destruction. In all probability, the clueless people's commissars, generals, and party secretaries from the provinces did not realize that they were walking into a trap from which there was no escape. The ramifications of the Stalinist choreography only became apparent on the second day of the plenum, when those present discovered that the arrest of Rykov and Bukharin did not mark the end of the violence and persecution but only the beginning. They too had all participated in the persecution of alleged enemies of the people in their provinces, and in doing so they had made themselves Stalin's accomplices. Moreover, by approving the arrests of Bukharin and Rykov, they had recognized the dictator's right to execute members of the Central Committee at will. Stalin now turned this weapon against them and ordered his people in the Politburo to begin leveling their accusations against the people's commissars and party secretaries, who were then forced to justify themselves.

Why did the Central Committee not put up a fight to avert its self-annihilation? The answer is simple: its members had no opportunity to agree upon a common strategy. Inside the party all communication was vertical. Although the party secretaries in the provinces and republics were connected to the dictator and his apparatus, they were unable to communicate with other party secretaries and discuss how to react to the center. Stalin, of course, exploited these circumstances to his own advantage.[89] The members of the Central Committee submitted to Stalin's choreography because obedience seemed to hold more promise than dissent and resistance. Disobedience is a luxury reserved for those who are not facing imprisonment or death upon defeat. The fate that befell Bukharin and Rykov had made this abundantly clear.

The production that Stalin had staged followed a model of escalation. Among the first to address the plenum was Andrei Zhdanov, who had not only succeeded Kirov as Leningrad party boss but had also taken his place in the Politburo. Zhdanov pointed to the potential dangers of the rights that the new Stalin Constitution extended to kulaks, clerics, and "former people." These class enemies, Zhdanov said, needed to be prevented from exploiting the upcoming Supreme Soviet elections as a chance to agitate against the socialist order. "It would be a big mistake to postpone the struggle against these remnants until the moment of the elections," he told the group. He also did not forget to add that the "organs of suppression" would be more necessary than ever to break enemy resistance. The capitalist powers that had encircled the Soviet Union, Zhdanov explained, were in a position to enlist the help of undiscovered enemies and destroy the socialist order—a fact that should never be lost sight of. Of course no one seriously believed that former oppositionists, priests, and kulaks were going to nominate candidates for the elections, let alone campaign for them. The party leadership never intended to hold free elections anyway, where opposition candidates would have been allowed to criticize the government.[90] And nobody, of course, truly believed that enemies of the Bolshevik order had disguised themselves as Communists to subvert state institutions either. But the members of the Central Committee affirmed all these fantastical notions as truth, and this was all that mattered.

The head of the Society of the Godless, Emelian Yaroslavsky, instantly drew the right conclusions from Zhdanov's remarks. "Don't forget," he told the listeners, "that the religious organizations throughout the country are presenting themselves as organizations for the preparation of anti-Soviet elections." The provincial party secretaries were quick to confirm that kulaks, popes, and mullahs were indeed agitating against Soviet power and invoking the constitution to justify their shameful acts. Levon Mirzoyan and Yakov Popok, the party bosses in Kazakhstan and Turkmenistan, claimed that the clergy there were organizing "crusades" and meeting in churches to discuss the significance of the new constitution.[91] But what had the party secretaries and people's commissars done about it? Next to nothing. Beyond that, they had failed to counter the enemy's attempts at subverting the party and sabotaging industrial production. "The party organizations do not know how to handle the sectarians," exclaimed Yefim Yevdokimov, who was both one of Stalin's most brutal Chekists and the Rostov party leader. "Not even the Chekists are monitoring them."[92]

What was to happen now? Sergo Ordzhonikidze, the people's commissar of heavy industry and a friend of Stalin's, was supposed to provide an answer. In January 1937, Stalin had ordered him to brief the Central Committee on the effects of "wrecking" in heavy industry and to discuss the failures of the party secretaries in the struggle against spies and saboteurs. But Ordzhonikidze refused. Although he was one of the despot's closest friends, he considered it nonsensical for him, as people's commissar of heavy industry, to participate in the self-destruction of the Soviet economy. Ordzhonikidze had remained silent while managers and factory directors were being arrested, but then his closest associates had begun to disappear. Then even his brother was arrested and killed, and finally Ordzhonikidze decided to speak up. Stalin responded to Ordzhonikidze's protests by pointing to the "confessions" of the accused, along with the "evidence" that Yezhov had supplied. "What close friends we once were," Ordzhonikidze reportedly lamented to Mikoyan. It was still inconceivable to him that his old companion Stalin really could have presided over the execution of his own brother. He could no longer stand by and watch his department self-destruct, and he told Stalin that he would no longer support him by handing over friends and clients. But Ordzhonikidze's attempts and protests were in vain. A heated argument in Stalin's office ensued, and Ordzhonikidze ended his own life that very same day.[93]

Stalin's loyal servants Molotov, Kaganovich, and Voroshilov, however, had no problem carrying out the orders that Ordzhonikidze had refused to execute. They spoke of "lessons" to be learned from the "wrecking activities" and from the "espionage of Japanese-German-Trotskyite agents," who had wormed their way into the railroad, the military, and the heavy industry of the Soviet Union. Agents disguised as Communists, they claimed, had carried out the attacks on behalf of Trotsky and the Gestapo, and Soviet industry and the Red Army had been taking heavy blows on a daily basis—it was years since there had been a day without attacks. "The distinguishing feature of the wrecking activities that have now been revealed," Molotov explained, "lay in the fact that the party organizations were exploited" and that "the party membership card was exploited to organize wrecking activities within our state apparatus, our industry. The distinguishing feature was that the bourgeois vermin, the bourgeois specialists, the former owners and the foreign agents, the agents of fascist espionage and foreign states, allied with the Trotskyites and other double-dealers that sit in our Party." Nowhere was it worse than in the armed forces, he claimed, because here the enemy had successfully enlisted high-ranking officers to his cause. According to Voroshilov, the saboteurs had "worked on Red Army soldiers and made enemies out of them." They had also destroyed airplanes and set fire to military air bases. Stalinist reality, as Voroshilov and Molotov painted it, existed in garish colors. "The bourgeoisie and our enemies are down to their last resort, they are gathering the last cadres that could help them." It was thus critical that everyone remain vigilant and make sure "not to forget" what they were "constantly being reminded of by Comrade Stalin."[94] And how was the enemy to be fended off? Kaganovich knew: "We must immediately remove all defects which allow the enemies to arm themselves in our midst, so that we can expose the enemy in time, since, as Comrade Stalin says, such cases can and will repeat themselves."[95] The message could not have been clearer. Had it not been for the weakness, indecision, and resistance of the party secretaries and People's Commissars, the enemies would never have been able to carry out their destructive work in the first place.

Beria and Bagirov, Stalin's men from the Caucasus, who were the party bosses in Georgia and Azerbaijan respectively, listened closely to the speeches of Molotov and Kaganovich and seemed to understand immediately what was expected of them. They reiterated the dictator's warnings multiple times and praised his foresight. Had it not been for Stalin's great foresight, they proclaimed, it would never have been possible to root out and reveal all those enemies who had been at work, trying to undermine the Soviet order in the Caucasus since the early 1930s.[96] All the other members of the Central Committee appeared to be in a state of shock, unsure of how to respond to the horrendous scenarios Stalin's people had just confronted them with. Those who were unwilling to join in and say something were in danger of arousing the suspicion that they too were enemies. And once one had become a suspect there was little hope of being able to defend oneself. Those who exposed potential traitors, on the other hand, proved their loyalty. Stalin's closest followers, it appears, had been given clear advance instructions on who would be placed under suspicion at this meeting and who was to be spared. "Allow me to move on to specifics." And with these words Yezhov unexpectedly descended upon the bewildered people's commissar of finance, Grigory Grinko. It was a well-known fact, Yezhov said, that both the State Bank and the Bank of Industry were being led by Trotskyite spies and saboteurs. And despite the wrecking activities that had been going on in his ministry Grinko had remained silent. Why? Apparently because he believed that "these matters were of no concern" to him. Grinko was evidently unprepared and could only blurt out the panicked words, "Who? Me?"

The circle of suspects also included Nikolai Pakhomov and Ivan Lyubimov, the people's commissars of water transport and light industry. Yezhov demanded that they speak, as their silence would betray them as friends of the enemy. "Lyubimov sits around here in silence," he exclaimed, although 141 of the "most active wreckers" in his ministry had already been arrested and most of them shot. Pakhomov conceded that he had committed errors, but now, after hearing Molotov and Kaganovich speak, he recognized that "after this plenum one will have to work in a new way." He also admitted that there had indeed been "spies, wreckers, and saboteurs" among his leading employees, who had, "as it turned out," enjoyed his "trust, even great trust." Molotov and Kaganovich went on to accuse Pakhomov of only screening his ministry for enemies after being prompted to do so. Employees who turned out to be spies, they said, had even been decorated with medals. "There have been many incidents and accidents on your watch," Kaganovich told the unfortunate Pakhomov. "Tell the plenum why these incidents and accidents keep happening and how you imagine you will combat them, how you imagine going about putting an end to the wrecking activities and work accidents." Pakhomov replied that he had overseen the arrest of several enemies and could even disclose their names: "I will not begin wasting your time by reading the whole long list, but I have here a list with the names of seventy-seven people (laughter), two-thirds of whom have been arrested." Stalin: "Precious few in my view." Pakhomov: "Comrade Stalin, I have told you that this is just the beginning (laughter throughout the room)."[97]

At the end of the plenum Stalin finally stepped in to offer up the lesson that the day's events were supposed to teach everyone. Neither the people's commissars nor the provincial party leaders, however, appeared to have understood what was at stake for them. Yezhov spoke openly on Stalin's behalf, explaining that admitting to shortcomings and errors would not suffice. All mistakes would have to be atoned for by taking ruthless action against the enemy, and functionaries would be required to present detailed plans explaining how they would do this. "Of course the enemies will mainly be exposed by the organs of the NKVD," Molotov told the Central Committee. But were they really incapable of figuring out for themselves what was going on? Could they really be missing all the signals coming from the organs of state security?[98]

In any case, the NKVD seemed to have learned the lesson that the other departments still needed to be taught. That was why Yezhov needed only mention the mistakes of the past to highlight the successes of the present day. "The enemy could no longer even appear in the open. He had to conspire, he had to mask his activity as a double-dealer, to conceal his vile acts with Soviet phraseology. The enemy was beginning to employ the methods of outward loyalty—typical for spies, deviators, and provocateurs—and was actually descending deep into the underground to damage our Soviet order clandestinely." But what had Stalin's Praetorian Guard done to counter these threats? Next to nothing, said Yezhov. They had failed. Although Stalin had been issuing warnings about spies and saboteurs since 1928 they had been ignoring him. They had not even been able to prevent the murder of Kirov, and had the Central Committee not intervened in time, the Trotskyites and Zinovievites who had planned and incited his assassination would have remained at large. Even the prisons of the GPU had been breeding grounds for anti-Soviet agitation, where prisoners could supposedly order books and food at will. In these places, which, according to Yezhov, were more like sanatoriums, prisoners could even receive vodka and flowers to decorate the windows of their pleasant and brightly lit cells. How could the secret police have turned a blind eye and a deaf ear to these dangers for so long? Had it not been their duty to reveal secrets, expose conspiracies, and punish without mercy? How could the Chekists have failed so miserably? Yezhov delivered Stalin's response: counterintelligence had fallen into the hands of Polish spies. And despite this, Yagoda and his deputy, Molchanov (director of the Secret Political Department of the GPU and the Belorussian branch of the NKVD), had ignored all signs. Enemies had been posing as Communists, and Yagoda and Molchanov had even protected them from persecution. "I think that what we have here is a simple case of treason. There is no other way to qualify this matter." And this was Stalin's cue to turn to Yagoda and his people. He asked whether Molchanov had been arrested in the meantime, knowing full well that the security organs had picked him up directly before the plenum. Stalin: "And what about Molchanov? What became of him? Was he arrested or not?" Yezhov: "Yes, he was arrested, Comrade Stalin, he's inside." A call from within the room: "Well done. Did he confess?" Yezhov: "He has confessed to many improprieties, but he has not confessed to these things, the investigation is currently underway."[99]

A prominent and powerful NKVD man was now sitting in prison and giving testimony. What could those gathered there have been thinking? Of course they knew that Molchanov would be tortured and that he would confess to whatever the Chekists could beat out of him. But who would be incriminated in the end? Had Stalin already decided who would be convicted and who would be spared? For Yagoda and his men, it seemed, the game was not yet over, so they were at pains to admit errors and promise betterment. Yagoda took responsibility for all past mistakes. He should have begun exterminating "fascist gangs" sooner. He should have started in 1931. He had failed to draw the right conclusions from Stalin's warnings. He had failed to recognize that the accidents caused by industrial workers were really acts of sabotage. Much of the GPU's operative work was not concentrated in his hands, and thus he knew little about it. He did not know which groups Molchanov belonged to and insisted, "I did not witness Molchanov's treason." Only now did he realize that Molchanov had been a traitor. "How he was connected, with whom he was connected—only an investigation would reveal this information." How could it have come to this? The Chekists, he claimed, had detached themselves from the party. They thought only of "the honor of the uniform" and of their own kind. They had been deaf to the warnings and blind to the signals, while he, Yagoda, had "fully and completely understood" the lesson that had been taught.[100]

Yagoda confirmed all the accusations Yezhov had made against the NKVD on Stalin's behalf. The dictator's reality, of course, could not be called into question. The other Chekists recognized this immediately and began coming forward to blame past mistakes on their superiors and try to save their own lives. Leonid Zakovsky confessed that the NKVD had violated all Bolshevik principles of cadre selection. Yagoda had surrounded himself with "his people" and was still protecting them from persecution, long after the Central Committee had called for their removal. He had reportedly refused to acknowledge the threat posed by Bukharin and the rightists, Polish spies, and Belorussian nationalists. Yagoda's deputy, Yakov Agranov, regretted that he and his colleagues had failed in the struggle against the enemy but insisted that he had urged Yagoda to coordinate all NKVD-related matters with Yezhov, the secretary of the Central Committee. Yagoda, he said, had refused as he considered such consultations to be an imposition. "You only run things by others if you are not master of the house," Yagoda had reportedly said. Moreover, he had delayed the investigation in the trial against Zinoviev and Kamenev because he doubted the existence of a Trotskyite terrorist center. Agranov accused himself of failing to notify the Central Committee about politically questionable orders issued by Yagoda. Vsevolod Balitsky and Stanislav Redens spoke of the shame that leading Chekists felt over their own failings. Redens, who was married to Stalin's sister-in-law, sought to prove his loyalty by claiming that he had informed the Politburo after Yagoda had declined to arrest Eismont in the aftermath of Kirov's murder. He had been considered a "traitor" in the NKVD ever since.[101]

Last to speak was Yefim Yevdokimov, Stalin's security apparatus stooge, who had presided over the worst of the violent excesses during forced collectivization. He asked whether Yagoda had not always been a wolf in sheep's clothing. In 1927 Stalin was said to have summoned him to his dacha in Sochi, where he had been given orders to seek out and punish wreckers and saboteurs in the Donbass. But even back then, he claimed, Yagoda had refused to believe the reports about spies and saboteurs.

> Comrades, after all that we here at the plenum have heard about the affairs of the NKVD, the address of Comrade Yezhov and the speeches of the comrades make it clear that the conditions that have been created in the organs of the NKVD within the last few years are good for nothing, and the main culprit in this matter is Yagoda. I think that this matter will not be settled with just Molchanov. (Yagoda: "Have you lost your mind?") I am deeply convinced of this. I think that the ex-leader of the NKVD has to be held responsible with all the strength of the law, just as we in the Cheka are used to being responsible for everything we are ordered to do. And we have to seriously think about the possibility of keeping him in the Central Committee. He has to be stripped of his rank as General Commissar of State Security, even if he is already out of service. He doesn't deserve it.

What was to become of Yagoda? Would he be expelled from the Central Committee? Would he be forgiven? Or would he be arrested?

Stalin allowed Ivan Zhukov, the people's commissar of local industry, to submit a supposedly spontaneous proposal:

> From all the materials that have been presented to us, from all the testimonies of the detainees we have read and all the speeches and discussions at the plenum, it is clear that this matter involved direct betrayal by an entire group of persons. Therefore this matter must be investigated, and this investigation must be handed over to the NKVD, to Comrade Yezhov. He will take excellent care of this matter. I think that the leadership of the NKVD cannot be bypassed in this matter. (Noise in the room. A call: "Unclear, what are you suggesting?") I know that all these Sosnovskys and the others have been arrested. (Yezhov: "They've all been arrested.") Why not arrest Yagoda? (Noise throughout the room.) Yes, yes, I'm convinced that it will come to this. (Kossior: "What do you propose?") That we get to the bottom of all this.[102]

Stalin emancipated himself from his cohorts by playing them off against each other, and he destroyed any sense of predictability and reliability, which people depend on in order to avoid dangers and risks In his concluding remarks to the plenum he informed the distressed Central Committee members that there were lessons to be learned from what had been said. Two days earlier, Stalin had declared that "under the current conditions," the "ability to recognize the enemies of the party, no matter how well they may mask themselves" was "an indispensable quality for every Bolshevik." But the party leaders in the republics had clearly failed in this task. They had cultivated inadmissible cults of personality and had maintained networks of camaraderie, willfully ignoring central directives and sparing enemies of the people from annihilation. Party and state employees were supposed to be devoted to the party—not wrapped up in personal devotion and loyalty. They were supposed to be selected on the basis of their political reliability and professional competence, not according to the principles of "personal acquaintance, personal devotion," as had been going on in the provinces.

Not even Stalin's companions from the Caucasus appeared to have understood that the dictator only tolerated one kind of loyalty—the kind that served to increase his own power. He had long since cautioned Levon Mirzoyan, the party leader of Kazakhstan, who had also worked in Azerbaijan and the Urals for many years, not to endow his "friends" from the Caucasus with offices and privileges. His staff,

Stalin told him, should be recruited from people native to the region. "What, then, does it mean to have an entire group of friends and companions from Azerbaijan in tow who are not connected to Kazakhstan from the ground up? What does it mean to have an entire group of friends from the Urals in tow who are not connected to Kazakhstan from the ground up? It means that you gain a certain degree of independence from the local organizations and, if you will, a certain degree of independence from the CC. You have your group, I have my group, they are personally devoted to me." For Stalin, loyalty to anyone but himself was treason. Mirzoyan had violated all the rules of Stalinist friendship, for friends that the dictator had not declared friends could quickly become enemies. "In general," said Stalin, "all these people are more or less under suspicion in the republics they were summoned from." Rzayev, Kuliyev, Aliyev—they had all been people's commissars in Azerbaijan. Following their removal from office, however, Mirzoian had given them ministerial posts in Kazakhstan. "How does that look? Is this the way to choose our people? Where does this lead, what good does it do? This I ask you. I warned Comrade Mirzoyan that this was not the way to behave, that the cadres have to be selected from local people. But you see, he created his group of personal devotees, he did not select these people according to the Bolshevik principle, and there are also Trotskyites among them. But he hopes that they will work with him forever once they are devoted to him. But what happens when he is finished?"[103]

Such methods of group cohesion were "hostile to the party" and needed to be terminated before it was "too late." The consequences of concealing suspicious activities were obvious. Ordzhonikidze had been receiving questionable letters from Lominadze for a long time, and although Stalin (according to himself) had demanded that these letters be handed over to the Politburo Ordzhonikidze had preferred to keep them under wraps, fearing that Lominadze would be shot. Apparently friendship had been more important to him than loyalty to the party, and what had this led to? Everybody knew that Lominadze was an enemy of the people, and even Ordzhonikidze eventually recognized this too when he demanded that his friend be shot. "You see, you come up with a nice story when you cover up and conceal the comrade's mistakes, when you don't hold him back in time but provide cover for him instead. You will drive him to ruin, to certain ruin." Stalin mistrusted the party secretaries who had deceived and lied to him in the past, and to be sure that such mistakes would never be repeated, he advised them to appoint two deputies who could replace them at any given moment.[104]

As soon as the plenum was over, Stalin put the terror machine into operation. Only a few survived the orgy of violence, which extended into the autumn of 1938. Almost all members of the Central Committee were killed. Genrikh Yagoda, his followers, and most of the people's commissars and provincial party secretaries who had spoken before the Central Committee died in the execution cellars of the NKVD. Some, such as Akmal Ikramov and Ivan Kabakov, party leaders in Uzbekistan and the Urals, were arrested in May 1937. Others, such as the Belorussian party boss, Nikolai Gikalo, and the second secretary of the Ukrainian party organization, Pavel Postyshev, were initially transferred to different regions but were then shot in 1938. Not even members of the Politburo could feel safe anymore. Stalin had the deputy premier Ian Rudzutak arrested in May 1937, and the West Siberian and Ukrainian party bosses Robert Eikhe and Stanislav Kossior were arrested in April and May 1938, while Vlas Chubar, the deputy head of government of the USSR, suffered the same fate in June. All of them had only recently become members of the Politburo.

Stalin's message could not have been clearer. Anyone could be arrested at any time, and even membership in the inner circle of leadership no longer afforded immunity. Eikhe, Chubar, and Rudzutak were tortured cruelly, but they refused to confess to crimes they had not committed. Beria and Rodos tortured Eikhe, and when they realized they would not be able to extract a confession they poked one of his eyes out and then shot him. "Rudzutak said he was terribly beaten and tortured. And still he remained steadfast. Indeed it seems that he was cruelly tortured." Molotov recalled this decades later, without showing even the faintest signs of empathy. Rudzutak was "a highly intelligent, perceptive fellow," he recalled, but there came a point when Stalin could not tolerate him anymore, as he was not a hard worker and rubbed shoulders with unsavory characters. "He never confessed to anything about himself. He was executed by firing squad. A Politburo member. I don't think he was a conscious member of any faction, but he was too easygoing about the opposition and considered it all nonsense, just about trifles. That was unforgivable. He didn't realize the danger of his attitude." Whether Chubar had really been an enemy or not had been impossible to determine. Once he had been tortured and abused, however, he could no longer be released from prison. "Stalin could no longer rely on Chubar. None of us could. "Yagoda gave in during his first interrogation because he knew Stalin would have him tortured if he refused to admit to everything he was accused of. "For my entire life I have been running around with a mask," he declared during his interrogation in the Lubianka, "and have been passing myself off as an irreconcilable Bolshevik." But in reality, he confessed, he had always been an enemy of the Soviet order.[105]

But what was being enacted here was by no means the product of a wildly deranged mind. It was all very much calculated. Stalin used the representational strategies of psychological and physical violence as a means of intimidating the elite, which allowed him to dispense with the necessity of coercing them into doing what he demanded. Once the surge of violence had subsided, Stalin never again needed to summon a Central Committee plenum to notify others of his intentions. From this point on everyone knew what was expected and what was forbidden. In their isolation, the provincial party secretaries were at the mercy of the violence. They learned quickly that their only chance of survival was to work toward the dictator in a manner that prevented him from suspecting them of deceit.

In Georgia and Azerbaijan, Stalin left it up to the local party leaders, Lavrenty Beria and Mir Jafar Bagirov, to spur on the self-destruction of the party. Beria and Bagirov belonged to the dictator's Caucasian clique. They imitated Stalin's style of rule, and they possessed the necessary instincts for survival in the dictator's court. They anticipated his every wish and committed murders with preemptive obedience. When it came to pleasing the tyrant in the Kremlin, old friendships had no weight for them. The party leadership in Azerbaijan, Georgia, and Armenia had surrendered to Stalin in its entirety. Bagirov had whole peasant villages wiped out. He ordered the shooting of twenty ministers from his administration, along with all the party secretaries in the republic. He had entire clans murdered and presented them to the dictator as enemies. The little despot in Baku imitated the methods of the big despot in Moscow. He had delinquents brought to his office and had them tortured in his presence. "Let the detainees really have it," he had said, "so that they have to be carried to the place where they're shot." Baku's former Komsomol chairman, Ostashko, recalled in 1956 how he had been arrested and taken to Bagirov's office. He had complained about the torture methods and confessions extorted by the state security organs. Bagirov, he recalled, had "laughed," punched him "hard in the face," and said cynically, "Show him Soviet state security." Ostashko was then dragged next door and "beaten half to death."[106]

Beria operated in a similar manner. In July 1937 he informed his lord and master of "counterrevolutionary centers" that had been unearthed throughout the Transcaucasian republics—in Armenia, Georgia, and Azerbaijan. Worse still, almost all notable national Communists apparently belonged to one of them. Beria listed the names of the "guilty" and recommended that they be arrested, along with their wives and children. Scruples were something Beria did not have. He shot the Armenian party leader Agassi Khanjian dead with his own revolver. He then poisoned the first secretary of the Abkhazian party organization, Nestor Lakoba, and had his entire family liquidated. His sadistic attendants Bogdan Kobulov and Avksenti Rapava took pleasure in beating and torturing detainees as well. This kind of brutal determination and loyalty was something that Stalin appreciated greatly, and so he rewarded his friends from the Caucasus richly with privileges and promotions. Beria and Bagirov were the only provincial potentates who survived the year 1938. When the mass terror was finally over, they entered into the party's inner circle of leadership, where they remained until after the demise of the despot, when Nikita Khrushchev had them arrested and shot.[107]

The provincial party secretaries took pains to outdo each other in demonstrating their subservience to the dictator. They wrote reports proclaiming their achievements in the struggle against spies and saboteurs, but although some managed to portray themselves better than others, merit alone was no protection against death. The dictator had already opened the floodgates for denouncers and provocateurs, and by this time no one was safe. "Every party member," Stalin proclaimed at a conference of the Military Council in early June 1937, "every honest partyless citizen of the USSR not only has the right, but also the duty, to report the faults that he notices. Even if just 5 percent is true, that's still something (*to i eto khleb*). They are obligated to write letters to their people's commissar, the CC too of course. However they please."

Stalin could take satisfaction, as he began to receive letters from simple Communists and functionaries throughout the Soviet Union denouncing party leaders as traitors and enemies of the people. That very same month he received an anonymous letter accusing State Prosecutor Vyshinsky of providing cover for public enemies and spies working in his vicinity. Although Vyshinsky survived, he remained under suspicion for the rest of his life. Others were less fortunate. According to an anonymous denouncer, the second secretary of the Communist Party of Ukraine, Mendel Khataevich, had also surrounded himself with enemies of the people in the past and even now he was retaining employees of questionable loyalty. Stalin underlined the names of the suspects that the denouncer had identified in his letter and ordered their arrest. Khataevich was taken by the NKVD only a short time later and then shot.[108] Kuibyshev's regional party committee was also consumed with the struggle between functionaries, all of whom realized that their lives were on the line. In September 1937 Stalin received a circular from Frenkel, the representative of the Party Control Commission, accusing the regional party leader, Postyshev, and the head of the NKVD, Popashenko, of impeding efforts to expose enemies. The "extermination" of enemies, he complained, was proceeding "rather slowly." Frenkel's explanation for this must have pleased Stalin because he underlined it in colored pencil. Postyshev, along with the district leaders of the NKVD, had "hampered the exposure of enemies" because they themselves were in league with them.[109]

It took some satraps longer than others to realize that their time was up. A demonstration in Alma Ata in May 1938 had featured posters of Kazakhstan's party boss, Levon Mirzoyan, which were significantly larger than the portraits of Stalin. When Stalin found out he immediately summoned Mirzoyan to Moscow. Mirzoyan, however, was arrested before he could even reach the capital and executed before the year was out. In April 1937 Rumiantsev, party boss of the Western Region, was ordered to have his deputy and second party secretary, Akim Shilman, arrested. Even by this time Rumiantsev had still not comprehended what duty he was expected to perform, and he refuted every allegation that his deputy was a foreign agent or a Trotskyite enemy of the people. Stalin pressed the matter, and Shilman was eventually expelled from the bureau of the Area Committee. Shortly thereafter Rumiantsev's own star began to wane.

In spring 1937 Stalin's old attack dog Kaganovich arrived in Smolensk to "expose" the party boss of the Western Region as a traitor and a spy. Rumiantsev, it was claimed, had ties to Polish and German intelligence, and after his return from a trip abroad, he had publicly praised the "foreign orders" and National Socialism in particular. The commander of the Western Military District, General Yeronim Uborevich, had reportedly been a welcome guest at Rumiantsev's house. Here, they had allegedly plotted conspiracies and entertained themselves with "card games and billiards." That was how Kaganovich understood it at least, and he promptly notified Stalin of his discoveries. In June 1937 Rumiantsev and his men were arrested and killed soon thereafter. The new party boss, Demyan Korotchenkov, came from Moscow and was one of Kaganovich's people. He had previously served as party secretary in the capital's Bauman Rayon. Just as his predecessors had done, Korotchenkov took his friends from the Moscow apparatus with him to Smolensk—but only after making sure that neither Stalin nor Kaganovich would object.[110]

Stalin might have relied on the apparatuses to destroy themselves, but that was not his nature. As Kaganovich recalled forty years later, Stalin had everyone he suspected of deceiving him closely monitored. "Stalin was extremely vigilant and very cautious."[111] In July 1937 the party secretaries of the republics and areas received instructions from Yezhov, alluding to the inefficiency of the security organs in dealing with "enemies of the people." Enemies were supposedly being detained under conditions that resembled "sanitariums." Repression needed to be intensified, and the number of arrests needed to increase. For this to happen, though, policing and punishment of the provincial party leaders needed to be stepped up. In September 1937 Stalin discovered that Amosov, secretary of the Kirghiz Communist Party, had been trying to protect his friends and followers from persecution. In response, Stalin sent him a telegram informing him that the Central Committee would resort to "extreme measures" unless he, Amosov, abandoned his "liberalism toward the enemies of the people" immediately. In summer and autumn 1937 Stalin dispatched his most trusted followers in the Politburo to the provinces, where they were to intensify the terror campaign and demonstrate how the bloody trade was supposed to be carried out. Anastas Mikoyan traveled to Armenia to oversee the self-destruction of the local party apparatus, while Georgy Malenkov and Andrei Andreyev were sent to Saratov, Voronezh, Rostov, the Urals, and Central Asia. Everywhere they went they brought terror with them—all per order of Stalin. Mikoyan later recalled how Stalin had handed him a letter just before his departure for Yerevan. "I was supposed to read out his letter to the plenum of the CC," Mikoyan reported, "and sign the list of persons due to be arrested, which had been prepared by the NKVD of the republic with Moscow's approval." From then on, everything had proceeded according to "Stalin's scenario." The list contained the names of three hundred people, and he, Mikoyan, signed it and sent them all to their doom.[112]

There were no objections. All of Stalin's confidants performed the tasks assigned to them. Some even did so with pleasure. At the end of May 1937 Andreyev sent Stalin a telegram from Sverdlovsk, reporting, "the general mood in the organization is good, the CC is thanked." He had exposed several functionaries as Trotskyites and enemies of the people, he said, but at least seven rayon party secretaries needed to be arrested. He would gladly see to it, as long as Stalin agreed. In July Andreyev showed up in the Republic of Volga Germans to expose "terror bands" and "saboteurs." These people were killed on the spot—with Stalin's consent, of course. Andreyev was also able to report the arrest of seven ministers and three party secretaries in Stalinabad. In Tajikistan, the arrested included "the chairman of the Council of People's Commissars, the deputies, the chairman of the Central Executive Committee and the secretary, almost all people's commissars, 15 secretaries of the Rayon Committees." After leaving Voronezh, Andreyev informed Stalin by telegraph that the bureau no longer existed and that "all cadres" had been "arrested as enemies of the people." He would now be moving on to Rostov. Sometimes Stalin even gave him detailed instructions on what to do with the party functionaries he had deposed. In April 1938 Andreyev telegraphed from Sverdlovsk that Morozov and Grachev, secretary of the local party committee and chairman of the soviets, had been relieved of their posts. Stalin replied that they should be summoned to Moscow to be placed at the CC's disposal. "On their way," they were to be "arrested and taken to the NKVD." Similar measures were taken against the Voronezh party leader, Ryabinin, who was sent to Moscow, interrogated by Stalin personally, and then shot.[113]

In summer 1937 Stalin's most trusted minion Lazar Kaganovich made his appearance in the Russian core provinces and the western areas of the Soviet Union. Mikhail Shreider, who was deputy leader of the NKVD in Ivanovo at the time, recalled how Kaganovich arrived in Ivanovo at the beginning of August 1937 to see that Stalin's will was being carried out. He was accompanied by Matvei Shkiriatov, the secretary of the Central Control Commission. Party functionaries and NKVD men were waiting for them at the train station. "When Kaganovich and Shkiriatov stepped out of the carriage," remembered Shreider, "Shkiriatov saw me, shook my hand and said, 'Ah, my dearest, you too are here! Now, that means that everything is all right.' And then he turned to Kaganovich and explained, 'I shared a room with him for two weeks in the Kazan Court hotel. We exterminated an entire regiment of thieves and wreckers there.'"[114] The local party and NKVD functionaries trembled with fear, for they knew that Kaganovich had destroyed the Yaroslavl party organization only a few days earlier and were probably also aware that Nefredov, the area party secretary, had recently been arrested and shot, on Kaganovich's orders, for his supposed involvement in an assassination plot against Kaganovich.[115] "Iron Lazar" was accompanied by several functionaries from the Central Committee and thirty NKVD officers as bodyguards. His group included three party secretaries from Moscow who had been designated to replace the local executive leadership. As elsewhere, however, this exchange of functionaries could not be performed without a certain amount of stage direction. Kaganovich cast Shreider in the role of the denouncer at the Area Committee plenum that he promptly convened and gave him the task of publicly unmasking the party secretary, Nossov, as an "enemy of the people." He was also to deliver the talking points for the reckoning with the old leadership.

Kaganovich then stepped up to the podium himself. He spoke to the members of the Area Committee for several hours, ranting and hurling threats at the functionaries, some of whom were taken outside while he was still speaking. The leadership in Moscow, he said, knew and saw everything that was taking place in the provinces, meaning that it was no longer possible to pretend or protect friends and followers from persecution. "There will be no special consideration for people's commissars, for their deputies, or for any kind of functionaries," Kaganovich announced. "We will remorselessly exterminate all those who are ruining our people. Stalin's hand has never trembled, and it will never tremble." Furthermore, he exclaimed, everyone should be thankful to the NKVD and to Nikolai Yezhov for their "great work" in the struggle against enemies of the people. Before being arrested, Nossov too had to sit through Kaganovich's rant. Nossov's attempts at self-justification were no match for the roaring and ranting of Stalin's vassals, who accused him of not having brought "a single scoundrel" under suspicion and of having left it up to the NKVD to expose the enemies lurking about. The party was "surrounded by a circle of enemies," saboteurs and spies, who were being financed by foreign powers. "Those in our state who fail to exert themselves with their entire souls are also wreckers. Sabotage and wrecking begin in places where people are not working with their entire souls." Furthermore, anyone who stood in the party's path would be "exterminated"—a historical fate reserved for all "wretches, scoundrels, and dregs of human society." Nossov's fate remained uncertain, as Stalin, it seems, had not yet decided what he wanted to do with him. It would, however, Kaganovich announced, by no means suffice to merely relieve Nossov of his post.[116]

"Everything went very quickly," Shreider recalled. "Kaganovich and Shkiriatov mentioned the names of a row of leading employees of the Regional Party Committee, accusing them of Trotskyism and other sins. They were all expelled from the party at the plenum and arrested on their way out. For this purpose, Radzivilovsky [the NKVD boss of Ivanovo] had previously summoned his employees to the building of the Regional Party Committee."[117] On the following day, Kaganovich confronted the members of the Committee with the testimony of the arrested party leaders to show them just how hopeless their situation was. "Look at Vasilev," said Kaganovich, "who was excluded from the party here at this plenum, who unburdened himself here, who was arrested here on the spot. He walked out of here and was arrested, and already after half an hour he said: give me paper. He sat down and wrote the following confession: 'To the Chairman of the Regional Administration of the NKVD. I confess that a rightist counterrevolutionary organization existed in Ivanovo, which was headed by Ageyev, Epanechnikov, Stupishin, and also myself between 1934 and 1935.' (Shkiriatov: 'Do you see, what a scoundrel!')"[118] Others, such as Epanechnikov, were evidently not prepared to submit so readily to the self-incrimination Kaganovich demanded of them. Kaganovich went on to discuss Epanechnikov's case: "Now, let's take Epanechnikov, he was arrested on the opening day of the plenum, at three o'clock. When he was arrested he was surprised. A misunderstanding, a misunderstanding. Now, we shall see. He confessed at four o'clock. . . . There you have your Epanechnikov! And didn't you believe in Epanechnikov's every word until the very last moment? How is that possible? Even on the day of his arrest they still believed him, and Nossov believed him. There you have your leader, a leading terrorist!" This was one big "band of terrorists," and the party was filled with "spies" and "beasts." Soon, though, they would be wiped out forever.[119]

Kaganovich then went on to tell the Regional Party Committee that it too should be able to function with fewer members. "I have already hired three hundred fighters," he explained. "Is this a small number for the Ivanovo organization?"[120] The committee members present were filled with dread, but they rose just the same and offered up the same hysterical applause when "Iron Lazar" uttered Stalin's name. At the end, Kaganovich had his Moscow secretaries "voted" into the local party leadership. The party boss, Nossov, was then deposed and expelled from the party as planned. Stalin, however, had made some special arrangements for him: he had him brought to Moscow to be shot.

Although Kaganovich presided over the events in Ivanovo, Stalin was always the master of the situation. Furthermore, never once in the whole course of the production did Stalin cease to be the master of all that was taking place. Shreider described the manner in which the dictator and his disciple spoke to each other:

> Kaganovich phoned Stalin from Ivanovo several times a day and briefed him on the number of arrested individuals and the progress of the investigations. After every conversation he approached Radzivilovsky and demanded that he take measures to speed up the extortion of confessions from this or that arrested staff member. And regardless of the fact that Radzivilovsky and his subordinates extracted arbitrary confessions from the detainees with exceptional speed and by means of cruel torture—mainly demanding that they implicate as many colleagues, friends, and acquaintances as possible and then accusing them of being enemies of the people, which in turn led to more arrests—Kaganovich and Shkiriatov were not satisfied with the achieved results. They continued to compel Radzivilovsky to increase the number of arrests even further.

In the meantime, Kaganovich called Stalin to inform him about the Regional Party Committee plenum and await further instructions. "After he ended the conversation about Nossov, Kaganovich informed Stalin about how many and which employees of the Regional Party Committee, the Executive Committee, and other organizations had been arrested and how many new enemies of the people he had exposed." Despite Kaganovich's efforts, however, Stalin did not seem pleased. Kaganovich's response, as Shreider recalled it, was, "I hear you, Comrade Stalin. I will increase the pressure on the employees of the NKVD, so that they don't liberalize but expose a maximum number of enemies of the people."[121]

Nothing remained of the party organization in Ivanovo. The prisons were filled with party members and employees of the state administration. Even mechanics from the train depot and grocers were arrested and shot as spies and saboteurs. Eventually the detention facilities became so overcrowded that the NKVD had to seize the city's kindergartens to accommodate further detainees. When Kaganovich left the dacha of the local NKVD boss, where he had stayed during his time in Ivanovo, he drove through empty streets, cordoned off by NKVD guards. When he arrived at the train station the new party leadership had gathered there to bid farewell to Stalin's trusted minion. Kaganovich was pleased. The party organization had been wiped out, and the prisons had been filled. His work here was done. As a parting gift, Kaganovich handed out generous tips to the servants and cooks who worked for the NKVD and had taken care of the esteemed guest from Moscow. Then, off he went to spread fear and dread elsewhere. The killings, which began directly after Kaganovich's departure, were presided over by the new party secretary of Ivanovo, Simochkin. He took part in the executions personally, using his own revolver.[122]

THE ANNIHILATION OF THE OFFICER CORPS

In spring 1937 the army leadership also became a target of the dictator's mistrust. After all, the Red Army officer corps not only had authority over the armory of the proletarian state, but was also closely connected with the party secretaries who wielded political power in their respective military districts. Some historians have wondered what could have ever compelled Stalin to wipe out the army leadership, especially when he was convinced that the Soviet Union was being encircled by military threats on all sides. Another question, though, is whether the dictator's logic of vengeance even allowed for an alternative to making the officer corps members into suspects as well. Could it really have been otherwise? This was, after all, an elite group that was in a position to take up arms against him. To spare a group like this was not Stalin's style. Although high-ranking officers were all being closely monitored by political commissars and the secret police, the dictator still questioned their loyalty and unconditional devotion. And he had good reason. Just as there had been dissenting party secretaries, there had been Red Army officers, too, who had criticized the excesses of collectivization. Some of the army units deployed in the pacification campaigns against village insurgency had refused orders or engaged in passive resistance. And of course Stalin and his simple-minded war commissar, Kliment Voroshilov, were well aware of the danger they faced if peasant soldiers were to give up battling insurgents and turn their weapons against the state. They had not forgotten the course of events leading up to the 1917 Revolution—which had only been possible because of the refusal of the soldiers to obey their superiors. What would happen if the officers themselves disobeyed? This question first arose during the collectivization of agriculture, when Stalin and his helpers tried to use the army against insurgent peasants.

At that time, officers suspected of having fought for the Whites during the Civil War were discharged from the armed forces and arrested. In such cases the party leadership did not even shy away from executions. In spring 1931 the GPU arrested and shot a highly decorated divisional commander who was accused of working for Czechoslovakia. That same year, the secret police uncovered a "counterrevolutionary organization" in the officer corps of the Black Sea Fleet, whose members had once been leaders in the tsarist navy. Year by year the number of military personnel arrested steadily increased. In 1932 3,889 "socially alien elements" were removed from the army. By 1933 the figure had risen to 22,308. Marshal Mikhail Tukhachevsky and other high-ranking generals were suspected of being in league with Bukharin and the critics of forced collectivization. When the Ukrainian party boss and the head of the Ukrainian government, Stanislav Kossior and Vlas Chubar, criticized the Politburo's utopian grain procurement quotas in the early 1930s, they could also point to the reluctance of several generals. As Stalin soon discovered, Iona Yakir and Fyodor Raskolnikov, commanders of the Kiev Military District and the Black Sea Fleet, had criticized the use of violence against insurgent peasants as well. Never before had generals obliged the leaders to question their loyalty, and

Stalin perceived this alliance of moderates as a conspiracy. In September 1930 he wrote to Ordzhonikidze that the chief of the General Staff, Mikhail Tukhachevsky, was in league with the "rightists," and that if Bukharin were to prevail in the power struggle against Stalin then it could result in a military dictatorship. Two years later, in 1932, Tukhachevsky was named in connection with the treasonous Eismont and Tolmachev and suspected of having known about their "plot." In 1932, however, Stalin could not yet do what cost him no trouble in 1937. The final hour of the generals had arrived, as Stalin embarked on his grand assault against high-ranking military functionaries and officials, and dealt deadly blows in all directions.

It began with the shooting of several tsarist officers, who had distinguished themselves during the Civil War on the side of the Reds but were now accused of having banded together with oppositionists and plotted against the party leadership. Executions of this kind were already being carried out in 1936, but it was only after the plenum in February–March 1937 that the persecution of Red Army members began to lose all sense of proportion. In May 1937 Stalin's war commissar, Voroshilov, informed leading employees in his ministry of the plenum's results and the lessons to be learned from them. Five-sixths of the world, he said, was in the hands of hostile capitalists. They had already encircled the Soviet Union and were simply waiting for their opportunity to destroy it. The enemy was particularly mischievous in areas where the security interests of the Soviet State were at stake. He was "deeply convinced" that the fire disasters and accidents affecting the troops in eastern Siberia had not been freak occurrences either. The enemy's handwriting was plain to see, and that is why he had personally sent out telegraphs to all departments, instructing them to initiate the hunt for "wreckers." His efforts, he reported, had resulted in the arrests of a divisional commander and a major only a short time later.

Voroshilov's signal triggered a wave of arrests in the Red Army. Wherever troop leaders and party secretaries were connected, they proceeded to drag each other into the abyss. Whenever party functionaries were exposed as German or Japanese spies or saboteurs, their downfall also spelled disaster for the colonels and generals associated with them. For who, if not the officers themselves, would even have been capable of overthrowing the dictator and his order? According to Stalin's logic, the annihilation of the Soviet officer corps was an inevitable progression of the terror against the party elite. As usual, Yezhov carried out his duties with particular zeal. He supplied Stalin with dossiers on conspiracies and plots, and he accused leading generals of being paid by German intelligence to divulge military secrets to the Wehrmacht. Although these allegations were completely fabricated, the close cooperation between the Red Army and the Reichswehr during the 1920s did lend them a certain degree of plausibility. Stalin decided against staging show trials for the arrested officers, as he evidently doubted that they would break down in court the way Kamenev and Pyatakov had done. But he still needed confessions of some sort that he could present to the rest of the leadership and to the foreign public.[123]

Tukhachevsky and Yakir were arrested in May 1937, and dozens of high-ranking officers followed them into prison in the weeks to come. Yezhov's deputy Frinovsky instructed the head of the Moscow NKVD to torture the detained officers until they confirmed the existence of a grand conspiracy. The Chekists had difficulty extracting confessions, however, as the generals were able to withstand the torture longer than the party secretaries who had been beaten and abused in the cellars of the NKVD. Konstantin Rokossovsky, who would later become a marshal himself, had his teeth knocked out and his ribs broken. Others were beaten half to death before they gave the confessions that Stalin wanted. Tukhachevsky, Uborevich, Yakir, and four other high-ranking generals were condemned to death in a secret trial before the Military Collegium of the Supreme Court in 1937 and were immediately shot. The newspapers announced to the public that the country's leading generals had been executed for high treason. Meetings were convened in companies and administrative agencies throughout the Soviet Union, and workers and employees were required to vilify the condemned generals as human dregs and scum. Zinaida Pasternak recalled how her husband had been approached by two NKVD men in June 1937, who had presented him with a declaration that they wanted him and other Soviet writers to sign. The declaration stated that the artists of the Soviet Union welcomed the death sentences that had been handed down to the treasonous generals, and although Pasternak refused, his name still appeared in the newspapers that published the declaration the following day.[124]

Immediately after the arrests of Tukhachevsky and Yakir, Stalin had the leading commanders and political commissars of the Red Army summoned to the Kremlin in early June 1937 to confront them with a series of new allegations that they had elicited from the imprisoned under torture. This was a game in which Stalin and the Central Committee had already rigged the deck. There was no hope of winning because, once again, Stalin had left the participants in the dark. Voroshilov had the task of making sure that they understood that the arrests of the past few weeks were merely the prelude to a great extermination campaign against enemies in the armed forces.[125] Once more, Stalin's stage directions followed a familiar pattern. Voroshilov opened, and then Molotov and Kaganovich made their entrances. They began shouting at the officers and ambushing them with questions—which was merely part of a performance intended to sow fear and insecurity. Even the legendary warhorse and founder of the Red Cavalry, Marshal Semyon Budyonny, struggled as he was forced to defend himself against accusations of having been friends with the arrested.[126] Quite early in the "debate," the exchanges drifted into the realm of the absurd. Red Army Chief of Staff Marshal Alexander Yegorov confirmed the dictator's conspiracy theories but protested that he was innocent and knew nothing about the conspiracy that Tukhachevsky, aided by his friends in German intelligence, had supposedly been organizing. He was willing to vouch for this with his own life, he insisted. Stalin's response was that the culprits would be shot anyway.[127]

Although we will never know for sure what Stalin genuinely considered possible, his remarks to the War Council on June 2, 1937, at least reveal something about the world in which he lived. His explanations for the generals' supposed treason were grotesque, but they were met without opposition. Those who had been shot, Stalin said, were no longer relevant to the discussion. What mattered now were the enemies who, until recently, had been at large. These included Yagoda, Tukhachevsky, Yakir, Uborevich, Kork, Eideman, Gamarnik, Rudzutak, and Enukidze—all of whom were accused of having worked for the German intelligence and military and of having leaked information from the innermost circle of the Soviet state to its enemies. Yakir had supposedly feigned a liver disease and used the pretext of traveling abroad for recovery to rendezvous with German intelligence operatives. "What kind of people are they?" Stalin asked rhetorically. It was an interesting question, he answered, but a difficult one. Anybody, no matter how well disguised, could potentially be a hidden enemy. Stalin continued:

> Of course one could ask how it is possible that people who were still Communists yesterday suddenly become the sharpest weapons in the hands of German espionage. Today comes the demand: Give us information. If you don't, then we have your signature that you allowed yourself to be recruited, we will make it public. Out of fear of being unmasked they provide information. Tomorrow comes the demand: No, that is too little, give more and take money, provide a signature. After that comes the demand: Begin with the conspiracy, the wrecking activity. First wrecking, then diversion; show us that you're working on our side. If you don't, we will expose you, we will hand you over to the agents of Soviet power tomorrow, and heads will roll. They begin with the diversion. Then they are told: No, you must somehow try to organize something in the Kremlin or take over the command post in the Moscow garrison. And they begin to do their best. Then that is not enough either. Provide real facts about something that is worth it. And they murder Kirov. Now, take it, they are told. And then they are told: keep going, why not overthrow the entire government? And they organize it through Enukidze, through Gorbachev, Yegorov, who was head of the school of the VTsIK [All-Union Central Executive Committee of the Soviets] at the time, and this school stood in the Kremlin, under Peterson. They tell them: organize a group to arrest the government. The messages fly back and forth, that there is a group, that we're finished, that we'll carry out arrests etc. But that isn't enough, just making arrests, exterminating a few—what about the people, the army!

Tukhachevsky and the other generals had been "marionettes" in the hands of the German Reichswehr and had "systematically" divulged all military secrets to the Germans. "The Reichswehr wanted to see the current government overthrown and smashed, and they took on the task, but without success. In case of a war the Reichswehr wanted everything to be prepared, for the army to commence with wrecking activities, so that the army loses its defensive capabilities. This was the Reichswehr's aim, and they made preparations for it."

But why were the traitors unable to resist the offers of the Reichswehr? Had they really turned their backs on communism? No. In Stalin's world, noble motives of this kind did not play a role. Instead, in his view, Enukidze, Rudzutak, even Yakir and Tukhachevsky had fallen victim to a "pretty woman," who reportedly seduced men and recruited them as spies for the Germans. "There is an experienced agent in Germany, in Berlin . . . Josephine Heinze, maybe one of you knows her. She is a beautiful woman. An old agent. She recruited Karakhan. She recruited him with the ways of a woman. She recruited Enukidze. She helped recruit Tukhachevsky. She also had Rudzutak in her hands. This Josephine Heinze is a very experienced agent. She is probably Danish and works for the German Reichswehr. A beautiful woman, who likes to cater to all men's desires." Stalin's world was rather simple. It was a world where men became spies because they were unable to resist the advances of a beautiful woman. "You see," he told his listeners, "this is what these people are like."[128]

And yet a number of army commanders still seemed to harbor the illusion that it mattered whether the accused were guilty or not. In August 1937, for example, at a gathering of Red Army political commissars, one leading commissar asked how they should explain the arrests of the generals to the soldiers. Stalin's response was that the generals' confessions were of a "certain significance." When some commanders still dared ask whether one could really speak of "enemies of the people," the dictator's response was, "We certainly must."[129]

The self-destruction of the army was not an end in itself. It was part of a terror with which Stalin and his cronies sought to punish disloyalty and spread fear. Of course Stalin believed none of the absurd confessions that were beaten out of the officers by the Chekists. After all, he was the one who had scripted the confessions. But he was able to exploit foreign tensions for his own purposes. The Soviet Union at this time was waging a propaganda war against Nazi Germany. It was militarily involved in the Spanish Civil War, and felt threatened from Finland, Poland, Romania, and Turkey. The Soviet Union was isolated, and it was indeed without a friend in the world. Was it not wise, under these circumstances, to mistrust even those who were closest? These circumstances allowed Stalin to lend a certain degree of plausibility to his paranoia. Although it was difficult to prove that Soviet generals were committing treason, it was plausible. Decades later, in an interview with the journalist Felix Chuev, Molotov would give his answer as to why Stalin had annihilated the army leadership. As he explained it, it was unavoidable that innocent people were killed, but the Soviet Union had been under serious threat. After the 1917 Revolution the party had "slashed right and left," but numerous "enemies of various stripes" had still gotten away. And in the face of "the growing danger of fascist aggression, they might have united." He said that it was "thanks to 1937 there was no fifth column in our country during the war." Furthermore, Molotov continued, there had been Bolsheviks who were "loyal and dedicated as long as the nation and the party face no danger." " But they would "switch sides" whenever the situation became "dangerous." It was unlikely, he conceded, that these people had been spies, but they had been "definitely linked with foreign intelligence services" and more importantly, "at the decisive moment they could not be depended on." Like Stalin, Molotov knew that those who had been killed had never been spies, but had they not been disposed of in a timely manner, then they might have become traitors. This is precisely the kind of mistrust that the Stalinist style of rule was based on. Should Molotov have told Chuev instead that thousands had been killed according to the mood of the dictator? Only an answer that invoked the constraints of war was an answer that still made sense forty years later.[130]

The terror against the officers of the Red Army was a frenzy of blood. The armed forces destroyed themselves. Not a week went by without a new slew of accusations and arrests. The detained officers were bestially tortured until they confessed and named their supposed aides and accomplices in treason. Prisoners were confined in hopelessly overcrowded cells and died under miserable conditions from disease or abuse. They were treated like animals. Scurvy ravaged their bodies, and their teeth fell out. At any rate, this is how one officer described the conditions in a March 1939 letter to Stalin. The henchmen of the NKVD gave their imaginations free reign when it came to devising new forms of abuse for their detainees. Victims had their ribs broken and their teeth knocked out. Some Chekists spat into the prisoners' mouths or defecated on them. Some of the officers stood firm and refused to confess. Marshal Vasily Bliukher, the supreme commander of Soviet troops in the Far East, for example, refused to confess to being a Japanese spy, so in 1938 Yezhov's lackeys beat him to death.[131]

The officer corps was a shadow of its former self. Almost nothing remained. More than ten thousand Red Army officers had become victims of Stalin's terror, and three of five Soviet marshals had been arrested. Among the victims were 15 army commanders, 15 army commissars, 63 corps commanders, 30 corps commissars, 151 division commanders, 86 division commissars, 243 brigade commanders, 143 brigade commissars, 318 regimental commanders, and 163 regimental commissars. In April 1938 the head of the "special department" of the 5th Mechanized Corps notified Voroshilov that "100 percent of the command personnel in the corps and all of its brigades" had been arrested.[132]

Already by autumn 1937 the terror's devastating effects on the army had become quite apparent. There were divisions under the command of majors. There were tank brigades under the command of captains. Command structures had collapsed, and military discipline was gone. Those who had been shot had been replaced by young officers who had little sense of responsibility and whose inexperience made them prone to mistakes. Above all, though, the commanders who remained could be denounced and arrested at any given moment. Everyone knew this, and thus they no longer had any authority. Why should anyone trust or obey an officer who might not even be there one week later? At any rate, in 1937 soldiers had a better chance of survival than their officers.

The army was destroyed piece by piece by its own leadership, and it would not recover from this killing spree until the beginning of the Second World War. The Red Army after 1938 was led by officers who were young, inexperienced, intimidated, and afraid of making decisions. The consequences became clear in 1939–40 and in the summer and autumn of 1941, when Soviet troops were decimated by Finnish and German forces—a state of affairs that might easily have been avoided, had Stalin been able to refrain from killing his military experts in 1937.

THE SELF-DESTRUCTION OF THE STATE APPARATUS

The terror did not remain confined to the party and the army. It raged throughout all institutions of the Soviet Union. Neither the state administration, nor the schools, nor the universities, nor the industrial enterprises, nor the artists' associations were spared. Factory directors, managers, and technicians were all punished with death for their associations with disgraced party leaders. They were blamed for the failure to meet quotas and for accidents that were really due to overloaded machinery and incompetent personnel. Whenever party secretaries and state functionaries were tried and shot, their subordinates were taken down with them. This was, after all, an integral part of the Stalinist logic of the personalized dictatorship: clients had to die with their patrons.

In March 1937 a wave of violence began to sweep through the Soviet Union. In many government agencies and business enterprises, offices and entire executive suites became empty. Anyone appointed secretary of a party committee or head of an NKVD branch during this period was in mortal danger. In some places people who had only recently been promoted were removed from office and shot. A targeted denunciation, the suspicion of the dictator, or even a functionary's incidental acquaintance with someone who had been arrested—any one of these things alone was enough to elicit a death sentence. Some functionaries realized this and did their best to maintain a low profile. Semyon Zhukovsky, for example, who belonged to the presidium of the Central Control Commission, tried to avoid being promoted to a leading position in the NKVD. Despite his best efforts he was appointed Yezhov's deputy in January 1938, only to be removed from office the following October and then executed in 1940. In Kuybyshev on the Volga, the havoc wrought by the terror in the summer of 1937 was so devastating that the local party leaders faced difficulties to find candidates who were willing to replace those who had been arrested. Stalin received a confidential report from Kuybyshev in September 1937, informing him that the local party boss, Pavel Postyshev, had started calling workers into his office and offering them posts as party secretaries and economic experts. The workers apparently knew better and tried to avoid being appointed, citing their inexperience and fear of responsibility. Postyshev, however, not only handed out promotions but also threatened functionaries with dire consequences if they failed. On September 10, 1937, Stalin sent a telegram to all party leaders in the provinces, calling for the organization of show trials against "wreckers" in every republic and region. These "wreckers" were supposedly responsible for a plague of ticks and needed to be shot. Postyshev read Stalin's directives to the attending functionaries and declared that violence was the only solution. "In this matter we will carry out shootings," he said. "We will shoot seven to ten people without fail."[133]

Others began to panic because their family members were being taken away, and they themselves were now suspected of having been accomplices. In June 1937, after his brother-in-law Ian Gamarnik committed suicide, Alexander Bogomolov, who belonged to the leadership circle of the Moscow party committee, wrote to Stalin. "Never, not in the slightest," he wrote, "was I ever connected to the enemy of the people Gamarnik, nor did I maintain any relations with him in general, I never spoke about political issues with him, which is why I knew nothing of his political views and therefore didn't suspect anything. My encounters with him were mostly purely coincidental, and the conversations lasted only a few minutes." He claimed that he had never been to Gamarnik's apartment. Not even his wife, Gamarnik's sister, had confided in her brother. Bogomolov insisted that he had never belonged to an oppositional faction. Words of naked fear lined the pages: "Comrade Stalin. I occupy a responsible position in the Moscow party organization. The party, the Central Committee, can trust me to the end . . ."[134]

Government offices and enterprises throughout the Soviet Union turned into madhouses. Their personnel trembled with fear and began denouncing each other in order to protect themselves from arrest and death. Not a day went by without somebody being picked up or simply disappearing forever. Departmental offices were emptied out. The functionaries who remained had no choice but to adapt to lives overshadowed by death. Some succumbed to the fear. Others committed suicide or accepted their fate, as though the daily terror was an inevitable natural disaster that could not be averted. In October 1937 Vyshinsky notified Stalin that Georgy Chazov, the state prosecutor of the Bashkir Republic, had been found dead by a riverbank outside of Ufa. He was said to have killed himself with two shots from his revolver after having been accused of "sneaking" Bukharinist views into a newspaper article.[135] Everyone became enemies. No one could be trusted or asked for help any longer. Anyone hoping to stay alive needed, under all circumstances, to avoid unknown persons, as they could turn out to be provocateurs or suddenly become "enemies of the people" at any given time. In Moscow the terror was particularly devastating because the functionaries were so closely connected and even lived within spitting distance of each other. As soon as one Communist was picked up by the "organs," dozens of other officials who knew or had worked with him disappeared as well. Moscow was hit harder than other major cities by the merciless terror. Apart from accommodating the most important functionaries of the Union agencies, scores of oppositional Communists from the Soviet republics, who had been deported by local party leaders, lived in the capital as well.[136] Yelena Bonner described the dismal atmosphere in 1937, when people sat in their homes hoping that the state security organs would come to take their neighbors away instead. "Conversation stopped when we heard the elevator and the door slamming," she recalled. "Then we would all resume talking. At once. Loudly. Or did it just seem loud? We were waiting in Lida's room, the way we did at the Luxe at night. The way everyone did everywhere. But the time for us hadn't come yet."[137]

In those days, the "house on the embankment," the large apartment complex near the Kremlin where the Soviet ministers and party functionaries lived, resembled a way station for future prisoners. Yuri Trifonov commemorated it in his autobiographical novel of the same name (*Dom na nabereshnoi*).[138] From his Kremlin window Stalin could watch as lights went out in the apartments when functionaries were picked up by the NKVD. He seemed to enjoy this role as master over life and death. He would sometimes call his victims and reassure them that everything would be fine, despite having just given the order to have them arrested. Others, such as the writers Boris Pasternak and Mikhail Bulgakov, were fortunate because, for although they received a phone call from the dictator, he also elected to spare their lives. In all likelihood he appreciated that they neither pretended nor cajoled him nor lied to him. Furthermore, what relevance did a writer possess if no one got to read his books anyway? If there was ever a time when the leadership exerted total control over the state and party apparatuses, this was it, and in the end it would be the functionaries' undoing. Apart from its chairman, Nikolai Bulganin, none of the leading representatives of the Moscow Soviet lived to see the end of 1937.[139]

It was not just the party and state agencies that were required to offer sacrifices in the year of the terror. The violence devoured the NKVD apparatus as well. Stalin's Praetorians were just as helpless as the victims they arrested and killed. Most Chekists were members of ethnic minorities—Jews, Latvians, and Georgians in particular—who were unable to forge alliances outside of the circle of power. Many Chekists had been members of other revolutionary parties before the revolution or had participated in morally reprehensible crimes of particular cruelty. Stalin knew that minorities or criminals, who were stained with blood from their services to the revolution, could not simply give up their murderous ways. They had no choice but to continue bringing the dictator the sacrifices he demanded. But this made them vulnerable since they had no weapons that they could have directed at their master. Stalin could have them removed at any moment. He needed only point out that they had been enemies before the revolution, suggest that they were working for foreign powers now, and that would be the end of them. Who would bother defending apolitical cynics and professional executioners who nobody liked anyway? And so, in spring 1937 Stalin let violence wreak havoc in the NKVD as well. Yezhov killed Yagoda's entire staff and had them replaced with his own people. He also ordered the arrest of all Chekists in the provinces who were suspected of having ties to former oppositionists. It was not long before loyal supporters of the new NKVD boss were also deployed to the provinces, but they faced the same dilemma as those who had been arrested. How were they supposed to do their work without ultimately becoming victims of the violence themselves?[140]

In March 1938 the Hungarian economist Eugen Varga dared to write Stalin a letter, apparently under the mistaken assumption that the dictator was unaware of what was happening. "Under the current conditions," his letter began, it would be "absolutely right to arrest two innocents rather than letting even a single spy get away." At the moment, however, people were being arrested without ever discovering the reason why. Some were being arrested, while others were being spared, and no one knew why. A "dangerous atmosphere of panic," he reported, had spread among the foreign Communists. Many had adopted the habit of collecting their belongings "every night in anticipation of their possible arrest." Others had "become partially insane due to the constant fear" and were "unable to work." Varga explained further, "This mood suggests that being arrested is no longer considered a disgrace—as it was one year ago—but rather a misfortune. Instead of despising them, they pity the detainees."[141]

THE OMNIPOTENCE OF THE DESPOT

Stalin was throughout the master of the process. He instigated Yezhov to provide him with new information about traitors and spies and supply him with lists containing the names of suspects. No one among Stalin's devotees walked in and out of his office during 1937 more often than Yezhov.[142] In the year of terror, the dictator preoccupied himself with techniques of violence and methods of killing. He had ceased to govern because his work of destruction was now more important. In June 1937, as the terror reached a climax, Yezhov presented his master with a daily collection of interrogation protocols, NKVD dossiers, denunciation letters, and lists containing the names of state and party functionaries destined for execution. Stalin read what he had been given avidly. He underlined passages in the letters and used the margins to make notes on those mentioned by name. He even decided what charges would be raised against those he condemned to death. In July 1937 when the party leader of Tajikistan informed Stalin that the chairman of the republic's Central Executive Committee, Shotemor, had been expelled from the party because of "counterrevolutionary activities," Stalin added a handwritten note to the bottom of the letter: "Shotemor must be expelled from the party as an English spy." No one will ever know for certain if Stalin read through every list of candidates for death, but it would seem contrary to his nature to sign them without verifying that the NKVD had carried out its assignments with due diligence. In some cases, he turned death sentences into prison sentences or crossed a name off the list. In most cases, however, all those whose names were on the lists were sent to their deaths with a stroke of Stalin's pen. On December 12, 1938 alone, Stalin signed death orders for 3,167 people. Between February 1937 and October 1938, he was given 383 lists with the names of 44,477 leading state functionaries, army officers, and state security personnel. Of these, 38,955 were shot with Stalin's personal approval.[143]

Convicting spies and traitors on the basis of evidence collected by the NKVD was not at the top of Stalin's list of priorities. Anyone could be a traitor, and the "organs" needed to kill as many people as possible to make sure that no potential enemy could escape. On June 2, 1937, Stalin told the Military Council that some people believed that only those with socially alien backgrounds or who had sided with Trotsky in the past could be enemies. This, however, was wrong. It was also un-Marxist and "biological." Was it not common knowledge that Lenin himself had been a nobleman, Engels a factory owner, and Chernyshevsky the son of a pope? Although Felix Dzerzhinsky and the Politburo member Andrei Andreyev had once supported Trotsky, they had never proven themselves disloyal. Others, however, had invoked their proletarian backgrounds but then turned out to be "villains." People, he declared, should not be judged by their background but by their actions.[144] The message could hardly have been clearer: anyone could be an enemy now—workers, peasants, nobility, kulaks, supporters of Stalin just as much as friends of Trotsky. There was only one way out of this dilemma. The terror had to cross all boundaries. It needed to spread like an ulcer into every corner of Soviet society to ensure that no enemy would survive the great cleansing tempest.

Stalin's absolute power grew out of the boundlessness of the terror. Wherever functionaries denounced each other and succumbed to fear, Stalin assumed the role of master of life and death. Stalin rarely convened the Central Committee and the Politburo anymore. He himself was now the Central Committee. Although he occasionally had the members of the Politburo countersign when he issued one of his terror orders, this was a mere formality by now. From now on, all important decisions were made in his office or at his dacha in Kuntsevo, outside of Moscow, where Politburo members met to dine and drink with the dictator. By mid-1937 Stalin could do things that, one year earlier, would have required the approval of others. He also stopped writing letters, as everyone knew what had to be done to satisfy him. Stalin's stooges were now at his beck and call. When Stalin grew tired of someone they had that person arrested and killed without delay. There was no need to even supply a reason anymore. When Stalin decided to remove Ian Rudzutak from the Politburo and have him executed he no longer needed anyone's approval. As Molotov recalled, Stalin had always been on good terms with Rudzutak. But then he ordered to have him shot.[145]

Stalin expected his cronies to submit to him unconditionally, and he demanded loyalty to the point of self-abandonment. Whoever betrayed this loyalty violated the code of brotherhood that Stalin had brought with him from his Georgian homeland. Friendship and personal loyalty had a different meaning for him than for the "European" Bolsheviks. His notions of friendship had been shaped in a perilous world of war and violence, where mistrust toward strangers, who were beyond one's control, was not just acceptable but was considered a virtue. In a world where nothing was stable, friendships needed to be secured with tokens of loyalty. "We have to respect each other and rely on each other," Stalin wrote to Ordzhonikidze in September 1937. "We may not only demand respect for ourselves, we also have to respect the others. I'm talking about the members of our circle of leadership, which did not emerge by coincidence and must remain unified and inseparable. Then everything will go well."[146]

Anyone who was disloyal forfeited his honor, because disloyalty was a betrayal of the most important principle of all—the unwavering friendship between men. Stalin's model of rule was similar to that of a band of robbers who conformed to the rules of the "Honorable Society." In summer 1932 Stalin invited the German Communist Heinz Neumann and some of his followers to dinner at his country retreat near Sochi, where he presented them with a grotesque drama. Neumann for his part would never forget the experience. His wife recalled it vividly:

> Many guests had already gathered in front of the villa when an old Caucasian stepped onto the terrace and was given a warm welcome by Stalin. Then, in accordance with the duties of a host, he introduced him to the others with the following words: "This is Comrade X, my assassin . . ." The bystanders looked up, astonished and bewildered, whereupon Stalin affably explained that the guest in question had forged a terrorist plot against him not so long ago, with no other intention than to murder him. This attack had failed however, thanks to the vigilance of the GPU, and the assassin had been condemned to death. But he, Stalin, deemed it proper to pardon this old man, who had, after all, simply acted out of nationalist infatuation, and in order for him to feel that the hatchet had been buried once and for all, he had invited him to Mazesta as his guest . . . During this lengthy exposition the old man stood before the flock of guests with a downcast gaze.[147]

Stalin could have people killed, or he could grant them the gift of life. Either way, the decision was based on his mood at the time. Those who were present to witness this spectacle realized that their own fate also rested in his hands. Five years later, in November 1937, Neumann was shot in Moscow. Stalin, in the meantime, had become master of life and death. Once no one contradicted him anymore his friends became clients who had no choice but to submit to their patron. The Stalinist ideology of loyalty became the ideology that his associates were forced to follow. Brotherhood and the covenant of loyalty became the ideals of the Stalinist order.

But the demand for loyalty also bred mistrust and suspicion. Stalin could not always be sure that his followers would surrender to him unconditionally and by their own volition. So to ensure that they behaved as he desired, he played them off against each other, entrusted them with the execution of heinous crimes, and subjected them to various tests. "Stalin was extremely vigilant and very careful," Kaganovich recalled forty years later, as he explained to the historian Kumanev why he had turned his own brother over to the despot. As Mikoyan recalled it, Stalin trusted no one, not even him, an old companion from the Caucasus. In summer 1937 when Mikoyan came to Yerevan to oversee the arrest of Armenian Communists he went before the Central Committee, and something very unusual happened: "To my complete surprise Beria suddenly appeared. He entered the room as I gave a speech at the podium. . . . I assumed that Stalin had ordered him to come and arrest me there at the plenum. However I hope that I was able to conceal my anxiety and he didn't notice it."[148]

Only those who were prepared to offer sacrifices to the dictator could gain his trust. The brothers of Ordzhonikidze and Kaganovich, both high-ranking officials in the Soviet economic bureaucracy, were arrested and killed on Stalin's orders. He had Nikita Khrushchev's daughter-in-law arrested; the son of the Finnish Communist leader and Comintern functionary Otto Kuusinen, was hauled off to prison too. The same fate befell the wife of Stalin's secretary Poskrebyshev. The wife of Kalinin, the nominal head of state, was thrown into a camp for having spoken ill of Stalin. In 1938 Stalin drove Yezhov's wife to suicide, before the almighty head of the NKVD fell from grace himself. Eventually even Molotov would be forced to make a similar sacrifice after the war, when Stalin had his wife arrested and taken to a camp; they would not be reunited until after the death of the tyrant. Kalinin, Kaganovich, and Molotov all passed the dictator's test because they had approved of the arrest of their wives and relatives without hesitation. Furthermore, they had recognized Stalin's right to test their loyalty in this manner. Kaganovich once wrote to Stalin, "You not only have an official, political right, but also a comradely-moral right to give orders to someone you have shaped politically—this also includes me, your pupil."[149] Those who were able to withstand the psychological violence that the dictator inflicted on those around him revealed that their loyalty to the leader meant more to them than their loyalty to their families. Only those who remained steadfast in the face of such terror would remain in the dictator's circle of friends.

No one could know in advance what Stalin's next move would be or what he would do with his followers, his friends, or his relatives. It was near impossible to expect or anticipate anything, and it was this very insecurity and unpredictability that the Stalinist style of despotism was based on. Stalin even gave orders to have his own close relatives killed. Stanislav Redens, one of the Soviet Union's highest-ranking NKVD officers and the husband of Stalin's sister-in-law Anna Alliluyeva, was killed for no apparent reason by order of Stalin. Sometimes, however, Stalin did remember his old friends from the Caucasus and sent them money or prevented their executions. In 1937 Stalin's longtime Georgian companion Sergei Kavtaradze was arrested, accused, along with Budu Mdivani, of having plotted against Stalin. Kavtaradze's wife was arrested too and then cruelly tortured. In the end, Mdivani, who had once been one of Stalin's closest friends, was shot. Kavtaradze, however, was more fortunate: the dictator put a horizontal line next to his name on the death list, and so he was spared.

Then in 1939 Stalin remembered his old friend again and had him summoned from the Lubianka. Kavtaradze was made deputy minister of foreign affairs and subsequently became Soviet ambassador to Romania. In Stalin's empire, it was possible to face doom one day and be appointed minister the next. More often than not, though, it was the other way round. If we are to believe Simon Sebag Montefiore, who later spoke to Kavtaradze's daughter Maya, then we must imagine Stalin as a cold-blooded psychopath. The Kavtaradzes had only just moved into their new Moscow apartment when they were paid a visit by Stalin and Beria late one evening. They dined and drank into the early morning, feasting on Georgian delicacies from the restaurant "Aragvi." Stalin asked who had tortured Kavtaradze's wife so severely—she had turned completely grey during her short-lived confinement. He then sat the young Maya on his lap and began to sing. "There he was short and pock-marked. Now he was singing!" Maya was enchanted and frightened to an equal degree. "He was so kind, so gentle—he kissed me on the cheek and I looked into his honey-coloured, hazel, gleaming eyes, . . . but I was so anxious." Kavtaradze himself remembered how Stalin had summoned him after his release from prison. Stalin's parting words to him had been, "Nevertheless, you all wanted to kill me." A cold shiver had run down his spine.[150]

According to the historian Robert Tucker, if Stalin had written memoirs, they would have amounted to nothing more than a second edition of the *Short Course of the History of the Communist Party.*[151] But there is nothing to suggest that Stalin was acting under ideological constraints when he ordered people tortured and killed. Stalin was a murderer who took pleasure in destruction and harm. The ideological framework provided by the canonical texts was simply a means of justifying his misdeeds. In the inner circle of power he spoke openly of repression. If Stalin had written memoirs, it probably would have been a long series of stories about conspiracies and traitors. It would have revealed nothing of the dictator's inner being, nothing of his intentions and his convictions—for Stalin never revealed his actual thoughts in public. But such knowledge is not essential for an understanding of Stalinist violence. Stalin's actions followed a pattern that was clearly recognizable to people both of his time and of years to come. While the pattern can be interpreted in various ways, it is a pattern that can be identified, and this alone is what counts.

Stalin was a violent criminal. His murderous excesses had to continuously increase in intensity because every misdeed performed compelled subsequent action. Once someone had been arrested and tortured, the chances of ever being released were slim. A survivor would have been a visible representation of Stalin's cruelty, a reminder to the dictator that there were people who would never forget what had been done to them. Stalin never forgot, and he assumed that it was the same for others. In his Georgian homeland, a murderer had to reckon with revenge from the victim's relatives, and a blood feud could only be averted if the perpetrator killed or incapacitated all of his opponent's kin. When it came to dealing with the enemies of the Soviet people and their families Stalin followed the same logic. In June 1937, after the fall of Genrikh Yagoda, Stalin ordered Yagoda's entire retinue as well as all his people in the NKVD shot in the Dmitrovsk labor camp. Their corpses were to be deposited near the former NKVD leader's dacha, as a reminder that clients rose and fell with their patrons. Genghis Khan was said to have claimed that the victor could not live in peace until he had killed the vanquished. Whether this is true or not it apparently struck a chord with Stalin, as he underlined it in a history of Eurasian conquest he had read.

In November 1937, on occasion of the anniversary of the October Revolution, Stalin, sitting with his closest confidants, raised his glass in a toast. He also used the occasion to speak of the extermination of clans and families. The Comintern chairman Georgi Dimitrov later recorded Stalin's words in his diary: "And we will destroy each and every such enemy, even if he was an old Bolshevik; we will destroy all his kin, his family. We will mercilessly destroy anyone who, by his deeds or his thoughts—yes, his thoughts—threatens the unity of the socialist state. To the complete destruction of all enemies, themselves and their kin!"[152]

Hostage-taking and collective punishment became an integral part of the system of fear in the years of the Great Terror. Families of the arrested were also taken hostage, as a further means of forcing confessions out of the accused. Even after an "enemy" had already been killed, his wife, children, and relatives were forced to continue his suffering. On June 19, 1937, Stalin ordered Yezhov to have the wives of Radek, Bukharin, Rudzutak, Yagoda, Tukhachevsky, and other arrested generals "deported from Moscow immediately." Days later, on July 5, he gave orders to arrest all the wives of Trotskyites and spies who had been convicted of treason and to lock them up in the camps near Narym in Siberia and Turgai in Kazakhstan for five to eight years. Their children were to be sent to NKVD orphanages. In November 1937 Yezhov, for the first time, supplied Stalin with a list that contained the names of not just arrested Communists, army officers, and NKVD personnel but their wives as well. He requested that the wives be executed as well, and not surprisingly Stalin gave his approval.

Over time, Stalin's followers slowly internalized his system until it became normality for them. "Why were the repressions extended to wives and children?" the journalist Felix Chuev asked Molotov. "What do you mean, why?" Molotov replied. "They had to be isolated somehow. Otherwise they would have served as conduits of all kinds of complaints."[153]

MASS TERROR

Terror raged throughout the land. It was not just Communists and generals who were struck down by it. It seeped into and corroded every stratum of Soviet society. From the very beginning, managers, factory directors, and kolkhoz chairmen had been blamed for unfulfilled plan

targets, damaged goods, and accidents. The terror made its first real de-
but during the early stages of the second Five Year Plan. Between 1933
and 1936, in the Donbass alone, more than fifteen hundred managers
and engineers were arrested as "saboteurs" or "wreckers" and were
either sent to concentration camps or shot.[154] In early 1937 the director of a textile factory in Smolensk, along with his closest associates,
was arrested and accused of falsifying plan quotas, failing to organize
work uniforms for sewing workers, and only paying upper-level employees. "Poloskov's activity," the NKVD reported to Moscow, "was
aimed at generating mass discontent among the workers." And was this
really a big surprise? The director was, after all, the head of a "terrorist,
Trotskyite group." This kind of stigmatization also served the purpose
of negative integration. Workers and peasants were in a position of
helplessness and powerlessness. Although they could do nothing about
their own condition they could at least denounce unpopular managers
and directors and have them arrested. Stalin's henchmen simply had to
wait for the workers to become disgruntled and turn their bosses in.
The so-called shock workers, in particular, were more than happy to
accept the offer to denounce enemies.[155]

In late August 1935 a miner in Irmino in the Donbass by the name
of Alexei Stakhanov extracted 102 tons of coal in a single shift. This
was a fourteenfold outperformance of the norm. In reality the local
party committee had helped out a bit. They had staged this socialist
competition in the first place and then allocated two additional workers to help Stakhanov set the record. News of Alexei Stakhanov's heroic deed spread like wildfire, and by September *Pravda* was already
speaking of a "Stakhanovite movement." Stalin and his people instantly
recognized the potential strength inherent in this movement. Ordzhonikidze, for example, understood very well that shock work and socialist competition were the perfect tools for countering managers when
they complained about unreasonable plan targets. Furthermore, this
was a means of demonstrating that technological backwardness could
be compensated for by iron will. Managers who opposed this lunacy
were also easy prey for proletarians seeking to rise in the ranks, as it
was easy to accuse them of having defeatist attitudes and lacking belief
in the victory of the common cause.

Before long, the Stakhanovite movement had become the organizing
principle of the Soviet economy. By winter 1935 it had taken hold of

all branches of industry and even the cotton plantations in the Caucasus and Central Asia. Stakhanovites moved mountains. They were Bolshevik men of action, and they paid no heed to the reservations of concerned bourgeois experts. The whole business pleased Stalin greatly, and in late November 1935 he announced in *Pravda* that the "struggle for high quotas" would have to be "developed in all branches of production." In order to demonstrate that the new style was commensurate with the dictator's will, Stalin appeared at shock workers' congresses, invited Stakhanovite heroes to the Kremlin, and posed with them on the front page of *Pravda*. Stakhanovites were granted privileges and bonuses. They were given exclusive access to shops that were normally reserved for Communist functionaries. Stakhanov himself was given a car and a luxurious apartment, and he became a living example of what could be achieved if one surrendered oneself completely to the rules of the Stalinist war economy. This, however, was also why Stakhanovites were met with rejection and hatred by the workers and peasants. The Stakhanovites increased the pressure on building sites and in the factories. They caused quotas to be raised, and they were given privileges that no one else had. And yet their achievements brought Soviet industry absolutely nothing. They were entrusted with machinery that they did not know how to handle, so they disrupted the production process and caused accidents. Furthermore, in the areas of industry where muscular strength did not matter shock work only resulted in damage and ultimately ruined production. What was the use of manufacturing a record number of products in a record amount of time if no one wanted them anyway? What good were harvested cotton and potatoes that decayed out in the open because there were no depots to store them in?[156]

But the production of useful goods was not what really mattered. The Stakhanovite movement mobilized resentments. It polarized, it caused strife, and it uncovered the hidden enemies who dared to doubt that the Bolshevik project would really succeed. As early as September 1935, within weeks of the first shock worker campaigns, Ordzhonikidze declared his certainty that the Stakhanov method would lure "saboteurs and wreckers" out of their hideouts. In November 1935 Stalin himself addressed the delegates at the first all-Union conference of Stakhanov workers. He warned them that there were saboteurs and wreckers about who opposed the class struggle. Managers and directors who resisted the new work methods, Stalin promised, would receive "little slaps in the face."

The Stakhanovite movement was a cadre revolution, and it provided a new recruitment pool from which to draw the party elite. In 1936, in the Donbass alone, more than three hundred Stakhanovite workers were promoted to leading positions. At the same time, the movement was a "political pogrom" directed against technicians, specialists, and directors. Those who protested the destructive acts of the shock workers could be arrested, prosecuted in show trials, or paraded through the streets as saboteurs. The regime could also blame them for accidents, production losses, and bad harvests—even when it was really the Stakhanovites who were at fault. By 1937, being a technician or a director had become a life-threatening profession. By April 1938, in the Donbass alone, a quarter of all engineers and managers had been arrested by the "organs." Some companies eventually had no specialists left at all. "They simply disappeared, and it was never clear whether they had been shot," recalled one foreign technician. Production slowly collapsed. Those who were arrested were replaced by younger workers, but they had no professional expertise and were also crippled by the fear of falling victim to the same fate as their predecessors.[157]

Denunciations spread like an epidemic through building sites, mines, and factories. In many cases, the Stakhanovites were the ones who proved their loyalty by denouncing directors who had opposed the ludicrous shock campaigns. Stalin took kindly to such vigilance, and anytime disgruntled workers were unsure of who was to blame for their misery, Stalin was happy to point them in the right direction. When Donbass miners complained about their wretched working and living conditions Stalin immediately let them know who was to blame, telling them, "The director is an enemy of the people." Although blunders and accidents were the fault of workers, the directors generally had to pay for these offenses by being denounced as "saboteurs." To make the difference between workers and enemies more visible, the regime continued staging show trials throughout the years of the Great Terror. The show trials gave men of the fist the opportunity to appear as witnesses and hurl all their stored up rage and hatred at their white-collar masters. But the extreme nature of the terror in the Soviet coal and steel region was also due in part to the local party secretary, who feared that

Stalin might have him arrested and killed and so did his best to personally spur on the violent excesses in the region.[158]

The year 1937 was also a year of dread in the villages. Peasants who lagged behind on their plan targets were accused of sabotage. In early summer 1937 "counterrevolutionary and socially harmful elements" were expelled from the collective farms in the Western Region. All peasants suspected of hiding their pasts from the authorities or sabotaging grain procurement were shot. "In the past two years," wrote the head of the NKVD in Smolensk to Kaganovich, "seventeen soviet and party activists of lower ranks were killed by counterrevolutionary elements, six were wounded, and eighty-three were attacked and beaten, including a significant percentage of Stakhanov people from the kolkhozy and sovkhozy. At the same time counterrevolutionary elements carried out three hundred arson attacks on kolkhoz property and the property of lower-ranking party and soviet activists."[159] Stalin demanded that Bagirov, party boss of Azerbaijan, rid the Nakhchivan border region of human "waste." Bagirov did as he was told and had the populations of entire villages wiped out. Peasants who failed to meet their cotton quotas were arrested and shot.

On August 3, 1937, Stalin sent a telegram to all provincial party secretaries, expressing his dissatisfaction with their repressions. It was impermissible, he wrote, to leave the task of exposing and exterminating agricultural saboteurs up to the NKVD alone. The kolkhoz farmers needed to be enlisted in the struggle against the enemy too. The party committees also needed to organize "two to three show trials" in every district to expose the "enemies of the people," who had allegedly infiltrated the party cells and soviets, trying to advance their malevolent aims. Both the trials and the verdicts would have to be given elaborate coverage in the local press. In the days that followed, Stalin sent dozens of telegrams to the provinces, prompting local party secretaries to address bad harvests, damaged machinery, and accidents in the collective farms by having the "culprits" shot. This reckoning with the enemies of the people would need to be reported in the press. Andrei Andreyev was commissioned by the Politburo to travel to Saratov and get the machine of terror there into gear. In a telegram from July 28, 1937, Stalin wrote to him, "The CC agrees with your proposal to put the former employees of the MTS [Machine-Tractor Stations] on trial and have them shot." Ten days later, he ordered the regional party boss to liquidate more functionaries in the villages: "The CC proposes organizing an accelerated court procedure in the matter of those accused of arson within seven days, condemning them all to death and announcing the shootings in the local press."

The regime gave the peasants the opportunity to seek revenge for injustices they had suffered in the past but without having to hold their true tormentors accountable. By April 1937, in the autonomous Republic of Chuvashia alone, 360 kolkhoz chairmen had been arrested and tried for beating up peasants and overstepping their authority. The Soviet press provided in-depth coverage of the trials and presented the courtroom dramas as acts of vengeance by working people, rising up against enemies and oppressors. Peasants were the avengers and accusers. They vilified the defendants as "crooks," "pigs," and "man-eaters," and wished death upon them. Where terror raged, Stalin saw success. In October 1937, when Siberia's party boss Robert Eikhe briefed the Central Committee on the achievements of Siberian agriculture, Stalin was well aware of the reason for the success. The kolkhoz farmers, of course, had freed themselves from saboteurs, and now "they are happy."[160]

Just as during the Civil War, workers who criticized the leadership or rebelled against disciplinary laws in the factories were met with violence. In early 1935, after Kirov's murder, some forty thousand people were deported from Leningrad. In the summer of that year the NKVD began shooting "kulaks" and "bandits" in the Donbass. Workers who had mocked the deceased Kirov in song or wished death upon Stalin were deported to Siberia on freight trains. Thousands of workers died at the hands of the NKVD execution squads in 1937. In one settlement in the Donbass, a roofer whose only offense had been poor workmanship was shot as a saboteur. Elsewhere, a worker had to die for having attended religious services. Thousands of workers in the Ivanovo district were taken into custody by the NKVD for allegedly having complained about their working and living conditions. In early August 1937 the NKVD in Alexandrovsk reported that the local radio factory contained 112 "socially alien" elements among its 2,000 workers. They had already been banished from Moscow and were now committing sabotage in the factories here. No one has counted the victims of this terror. According to Hiroaki Kuromiya, 50,000 people were shot between 1937 and 1938 just in the Donbass, the steel and coal region of the Soviet Union. These people were workers and peasants.[161]

The mass terror, which began in summer 1937 and continued into the autumn of 1938, was an attempt to intimidate Soviet society, to instill fear and dread, and to remove all potential opponents of the regime. This was what Stalin had in mind in July 1937 when he introduced the resolution to start having people killed by quota. Although it was July when Stalin first announced his plans for mass murder, in all likelihood he had reached the decision much earlier in the year, when a wave of bad news had swept in from the provinces. The bad news was that things were happening that, in the eyes of the party leadership, should not be happening. In many places, citizens were making use of the rights conferred by the new constitution and voiced their opinions regarding their miserable living conditions. What no one had dared to address before was now coming to the surface. In their requests and petitions, peasants invoked the basic tenets of the Stalin Constitution and implored the leadership to reopen the churches and grant the religious freedom that had been promised. In January 1937, immediately before the start of the Central Committee plenum, Kaganovich, Andreyev, and Yezhov received a report from Tamarkin, deputy leader of the Department of Culture and Education, informing them that the priesthood was organizing itself and that no one was preventing its members from conducting anti-Soviet propaganda. Clerics in Ukraine had even dared to send a delegation to Kiev and petition the government to reopen their churches for the faithful. Moreover, priests had organized "processions and demonstrations" on the streets in some areas of the central Volga region. The clerics apparently claimed that such demonstrations were permissible because they were guaranteed by the constitution. In the Black Sea Area, Dukhobors—members of a Christian sect—had reportedly refused to follow the army's draft order and had thrown away their draft cards. Not even the League of the Godless was a refuge of socialist convictions anymore. It too was now "full of Trotskyites and other criminals in a number of places."[162]

Similar information emerged from the second Union-wide census in January 1937. Evidently no one in the party leadership had imagined that peasants and workers would publicly acknowledge that they observed religious practices. The leaders in Moscow were shocked by the answers that more than half of all respondents gave to the census collectors. Surprising news also reached them from the empire's western regions. According to one report Kaganovich received from the local

NKVD leader in Smolensk, 69.9 percent of all adult villagers in the region had described themselves as "people of faith."[163] Stalin had the option of killing the bearers of the bad news—the census organizers— and he did this, but he was still faced with some unpleasant facts.[164] How was it possible that people who supposedly feared the security organs and their violence were willing to speak so openly about the meaning of religion in their lives? Stalin's followers quickly found a Stalinist answer. The reason was that enemies of Soviet power had instigated and indoctrinated the population. The regional party secretaries provided the usual explanations at the Central Committee plenum in March 1937. They spoke of "hostile elements," kulaks and clerics who had exploited the recent campaign for the popularization of the new constitution and the census as a means of spreading their anti-Soviet propaganda. Emelian Yaroslavsky, the chairman of the League of the Godless, conjured up a retinue of powerful enemies who were lying in wait, about to organize "anti-Soviet elections" and subvert the political order. Even in the area near Smolensk, which was only a few hundred miles from Moscow, there were still more than 1,000 churches and 836 clerics. Apparently not even the Baptists or other Protestant sects were afraid of the regime's violence. More than 6,000 sectarians lived in the Smolensk region, and according to the Chekists, they were organized into 200 separate groups, all of which posed a threat to the Soviet order. The only answer, Kaganovich determined, was to have the popes and sectarians arrested and exterminated.

Since 1935, scores of kulaks and clergy had also been returning to their villages from which they had been banished. More than seventy-eight thousand people were covered by the amnesty declared by the regime in August 1935. What reason should they have had for voluntarily submitting to the regime? Those who had lost their homes, their wives and children, who had survived the hunger and the cold—they were forever lost to the socialist experiment. The provincial potentates were forced to face this truth as increasing numbers of peasants returned, demanding to be rehabilitated and given back their property. In March 1937 Yakov Popok, first secretary of the Communist Party of Turkmenistan, delivered the alarming news to the Central Committee that clan leaders who had returned to their villages were invoking their constitutional rights to reclaim their confiscated property. In some villages, the returning kulaks were even allowed to join the collective farms, as there was no longer any reason to deny them membership. In the Siberian countryside, released convicts who were unable to return home had formed robber bands. Not even the cities were safe, as between 1931 and 1937 almost 400,000 former kulaks had fled the villages and special settlements in Siberia and gone into hiding in the cities. Ivan Kabakov, party boss of the Urals, spoke of thousands of "alien elements" that had escaped to the cities during dekulakization and were now seeking rehabilitation. Nowhere did the threat seem greater than in Siberia, the land of camps and special settlements. According to the regional party boss, Robert Eikhe, "passionate enemies" lurked everywhere and were "trying to continue the struggle against the Soviet state by all means." Siberia's villages and cities were supposedly ruled by "backward views and hostile sentiments" that needed to be stamped out. The "flotsam and jetsam" of the revolution—thieves, vagabonds, beggars, orphans, and prostitutes—needed to be countered with the same measures, as the new order needed to be represented by new and obedient men and women only.[165]

As Stalin and his followers saw it, all the people who had been marginalized by the great social upheavals needed to be wiped out. The systematic stigmatization and violence of the regime had produced these outcasts in the first place, but the Stalinist scenario of looming threats was not always based on fantasy alone. In Siberia, bands of thieves composed of released or escaped convicts raided collective farms, trains, and police stations. Cities throughout the Soviet Union were filled with homeless people, violent working-class youths, and criminals who terrorized their surroundings. In the city of Omsk, rapes, lootings, murders, and manslaughter were daily public occurrences, and there was little that the inferior policemen of the Soviet state could do about it. As late as the mid-1930s, the regime was still at war with armed Chechens and Ingushes in the northern Caucasus, who operated from the impassable mountains and carried out raids on outposts of the socialist order. Indeed, Stalin had several concrete examples of genuine threats that could be used to justify his program of murder.

In the northern Caucasus, in eastern Ukraine, and in Siberia, the mass operations to exterminate "bandits," "socially harmful elements," and criminals had already begun in 1933. The railway police had concentrated on rail routes and junctions of major roadways in an attempt at recapturing runaway peasants and arresting criminals who could otherwise have gotten away amid the chaos of collectivization. In spring 1935 the GPU began hunting down "hooligans" and homeless children. 160,000 were ferreted out, and 60,000 were sent to NKVD orphanages. In his commentary on the situation Voroshilov wrote to Stalin, "Why don't we have these rascals shot? Should we wait for them to become grown-up criminals?" The internal passports introduced in 1932 helped the secret police control the movement of subjects and distinguish between friend and foe. But rather than solving the power holders' dilemma, their violent campaigns merely made it visible, as they multiplied the number of outcasts. In early 1937 the head of the NKVD in western Siberia, Sergei Mironov, highlighted the threat once more. Over 9,000 "socially harmful elements," including kulaks, bandits, White Guards, and clergymen, had been registered in the mining district of Kemerovo. Another 200,000 banished kulaks, bandits, vagrants, and beggars were also living in Kusbass and in the Narym area. As Mironov saw it, they posed a threat to the public order. They were all potential spies and saboteurs, ready to pounce at the first available opportunity to forge an alliance with the Japanese against Soviet power, and thus they needed to be eradicated for good.[166]

Reports of this kind pleased Stalin, as they allowed him to give free rein to his lust for destruction. On July 3, 1937, the party organizations of the Soviet republics and regions received a telegram from the dictator, preparing them for the impending violence:

> It has become apparent that the majority of the former kulaks and criminals, who were once banished from various regions into the northern and Siberian regions and returned after the end of their banishment, are the main instigators of all kinds of anti-Soviet and subversive crimes, both in the kolkhozy and sovkhozy as well as in transport and in some areas of industry. The CC of the VKP advises all secretaries of the regional organizations and all representatives of the NKVD in the regions and republics to register all returning kulaks and criminals, so that the most dangerous among them are immediately arrested and shot in an administrative manner by the troikas, and the remaining, less active but equally dangerous elements can be catalogued and banished to regions determined by the NKVD. The CC of the VKP proposes that it be notified of the names of the members of the troikas and also the number of those due to be shot and banished within five days.[167]

As was customary whenever Stalin decided to speak through violence, he left it up to his followers and satraps to decide who would
live and who would die. The death of many ensured the survival of the
few. The dictator's telegram unleashed a torrent of hectic activity in the
provincial party committees and NKVD branches. Within days, Stalin
received the first proposals from party secretaries detailing how they
envisioned the practical implementation of the murder program. The
Moscow party boss Nikita Khrushchev recommended arresting 41,805
people, having 8,500 of them shot, and having the remainder interned
in concentration camps. The head of the NKVD in western Siberia also
indulged in some exorbitant exaggerations. He reported having registered 26,000 people and believed that 11,000 of them should be shot,
while the remaining 15,000 should be sent to camps. On July 9 and
10 the Politburo convened to discuss the proposals from the party secretaries of western Siberia, Bashkiria, North Ossetia, Chuvashia, the
Black Sea Area, the Far Eastern Region, and Azerbaijan. The decision
was made to shoot 6,600 kulaks and 4,200 criminals in western Siberia. In the Black Sea Area 5,721 kulaks and 923 criminals would be
put to death. A further 7,000 would be sent to camps. The plan for
Azerbaijan included the murder of 1,000 kulaks and criminals, along
with the deportation of the families of "bandits" and robbers to camps.
The regime installed troikas in all regions, which were made up of the
regional party secretary, the local NKVD boss, and the prosecutor of
the region. Changes in personnel required Stalin's prior approval, and
he would decide whether to accept the proposals of his people or alter
the composition of the troikas as he best saw fit.

The numbers that the Politburo received from the provincial party
committees served the NKVD as a template for drawing up an operational blueprint. On July 31, 1937, this blueprint was confirmed by the
Politburo as "Order 00447." No one was supposed to know about it,
though, which is why the security organs and party committees that received it in early August were instructed that it was strictly confidential.
In the meantime, Stalin had apparently decided to expand the circle of
victims. The order no longer included just the kulaks who had returned
from banishment or gone into hiding in the cities and major construction sites. Now, the order also included members of former "anti-Soviet
parties," clergymen, sectarians, former White officers and tsarist state
officials, bandits, and criminals. It failed to mention, however, who was

to be shot and who was to be imprisoned. The order merely contained a vague guideline stating that 72,950 people would have to be killed and that 194,000 would have to be interned in concentration camps—differentiated according to region. Relatives of "active" enemies were to be sent to camps, and the family members of the remaining victims were to be deported from their homes and placed under "systematic observation." Although the directive determined how many executions and how many camp detentions each region was supposed to have, the local NKVD bosses could decide at their own discretion how to categorize their prisoners—with those in the first category being destined for death and those in the second category being destined for camp internment: "The state security organs are entrusted with the task of annihilating this entire band of anti-Soviet elements in the most merciless manner." Once again Stalin preferred to limit himself to insinuations, rather than tell his vassals directly what he expected of them. This was not, however, a sign of indecisiveness or lack of direction on Stalin's part. Instead, it represented the very essence of Stalin's technique of governance. He purposely created ambiguity and uncertainty, and the result was always that the violence increased.

The murder campaign was set to begin on August 5, 1937 and was to be concluded in early December of the same year. The previously deployed troikas were to preside over the process. Their task was to decide who would be executed and who would be imprisoned. They were to brief the NKVD leadership on their progress every five days. Yezhov and Stalin nevertheless remained in control of the exterminatory procedure, for although the directive merely set "guideline figures," it prohibited local NKVD leaders from lowering or raising the number of victims at their own discretion. Stalin expected to be given the final say in this matter also.[168]

On July 16, 1937, before the official order was issued, Yezhov summoned the regional NKVD bosses to Moscow to fill them in on the aims of the operation ahead. They were expected to exterminate as many enemies of the people as possible within the coming months. "Strike, annihilate without distinction," he told them. "Better too many than too few." Everyone, he proclaimed, knew that the enemy needed to be annihilated forever. Restraint was therefore ill-advised. Wherever possible the central guidelines were to be improved and if possible surpassed. If this meant shooting "a thousand additional people," this was "no big deal." No one dared to criticize the leadership's plans. Mikhail Shreider recalled how Salygin, the NKVD boss of Omsk, had raised doubts concerning the quota system. Yezhov's response had been to have him arrested immediately. A short time later other NKVD leaders had also been relieved of their posts and shot. Did the remaining regional NKVD leaders really have much choice but to obey, and to carry out the orders given by Stalin and Yezhov?[169]

On July 25 Sergei Mironov called the NKVD bosses of western Siberia to Novosibirsk to prepare them for their future assignment. More than ten thousand people were slated for execution in Siberia, he explained, but the NKVD leaders had permission to shoot up to twenty thousand if they desired. The Chekists, Mironov said, were to seek out remote forest areas, where victims could be shot and buried on the spot. He explained in detail how and where the murders were to be carried out:

> A number of technical questions remain. If we take the operative sector of Tomsk and a few other sectors, then an average of 1,000, in some cases up to 2,000 sentences should be executed in each of these sectors, for example. What is the head of the operative sector to do when he goes there? He must find a place to execute the sentences and a place to bury the bodies. If this happens to be in the forest, then you must mow the grass first and cover up the spot with this grass later, and meanwhile the place where the executions are carried out must remain a secret in every respect, because all these places can become sites of religious fanaticism for counterrevolutionaries and men of faith. The apparatus must be kept in the dark about the place of the executions and the number of condemned whose sentences were being carried out, there is to be no knowledge of this, as our own apparatus could pass on this information.

Those present apparently understood what was expected of them, as their leader's presentation was met with "stormy" applause.[170]

Although the systematic mass murder would not officially begin until early August, the NKVD bosses in western Siberia and the northern Caucasus took the opportunity a bit earlier to demonstrate what they were capable of. They began with their first arrests and shootings at the end of July, while the NKVD in the remaining regions did not begin until after they had received their orders from Yezhov. By September 1937 the security organs throughout the Soviet Union had already arrested 100,000 individuals. In some regions the quotas were maxed out within a matter of weeks. Although the NKVD in western Siberia initially was to shoot "only" 5,000 people, by October they had arrested and assigned almost 14,000 people to the first category (death). While Omsk was not supposed to murder any more than 1,000 people, in December 1937 the local NKVD boss, Gorbach, notified Yezhov that over 11,000 people had already been killed. Gorbach had no other choice. He did not know how many people were being killed in other regions of the Soviet Union, as neither Stalin nor Yezhov told the provincial functionaries what was happening elsewhere, and he, like the other local secretaries and Chekists, was under intense pressure not to "underperform." That is why Gorbach and the other clueless NKVD bosses sought to liquidate as many people as possible—to avoid coming across as underachievers and to avoid falling out of favor.

In the second half of 1937 and in early 1938, regional party secretaries throughout the Soviet Union petitioned Stalin to raise the quotas, in the belief that such displays of zeal would help them win his favor. On February 4, 1938, the party boss of Gorky (formerly Nizhny Novgorod) sent out a telegram informing the leadership that all enemies of the people in his region had already been killed but that an additional 9,000 "anti-Soviet elements" had been discovered. Of these 3,000 would need to be shot and 2,000 interned in camps. Stalin did not disappoint, and in most cases he approved such requests. Although he sometimes informed his functionaries of his decisions orally, quota increases were generally authorized in writing. On August 20, 1937, Stalin sent a telegram to the local party boss in Krasnoyarsk, granting his request to raise the quotas there to include an additional 6,600 shootings. In most cases, he wrote on the requests that he was "in favor" (za) and forwarded them to Yezhov, who was responsible for seeing that the murders were carried out. By December 1937 the Politburo had raised the quotas to include 22,500 additional victims in the first category and 16,800 in the second category. In late January 1938 Stalin gave the order to arrest an additional 57,200 enemies of the people and have 48,000 of them shot by mid-March.[171]

The regime staggered into a frenzy of blood. Although Order 00447 had imposed certain procedural regulations on the organs no one observed them anymore. In most regions, the troikas existed only on paper, and in practice, local party secretaries and NKVD leaders made their own decisions regarding quotas. In most cases, detainees saw neither a judge nor a prosecutor, as their fate was decided upon in their absence. The NKVD bosses in charge amassed fictitious investigation files detailing the offenses and punishments of the accused. Those whose names ended up on the NKVD death lists were simply shot. In this vein the troikas decided people's fates at an astonishing rate. In Omsk on October 10 1937, for example, the local troika managed to condemn 1,301 people to death in a single day. The NKVD officers were under immense pressure to prove their loyalty and determination to their superiors and attempted this by way of anticipatory obedience. Mikhail Shreider and other Chekists who were arrested after the end of the terror remembered how Yezhov had commended Ivanovo's NKVD boss Radzivilovsky for his zeal. As a token of gratitude for his exceptional performance, he had been given permission to raise the arrest quotas in his region. In Moscow, the NKVD officers Semyonov and Yakubovsky engaged in an absurd competition that daily claimed the lives of several hundred victims. Isaya Berg, who was a lieutenant of state security, presided over the executions at the Butovo firing range outside of Moscow, before being arrested himself in August 1938. After his arrest he described his former activities in this manner: "All cases were waved through by Semyonov without the slightest regard for procedural requirements, 400 to 500 cases daily in the troika, where two cases were processed per minute. I must say that Semyonov and Yakubovich competed with each other when it came to the speed of processing the cases. After the meetings Semyonov always went to Yakubovich in his office and gloated over the fact that he had worked through fifty more cases than the latter in the same amount of time, and both laughed about how quickly they had condemned the accused without examining the cases."[172]

In Belorussia, too, the NKVD staged bouts of socialist emulation over who could physically annihilate the most enemies. More than ten thousand prisoners held in the concentration camps were murdered by the security organs. In February 1938 the Politburo issued a directive ordering the NKVD in the Far Eastern Region to shoot an additional twelve thousand people to reduce the number of camp inmates. This murderous measure ultimately claimed the lives of over thirty thousand people, most of whom were prisoners, who had been convicted for political reasons or had defied camp regulations. There could be no camp or prison large enough to accommodate everyone whom the terror campaign had deemed unfit for society. Stalin, however, had a simple solution to this dilemma, and that was to free up space in the prisons and in the camps by allowing the machine of death to power ahead. Those too weak to perform hard labor either starved to death or were killed upon arrest. In some regions, Chekists looked for "pragmatic" solutions to fulfill their quotas. In autumn 1937 the security organs in Yaroslavl began targeting the homeless, thieves, and criminals. The regional NKVD boss Andrei Yershov notified Moscow in January 1938 that his cities had all been "cleansed" of "bandits" and criminals and that the crime rate in the entire region had dropped significantly. In Moscow in 1938 invalids, amputees, and people who were blind or suffering from tuberculosis were also put to death. In Leningrad deaf-mutes were murdered. In February and March 1938 alone, the henchmen of the Moscow NKVD murdered 1,160 people with physical disabilities. As early as September 3, 1937, Stalin had already commissioned an additional troika for the city of Moscow to hasten the reckoning with "kulaks and criminal elements" there.[173]

The Chekists executed people who had always been enemies—former oppositionists, members of the tsarist aristocracy, kulaks returning home from exile, and criminals. In many regions, however, the boundary between friend and foe remained unclear. And even after targets had already been reached, the Chekists still sought out new victims as a means of showing the leadership that they were loyal and reliable. The NKVD in Turkmenistan went to the bazaars and arrested males with long beards who looked as if they could have been Islamic clerics. In some areas, local NKVD leaders decided at their own discretion to expand the circle of victims. In western Siberia, in August 1937, the NKVD boss, Gorbach, ordered the liquidation of everyone who had ever been a soldier or officer in the tsarist army and had been in German captivity. This applied to at least twenty-five thousand people.[174]

Although the victims in NKVD interrogation centers saw neither prosecutor nor judge, they were forced to sign confessions and admit to their involvement in conspiracies and spy rings. Stalin expected the security organs to seek out monarchists and former White officers and prove their involvement in antigovernment plots. The victims were tortured, beaten half to death, confined in cold and narrow cells, and deprived of sleep. The NKVD henchmen broke their ribs and bones or administered electric shocks until the desired confessions could be extracted. Nikolai Kazartsev, who interrogated detainees in 1937, recalled how the deputy people's commissar, Leonid Zakovsky, had not only given detailed instructions on how to treat the victims but also enjoyed beating them personally. "During the interrogation in the Taganka prison Deputy People's Commisar Zakovsky and the deputy boss of the NKVD administration Yakubovich suddenly came to me in the interrogation room, as the culprit was standing against the wall. Zakovsky approached me and yelled at me with obscene curse words: 'Why are you making speeches to him?' and as he kicked the detainee in the stomach he said: 'This is how you interrogate him without encouraging him.' Yakubovich added: 'Show him the ABCs of Communism.' And then they left."[175]

Dmitrii Goichenko, a peasant who had risen within the party and participated in the persecution and terrorization of kulaks in 1930, was later arrested as a "Polish spy" in western Ukraine in November 1937. Upon his arrest he was tortured until he admitted to having plotted to kill the great leader. He described his confinement and interrogation vividly:

> On the morning of July 7 they took me to interrogation. It was already the eighty-first time. They led me into the cellar, and I thought: into the ice cellar again. But after a few zig-zag curves in the cellar labyrinth they led me into a bright room. . . . There were telephones on the table, and a box with signal sounds. From this room you were led through a number of narrow doors in the side walls. Next to that there was another opening, which was locked by an iron grille that led into an even deeper cellar, where, as it turned out, the detainees were shot. Through one of these doors they took me into a very narrow corridor, from where I was led into torture chamber No. 26. It was a small room with small arches toward the ceiling. The walls had been painted a bright yellow and were spattered with blood. They were covered in marks of bloody hands that had tried to hold on to them but had slipped off. The floor was also covered with large bloodstains. The torture chamber strongly smelled of blood.

Goichenko was interrogated by an NKVD man of heavy build who had honed his torture skills from beating and killing people as part of his daily routine:

> With the tremendous might of his heavy fists he punched me on the chest, in the face, in the stomach. Without end he beat the head and

the neck. He held my head down and hit the back of my neck with his hollow hand, so forcefully that I became dizzy and thought my head would fall off. He "worked" almost uninterruptedly and only took short breaks to have a smoke and say a few "amicable" sentences like "Get on the right track, bandit." He pulled out the hairs of my beard, burnt my lips with cigarettes, he pressed his large index finger behind my ears, broke my collar bone. He forced me to stare for hours into the lamp that was directly in front of my head, while he tirelessly continued to punch me in the chest, my throat and between the ribs. I was made to stand throughout the procedure. Even though I no longer even know where it hurt and where it didn't, the pain that was deliberately induced by the executioners was impossible to bear. As inhuman as the punches in the face, on the head or the legs may have been, they proved to be a hundred times less agonizing that the blows to the heart or the left hand, which became completely swollen, discolored and, the longer it took, eventually took on a dark, crimson-blue color. It looked like a gigantic boil. Touching it alone made me dizzy and feel sick. . . . Kostomolov tried to find out where it hurt me the most. This is why I focused all my will-power on not showing him where I was most sensitive.[176]

Goichenko escaped alive, despite all the abuse that Stalin's torturers had devised for him. Such good fortune, however, was rare. Hundreds of thousands were beaten to death or shot because they had fallen into the hands of the NKVD terror apparatus purely by coincidence.

The fate of those condemned to death by the troikas had to be kept under wraps at all costs. The victims were not told what awaited them until their execution was imminent, and relatives who asked the NKVD where their liquidated family members had gone were told that they had been sentenced to "ten years' camp detention without the right to write letters." It was not until much later that the petitioners came to realize what this actually meant. Nonetheless, the henchmen could not conceal the murder program from the public everywhere. By late summer 1937 the NKVD in Ivanovo was already killing people at such a pace that it became increasingly difficult to dispose of all the bodies without arousing unwanted attention. Shreider recalled how the NKVD men shot naked detainees "by the hundreds" in the washrooms of the prison, piling up their bodies before they were hastily buried on the compound. The NKVD henchmen in Oryol shot their victims in the forests outside the city, but they lacked due diligence in their task, as kolkhoz farmers discovered limbs protruding from the topsoil shortly after the shootings. In Kuybyshev on the Volga, too, peasants found corpses scattered through the forest that had been left the previous September (1937) by the NKVD death squads. This, however, was not acceptable. The regional NKVD boss informed Stalin that the leader of the death squad responsible for this "provocative hostile act" had been arrested. Whoever failed to master the craft of killing deserved to die like the others.

The NKVD executioners "worked" without interruption, as each victim had to be executed individually via revolver shot. These murder assignments were not carried out in the prisons but in secluded areas, in graveyards or on shooting ranges outside the cities. Between August 1937 and October 1938 a four-man NKVD execution squad on the Butovo firing range near Moscow shot more than twenty thousand people dead, and in Leningrad the Chekists murdered forty-seven thousand people just outside the city limits. As soon as the Moscow troikas had reached their "verdicts," the prisoners were loaded onto trucks and driven out to Butovo. They usually reached their destination around midnight and would then be led to barracks where the executioners were waiting for them. Only then were they told what fate awaited them. They were forced to undress and stand in front of trenches and were then shot in the neck by the NKVD men. Sometimes the victims were beaten before their execution so that they would not call out Stalin's name in their final moments. The executioners worked into the early morning hours, shooting between three hundred and five hundred prisoners each night. In order to endure what was demanded of them, they drank vodka, ladled out of buckets. Once their bloody task was complete, they washed themselves of the blood of their victims with eau de Cologne, ate a good meal, and drove back to Moscow still drunk. Peasants from the surrounding villages descended upon the shooting range in the evening to bury the corpses and dig new trenches. This bloody spectacle was repeated night after night and day after day. By early summer 1937, however, the Chekists had to order a bulldozer because the trenches that had been dug manually could no longer hold all the corpses.[177]

This is what it was like throughout the Soviet Union where people were shot by the thousands. In the Bikin death camp, which was located along the Khabarovsk-Vladivostok rail route in the far east of the Soviet Union, the murders were also carried out by only a small group of Chekists. One of them recalled how four cars with six camp inmates each would be driven out to a hilltop near the camp every morning. This was where the prisoners were shot. Their bodies were then buried by specially assigned criminal convicts, who also dug new trenches for the next batch of victims. "We yelled: 'Get out! Get in line!' They crawl out, and the trench before them has already been dug out. They stand there, squirming, and we shoot at them immediately. . . . We drove back to the camp, turned in our rifles, and then we drank at the state's expense, as much as we wanted." More than fifteen thousand people were killed in this particular manner. In Kuybyshev, the perpetrators alternated between various different execution scenarios. Over six hundred victims were strangled with thick ropes, and in the camps of Magadan, twenty-five hundred prisoners were shot with machine guns. In Kharkov Chekists beat their victims to death. In Zhitomir a sixty-seven-year-old woman was slain by an NKVD officer using a spade, and in the small town of Kansk, near Krasnoyarsk, the perpetrators chopped their victims into pieces with sabers to make room for more bodies in the trenches. NKVD officers in Moscow were apparently so overextended that they had to deploy gas wagons in which the prisoners were killed on the way to Butovo. The Chekists reportedly filled the cargo space with poison gas, until the victims, who had been stripped naked and tied up, choked to death.[178]

How did the Chekists cope with having to do such horrible things to their victims? For violent criminals, men who had been trained in the craft of killing, these circumstances were a dream come true. The project of mass terror gave them the opportunity to demonstrate everything they had learned in the NKVD. Stanislav Redens, the husband of Stalin's sister-in-law and head of the Moscow NKVD, selected the executioners himself. He would occasionally take lists of the condemned home with him, where he would enjoy a cup of tea while marking out the designated killing zones in Butovo and deciding the order in which the victims were to be shot. Although neither Redens nor Yezhov's deputy were obligated to torture and kill their victims themselves they enjoyed doing so. Vasili Blokhin, the commandant of the Lubianka, also took part in the mass executions on the Butovo firing range. Blokhin, after all, was a professional killer; he murdered without remorse, and he took nothing but satisfaction in his work. As his colleagues recalled, he had a habit of putting on a cinnamon-colored leather apron, leather gaiters, and rubber boots before setting off to kill his victims. Stalin thought highly of Blokhin. In autumn 1938, when the mass killings finally ended, Stalin had Blokhin spared, and in 1940 Stalin sent him to Kalinin (formerly Tver) where he was commissioned to shoot several thousand Polish officers. The Stalinist system needed these sadistic and violent perpetrators. They accomplished the bloody tasks that the office desk perpetrators were capable of imagining but not actually carrying out. Without them, the practical implementation of the Stalinist murder program would never have been possible. These were men who, when allowed to murder, were very much in their element. And as long as it pleased the dictator they remained there.[179]

By 1937 there was no escaping the violence, neither for the psychopaths nor for the careerists. All those with blood on their hands found themselves in the predicament that they had to continue the killing if they wanted to avoid being killed themselves. Stalin's executioners had no choice, for they knew full well that the torturer of today could easily become the victim of tomorrow. They were confronted with this reality on a daily basis, as they watched colleagues fall out of favor, be arrested, and then disappear into the NKVD dungeons to be tortured and shot. This made for a kind of psychological pressure that only hardened psychopaths and violent perpetrators could tolerate. At the same time, however, there were also Chekists who despaired. They were traumatized, they lost their minds, or they took their own lives. In October 1937 all "Trotskyites" in the Magadan concentration camp were taken from their barracks and shot in the nearby forests. A member of the death squad present recalled how this experience "left such a strong impression on me and my comrades that I literally walked around in a daze for several days." One driver tasked with burying the dead on the Butovo firing range described becoming unable to sleep at night. His wife recalled how he would sit on his bed with a loaded revolver, night after night, muttering to himself, "They will take revenge on me."[180]

The perpetrators did not forgot what they had done to their victims either. "When I got posted to the NKVD, I was incredibly proud," one former NKVD officer recalled years later during perestroika:

From my first salary I bought myself a good suit. . . . Whenever I shot a German, he would yell in German, whereas the others, they yelled in

Russian. . . . They were our own people somehow. . . . Shooting at Lithuanians and Poles was easier. But the Russians, they yelled in Russian. . . .
At the end we were always covered in blood, we wiped our hands clean
on our own hair. . . . Sometimes we were given leather aprons. . . . Our
work was no picnic! Whenever someone wasn't dead immediately, he fell
over and squealed like a pig. . . . spitting blood. . . . Screaming and cursing on both sides. . . . You weren't allowed to eat anything beforehand.
. . . I for one couldn't do it. At the end of the shift they always brought
us two buckets—one full of Vodka and one full of eau de Cologne. . . .
With the Cologne we would wash our entire upper bodies. Blood has an
intense smell. . . . a very specific smell. . . . Sort of like sperm. . . . I had
a dog, a shepherd, he would always avoid me when I came home from
work. . . . If one of the soldiers was found to enjoy the killing, he was removed from the firing squad and transferred. We didn't like such people.
But they existed too. . . . Many of us came from the countryside, like
me, people from the countryside are tougher than city folk. . . . But we
were slowly introduced to this task. . . . The first days the newcomer just
watched the executions or guarded the condemned. Sometimes someone
lost his mind. It isn't so simple, after all. . . . Even when you're killing a
rabbit, you need practice, not everybody can do it. . . . You let the condemned get down on his knees, then a shot from up close in the head, to
the left above the ear. . . . We had Nagant pistols. I'm almost deaf on the
right ear. . . . You shoot with the right hand, you see. . . . I pushed through
my demand for a massage of the right arm and the right index finger
twice a week with my superiors. Compulsory, for everyone. We were
given certificates. . . . They were awarded for the "fulfillment of a special
assignment for the party." I have a whole cabinet full of these certificates,
printed on the best kind of paper. Twice a year we were sent to a good
sanitarium with our families. The food there was excellent. . . . Lots of
meat. . . . Good treatments. . . . One time we loaded the condemned onto
boats and steered out to the open seas with them. . . . On the way back
the boats were empty. . . . There was a deathly hush. Everyone had only
one thought: When we get back on land, we too will. . . . This is how we
lived. I always had a packed plywood suitcase under my bed: a change of
clothes, toothbrush, razor. And a pistol under my pillow. To put a bullet
in my head. This is how we lived. . . . Everybody lived like this! Whether
soldier or marshal. . . . We were all equal in that respect. . . . I was arrested after the victory. The NKVD people had special lists. . . . I got
seven years! I served the whole term. To this day . . . I wake up early at
six in the morning, like in the camp. What I was inside for? They didn't
tell me what I was inside for. . . . What for? . . . They will call Stalin a
great man someday. The hatchet outlives its master.[181]

THE NATIONAL OPERATIONS

The terror spared no one, neither Communists nor the partyless, neither workers nor peasants. It was the hallmark of Stalinist terror that it respected no boundaries and that it no longer distinguished between friend and foe. In the second half of 1937 Stalin and his cronies also began targeting ethnic minorities. Poles, Germans, Finns, Latvians, Estonians, or Iranians were no longer just members of a nation. They were now agents of foreign powers and threats to the security of the Bolshevik state. Indifference to the nation of origin was no longer a valid excuse, as it was not for the victims to decide who they wanted to be and what life they wanted to live. It was not possible to simply opt out of one's national background, just as affirmations of loyalty to Soviet power were of no help to the kulaks or priests. Most Bolsheviks understood very well that workers and Communists were also members of nations. Otherwise they would never have divided the Soviet Union into national republics and regions, indigenized the administration, or established social hierarchies along ethnic lines. It would be fully erroneous to claim that the concept of the nation was irrelevant to the Bolsheviks. On the contrary, Stalin and his followers were in fact prisoners of their own essentialist notions and animosities. They had very clear conceptions regarding the reliability of national collectives. Jews, Stalin believed, were "cowards" and "parasites." Americans meanwhile belonged to a nation of "dealers." Poles and Germans made "good soldiers."[182] Sometimes Stalin's characterizations were particularly absurd. On April 22, 1941, he told a group of Tajik artists who had been invited to the Kremlin, "The Tajik people are a special people, they possess an old, rich culture. They tower above the Uzbeks and Kazakhs." In an exchange with a number of *Pravda* journalists, Stalin described the Tajiks as "the most ancient people of all peoples in Central Asia." Further, he told the reporters, "They are people with an ancient culture. You have probably noticed that the art by these people is finer, that they understand and feel art in a more subtle way. They are a people whose intelligentsia has brought forth a Ferdowsi, and it is not for nothing that the Tajiks trace their cultural traditions back to him."

The dictator described himself as anything but a rootless Communist. Stalin could not have been one even if he had wanted to be. His appearance and manner of speech very much betrayed his origins as

Georgian. As Stalin's interpreter, Vladimir Yerofeyev, recalled it was difficult to understand the despot, as he spoke with a toneless voice and made "many grammatical errors." Stalin was neither a Russian nor a European, and he made it a point not to be a cosmopolitan, but a Georgian. At a Kremlin reception on November 7, 1938, in celebration of the anniversary of the revolution, Georgi Dimitrov, chairman of the Comintern, made the mistake, while speaking in praise of Stalin, of failing to pay heed to the dictator's origins. "Comrade Dimitrov, pardon me for interrupting you, but I am no European," he said. "I am a Russified Georgian-Asian."[183]

Stalin represented the national obsessions of the multiethnic Bolshevik elite, who could only conceive of social realities in national forms. Mikoyan, Ordzhonikidze, Beria, Kaganovich, Rudzutak, Yezhov, and several other members of the inner circle of leadership were either members of ethnic minorities themselves, had grown up in the multiethnic border regions of the tsarist empire, or had acquired political experience there. As they understood it, there was no contradiction between social and ethnic conflicts because at the periphery, social antagonisms were reduced to national antagonisms. If all Ukrainians and Georgians were peasants, then the protests against collectivization could also be interpreted as acts of national defiance. The national obsessions of the Stalinist elite stemmed from these experiences. Yezhov, who came from Lithuania, was deeply apprehensive toward Poles. Kaganovich, a Jew, detested the anti-Semitism prevalent among Ukrainian and Polish peasants in western Ukraine. Beria was mistrustful of Abkhazians and Armenians, and Stalin considered the mountain peoples of the Caucasus to be disloyal and unreliable.

People were not only members of their classes but eternal hostages of their nations as well. Commitment to one's ethnic heritage was not merely an act of self-assurance. It could also be employed in the daily struggle over scarce resources and privileges. In this regard, the Bolsheviks reaped what they sowed. Mary Leder, an American citizen of Jewish descent, who immigrated to the Soviet Union with her parents in the early 1930s, recalls the residents of Moscow being downright obsessed with the ethnic origin of their neighbors and colleagues. "This obsession extended to all nationalities. 'Do you know the Armenian who lives on the second floor?' 'The Tatar in the foundry?' 'The Assyrian shoe-cleaner?' 'The Georgian teacher?' and so on." According to her, she had not met a single Russian who did not consider the Jews to be a nation and the United States a conglomerate of nationalities.[184]

The public use of ethnic stereotypes is dangerous, as it insinuates that people affiliated with a particular collective also act on behalf of this collective. An Azerbaijani who invoked the "backwardness" of his nation in order to secure advantages at the expense of Armenians and Russians had to reckon with others bringing their ethnicity into play as well. Under these circumstances, citizens could become enemies, especially when the political leadership started to worry that certain ethnic groups were dangerous or disloyal. Of course the ethnic mapping of the empire also altered the perceptions of the Bolshevik leaders. When Lazar Kaganovich visited the Ukrainian-Polish border region on Stalin's orders in 1927, he was indignant over the hatred directed against Communists and Jews by the Ukrainian and Polish peasants. In the Berdichev sugar factory, workers had supposedly openly proclaimed that it was "necessary to settle score with the Communists and Jews." How could the workers of a Soviet state have hated Jews so much? Kaganovich found an explanation that fed off the same resentments as the anti-Semitism of the Ukrainian workers: Polish spies had infiltrated the region and were inciting the workers to revolt against Soviet power. After all, the Ukrainian Poles were "anti-Soviet" and "defeatist" in their attitudes, making them easy prey for Polish intelligence. Polish villages were supposedly in the hands of Catholic clergymen and small groups of "faithful patriots." "These circles are set against the Soviet civil organizations in the Polish settlements, and their influence is exceptionally strong at every turn. They openly agitate among the Polish youth for them to join the Polish Army in case of a war, and the great majority of Polish teachers, who are also under the influence of the clergy, enthusiastically support this agitation." The Soviet authorities had thus far been unable to disrupt contacts between Poles on either side of the border. Almost all Polish residents maintained close relations with their relatives in the neighboring country, and this had led people to spread the rumor that the border region would have to be ceded to Poland in the next war. While Kaganovich never said it directly, his report made it very clear that he was very much in support of a displacement of the Poles from the border region.[185]

However, the romantic conception of nations as communities of fate was far removed from the biological racism of the National Socialists.

At the most, one could speak of a cultural form of racism, prevalent among the Bolsheviks, which legitimized violence whenever national minorities came under suspicion of disloyalty. How else is it possible to explain that Stalin had Armenians and Germans deported from Ukraine, but refrained from such national consolidations in Armenia or in the Republic of Volga Germans? One explanation is that national minorities only posed a threat when they failed to integrate into ethnically homogenous landscapes or when fears arose that they were destabilizing Soviet order. For in the minds of Bolshevik leaders, the true homelands of Germans, Poles, and Finns lay beyond the borders of the Soviet Union. To Stalin and his followers, these dangers could only be averted by violent means.[186]

As early as February 1927 the Politburo ordered the party leadership in Azerbaijan to register all "nationalists," as well as all members of the former ruling party, Musavat, which had been disbanded in 1920. These people were to be classified as traitors and Turkish spies and then eliminated. In the years of collectivization the regime showed no restraints in terms of the brutality it was willing to exhibit. Meanwhile, the Bolsheviks feared that the governments of neighboring countries could exploit the discontent of peasants in Ukraine and other border republics for their own ends, and these fears were not unfounded. Not only did peasants revolt against the regime, but in Ukraine, Karelia, the Caucasus, and in central Asia they also tried to cross the border and flee abroad. Word spread quickly among the German colonists that the German government would help them escape from the Soviet Union. Thousands besieged the German embassy in Moscow in summer 1929, and the German consulates in Kiev, Kharkov, and Odessa also struggled to manage the onslaught. But travel permits required the approval of the Soviet authorities, which is why peasants also petitioned Mikhail Kalinin, the nominal head of state of the Soviet Union, to obtain permission to emigrate to Germany or Canada.[187]

Stalin and his aides saw these movements as acts of treason and expressions of disloyalty. They also suspected the governments of neighboring states of attempting to destabilize the border region. In response they had the borders of the Soviet Union closed, so that now no one could leave without permission and no one could enter unnoticed. The borders were secured with barricades, and military force was also employed to prevent peasants and nomads from getting across. By this time, the Politburo had already ordered local authorities to register all foreign nationals in the border areas and examine their ties. In the early 1930s, Iranians and Turks in the Transcaucasian republics were forced to choose between becoming Soviet citizens or leaving the country. Forced emigration, it later turned out, may have been the better choice, because in January 1938 Stalin announced to the party boss of Azerbaijan that he had one month to deport all Iranians who had taken on Soviet citizenship to Kazakhstan. Iranians who preferred to remain Iranian citizens, however, were to be banished to Iran "immediately," just as had been done with the Kurds from Nakhchivan one year earlier. Soviet citizenship was the entry ticket to a slave state.[188]

By the early 1930s the removal of ethnic minorities from the border areas was well underway. On February 20, 1930, the Politburo decided to place the border regions in the Caucasus and central Asia under military supervision and also to expel all "kulak families of nonindigenous nationality."[189] In March, Stalin ordered the GPU to widen its search for Polish "bandits," "spies," "counterrevolutionaries," and smugglers in western border regions of the Soviet Union. Anyone who appeared to fit one of these categories was to be arrested and consigned to a camp. Between three thousand and thirty-five hundred families were slated to be removed from the Belorussian border region, along with another ten to fifteen thousand families from the Ukrainian border region.[190] In 1928, when violent interethnic conflicts broke out between Chinese, Korean, and Russian settlers in the Far Eastern Region, the local Bolsheviks once again did not hesitate to propose radical solutions. All Koreans living in the strategically important region of Vladivostok were marked for deportation, and although this eliminatory program was not implemented for another ten years, the leadership in Moscow felt confirmed in its verdict that the border regions were inhabited by unreliable ethnic groups. Borders, it seemed, turned into front lines. They needed to be held and defended by soldiers.[191]

Beyond the borders, however, Stalin and his cronies had no inkling of what life was like. In their minds, what went on elsewhere was all just part of one grand conspiracy against the Soviet Union. The National Socialist seizure of power in Germany, the emergence of authoritarian, fascist regimes in east-central Europe and on the southern flank of the empire, and the Spanish Civil War—all of this simply confirmed the leadership's paranoia that the Soviet Union was being encircled by hostile forces. In late 1932 the Politburo received word that thousands of peasants from southern Ukraine and the Donbass had abandoned their kolkhozy and descended into the Soviet heartland. As soon as he heard this news Stalin knew immediately that it was "Polish agents" who were at work causing this exodus. They were plotting to use these refugees to destabilize collective farms elsewhere in the Soviet Union too. And for that reason, all peasants attempting to escape needed to be caught and deported. At least this was how Stalin formulated it in his January 1933 directive, which he sent to the party bosses in Rostov, Kharkov, Stalingrad, Samara, Voronezh, Minsk, and Smolensk.[192]

The 1933 deportation of the Kuban Cossacks ushered in the Soviet era of ethnic cleansing. On December 14, 1932, Stalin ordered the GPU to deport "all residents" of the Cossack Stanitsa of Poltava "into the northern areas of the USSR." "Conscientious Red Army soldier-kolkhoz farmers" would then settle the vacant territory. Cossacks in the remaining cities and villages of the Kuban area were arrested and deported soon thereafter. Ultimately this amounted to more than sixty thousand people in total—including the poor and landless, women and children.[193] Back during collectivization the Cossacks had violently resisted being forced to join collective farms. Now they were to be punished for it, and the regime's retribution was cruel. To Kaganovich, every Cossack was a potential traitor and thus needed to be dealt with violently. "Everyone must be held liable for their neighbor," Kaganovich said.[194]

The murder of Sergei Kirov in December 1934 was also an occasion for the state security organs to begin targeting national minorities in Leningrad and the surrounding area. More than twenty-two thousand Germans, Latvians, Estonians, and Finns were taken from their homes, arrested, and deported. In early 1935 over forty-five thousand people in Vinnitsa and Kiev were arrested and handed over to the GPU because they had been deemed "socially alien" or "unreliable elements." Over 57 percent of them were Germans or Poles. In Belorussia the secret police began searching for "Polish spies" who, according to the local NKVD director, Leplevsky, had infiltrated all levels of the party and the Komsomol in order to destabilize it. The result was that the security organs smashed 104 "Polish agents" and thirty spy rings within only a few months at the start of 1935. Throughout all the larger areas of the country Polish emigrants were taken into NKVD custody. In

Ukraine the expulsions continued into January 1936, and by the following autumn more than half of the German and Polish populations had been deported. According to the final NKVD report, by October 1936, sixty-nine thousand people had been removed from Ukraine and resettled in Kazakhstan.[195]

A couple of months later, in July 1936, the Regional Committee of the Far Eastern Region requested permission to arrest the supposed Japanese spies and saboteurs lurking in the border areas. For Stalin, however, this did not go far enough, and in August 1937 he demanded that all Koreans living in the region be deported to Kazakhstan. According to his calculations this resettlement project made economic sense as well: at least, the September 21, 1937 Politburo protocol laconically notes that "transportation for one family in a freight car costs 750 rubles."[196] By October 1937, the security organs had driven 172,000 Koreans out of their homeland and deported them to Kazakhstan—a project that was overseen by Stalin personally. On September 11, 1937, Stalin sent a telegram to the local party secretary and the chief of the NKVD in Khabarovsk, warning against deviating from the planned resettlement schedule. "People sabotaging the operation, regardless of who they may be," Stalin cautioned them, "are to be arrested immediately and punished by example." Furthermore, Stalin instructed, "Don't just arrest Volsky [party boss of the Far Eastern Region, who was arrested shortly afterwards], but dozens of Volskys."[197]

In summer 1937 the floodgates were opened in this regard too. To Stalin and his agents, all border regions were now places of hazard and front lines of battle that needed to be cleansed of their disloyal minorities. That is what happened in autumn 1937 and spring 1938 in the Caucasus, when Stalin ordered the NKVD to remove all Kurds from Nakhchivan and deport them to Kazakhstan. Even in this distant reach of the empire, far removed from Moscow, the expulsions were carried out to the dictator's satisfaction. More than a thousand Kurdish families were gathered at various collection points, registered, and placed under surveillance. Since the lack of rail lines and streets made it difficult to carry out the expulsions quickly, the Kurds were escorted on foot from Nakhchivan to the Caspian Sea, where they were loaded onto ships and taken to Kazakhstan.[198] In late summer 1937, about the same time that the resettlement of the Kurds was beginning, Stalin also demanded that the borders of Ukraine, the Caucasus, the Far East, and

Mongolia be depopulated, as a means of suppressing communication across the borders. Soldiers could no longer even patrol the borders of their native regions. On Stalin's orders, all Armenian regiments were withdrawn from the Soviet-Turkish border and replaced with Russian troops.

At times the lines between ethnic and social categories could blur in the terror orders. In August 1938 Stalin ordered the party boss of Tajikistan to arrest thirty thousand nomads living near the Afghan-Soviet border and detain them in concentration camps. Stalin's justification was that if they were not removed they could join up with Afghan warlords and form an alliance against Soviet power. His order spoke of kulaks and bandits who needed to be exterminated, but one should not be misled by Stalin's words. His main concern in this corner of the empire was to expel a disloyal ethnic group from a border area.[199]

By summer 1937 Stalin had found an alternative to deportation, namely organized murder. Deportation was really only a viable option when a territory was inhabited by a clearly identifiable minority group. But what about all the non-Russians who did not live in clusters with their countrymen but were instead dispersed among the Russians? The Russian cities were filled with Germans, Poles, Latvians, Greeks, and Armenians for whom this was the case. From Stalin's point of view, the simplest and most efficient solution was to have these people killed. First there was the "German operation." On July 20, 1937, Stalin instructed Yezhov to arrest all Germans working in the Soviet defense industry. Whether they were citizens of the German Reich or German Communists was irrelevant. Simply by being German, one had the potential to be a spy and could now be arrested, imprisoned, or shot as such. The "German operation" claimed the lives of some forty-two thousand people and included not just ethnic Germans but also anyone who had ties to German diplomats or had been in German captivity during the First World War.

Shortly afterward, on August 11, 1937, Stalin ordered the arrest of all Polish "spies." Rings of Polish spies had supposedly already been uncovered throughout the Soviet Union, and even those who were not currently making mischief could always become a threat in the future. Thus, as a preventive measure, the NKVD needed to arrest all members of the "Polish military organization," former Polish prisoners of war, Polish immigrants, members of the Polish Socialist Party, and all "anti-Soviet and nationalist elements in the Polish rayons." Anyone convicted of espionage or sabotage would be shot, and all remaining detainees were to be sent to camps. This order, however, did not specify who was to be shot and who was to be imprisoned, and once again this very lack of clarity helped unleash an orgy of violence that was even greater than it might otherwise have been. On September 14 Yezhov sent his master a preliminary report on the "Polish operation," informing him that Poles guilty of military espionage and organized anti-Soviet revolts had been discovered in all regions of the Soviet Union. The NKVD had already arrested 23,216 people, Yezhov reported, and they had already confessed to their crimes. Stalin was evidently pleased. He underlined the number of detainees in pencil and wrote Yezhov a short response: "To Comrade Yezhov: Very good. Dig up this Polish spy filth and get rid of it in the future too, exterminate them for the sake of the USSR. J. Stalin, 14.9.1937."[200]

Initially, the Polish murder campaign was somewhat directed. It targeted Polish prisoners of war who had remained in the Soviet Union after 1920, political émigrés, members of Polish parties, and the Polish population in the western border regions of the Soviet Union. A few weeks later, however, Yezhov made the announcement, "The Poles must be completely destroyed," and proclaimed that this would now include "all Poles." Poles taken into NKVD custody could now expect the worst. Whether they considered themselves communists or nationalists was irrelevant. Nearly the entire Polish section of the Communist International was killed, and in August 1938 the Polish Communist Party had to be dissolved because almost all of its members had been either imprisoned or killed. More than thirty-five thousand Poles were expelled from the Polish-Ukrainian border region, and Stalin's henchmen even ventured into the Far Eastern Region, to the Amur area and to Kamchatka, to search for Polish "White Guards." There were supposedly Poles living there who maintained ties with the Japanese consul in Khabarovsk and with Russian nobility who had settled beyond the border after the revolution. In July 1938 Molotov received a report from his plenipotentiary in the Far Eastern Region, informing him that enemies and spies had subverted all institutions there and that a "half-Polish" woman was working at the Geological Institute in Khabarovsk.[201]

Yezhov's henchmen combed the cities of the Soviet Union looking for members of national minorities. Latvians, Estonians, Koreans,

Finns, Kurds, Greeks, Armenians, Bulgarians, Chinese, and Turks living outside their "homelands" all posed a threat to the Soviet order. Internationalism, which the Bolsheviks had once celebrated, was now a thing of the past. As Sobolev, party secretary of Krasnoyarsk, put it, the time had come to end the internationalist "game." All national minorities needed to be "captured, forced to their knees, and exterminated like rabid dogs." Radzivilovsky, head of the Moscow NKVD, recalled how Yezhov had assigned him the task of constructing an "anti-Soviet underground organization of Latvians," by arresting a number of Latvian Communists and then "beating the necessary confessions out of them." Poles and Latvians were spies—of this Yezhov was certain. There was no longer need for any further proof: "No need to trouble ourselves with this crowd. . . . We have to prove that the Latvians, Poles and others inside the VKP [All-Union Communist Party] are spies and diversionists."[202]

In November 1937, five thousand German families were taken from their homes in Kiev and deported. All the Chinese who still lived in the city were picked up by the state security organs as well. In Kharkov the NKVD began arresting Armenians, Greeks, Bulgarians, Poles, Germans, and Latvians—all members of national minorities whose compatriots lived in neighboring countries. Their clubs were closed, and their newspapers were banned. Chekists reportedly scoured telephone books and census records to seek out suspects. The German settlements near Kharkov and the Estonian and Finnish settlements near Leningrad were also emptied out during these autumn weeks. Even the Red Army units in Siberia were screened for Germans and Poles, and all soldiers and officers with the wrong ethnic background were arrested. Nowhere did the terror rage more cruelly and relentlessly than in the Donbass, the coal and steel region of the Soviet Union, where nearly the entire German, Polish, and Latvian populations were simply put to death. Around the same time Yezhov ordered all Greeks living in the Donbass arrested, so the Chekists removed another 3,628 people from their homes and within the next four months had 3,470 of them killed.[203]

Sometimes not even the victims understood what was happening to them. They simply could not fathom that their ethnic background would decide whether they were to live or die. Alexander Weissberg-Cybulski was an Austrian scientist living in Kharkov who was arrested by the NKVD. He recalled how strange the national waves of new prisoners had seemed to him during his internment in autumn 1937: "Already during September the rumor began to spread that the Latvians were being arrested, and that the Armenians would be next. We couldn't understand what this meant. We considered it impossible that the GPU would use criteria such as ethnicity—so insignificant when it comes to a man's political disposition—as a pretext for their repressions. Still we couldn't help but notice that on one particular day, all the new arrivals were prisoners of Latvian nationality. On another—all Armenian. We're talking about hundreds of people in both cases."[204]

The "national operations" did not follow any kind of carefully engineered plan. The NKVD was not even given guideline figures of how many people to arrest. Never before had the state security organs organized a "national operation," and when the Chekists received the order to murder Poles and Germans, they had no other choice but to sift through census records and internal passports to find them. The problem, though, was that until 1938 citizens could still decide for themselves which nationality was to be entered in their passports. This meant that it was up to authorities to select their victims, and in some regions, the party secretaries disposed of their national minorities, even if their passports did not identify them as such, by having them registered as "socially alien elements." The final decisions, however, were made in Moscow. Yezhov and the state prosecutor, Vyshinsky, received the death lists from the provinces and then confirmed or amended them to determine how many people would be killed and how many would be sent to concentration camps. In an evening they could process anywhere between 1,000 and 2,000 cases. On December 29, 1937, Yezhov and Vyshinsky "sentenced" 992 Latvians from the Leningrad area to death.[205]

The reason these murderous excesses took on such monstrous proportions was that there were never any clear guidelines from the central command. In early 1938, after the killing campaigns against party members and kulaks had already reached a peak, Stalin extended the deadline for the execution of the national operations because, in his estimation, the security organs had not yet arrested as many people as necessary. On January 31 he ordered the NKVD to continue "smashing the espionage and sabotage contingents of the Poles, Latvians, Germans, Estonians, Finns, Greeks, Iranians, Harbin people [*Kharbintsy*— railway workers who had been employed in Japanese-controlled Manchuria], Chinese, and Romanians," as part of an effort that would continue until April 15. All detainees—Soviet citizens and foreign nationals alike—were to be shot, and to ensure that no one was spared, the despot also gave orders to "crush the cadres of Bulgarians and Macedonians, both foreign nationals as well as citizens of the USSR."[206] The national operations, which actually continued until November 1938, claimed more than 350,000 victims. 144,000 people were arrested as part of the Polish operation alone. Almost 250,000 people—nearly 70 percent of those arrested during the national campaigns—died by way of NKVD firing squad. If 1937 was the year of social cleansing, then 1938 was the year of ethnic cleansing.

The final body count was horrific. If the internal statistics of the NKVD are to be believed, the security organs arrested 1,575,259 people between October 1, 1936 and November 1, 1938. 1,344,923 people were sentenced: 681,692 of them were condemned to death, and the remainder were imprisoned in camps. 767,000 people were arrested as "anti-Soviet elements," and of these 387,000 were shot. 328,000 were victims of the national operations. But these were only the figures as of November 1, 1938. We will never know for sure how many people actually died during these destructive excesses because after November 1, 1938 the NKVD records provide no more data and only include victims who were condemned to death by the troikas.[207]

What initially began at the beginning of 1937 as a bloody "self-cleansing" of the Communist Party culminated in organized mass murder. The killing and torturing continued into the winter of 1938, and never once did it cross Stalin's mind to put a stop to it. In the Soviet Union of 1937 the world was out of joint. The apocalyptic drama of dread, however, was centrally devised and directed. Stalin and his associates controlled the terror. They directed the show, and they were the ones who forced local party and security organs to reach new extremes of extremism. The mass murder was not the work of ingenuous provincial satraps who imposed their extermination strategies on the center. It was the work of Stalin. In his mind, what he did unto others was not senseless chaos but was instead a purifying storm that would forever cleanse the earth of its refuse. No terror could ever be cruel enough to achieve this goal.[208]

THE END OF MASS TERROR

The end of mass terror came in stages. At a Central Committee plenum on January 18, 1938, Stalin, for the first time ever, expressed some
criticism of the excesses that had been committed during the expulsions
and arrests of party members. It was Pavel Postyshev, however, who
Stalin evidently decided should take the blame. Postyshev had served
as second secretary of the Ukrainian Communist Party before being
appointed party boss of Kuybyshev in 1937. Now, in front of everyone,
Stalin's henchmen turned to Postyshev and accused him of having expelled and persecuted innocent party members in Kiev and Kuybyshev.
Violent though his acts may have been, Postyshev had carried them out
on Stalin's orders and failed to understand why he was now being held
responsible for them. "Of all the leading secretaries of the rayon committees and of all the chairmen of the rayon executive committees,"
asserted Postyshev, "barely a single person has turned out to be honest.
Why does this surprise you?" Molotov, however, made clear that Stalin did not want to hear these kind of answers anymore, "Aren't you
exaggerating a little, Comrade Postyshev?" Postyshev pointed to the
confessions extracted and the NKVD case files that had been used to
prove the guilt of those arrested. He soon saw, however, that his situation was hopeless and admitted to having committed "serious errors."
Soon thereafter, he was relieved of all posts, arrested, and shot.[209]

While the sacrifice of Postyshev did not mark the end of the Great
Terror, it sent a signal to the functionaries that Communists at least
could expect some protection against arbitrary persecution. Stalin, it
seemed, had finally achieved what he had set out to do. He had had
all potentially disloyal and unreliable functionaries removed, and he
had created a ruling apparatus that was staffed entirely by a new, sub-
servient elite. Now Stalin could even afford noble gestures once again.
Immediately after the January 1938 plenum members who had been
expelled from the party were readmitted, and arrest warrants against
Communists were rescinded. The national operations and the mass terror against "socially alien elements" would continue, however, before
reaching a final climax in spring 1938. In fact, Stalin made it clear to
Yezhov that the operations were not proceeding as quickly as he would
have liked. The prisons were overcrowded, and the NKVD seemed to
be incapable of killing the remaining enemies within the appropriate

time frame. There were more than 100,000 people whose names were on lists but whose cases had not yet been processed. The killing machine, Stalin demanded of Yezhov, needed to be accelerated. All cases needed to be concluded, and every last enemy needed to be exterminated by November 15. To ensure that Stalin's demands could be met, in September 1938 the national operations were handed over to the provincial troikas, who would now decide for themselves who would live and who would die. And so in the autumn of 1938 another 72,000 people died in the killing compounds of the NKVD, before Stalin officially declared an end to the terror on November 17.

No one will ever know why exactly the dictator finally elected to end the killings. Did he and his associates really believe they had achieved their dream of cleansing the world of enemies? This seems unlikely, as the terror started up again during Second World War and then carried over into postwar period too. In all probability, Stalin had simply achieved another dream: he had cleansed the Soviet Union of anyone who could contradict him. His functionaries trembled with fear, and those who had risen to achieve positions of power obeyed because they owed everything they had attained to the demise of the old elite. The widespread creation of fear and dread had caused all potential sources of resistance to dry up forever. The terror, wrote Hannah Arendt, was meant "to take away man's liberties and destroy freedom as a living political reality."[210] What goals still remained for Stalin and his associates? It was imperative that the violence not lose its extraordinary quality, as its horror-provoking effects were only possible in the context of the suddenness of the terror. Victims and survivors needed to remember the violence and always bear in mind that everything that happened could happen again—at any given time.

Now was not the time to "throw popes into prison," the head of the Novosibirsk NKVD told his deputy in winter 1938. This was in response to the deputy's request to arrest another hundred clergymen as counterrevolutionaries. In December 1938 the head of the Crimean NKVD was arrested for having continued mass operations even after the disbandment of the troikas. On November 28 and 29 Chekists there had murdered another 700 people. In Leningrad, meanwhile, over 10,000 prisoners, who had been condemned to death and were awaiting execution, were able to go free because the news reached the prison in time that their sentences had been rescinded.[211] Vyshinsky, Stalin's zealous and servile henchman, now discovered that a great number of innocent people had been wrongly condemned. In 1938, in the camps of Kolyma, the troikas had reportedly sentenced 12,566 people and had 5,866 of them shot. In September 1939 Vyshinsky informed Stalin that a judicial review of the situation in Kolyma had revealed "a massive number of false verdicts, which were applied to acts that in no way represented punishable crimes." In one particular case, the testimony of a single witness had led to the condemnation of fifty individuals. He, Vyshinsky, had removed the responsible prosecutor from his post and indicted him.[212] The period of murderous excesses was over, and it was Stalin himself who brought it to an end. As the terror ended the final hour of the executioners was also ushered in.

When the dictator announced the end of the *Yezhovshchina*, as the mass terror was colloquially referred to, it was clear that Yezhov's days were numbered. In summer 1937 the notion that the thoroughly loyal Yezhov might one day fall out of favor would have been nearly inconceivable. Stalin had decorated him with the Lenin Medal in June, and in October of that same year he had been accepted as a candidate for the Politburo. In public, Stalin had always presented Yezhov as his most trusted aide and had forced his selfless servant to go on vacation in December 1937 to recover from the stresses and strains of his murderous work. At a January 21, 1938 Kremlin reception for representatives of the Supreme Soviet, Stalin had even proposed a toast to state security and its foremost servant. He had bid all those gathered to express their thanks for the "tens of thousands of heroes," and their daily "humble, useful work" for state security. "To all Chekists and the organizer and head of all Chekists," Stalin had proclaimed, "to Comrade Yezhov!"[213]

But Stalin would not have been Stalin if he had trusted Yezhov blindly. Yezhov too was put to the test. In April 1938 Stalin made him head of the People's Commissariat of Water Transport and had his predecessor, Pakhomov, shot. Soon, rumors began to spread that Yezhov had fallen from grace and that his overthrow was imminent. While it is unknown whether Stalin started these rumors, one thing that is clear is that he did nothing to suppress them. Yezhov knew that he was in danger and did everything he could to demonstrate his devotion. Mostly, that meant exercising all the violence he could. He unleashed merciless terror in the People's Commissariat of Water Transport. He had leading employees arrested and shot and then had them replaced with people he knew and trusted from the NKVD. But this was also a mistake. To have adversaries killed and then replaced with one's own people, but without obtaining Stalin's permission, was never advisable.

Yezhov had more power in his hands than he was able to deal with. He became megalomaniacal. He lost all self-control. There was talk of his inviting friends and colleagues to lavish celebrations at his dacha. There was talk of sexual orgies taking place in his offices. Even on official trips to the provinces Yezhov was apparently unable to rein in his excessive drinking habits. In February 1938 he traveled to Kiev with Alexander Uspensky, head of the Ukrainian NKVD, and several other high-ranking state security officials to oversee the execution of Stalin's terror orders. Yezhov ordered arbitrary mass arrests and signed death warrants without reading them. Everyone could tell when Yezhov was drinking on the job, as the alcohol loosened his tongue. During a party committee reception in Kiev he lost all self-control and began proclaiming that he was all-powerful, that he had everyone in his grip, and that he could have the entire Politburo arrested if he wanted. And indeed, he had complied extensive dossiers on members of the Politburo. None of this, however, remained a secret to Stalin. He knew about the dossiers on the Politburo members, and he knew about Yezhov's boasting. Yezhov was on shaky footing.

In early summer 1938 Yezhov's star began to fade. In June Genrikh Lyushkov, NKVD boss of the Far Eastern Region and Yezhov's close confidant, fled to Japan in fear of being arrested and shot if he remained in the Soviet Union. Lyushkov's deputy Moisei Kagan had already been arrested and murdered in April, and in May Yezhov had informed his protégé that he was slated to be transferred to the central NKVD apparatus in Moscow. Lyushkov had understood what this "promotion" meant and what fate awaited him in Moscow. Frinovsky, Yezhov's deputy in the NKVD, had wanted to have Lyushkov arrested at once, before Lyushkov would be able to divulge secrets about all the horrors committed by the terror apparatus. Yezhov, however, had chosen to protect his minion and had urged him to take his own life before he could be executed. A short time later Lyushkov fled abroad across the Manchurian border. Now that Lyushkov was gone Stalin suspected Yezhov of having warned him, and fear rapidly came to be Yezhov's closest companion as well. Yezhov's most faithful employees in the NKVD, Leonid Zakovsky and Lev Mironov, were arrested in early summer 1938, and then, in August, Stalin appointed the Georgian Lavrenty Beria to be Yezhov's deputy. At the thought that the brutal and unscrupulous Beria would now be at his side, Yezhov began to panic. He then ordered the execution of Zakovsky, Mironov, and several other fallen confidants of his so that they would be gone before Beria would have a chance to interrogate them.

Beria fulfilled all of Stalin's expectations. He had Yezhov's friends and colleagues arrested, and he supplied the dictator with dossiers detailing the transgressions of the NKVD boss. Yezhov in the meantime tried to regain Stalin's favor. On September 23, 1938, he wrote Stalin a letter in which he conceded his errors and shortcomings and admitted to having failed to recognize in a timely manner that he had been surrounded by "traitors" and enemies of the people. Moreover, he claimed to have neglected the personal protection of Stalin and the members of the Politburo. "I give my Bolshevik word and pledge my commitment before the CC of the VKP and Comrade Stalin to learn all these lessons in my future work, to learn from mistakes and to remedy them wherever the CC wishes to deploy me, so that I can justify the trust of the CC." But it was too late for any of this. Yezhov's time ran out on November 14, 1938, when Uspensky, head of the Ukrainian NKVD, went into hiding for several months to avoid being arrested. Yezhov was forced to submit his resignation to the Politburo. Then, on November 23, he was called into the dictator's office to account for Uspensky's escape, and the following day he was relieved of all duties in the NKVD. But the writing had already been on the wall a few weeks earlier when the regime had celebrated the anniversary of the revolution. Instead of Yezhov next to him on the podium, Stalin had invited Beria, Yezhov's deputy and successor, to preside over the military parade with him.

Yezhov's agony lasted for over a year. Although Stalin kept him in the Politburo, he banished him from his court. Yezhov no longer had either influence or power and was now forced to stand by and watch while his successor mocked and discredited him. Beria presented Stalin with all the dossiers that Yezhov had compiled on the members of the Politburo, and Yezhov ultimately received the blame for the NKVD's murderous excesses. Yezhov's NKVD had arrested innocent people, and Yezhov had withheld information on spies and saboteurs. In December

Stalin received a message from the party boss of Oryol, complaining that the Chekists had blackmailed people into giving false testimonies. Stalin replied that he had received "analogous messages" from other regions as well but that Yezhov had failed to react to these signals. That, Stalin lied, was why he had been removed.[214]

Yezhov drank heavily and only sporadically appeared for work in the People's Commissariat of Water Transport. Day after day he waited to be arrested and taken to the Lubianka, but day after day nothing of the kind happened. In January he even took part in a Politburo meeting one more time, despite the fact that Beria had had his brother arrested in the meantime. Yezhov made his last public appearance at the inauguration of the Eighteenth Party Congress in March 1939. He tried to contact Stalin and sent him a handwritten note that read, "I implore you: speak to me, only for one minute. Give me this opportunity." But Stalin refused. In between sessions, the Central Committee discussed which of its members would be up for reelection. Stalin took the opportunity to humiliate Yezhov by asking him, in front of everyone, what reasons he might have to justify his candidacy. Hadn't he wanted to kill Stalin? Stalin asked. At this Yezhov turned pale, and his voice broke as he conceded that although he had made mistakes he loved Stalin more than his own wife. Stalin left it to the members of the Central Committee to decide Yezhov's fate, noting that he for one, however, had his "doubts." Yezhov was expelled from the Central Committee but remained People's Commissar of Water Transport. Then, on April 9, 1939, Stalin dissolved the People's Commissariat, and Yezhov—now a minister without a ministry—was arrested the following day.

Yezhov remained in prison for almost a year, despite having confessed, almost immediately after his arrest, to having been a spy for both Polish and German intelligence. On April 26, Beria sent Stalin the transcript of the first interrogation, during which Yezhov had been forced to degrade himself and confess that he, of all people, was a friend of the Poles:

> KOBULOV: During the last interrogation you said that you carried out espionage activities for Poland over the last ten years. However you concealed a number of other espionage connections. The bureau of investigation demands truthful and exhaustive statements from you in this matter.

YEZHOV: I must confess that when I provided truthful statements about my espionage activities for Poland, I actually concealed my espionage ties to the Germans from the bureau of investigation.

KOBULOV: What were your purposes in trying to divert the investigation from your espionage ties with the Germans?

YEZHOV: I did not want to reveal my direct espionage ties with the Germans during the investigation, particularly since my cooperation with German counterintelligence was not merely limited to espionage on behalf of German counterintelligence. I organized an anti-Soviet conspiracy and prepared a coup d'état, which was meant to be realized by means of terrorist attacks against the leaders of the party and the government.[215]

Frinovsky preferred to sign all testimonies that were prepared for him. Only Yezhov's deputy, Yefim Yevdokimov, who had been arrested in autumn 1938, endured the torture for five months, until he too was broken and confessed to everything that Stalin demanded to hear. Stalin received regular reports on the physical condition of his prominent prisoner, the last of them being from January 11, 1940, when Beria informed him that Yezhov was suffering from headaches and pneumonia. The end finally came on February 3, 1940, when the Military Collegium of the Supreme Court condemned the former head of the NKVD to death in a secret trial. In the opinion of the court, Yezhov had been the leader of a foreign conspiracy within the NKVD and had planned to kill Stalin and Beria. Everyone connected with Yezhov died with him. This included his employees, followers, and their relatives—346 people altogether, with women and children among them. Yezhov called the state prosecutor, Vyshinsky, a "whore" and a criminal and cursed him for trying to shift the blame for all his misdeeds onto him. Yezhov insisted that he had done no wrong in "cleansing" the NKVD of fourteen thousand Chekists and that his "greatest fault" was only that he "did not purge enough of them." At his trial he retracted his previous statement that he had been a Polish spy and implored the court not to "torture" him but to "go ahead and shoot" him. Yezhov screamed hysterically as he was taken from his cell to be shot. Chekists grabbed him by the arms and dragged him to the execution cellar where Vasily Blokhin, Stalin's chief executioner, ended his life. That very same day, Stalin met with Beria and Mikoyan to discuss economic matters. Did he and Beria, who had witnessed the execution, also speak about Yezhov's final moments? No one will ever know for certain, but Stalin would not have been Stalin if he had not insisted on that.[216]

Yezhov became an unperson. His name vanished from the public eye as though he had never existed, and Stalin rarely even mentioned it anymore. The airplane builder Alexander Yakovlev recalled, years later after the war, how Stalin spoke of past events. "Yezhov is a scoundrel!" Stalin had said. "A sordid individual. If you phone the Central Committee, they'll say he's gone to work. If you send someone to his house, they find him lying on his bed, drunk and unconscious. He killed many innocents. We shot him for that."[217]

VIOLENCE AND ITS SITUATIONS

Ideas do not kill, but people who dream of killing are capable of acting on the things they imagine. To men of violence, who are intimately acquainted with killing, ideas are only a means of legitimizing their lust for murder to those for whom violence is not a natural course of action. Neither Stalin nor Yezhov were guided by Marxism or its promises when they had people arrested, tortured, and killed. Stalin and many of his associates did indeed think of bloody terror as an unavoidable surgical intervention in a society that they believed was beyond their control. This was only possible, however, because violence was a self-evident means of securing power for Stalin and his henchmen. It had absolutely nothing to do with the writings of European Marxism. It arose from the experiences and mental dispositions of the perpetrators. Stalin was a man of violence. What he did to others was a matter of cold calculation, and the game with death was simply part of his technique of rule. He never lost control of himself, nor did he suffer from depression or hallucinations. One should bear in mind that he also took pleasure in eliminating people. "One thing's certain," the prominent Polish Communist Roman Werfel recalled during the 1970s,

> Stalin was a double-dealing hypocrite. I'll give you an example. There was an estate in the suburbs of Moscow where old Bolsheviks live; each of them had their own little Finnish house. Stalin had one there as well, not a very grand one as yet, and Vera Kostrzewa lived next door to him. One day she was pruning roses in her garden. Stalin came up to her and said "What beautiful roses." That same evening she was taken away and shot; Stalin knew about it. But in 1944, when our delegation came to

see him, he suddenly asked, "You used to have such nice people. Vera Kostrzewa, for instance—do you know what's become of her?"[218]

Anyone who maims and kills large numbers of people has to reckon with retribution. Violence destroys trust, and it creates a set of conditions in which no one can be certain of anything. Ultimately, however, it also undermines the sovereignty of the violent perpetrator himself. Once Stalin had established a role for himself as a violent and fearsome despot he could not simply quit his role. When fear subsides, the rule of the despot—a rule based on fear—is in jeopardy. That is why he mistrusted even his closest confidants, surrounded himself with armed bodyguards, and even had his dacha sealed off with several fences. He forced his assistants to taste his food for him and hired his in-house staff personally. To Stalin, the violence was eventually justified because it was the only thing guaranteeing his singular position of power. Had Stalin been confronted with the accusation that he was a conscienceless murderer, he may well have simply not understood. How else is it possible to explain the fact that he not only signed off on all terror orders himself, but that he also stored them in his personal archive?

The world of Stalin was the state of emergency. The state of emergency allowed him to transform political space into a space of violence. In this regard Stalin was both the creator and the beneficiary of the state of emergency, as it enabled him to not only terrorize Soviet society, but also to discipline his retinue through the controlled use of violence. Stalin, however, was not a man who only used violence strategically. Murder did not bother him. Furthermore, he despised weaklings who spoke of violence but were unwilling to expose themselves to its consequences. Even during the Civil War he had villages burnt to the ground and had people shot for no apparent reason—other than that he took pleasure in exercising violence against defenseless individuals. The Civil War marked one of the happiest times of Stalin's life because it was a time when Stalin was allowed to be nothing but Stalin.[219] "There are weaklings," he declared at a November 1938 celebration of the October Revolution. "They are afraid of grenades, they crawl around on the ground, they are a laughing stock." But in Stalin's homeland even minor incidents tended to end in violence. Blood feuds, violent disputes between peasant villages, and raids by bandits were normal parts of the young Stalin's daily life. Only those who could threaten violence and use it to assert themselves were able to survive in this hostile environment. Threats of violence, however, required friends and protégés. Otherwise they remained empty. Men needed other men who they could depend on under all circumstances, especially when they had performed acts of violence together.[220]

In Stalin's Georgian homeland friendship and honor carried different connotations than they did in the Russian center of the empire. Stalin's idols were the leaders of robber bands, not only because they were persecuted by the autocratic state and its officials, but also because, for someone like Stalin, they embodied the masculine ideal. Men were warriors, and they joined forces with other warriors. They fought their enemies, and they submitted to their leaders unconditionally. A man's sense of self-worth and his status were based on honor. In the "Honorable Society," betrayal was punished with disgrace or death. Whoever failed as a man lost his honor and ceased to be a man. Stalin's conception of rule resembled the Mafia's code of honor. "I was born in the Land of the Camorra," writes the Italian journalist Roberto Saviano, "in the territory with the most homicides in Europe, where savagery is interwoven with commerce, where nothing has value except what generates power. Where everything has the taste of a final battle. It seemed impossible to have a moment of peace, not to live constantly in a war where every gesture is a surrender, where every necessity is transformed into weakness, where everything needs to be fought for tooth and nail."[221]

Try seeing the world through Stalin's eyes, and everything that we would never expect of ourselves instantly becomes normal. The same can be said of his friends who knew what it meant to live with violence. Ordzhonikidze, Beria, Mikoyan, Voroshilov, Molotov, and Kaganovich all understood what a man with a gun meant in Stalin's orbit. They had internalized the dictator's violent style to such a degree that, for them, an alternate nonviolent reality was inconceivable. At the November 1938 celebration of the anniversary of the revolution, Voroshilov declared that if Trotsky and Zinoviev, instead of Stalin, had won the intraparty power struggle after Lenin's death then "they would have slaughtered us all."[222]

The Bolsheviks were men of violence. They publicly celebrated a macho cult of killing, and they surrounded themselves with the insignia of military violence. They dressed in military boots, black leather jackets, uniforms, and gun holsters. Stalin was never seen without his boots and military cap. The cult of violence also included a brutalization of language and a contempt for tolerance, pity, and empathy. This became normality for perpetrators and victims alike, and they adapted themselves accordingly. Several weeks after the execution of Zinoviev and Kamenev, the Chekist Karl Pauker, who was in charge of the dictator's bodyguards, decided to show Stalin and Yezhov how Zinoviev had pleaded for his life as he was taken to the execution cellar. Two bodyguards dragged him into the room by his arms while he imitated Zinoviev's screams. "Hear oh Israel the Lord is our God, the Lord is one," Pauker cried with a Jewish accent as he raised his arms toward the sky. Stalin and Yezhov hooted. Pauker then replayed the scene a second time, and Stalin convulsed with laughter. He laughed so hard that he had to hold his belly and beg his bodyguards to stop.[223]

At Stalin's request, those who had been beaten and tortured were presented in his office. He also gave detailed instructions on how the prisoners were to be abused. He even beat his own personal secretary, Poskrebyshev. "How he beat me. He grabbed me by the hair and slammed my head on the table," Poskrebyshev later told the writer Alexander Tvardovsky, after the tyrant's death. "Beat, beat," Stalin would write on the reports he received of arrested "enemies of the people." Stalin's henchmen not only participated in interrogations, they also took to wielding the baton themselves. Yezhov personally tortured and shot his prisoners; he also prompted the executioners to beat his predecessor Yagoda before they shot him. In May 1939 Chekists found a collection of empty revolver casings in his desk drawer. Yezhov had had the names of Old Bolsheviks who had been killed with these cartridges engraved on them. Nikita Khrushchev remembered one time in 1937 when the NKVD boss had showed up for a meeting with bloodstains on the shirt, explaining that this was the blood of "enemies of the people."

Lavrenty Beria, Yezhov's successor, was an equally unscrupulous and violent perpetrator. He surrounded himself with psychopaths and sadists, who tortured and killed in his name. His confidants from the Caucasus—Bogdan Kobulov, Avxenti Rapava, and Iuvelian Sumbatov-Topuridze—who received influential posts in the NKVD were also brutal butchers, killers for whom no act of violence was too awful. According to one of his subordinates, Beria had told the henchmen of the NKVD to "punch [the victims] in the face before sending them to kingdom come." Kobulov and his cronies bound their victims with rope and then slugged them a few times with their revolvers before shooting them. When Robert Eikhe, previous Politburo member and Siberian party boss, was being led to his execution, Beria ordered his cronies Rodov and Esaulov to first beat him. In Beria's presence, they beat him with truncheons and kicked him—knocking one of his eyes out of its socket—before finally shooting him. Beria killed his adversaries and rivals himself. He shot people with his own revolver and raped underage girls. But he never made the mistake of deceiving his lord and master. Stalin had always been adept at finding executioners of this kind.[224]

What choice did men like Yefim Yevdokimov, Nikolai Yezhov, or Lavrenty Beria even have? They had murdered for Stalin and caused his followers to tremble. Without the dictator's protection they would have been exposed to the wrath of the elite without a help in the world. Nobody mourned Yezhov's fate, and when Khrushchev had Beria shot in June 1953 no one mourned him either. Stalin was an ingenious power strategist. As long as criminals and psychopaths were prepared to kill at his behest, he had no one to fear—neither the followers who feared the Chekists nor the Chekists themselves, who so desperately depended on protection from their patron.

The Bolshevik revolution was an attempt at subjugating, controlling, and reshaping the population of the empire. Steelworks and tanks were supposed to replace huts and icons. Peasants were supposed to become communists. Under Stalinist conditions, however, the attempt at creating New Men through the physical annihilation of the old led to the development of a system based on organized mass murder. The dream of the New Man turned into a nightmare. Peasants became slaves, and Socialism degenerated into despotism.

"I assumed," remembers Jakub Berman, who belonged to the Polish Communist Party's leadership after the Second World War, "the terror of the Great Purge was a side effect of the search for a solution to the Soviet Union's extremely difficult international situation, and possibly also a result of Stalin's own internal struggles and contradictions; they in turn may well have been connected with his extreme suspiciousness, which had become pathological. I didn't try to justify what was happening; rather I accepted that it was a tragic web of circumstance which drew an enormous number of victims into it." Berman searched desperately for a meaning behind the mass killings, and ultimately he fooled himself into believing that "you can't make omelettes without breaking eggs." At some point, however, Berman, seems to have lacked the strength to believe what he had tried to convince himself of day after day.[225]

All that remained for the survivors was the hope that the madness they had fallen victim to served a higher purpose. This hope, however, could not offer consolation to everyone. A fifty-nine-year-old architect from Moscow by the name of Anna looked back with rage after the collapse of the Soviet Union. Her father had been shot, her mother had been sent to a concentration camp. She herself had survived the hell of an NKVD orphanage. What higher purpose could this nightmare possibly have served?

> Evil fascinates us . . . It's like hypnosis . . . There are dozens of books about Hitler, dozens of books about Stalin—about his family life, about the women he loved, which wine he drank, what he liked to read, . . . it interests us to this day! The devil's favorite wine . . . , his favorite cigarettes. . . . Who were these men—Tamerlane, Genghis Khan? . . . What kind of people were they? And the millions who were just like them, only much smaller, who did dreadful things. Only a few of them lost their minds over it. All the others led a completely normal life. Kissed women, rode the bus, bought toys for their children. . . . Everyone thought: it wasn't me. . . . I was not the one who strung people up by their feet and beat the brains out of people's heads so that it splattered onto the ceiling, I was not the one drilling a sharpened pencil into a woman's bosom. . . . It wasn't me, it was the system. . . . Even Stalin. . . . He himself would always say: I am not the one who decides, the party does. To his son he said: You think I am Stalin? No! Stalin, that is him! And he pointed to his picture on the wall. The machinery of death, the devil's machinery was uninterruptedly in operation. . . . For decades. . . . The logic was simple and ingenious: victims and executioners, and in the end the executioner became a victim himself. . . . No human being could have devised this. . . . The wheel keeps turning and it's nobody's fault. . . . Man spends his entire life wavering between good and evil. Either you drill a pencil into someone's nipples or someone does it to you.[226]

6 Wars

THE EXPANSION OF VIOLENCE

THE END OF the exterminatory violence did not mean an end to the terror. It changed, because the system of power was transformed. Stalin no longer needed to kill prominent party leaders to make examples of them. His underlings were prepared to do his bidding without being forced. True power is built on the willingness of subordinates to regularly and voluntarily perform the leader's will, even without the threat of torture or death. It arises from the routine of repeatable situations in which those who are dependent on power instinctively do what is expected of them. The exercise of power in individual cases only has temporary effects, but it is the voluntary and repeatable performance of the ruler's will that serves to assure him of his power. "Compliance in the here and now becomes compliance in every case," wrote Heinrich Popitz, regarding the establishment of permanent power. "Conformity on a case-by-case basis gives way to norm-setting behavior." The ruler saves time, for when compliance is the norm, the amount of effort required to secure his power is reduced. He no longer needs to issue directives in every case, and he does not even have to be present for his will to be done. "The right behavior is known, it is deducible from the situation."[1]

This shift is well illustrated by two incidents—one in 1939 and one in 1941—that contrast the changing approaches to terror. The first-incident was in September 1939, when Nikita Khrushchev traveled with Marshal Timoshenko to Vynnyky, a small town near Lwów, which the Red Army had been occupying since the signing of the Hitler-Stalin Pact. The purpose of their visit was to confront the local NKVD boss, Mikheyev, about his lack of visible achievements there. Mikheyev tried to justify himself, pointing to all the violent measures that had already been taken, but Khrushchev was not interested in excuses and de-manded to know, "What kind of work is this? No one has been shot." Two years later, in April 1941, this kind of prodding and justification were no longer necessary. Khrushchev informed his master that six hundred people had been shot at while attempting to flee across the border near Chernivtsi into Romania. Fifty of them had been killed.[2] No one had ordered Khrushchev to carry out this attack, nor had any-one forced him to notify Stalin. But Khrushchev, like everyone else in the dictator's vicinity, now knew what needed to be done to appease the despot in the Kremlin. The threat of death was unnecessary. Those within Stalin's inner circle were not alone in understanding what sur-vival in his despotic regime required. The young functionaries who had been promoted after 1938 to replace those shot were also well aware of what power demanded of them.

But the regime could not expect its subjects to voluntarily subdue to its power. It had, after all, made slaves of them, without provid-ing any sort of material wealth as compensation. A despotic regime, which offers benefits to the functionaries but not the peasantry, must rely on coercion instead. And so the Stalinist dictatorship remained a slaveholders' regime, keeping peasants confined to collective farms and stigmatizing prisoners and special settlers as second-class humans. Even after the end of the Great Terror, not a single year went by with-out campaigns against enemies, in which vagrants, gypsies, prostitutes, runaway peasants, and people without work and residential permits were banished from the cities and deported to Siberia. In June 1940 the regime introduced a new set of draconian laws in an effort to disci-pline the industrial workforce. Anyone who arrived late for work or re-mained absent could be sent to prison. Within a period of eight months 150,000 workers were tried under these laws in Leningrad alone, and by October 1940 Soviet courts had sent 1,349,560 workers to prison. On September 3, 1940, the Soviet state prosecutor, Viktor Bochkov, informed Stalin that although the courts had been lenient in many cases, the new laws were proving effective. Factory directors were apparently reporting workers at random in order to avoid coming under suspicion themselves of protecting idlers and drunkards from criminal prosecution: "In the past, late arrivals of one, two, three minutes would not always garner attention, but now such late arrivals are being registered. Cases of people leaving work early and not getting to lunch on time are also being registered. There were cases in the past where drunken workers were allowed to work, nowadays this is no longer allowed, and they are held to account for idleness (*progul*)."

The state security organs also began targeting juvenile criminals and hooligans. Tens of thousands were condemned extrajudicially and thrown into camps. The secret police embarked on a daily manhunt for suspects who might have surreptitiously obtained residence permits in Moscow, and in most cases they found these outlaws waiting in line for bread in the early morning hours. In June 1940 Beria informed Stalin that the state security service had expelled 1,120 people who had been living in Moscow without a residence permit and recommended that anyone caught selling goods on the black market, living in a city illegally, or having no regular employment be arrested and locked up. Indeed, the regime soon took action and imposed a travel ban affecting all major cities and most of the Soviet Union's border regions. The secret police also intensified their campaign against the underground economy, and in the first six months of 1940 they arrested more than 50,000 individuals for selling food on the black market.[3]

Stalin and his cronies harbored no illusions regarding the loyalty of the population. It was clear that the third decade of Bolshevik rule would require violence as well. Stalin knew better than anyone that people forced to make public declarations of their great good fortune and joy, while leading private lives of misery, would rise up in revolt if given the opportunity. To prevent this from happening, the state needed to gather information, monitor contacts, and intimidate disloyal groups. It needed to remind the people that the rulers could mete out punishment at any time and in any place. Nevertheless, everything that had been essential for Stalin and his henchmen in 1937 was now, in 1940, no longer quite so critical. The terror did not go away, but it was no longer quite so unpredictable. Who, in 1939, could still make a serious claim that the Soviet Union was being threatened by nobility, kulaks, White Guards, or Socialist Revolutionaries? Stalin's regime abandoned arbitrary mass killings and instead defined both the circle of possible victims and the severity of potential punishments. Stalin and his followers, it seemed, finally felt secure in their power. To them, the mass terror had fulfilled its purpose. It had paralyzed and intimidated Soviet society, prevented all resistance from even forming, and forever removed all enemies.

But then, as soon as the regime's power was again at stake, it returned to its old ways of terror. When Hitler presented Stalin with the opportunity to occupy eastern Poland, annex the Baltic states of Estonia, Latvia, and Lithuania, and force the Romanian government to cede the province of Bessarabia, the territory of the Soviet Union grew but the power of the Bolsheviks did not. It would have been absurd for Stalin to expect the underclasses in the occupied countries to rise up against the elites and join the Soviet occupiers. What, after all, could the impoverished Soviets offer the people they were occupying? Stalin's army looked more like a disorderly bunch of ragged, hungry peasants than the military force of a powerful state with claims to world domination. The bearers of the revolution did not even have enough shoes and clothing for themselves. Although some of the soldiers had boots, others walked around with rags wrapped around their feet. Some had coats, but others had only short jackets, and the clothes worn by almost all of them were threadbare and tattered. "Torn uniforms, dirty coats, hands, and faces, they washed their boots in puddles, they picked papers off the streets and rolled cigarettes, they were pitiful." This was how a ten-year-old boy recalled the Red Army's arrival in Lwów in September 1939.[4] The Polish writer Aleksander Wat, who witnessed the Red Army marching into the city of Łuck, was bewildered:

> You know, those Mongol-like faces, those shoddy uniforms, those raggedy Mongolian peaked caps. It was Asia but in such mass amounts, Asia at its most Asian. I met a friend there, and we went to the movies to see *Ivan the Terrible*. We had to run out of the theater—the stench was unbearable. Boots and more boots and that smell of birch tar and sweaty feet and cheap rolling tobacco. When I had been moving toward communism, I had accepted those Asiatic faces as a fact of life, and I didn't think about them when I was moving away from communism either. I thought that to oppose the European and Asian was merely empty anti-Soviet propaganda, a nineteenth-century issue. Very superficial stuff. But there it was—pure Asia.[5]

As Stalin's peasant soldiers left the Soviet Union and marched into the occupied territories, they discovered again and again that all sorts of things that were absent in the Soviet Union were not only available here, in Poland and in the Baltic states, but that the people took them for granted: shop windows filled with goods, peasants who wore leather boots and lived in solid houses, city dwellers with wristwatches and bicycles. Sandra Kalniete, who became the Latvian foreign minister after the collapse of the Soviet Union, remembered how Red Army soldiers in Riga were sighted on multiple occasions, asking shopkeepers whether one could really buy "white bread and butter in a shop each day and without limitation." For peasants and workers from the Soviet Union such a luxury would have been unthinkable, and so the soldiers took everything that had been unavailable to them back home. In Lwów, even Russian officers and Communist functionaries were observed elbowing their way into local shops to buy or loot watches, edible delicacies, and other luxury items. For the first time in their lives, peasants saw other peasants who were not plagued by hunger. But the encounter with Estonians, Latvians, and Poles was a humbling experience, and it made the "victors" see with their own eyes that the defeated lived better lives than they did. According to Jan Gross, this was the major difference between National Socialist and Stalinist occupation policies. "What was lacking under the Soviet occupation was the sense of pervasive discriminatory contempt, the *Übermensch* airs, so forcefully projected by the Germans. If anything, initially at least, the Soviets were themselves somewhat awed, insecure, and intimidated."[6] Vanquished though the Poles and Baltic peoples were, why would they have looked to the social order of a poorhouse as their shining example?

In winter 1939 the soldiers also discovered that the military supremacy of the Red Army was nothing but an illusion, a product of the regime's relentless propaganda efforts. In November 1939, when Stalin ordered his generals to attack Finland, the expectation was that the Soviet Army would subdue its neighbor within a matter of days. It was the first time, however, that Stalin's threats did not lead to the immediate surrender of those on the receiving end. The Finnish Army defended itself valiantly. It encircled the Soviet units, wore them down, and even forced them to retreat in some places. In January 1940, directly before the start of a second Soviet offensive, Stalin announced to his circle of followers that Finland would not survive the war: "There are 150,000 Finnish *Schutzkorpists*—that's where the White Finns are strongest. We have killed sixty thousand of them; we shall have to kill the rest, and that will be the end of it."[7] In reality, though, it ended up taking the Red Army another two months to make even modest territorial gains and force the Finnish government to cede parts of Karelia to the Soviet Union. The warring parties ended the conflict in March, and although the Soviet Union had expanded its territory, Finland had retained its sovereignty. Over 125,000 Soviet soldiers had died for this achievement, and another 265,000 plus had come home wounded.

What was initially supposed to be an easy, short-lived campaign had turned into a bloody war. It demonstrated quite clearly to the political leadership that its military capabilities were limited. The Red Army's officers lacked experience, and its soldiers lacked motivation. Generals sent their soldiers by the thousands into the line of Finnish machine-gun fire, and they let them die in droves in militarily pointless battles. After the war, Red Army soldiers could no longer believe the regime's propaganda that the armed forces of the proletarian state were invincible or that they would be greeted as liberators by the oppressed peoples of the world. Quite the opposite seemed to be the case. Furthermore, the leadership in Moscow apparently shared this view, because when the first Soviet prisoners of war returned home from Finland they were immediately arrested and taken to filtration camps under suspicion of being spies. In July 1940, 232 former Soviet prisoners of war were put to death. The justification, as Beria told Stalin, was that they had been Finish intelligence operatives.[8]

The Bolsheviks gained territory, but they made no friends. Furthermore, they had good reason to doubt the loyalty of the subdued and to be mistrustful of their own soldiers, whose experiences abroad and in the military contradicted everything that Soviet propaganda had told them. What, then, was to be done? For Stalin and his followers it was clear. The new socialist order could only prevail if the old order was wiped out violently. In other words, the occupied territories needed to catch up. They still needed to experience everything that the Soviet Union had already undergone.

The terror returned, but it sought out new victims. Beyond the borders of the Soviet Union the concept of social mobilization encountered its limits. After the experiences of collectivization and mass terror, the nationality policy of the Bolsheviks had lost all appeal in the neighboring countries, meaning that the Bolsheviks could not count on the support of workers and peasants in Estonia, Latvia, or Lithuania. Poland and the Baltic republics had escaped the 1930s without collectivization, famine, or terror, while in the Soviet Union ethnic minorities had been deported or shot. Inside the Soviet Union, the Bolshevik dictatorship encountered resistance everywhere and had to assert itself against the will of the people. Why should it have been any different in the occupied territories? What did Polish workers and peasants stand to gain from a victory of Soviet power? Had the Poles been given a choice, the Soviet order surely would not have been it.

Stalin understood this very well, and he harbored no illusions that it might ever be otherwise. The Polish state, however, was also on a weak footing. In the Kresy, the country's eastern territories, which were inhabited by Ukrainians, Belorussians, and Jews, the Polish state had never amounted to much more than a small conglomeration of Polish elites. In the event of a Red Army occupation there was no reason to believe that anyone—neither the native peasant population nor a foreign power—would come to the aid of the Polish upper classes. Stalin was aware of this predicament too, and it would have been contrary to his nature to miss the opportunity to exploit it. Thus, in August 1939, when Hitler approached Stalin to suggest that the two nations carve up Poland between them, Stalin had no reservations. On September 17, 1939, the Polish ambassador to the USSR, Grzybowski, was summoned to the Foreign Ministry, where Molotov's deputy Vladimir Potyomkin handed him a note, informing him that the Red Army would be occupying the eastern part of Poland. As Potyomkin later wrote in his diary, the Polish ambassador was beside himself. He refused to accept the note and reportedly exclaimed that if this were to happen it would mean the "fourth partition of Poland and its destruction." When he protested that the Soviet Union was helping Germany "destroy" Poland, Potyomkin's response was that the Polish state was done for anyway and there was no use in opposing the inevitable. Soon thereafter, Molotov addressed the Supreme Soviet, declaring that "one swift blow" by the Wehrmacht and the Red Army was all that would be needed to rid the world forever of "this ugly offspring of the Versailles Treaty."[9]

When Soviet troops marched across the border into Poland in mid-September 1939 Stalin presented it as a liberation of Ukrainian and

Belorussian peasants from the Polish yoke. The Soviet press celebrated the annexation as a "reunification" of separated peoples, who would now be reunited with their compatriots in the Soviet Union and brought under the protective roof of the multiethnic empire. The regime's claim to being the advocate of oppressed nations did not remain without consequences for the occupied territories. On September 22 Lev Mekhlis, the head of the political administration of the Red Army, informed Stalin that the Polish Army was no longer offering any resistance and that Ukrainians and Belorussians who had been resisting the Germans had now "laid down their arms" and surrendered. Soviet troops, he reported, were being greeted as liberators by the Ukrainians and Belorussians, and when the first Red Army soldiers had appeared in the villages of Ukraine, the women had even cried "tears of joy." In some areas, however, the violence had spiraled out of control. There had been reports of Ukrainians raiding Polish villages, setting houses on fire, and killing local residents. In some places the rage was so great that the Red Army had been forced to protect captured Polish officers from angry peasant mobs. In other villages, though, the Ukrainian peasants had been permitted to torture and kill Polish officers and settlers while Red Army soldiers watched. In the Novogrod district, Polish policemen were slain with axes, and three hundred prisoners were bludgeoned to death with hammers. In Łuck twenty-four Polish settlers were tied up with barbed wire by Ukrainian peasants and drowned. In Pruzana, meanwhile, Belorussian peasants had stoned a Polish Army captain to death. In almost every case the Soviet occupiers exercised restraint and allowed the peasant committees to proceed with the punishment of the Polish settlers as they desired.

Sometimes, however, Red Army soldiers participated in the massacres themselves. When Polish soldiers near Grodno resisted, the Soviet victors had 300 Polish prisoners, including a regimental commander, shot dead. In Polesia, another 150 officers were murdered. On September 27, 1939, near Grabowiec, a locality between Hrubieszów and Zamość, more than 5,000 Polish soldiers were taken into Soviet captivity. 164 of the men, who were identified as Polish officers or policemen, were shot by the Ukrainian militia and Bolshevik commissars. In Podhorce, in the district of Złoczów, the occupiers also identified 500 residents as "policemen," gathered them in the town center, and let the Red Army soldiers gun them down. Elsewhere, Chekists killed

Catholic priests and Polish Army soldiers, simply because they found the skin on their hands too soft, which supposedly betrayed them as members of the elite.

This violence no doubt pleased the new masters, as it helped them present themselves as friends of the oppressed peoples in these regions. Mekhlis wrote to Stalin that it was an axiom of political wisdom that interethnic conflicts should be redirected to target Polish landowners and state officials. It would also be wise, he said, to release all Ukrainian and Belorussian prisoners of war, as they were perhaps the only potential friends that Soviet power might have in the occupied territories. Mekhlis made no mention of the Jews. He himself was a Jew, and probably thought it wise to avoid mentioning the Jews in Stalin's presence, lest he gives the impression that he was trying to champion the cause of his own people. But Jews were raiding Polish estates and police stations. Jewish self-defense units had also attacked scattered units of the Polish Army. Although Mekhlis was certainly exaggerating when he spoke of the joy with which Ukrainian peasants had welcomed the Red Army into their villages, he was not exaggerating when he spoke of the ethnic conflicts that had broken out throughout eastern Poland. These conflicts allowed the occupiers to play Poles, Ukrainians, and Jews off against each other and poison relations between the different ethnic groups in this corner of the world in a way that would be felt for years to come.[10]

In late September more than 250,000 soldiers from the defeated Polish Army were taken into Soviet captivity. Tens of thousands of them were left to wander aimlessly, as the Red Army could neither imprison them nor provide for them. Lavrenty Tsanava, the Belorussian NKVD boss and a close confidant of Beria, suggested setting up collection points and filtration camps to weed out potentially hostile soldiers. He also proposed releasing all Belorussians and Ukrainians from captivity. On September 20 the first prisoners were taken to camps beyond the former border in Belorussia, Ukraine, and the Vologda region. On October 3, 1939, Stalin ordered the NKVD to deploy 25,000 Polish prisoners of war to build roads. He also ordered the release of all Belorussian and Ukrainian soldiers, who were to be taught the "slogans" of the Soviet state and mobilized for the upcoming "elections."

There was to be no mercy for the Polish prisoners of war. Stalin instructed the NKVD to transfer Polish officers and state officials to special camps and separate them from lower-ranking military personnel. High-ranking Polish officers and state officials were to be taken to the NKVD camp in Starobilsk, while policemen and Polish intelligence operatives were to be detained in Ostashkov. All prisoners who had lived in the western part of Poland before the war would be interned in the camps of Kozelsk and Putivl and subsequently deported to German-occupied Poland. Whether they were Poles, Jews, or Communists was irrelevant. Over ten thousand Poles were sent to prisons in Vilnius, Lwów, Pinsk, Tarnopol, Baranovichi, and Brest, and between October 24 and November 23, 1939, the Soviet authorities handed 42,492 prisoners over to the German occupiers. Of course this also included all the Jews they had captured, despite their pleas to not be surrendered to the mercy of the National Socialists.[11]

Stalin also employed this strategy of divide and rule in his effort to destabilize the Baltic republics. The Baltic annexation was based on a cynical model of blackmail. Hitler had used it successfully against Austria and Czechoslovakia one year earlier, and Stalin found it worthy of emulation. Immediately after the attack on Poland, Stalin demanded that the governments of Estonia, Latvia, and Lithuania approve the stationing of Soviet troops on their soil. Molotov even threatened to have the Latvian foreign minister arrested if he dared to resist: "You're not going to return home," he told him, "until you give your signature to your self-inclusion in the USSR."[12] Six months later, in June 1940, the moment had arrived for Stalin to annex the neighboring countries. The foreign ministers of the Baltic republics were summoned to Moscow, where Molotov informed them that their countries would be occupied, and a short time later the invasion began. The Red Army encountered no resistance, as the governing administrations in Tallinn, Riga, and Kaunas had instructed their citizens to bow to the inevitable. In Latvia, the Red Army's arrival even came as a surprise, as the government had already expressed its willingness to accept Stalin's demands without even informing its citizens of the looming threat.

The Red Army arrived with tanks, heavy equipment, and NKVD units in tow. Following the Finnish disaster, no efforts were spared in bringing the operation to a successful conclusion. Over 200,000 soldiers were sent to Latvia alone, where they occupied the capital and the most important areas of the country. And since those who were caught off guard offered no resistance, the occupation in Estonia and Lithuania was achieved effortlessly as well.

As was usual for Stalin, once he had decided to apply coercion but was uncertain as to whether those under threat would obey voluntarily, he sent one of his people to the scene of events. Leningrad's party boss, Andrei Zhdanov, was dispatched to Tallinn. Former State Prosecutor Andrei Vyshinsky, traveled to Riga. And the deputy leader of the NKVD, Vladimir Dekanozov, arrived in Kaunas. Stalin's satraps in the Baltics fortified themselves in the Soviet embassies and made their important decisions from there. As a first order of business, they demanded that the governing administrations initiate the transition to the new order themselves. They organized rigged elections, in which the supporters of the Bolsheviks naturally emerged victorious. They also made an effort to pit the national minorities against the majority, and bloody clashes soon broke out as Russian and Jewish workers from the harbor district descended upon the center of Riga to besiege government buildings and hunt down Latvian policemen. Even in Liepāja and other small Latvian towns Soviet intelligence organized "committees of the poor" to help the occupiers spread fear. There were Russian National Bolsheviks in Riga and "Red Guards" in Liepāja. Both of these groups—which had particularly large Jewish memberships—looted, ransacked houses, searched out "enemies of the people," and beat up Latvian policemen. Although the Russian and Jewish press lauded the occupation of Latvia as an act of national liberation, most Latvians felt deep humiliation about the obliteration of their state.

Zhdanov and Dekanozov helped organize similar takeovers in Estonia and Lithuania. Their task was to convince the rest of the world that the Bolsheviks had also arrived as liberators of oppressed minorities. On July 18, 1940, Zhdanov stepped out onto the balcony of the Soviet embassy in Tallinn to greet a crowd of communist demonstrators, who had gathered in the forecourt to celebrate the viceroy of Stalin. Latvians, Estonians, and Lithuanians, however, had no reason to celebrate. In the course of July and August 1940 the Baltic republics were transformed into Soviet socialist republics and subsequently joined to the Soviet Union.[13] The presidents of Estonia and Latvia, Konstantin Päts and Kārlis Ulmanis, were arrested and deported. Päts died in 1956 in a psychiatric hospital in Burashevo near Kalinin, and Ulmanis lived out his last days in a prison in Turkmenistan, before perishing in 1942.

Latvia's president, Antanas Smetona, was the only one who managed to escape and later died in the United States.

For Stalin, this was all rather easy. No one came to the aid of the invaded, and the authoritarian regimes of the Baltic states did everything necessary to help the occupiers contain the people's rage. Within a relatively short period of time, several million people had become Soviet subjects against their will, and to ensure that they remain so Stalin and his henchmen turned to their proven repertoire of repression. The terror, however, could only be successful if it was directed by the dictator's own people, whom he trusted. Nothing could be expected of the native Communists. In December 1940 the Latvian Communist Party had 2,800 members, 1,099 of whom lived in the capital, Riga. Only 28 percent of them were Latvians, however, while the rest were Russians or Jews. Furthermore, during the 1930s most of Latvia's Communists were either in prison or in exile in Moscow. Communist rule in Latvia was equivalent to foreign rule, and it would remain so for a long time to come. But for Stalin's style of rule, the advantages of this situation outweighed its disadvantages, as the loyalty of Russian and Jewish Communists had never been in question. They would never collude with their would-be overlords—the Latvians—and Stalin knew this. The Soviet Union did have collaborators in the Baltic republics, and although they remained an insignificant minority, with no chance of influencing the course of events either in their homelands or in Moscow, this very lack of influence was exactly what Stalin needed. As the dictator, Stalin could trust marginalized collaborators just as blindly as he could trust the Russian and Jewish Communists he had sent to the occupied areas. Everyone knew that their position in the power hierarchy was solely dependent on the mercy of the occupiers and that a collapse of Soviet power would mean their downfall as well. Every violent act they committed in the name of the dictatorship increased their dependence on the good will of the dictator, and the dictator in turn made them hostages of his strategy of violence.[14]

But what of those who had never attended a Soviet school or served in the Red Army and had no idea what the dictator expected of them? How were Estonians and Latvians supposed to become Soviet citizens who would submit and obey voluntarily? The regime's response to such difficulties was always the same. It limited the people's freedom of movement, restricted the flow of information, confined them to collective farms or factories, drafted them into the Red Army, and took every available opportunity to remind them that they were powerless. People only accustom themselves to life in a dictatorship when they no longer believe that alternatives are possible, when they believe that they have no choice but to reconcile themselves to a life without freedom. But the triumph of slavery is not complete until all hope has been abandoned that the dictatorship will one day end. "You'll get used to it, or else you'll croak," was a common response that Soviet soldiers gave residents in the occupied territories when they failed to understand what was happening to them. These soldiers had experienced what it meant to submit to a reign of violence, and now it was time for a new set of subjects to get used to it too.[15]

Within weeks of the occupation, border fortifications had been erected on the demarcation line between Soviet and German occupied territory. NKVD border troops were given orders to remove all suspicious persons from the border areas, to destroy their houses, and to use force to prevent all attempts at escape. Nobody was to leave or enter the Soviet Union without permission. On April 4, 1940, Stalin instructed the Red Army General Staff to distribute eighteen hundred revolvers throughout western Ukraine to the secretaries of party committees there. The idea was that they be able to command more respect in the occupied territories. One day earlier, Stalin had ordered the confiscation of all privately owned radios in the Finnish-Soviet border region. From now on, the only information to reach the new subjects was to come from the world of lies. Peasants and city dwellers in the occupied areas were now required to participate in "elections," which served no other purpose than to stigmatize outcasts and enemies and impose the will of the new masters. People who could be forced to take part in elections that followed no democratic procedure whatsoever could also be ruled at will. In October 1939 NKVD men reportedly appeared in Polish and Ukrainian villages on horseback and forced the locals to join gatherings where they had to praise Stalin and his constitution. This was how many peasants would later remember the farce of what was known in the Soviet jargon as "election campaigns."[16]

The Stalinist terror was not merely a successful attempt at beating people into submission by spreading fear and dread. It was also an instrument of ethnic cleansing with which the Stalinist regime did its best to poison relations between the various ethnic groups of Eastern Europe. Furthermore, it was an elegant means of strengthening the power of the Soviet regime, for wherever minorities lived in fear of majorities, the dictator's power was limitless. The ultimate goal was to break all resistance and eliminate the power of the old elites forever. The project of terror began in Poland, where it was also the most ruthless. Stalin left no doubt about his intention to destroy the Polish state and its elite. All traces of the Kresy, which once belonged to Poland, were to be erased. The Bolsheviks had lost the former western provinces of the tsarist empire in the Russo-Polish War of 1920. As a political commissar, Stalin himself had witnessed the Bolshevik army being stopped at the gates of Warsaw by Polish troops and forced to retreat. The defeat had been dishonorable, and now Stalin was prepared to take revenge. The conquered territories were soon remapped, the population was registered and categorized, and all able-bodied men were forced to join the Red Army. This included Poles, Ukrainians, Belorussians, and Jews, who already fought in the struggle against Finland in the autumn of 1939.

In December 1939 Stalin ordered Beria to have all Polish settlers and foresters, who had entered the region after the Russo-Polish War, deported to the Urals and Western Siberia. Their families, of course, were to be deported along with them, while the most "malevolent" elements were to be handed over to the NKVD. On February 10, 1940, Beria's subordinate Bogdan Kobulov, who was in charge of the operation, was able to report that the deportations had begun at seven that morning. "The operation is proceeding normally," Kobulov reported. Temperatures had dropped to thirty degrees below zero, and a number of soldiers were suffering from frostbite, but other than that there had been no noteworthy incidents. He apparently did however, consider it worth mentioning that an unruly detainee had "bitten" an NKVD officer. The following day Beria informed Stalin that the operation had been brought to a successful conclusion. In the space of two day 146,375 people had been loaded onto freight trains and taken away. Over 50,000 Chekists, militia members, and Red Army soldiers had been in action, and not a single settler had escaped. "During the execution of the operation," Beria reported, "there were no incidents that deserve any sort of attention." Some settlers had reportedly tried to escape, but their attempts had been foiled by the NKVD. In some places, peasants had reportedly helped the Chekists round up Polish settlers at the collection points in order to be able to loot the prisoners' homes once they were gone.[17]

In April 1940 the relatives of Polish officers and state officials in Soviet captivity were deported. This included more than 22,000 families with over 65,000 people. The next wave of terror followed in June and July 1940 when 78,000 people, many of them Jews who had fled the German occupation zone, were taken from their homes and deported to Siberia. One year later, in April 1941, violence returned to the region once again. This time Stalin ordered Merkulov, the minister of state security to arrest and deport the family members of people who had fled, gone into hiding, been sent to prison, or been shot on account of their membership in a Polish, Ukrainian, or Belorussian "counter-revolutionary organization." The result of this order was that another 61,000 people were taken from their homes and deported within a matter of weeks.

This terror was not directed at the Polish elite alone. In the second year of occupation, the regime took the opportunity to settle scores with defiant Ukrainian peasants and nationalists who opposed the Bolshevik dictatorship. Just before the Wehrmacht's attack on the Soviet Union, Stalin demanded that the NKVD violently suppress all resistance from Ukrainian partisans and rebellious peasants. The population was to be disarmed, and anyone in possession of a weapon was to be arrested. The family members of "bandits," Polish officers, and "counter-revolutionaries" who had already been executed were to be deported to "distant areas of the Soviet Union" for the duration of twenty years. This operation, which was carried out in June 1941, claimed another 90,000 victims.

Between February 1940 and June 1941 more than 381,000 people were deported from the Soviet occupation zone in eastern Poland and taken to Siberia or central Asia. The statistics kept by the state security organs, however, only account for victims deported after February 1940. They provide no information about the arbitrary arrests and shootings that followed the Red Army's invasion in autumn 1939, and they make no mention of the thousands of Polish and Ukrainian peasants who were forced to join the Red Army against their will or become slave laborers in the coal mines of the Donbass. These numbers have never been counted. Tens of thousands of people were also forced to leave their homelands because Stalin and his cronies had decided that Lithuanians should not live in Belorussia and that Belorussians did not belong in Lithuania. Over 100,000 people, who were forced to leave eastern Ukraine, were resettled in the occupied areas of Poland and housed in the homes of Poles who had been deported to Siberia. In one way or another, probably more than a million people were expelled from the territories of eastern Poland.[18]

Although the terror in the Baltic republics set in later, it was no less cruel than in occupied Poland. Here, too, terror was the regime's attempt at asserting itself against national resistance, and nowhere on their path to total power were the Bolsheviks met with greater resistance than in Estonia, Latvia, and Lithuania. In January 1941 a decree went out that all Estonian, Latvian, and Lithuanian conscripts serving in the national units of the Red Army were to swear an oath and pledge their allegiance to the new Soviet order. According to state security agents, however, in many places soldiers and officers outright refused, and when pressed they had simply grown excited and begun speaking about the poverty and backwardness of the Soviet Union. "Under Smetona," a Lithuanian officer was said to have claimed, "they gave us good food to eat, but since the arrival of Soviet power, we are being fed like dogs, and now there is even talk of an oath. I will not take an oath." A battery commander reportedly told his soldiers that there was "nothing" for them in the Soviet Union, and, indeed, this was one reason why the authorities prohibited Lithuanians from traveling to Russia and seeing life under socialism for themselves. According to one Latvian soldier who had been to Leningrad, the workers there were treated like slaves. He also told his comrades of a hungry worker being shot for selling a sheepskin on the black market. Soviet informants, too, reported to Moscow that the standing of Soviet power in the Baltic states was particularly poor. In Latvia, informants reported, political leaflets were circulating that urged soldiers to resist their officers and refuse the oath. The leaflets also claimed that Hitler's forces would soon attack the Soviet Union and "cleanse Europe of Jews and Communists." Finland already stood under the protection of the German army, and Latvia, it promised, would soon be free as well.

How was it possible for people to speak truths that had not been officially authorized by the government? The Chekists who had the task of reporting this outrage also had a simple explanation: "The hostile elements have greatly increased their counterrevolutionary activities in the recent past, not only by trying to interfere with the taking of oath, but also by establishing cadres of spies and diversionists in the territorial units." This was what Ryabshin, the political commissar of the Baltic Military District, reported at any rate. One soldier was found in possession of a Latvian national flag, and another soldier had a portrait of the deposed President Ulmanis. Several Latvians had been seized at the border while attempting to flee to Germany. It was quite clear that German intelligence was recruiting soldiers to infiltrate the Red Army in the Baltic republics and destabilize the Soviet order there. Between October 1940 and May 1941 courts martial in the Baltic Military District condemned 1,058 soldiers for "counterrevolutionary agitation." This, however, was far from sufficient. Ryabshin recommended searching all military units for enemies and spies and also replenishing the national units with soldiers from other Soviet republics. In this way, all potential future resistance would be crushed before it could even form.[19]

For Stalin and his cronies, violence was once again the only solution. On May 16, 1941, the dictator ordered the Ministry of State Security to arrest all members of "counterrevolutionary parties," along with everyone in Lithuania, Latvia, and Estonia who had ever been a policeman, officer, state official, landlord, or factory owner. Once arrested, they were to be taken to concentration camps. Their family members and household employees would be deported to Siberia or Kazakhstan and kept there for twenty years. This applied to Germans living in the Baltic states, as well as to Estonians, Latvians, and Lithuanians who had lived in Germany and returned to their homeland after the Hitler-Stalin Pact. Stalin also decided that it was not enough to deport the Baltic elites, and that all prostitutes, who were registered by the police as such, should be deported as well. Within a matter of two days, more than forty thousand people had been taken away. On June 12 and 13, 1941, only one week before the Wehrmacht's attack on the Soviet Union, the dictator declared that Moldavia would be the next target and that it too would have to endure everything the Baltic republics already had endured. This was a decision that resulted in the loss of freedom and homeland for another thirty-three thousand people. The deportations from the Baltics and from Moldavia apparently proceeded according to plan as well, and on June 17 the minister of state security, Merkulov, reported that there had been almost no resistance. Only seven people had had to be killed.[20]

We should not be misled by the state security reports, which present the expulsions as simple, orderly affairs. In reality they were murderous terror campaigns that claimed the lives of thousands. NKVD squads and their civilian auxiliaries, consisting of Jews or Ukrainians, employed a strategy of taking their victims by surprise. On February 10, 1940, seemingly out of nowhere, they appeared in the villages of the annexed areas of eastern Poland, catching the unsuspecting victims completely off guard. Only when the Chekists arrived at their doors did they learn that they would be deported. There was scarcely time to dress and pack the most essential of belongings before being led away. In some areas, children came home from school to find their parents gone. In the course of deportation, families, friends, and relatives were all separated. Victims only rarely discovered why they had been picked up or where they were being taken. While the victims in Poland may have had some suspicion of what the Bolshevik state had in store for them, in the Baltic republics the terror came as a complete surprise. In Riga, in the spring of 1941, apparently no one had believed it was possible for the occupiers to take people from their homes and deport them without trial. Sandra Kalniete, whose parents were deported during this period, recalls how in Latvia "people had been accustomed to living in a state of justice, where an innocent person could not, like a criminal, be pulled from his or her house at night and put in a cattle car to be sent into unknown exile." Now, though, the violence had paralyzed them with its suddenness, and thus the Latvians could offer no resistance.

The expulsions in the annexed territories led to an unforeseen traffic chaos. Thousands of trucks and horse carts rumbled through the streets of Lwów, the center of western Ukraine. A woman, who would go on to survive the whole ordeal, recalled how all one could hear in the early morning hours was children crying, dogs howling, and the occasional gunshot being fired by the NKVD men. "When we reached the road a very unpleasant sight opened before our eyes. Well, some two hundred sleds with Polish families were already standing there. Children were crying. Along the column, mounted Red Army soldiers kept riding back and forth. It was a moving spectacle."[21]

Villagers were escorted through the freezing cold to train stations and loaded onto freight cars. In many cases, small children would not even survive the journey to the station. A survivor remembered seeing babies in Przemyśl that had frozen to death, whose mothers had left them by the roadsides or thrown them out of the trains. The stations were sites of dreadful scenes. People were penned into crowded cattle cars, where they often spent several days in the freezing cold, before the trains started rolling. Frequently, people perished while still at the station or while waiting in the unheated carriages. Many more were dead upon arrival at their destinations. One eyewitness recalled that in the train station in Łomża, people spent three days waiting in unheated rail cars before the train finally departed. Many of the children were already dead by then. He later saw a picture of the train in a Soviet newspaper, with teary-eyed people chasing after it. "Weeping families who are not going to Russia," read the caption below the image.[22]

The very young and the very old died from hunger, cold, thirst, or exhaustion before they reached Siberia. Even the heads of the Gulag administration, who were in charge of allocating prisoners to various slave labor settlements, complained about the ruthlessness with which the deportations had been carried out. There were reports of people arriving at their destinations without any belongings or clothes. Children arrived without parents, and infants arrived without mothers. Aged people without teeth, epileptics, people who were blind or missing limbs, and even American citizens—they were all taken to Siberia.[23]

Stalin did not shy away from murder either. As was usual for when he decided he wanted people killed, he prompted his followers to request the necessary orders. For him it was important that his devotees stained themselves with blood. On March 5, 1940, Beria sent Stalin a letter in which he proposed shooting 25,700 Polish "officers, officials, landowners, policemen, spies, gendarmes, and prison guards," who were currently being held in the prisoner of war camps and prisons. There would be no need for an investigation or an indictment, as they were all "sworn enemies of Soviet power, filled with hatred for the Soviet system of government." Beria reported, "Officer and police prisoners of war in the camps are attempting to continue their counterrevolutionary work and are conducting anti-Soviet agitation. Each one of them is just waiting to be released in order to be able to enter actively into the battle against Soviet power." And since the NKVD had discovered organized insurgencies throughout the occupied territories, Polish officers posed a potential threat to the new order too.

This would make the summary execution of all "irremediable enemies" unavoidable. Among these irremediable enemies were 14,700 officers and state officials who were being held in camps, along with 11,000 "members of counterrevolutionary espionage and sabotage organizations" who were imprisoned in Belorussia and Ukraine. Although this was presented as a request, the decision, of course, had already been made long before. After receiving Beria's letter, Stalin gave his approval that very same day. "I'm in favor," he wrote on the letter, and then instructed Molotov, Voroshilov, and Mikoyan to add their signatures. Kalinin and Kaganovich had their names inserted by Stalin's secretary, Poskrebyshev.[24]

The reasons that Stalin gave Beria, when he decided that the Polish officers would die, will most likely remain unknown. Were the camps supposed to be cleared out to make room for Finnish or Baltic prisoners? Was he recalling the humiliation of the Civil War, when the Red Army had been defeated by the Poles? Did he plan to use the officers as collateral to prevent the Polish government in exile in London from sending soldiers to resist the Red Army on the Finnish front? Did he only give the order to kill after the Finnish defeat had become inevitable and the prisoners were no longer of any value to him? Or did he really fear that the Polish officers, if released, could one day pose a threat to the Soviet order? Stalin's motives were probably quite simple. In all likelihood he imagined that, without an elite, Poland would cease to exist as an independent state. There would be no one to represent Polish interests and no one to question Stalin's plans for shifting national borders. As George Sanford writes in his book on the Katyn massacre, the Polish officers "laughed off" the Bolshevik attempts at winning them over with their crude propaganda. No one in Poland considered the Soviet order of violence an exemplary model for society. "Their national, patriotic, and religious values and behavior as well as their individualism and autonomous self-organization were a continuous affront to NKVD ideas of camp discipline." It cannot be ruled out that Beria had spoken with Stalin about this rebelliousness and presented him with reports on prisoner behavior. Stalin was in need of loyal Polish collaborators. Although he could have had the Polish officers deported or exiled abroad, in light of everything else he had inflicted on others why would he have behaved differently in this situation and spared them? Stalin was a despot, and he killed because he took pleasure in killing. He did not require a moral justification for his acts of violence, and although he was well aware that killing prisoners of war violated international law and the Geneva Convention, this did not interest him.[25]

Stalin entrusted an NKVD troika with the task of carrying out the executions. This troika, which was made up of Beria's friends Bogdan Kobulov, Vsevolod Merkulov, and Leonid Bashtakov, was allowed to decide which victims would be shot. On March 15, 1940, the commanders of the prisoner of war camps in Kozelsk, Ostashkov, and Starobilsk were summoned to Moscow, where they were briefed on the planned executions and instructed to organize the transportation of the prisoners to the execution sites. The executions began in early April, and the last victims were shot in mid-May. Detainees were taken to the places of execution by train—from Ostashkov to Kalinin (Tver), from Starobilsk to Kharkov, and from Kozelsk via Smolensk to Koze Gory in the Katyn Forest. In order to prevent the condemned from becoming suspicious, the NKVD began a rumor that a release of prisoners of war was imminent. On the day before they were taken to their places of execution the condemned were given food supplies and typhus vaccinations. As Salomon Slowes, a prisoner at the Kozelsk camp, recalled, the condemned were fully unaware of the fate that awaited them: "After painstaking examination, the happy men bounded down the entrance stairs, beaming from ear to ear and clutching portions of bread and dry herring wrapped in white paper. This latter was considered a luxury in the camp. Observing the precautions taken and the way the men were examined, we were more convinced than ever that the rumors were true, and that our comrades were about to be repatriated."[26]

In March 1991 the Military Prosecutor's Office in Moscow managed to track down an NKVD officer who had participated in the executions in Kalinin. He provided the investigators with a detailed account of the murder campaign. Thirty NKVD men had arrived from Moscow. Most of them had been drivers and guards, while only a few men had been in charge of the executions. Vasily Blokhin, Stalin's executioner for special assignments, had reportedly appeared in Kalinin, along with two of his helpers and a suitcase full of German-made Walther pistols for the executioners to use in carrying out their "work." Each day, 250 detainees were brought to the prison and led down into the cellar. Their identities were verified in an entryway, and then, one after another, they were taken to a soundproofed room where Blokhin and his henchmen shot them. Blokhin, as the eyewitness recalled, would wear leather gaiters and a leather apron. "Two men held [the prisoner's] arms and the third shot him in the base of the skull. They led him into the cell and shot him in the base of the skull. That's all."[27] More than 6,800 men were killed in this manner. Blokhin needed less than two minutes to send each prisoner to his death. The bodies were then taken from the prison to be buried in a forest twenty miles outside the city that very same night.

In the Kharkov prison 3,896 Polish officers from the Starobilsk camp were murdered in the same manner. In the case of this massacre too, the Russian Military Prosecutor's Office was supplied with information by one of the perpetrators in spring 1990. According to his testimony, the detainees were shot in the prison cellar in the presence of the prison director and the state prosecutor—100 a night, sometimes as many as 250. The dead were loaded onto trucks and thrown into a pit in a forest outside of Kharkov. The perpetrators were under intense pressure. As the NKVD man recalled, they were required to kill without interruption because the next batch of prisoners was always due to arrive the following morning. Not a single victim was allowed to survive the night, so the executioners "worked" without respite. In the early morning hours, they followed the usual procedure of cleaning up with eau de cologne and drinking themselves into a stupor with vodka.

In all probability the 4,410 prisoners who were taken from Kozelsk via Smolensk to Koze Gory in the Katyn Forest died in this manner as well. To this day, however, it remains unclear where exactly the Polish officers were murdered—whether it was in the prison basement or in the forest, where the bodies were later found. The victims were probably shot in front of trenches that had been dug, and then thrown into them. Some appeared to have offered resistance as they were being led to the trenches, as some of the bodies later discovered had their hands tied together with barbed wire. Similar procedures appear to have been applied elsewhere as well. What became of the 18,632 Poles who were imprisoned in western Ukraine and Belorussia, however, has remained unclear to this day. 7,305 of them, in any case, were taken to Kiev, Kharkov, Kherson, and Minsk to be killed there. The precise location of their execution and burial remains unknown.

For their service of having shot several thousand people, Beria saw to it that Blokhin and his henchmen received an additional month's wage—an absurdly low sum, considering everything they had done. But Blokhin at least would not regret his role as Stalin's loyal servant for so many years. Stalin held him in high regard and showered him with privileges and decorations, and ultimately he outlived his master by two years. Not all NKVD leaders enjoyed Stalin's trust, however. Stalin apparently mistrusted the Kharkov NKVD, for example, as he sent inspectors there to confirm that the "condemned" had in fact been shot. Roman Rudenko, the deputy state prosecutor of Ukraine, appeared in the execution cellar to read out the "verdicts" and supervise the killings. Six years later, as Soviet chief prosecutor at Nuremberg, he tried to blame the mass murder he had witnessed on the National Socialists.[28]

THE STALINIST WAR

Hitler's attack on the Soviet Union transformed the nature of the war that Germany had unleashed on Europe. It became a merciless war, a war of annihilation, and all previous boundaries were crossed. As Goebbels noted in his diary, Hitler was euphoric and relieved once the attack order had finally been issued to the troops. "The Führer seems to be losing his fear as the decision comes nearer. . . . He is relaxing visibly. All the exhaustion seems to be dropping away." Indeed, the war against the Soviet Union gave him the opportunity to finally, completely turn his back on international law and the rules of conventional warfare and do what he had been plotting for years but had not yet been able to do: the annihilation of the Jews of Europe and the enslavement of several million people.[29]

Like Stalin, Hitler too made his generals hostages to his strategy of violence. They were dragged into a war of annihilation with an uncertain outcome and no end in sight. Although they justified their great slaughter by claiming to be defenders of civilization, in reality they had burnt all bridges to the civilized world behind them. They had embarked on this gruesome project together and thus had to stay and see it through. By the winter of 1942 at the latest, however, Hitler must have sensed that Stalin's conceptions of the rules of war were no different from his own. After everything that had happened, peaceful compromise was out of the question. The only possibility was for the defeated to be destroyed. "We will deal with them," wrote Goebbels in his diary on August 1, 1941, "mainly because we have to deal with them."[30]

To Hitler, anything that led to the ultimate annihilation of the enemy was permissible. His war broke with all traditions of civilized warfare and all military virtues that had once distinguished the German army. The Bolsheviks, however, were better mentally prepared for a war of annihilation than Hitler and his generals had assumed. In Germany and in western Europe there were certain barriers that Hitler had to break down in order to achieve his criminal aims. In the Soviet Union none of these barriers existed. When Hitler's soldiers invaded the Soviet Union they entered a space of violence and were confronted with a population that had already seen and experienced horror. To many, the National Socialist reign of terror merely marked yet another chapter in a tale of woe that had started ten years earlier. This was how the Stalinist functionaries, Chekists, and commissars saw it as well. For them, the war of annihilation was a chance to put their skills to use. They had been waging war for a long time, but only now could the truly violent and terroristic practices of the state fully unfold. No system was better prepared for war than Stalin's. It had had no regard for human life before the war, and there was no reason to suspect that the conditions of war would change this. Stalin and his followers were at last truly in their element. There was nothing the dictator enjoyed more than waging wars that he could win, and since the attackers were threatening him with annihilation, he could respond with annihilation in turn. For the first time ever, all the propagandistic claims about the enemy were actually confirmed by the experiences of several million Soviet citizens. At last, Hitler and Stalin both had an enemy that was more than just the product of their own imaginations and propaganda efforts. In the end, Stalinism triumphed because it was better equipped for this murderous confrontation than Hitler's forces. In the first months of the war, however, no one would have imagined that a Soviet victory could be possible.[31]

In the early morning hours of June 22, 1941, several million German Wehrmacht soldiers crossed the border into the Soviet Union. The days of the Stalinist regime appeared to be numbered. At the beginning of the war, no one imagined that the Red Army would ever survive the conflict, and by late summer 1941 it seemed to be collapsing under the Wehrmacht's heavy blows. The troops had not been prepared for the German onslaught, and they had not even been placed on alert. Although Stalin had received multiple intelligence reports warning him of the German threat he had been unwilling to believe them.

Stalin knew that the Soviet Union was not yet ready for war, which was why he wanted to avoid giving Hitler a reason to attack. Stalin would never have voluntarily entered into a war he could not win, and he assumed that Hitler was as smart as he was and would refrain from initiating a risky two-front war. Therefore Stalin ignored all the warnings, even from his most loyal Chekists. He mistrusted many of the agents and diplomats who were supplying him with information and warnings, especially his ambassador in London, Ivan Maisky. An agent of state security who had been traveling from Berlin to Moscow via Poland in June had seen streets near the Soviet border being repaired and train tracks being refitted to match the Russian track gauge. He reported having seen convoys of military vehicles and marching columns of German soldiers in assault gear as well. But this, too, Stalin chose to ignore. The minister of state security, Merkulov, and his deputy, Kobulov, both advised Stalin to anticipate the Wehrmacht's attack with a preemptive strike. Then, on June 9 Kobulov reported that Hitler had already ordered the attack some time ago and that Göring's staff was already in Romania to coordinate Luftwaffe operations from there. Stalin was advised to "consider the possibility of a surprise attack." On June 16 Merkulov notified Stalin that he had received confirmation from one of his trusted agents that the Wehrmacht's preparations for an attack were complete. Stalin's response was to tell him, "This is not a 'source,' but a disinformer." He then advised Merkulov to send this agent, who was supposedly in the Luftwaffe headquarters, back to his "whore mother." Unless something was declared reality by Stalin himself, it simply did not exist.

On June 18, 1941, the minister of defense, Marshal Timoshenko, and the chief of the general staff, Georgy Zhukov, made one final attempt at changing Stalin's mind. They told the dictator explicitly that a Wehrmacht attack was imminent and that the armed forces needed to be placed on high alert immediately. Stalin was still not open to any such suggestions, and as Timoshenko later recalled, Stalin grew angry and threatened him:

> Stalin returned to the table and spoke harshly: "It's all Timoshenko's work, he's preparing everyone for war, he ought to have been shot. . . ." I told Stalin what he had told everyone at the meeting with the Academy graduates, that war is inevitable. "So you see," Stalin said addressing the Politburo, "Timoshenko is a fine man, with a big head, but apparently a

small brain"—at this he showed his thumb. "I said it for the people, we have to raise their alertness, while you have to realize that Germany on her own will never fight Russia. You must understand this." And he left. Then he opened the door and stuck his pock-marked face round it and uttered in a loud voice: "If you're going to provoke the Germans on the frontier by moving troops there without our permission, then heads will roll, mark my words," and he slammed the door.[32]

Even as the attack was already underway, Stalin and Molotov chose to ignore what was happening. As late as June 22 they still expected Hitler to offer negotiations or simply demand concessions from them. Neither, it seemed, could imagine that Hitler would dare invade the Soviet Union and draw it into a war of annihilation. Mikoyan in any case remembered that Stalin, even on June 22, was still convinced that Hitler would not begin a war. Anyone who dared raise doubts or point out errors to the dictator could only expect the worst. Pavel Rychagov, head of the Soviet Air Force, told Stalin that the air force's aircraft were not ready for combat and that they were repeatedly crashing because the political leadership was forcing the pilots to fly in "coffins." Stalin's only response was, "You should not have said that." On June 24, two days into the invasion, Stalin had Rychagov arrested and tortured. In October of that year he was shot as a traitor. From this point on, no military leader would ever dare oppose Stalin again or make any suggestion that was not to his liking. The soldiers of the Red Army would pay dearly for this.[33]

Hitler's campaign was threatening to be a military catastrophe for the unprepared and panic-stricken Red Army. It now seemed as though the Blitzkrieg, which had already led the Wehrmacht to victory in Poland and France, would triumph once again. Vilnius and Minsk fell into German hands within the first few weeks, and by September 1941 the Germans were at the gates of Leningrad. Hitler, in the meantime, had given orders to postpone the attack on Moscow. Instead, he instructed his generals to concentrate the offensive on Ukraine in order to take possession of the economically important grain-producing regions and protect the Romanian oil fields from the Russians. Although they did not agree with Hitler's plans to delay the attack on Moscow the Wehrmacht generals consented to this. Meanwhile, Hitler's armies made rapid advances in the south. Kiev was captured in mid-September, and by October the Germans had occupied Kharkov in eastern Ukraine.

More than 650,000 Soviet soldiers were taken into German captivity in the battle for Kiev alone. At this point the Wehrmacht also resumed its offensive against Moscow.

The first weeks of war seemed to confirm the German generals in their belief that the Soviet Army had little in the way of fighting strength to offer. The officers of the Red Army were out of their league. The generals were incompetent and, with few exceptions, were more focused on winning the dictator's favor than on making strategically sound decisions. Only a small number of the climbers and party members who had risen to the upper ranks of the army after the terror of 1937 proved able to handle their tasks. On the front, it was Stalin's system of fear and dread that was on everyone's mind. The dictator and his military advisers were mistrustful of their troop leaders and forbade them from making their own decisions. They were ordered to wait for instructions from the central command. Within the first weeks of war, however, the German attackers had disabled all the Red Army's system of communications. The links between units were severed, and this created such confusion that orders no longer even reached the troop leaders.

In Moscow too, the commanders lost sight of what was happening on the front, as they were unable to establish regular channels of communication with their men in the field. Either their orders reached nobody at all, or they arrived in such a garbled form that they only led to more disorder. Even Stalin seemed to realize that his generals had lost control of the situation. On June 28, after the Wehrmacht had captured Minsk, Stalin and his people in the Politburo went to the Ministry of Defense to confront Timoshenko and Zhukov. Zhukov insisted that his generals would bring the situation under control and organize the defense to the leadership's satisfaction. Stalin, however, could not be placated and demanded of Zhukov, "What kind of General Staff is this? What sort of Chief of Staff are you, who on the first day of the war gets flustered, loses contact with the troops, represents no one, and commands no one?"[34]

Stalin apparently believed that he had no option than to issue the pointless order to stay the course—a strategy that would cost hundreds of thousands of soldiers their lives. Attack was the best defense. Back during the Civil War, the Bolsheviks had supposedly prevailed on account of this strategy, and Stalin believed in it still. He prohibited his generals from withdrawing their troops from Kiev, although the

Germans were expected to outflank and surround them. The result was a military disaster. Stalin's armies were beaten down by the technically and strategically superior war machine of the German Wehrmacht, suffering defeats so crushing that no one believed they would be able to offer resistance anymore. Initially, Stalin could not even rely on the willingness of his soldiers to sacrifice themselves. In some sections of the front the Red Army soldiers did offer fierce resistance. Many hundreds of thousands of others, however, deserted and ran away from their units. The self-confidence of the National Socialist regime, meanwhile, had reached an all-time high, and its civilian and military representatives did not recognize that Operation Barbarossa posed some serious dangers. After just a few weeks of war, the chief of the General Staff, Halder, was of the opinion that the outcome had already been decided. Although Goebbels did not share quite the same degree of optimism, he too had no initial doubts that Germany would triumph in the end. His diary entry from July 9, 1941 reads, "There can no longer be any doubt that the Kremlin will fall sooner or later."[35]

After several more weeks, however, even Hitler and his generals were forced to admit that they had underestimated the enemy's capabilities. During the battle for Smolensk in July 1941, the Wehrmacht sustained heavy losses. The enemy refused to surrender the territory, defending it tooth and nail. "The resistance of the Bolshevists," wrote Goebbels in his diary on August 1, "appears to be stronger than we expected, and particularly the material means at their disposal are greater than we had assumed." Had the Führer known the extent of the enemy's armory he probably would have thought more carefully before deciding to attack the Soviet Union. Goebbels believed that the resilience of the Red Army could be traced back to the terror that the political commissars and commanders exercised in their units. A soldier's life, he wrote, was "worth less than a glass of lemonade." This alone made it possible for the Red Army to resist so stubbornly. Goebbels realized that although Stalin's strategy resulted in heavy losses for the Soviet Union, it also meant heavy losses for the Wehrmacht. It meant that this was now a war that Germany could not win without heavy losses. By autumn 1941 at the latest, no one in the German army leadership harbored any illusions about the nature of the war. The Blitzkrieg had failed, and the Wehrmacht, it turned out, was not as well prepared for a war of attrition as its enemy—which had the additional advantage of fighting on familiar territory. In July alone 63,000 German soldiers were killed in action. By early September over 400,000 Wehrmacht soldiers were either dead or wounded and not a single military aim had been achieved. The German Reich was not prepared for a prolonged and strenuous military campaign of this sort. It lacked not only the manpower but also the material resources. The Wehrmacht simply could not continue the same level of war into 1942 that it needed to so as to bring the war to a successful conclusion. The end of the Blitzkrieg in winter 1941 marked the end of the National Socialist conquest. No one knew this better than Hitler, and now he could only hope that the iron will of his soldiers would compensate for the economic and technological superiority of the Allies.[36]

"It must be clear to us," commented Goebbels on October 30, 1941, "that the war against the Soviet Union will thus come to experience a far-reaching delay." The belief in rapid victory had been erroneous. "Whenever we wrest victories in spite of this, it owes everything to the insurmountable tenacity of our troops and the inventive imagination of their leadership in overcoming difficulties." A war against a military force that fought so "dull-wittedly" and with so little concern for strategies and tactics was "much more difficult than war against an army that operates according to modern western European viewpoints."[37] Ultimately, the Wehrmacht could not triumph over this "dull-wittedness"—not unless its own soldiers became dull-witted themselves. Once the Blitzkrieg strategy had to be abandoned, the German army lost its mobility and vigor. In France, Hitler's soldiers had marched down paved roads. Here, though, they were forced to wind their way along uneven, unpaved paths that by autumn had become wastelands of mud. Although the generals dreamed of Blitzkrieg, what they neglected to remember was that motorized units are of little value in areas with no paved roads. Therefore, the armored Wehrmacht units were confined to the highways linking the major cities of the Soviet Union, and since they never ventured off the major roads they never achieved any military control over the hinterland. The result was a military disaster for the Germans.

In October 1941, when the Soviet campaign first began to stall, the triumphant officers of the Wehrmacht's General Staff, who had been spoiled by success, suddenly became aware of several deficits that had previously not concerned them. Their soldiers lacked winter clothing and gear, and their technical equipment was failing due to the harsh climate. Also, when temperatures dropped below freezing, the engines in the tanks no longer worked. At no point in time was the German war economy in a position to make up for all these losses and keep producing enough trucks to maintain the army's maneuverability and prowess. The German army on the Eastern Front was starving and slowly freezing. Already during the battle for Moscow in winter 1941 German soldiers could be observed running about in looted furs and lady's coats, akin to "thickly padded vagrants."

In December 1941 and January 1942 Stalin ordered several Siberian divisions to be sent into battle to defend Moscow. The defense was successful, and for the first time in the war, German troops were forced to retreat. The military leadership struggled to rally its troops and prevent the front from collapsing. The Wehrmacht had lost its aura of invincibility. Its numbers were thinned by costly battles, and some front-line sections had only a handful of soldiers facing down an overwhelming Soviet force. The decimated and demoralized Wehrmacht units had lost the will to win. Now, all that remained was the desire to survive at all costs. By this time, there was scarcely a soldier who still understood why he had been sent to fight a war in which there was nothing to gain and everything to lose. No one, apart from the National Socialist ideologues, seriously believed that the Soviet Union could ever become a home to German colonists. Who, after all, would want to live in a land that had nothing to offer but poverty and privation? The German soldiers fought for nothing but their own survival. "We increased the number of birchwood crosses on which a steel helmet was placed," wrote the soldier Willy Peter Reese, "and where a human decayed who had turned into a brute. This was the meaning of the war." They were unwashed and full of lice, "mentally depraved," nothing but jaded bodies. "We had no faith to sustain us. . . . The fact that we were soldiers was enough to justify the crimes and depravities, and a sufficient basis for an existence in hell."[38]

In any war, such conditions are reason enough to resist the enemy and commit acts of cruelty. Such behavior can in no way be explained by ideological convictions. Hitler's soldiers did not wage a war of Weltanschauung. They were trapped in a war that had its own inescapable dynamic. They had unleashed a war of annihilation that they could no longer control. The soldiers became brutalized, not because they had convictions, but because the circumstances left them with no other choice. The Wehrmacht defied all existing conventions of war, and the Red Army paid it back in kind. Under these conditions, technology and military skill were meaningless. Those exercising the violence were so constrained by circumstances that they had no other solution than to destroy the enemy completely. This was precisely the meaning that the war of annihilation held for both the National Socialists and the Bolsheviks. War of this sort suited both Hitler and Stalin, as it demanded not just the defeat of the enemy but also his extermination. Furthermore, it allowed them to justify their misdeeds and crimes as necessities of the war. The war of annihilation took place in spaces of violence, and the peasant soldiers of the Red Army were better prepared for it than their enemies, who were fighting not only on unfamiliar territory but for a cause that did not concern them. Hitler was ill-advised in his decision to wage war against a regime for which mass violence had become second nature and whose soldiers knew how to handle this violence. Ultimately, this was an adversary that the Wehrmacht had no hope of vanquishing.[39]

In summer 1942 the Wehrmacht was able to take the offensive once more as it advanced toward Stalingrad and into the Caucasus. But after the defeat at Stalingrad and the failed Kursk offensive in July 1943 the Wehrmacht's offensive capabilities were exhausted. In September 1943 the Red Army recaptured Kiev, and in summer 1944 Soviet troops wiped out the entire Central Army Group near Minsk. By autumn the Germans had been pushed back as far as the former frontier of the Soviet state. The westward offensive of the Red Army was much more difficult now, as the resistance of the German defenders grew stronger. The struggle dragged on until the conquest of Berlin in May 1945, and this final phase of the war cost the Soviet Union more than a million soldiers. Nonetheless, the Soviet armies had won a victory that, in 1941, no one had imagined possible.[40]

At the beginning of the war, after the Wehrmacht's first devastating blows, hardly anyone expected the Bolshevik regime to recover. By October 1941 more than a million Soviet soldiers had been taken captive by the Germans. In western Ukraine, in the former Baltic republics, in Moldavia, and in many regions of the Russian countryside, the Wehrmacht soldiers were greeted as liberators from the Stalinist yoke. In Lwów, which had belonged to Poland before the Hitler-Stalin Pact and had suffered greatly under the NKVD's reign of terror, the population revolted against the Red Army before the German troops even arrived. On June 28 the Communist functionaries abandoned the city under the protection of NKVD troops. Red Army officers fled the city, escorted by tanks. The Red Army soldiers who remained in Lwów were shot at by Ukrainians from the rooftops of their houses. The end of Bolshevik power there seemed certain.[41]

Before leaving the city, however, the Chekists murdered the detainees who were still in their prisons. Elsewhere too, the NKVD slaughtered their prisoners by the thousands before fleeing. When the first German soldiers arrived in Lwów, on July 1 and 2, they witnessed the outbreak of an unrestrained orgy of violence. Ukrainians and Poles whose relatives had been abducted or shot by the NKVD, took the opportunity to attack and kill anyone they suspected of belonging to the old regime. Jews were particular targets of the mass rage, as they had allegedly supported the Stalinist system. A Polish locksmith who lived in Lwów at the time recalled how Jews were forced to stand in rows of four and cheer for Stalin, before a furious mob was unleashed on them. Those who survived the massacre had the task of removing corpses from the NKVD prisons and burying them.[42]

In Moldavia, Lithuania, and Latvia the victims of the regime also took their anger out on Communists, Jews, and Soviet collaborators. Only rarely, however, did these pogroms begin spontaneously. Einsatzgruppe A shot Jewish males immediately after arriving in Latvia. In July 1941 Walter Stahlecker, who was in charge of the Einsatzgruppe, recruited Latvian men to establish pogrom units and ordered the Latvian police to participate in the killings. Pogroms also broke out in Moldavia when the Romanian army occupied the region. There were cases of spontaneous and cruel attacks on Jews and supposed profiteers of the Communist regime here. But the Moldavian peasants did not kill out of rage alone. They also killed because the Romanian occupiers had promised them their victims' possessions. Whatever the motives might have been, this violence would not have occurred if the new masters had made it a punishable offense. But this was not the case. Everyone knew that Communists and Jews could be killed with impunity, and many seized the opportunity to take revenge for the humiliation and terror they had endured under Soviet rule. In July 1941 it seemed impossible that the Bolsheviks would ever return, and people acted in the certainty that they would never be punished for their actions.[43]

One German soldier in the Lithuanian capital of Kaunas watched as a young Lithuanian beat people to death with an iron rod. At the end of his violent frenzy, when forty-five people were dead, he pulled a harmonica from his pocket and played the Lithuanian national anthem. Several Lithuanian civilians had gathered round to watch the cruel event, and not only did they refrain from attempting to stop the aggressor but they actively cheered him on. "I asked the German speakers what was happening here, and they told me the following: The parents of the boy who beat the others to death had been dragged out of their beds, arrested, and shot on the spot two days earlier because they were suspected of being nationalists, and this here was the young man's revenge. There was a row of dead bodies nearby; according to the civilians, they had been killed by retreating commissars and Communists two days previously."[44]

Even in the heart of the Soviet empire people's fear of their Bolshevik masters slowly receded as news of the German advance began to spread. For years the regime had preached that the Red Army was invincible and capable of annihilating any enemy within a matter of days. But as early as the Finnish-Soviet War this had been exposed as a lie. The soldiers of the Red Army were now fleeing from an apparently all-powerful adversary, and not a day went by without new reports of fallen cities and abandoned lines of defense. Within a matter of weeks only a small minority of enthusiasts still believed in the possibility of a Soviet victory. Most others assumed that defeat was inevitable. In the streets of Rostov-on-Don people could be heard discussing the impending collapse of the regime. This was what Mary Leder, a young American who had moved to the Soviet Union in the early 1930s, recalled. For the first time ever, she met people who were no longer willing to pretend. "It will be over soon," one young woman predicted. The Germans were on their way, and then they would "take care of the Communists and the Jews."

The Polish Army officer Salomon Slowes also recalled such sentiments during his September 1941 train ride with other Polish soldiers to join the army in exile of General Anders in southern Russia. Slowes saw ragged soldiers and famished refugees at every station the train passed through. In Moscow, the train stopped at a switch yard in the city outskirts, and there he witnessed the breakdown of authority with his own eyes:

On the stone floor in the unlit waiting room, hundreds of women and children, with their belongings, sprawled or sat in various postures for days and nights, waiting for a train heading south. The place was awash with filth, poverty, and despairing, hopeless people. The disgruntled mob raged, fumed, and cursed. They fearlessly disregarded the security police, who kept themselves at a safe distance. Now and then somebody uttered sympathetic remarks about the Nazi occupier, intimating that he was preferable to the existing Soviet regime. Refugees from the front delivered shocking accounts about the Red Army's crushing defeat. Their critical and heretical comments spurred many of the Poles to seek revenge.[45]

Under these conditions it became impossible for the regime to defend its version of reality against the reality experienced by so many millions. Untold numbers of Soviet subjects had seen a radically different world and could no longer be forced to live in the world of the lie. Whatever impact the regime's crude propaganda had ever had, it was all gone by now. None but a small minority still took it seriously. A perpetual liar will never be believed, even when he starts telling the truth, and every reference to atrocities committed by the conquerors was considered a lie by everyone who had learned to mistrust the Bolsheviks. Not even the Jews believed what they read in the Soviet papers anymore. The reports of crimes committed by the Einsatzgruppen were largely ignored. In late June 1941 the newspapers began reporting that the conquerors were shooting Jews for no apparent reason, but still very few believed it. Most of the Jews in Kiev were convinced that the arrival of the Germans would mean an improvement in their situation and would bring an end to the terror. Some still remembered 1918, when the German Kaiser's troops had marched into Kiev and were welcomed with open arms by the Jewish population. "It can't get any worse" was the conviction that seemed to be shared by almost all Jews who refused to flee the city. For all those who had not seen the SS murder squads with their own eyes the Communist propaganda made little impression. Leder recalled how her father-in-law, a Russian Jew from Rostov-on-Don, had refused to leave the city because he believed that the German atrocities being reported in the Soviet press were just more lies. He paid for his naivety with his life, as did thirty-three thousand other Jews in Kiev who were shot by SS units in the ravine of Babi Yar in late September 1941.[46]

In some regions Soviet authority was collapsing faster than elsewhere—especially in the areas where Stalinist terror had wreaked the most havoc. Workers in the Donbass rose up in revolt when they heard that party functionaries and industrial managers were fleeing the region but planning to leave the workforce behind. Throughout autumn 1941 looting took place and bloody clashes between workers and NKVD units ensued. A worker from Stalino (today's Donetsk) later recalled the events: "The city was in a state of powerlessness. Nothing remained, no police, no one. Then the general looting began, which meant that everyone took as much as they could get their hands on. It was a wicked thing. They took away whatever they could, from the businesses and factories, the meat-packing plants, the flour mills and the shops. . . . Dreadful anarchy stretching over two days. Powerlessness. Our people were gone, there was no militia, and the Germans had not yet arrived."[47]

Wherever authority showed signs of weakness, power quickly waned. In October 1941 riots broke out among workers to the northeast of Moscow in Ivanovo when party functionaries and factory directors tried to leave the city. In Zhitomir and Berdichev peasants took possession of the apartments that fleeing Communist functionaries had left behind, and in Kherson disgruntled city dwellers raided the bread factory and food warehouses after the NKVD had abandoned the city in panic. Years of pent-up rage exploded in one more orgy of violence. "They destroyed, beat, pillaged, and plundered," recalled a witness to the riots in Kherson. Even in faraway Vologda, the mood of the population was darkening. In January 1942 the Polish officer Gustav Herling watched as women waited for bread in front of the state shops, complaining about the cuts in food rations and damning the war that had taken their husbands from them. "Twice I even heard the whispered question: 'When are these Germans coming?'"[48]

Even in Moscow and Leningrad, the capitals of the revolution, the pressure on the regime was mounting. On October 15, 1941, with German troops just a few miles from Moscow, Stalin gave the order to evacuate the ministries from the capital. Panic ensued. Party functionaries, state officials, and factory directors hastily gathered their files and left Moscow in motorcades. Some Communists burned their party membership cards before fleeing. Other Muscovites soon joined the exodus, forming long columns of people that could only inch along at a snail's pace down the main road to Ryazan. Probably more than a fifth of all residents abandoned the capital during these days. Andrei Sakharov, who was a student at Moscow University at the time, recalled the panic seizing the functionaries as the Germans approached: "As office after office set fire to their files, clouds of soot swirled through streets clogged with trucks, carts, and people on foot carrying household possessions, baggage, and young children." When Sakharov and other students gathered at the university to help organize its defense, the functionaries were already on their way out. "I went with a few others to the party committee office, where we found the party secretary at his desk; when we asked whether there was anything useful we could do, he stared at us wildly and blurted out: 'It's every man for himself!'"[49]

The Bolshevik mystique as the invincible perpetrators of violence was rapidly crumbling. And as the Bolsheviks' authority waned, so did the people's fear of them. In the center of Moscow party functionaries, trying to flee, were attacked by pedestrians. In some factories there were even reports of workers attacking and beating their managers and directors. Amid the chaos looters soon took to the streets, raiding shops and stealing vehicles. According to NKVD agents, an angry mass of "tens of thousands of people" gathered in the center of Moscow and went about looting bread shops and kiosks. The militia had long since lost control of the situation. In Leningrad the regime's loss of authority set in sooner and lasted longer. On November 7, the anniversary of the revolution, women and children assembled in the city center with leaflets and banners, demanding that Leningrad be declared an open city and surrendered to the German troops. One leaflet circulating through Leningrad at this time declared that the end of the "hated Kremlin and Smolny executioners" was near. Most Soviet subjects had only a vague idea of the political aims and violent practices of the National Socialists. Many people—particularly at the beginning of the war—believed that the Wehrmacht's war against the Soviet Union was only directed against Jews and Communists and that the rest of the population had nothing to fear. As Irina Ehrenburg, the daughter of the writer Ilya Ehrenburg, later recalled, in Moscow, anti-Semitism once again became socially acceptable.[50]

German troops marching into Kiev were greeted as liberators. A Ukrainian patriot and a founding member of the first Ukrainian parliament who had suffered under Bolshevik rule felt reborn: "The devil's regime was gone and I had become a human being. I thought to myself, what a fatal tragedy for a citizen to wish the defeat in war of his own state." When the Germans rolled into the city the sun was shining and joyful people were standing along the Khreshchatyk, the main road, jubilantly welcoming the conquerors. As one witness recalled, "many women were holding bouquets of flowers, which they threw at the soldiers and officers passing by. It was a rare case in history when the defeated rejoiced about the arrival of the victors."[51]

Nowhere was the collapse of the Bolshevik reign of violence more widely celebrated than in the villages conquered by the Wehrmacht, where the peasants believed that Hitler would free them from Bolshevism and its collective farms forever. To the astonishment of Wehrmacht soldiers, peasants approached them, offering welcome gifts of bread and salt. "We were welcomed as liberators by the Ukrainian people," one Wehrmacht lieutenant remembered. "It is a great joy," he wrote, "for us to experience this warmth on a daily basis. Friendly faces everywhere, with flowers they stand at the roadside, the entire village flocks to our bivouacs, readily giving us all the support we need."[52] Not even the mass shootings of Jews behind the front line seemed to faze the peasants. Initially at least the Einsatzgruppen carried out their killings in a manner that was neither random nor indiscriminate but was instead selective and purposeful. And what did it matter to the Ukrainian and Russian peasants anyway if the SS wanted to kill Communists and Jews? The Stalinist reign of terror seemed to be gone from village life for good, and for this no price could be too high. Only in the second year of war did it become clear that a German conquest meant death and disaster for the villages of Russia and Ukraine as well. The rejoicing over the liberation soon began to fade. Like the Bolsheviks before them the German occupiers had nothing to offer the peasants but poverty and enslavement.[53]

Initially, many peasant soldiers serving in the Red Army also believed that captivity was preferable to battle. The troops were poorly led. They had only the barest of essentials. And whenever the enemy appeared, the lines of defense quickly collapsed. So severe was the demoralization that in many cases entire battalions of soldiers surrendered willingly. In some sections of the front Red Army units fought to the death, but as the command authority of the officers and commissars slipped away the soldiers also stopped fighting. Few were prepared to give their lives for a war that had largely been considered a lost cause since the first few weeks after the Wehrmacht's attack. In summer and autumn 1941, as the authority of the regime crumbled further, it became difficult to maintain any kind of respect for authority in the army either. The commanders in the hinterland were often unable to get their recruits to their designated units, and even in Moscow, the number of deserters rose to menacingly high levels. In the capital's October Rayon alone, out of 1,800 drafted recruits, only 814 reported for duty in June 1941. By October 1941 more than 650,000 Soviet soldiers had either deserted or abandoned their units.

No other army in the Second World War suffered such high rates of desertions and defections. In the first year of the war, Ukrainians, Cossacks, and soldiers from the Caucasus surrendered in large numbers, as rumors spread that although the Wehrmacht abused Russians and Jews, they could be expected to be kinder to Ukrainians, Estonians, Latvians, and Lithuanians. Soldiers from western Ukraine or the Baltic republics had no reason not to desert, as they were serving in a foreign army against their will anyway. More than a million captured soldiers were enlisted by the SS or the Wehrmacht. Cossacks and Ukrainians served as "voluntary helpers" alongside German units, and tens of thousands of Turkmens, Azerbaijanis, Kalmyks, Tatars, and Bashkirs joined the German military effort as well. Even the Soviet General Vlasov, who was captured in 1942, joined forces with the Baltic German Nazi functionaries and assembled Russian national units to fight for the Wehrmacht against the Communists. But Vlasov's dream of Russia's national rebirth was not Hitler's dream. Hitler's war was one of extermination, and in Hitler's designs the needs of the Russian people counted for absolutely nothing. And so the fragile alliance between the Russian people and the German occupiers crumbled in the second year of the war.[54]

Had Hitler not done Stalin the favor of terrorizing the territories his troops occupied, then Stalin's regime might well have collapsed. For Hitler, the war was not a struggle between National Socialists and Communists but was instead about the conquest of *Lebensraum*—a vision that allotted no place for the Russian people. This war of conquest had no regard either for the military opponent or for the civilian population. To Hitler, the vanquished were nothing more than a mass of inferior slaves, meant only to serve the glory of the Reich, and there could thus be no mercy for them—either as political or as military adversaries. By March 1941 at the latest Hitler had made certain that his generals understood that in the fight against the Red Army all rules of civilized warfare were suspended. The chief of the General Staff, Halder, made a note of Hitler's comments in his diary: "We must abolish the use of the term camaraderie among soldiers. A Communist is not a comrade, neither before nor after battle. This is a war of annihilation. . . . We are not waging war to preserve the enemy. . . . Commissars and GPU people are criminals and must be treated as such." In May 1941, the Wehrmacht High Command devised a draft proposal that, in June, was handed down to the troop leaders as the "Commissar Order." It committed Wehrmacht officers to kill captured political commissars and high-ranking representatives of the Bolshevik state immediately. "The barbaric, Asiatic fighting methods are originated by the political commissars," read the order. "Therefore, when they are picked up in battle or in the resistance, they are, as a matter of principle, to be finished immediately with a weapon."

Wehrmacht soldiers were advised that they should not even exercise restraint toward the civilian population. Civilians who were found in possession of weapons or were suspected of colluding with partisans could now be shot. Every German soldier knew that he would not face repercussions for obeying these orders. Soldiers were free to murder out of "bitterness against atrocities or subversive work of carriers of the Jewish-Bolshevik system," and they would now go unpunished. In every unit there were always a few officers who defied these murder orders, but in large part the directives were adhered to. In October 1941 Field Marshal von Reichenau, who was among the staunchest National Socialists in the military leadership, issued an order assuring his soldiers that any atrocities they committed would be exempt from future prosecution: "The soldier in the East is not only a fighter in accordance with the art of war, he is likewise the bearer of an inexorable *völkisch* concept, and the avenger of all the bestialities committed against the Germans and those of related stock. Therefore the soldier must have a full understanding of the necessity of the just punishment inflicted upon subhuman Jewry."[55]

The treatment of Soviet prisoners of war also violated basic rules of international law. They were not treated like combatants but like slaves, who could be forced to perform hard and heavy labor or left to starve. In the National Socialists' prisoner of war and extermination camps millions died of exhaustion or hunger or were simply murdered. Of the 5.7 million soldiers who entered German captivity between 1941 and 1945, only 930,000 still remained in the camps when the war was over. A million or so captured soldiers served in the Wehrmacht, and another million either escaped or were liberated by the Red Army. But the remaining 3.3 million Soviet prisoners of war—more than half of all soldiers to surrender—either starved to death or lost their lives by other inhuman means.[56] "It was truly horrendous," recalled a Wehrmacht soldier, speaking of the transport of Soviet prisoners of war after the battle of Vyazma in October 1941:

> I was there during the transport from Korosten to just outside Lwów. Like animals they were thrown out of the cars and beaten with canes on their way to the trough to keep them in line. There were these troughs at the train stations, and they pounced on them and began guzzling like beasts, then they were given just a little something to eat. Then they were herded back into the carriages—there were between sixty and seventy men in a single cattle car! They pulled out ten corpses at every stop, as the people had suffocated for lack of oxygen. . . . At the stations the Russians peered out of these narrow hatches and shouted like animals in Russian to the residents who stood there: 'Bread! God will bless you,' and so on, and they threw out their old shirts and shoes, and there were children who came and brought them pumpkins to eat. The pumpkins were thrown into the carriages, and then all you could hear was rumbling and beastly shouting—they were probably beating each other to death. I was finished; I sat in a corner and pulled my coat over my head.[57]

Two years into the war, no Soviet soldier still believed that survival in German captivity was possible. Hitler's Wehrmacht left the soldiers of their adversary no choice and turned them into bitter enemies.

The German occupiers did not simply fight the Soviet soldiers. They harassed the civilian population in the occupied territories as well, and within the first weeks of the Russian campaign it was clear that the National Socialists had no interest in working with those who had welcomed them as liberators. To Hitler, the peoples of the Soviet Union could only be helots, subdued and exploited to serve the economic interests of the Reich. Alfred Rosenberg, Hitler's chief ideologue and Reich minister for the Occupied Eastern Territories, spoke in favor of an alliance between the Germans and the non-Russian peoples of the Soviet Union, but his proposals were all rejected by the powerful Reich commissars Erich Koch and Wilhelm Kube. The National Socialist occupation regime had no regard for the interests of either Ukrainian and Latvian nationalist leaders or the civilian populations in the occupied territories. Hitler's intention was to raze Moscow and to blockade Leningrad to starve it out. The Wehrmacht lived off the land it occupied, and its soldiers took what they needed to survive from the peasants they encountered. Furthermore, the Germans, in whom so many had placed their hope, had no reason to dissolve the much-hated collective farms. Their main concern was to supply their own troops with whatever they could salvage from the villages, but the Reich needed a workforce too, so in 1942 the occupational authorities began registering peasants in Ukrainian and Belorussian villages and making them into slave laborers. While some went voluntarily, most *Ostarbeiter* (forced laborers) were deported to Germany against their will.

During the first year of the war the people in the occupied territories refrained from acts of resistance against the occupiers. They even helped direct them to escaped Red Army soldiers who were now hiding in the forests. Not until summer 1942 did the partisan war become a serious challenge to the German occupiers, when the partisan bands no longer needed to rely on force alone to get the peasants to cooperate with them. The partisans raided villages and killed anyone suspected of collaborating with the Germans, so it became necessary for the Wehrmacht to carry its death and destruction into the villages as well. Its security divisions burned villages to the ground, shot hostages, and did their best to transform vast swaths of land into inhospitable "dead zones," in which no partisan would ever be able to survive. Despite all efforts, however, the Germans failed to establish control over the situation. A twelve-year-old boy witnessed SS units coming to his village in search of partisans and shooting everyone they considered a suspect—which included old people, women, and children.

They always shot three at once, stood them at the edge of the pit and shot directly from the front. The rest watched. I don't remember the children saying goodbye to their parents or the parents to their children. A mother lifted the hem of her dress and covered her daughter's eyes. They shot fourteen people, then they closed up the pit. Again we stood by and watched how they heaped up the soil and trampled on it with their boots. Then they patted it down with a spade, so that it looked nice and proper. They even straightened out the edges, you see? Neat and tidy. An older German wiped the sweat off his forehead afterward, as though he had worked on the field. Do you understand? You don't forget something like that.[58]

If the National Socialists were to permanently break all resistance to their occupation, their terror needed to be all-encompassing. In 1943, after all, their physical presence was limited to a few major cities. Off the main roads and outside of the cities, the Germans' only means of making themselves known to the peasantry was by way of intermittent raids carried out by the security divisions. In the rural areas it was a fight of all against all. Ukrainian partisans fought Bolsheviks and Poles, while Jewish partisans fought Ukrainians and Poles. The Wehrmacht was no longer the referee in this chaos but was instead one more party in the conflict. As such, it attempted to subdue everyone else, and in the midst of this space of violence the Wehrmacht was unable to subdue anyone.

Partisans killed, tortured, raped, and pillaged, showing no regard for whether the victim was friend or foe. Ukrainians killed Poles, Poles killed Ukrainians, and Soviet partisans murdered collaborators and auxiliary police. The peasants, in any case, were the perpetual victims of a boundless terror. "The population is fleeing from both the Reds and the Germans," noted an August 1943 report by the Ukrainian partisan movement. In this war of annihilation the peasants had nothing to gain and nothing to lose, apart from their own lives. By spring 1943 at the latest, however, they were forced to face the prospect that the former masters could very well return, and with vengeance. The Germans—by this point it was clear—would not be staying. And if they would be leaving anyway, what reason did the peasants have to cooperate with them any further? Every village the German security divisions burned down meant a new flood of fighters for the ranks of the partisans. When the Red Army returned to Belorussia in summer 1944, it discovered a land that had been ravaged and depopulated by war.[59]

Stalinism survived. It survived because the National Socialists brought a terror with them that caused the horrors of Stalinism to fade into obscurity and be forgotten. Beyond that, Stalinism succeeded because its representatives reclaimed their power with an iron fist. In the first days of the war, even Stalin seemed to doubt whether the Soviet Union could really win. None of his predictions had been fulfilled, and for the first time ever Stalin truly appeared uncertain. Hitler had outsmarted him, and there was nothing he could do about it. Stalin was not accustomed to such powerlessness. He refused to appear in public. Molotov was given the task of informing the population via radio broadcast that the Soviet Union was under attack. According to Mikoyan's memoirs, in those days Stalin "was not interested in anything" and did not "show any initiative." The legacy of Lenin seemed to be over, he lamented. Everything seemed to be lost. On July 1 the members of the Politburo reportedly gathered in the Kremlin to discuss the events in Stalin's absence. Beria proposed the establishment of a State Defense Committee to handle government affairs with Stalin at its helm. They then drove out to Stalin's dacha in the outskirts of Moscow to summon the dictator back to work. Never before had they dared meet without his knowledge or visit him unannounced. Stalin, sitting on a sofa, seemed surprised, and eyed them suspiciously. "Why have you come?" he reportedly asked them. "I had no doubt," Mikoyan wrote, "that he thought we were coming to arrest him."[60] Did Stalin really believe they had come to arrest him? This was Mikoyan's interpretation, but there are reasons to question his portrayal of events. According to the dictator's log, on July 1, 1941 he met with Molotov, Malenkov, and Beria at 4:40 P.M., and then at 5:45 P.M. he spoke with Mikoyan. According to the log, Beria and Molotov even visited Stalin's office twice that day, and it was not until 1:30 the next morning that the last visitors left the Kremlin. From the day of the German attack not a single day went by without Stalin driving to the Kremlin. Apart from July 29 and 30 his office never remained empty.[61]

Stalin evidently returned to his usual routine rather quickly. He ordered the establishment of a State Defense Committee consisting of the most important members of the Politburo, and he initiated the evacuation of heavy industry to the Far Eastern Region of the Soviet Union. On July 3 Stalin personally addressed the public in a radio broadcast. Addressing his "comrades, citizens, brothers and sisters," he sought to strengthen the will to resistance. He spoke of defending the homeland and of the "patriotic people's war" that was to be waged against the German aggressors. In November 1941, on the anniversary of the revolution, Stalin addressed a group of soldiers who were about to be sent to the front. He spoke of the shared legacy of the tsarist past, of the land of Pushkin and Tolstoy, and of the war heroes Alexander Nevsky, Alexander Suvorov, and Mikhail Kutuzov. When had the dictator ever spoken of the people as "brothers and sisters"? When had there ever been any mention of the "motherland"? Stalin's speech had a profound impact. The writer Konstantin Simonov was greatly moved by Stalin's words of reconciliation. "I hate war, yet I see a sense in defending your country, whatever it's like, when it's a matter of defending against the invasion of the enemies," wrote Dmitri Shostakovich.[62]

Now, in the hour of crisis, was the regime going to put an end to the terror of the previous years? Were Stalin and his cronies going to lay down their arms that, for so long, had been directed against their own people? There were certainly signs pointing in this direction. After the crushing defeats of the first two years, Stalin began to realize that his generals were better versed in warfare than he was. In autumn 1941 he had the incapable political generals Voroshilov and Budyonny relieved of their commands and replaced with competent leaders. Stalin did everything possible to boost the confidence of the officer corps and motivate his generals. He introduced guard regiments, uniforms, and medals, as they had existed during the time of the tsar. From now on, soldiers would not be fighting and dying for communism but for their homeland instead. The Red Army was now engaged in a "patriotic war," just as the Russian Army had been in 1812 when it fought back Napoleon. As Stalin had proclaimed in his July 1941 address, this was a cause that all peoples of the Soviet Union should be able to relate to.

As the war entered another critical phase, Stalin sought new means of legitimating his rule. References to Marxism and its empty promises of salvation did nothing to mobilize the army or the home front for the struggle. Stalin himself seemed to have little faith in the persuasive powers of communist teachings anyway, which is why he called for a moratorium on the persecution of the church. The hope was that the dictatorship would be able to enter into a partnership with the church and harness its galvanizing powers for its own ends. This strategy soon proved to be a great success. The high clergy of the Orthodox Church accepted the state's offer of reconciliation and came to its aid. On June 22, 1941, Metropolitan Sergey addressed the people and called them to support their country: "The church of Christ blesses all Orthodox fighters defending the holy borders of our motherland." Stalin could hardly have asked for more. Not only did the Metropolitan submit to him unconditionally, but he also legitimized the war and condemned clergymen who collaborated with the German occupiers.

The Red Army ceased to be the military force of the world proletariat, fighting for the victory of communism. It was now engaged in a national war, waged in the name of Russia.[63]

"And the truth," wrote the Russian composer Dmitri Shostakovich in his memoirs,

> is that the war helped. The war brought great sorrow and made life very, very hard. Much sorrow, many tears. But it had been even harder before the war, because then everyone was alone in his sorrow. Even before the war, in Leningrad there probably wasn't a single family who hadn't lost someone, a father, a brother, or if not a relative, then a close friend. Everyone had someone to cry over, but you had to cry silently, under your blanket, so that no one would see. Everyone feared everyone else, and the sorrow oppressed and suffocated us. It suffocated me too. I had to write about it, I felt that it was my responsibility, my duty. I had to write a requiem for all those who died, who had suffered. I had to describe the horrible extermination machine and express protest against it. But how could I do it? I was constantly under suspicion then. . . . And then the war came and the sorrow became a common one. We could talk about it, we could cry openly, cry for our lost ones. . . . To be able to grieve is also a right. . . . I wasn't the only one who had an opportunity to express himself because of the war. Everyone felt it. Spiritual life, which had been almost completely squelched before the war, became saturated and tense, everything took on acuity, took on meaning.[64]

Much of the war—which was a nightmare for people in western Europe—brought Soviet citizens a certain relief. For the first time, people were able to speak openly about the violence they had suffered. The Wehrmacht's invasion opened up a new space of freedom in which people could express themselves in ways that previously—under the despot's reign of terror—had been impossible. By the second year of the war it was possible for artists and writers to deviate from the dogmas of the past—as long as they refrained from unflattering portrayals of the dictator himself. In the early years of the war, at least, it was no longer compulsory—everywhere and at all times—to praise the Red Army's achievements as a gift from the party and its leaders. Even the hateful propaganda penned by the writers Ilya Ehrenburg and Konstantin Simonov, which called on the people to murder the German foes—those "fish-eyed idiots" and "gray-green snails"—and "bury them in the ground," could get away with not making references to the party and its leader. At the beginning of the war Stalin also limited his own appearances in public, since he wanted to avoid being associated with the Red Army's most devastating defeats. The cult of Stalin would only return in its most monstrous form once the tide of the war began to turn.[65]

The regime mobilized all available resources for the war effort. Its ability to survive the crisis of 1941 was not least due to the invoking of patriotic zeal and the moral right to self-defense. In mid-October 1941, with German troops approaching Moscow, news began to spread that Stalin and Molotov had resolved to not abandon the city. The panic suddenly seemed to calm, and the looting stopped when NKVD units arrived. The state and its leaders had not given up after all. On the anniversary of the revolution Stalin went to Moscow's Mayakovskaya metro station to address a group of soldiers that was about to be deployed for battle. The purpose of the appearance was to assure the people that the dictator and his followers would persevere. Stalin was well aware of the psychological effect of his presence, and he knew that if he were to flee Moscow his regime would be relinquishing all power. Whatever doubts in the Soviet Union may still have remained, they were dispelled when the German advance came to a grinding halt at the gates of Moscow.

In addition to its gains in terms of propaganda, the regime also improved its organizational and military capabilities. The generals began to learn from past mistakes, and the war economy began producing tanks and artillery in such large numbers that the military balance of power soon shifted in the Red Army's favor. The relocation of industry to the Far East of the Soviet Union was a logistical feat that, at the start of the war, no one would have considered possible. It was, of course, only possible because of the regime's failure to show any regard whatsoever for the needs or lives of its own people in the process.[66]

The Soviet Union in 1942 was not what it had been in 1937. In the face of war it could not have been otherwise. People gave their lives to protect their homeland, and some did so voluntarily, not in defense of the dictatorship but as patriots. Now that the war had caused them to forget everything he had inflicted on them and their country, it is possible that many saw the bloodthirsty despot in a different light. The myth of the Great Patriotic War, however, which reinvented the Soviet Union as a shared experience, only emerged two decades later. It was not until the 1960s that the Red Army's victory could and had to be hailed as a people's victory, when the regime had no other sources of legitimization to fall back on. The Second World War was subsequently celebrated as a heroic joint experience that united the peoples of the Soviet Union, and no offer of integration was taken up with greater enthusiasm by the Soviet citizens. At the time, however, the myth did not match the experiences of most people. For them, the war was chiefly a violent orgy of apocalyptic proportions. Far from marking the end of Stalinism, the war allowed Stalinism to unfold its full potential. In the midst of war the regime lost all inhibitions, not only when it came to exercising excessive violence against the enemy, but also when it came to the merciless use of terror against its own soldiers and civilians.

When the war started Stalin began to sense that his power was at stake, just as it had been during the peasants' revolt. Stalin would not have been Stalin if he had trusted his officers and soldiers. He was well aware of the havoc his regime had wreaked in the past, and he knew that the peasant soldiers had no reason to sacrifice themselves for him or his state. "They want us to die for them—no, we are not as stupid as they think," Slovak soldiers overheard captured Red Army soldiers saying after they had surrendered near Kiev in September 1941. "They left our children without bread, to starve to death, but they force us to defend Stalin and his Commissars."[67] Stalin received news of the desertions and the jubilation over the Wehrmacht's arrival in the Ukrainian countryside, and he knew better than to trust the generals who were supposed to lead these peasants into battle. In Stalin's empire there was only one conceivable solution to this problem: the spread of fear and dread. Only those in mortal fear would yield to the dictator's orders. And once the Red Army officers and soldiers realized that the Germans, too, had nothing but misery and death to offer them, Stalin's strategy began to work.

Stalin issued the first terror orders within days of the Wehrmacht's attack. He instructed the Red Army General Staff to punish every officer caught supplying headquarters with false information. From day one, generals who failed the despot on the battlefield stood to be executed. In December 1941 Stalin sent Lev Mekhlis, the director of the Red Army's political administration and one of the dictator's most brutal henchmen, to the Northwestern Front. Mekhlis was not a military expert, but he had proven in the past that he had no difficulty taking action whenever Stalin's officers needed intimidating. This time, too, he did not disappoint. He interrogated the unit commanders thoroughly and threatened to shoot them if they voiced any opposition. In March 1942 Stalin assigned his trusted crony to coordinate Soviet Army operations in Sevastopol on the Crimean Peninsula. Due to his lack of knowledge of military tactics Mekhlis was a miserable failure there. To compensate, he terrorized the Red Army General Kozlov, drove around the front carrying a pistol, and issued all the ludicrous orders he could think of. He forbade the officers to dig trenches, as this would supposedly undermine the troops' offensive spirit. Meanwhile, he sent telegrams to Stalin, demanding that panicmongers and cowards be shot. On one of these telegrams Stalin wrote, "Comrade Beria, right! In Novorossiysk, make sure that not one scum, not one scoundrel is breathing." Tens of thousands of Soviet soldiers lost their lives in the carnage of the Crimean campaign, and an additional 176,000 plus were captured. This was all thanks to their having been led into battle by a military amateur and a terrorist. In the end, the Crimean Peninsula was lost.[68]

Those who failed to submit unconditionally to Stalin's directives were toying with death. Even the popular and successful General Zhukov was confronted with this reality. After he was appointed supreme commander of the Leningrad Front, Molotov told him he would have him shot if he failed to fend off the German tanks. In early July 1941, after the fall of Minsk, Stalin had the supreme commander of the Western Front, General Dmitri Pavlov, and three other generals from his staff arrested. The charges against Pavlov could hardly have been more absurd. He was accused of hampering the expansion of fortifications and failing to alert the troops, although the threat had supposedly been obvious. When the war had first broken out, Stalin and his people's commissar of defense, Timoshenko, had urged Pavlov to "stay calm" and "not panic." At that time they had still been insisting that the reports of an impending Wehrmacht attack were all fabricated. "Make sure not to yield to German provocations. Call me if something happens," was the last message Pavlov received from the Kremlin before communications broke down.

Now Pavlov was supposed to take the blame for what was very much Stalin's error. Stalin gave the order to have him and his subordinates arrested. Pavlov was tortured and forced to make the absurd confession that he had been a traitor and a spy for German intelligence all along and that he had been involved in Marshal Tukhachevsky's "military conspiracy" but had remained undiscovered. Accordingly, Pavlov had not failed, but had actually been working on the enemy's behalf. Then, on July 22, 1941, the generals were tried before a secret military tribunal. Although they withdrew their confessions, this was irrelevant to Stalin's decision, and they were condemned to death. Whether or not Pavlov and his commanders had really neglected their duties was of no interest to him. Their execution was a message to the living: anyone who retreated from the enemy had signed his own death warrant. Two days into the invasion, Stalin ordered the arrest of the former head of the General Staff, Kyrill Meretskov, who had been put in charge of the inspection of the Northwestern Front just days before. Boris Vannikov, the people's commissar of armament, was arrested too. Both were taken to the Lubianka where Beria had them tortured. Beria's butchers broke Meretskov's bones and beat his face to a bloody pulp, leaving him little more than a shadow of his former self. Following Pavlov's arrest, Beria began piecing together the "evidence" pointing to a grand military conspiracy. He had the detained generals tortured to extract confessions that could be used to incriminate the others. For a short time Timoshenko and Zhukov feared that Stalin would have them killed as well. In this particular case, however, the dictator reached an unusual decision. Meretskov was released three months later and allowed to command an army division. Although he was not excluded from the circle of power, he was never again allowed to speak of his ordeal. In Stalin's presence it was as though this episode in his life had never taken place. Other commanders were less fortunate, and in the course of 1941 and 1942 fifteen generals were arrested and shot by the state security organs.[69]

Stalin set the tone for action with an order from August 16, 1941: "Can the Red Army tolerate in its ranks cowards and deserters who surrender to the enemy, or faint-hearted commanders who exhibit indifference at the first sign of difficulty at the front and desert into the hinterland? No, Never! If these cowards and deserters are given free rein, they will break our army's back and ruin our motherland in no time. Cowards and deserters must be annihilated." And so it came to be. All commanders and commissars who retreated from the enemy or surrendered were "malevolent deserters" who should be shot "on the spot." Their families were to be arrested as well.[70]

Death was everywhere, and anyone who wanted to survive this inferno was well advised to do as the dictator expected. Stalin's generals lived in the shadow of fear and passed this fear on to their subordinates. In autumn 1941 Zhukov announced to the staff commander of the Northwestern Front that Stalin was "dissatisfied" with his work. Further, Zhukov told him: "Until now the commanders who have disobeyed their orders and retreated from the lines of defense have not been punished. With such a liberal attitude toward the cowards, your defense will amount to nothing." The only solution, Zhukov said, was for him to begin punishing the "cowards and traitors" immediately.[71] In late 1942 the future Marshal Chuikov arrived in Stalingrad on Stalin's orders to defend the city and hold it at all costs. His first order of business in the city was to shoot several officers as a means of demonstrating the price of disobedience to the soldiers. "We immediately applied the most severe measures against the cowards. On the 14th I shot the commander and the commissar of a regiment, soon afterwards I also shot two more brigade commanders and the commissars. Everyone was totally bewildered. We made all the fighters, but the officers in particular, aware of this."[72] Stalin had not ordered this act of violence, but Chuikov had internalized Stalin's style and knew what the dictator wanted. He was unable, in fact, to even imagine that the dictator could have expected anything less. Violence had become the norm, and this applied to the relationships between generals and officers too. Marshals Budyonny and Yeremenko shot subordinates who committed errors, and they even beat members of their own military council to intimidate them. Yeremenko took to carrying a cudgel with him to discipline his subordinates. Whenever commanders notified Stalin that their officers had failed in one way or another, wrote Khrushchev in his memoirs, Stalin's response was always the same: "But did you smash him in the face? You've got to let him have it in the kisser! Right in the kisser!"[73]

The relationship between commanders and officers was positively poisoned by Stalin's terror. Not even the political commissars, who were responsible for keeping officers in check, could be sure of their safety. In late June 1941 a bitter conflict broke out on the Southwestern Front between the corps commander, Riabyshev, and his political commissar, Nikolai Vashugin. The two men mistrusted each other deeply, but in the end the commander emerged victorious because the commissar had made the mistake of issuing orders that contradicted the written instructions from the headquarters. When Riabyshev's motorized corps was encircled and destroyed by the Germans Vashugin was held responsible. Realizing that he had broken Stalin's rules, he became so terrified that he lost control of his bowels. He drove to Kiev in a panic to speak with Nikita Khrushchev, who at that time was political commissar of the Southwestern Front. What should he do now, he begged Khrushchev to tell him. "If you've decided to shoot yourself," Khrushchev replied, "what are you waiting for?" And Vashugin drew his pistol and blew his brains out.[74]

Stalin's system of terror was simple but effective: the commanders feared the dictator, and the soldiers feared their commanders. The army leadership had no other choice than to pass the violence they were threatened with on to their subordinates. The soldiers, accordingly, were expected to defy death. The lives of the officers depended on it. In October 1942 Marshal Chuikov ordered the commander of the 138th Rifle Division, which was battling the Germans in the center of Stalingrad, to recapture the train station. "I'm warning you," Chuikov added, "if you fail to carry out my military order, you will be put on trial." The commander had no choice but to execute the order and in doing so sent several thousand of his soldiers to a completely pointless death.[75]

"Our superiors," wrote the soldier Gabriel Temkin, "had little regard for the lives of their soldiers, they did not count their losses."[76] Food was scarce. In the first two years of the war, soldiers ate the provisions of fallen enemies or meat from dead horses. Some wore neither helmets nor boots, and even in this wretched condition they were led into battle like cattle to the slaughter. The losses that the Red Army sustained in the first years of the war were so severe that any given new recruit had only a very slim chance of surviving more than a few weeks. One Red Army soldier recalled how the soldiers stumbled along the road near Stalingrad in summer 1942 like "sleepwalkers." They had "black faces with a tortured look, uniform jackets white with salt, bloody feet cut to ribbons that refused to do further service."[77] To Stalin and his generals, the peasant soldiers called to defend the country were fully expendable. They were nothing but numbers, serfs, and they could easily be replaced. One after another they were sent charging into German machine-gun fire by incompetent and frightened commanders, to die by the thousands in strategically pointless attacks. In a series of suicidal attacks in Stalingrad in the autumn of 1942, Uzbek, Kirghiz, and Tatar soldiers, who neither understood the Russian commands being given by their officers nor the sense behind the slaughter, were sacrificed by the thousands. In some sections of the front soldiers were forced to charge enemy lines without weapons. Their only chance was to scavenge for the rifles of their fallen comrades. In Stalingrad and other fronts soldiers did not get their uniforms from the quartermaster but from their dead and bloodied comrades. "They sent us to the front without rifles," complained a wounded corporal who was taken to the military hospital in Sochi in September 1941. Soldiers who asked their commanders for weapons were told, "Well, when someone is killed, then you take his rifle." Even during the battle of Kursk, in July 1943, Soviet generals sacrificed their tank divisions in strategically senseless frontal assaults, as the only tactic accepted by the dictator was that of all-out attack. The "four-stage strategy" was Zhukov's description for the unimaginative and reckless manner in which the war was being conducted by the Soviet High Command. Three waves of attack were to level the ground, and the fourth wave was to charge across it. How many soldiers perished in the process was of no consequence, either to the generals or to the officers.[78]

When Soviet holidays rolled around, Stalin expected to be given military victories as presents. Kiev, Königsberg, and Berlin were all taken by the Red Army at terrible cost—which could have been avoided if the despot had tempered his demands. Those who failed became victims of his vengeance. In May 1944, when the Third Belorussian Front failed to break through German lines and its units near Orsha were forced to retreat with heavy losses, the soldiers were expected to pay for their generals' ineptitude. "On May 29," remembered the soldier Leonid Rabichev, "our offensive collapsed once again. We did not make it past the third line of German fortifications and suffered enormous losses. One day later they read a terrible letter from the High Command to the commander of the Third Belorussian Front, General Cherniakhovsky, out loud to us at the front. It said that the Third Belorussian Front had forfeited the confidence of the party and the people, and would be obligated to pay for its guilt in blood."[79]

In war as in peace Stalin apparently knew no means of establishing discipline and obedience that did not involve the dissemination of mass fear. Commissars and officers responded to disciplinary violations with merciless terror. Not only deserters but also soldiers who had retreated from the enemy or simply voiced discontent were summarily shot. In September 1942 soldiers from the 64th Rifle Division on the outskirts of Stalingrad discovered that the German Luftwaffe had not only wiped out an entire army unit nearby but had also destroyed the field hospitals. The soldiers began to panic. The wounded flooding back alongside the defeated troops told of the inferno from which they had escaped, and the following day soldiers began deserting in droves. In response, the commander lined up the weakest units in his division, hurled abuse at the soldiers, and cursed them as cowards. He then marched down the rows and shot every tenth man in the face with his revolver. A similar incident occurred in mid-October 1942 when two soldiers from the 204th Rifle Division in Stalingrad disappeared without a trace. The response of the regimental commander was to have their superior officer executed—despite the fact that this was a nineteen-year-old second lieutenant who had only been assigned to the regiment five days earlier and knew nothing about deserting soldiers. But this kind of terror had a tremendous impact: the fear of being shot encouraged soldiers to try to prevent each other from deserting.

In the midst of war, no terror could be cruel enough. In late summer 1941 NKVD units posted on the Leningrad front began shooting up to 400 soldiers a week for desertion. By the end of 1941 almost 4,000 people serving in the Baltic Fleet had been executed. Between August and October 1941 more than 20,000 Red Army soldiers were court-martialed and shot. In the battle for Stalingrad alone, more than 13,500 Soviet soldiers were shot as deserters or cowards. In winter 1942 soldiers in one particular unit on the Stalingrad front were accused of criticizing the political leadership and questioning the competence of the generals. The delinquents were seized by NKVD officers and "sentenced" by the political commissar of the unit. They were then forced to undress before being shot in front of their comrades.[80]

The soldier Pyotr Astakhov witnessed a similar execution near Voronezh. He and his comrades from the regiment had been ordered to line up in a row. Even from a distance they could hear the screams of the condemned soldier being dragged before them by two guards. The regimental commander was reportedly leafing through his papers in boredom when the procedure began. "Forgive me, don't kill me,

Comrade Commissar," the soldier was yelling. Astakhov described the experience further:

> The tears, the wailing, the screaming and the attempts to break away from the armed guards made a strong impression on the men who saw the procedure of an execution for the first time with their own eyes. Our people were shooting their own kind. A young man was killed as though it were a lesson for the living. The guard soldiers waited for the last words, after which the sentence had to be executed. The commissar uttered the words "to the shooting," shots were fired into the back of the condemned, and like a sheaf he fell face first into the dirt. Both guard soldiers approached the corpse, tested the head with their bayonets, and then shot the dead man one more time. This inhumane act marked the conclusion of our first day at the front. The goal of this dreadful tribunal had been reached—this image would not only remain lodged in my own memory, but probably also in the memories of everyone else who witnessed this terrible execution that day.

Sometimes officers would also make their soldiers walk past the graves, as a reminder of where "treason" against the homeland would lead them.[81]

By mid-August 1941 Stalin had given orders to sweep the army for spies and traitors. The army staff was also required to report the names of soldiers who had surrendered or deserted, to the regional NKVD branches, so that their families could be taken hostage. Thus, Soviet soldiers not only died in defense of the motherland, but also out of fear that if they surrendered the Stalinist terror apparatus would take revenge on their families. Stalin led by example and disowned his own son, Yakov, after he had allowed himself to be captured by the Germans. Stalin condemned him as a "coward" and a "traitor" and declined to exchange him for the German Field Marshal Paulus. Yakov was taken to a German prisoner of war camp in Sachsenhausen, where he was later shot by guards while trying to escape.[82]

"Not one step back" (*Ni shagu nazad*) was Stalin's infamous "Order No. 227" from July 28, 1942. It was a warning for anyone who might consider retreating that the punishment would be cruel. "Panicmongers and cowards must be exterminated on the spot."[83] Retreat or surrender amounted to treason. NKVD and Red Army units armed with machine guns waited in the rear to fire volleys at retreating soldiers and chase them back to the front. A Red Army soldier who came in contact with the "extermination units" described the NKVD soldiers as being "well-fed" and "well-clothed." They wore new helmets and "waterproofed raincoats," a "luxury that was not even available to every officer."[84] Stalin could depend on such warriors as they received high pay and ample provisions. Furthermore, they were waging a war they could only win, since in combat with their own countrymen they were running little risk to life and limb. In August 1942 the head of the Red Army political administration informed headquarters in Moscow that although there had been cases of panicked soldiers deserting or fleeing from the Germans in the past year, this was becoming increasingly rare, as "the cowards" had all been "cruelly liquidated." The political commissar of the 62nd Army, which was deployed outside of Stalingrad, reported that the general in command had already begun executing Stalin's order. Cowards and panicmongers who tried to flee the attacker were shot in the presence of their comrades.[85] Lieutenant Zia Bunyatov witnessed how NKVD units near Rostov-on-Don blocked his unit's retreat: "Our retreat was barred by a special purpose detachment [of the NKVD]. A few hundred officers of retreating units were driven to a large farm. They were escorted one at a time, into a house. Three men sat at a table. They asked us about our rank and where our personnel were. . . . The trial was short. The sentence was passed then and there. The accused were led behind a pigsty and shot." Bunyatov survived by a fluke, as Marshal Semyon Budyonny had arrived in the meantime and sent the remaining officers back to their units.[86]

Not even the courts-martial of the army divisions were able to elude the pressure of the Chekists. Operatives of the military intelligence service Smersh (Smert Shpionam, Death to Spies) monitored the officers who were in charge of condemning "traitors" and "cowards" in their units. The secretary of a court martial remembered how a high-ranking Smersh functionary had complained, "There are too few arrests. There are no signs of work." In order to meet the expectations of the intelligence service, the courts martial necessarily had to adopt Stalin's violent style: "In order to make the work 'visible,' one had to provide the superior who demanded something and checked on the orders with reports of gleaming successes; you constantly needed to show signs of activity and arrest enemies, spies, terrorists, and anti-Soviet elements, and transfer their cases to the courts martial."[87]

The system of terror also included the political commissars, who kept tabs on officers and soldiers in all regiments of the Red Army.

So great was the regime's mistrust that up until October 1942, all the decisions officers made required the prior approval of the commissars. In the first two years of war the results were calamitous, as sending soldiers to pointless deaths seemed to be the only politically acceptable course of action. The soldiers were resentful of the well-fed political officers who spoke of a struggle they themselves were never forced to face. "The political commissar with his new epaulettes and shiny boots," recalled the soldier Yelena Romanova, "parades about in front of the unshaven men in their ragged clothes and worn-out shoes, delivering a speech." In some units, the commissars took to celebrating lavish feasts with vodka, greasy food, and women who offered themselves up for money and gifts. Ordinary soldiers meanwhile were dying on the battlefield.[88] In Stalin's cosmos of violence, however, the commissars rendered an indispensable service to the regime, as they reported cases of disobedience, denounced critics, and fostered an atmosphere of fear and mistrust that even pervaded the front lines. They not only denounced soldiers to the military intelligence service but also performed the executions themselves when they believed this would restore discipline within their unit. "The boys understood," wrote the commissar Nikolai Moskvin in his diary after having shot a disobedient subordinate in front of his comrades. "A dog's death for a dog."[89] Some soldiers wished the same for their commissars, and in November 1941 the head of the NKVD's "special department" in the 43rd Army reported that soldiers had been conspiring against their commissars. "All political commissars should be shot," one soldier reportedly told his comrades. "If I had to go into battle with a political commissar, then I'd shoot him for sure."[90]

For the Wehrmacht soldiers observing everything, this was beyond comprehension. Why were officers and Chekists firing at their own soldiers? Was the war against the invading army not demanding enough? In September 1942 when a Soviet Army unit near Stalingrad wanted to abandon the futile struggle and surrender, a German panzer unit actually prevented the soldiers from being shot by NKVD extermination units stationed in the rear. Between July and October more than 650,000 Soviet soldiers were arrested for deserting or being away from their units. In Mozhaysk, a town to the west of Moscow, 23,000 soldiers, including more than 2,000 officers, were arrested in a period of just five days in October. The Red Army was a stranger to retreat because its soldiers had only two choices. They could either be shot and captured by the Germans, or they could die at the hands of the NKVD units. Charging ahead generally offered them greater chances of survival than retreat.[91]

Soviet soldiers who had been taken prisoner in the Finnish-Russian Winter War were sent to concentration camps beginning in spring 1940. Gustav Herling remembered how soldiers returning from war were marched proudly through the streets of Leningrad, only to be loaded onto trains and taken to penal camps immediately afterward.[92] After the German attacks, little changed in terms of how returning prisoners of war were dealt with. NKVD units searched for "spies" and "traitors" among the retreating troops and arrested anyone who had managed to escape the Wehrmacht during the great battles of encirclement. Behind the front, the NKVD extermination units not only prevented soldiers from retreating but also took immediate action against "cowards" and "malingerers." This of course was simply a means of frightening other soldiers and discouraging them from backing down. The Russian medic Vera Yukina witnessed soldiers, who had escaped the Germans after several weeks of heavy fighting near Bobruysk, being taken away by the NKVD. "What kind of society must this be for millions of armed soldiers to treacherously turn their backs on it?" she wondered.[93]

A female Russian soldier who was stationed at the Moscow front in December 1941 saw no way out of this dilemma. "I carry an automatic weapon," she explained, "and I always keep a spare bullet for myself. It is bad to get captured by the Germans, and if you run away from the front, they will throw you into Stalin's camps—you will be lost." As of October 1, 1944 over 355,000 Soviet soldiers who had broken out of German encirclement were processed through NKVD filtration camps. By May 1945, 994,000 soldiers had been court-martialed, and of them 157,000 had been condemned to death. The others had been sent to camps or penal battalions where their chances of survival were grim. Penal battalions were death units, and the soldiers usually fell in battle within a matter of days or weeks. In the course of the war more than 1.5 million Soviet soldiers served in such units, which contained not just soldiers who had been court-martialed but also professional criminals and "class enemies" who were supposed to pay their "debt" in blood. They were assigned tasks such as clearing minefields with their bodies or charging at enemy lines across open terrain. In the battalions the officers were masters over life and death, and there was no law to prevent them from treating the soldiers as they pleased. When they felt like killing someone they did so, and no one asked why. The penal battalions were walking death camps, and everyone forced to serve in them eventually understood this. "We thought," said one *shtrafnik* after the war, "that it would be better than a prisoner of war camp. We didn't know at the time that it was nothing but a death sentence." Soldiers who survived this nightmare remembered how even the wounded who survived a failed attack were promptly shot by the waiting NKVD units when they returned. In Stalingrad, the commanders were able to employ their *shtrafniki* with considerable success in house-to-house "rat war" combat.[94] The reason was that in any place a punishment battalion was deployed the enemy had no choice but to fight to the death as well. A Hungarian officer who witnessed the assault on Budapest recalled how the Red Army employed these battalions:

> Towards evening the Russian so-called penal battalion (political prisoners) attacked our positions. A horrible bombardment awaited them, with concerted salvoes from machine guns, mortars and dug-in tanks, and even the speedboats on the Danube were showering bullets on them. . . . The attack collapsed after a little while with huge losses. Hundreds of dying and wounded were lying in front of our positions. We could often hear shouts of '*bozhe moi*' [my God] together with loud, but weakening, calls for help. Our stretcher-bearers tried to bring them in, but each time their efforts were rewarded with machine-gun fire. These people simply had to die. We were unable to help them, and by the next day they were silent.[95]

Of all the armies in the Second World War, Soviet soldiers experienced the worst treatment by far. Their chances of survival were slim—soldiers fighting in Stalingrad usually died in battle within a few days. Red Army commanders stubbornly dismissed tactical and strategic considerations, as Stalin and his cronies considered full frontal assaults to be the only acceptable method for fighting battles. Even as the war neared its end they continued to insist on it. Tacticians were cowards, whereas attackers were heroes, and their success proved them right. Since there was no shortage of manpower and no public opinion to take into consideration, the number of casualties was irrelevant. In December 1944, when regular Red Army units reached the Danube near Budapest, officers drove their soldiers into the freezing water, letting them drown or be killed by enemy machine-gun fire and dive bombers. Although soldier after soldier was dying and no one was coming near the opposite shore, the officers still continued driving their soldiers into the river. In the end not a single soldier from the first assault company was left. "Sir, if this is how they treat their own men," a Hungarian soldier asked his superior officer, "what would they do to their enemies?"[96] Almost nine million Soviet soldiers died in battle between June 1941 and May 1945. In the final six months of the war, when Soviet troops had already advanced onto German territory, Red Army soldiers continued to die at excessive rates. In these last six months alone more than a million Red Army soldiers lost their lives in attacks that looked impressive but were strategically pointless. Among the last of them were the offensive on the Seelow Heights in April 1945 and the capture of Berlin.[97]

The front-line soldiers of the Red Army were trapped in a cycle of violence from which there was no escape. They were given no leave, and they had no contact with women or anyone else from the outside world. For the men, wrote a female medic, "it was difficult, four years without women." They had nothing of the life that the officers took for granted. Officers protected female soldiers and civilians from being assaulted by their troops in exchange for sexual favors. The peasants in uniform, meanwhile, were left to their own devices. "There were no brothels in our army, and the soldiers were not given pills either. Perhaps they took care of this elsewhere, but not in our unit."[98]

Life, as it existed beyond and behind the front, was unknown to the soldiers. Their reality was confined to the small cosmos of the front, which was based on the whims of the officers and commissars and their proclivity for violence. Week after week, the units were supplied with new soldiers as the number of casualties steadily increased. Under these circumstances it became impossible to resist the system of terror. The soldiers became isolated, and in their mortal fear their lives were reduced to the bare struggle to survive one more day. The soldier Pyotr Astakhov later related that it was the "instinct of self-preservation and the feeling of fear" alone that had allowed him to survive this war. In combat, soldiers became bodies that mechanically obeyed commands. Their existences as individuals were erased, and their wills were broken. The war was what transformed people into atoms—isolated, egotistical, deadened creatures, defined by nothing other than violence.[99] This also helps to explain the brutality with which the soldiers of the Red Army attacked the civilian populations of Germany and the rest of central and eastern Europe. They killed and they raped, not for revenge, but because it allowed them to overcome the humiliation that they themselves had been forced to endure for so long. For fleeting moments, even the powerless could force others to feel their power. When the Red Army advanced into Poland, Hungary, and Germany the officers informed the peasant soldiers that they were free to take whatever they wanted and do whatever they pleased—a privilege that was normally reserved for their masters. Peasants were now free to rape, kill, and take possession of women, without requiring any authorization from above. The result was a wave of violence that swept across the conquered territories. In Budapest alone some 100,000 women were reportedly raped.

"We attacked. The first German villages. We were young. Strong. Four years without women. Cellars full of wine and food. We grabbed the German girls," one Red Army soldier recalled decades later. "Ten men raped one girl. There were not enough women, the population had fled from the Soviet Army. We grabbed really young ones. Twelve-year-olds. If one of them cried, we would beat her or gag her mouth. It hurt her, but we found it amusing. Today I no longer understand how I could take part in something like this. But that was me." For once in their lives, slaves could be victors. They had triumphed over the "master race," and they had proven to each other that they were the all-powerful and that their victims were the powerless.[100] "Women, mothers and their daughters lying all across the side of the road," was how the soldier Leonid Rabichev remembered the Red Army's advance into East Prussia.

> And in front of each of them stood an armada of laughing peasants with their pants down. They cast them aside, covered in blood and unconscious; the children rushing to their aid were shot. Crying, bawling, laughing, screaming and moaning. And their commanders, their majors and colonels stand by the roadside, one of them laughs, the other issues instructions,—no, he's in charge. To make sure that really all of their soldiers participate without exception. No, this was not collective solidarity [*krugovaia poruka*], much less revenge on the damned occupiers, but remorseless, deadly group sex.

Rabichev too abused defenseless women. He did not, after all, want to be seen as a "coward" or considered "impotent" by his comrades.[101]

The Hungarian Jewish writer Ephraim Kishon, who witnessed the Red Army's arrival in Budapest in 1945, also documented the cruelty and rapes committed by the Red Army: "After the many millions of victims of Lenin, Trotsky and Stalin, as well as the millions of war dead, death had become second nature to them. They killed without hate, and faced their own death without objection."[102] People who had already spent several decades living in spaces of violence approached war in a different manner than people who came from parts of the world where civil protection existed—people who had been thrown into battles of annihilation without any preparation. Amir Weiner summed this up nicely: "Simply put, the relentless and harsh experiences of collectivisation, famine, and terror produced a tough people who could and did endure difficulties that had defeated others."[103]

We must abandon the idea that wars can only end in victory when soldiers go into battle inspired by notions of freedom and motherland. The opposite is true. In the heat of battle, ideas are irrelevant. As one soldier who had survived the battle of Stalingrad recalled, whenever an assault was launched on the German trenches, officers were required to call out Stalin's name. After that, though, nobody ever wasted any thoughts on the dictator during combat. Soldiers reduced to a struggle for survival weigh the costs of one course of action against the benefits. What are the chances of survival in the cases of desertion, insubordination, or captivity? The risks are substantial, and the consequences of the decision are impossible to estimate. Ultimately, soldiers generally prefer conditions of reliability, provided by staying, to the uncertainty of desertion. They decide against desertion because the chances of survival offered by staying and fighting seem greater.[104]

Ideologies only come into play after the war when it becomes necessary to find meaning in the sacrifices. Military achievements require moral justification because the thought of death and annihilation is unbearable without moral justification. Comrades cannot have suffered and died in vain. Accordingly, memories from the postwar period are often misleading guides for historians of war. In his memoirs, the writer Anatoly Rybakov provides an answer to the riddle of why soldiers who were treated so badly not only obeyed, but could also become victors:

In the three decades of Stalin's rule, the war was probably our only just cause. And it demanded a different moral compass. You cannot fight if you do not trust the man next to you, the perils of war and the closeness of death bind the people together. The dictatorship was as brutal as ever, the reckoning followed in no time, the people were not spared, the victims counted for nothing, for every dead German soldier we paid with the lives of four of our own. The system still saw the life of the individual as worthless, but within themselves people had broken out of its killing shell. The enemy stood on their soil, burned cities and villages to the ground, exterminated friends and relatives, brought humiliation and slavery. The soldier conceived of himself as a defender of his people and his motherland. He not only defended his own country, but also entered the country of the enemy. This exalted him in his own eyes, waking the human dignity that the regime had trodden down.[105]

It was not just the German occupiers who brought terror to the civilian population. From the very first day until the very last day of the war the Soviet people were forced to endure the violence of their own regime as well. In June 1941 Stalin issued a directive to destroy all streets, roads, and villages, as a means of making sure that the advancing enemies would find nothing but an empty and devastated wasteland. Peasants' livestock and harvests were to be wiped out, and their huts were to be burnt to the ground. "During the retreat," ordered Stalin, "all valuable military items and all sick and wounded soldiers are to be evacuated in a timely manner. Anything that cannot be salvaged is to be destroyed. The retreat will be secured by blocking detachments, which will destroy streets, communication links, and bridges, set up tank barriers and lay mines." During the Soviet retreat from the Dniestr, wrote the soldier Dmitri Levinsky, soldiers were instructed to shoot Romanian prisoners and, as Stalin had ordered, "leave nothing to the enemy." Any food warehouses, factories, or shops that the NKVD troops and the Red Army came upon were demolished, leaving the townspeople with nothing but destitution. Before departing from Kiev in September 1941 the NKVD planted mines in buildings throughout the city center and equipped them with timed fuses that were meant to explode at intervals. Wehrmacht soldiers marched into Kiev on September 19, but the mines only exploded five days later, turning the city into a smoking pile of rubble. More than twenty thousand people were left homeless, and the city center was rendered uninhabitable.

Stalin wanted to make sure that the German occupiers, making their way eastward, would have nothing but scorched earth to occupy. Furthermore, he wanted them to be confronted with the rage of famished peasants and city dwellers when they arrived. Cities that were captured by Hitler's armies were sealed off so that people could not flee. Densely populated cities, Stalin assumed, would be more difficult for the occupiers to manage and keep supplied. Only able-bodied men, functionaries, scientists, artists, and other privileged persons were allowed to be evacuated from the cities by the security organs. According to Stalin's calculations, people caught in the crossfire would blame the aggressors rather than the defenders for their misery. This is also why the residents of Stalingrad were forced to remain in their city even after autumn 1942 when it became a bloody battlefield. Stalin's plan worked. The Germans did not want to feed the population in the occupied areas and only wanted to plunder them. But the less that was available to plunder, the worse the occupiers' chances of living off the land, as the German leaders had originally intended, became. The area in direct proximity to the front was to be made uninhabitable. On November 17, 1941, Stalin ordered the army leadership to destroy and burn "all villages situated in the hinterland of the German forces, to a depth of 40 to 60 kilometers from the front line and 20 to 30 kilometers to the left and right of the roads." Everything here was "to be destroyed and reduced to rubble." Airplanes were to destroy from above and leave nothing behind that the invaders could use. The Germans had no winter clothing and were defenseless against the cold. With neither shelter nor provisions they were easy targets for the Red Army. Stalin's order from January 11, 1942, which called for the city of Rzhev to be "completely destroyed" by artillery fire, followed the same logic. What would happen to the civilian populations in these cities was not part of Stalin's calculations.[106]

When Stalin's forces retreated, they left not only devastated landscapes but also the corpses of their internal enemies in their wake. On June 24, 1941, Beria instructed the state security organs to shoot all "counterrevolutionaries" in the abandoned areas. Before their withdrawal from the cities in the Baltic republics, Ukraine, and Belorussia, NKVD units murdered or deported the detainees still in their prisons. Tens of thousands were either massacred or deported during the summer of 1941. The death marches into the Soviet heartland, meanwhile, claimed over forty thousand lives. As the Wehrmacht approached the city of Lwów, Stalin's executioners murdered more than twelve thousand prisoners still in their custody before fleeing. By the time the Germans arrived all of the prisoners were dead. It is difficult to imagine the horror that the family members of the victims experienced when they saw what the Chekists had done. Stalin's murderous forces had nailed children to the walls in the city orphanages, and tortured prisoners to death in the NKVD's dungeons. They had cut the ears and noses from their victims' faces, sliced their stomachs open, and disemboweled them. When time was running out—the Germans were already at the city gates—the Chekists had thrown hand grenades into the cells or used machine guns to execute the remaining prisoners that they did not have time to finish as part of their violent work. In Lithuania too the NKVD units left a trail of blood behind them as they retreated. Most Wehrmacht soldiers had never before seen such images. One German officer, passing through the deserted localities of Lithuania after the Red Army's ravages, wrote to his family that there were "only corpses piled up everywhere, or mutilated and wounded Lithuanians crawling about." There were "horrible, dreadful images to see."[107] In the haste of retreat, the Chekists had been unable to cover their crimes and dispose of the bodies as they usually did. For the first time, the manner in which Stalin's executioners carried out their murderous assaults came into plain view.

The regime's terror raged not only in the western periphery but in the hinterland as well. In the final weeks before the collapse of Bolshevik rule in Kiev, NKVD extermination battalions patrolled the city streets and shot anyone they deemed suspicious. As Victor Kravchenko remembered, such murders took place everywhere:

> Some of us . . . knew of episodes in which prisoners were killed on a mass scale when it became clear that they could not be evacuated. This happened in Minsk, Smolensk, Kiev, Kharkov, in my native Dniepropetrovsk, in Zaporozhe. One such episode has remained with me in detail. In the tiny Kabardino-Balkar Soviet "autonomous republic" in the Caucasus, near the city of Nalchik, there was a molybdenum *combinat* of the N.K.V.D. operated with convict labor. When the Red Army retreated from this area, several hundred prisoners, for technical transport reasons, could not be evacuated in time. The director of the *combinat,* by order of the Commissar of the Kabardino-Balkar N.K.V.D., Comrade Anokhov, machine-gunned the unfortunates to the last man and woman.[108]

Nowhere was the regime able to dispense with its brutalities, not even in places where no one expected the Germans to arrive. The terror was supposed to have a prophylactic effect. It was to remind people that the regime—even in the midst of turmoil and war—still knew how to punish disobedience. Those in a position to kill people without having to expect any resistance could be sure of their power. Just like during the Civil War and the time after Kirov's murder in December 1934, the regime once again adopted a system of shooting hostages. People were arrested, and if need be they were shot as a deterrent to others. Often they were not guilty of anything, but in murdering them the regime was able to demonstrate to the living what it was still capable of. When the war began Beria gave the order not only to kill all enemies in the western regions but to bring the violence to Moscow as well. As a preventive measure, 1,700 people were to be arrested as spies and saboteurs. On October 15, 1941, when defeat seemed inevitable and the functionaries were fleeing the city in panic, Stalin ordered the NKVD to evacuate the remaining relatives of executed "enemies of the people" from Moscow. They were to be taken to Kuybyshev, where the government had also escaped, and shot on arrival. Trotsky's sister and Kamenev's widow died in this manner in early October, and at the end of the month an additional 4,905 prominent prisoners met the same fate. Among them was the former Supreme Commander of the Air Force, Rychagov, who had dared complain, in Stalin's presence, about the "flying coffins" his pilots were forced to fly in. In November 1941 another 10,000 detainees in NKVD custody were murdered on Stalin's orders.

The security apparatus swiftly regained control of the capital. Looters, protesters, and army deserters were arrested or shot on the spot. Houses and public buildings were combed for spies and saboteurs who might be hiding there. In just three days NKVD battalions arrested 23,064 "deserters" on the Moscow front. Between October 1941 and July 1942 more than 830,000 people were arrested by the Chekists in the capital alone. Of them, 900 were shot, and 44,000 sent to prisons or camps. Chekists in the Donbass shot workers who criticized the government or objected to having their factories dismantled and destroyed. Here too, as the Germans approached, they hastily killed all suspects before fleeing. In the prisons of Stalino the prisoners were summarily executed by the Chekists. Directly before the Wehrmacht's arrival, the NKVD took the last remaining prisoners out of the city, forced them to dig their own graves, and shot them. In March 1943, Stalin ordered the party boss of Uzbekistan, Yusupov, to have fifty people shot "by extrajudicial means" as a deterrent. Kirghizstan's party leader received a similar order two months later: 150 bandits and hooligans needed to be shot. Even in the camps of Siberia, violence still had the final say. During the first months of the war, whenever the Wehrmacht captured another Soviet city, prisoners were killed in retaliation.[109]

The civilian population suffered the deprivations and violence of the war just as much as the soldiers. With the German conquest of Stalingrad the city became a slaughterhouse. Due in large part to Stalin's ban on leaving the city thousands of civilians, most of them women and children, died under miserable conditions. No city suffered more, however, than Leningrad. German soldiers reached the city's outer districts in September 1941 but were under orders to encircle rather than invade it. At the beginning of the war, Hitler had still spoken of razing Leningrad to the ground, but now he decided it would be preferable to starve it out instead. And indeed, the blockade lasted until January 1944. By April 1942 the Soviet regime had evacuated more than a million people across the frozen Lake Ladoga. Those who remained behind, however, had several more months of hunger and violence to endure. Not since the Civil War had the situation in one of Russia's major cities been so grim. "Corpses littered the streets," wrote the literary scholar Dmitry Likhachev in his memoirs, "and no one gathered them up. . . . The soft parts were cut off corpses that had fallen in the streets. Cannibalism had begun! First the corpses were stripped, then sliced to the bone, but there was scarcely any flesh on them; these naked, dissected corpses were a terrible sight. . . . When your child is dying and you know that only meat will save it—you'll cut some off a corpse . . ."

For the residents of Leningrad there was no escape from the violence. "We were doubly besieged," Likhachev recalled, "within and without."[110] Leningrad's residents were tormented and worn down by hunger, disease, and German artillery fire. Beyond that, they were victims of the terror of their own regime, which meted out draconian punishments in order to enforce obedience and discipline. In December 1941 Stalin proceeded to toughen the labor laws of June 1940. Workers could now be drafted into the army and punished according to the laws of war if they showed up late for work or violated the rules of workplace discipline. An uninterrupted work week was instituted in Leningrad, and anyone caught leaving work was tried as a deserter. In 1941 some 1.4 million people were imprisoned in the Soviet Union for arriving late to work. By summer 1942 the number was more than 21,000 in Leningrad alone.

Without such draconian disciplinary measures, public order in the starving city would have collapsed. Under such conditions any government would have punished looters, bread thieves, and prowling cannibals. Stalin's regime, however, exercised terror because the dictator was unable to conceive of any other disciplinary methods whatsoever. What mattered to him was that the state security organs remain in control during the blockade and that traitors and spies be seized and executed. Stalin was a stranger to pity and empathy, and the plight of Leningrad's starving civilians was of no interest to him. He expected his representatives in this besieged city to wield power in the same merciless Stalinist manner as always. In December 1941 Andrei Zhdanov, the Leningrad party boss, became the target of Stalin's suspicion. Stalin accused Zhdanov of withholding information about events in the city and at the front. "One might conclude that Comrade Zhdanov's Leningrad is not located in the USSR but in the Pacific Ocean," Stalin accused him. The previous August, before the Germans had reached Leningrad, Stalin had sent Molotov, Malenkov, and Kosygin to the city to put pressure on Zhdanov and his people. For the first time since 1935 Zhdanov had been in serious danger, as Molotov and Malenkov had uncovered "shortcomings" and "errors," and denounced him at the despot's court as an unreliable devotee. Zhdanov, so they had told Stalin, was not keeping the party leadership adequately informed about events in Leningrad and had retreated from the enemy. Zhdanov remained in office, but he now understood that he needed to make every effort to carry out Stalin's will if he wanted to counter these suspicions.[111]

In September 1941 Stalin expressed his vision of the defense of Leningrad. When told about German soldiers using civilians as human shields, Stalin recommended that the shields be shot at as well. "My answer is—no sentimentality. Instead smash the enemy and his accomplices, sick or healthy, in the teeth. War is inexorable, and those who show weakness and allow wavering are the first to suffer defeat. Whoever in our ranks permits wavering will be responsible for the fall of Leningrad."[112]

Police and the NKVD shot thieves for stealing loaves of bread and arrested anyone they considered a potential enemy of the regime. By October 1942 the security organs had exposed more than six hundred "counterrevolutionary organizations" in the city. Professors at Leningrad University were accused of being involved in conspiracies, and over ninety-five hundred people were arrested as spies and terrorists. In March 1942, at a point in time when no one expected the Wehrmacht to still be able to capture Leningrad, state security arrested all Finnish and German residents of the city—almost sixty thousand people in total—and had them deported to Kazakhstan. In their search for enemies and spies, the authorities relied on informers and agents. The campaigns for vigilance had left their mark. There were no reliable sources of information, and no one really knew how to distinguish between true stories and invented ones. People, grasping for bits of information, began to accept sources that, under normal circumstances, never would have been considered trustworthy. When the rumor spread that there were German agents wearing Soviet police uniforms, a series of violent attacks on the well-nourished militiamen carrying out their duties on the streets of Leningrad ensued.[113]

As Sergei Likhachev recalled, although the number of arrests did not decrease during the war, they became easier to endure because at some point the fear had simply vanished. Police terror lost its psychological effect because people inside and outside of prison were starving in equal measure. Lydia Ginzburg, like others who lived through the blockade, suffered hunger and cold but took satisfaction in knowing that the informers and little despots in her neighborhood were no better off. "The malnourished block manager could no longer get to his office. The dialectics of the varieties of evil."[114]

In late summer 1941 the regime also resumed its war against ethnic minorities that were accused of colluding with the enemy. On August 26, 1941, Stalin gave the order to have 479,841 Germans from the Republic of Volga Germans and the areas of Saratov and Stalingrad deported to Siberia and Kazakhstan. The Autonomous Republic of Volga Germans was dissolved, and everything that served as a reminder that Germans had once lived there was destroyed. According to the order, the "relocation" applied to "all Germans without exception." It was thus completely irrelevant whether the Germans in question supported or opposed Soviet power. All that mattered was their ethnicity. The decree of the Supreme Soviet, which authorized Stalin's terror order, spoke of "saboteurs and spies." These "enemies of the people" needed to be removed, as they posed a threat to the order and could potentially cause strife in the hinterland. On August 30 Ivan Serov, Beria's deputy and an expert when it came to displacing populations, reported that the deportation order had been read out to the party leadership in the Volga Republic. Even the chairman of the Council of People's Commissars in the Volga Republic, Gekman, had read the order and declared that he also believed it was the right decision. There were, indeed, "many villains" about. As a German himself, however, he also had to "resign" when his republic disappeared from the map. Russian workers in the city of Engels reportedly greeted the order with satisfaction. One worker declared, "Now I can go to the front in peace, because I know that my family is safe from the enemy within." Moreover, he explained, the government had been right in having the Germans deported, as there were "many spies among the Germans" who were known to "provide cover for each other." On September 8 Serov was able to notify Beria that 33,406 people had been removed from the republic on twelve trains.[115]

Between November 1943 and December 1944, at a time when the German Wehrmacht no longer posed a serious threat, Stalin and Beria had all Tatars from the Crimean Peninsula and peoples from the Caucasus—Chechens, Ingushes, Karachays, Balkars, Kalmyks, and Turkic Meskhetians—deported to central Asia. In the early summer of 1944 more "suspicious" peoples followed them into exile. This included 25,000 Greeks, Bulgarians, and Armenians from the Crimean Peninsula; Turkic Meskhetians and Kurds from the Caucasus; and 225,000 Crimean Tatars. Over three million people were expelled from their homelands during the war, including more than one million Germans and 470,000 Chechens and Ingushes. Decades later Molotov would continue justify the expulsions and told the Soviet journalist Felix Chuev, "The fact is that during the war we received reports about mass treason. Battalions of Caucasians opposed us at the fronts and attacked us from the rear. It was a matter of life and death; there was no time to investigate the details. Of course innocents suffered. But I hold that given the circumstances, we acted correctly."[116]

No efforts were spared in driving the enemies out of their homelands. In the northern Caucasus, three Red Army divisions, 100,000 NKVD soldiers, and 40,000 trucks and freight cars—all urgently needed at the front—were deployed to help deport the Chechens and Ingushes. Beria's enforcers, who organized the deportation between February and May 1944, were told to be thorough and to not "leave a single soul." The NKVD troops arrived without warning and surrounded the villages with trucks and tanks. The Chechen residents were given one hour to prepare for their departure and were then taken to the nearest station, loaded onto trains, and taken to their final destination.

The deportations went just as Stalin had hoped for. On February 22, 1944, Beria informed him that he had notified the leading party functionaries in the Autonomous Republic of Chechens and Ingushes that Stalin was planning to have the resident populations deported. The chairman of the Council of People's Commissars in Grozny, Supyan Mollayev, reportedly burst into tears but eventually "pulled himself together and promised to carry out all instructions." Beria then summoned the higher Islamic dignitaries and forced them to cooperate with the state security organs so that the victims would offer no resistance. The operation began the next day. "Today on February 23 at sunrise," wrote Beria to Stalin, "we began with the operation for the resettlement of the Ingushes and Chechens." By noon more than 90,000 people had been loaded onto freight trains. Beria's henchmen evidently encountered minimal resistance, and when they did, they shot their victims dead. In the village of Khaibakh Red Army soldiers rounded up more than 700 people, locked them in a barn, and burned them alive. Sure enough, however, Beria's report made no mention of this. He telegraphed Moscow that the deportations had proceeded "normally," that resistance had been crushed, and that more than 20,000 rifles had been confiscated. On February 25 Beria reported that the deportations had been completed successfully. 352,647 people had been taken away on eighty-six trains. The last train departing from the republic took the Chechen Communists away into exile.

Beria, who remained at the scene after the operation, immediately began making further plans. Now, he suggested, it might be a good idea to expel the neighboring Balkars as well. The Balkars, he told Stalin on February 25, had come into contact with German troops in 1942 and had forged an alliance with them. Once the Chechen operation was finished he would also have plenty of spare NKVD units at his disposal. These, he explained, could be deployed at a moment's notice to remove the forty thousand suspect Balkars living in the villages of the Caucasus Mountains. Beria wrote to Stalin, "If you are in agreement, I could, before my return to Moscow, make all the necessary arrangements on the spot for the removal of the Balkars." At his master's behest, Beria had already prepared the necessary documents. The Chechens, Crimean Tatars, and Germans serving in the Red Army became victims of Stalin's vindictiveness as well. As late as 1944, when the Soviet victory was almost certain, the dictator was still having his troops screened for national enemies. Soldiers and officers with the wrong ethnicity were disarmed, arrested and, like their compatriots, deported to central Asia.

The Chechen-Ingush Autonomous Republic disappeared, just as the republics of the Crimean Tatars and the Volga Germans had done. But for Stalin the mere expulsion of the people was not enough. He wanted instead to erase every trace of their existence from the memory of future generations. This meant ridding the cities and villages of anything that might serve as a reminder of their former presence. Stalin gave the order to purge the names of all places where the deportees had lived and to change the names of streets, squares, and buildings. Memorials and cemeteries were also destroyed. Russian peasants and refugees who had lost their homes in the turmoil of the war took up residence in the homes of the deported a short time later. And soon it was as though the Chechens, Crimean Tatars, and Germans had never lived here.

Nearly one-quarter of all Chechens and Ingushes lost their lives between 1944 and 1948. Many of the very young and the very old died of hunger or cold while still on the trains. Once they were in Kazakhstan, thousands more continued to perish from hunger or cold or typhus as there was neither food nor shelter available, and the bitterly poor peasants already living there refused to accept Chechens into the collective farm. With neither food nor clothing nor shoes, the deportees had no chance of survival. The regime's war became a war between its victims. The exiled were forced to compete with each other for scarce resources, living space, work, and food. Kazakhstan became a giant dumping ground for expelled individuals whose only concerns were to secure their own survival and to make life difficult for others. In these disputes, newcomers had the worst chances of success. In July 1944 bloody conflicts erupted between Chechen special settlers and other nationalities who had been deported to the region. Within a matter of days, the clashes had spread and developed into a protest against the local authorities, whom the deportees blamed for their misery. As usual, the regime crushed the revolt with brutal violence. NKVD units were deployed to the region to search for "saboteurs, shirkers, and malingerers," and in July 1944 Beria could notify Stalin that over two thousand "bandit elements" and robbers had been arrested.[117] To finalize the stigmatization of its victims, the regime decreed that the expelled would never again be allowed to return to their homelands. Germans, Chechens, and Crimean Tatars now bore the mark of the enemies. They were second-class people and would remain so for decades to come.

Gustav Herling, a Polish officer who had been sent to a Soviet camp after the signing of the Hitler-Stalin Pact, was released from detention in early 1942. On his way home he passed through the city of Vologda in northern Russia. He had intended to travel to Moscow by train but had to wait for the next four days in the city. He recalled how hundreds of released prisoners lay about on the train station floors, waiting for days for their train to arrive:

> In the daytime they were driven out into the town, where they spent their time looking for food, and in the evening the enormous waiting-room, by permission of the N.K.V.D., served as a dormitory for them. I hesitate before describing the four nights which I spent in Vologda, for I do not believe that literature could sink so low without losing some of its character as the artistic expression of things commonly known and experienced. Enough, then, to say that we slept next to each other, lying on our sides packed together like herrings in a barrel, and giving out an inhuman stench. . . . Every attempt to wade through the mass of bodies at night to reach the nearest bucket usually ended in someone's death. . . . I myself, still half-conscious after waking up suddenly, once stepped on someone's face. One of my legs was wedged between two bodies, and trying to free it I moved my whole weight onto my other leg and felt a spongy mass splintering and crackling under my heavy boot, while blood spurted from under the sole. A moment later I was sick into the bucket, though I had not come to it for that. Every morning at least ten bodies, stripped naked by their fellow-guests in the waiting-room, were carried out and laid on the open trucks.

Beyond the station, too, Herling encountered nothing but embittered and miserable beings, fighting over the last remaining scraps of food. "Thus the contempt for a damaged machine which is out of circulation has permeated all strata of the Russian people and has polluted fundamentally honest hearts."[118]

WAR IN PEACETIME

The Great Patriotic War did not mark the end of Stalinism. In many ways it was what allowed Stalinism to develop to its full potential. Under the conditions of war the regime was able to unfold all its lethal possibilities without any restraints. It was not until the war drew to a close that the regime again became uncertain, as millions of Red Army soldiers, forced laborers, and prisoners of war, who had been outside the Soviet Union for the first time in their lives, slowly returned home. They had conquered foreign nations where the people were living better lives than they were. They had seen whole worlds that had contradicted everything they had been told by the regime's propaganda. The edifice of lies was crumbling, and everyone knew it. How could anyone still possibly be convinced that the Soviet Union was a place of prosperity and abundance? The message runner Aglaya Nesteruk recalled her passage into Germany in 1945. She and her comrades could not believe what they saw: "And now we were on their soil. . . . The first thing to take us aback was the good roads. The big peasant houses. Tulle, white curtains. . . . flowerpots, even in sheds, and pretty curtains. White tablecloths. . . . Expensive dishes. . . . We couldn't understand: why had they gone to war if they lived this well? Our people lived in dugouts (*zemlianky*), whereas they had white tablecloths and drank from porcelain cups."[119]

Under the conditions of war it was irrelevant what people thought or experienced because there was no alternative to the order of the war. But when the guns fell silent in May 1945, the conditions of action for the regime changed entirely. What was to be done with those who had seen a new world and were now due to return to the old one? How would demobilized Red Army soldiers behave once they had been discharged and sent home? How was one to turn officers who had made independent decisions under adverse conditions into feeble slaves once again? "No one that had survived the horrors of the blockade," wrote Likhachev, "was frightened of anything anymore. It was hard to put the wind up us."[120] It was impossible to erase everything that people had seen and experienced. At most, the regime could try to prevent people from answering back and force them into obedience.

Rather than washing away the "barren and bitter reality" of which Maxim Gorky had once written, the Bolsheviks would reproduce it again and again. And yet most people hoped that the end of the war would make for a more relaxed political climate in their country. "After all that we have lived through, the government must change its policy," the university professor Tereshchenko confided to his diary in 1943, after the liberation of Kharkov ended his war. Like many of his contemporaries, he simply could not believe that all the horrors and privations of the war had been in vain. Intellectuals hoped for a more relaxed creative atmosphere, soldiers wished for peace, and peasants yearned for a world without collective farms and hunger. Andrei Sakharov later recalled his thoughts during the bitter experiences of the postwar period: "We all believed—or at least hoped—that the postwar world would be decent and humane. How could it be otherwise? But instead Soviet victory seemed only to intensify the regime's severity: soldiers returning from German POW camps were the first to feel the tightening of the screws. As the illusions faded, the nation disintegrated into separate atoms and melted away."[121]

Although the Soviet Union belonged to the club of victors in the Second World War, its people suffered far more in the war than the defeated. The war claimed over twenty million Soviet lives, and it left behind two million invalids, cripples, and homeless people, who could neither make their way in civilian life nor expect any help from the state they had served. Throughout the Soviet Union demobilized Red Army soldiers and refugees drifted about aimlessly. In Bryansk, as late as 1948, more than 9,000 families, invalids, and orphans were still living in holes in the ground. Living conditions elsewhere were hardly any better. In June 1947 Molotov received a circular from the minister of internal affairs, Sergei Kruglov, complaining that refugees and demobilized soldiers were disturbing the peace and refusing to work. More than 200,000 refugees from all regions of the Soviet Union had gathered in Krasnodar in southern Russia, starving and wasting away. Some 18,000 of the most unfortunate were effectively living "under the open sky," as the minister of internal affairs reported, and it was thus only a matter of time before plagues and epidemics would begin to spread. The local state authorities, meanwhile, were struggling to cope with the endless stream of new refugees, while at the same time trying to contain the massive wave of crime that the influx of refugees, demobilized soldiers, and homeless orphans had brought to the region. The refugees not only begged but also stole, robbed, and hijacked trains. In

Krasnodar, an old lady carrying a pair of chicken eggs was killed by a hungry demobilized soldier. The authorities tried to forestall the arrival of new refugees. In April 1947 they began to expel demobilized soldiers and homeless orphans from Krasnodar and stopped new refugees from entering the region. NKVD units were posted at the train stations and on the main roads, arresting anyone attempting to enter Krasnodar without valid identification. Within a matter of weeks the criminals had taken root in the neighboring regions instead. Such a practice, as the minister of internal affairs complained, simply caused the refugees to "move from one district to the other all the time."[122]

Not even the capital could offer bearable living conditions. When the young Pole Janusz Bardach returned to Moscow from a prison camp after the war he saw nothing but misery and poverty:

> Ramshackle buildings with tiny grated windows and broken front doors marked the fringes of Moscow. Feral cats yowled in the alleyways, and drunkards slept on the bare ground, covering themselves with newspapers. Fetid kitchen scraps clogged the gutters. Lampposts were scarce, and no policemen were in sight. Some people frightened me. Shadowy figures lurked between buildings, and heavily made-up women invited me into doorways. On street corners and outside taverns gangs of young, bare-chested men laughed loudly and shared a bottle, hurling insults and making catcalls as if the street belonged to them.[123]

The homecoming could hardly have been more dismal. People were forced to live in sheds and in cellars, amid rats and garbage, the physicist Yuri Orlov recalled. "And all this was in the heart of the capital of a nation that wished to teach the rest of the world how to live!"[124]

Indeed, many former officers and soldiers also gained new perspectives on life after the war. But Soviet reality had nothing to offer people who were now traumatized and uprooted or who had become invalids. No one could claim their rights in peacetime by invoking their heroic deeds during the war. In the struggle for survival, one could count on oneself alone. "I remember, for instance," wrote Joseph Brodsky,

> how in 1945 my mother and I were waiting for a train at some railway station near Leningrad. The war was just over, twenty million Russians were decaying in makeshift graves across the continent, and the rest, dispersed by war, were returning to their homes or what was left of their homes. The railway station was a picture of primeval chaos. People were besieging the cattle trains like mad insects; they were climbing on

the roofs of cars, squeezing between them, and so on. For some reason, my eye caught sight of an old, bald, crippled man with a wooden leg, who was trying to get into car after car, but each time was pushed away by the people who were already hanging on the footboards. The train started to move and the old man hopped along. At one point he managed to grab a handle of one of the cars, and then I saw a woman in the doorway lift a kettle and pour boiling water straight on the old man's bald crown. The man fell—the Brownian movement of a thousand legs swallowed him and I lost sight of him.[125]

Some hapless individuals even appealed to Stalin in their despair, hoping that he might deliver them from their distress. In August 1945 one soldier wrote to Stalin that he had lost both his legs and that neither he nor his family knew how they were to survive without food or shelter. All attempts to acquire an apartment had failed. "I'm lying in hospital, I'm completely helpless," he wrote.[126] Millions of people were forced to come to terms with a postwar life of misery, hunger, and cold. By now, however, they only submitted with great reluctance. Soldiers and officers had seen and experienced dreadful things during the war. Death and violence had become part of their daily existence, so much so that they were no longer afraid of speaking up. Officers who had been arrested by the state security organs were undeterred by the violence and death that awaited them. They despised the obese security police officers sitting behind office desks who dared interrogate officers who had offered themselves up for the motherland. Lev Kopelev, who was arrested by state security in early 1945 under the pretext of having shown pity for German civilians, expressed this sentiment. He had been a major, he had fought on the front lines of battle, and his only thanks had been arrest and interrogation:

> I saw his white, smoothly shaven, contemptuous face above me; the rubber hose in the white glove. Suddenly, without being fully aware of my actions, I reared up and swung the chair over my head . . . With a thrill of exultation, I saw him cower, an arm over his face. I heard myself bellowing hoarsely . . . "So you're going to strike me, fuck your mother, are you? Then do it right, you rear-echelon rat! Strike me dead with a bullet, not with that rubber shit! Or else you'll get your own back, in your clean-shaven snout, goddamn your fucking soul! German shells didn't scare me, and you're going to scare me with your little piece of rubber? Kill me, you worm! But the Soviet government will pay you back for it![127]

Kopelev spoke of Soviet power and how it would avenge him, but he spoke of it in a manner which would have been unthinkable before the war. During the war the concept of Soviet power had become a force that was no longer represented by the repressive state alone. Now it was embodied by the soldiers as well. Millions of soldiers had managed to avoid the daily encroachments of the party apparatus, and they had learned that nothing would change unless they took matters into their own hands. Why should the party and its leaders receive all the credit for everything that the soldiers on the front lines had accomplished? They had set foot on foreign soil as conquerors, and they had seen with their own eyes that even the defeated lived better lives than they did. There was no longer any lie that could convince them of the superiority of their state and its social order. Regardless of all the propaganda still being churned out, "the suffering and poverty were visible all around," as Brodsky later remembered life in Leningrad after the war when he was a student there. After all, he wrote, "you cannot cover a ruin with a page of *Pravda.*"[128] The regime was well aware that it would lose control of the situation if resistance and dissent were not crushed immediately. No one knew better than Stalin that the floodgates of criticism needed to be barred shut once again. Although soldiers and officers hoped the regime would reward them for their service to the motherland, for Stalin that was too much to ask. Anyone showing signs of weakness risked losing power, and Stalin was not prepared to concede an inch. Stalin decided that he alone deserved the credit for the war's outcome, and from now on the war would not be celebrated as a people's victory but as one more of the leader's wonderful feats. The subjects, however, were not prepared to submit voluntarily, so the postwar period too was marked by the regime's continued reliance on violence as a means of discipline.

In 1946 the dictator decided to reintroduce the kolkhoz system to peasant life. Even the German occupiers had been unwilling to give up the collective farms, as they were the only instrument of state control and subjugation in the village. The Bolsheviks too were determined to defend it. Although the peasantry lived in misery, in villages that were decrepit and devastated, with neither machinery nor draft cattle, the despotic regime still insisted that they offer tribute to the regime and expend their last bits of strength performing heavy labor. Against all economic rationale, Stalin gave orders to increase the number of working days on collective farms and to mercilessly punish farmers who failed to perform their duties. Peasants who cultivated kolkhoz land for private use or traded goods on the black market now faced criminal prosecution. The August 1932 law on "socialist property" was also reinstated, and peasants could now be imprisoned or banished for minor violations. The levies imposed on collective farms were such a heavy burden that peasants were forced to avail themselves of the meager yields from their own private patches of land. Penalty taxes, tribute, and forced labor drove them to ruin. Peasants were reduced to serfdom and forced to produce whatever the state authorities demanded of them. Village life offered them little in the way of opportunities, so just as before the war, many fled the villages for the cities. Even late into Stalin's reign peasants continued to flee the countryside. Between 1950 and 1954 over nine million peasants left their villages and went into hiding in the cities, in an attempt at escaping their lives of hunger and misery.

The regime was well aware of the miserable conditions the peasantry faced. Stalin received regular reports and petitions documenting hunger and violence in the countryside. In July 1945 a Red Army major approached the dictator to inform him of what he had witnessed while on vacation in the Chernigov region. Wherever he went, he reported, peasants were starving. Furthermore, no one was willing to work on the collective farms anymore as they offered the peasants nothing but misery. Peasants were frequently heard to complain, "Why should we go to work? They won't give us anything for it anyway." Beyond that, the major lamented, the responsible Communist functionaries did nothing to help the situation as they were all drunkards who took bribes and also treated the peasants inhumanely. The local authorities intercepted all letters of complaint and arrested all critics. Not even the soldiers who returned to their villages after the war were left in peace. Those who had criticized the living conditions had been deported to western Ukraine or sent back to the army. Functionaries reportedly even inflicted violence on war invalids. It was thus necessary, the major said, to "cleanse" the entire party and state apparatus of "servants to the Germans, cowards, and panicmongers" and to remove all "foreigners" and replace them with heroes who had "passed through the school of war."[129] The major knew that his only hope of getting the dictator's attention was to draw a connection between the targets of his criticism and the hated Germans. When, however, had anyone last dared to write Stalin such a letter?

Rebelliousness and resistance were punished mercilessly by the regime. Stalin expected his people in the provinces to do what was necessary to keep the peasants in check—no matter how ruthless. In this regard they did not disappoint him. Life after the war was no gentler than before. In 1946 and 1947 a famine, in which Ukraine was particularly hard hit, ravaged the land. It claimed over 1.5 million lives. In the course of the famine 12,000 kolkhoz chairmen were tried and several thousand peasants were sent to prison camps for having taken fallen ears of grain from the field. Peasants and workers whose sole focus was on survival had no strength to resist the regime's terror, even after the war. "We don't live, we exist," a peasant from the Stalingrad area wrote to the party leadership. "When will the agony finally end? We are already bloated, we are experiencing a terrible famine, and death will soon wipe us out." "The children don't go to school, there is no bread," wrote another peasant from the same region. "I will commit suicide, so I don't need to see this agony any longer." The intelligence services were also becoming aware of what the peasants were suffering. In December 1946 Moldavia's minister of state security, Mordovets, reported to Moscow that there were more and more people dying of hunger or exhaustion every day. Corpses littered the streets, and exhausted, dehydrated children lay starving in the hospitals. People everywhere could be heard lamenting that no one had ever starved under Romanian rule. Mordovets's solution was to summon the state security organs to pursue the "anti-Soviet elements" that were spreading these rumors, and also to have them take necessary steps to prevent peasants from fleeing to Romania.[130]

The intelligence service supplied Stalin with detailed reports on the misery in the villages, and still he turned a deaf ear. He demanded instead that state security suppress all criticism with violence. In January 1948 the Ukrainian party boss, Nikita Khrushchev, presented Stalin with a proposal on how to deal with insubordinate peasants. The failure to meet the grain quotas, he said, was due to acts of sabotage by "parasitic and criminal elements." The peasants were using the collective farms as a "shield" to engage in "speculation" and "thievery." In 1947 more than eighty-six thousand peasants had been working for themselves alone and had not spent a single day on the collective farms.

There were also multiple reports of violence. Peasants had reportedly killed Communist activists and set fire to their houses. It was possible to try the peasants who refused to work on the kolkhozy, but this, Khrushchev complained, had proven ineffective in the past, as the sentences at the judiciary's disposal—a maximum of six months in prison—were wholly inadequate. Khrushchev's solution was to reintroduce the principle of collective solidarity, as it had existed under the tsar, and grant kolkhozy the right to have "irremediable felons and parasitic elements" deported from the villages. Stalin approved the proposal immediately, and in February 1948 the Supreme Soviet issued a law regulating the deportation from the villages of "asocials" and "parasites." The kolkhoz leadership could now have rebellious peasants deported to Siberia for eight years. In May 1948 Khrushchev briefed Moscow on the initial progress. The "first cars" of condemned peasants had been sent north on April 10, and within the first month more than four thousand peasants had been removed from collective farms in eastern Ukraine. According to Khrushchev, the peasants had welcomed the law with great satisfaction. "Thanks to the state and our father Stalin for creating this law for us all, for us kolkhoz farmers," they had allegedly proclaimed.[131] Stalin was not simply a cruel tyrant. He also demanded that the people thank him for his cruelty.

For Stalin and his people, everyone in the Soviet Union was a suspect. Even in their hour of victory there was no room for generosity. When the war ended the state security organs unleashed a wave of merciless terror in the areas formerly occupied by the Germans. Collaborators and "spies" were arrested, people were publicly executed, and minorities accused of having colluded with the enemy were deported. Those who had lived under German occupation during the war were pursued by the NKVD, and many were eventually sent to filtration camps, where the decision was made to either release them or deport them to Siberia. But even those who remained free were still suspects. To make certain that the stigma of having lived under German occupation was permanent, citizens for whom this was the case received special stamps in their passports.

For collaborators, of course, there could be no forgiveness. Vlasov and his officer corps were condemned in a secret trial in Moscow and executed. Tens of thousands of his soldiers were deported to camps in Siberia. Anyone who was suspected of having sided with the Germans or served in their armies, of course, shared the same fate. This included the Kalmyks, who were deported from their homeland in southern Ukraine because they had supposedly aided the German occupiers. It also included Ukrainian volunteers and Cossacks who had fought alongside the Wehrmacht. Following Germany's surrender, all Cossacks who had served in the Wehrmacht were interned by the Allies and duly extradited to the Soviet Union. Harrowing scenes occurred in June 1945 in Austria's Carinthia and East Tyrol as the British prepared to hand over some fifty thousand Cossack prisoners to the NKVD. The prisoners began throwing themselves off bridges, slitting their wrists, or attacking the soldiers guarding them. Entire companies committed suicide together. Similar scenes could be witnessed on the British ships taking detainees in German uniforms from Liverpool to Odessa. Prisoners could be seen jumping overboard or ending their lives in any other number of gruesome ways. For those still alive when the ship arrived in Odessa, NKVD men were already waiting in the harbor, ready to gun them down as soon as they stepped off the ship. Never before had the British soldiers witnessed scenes like this. A British Army major who oversaw the extradition of twenty-two hundred Vlasov soldiers to the NKVD in Judenburg in Austria broke down in tears when he saw how the Soviet officers treated their own people. In a number of British units a mutiny nearly broke out. As one American general recalled, without using violence it was nearly impossible to extradite people from the Bavarian camps for "displaced persons." For decades to come he would be haunted by the screams of men who preferred suicide to repatriation.[132]

The circle of suspects also included the four million people who had entered German captivity or been taken to Germany as slave laborers during the war. Soldiers who had surrendered to the Germans were treated like traitors, and their suffering would continue after their release. By July 11, 1945, more than 800,000 former Soviet soldiers had passed through NKVD filtration camps. Over 600,000 of them were forced to perform slave labor in the "labor army" of the NKVD, and tens of thousands more were deported to camps in Siberia. Captured officers could expect no mercy either, as they had violated the basic Stalinist principle that only those capable of victory deserved to live. Officers were supposed to be examples for their soldiers, and if they were prepared to surrender then why would their soldiers continue fighting? That was why, in Stalin's eyes, they deserved no mercy. Stalin himself had disowned his own eldest son, a lieutenant in the Red Army, after he had been captured by the Germans. Why would anyone else expect better treatment? Over 120,000 Soviet officers were interrogated by the NKVD. Most of them then spent six years in camps and were then, upon their release, placed under observation.[133]

At the end of the war camps for "displaced persons" still held more than two million people who had been taken to Germany as "Ostarbeiter." The Western allies had a contractual obligation to return all slave laborers and stateless refugees in their custody to the Soviet Union. Initially, slave workers had hoped that the Red Army would liberate them and they would return home triumphantly. By early 1945, however, as hostilities in East Prussia and Brandenburg wore on, the freed prisoners slowly realized that all their suffering had been for naught. There were cases of arbitrary attacks—women who had worked as maids on German farms were ridiculed as "whores" and raped by Red Army soldiers—and many of the Ostarbeiter were shot or abused by the Chekists. "I cried, I pulled away," recalled a female slave worker who was raped by Soviet soldiers in East Prussia, "and told the leader of the group that my brothers were also fighting, but he beat and raped me. If only he had shot me instead."

The Americans and the British soon discovered that Soviet citizens were being treated worse by the security organs of their own government than by the Germans. Tens of thousands of Russian and Ukrainian slave laborers who had been taken to France by the Germans roamed about aimlessly during the winter of 1944. They raided farms and looted food. The American occupation authorities, who were struggling to cope with the situation, urged their Soviet allies to take care of their own people, and in response a high-ranking NKVD officer traveled to France to pay the Americans a surprise visit and show them how they dealt with troublemakers in the Soviet Union. He appeared at the scene personally and shot his defiant compatriots with his own revolver.[134]

In Stalin's empire problems were solved with the revolver. The allies became aware of this by spring 1945 at the latest. This was when Soviet repatriation officers started showing up in the internment camps of the Western allies to register all "displaced persons" who had lived in the Soviet Union before the war or in the territories annexed after the Hitler-Stalin Pact. As American officers recalled, the repatriation officers urged them to employ violence against detainees who refused to return home. In some cases, though, violence was not necessary. It sufficed for the Chekists to tell the detainees that they knew where their family members lived. Before being forced to march home on foot, displaced persons were used to dismantle industrial plants. Those who were registered by Soviet repatriation officers were essentially state property and were thus treated like slaves. Not even Latvians, Estonians, Lithuanians, and Poles, who had once been citizens of sovereign states, could avoid repatriation to the Soviet territories. The regime insisted that they too were citizens of the Soviet Union and would be treated accordingly.[135]

Those prisoners of war and forced laborers returning home after the war left one scene of desolation only to arrive at another. "When I set foot on Soviet territory again," remembered a female kolkhoz farmer, "it was as though I had fallen into a filthy pit." Nothing awaited them in their homeland but poverty, accusations, and shame. An American diplomat witnessed a group of returning Soviet citizens being welcomed back by a brass band as they arrived in the harbor of Murmansk—only to be led away, directly afterwards, by armed Chekists. Irina Ehrenburg expected that the Soviet prisoners of war who were arriving in Odessa in spring 1945 would receive a jubilant welcome with military honors. Instead she saw cheerless faces with portraits of Stalin in their hands, standing on a quay that resembled a "garbage dump." Following a short speech by a Communist functionary, they were led away to a nearby military academy to be interrogated. The next day, writes Ehrenburg, French and Belgian prisoners of war who had been liberated by Soviet troops returned home on the same ship. "There I saw joyful faces. . . . They sang, whistled, and laughed."[136]

Everyone returning home from German captivity was forced to live with the stigma of having betrayed the motherland. They would remain under suspicion for decades, for they had glimpsed the land of the enemy and they had seen all its wealth. They now knew how the Germans, Americans, and British lived, and they were no longer receptive to the lies of the regime. Although they could be forced to go through the motions of praising all manner of lies as truth, they could no longer be made to believe that the misery they had left behind and then returned to was truly the best of all possible worlds. Everyone knew that the victors were significantly worse off than the defeated and that their own people treated them no better than their enemies did. The Second World War shifted the borders of the Soviet Union toward Europe and ended the isolation of the Red empire. But this shift came at a high price for those in power, so Stalin and his people spared no effort in resealing open borders and stifling newly won freedoms. American and British military personnel were shocked and appalled when they saw how the Soviet authorities treated people in their German and Austrian occupation zones. The things they witnessed were so inhuman, so barbaric, that it even seemed justifiable to break off their friendship with their wartime ally. To Stalin, however, the use of excessive violence was nothing more than a power strategy, a means of disciplining the general population. Stalin and his cronies had again become insecure, so they had begun punishing with particular ruthlessness and cruelty. The torrent of death and destruction they unleashed was not just intended as a punishment for disloyalty but also as a deterrent, a reminder to the living that there would be no mercy for traitors. The message could hardly have been clearer: anyone who colluded with enemies of the regime and anyone who switched sides in war would have to pay dearly.

In many regions the expulsion of the German conquerors did not mark the end of the war. This was particularly the case in Poland, in western Ukraine, and in the Baltic republics, where the partisan struggle against the Red Army continued on. Into the late 1940s units of the national Polish underground army, the Armia Krajowa, were engaged in bloody skirmishes with NKVD troops. In Ukraine the Red Army and the NKVD waged a bitter war against nationalist partisans and peasant rebels who opposed the return of the Bolshevik regime. After the end of the war the strike capability of Ukrainian Bandera units grew to threatening levels, as they were joined by deserters and demobilized soldiers from the Red Army, the Waffen SS, and the security police—all of whom also supplied the partisans with weapons. In July 1945 alone eleven thousand Soviet soldiers deserted and defected to the partisans. Both sides knew full well that if they were defeated they could expect no mercy, and so they fought with a tenacity and cruelty reminiscent of the Civil War. The Red Army deployed tanks and planes. It destroyed villages and tried to cut the supply lines to the Bandera partisans. The partisans in turn responded with the weapons of the weak: they destroyed streets, bridges, and telegraph lines, and they spread fear and terror by killing every functionary of the hated regime they could get their hands on. The German occupiers had practiced a strategy of taking hostages, burning villages to the ground, and violently forcing peasants to reveal the whereabouts of partisans. Although the strategy had failed for the Germans, Stalin's henchmen continued to employ it.

Just as during the Civil War, the regime tried to foment unrest among the peasants as a means of fighting resistance. Over 60,000 peasants were recruited as "volunteers" and made to serve in so-called destruction battalions (*istrebitel'nye bataliony*). These were intended to terrorize villages on behalf of the NKVD. Nowhere was the blood toll after the war higher than in Ukraine. Between 1944 and 1953 more than 150,000 partisans were killed in combat or captivity by state security forces. 130,000 people were arrested as "spies" and "anti-Soviet nationalists" and thrown into prisons or camps, and over 200,000 partisan "supporters" were deported to central Asia. As late as May 1953, two months after the despot's demise, partisans and units of the Ukrainian Interior Ministry were still engaged in bloody skirmishes. But in the end, the Chekists prevailed, as everyone came to realize that there would be no help from abroad, and that any system, no matter how cruel, was preferable to the uncertainty of war.[137]

War also continued to rage in the Baltic republics, which were reclaimed by the Red Army in the autumn of 1944. In Riga, writes Sandra Kalniete in her memoirs, "armed bandits" and Red Army soldiers, arriving in October 1944, looted, robbed, and raped for days. In November state security units appeared in the city and systematically removed people from their homes. In Lithuania the state security organs arrested Catholic bishops and clergymen, along with intellectuals and officials who had served under the old administration or the German occupation administration. They and their relatives were all deported to Siberia. But by the time the new masters arrived in autumn 1944, resistance had already begun to take shape. Small guerrilla units were everywhere, raiding outposts of Soviet power and killing Communist functionaries. Between 1944 and 1953 more than thirteen thousand Communists and Soviet functionaries were killed by insurgents in Lithuania alone. As usual, terror was the regime's method of choice in attempting to break the resistance. The Soviet leaders dispatched the NKVD's 4th Rifle Division, which had previously been deployed to spread fear and dread on the Crimean Peninsula and in the northern Caucasus. Troops from the Ministry of Internal Affairs were also sent to Estonia and Latvia, where they engaged in bloody skirmishes with the partisans in remote areas. As late as spring 1953 there were still over twenty-eight thousand NKVD soldiers operating on Lithuanian territory.

The resistance was not broken until March 1949, when state security forces completed what they had begun in May and June 1941. Never again would the subdued, aided by foreign powers, be allowed to take up arms against the Soviet Union, as had happened in July 1941. The secret police ordered the deportation of all "fascist" agents who had received training and financial backing from the Americans. The terror raged relentlessly. More than 40,000 people, numerous Catholic priests and bishops among them, were arrested in Lithuania in May 1948. One year later the expulsions were extended to the Baltic republics. Between March and May 1949 the regime expelled 33,496 people from Lithuania, 41,445 from Latvia, and 20,660 from Estonia. They were all deported to Siberia. A short time later, in July 1949, Stalin ordered the expulsion of 35,000 "kulaks" from Moldavia. Thousands of peasants abandoned their villages and fled from the regime's enforcers. The terror plunged these societies into states of paralysis, wiped out their elites, and smothered all resistance. And Stalin reaped the benefits. Never again would anyone dare join an oppositional group and, indeed, all resistance gradually withered away. Between 1944 and 1953 in Lithuania alone more than 20,000 people were killed and over 240,000 were jailed or deported to Siberian penal camps. This amounted to more than a tenth of Lithuania's population.

But never again would it be enough for Stalin and his followers to simply terrorize the subjugated nations. The lack of freedom would now be institutionalized via the socialist command economy and the kolkhoz system of agriculture. These would make it particularly difficult to organize resistance. Soon, the regime was also sending Russians from throughout the Soviet Union to settle in the Baltic republics—to Estonia and Latvia in particular. Between 1945 and 1949 over 180,000 Russians were resettled to Estonia alone, and this in a nation where the postwar population had been barely over a million. Stalin's simple and primitive rationale was that the native population would become a minority in its own country and abandon all hope of ever freeing itself from foreign rule. The Russian settlers, meanwhile, would loyally enforce Moscow's will, since they had no hope of returning to their homes.[138]

TWILIGHT OF THE GOD

In May 1946 the Polish student Janusz Bardach was require to participate in the official May Day parade. He and his fellow students marched through Moscow in a gray, silent column for six hours before reaching Red Square. "When a particular group passed the central stage in Red Square, cheers of 'Long Live Stalin' blasted through the loudspeakers. The Party organizers waved their hands for everyone to join in, and we shouted 'HOORAY! HOORAY! HOORAY!' Then we broke into staccato, crying, 'STA-LIN! STA-LIN! STA-LIN!'" Stalin stood on the tribune and waved graciously to the passing crowd, as though he wanted to offer them his blessing. The masses, meanwhile, were herded across Red Square like cattle. It was raining, Bardach recalled, and NKVD men were barking orders, hurrying them quickly past the podium. "For as far as I could see, identical portraits of Stalin bobbed up and down above the sea of shouting marchers, and I pictured them stretching all the way across the Soviet Union to Kolyma."[139] The victors of Berlin were once again the vanquished. They had won the war, but they were still slaves to a despot who could not forgive their experiences or their success.

The Soviet Union had become a world power. It ruled the eastern half of Europe, and yet it could offer its subjects nothing but misery and slavery. Stalin and his aides were well aware that their dictatorship was not particularly popular. They felt the rejection, not just from the Western democracies but also from their own people. What other reasons did they have for punishing former slave workers and prisoners of war or deporting entire peoples? Obedience, they knew, could only thrive if fear once again became an integral component of their subjects' lives. No expressions of doubt or dissent would be allowed, and, once again, the worst of all worlds would officially be proclaimed the best of all worlds. The task of disseminating this lie was assigned to Andrei Zhdanov, the Leningrad party boss and head of the CC Department for Culture and Propaganda. Zhdanov had proven his worth during the siege of Leningrad, and he was now entrusted with a number of new assignments, all of which he carried out just as reliably. Zhdanov's task was to rid the Soviet Union of all the pernicious foreign influences that had found their way in. From now on, no one would be allowed to read books, watch films, or listen to records that evoked a world that was not allowed to exist. The Soviet Union would now be sealed off from the rest of the world and perfused with the poison of Stalinist xenophobia.

Stalin could not have chosen a more talented disciple for this program. In August 1946 Zhdanov launched a centrally orchestrated campaign against "scum" and "hacks" in Soviet culture and reviled and ridiculed the lyricist Anna Akhmatova and the satirist Mikhail Zoshchenko in front of a group of Leningrad artists. Anyone still clinging to the hope that the postwar period might bring more freedom and tolerance in the cultural realm was sorely mistaken. The regime condemned foreign plays, modern music, and modern paintings. It even forced Dmitri Shostakovich, Sergei Prokofiev, and other prominent Soviet artists to practice self-criticism and drag their own work through the mud. Not only modern classical music but also jazz disappeared from the cultural repertoire. Popular folklore moved onto center stage: art and literature were required to use simple images and sing the praises of the native culture. All traces of "rootless cosmopolitanism" were to be purged. At Stalin's behest, the cultural functionaries staged a grotesque national cult. It was characterized by a xenophobia that reached new extremes, but ultimately all the boasting was little more than a response to a deeply rooted inferiority complex. From this point on, the Soviet Union and its Socialist Republics were the creative center for everything that was great and exalted in the world. There was nothing in the world that had not been invented or designed by Soviet geniuses.[140]

Although the fear of persecution and arrest returned to daily life, the terror would never again reach the pitch of 1937. Violence was directed above all against artists, intellectuals, and scientists suspected of defying cultural dictates. Everything that came from abroad was to be condemned, while the simplicity of domestic cultural productions was to be praised. Literature, art, and science were separated from the Western world and would remain so for decades to come. Some of the natural sciences—biology, genetics, and psychoanalysis—were hit particularly hard by the effects of this xenophobic campaign because Stalin trusted charlatans and dilettantes more than respected scientists.

Beginning in 1946 cultural life and the natural sciences were again overshadowed by fear and subject to a system of denunciation and intellectual self-surveillance. Bardach remembered how he and other students were welcomed by the first secretary of the party at the Medical Institute: "We need to be aware that there are still enemies outside and inside our country. Now more than ever we need to watch our neighbors, our friends, and even our families. We need to unite around the Party and our leadership, and most of all we need to follow the guidance and teaching of our Great Leader, Stalin. Death to all the capitalists and imperialists in the world. Long live Comrade Stalin!" The students chanted Stalin's name for several minutes, rhythmically stomping on the ground with their shoes and clapping continuously. "My hands burned from the continuous clapping."[141]

Even in the postwar years, the unmasking of "spies" and "enemies" continued to be a daily occurrence. Anyone who published foreign literature or translated English books, anyone who had been in contact with influential Americans or Englishmen during the war could at any time fall victim to the paranoia. In September 1947 the security organs arrested the director of the state publishing house for foreign literature, as well as the American ambassador's chauffeur. Before long, public broadcasters and translators also began to fill the prison cells. They had been spies, the Chekists told Stalin, and they had been supplying the American ambassador in Moscow with state secrets: "At that time the Americans showed a heightened interest in the supply situation in the Soviet Union, as Minsche [one of the accused] testified. In this matter, Minsche had compiled reports on two occasions, in which he disclosed the food norms for different categories of the population, the prices in shops and on markets, and facts on the supply of industrial products to workers and employees." Two months later, Chekists arrested the deputy minister of telecommunications, Fortushenko, who was accused of establishing "criminal ties" to American intelligence and revealing the locations of Soviet radio stations in late 1945.[142] Something that was a matter of public knowledge in the United States was treated as an object of national security in the Soviet Union. Stalin's message could not have been clearer. All foreigners were suspects, and anyone who became involved with them would regret it.

Jews were a particular target of the regime's xenophobia as they were viewed as living examples of "rootless cosmopolitanism." After the

Great Patriotic War the aversion to foreigners was elevated to the level of official state ideology, as this was the first time ever that the phobias of the power holders accorded somewhat with the experiences of their subjects. During the war all conflicts had been reduced to antagonisms of "us" versus "them." Why would it have been any different after the war? All that remained of the Bolsheviks' revolutionary-era internationalism was the memory that the Bolsheviks had once condemned anti-Semitism. But now that Germans, Crimean Tatars, and Chechens were no longer part of daily public life, anti-Semitism once again became socially acceptable. After everything the Jews had suffered in the Second World War the return of anti-Semitism to the Soviet Union was a harsh blow—for there was probably no other ethnic group that had been better integrated into the Soviet system than the Jews. Those who had once been Jews were perhaps still aware of it, but the Jewish tradition was not an integral part of their lives, at least not for the intelligentsia. Their homeland was the Soviet Union. But affirmations of Soviet loyalty were of no interest to the National Socialists who had decided it was up to them to decide who was a Jew or not. Jews had no choice but to accept their identity as Jews, as nothing reduces people to themselves quite like the rejections they are made to face. For most of those affected, however, this affirmation of Jewishness was inextricably linked with the fate of the Soviet Union as their protector and homeland.

This view was also shared by the members of the "Jewish Antifascist Committee," founded in 1942, and its leader, the actor Solomon Mikhoels. The committee defended the Jewish cause, but with the express approval and under the strict control of the party leadership. Ilya Ehrenburg and Molotov's wife, Polina Zhemchuzhina, were even among its members. As the war against the German aggressors dragged on, the committee proved itself useful to Stalin by mobilizing support for the regime and it aims and improving the Soviet Union's image abroad. Thus, Stalin was able to tolerate Mikhoels and his committee advocating for the Jews. Mikhoels traveled to the United States and collected donations, and in February 1944 committee members even mustered the courage to approach Stalin about the possibility of establishing a Jewish Soviet Republic on the Crimean Peninsula. They also put together a study documenting the murder of Soviet Jewry, but the *Black Book,* as the authors Ehrenburg and Grossmann called it, was denied publication. The entire print run was confiscated and destroyed by the state security organs. In the official, state-sponsored version of events, the National Socialists were waging war against all peoples of the Soviet Union. A story that allotted a special place for the genocide of Soviet Jews could have no place in this historical narrative. Stalin was willing to tolerate the committee as long as it served his purposes. Ultimately, though, it needed to submit to the official interpretation of the war.

As the confidence of the Jewish Antifascist Committee and other champions of the Jewish cause grew, Stalin and his companions grew more and more mistrustful. The Soviet Union was among the first countries to officially recognize the state of Israel, but it also made Stalin wary. Now there was a Jewish "motherland," and he was well aware of its growing appeal among Jews in the Soviet Union. When Golda Meir, the first Israeli ambassador to the Soviet Union, arrived in Moscow in September 1948, she was welcomed enthusiastically by many Jews there. Several spontaneous rallies even took place. Jews began pledging their allegiance to the state of Israel, and some even expressed their desire to emigrate there. When was the last time the Soviet Union had experienced such spontaneous displays of enthusiasm—not orchestrated by the state or party leadership?[143]

The taking of such liberties was too much for Stalin to tolerate. In January 1948 he had Mikhoels killed by a hired assassin. The following November the Jewish Antifascist Committee was dissolved and most of its members were arrested. According to the official statement, the committee had been "a center of anti-Soviet propaganda" and had been funneling information about the Soviet Union to foreign intelligence agencies. In December 1948 Polina Zhemchuzhina, Molotov's wife, ran into trouble with the regime too. Viktor Abakumov, the minister of state security, informed Stalin that she had been a confidant of Mikhoels and had also attended his funeral. Furthermore, she had been to a Moscow synagogue on more than one occasion. Within days of receiving the report, Stalin had Molotov's wife expelled from the party and arrested by the secret police.[144] Not until July 1952, however, when the campaign against "rootless cosmopolitanism" reached its climax, were the prisoners condemned to death in a secret trial and shot. The Jewish Antifascist Committee was deemed an agent of American Zionism. The *Black Book* was condemned for attempting to "exaggerate the Jewish contribution to world civilization" and for attempting to demonstrate the "singularity of the Jewish people" and place them above all other victims of fascism. In their concluding remarks, the defendants repudiated the charges. "I would just like to tell the court," said the defendant Chaika Wattenberg-Ostrovskaya, "that all my statements from the preliminary investigation are a product of the interrogators' imaginations and do not correspond with reality." But since nobody, apart from the judges and the accused, heard what was being said here anyway, it did not matter whether the accused withdrew their confessions or not.[145]

The despot's representatives in the provinces recognized the signals and understood immediately what was expected of them. In April 1948, after the murder of Mikhoels, the party boss of Belorussia, Nikolai Gussarov, reported that he too had uncovered a plot involving "Jewish nationalist elements." The Jewish nationalists, he said, were filled with hatred for the "Russian and Belorussian people" and intent on damaging the Soviet order. There was no doubt, wrote Gussarov, that these nationalists enjoyed the backing of Jewish committees from the United States and Palestine. It had also emerged that the Jewish committees in the United States were operating on behalf of American intelligence. The Jews, Gussarov concluded, were "conspiring" against the Soviet Union on behalf of foreign capitalist powers. The inner security of the Soviet Union was in danger, and thus it was crucial that all Jews be removed from the party and state organs in Belorussia. He awaited instructions from Moscow, however, on how to proceed.[146] Earlier that year, Gussarov had submissively requested Malenkov's permission to close the Jewish theater in Minsk. "Nationalist sentiments," the party boss had explained, had been "prevalent among the theater's staff for some time." They had been promoting the idea "that the Russians and Belorussians were responsible for the death of thousands of Jews" because they "had not protected them from the Germans" and had instead "aided them in the extermination of the Jews." When Mikhoels, the "leader of Jewish nationalists," had visited Minsk, these "slanderous fantasies" had spiraled out of control.[147]

In January 1953, shortly before the dictator's demise, the campaign against the Jews reached a new pitch. The security apparatus unearthed a monstrous conspiracy masterminded by doctors, who had supposedly been responsible for the death of the Leningrad party boss, Andrei Zhdanov, and were now plotting to kill Stalin. British intelligence and American Jewish organizations were behind the assassination plots, but the doctors were the agents carrying them out. The circle of suspects also included Stalin's personal doctors who were banished from his court and arrested. As *Pravda* informed its readership, the "criminals" had confessed to having intentionally "undermined" the health of Zhdanov and the Moscow party boss Andrei Shcherbakov and killed them by giving them the wrong treatment. The newspaper explained further: "The majority of participants in the terrorist group, Vovsi, B. Kogan, Feldman, Grinshtein, Etinger, and others, were bought by American secret service. They were enlisted by a branch of the American secret service—the international Jewish bourgeois nationalist organization *Joint*. The dirty face of this Zionist organization, which masks its rotten activities with philanthropy, is completely revealed." All the accused admitted to having been hired by American intelligence to kill the leaders of the Soviet Union.[148] So strong was Stalin's desire for punishment and beatings that he threatened the Chekists with consequences if they failed him in this matter. Khrushchev overheard and later recalled Stalin's telephone conversation with the minister of state security, Ignatiev. "Stalin was crazy with rage, yelling at Ignatiev and threatening him, demanding that he throw the doctors in chains, beat them to a pulp, and grind them into powder."[149]

Stalin's campaign triggered a wave of anti-Semitic attacks throughout the Soviet Union. Jews were removed from public office, stigmatized, and branded enemies of the Soviet state. No affirmation of loyalty to the Communist Party could protect Jews from persecution now. "Well, quite simply," as Jakub Berman recalled the anti-Semitic campaign, "when you mentioned a Jewish activist who had a Russian pseudonym, you would give his real name in brackets, and that was a sign that the man had been marked down for removal and his post was going to be filled by someone else."[150] Throughout the Soviet Union Jews were denounced by neighbors and colleagues and fired from their jobs. And yet, there were still people who could not bear this outbreak of blind hatred. In February 1953 Stalin received an anonymous letter from a student, complaining about the daily discrimination and violence against Jews that she witnessed. Jewish children, she wrote indignantly, were being beaten, and Jews were being ousted from public office and universities. She simply could not understand why it was acceptable to treat Jews any differently than Russians. "Is it their fault that they were born as Jews? And can there even be a difference between the nations?" This patent disregard for humanity was more than she could bear. "What sort of life is this where there is no real justice?" she complained. But such pleas were irrelevant. Stalin and his helpers were not receptive to human empathy. It was only the death of the dictator that prevented a new wave of terror from engulfing the country. In March 1953, when Stalin finally died, the anti-Semitic campaign could finally no longer sustain itself, and all the "murderer doctors" who had not yet been killed were released.[151]

"The final period of Stalin's live was marked by a desperate need to expose 'terrorists,' 'poisoners,' and 'conspirators.' This need was just as desperate as the need a 'hardened alcoholic' has for vodka." This was how Dmitri Shepilov, *Pravda's* editor in chief and the secretary of the Central Committee, summed it up. Everyone who had contact with Stalin during his final years of life noticed this.[152] Stalin was a malevolent psychopath, and for him, violence was every bit as critical to life as air. Although he never employed violence for nonstrategic purposes, a life without death and annihilation was simply not conceivable to him. It had, however, become more difficult for the dictator to intervene in the bureaucratic structures that had developed during the war. In a sense, the postwar period imposed constraints on his arbitrariness that had not been there before. The apparatus had become so large that Stalin could no longer control it and all its functionaries in the same way. And yet the despot's disciples and satraps feared him more than ever. Stalin withdrew from official political life, but his pathological mistrust remained. In December 1945 Mikoyan traveled to Sakhalin and the Kuril Islands at the dictator's behest. His assignment was to assess the situation and report back to the dictator on what the occupying forces in the annexed territories were doing. When Mikoyan arrived he was welcomed with a telegram from the suspicious dictator, warning him, "We didn't send you to the Far East for you to keep your mouth shut and not pass anything on to Moscow. I demand that you report your impressions systematically, either daily or at least every two days."[153] On August 18, 1946, Stalin complained that the weather in Moscow had turned out differently than the weather report had predicted. So of course his aides had to take immediate action. Some days later, Voroshilov sent him an apologetic letter: "One day after your instructions of August 18, I called the deputy head administrator of the weather service, Comrade Libin (Comrade Federov is on vacation), to my office and demanded an explanation as to why the weather forecast for August 18 did not correspond to the actual weather."[154] Everyone was aware that anytime the dictator began asking questions this could lead to a new round of denunciations. And no one could be certain of who would be spared or not. When they discovered that something was afoot at the court of the despot, his devotees, satraps, and ministers could only prepare for the worst. What had the despot been saying and to whom? Who had been on vacation with him? Who had dined at his table? Did competitors and adversaries have access to the court? Such details were only disclosed to those who managed to get within earshot of the dictator.

But Stalin was an absentee dictator. He rarely appeared in public anymore and spent more and more time sequestered at his summer house on the Black Sea coast in Abkhazia. At times he would stay there for weeks or even months on end. In both 1950 and 1951 he spent four uninterrupted months there, and from August 1951 to February 1952 he was there once again. He had emancipated himself from his inner circle during the Great Terror, and now he no longer needed their affirmations of support. He no longer needed to ask anyone's advice, and his letter writing stopped. Now it was enough for him to play his cronies off against each other. Stalin would share a secret with one of them and then wait and to see whether or not he revealed it to the others. He chose heirs and successors, only to abandon them again in due time. Stalin still selected favorites, but they could still easily fall from grace. Everyone in his innermost circle knew that the dictator watched them closely and had their apartments bugged. They were not allowed to meet without his knowledge or make arrangements without his permission. Most importantly they were steadfastly bound to the rule that any secret they discovered had to be shared with him immediately.[155]

Whenever Stalin suspected someone of deceiving him, the secret police were dispatched to pursue that person immediately. Georgy Zhukov became a target of the dictator's suspicion after the end of the war. It angered Stalin to see the conqueror of Berlin bask in glory that was supposed to be reserved for him. Zhukov had accepted honors for his triumph in Berlin without paying deference to the great Generalissimo in the Kremlin, and this was something Stalin would never forget. So in 1946 Stalin demoted the marshal to become commander of the Odessa Military District. Even in faraway Odessa, however, Zhukov continued to accept tokens of homage for his military successes, and Stalin became progressively more mistrustful. Stalin ordered Victor Abakumov to search Zhukov's Moscow apartment and country retreat. Abakumov's men were instructed to return everything to its proper place so that Zhukov would not suspect that he was being spied on. Abakumov's agents found gold watches, carpets, furniture, valuable paintings, and costly fabrics, all of which the general had apparently confiscated from homes in Germany and taken back to Russia with him. Zhukov's country home, it was reported, contained "not a single product of Soviet origin." That same month, Abakumov's men also searched Zhukov's house in Odessa, where they discovered even more trophies of war and stolen goods. The general was fortunate in that he got off with a fright, but he was required to hand over the spoils and was publically humiliated. The once great general—conqueror of the Germans—was no more than a common thief. He had been reduced to absurdity. He was then shunted off to the Urals as a local military commander. Stalin, of course, surely took great pleasure in watching the hero be humiliated, and just as importantly, he had made Zhukov into a living warning against pride.[156]

Who could ever feel safe with the dictator watching over each and every move? Stalin's secretary, Poskrebyshev, was responsible for monitoring the bugging devices in the apartments of Stalin's suspects, but Stalin, it is likely, listened in on the conversations himself. In September 1945, at any rate, Stalin complained that the bugging device in the apartment of Andrei Vyshinsky, deputy foreign minister, was malfunctioning. And that same month, Beria also informed Stalin that high-quality microphones had now been installed in Vyshinsky's telephone. In 1950 Stalin gave orders to install bugging devices in the apartments of Molotov and Mikoyan as well.[157] In his final years, there was probably not a single member of the dictator's circle who had not been placed under surveillance. All Stalin needed to do now was lean back and watch the atmosphere of mistrust poison all remaining relationships among his servants. And indeed, as late as four years after the despot's demise, at the Central Committee meeting in July 1957, they were still accusing each other of spying:

> KHRUSHCHEV: Comrade Malenkov, you were not bugged. You and I lived in the same building. You were on the fourth floor, I was on the fifth, and Comrade Timoshenko lived on the third, and the listening

device was installed higher up, above my apartment, but Timoshenko
was bugged.

MALENKOV: No. Both Budyonny and I were bugged via my apartment.
When we agreed with you to arrest Beria, you came to my place, and
we were afraid to talk there because we were being bugged.

KHRUSHCHEV: But then it turned out that you weren't being bugged.

MALENKOV: So, I wasn't bugged, what does that matter?

KHRUSHCHEV: It does matter. You acted as though you were the aggrieved party, along with Comrades Zhukov and Timoshenko, but
factually it wasn't so.[158]

In Stalin's final years the party gradually lost its potential for mobilization and decision making. Between 1939 and 1952 there were
no party congresses at all, and even the members of the Central Committee only assembled on only three occasions—in 1946 and in 1947.
After that the party did not convene again until the autumn of August
1952, but even this, the Nineteenth Party Congress, amounted to little
more than a pep rally for the delegates to pay homage to the aging
despot. Not even the Politburo met regularly anymore, as Stalin had
stripped it of all power and appointed only his closest confidants to so-
called "commissions," where all matters of importance were discussed.
By this time Stalin made all decisions himself, which would then be
written out by his secretary and forwarded to the members of the Presidium, who would then have the privilege of countersigning them.

The decision-making center of the Stalinist dictatorship had shifted
into the despot's private space. Access to the decision-making process
meant obtaining access to the despot's court—by any means possible. It
meant dining with Stalin and accompanying him on his vacations. Life
in Stalin's vicinity, however, was a life on call. Mikoyan's daughter-in-
law, Nami, who moved into the Kremlin with her family in 1950, spoke
of life in the immediate vicinity of the despot as a "silent prison," where
no one looked anyone else in the eye.[159] In his memoirs, Khrushchev
also described the nightmarish atmosphere at the tyrant's court:

Those last years with Stalin were hard times. The government virtually
ceased to function. Stalin selected a small group which he kept close to
him at all times, and then there was always another group of people who
he didn't invite for an indefinite period in order to punish them. Any one
of us could find himself in one group one day and in the other group the
next. After the Nineteenth Party Congress, Stalin created among the new

Presidium members some wide-ranging commissions to look into various matters. In practice these commissions turned out to be completely ineffectual because everyone was left to his own devices. There was no guidance. There was nothing assigned for the commissions to look into, so they made up their own assignments. Everyone in the orchestra was playing on his own instrument anytime he felt like it, and there was no direction from the conductor."[160]

Stalin slept in late and often only appeared in the Kremlin in the late afternoon. He read files in his office, and in the early evening he received ministers and important functionaries in his study. As soon as the talks were finished, he had his secretary summon the members of the Presidium, who were forced to accompany him to the Kremlin's movie theater. If Khrushchev's recollections are to be believed, these gatherings were not for discussing political matters. They served no other purpose than to discipline the retinue:

> Stalin would get up from an afternoon nap around seven or eight o'clock in the evening and drive to the Kremlin. We would meet him there. He used to select the movies himself. The films were usually what you might call captured trophies—we got them from the West. Many of them were American pictures. He liked cowboy movies especially. . . . As a rule, when a movie ended, Stalin would suggest, "Well, let's go get something to eat, why don't we?" The rest of us weren't hungry. By now it was usually one or two o'clock in the morning. It was time to go to bed, and the next day we had to go to work. But Stalin didn't have to work in the morning, and he didn't think about us. Everyone would say, yes, he was hungry, too. This lie about being hungry was like a reflex. We would all get into our cars and drive out to the Nearby Dacha.

They would have to eat and drink with Stalin into the early morning hours, and the dictator apparently enjoyed seeing his people in degrading poses. The Polish Communist leader Jakub Berman recalled an incident in 1948, when Stalin put on Georgian music during dinner and made him dance with Molotov. Stalin sat back and watched as Molotov "led" him about. Berman felt an "inner tension," but at least "these dancing sessions were a good opportunity to whisper to each other things that couldn't be said out loud." It was not just his guests whom Stalin tried to humiliate. He forced Zhdanov and Malenkov to get drunk. He ordered Khrushchev to perform the gopak, a Ukrainian folk dance, in his presence. He made Mikoyan sample every dish served at his table, and he closely observed the facial expressions and gestures of his fellow diners. When Stalin gave an order, those around him obeyed without delay. As Khrushchev once told Mikoyan, "When Stalin says dance, a wise man dances."[161]

Stalin's retinue suffered, but they had no other choice than to play Stalin's game on Stalin's terms. During the war, he had had his Georgian head chef elevated to the rank of major general, and it seemed to amuse him when the chef served them meals in his military uniform. Stalin knew that his people found this joke humiliating, but he also knew that no one would dare even mention the rank of the chef. To do so might well have meant immediate death. As Khrushchev recalled, the Caucasus vacations that he and the others had to spend with the dictator were even worse than the nightly carousals. He once had to spend an entire month with Stalin, even sleeping in the room next to him. "It was sheer torture. I had to spend all my time with him, sitting over endless meals." This, however, was a necessary sacrifice, as being in Stalin's presence meant being privy to conversations "which you could use profitably and from which you could draw useful conclusions for your own purposes."[162]

Sitting at Stalin's table required a robust physical and mental condition, as anyone who aroused the dictator's mistrust or committed errors could expect to die from one day to the next. Those in Stalin's court lived a life on call, knowing that every day could be their last. "In those days anything could have happened to any one of us. Everything depended on what Stalin happened to be thinking when he glanced in your direction. Sometimes he would glare at you and say, 'Why don't you look me in the eye today? Why are you averting your eyes from mine?' or some other such stupidity. Without warning he would turn on you with real viciousness." Those who were no longer invited to the movies and nightly carousals took this gesture of disfavor to be a bad omen. The older the dictator became, the more unpredictable his style of rule became. Nikolai Bulganin described it this way: "You sit down at Stalin's table as a friend, but you never know whether you will be driving home or whether you will be taken—to prison!" Those in Stalin's inner circle needed to defend their places in his despotic court by all means possible.[163]

Stalin was aging visibly. The dictator's physical and mental decline was plain for all to see. In October 1945 he suffered a stroke, causing him to disappear from public life for some time. One year later, in

December 1946, he developed a high fever and was once again confined to his bed for quite a long stretch of time. He was diagnosed with high blood pressure, arteriosclerosis, an enlarged liver, congestive heart failure, and chronic hepatitis. Stalin was a sick man. He had become a mere shadow of his former self. As NKVD General Pavel Sudoplatov recalled, "Stalin had changed greatly. His hair was thinner, and although he had always spoken calmly and slowly now he spoke with difficulty and with longer pauses between his sentences."[164] At no point in time, however, did he ever seriously consider transferring power to anyone else. He toyed with the idea at times and even occasionally voiced it publicly, but more as a means of seeing how his crown princes and their rivals would respond than anything else. Time and again they all urged him to remain in office. The crown princes—Zhdanov, Malenkov, Bulganin, and Voznesensky—would have been putting themselves in mortal danger if they had dared to suggest that they themselves might succeed Stalin. In the end they were nothing more than marionettes in an ill-fated game of intrigue.

In December 1945 even the loyal Molotov found himself on the receiving end of the despot's mistrust. Rumors of conflict within the Soviet leadership had begun circulating in the American press early that month—despite Stalin's demand to Molotov the previous November that the correspondence of foreign journalists be monitored closely. Stalin, who was at his dacha in Sochi by the Black Sea at the time, discovered that the inner circle of Soviet power had become an object of interest for the American press. He also learned that the American newspapers were now consumed with the question of who would succeed him one day. Stalin, of course, did not fail to notice that Molotov, considered by everyone to be the second man in the state, was persistently silent on the matter. On December 6 he sent Malenkov, Beria, and Mikoyan a telegram in which he blamed Molotov for not immediately denying the rumors that he would succeed Stalin. Furthermore, he accused the foreign minister of being an agent of Western powers and said he could no longer be trusted: "I am convinced that Molotov does not much value the interests of our state and the prestige of our government, so long as he gains popularity among certain foreign circles. I can no longer regard this comrade as my first deputy. I send this only to the three of you. I have not sent it to Molotov, as I do not trust the conscientiousness of some of those around him. I ask you to summon Molotov and to read him this telegram in full, but not to present him with a copy of it." Malenkov, Beria, and Mikoyan replied immediately the following day. The telegram had reportedly been read out to Molotov, who admitted that he had made mistakes and had then "burst into tears."[165] The day after Molotov sent Stalin a telegram in which he admitted his guilt. The "iron ass" lamented that he had committed "serious political errors," but he assured Stalin that he would never again show leniency toward foreign correspondents. Molotov had understood immediately what it meant when Stalin suspected one of his people of not telling him the truth. "I will make an effort," he wrote, "to earn your trust in this matter, a trust in which every honest Bolshevik sees not just a personal confidence but also the confidence of the party, which is more precious to me than my own life."[166]

After the war Stalin anointed Andrei Zhdanov to be his successor. Zhdanov had proven his unconditional loyalty on several occasions but most recently during the campaign against "rootless cosmopolitanism" in Soviet culture. Georgi Malenkov and Lavrenty Beria had both risen in the ranks of the political leadership in the years after the Great Terror, and they had been among the dictator's closest confidants. They, however, fell out of favor and temporarily lost their posts, although Stalin allowed them to remain in the Politburo. Then in early 1948, despite his initial promise, Zhdanov's star also began to wane. By spring Stalin had ousted him from the inner circle of power, and in August 1948 he died under mysterious circumstances. Malenkov and Beria were returned to the core of the leadership and immediately began to pursue Zhdanov's Leningrad group. This group included, among others, the Central Committee secretary Alexei Kuznetsov, the Leningrad party boss Pyotr Popkov, and the head of the State Planning Commission, Nikolai Voznesensky, who had also been a Politburo member since the early 1940s.

Kuznetsov and Voznesensky were young, ambitious, and power-hungry, and for a time it appeared that Stalin had chosen Voznesensky as his successor. After the death of Zhdanov, however, these two also fell out of favor—not only because they had been Zhdanov's protégés but also because their apparent inability to temper their lust for power and influence had aroused Stalin's suspicion. They made mistakes, they talked too much, and they confided in other Politburo members without considering that their chatter might be reported to Stalin. In summer 1949 Malenkov and Beria began plotting to bring Voznesensky down. They forwarded Stalin a report from a functionary of the Planning Commission that criticized Voznesensky's professional conduct. According to the report, secret documents had gone missing, and Voznesensky had allegedly tried to conceal this. Kuznetsov first came under suspicion in 1948, when the minister of state security, Victor Abakumov, had two higher-ranking officers from his ministry tried in a "court of honor" without the dictator's knowledge. When called before Stalin to explain himself, Abakumov said that Kuznetsov had given him permission. Soon thereafter Kuznetsov and Voznesensky submitted an ill-fated proposal. All the other republics in the Soviet Union had their own Communist Party, so why should the Russian Soviet Republic be any different? Stalin was notified of this proposal, but he mistrusted any ideas he had not authorized himself. Mikoyan heard Stalin call Voznesensky a "great power chauvinist" and accuse him of believing that "not only the Georgians and Armenians, but also the Ukrainians were not human beings." The Leningrader's fate had thus been sealed. On April 7, 1949, Voznesensky was allowed to participate in one final discussion in Stalin's office. He could sense that his end was drawing near: he was allowed to keep his post but was no longer allowed access to the dictator's court. In August he wrote Stalin a letter, pleading for forgiveness for all the errors he had committed in the past. "I am appealing to the Central Committee and to you, Comrade Stalin, and I am begging you to pardon me." He was a man who had "learned his lesson" and who now understood "how one must observe Soviet and party laws." Stalin had already decided to have Voznesensky and Kuznetsov killed, but he waited until the end of October to have them arrested and tortured, so that they could confess to being English spies and traitors.[167] Their confidants, Yakov Kapustin and Yossif Turko, who had been second secretary of the Leningrad party organization, were also arrested and then beaten and abused until they too confessed to having betrayed the people and the motherland on behalf of English intelligence. Turko's legs were broken, and his head was beaten until blood streamed from his ears. And in the end they both gave Stalin the confessions he demanded. The great reckoning with the "Leningraders" was set to begin.[168]

Between 1949 and 1952 thousands of party and state functionaries were arrested for their suspected involvement with Zhdanov and his protégés. In January 1950, in Leningrad alone, more than fifteen hundred people were arrested as "spies" and "Trotskyites." Most of the victims were shot, not just in Leningrad, but everywhere that state security was at work tracking down friends and confidants of the disgraced functionaries. In February 1949 Stalin sent Malenkov to Leningrad to brief the party committee there on the allegations against Voznesensky, Kuznetsov, Popkov, and their friends in the Leningrad party organization—and also to warn them that treason and disobedience would be punished. Malenkov spoke against arbitrary actions and against nepotism, and he exposed the deposed functionaries as spies and traitors. He left no room for doubt that anyone failing to bow to the leader's will would have to be killed. Kuznetsov, Voznesensky, Popkov, and other high-ranking functionaries were condemned to death in a secret trial and shot in September 1950. In the courtroom they were made to confess that they had been chauvinists and careerists. More than six hundred members of the Leningrad Communist Party were required to attend the trial so they could see what disloyalty and treason in Stalin's empire could bring. Four weeks later the dictator ordered the family members of the condemned arrested and had them deported to Siberia.[169]

The fear made people into soulless automatons, who instinctively did what was expected of them. "The year 1949 steamrolled across all areas of science, ideology, across the whole of societal life, crushing everything in its path," remembered the literary scholar Raisa Orlova Kopelev. "But when I compare what I myself experienced—the years 1937 and 1949—then it would seem to me that the chances for demise were 'more equal' in 1937. The year 1949 claimed fewer victims, and random arrests were relatively less frequent. 1949 was not better, but somewhat different."[170] Party gatherings had to be held throughout the country, self-criticism had to be practiced, and sins had to be lamented. The wave of repression swept across the Soviet Union like a hurricane. "I do not only consider the Central Committee's decision to be right," declared the disgraced Moscow party leader Georgi Mikhailovich Popov in Malenkov's presence at a regional committee meeting in December 1949, "but absolutely right, I have taken it in and drawn the right Bolshevik conclusions for myself. I will strive to carry out any task given to me by the CC, and I am determined to overcome my mistakes, as it is demanded by the Politburo of the CC." Popov survived, at least in part because he was willing to perform the drama of public self-degradation to the despot's satisfaction. Not one sentence, not one single example that did not refer to the dictator, who had taught the party to practice self-criticism and to live in humility. "I believe," said Popov, "that things would be different here if self-criticism had been practiced." He himself had failed to recognize his poor "education" in time, and he was grateful to Stalin for having opened the "fire of criticism."[171]

In 1948 Stalin's mistrust took on pathological proportions. Even his loyal devotees Molotov and Mikoyan were now suspects, accused of having plotted against him and working for foreign powers. In late 1948 Stalin forced Molotov to divorce his wife, Polina Zhemchuzhina, as he considered her a Jewish nationalist and a Zionist agent. Molotov would later recall, "At the session of the Politburo when he read out the material on Polina Semenova supplied by the security people, my knees began to knock." But still he bowed to the inevitable. He wrote the despot a letter in which he admitted his "deep guilt" for having failed to prevent his wife from becoming involved with the "anti-Soviet Jewish nationalists."[172] Zhemchuzhina was arrested and imprisoned in a camp, and Molotov would not see her again until after the dictator's death. This was not all the "iron ass" had to endure. At the Nineteenth Party Congress Stalin also humiliated his loyal aide by announcing his fall from grace in front of all the delegates. In March 1949 Molotov lost his position as foreign minister when Stalin replaced him with Vyshinsky, and in 1952 he was ousted from the Politburo. Mikoyan, who suffered the same fate and lost his position as minister of foreign trade, could not fathom why Stalin had banished him from the inner circle of power after so many years of loyal service. No intrigue was too crude for Stalin. Anything that served to intimidate his former companions was fair game. Mikoyan recalled how Stalin invited him and Molotov to his holiday home by the Black Sea in 1948. They were sitting around the table, engaged in casual conversation, when Stalin's secretary Poskrebyshev suddenly rose from his seat and announced, "Comrade Stalin, while you are relaxing here in the south, Molotov and Mikoyan have prepared a plot against you in Moscow." Never would Poskrebyshev have dared to voice an accusation at Stalin's table unless his master had prompted him to do so. From that point on—despite their best efforts to dispel Stalin's mistrust—Molotov and Mikoyan were suspects. By 1949, for them the game was over. Although they would still be permitted to take part in office discussions, Molotov and Mikoyan would no longer be permitted to join Stalin for dinner. When Molotov discovered that Stalin did not want to see him anymore he suffered a nervous breakdown.

Mikoyan later recalled an incident in the autumn of 1951 when Stalin turned to his companions during dinner and said, "You've grown old! I'll replace you all!" Those present, Mikoyan remembered, "were so surprised that no one said a word." One year later, in October 1952, the ageing despot submitted a proposal to the delegates of the Nineteenth Party Congress that the members of the Politburo recognized as an ominous sign of things to come. Stalin recommended twenty-five candidates for the Politburo, which would now be known as the "Presidium." A governing body of this sort would be incapable of taking action, but just as importantly, the old guard would lose influence and power. Everyone understood the despot's intentions when he subsequently announced at a Central Committee meeting that it would be necessary to "vote," not just for a Presidium but also for a Bureau of the Presidium—which would have only nine members. Stalin had written the names of the chosen ones on a slip of paper. Mikoyan and Molotov were not on the list. The members of the Central Committee received an absurd explanation for Stalin's decision to isolate his old companions:

> Molotov and Mikoyan, who have both been to America, have returned from there under the strong impression of the power of the American economy. I know that both Molotov and Mikoyan are courageous men, but they appear to have been intimidated by the overwhelming strength they have seen in America. It is a fact that Molotov and Mikoyan have sent directives to our ambassador in Washington behind the Politburo's back, and that they made serious concessions to the Americans for the upcoming negotiations. Losovsky, who has been exposed as a traitor and an enemy of the people, was also involved.

When Mikoyan attempted to defend himself, Stalin responded to him, "It would be better for you to keep quiet."

In December 1952 the despot forced his most trusted henchman Kaganovich to publish an anti-Semitic article in *Pravda*. Kaganovich the Jew was not only meant to publicly condemn the "murderer doctors" but also to denounce "Zionism." Now even "Iron Lazar" was uncomfortable. He was appalled by the demand. He was "sick" with pain, as he told Mikoyan, because he had spent his life fighting anti-Semitism. But these were difficult years. Not even Khrushchev—who never talked back—and not even Kliment Voroshilov—Stalin's comrade from the Civil War—could be sure of where they stood in those years.[173] In March 1951 Khrushchev was publically humiliated. It began on March 4, 1951, when he had an article on the organization of the kolkhoz system published in *Pravda*. Unfortunately for him it was not to Stalin's liking, and two days later Khrushchev was forced to publicly express his regret and admit his "errors." "Following your instructions," he wrote to Stalin, "I have tried to give all questions more consideration. After thinking about it I realized that all my statements were wrong both generally and fundamentally." He was prepared to write a public criticism of his own article in *Pravda* and "thoroughly work out" his "false assumptions." "I implore you, Comrade Stalin, to help me correct my fundamental errors and thereby reduce the damage I have caused the party with my false statements."[174]

During his final years, Stalin also abandoned all inhibitions in his dealings with the security apparatus. He purposely set the deputy minister of internal affairs, Ivan Serov, against the minister of state security, Victor Abakumov, and then took pleasure in reading their letters, in which they accused each other of being enemies of Soviet power. In February 1948 Serov wrote to Stalin to complain that Abakumov had arrested ten of his employees for no particular reason. The minister of state security, he said, was a dubious figure, interested in nothing but his own gain. Furthermore, Serov accused Abakumov of having used the war as an opportunity to shamelessly enrich himself by seizing loot and trophies from the battlefield. The battle of Sebastopol, he said, had still been raging when Abakumov's military intelligence operatives appeared at the front to load trophies onto freight cars. It was clear that Abakumov had ordered them because it said "For Abakumov" on one of the carriages. "The conditions for the cooperation between the organs of the Ministry of State Security and the Ministry of Internal Affairs that have now been created under Abakumov's leadership are intolerable. Both in the center as well as at the periphery the employees of the Ministry of State Security are trying to compromise the organs of the Internal Affairs Ministry as far as possible."[175]

Stalin read Serov's letter but declined to help him. Abakumov's star did not begin to fade until he made mistakes that the dictator himself took notice of. In March 1948 Abakumov was reprimanded for the "court of honor" that he had held without informing Stalin.[176] The boisterous and industrious minister still believed that his merits for his role in the September 1950 execution of the "Leningraders" would secure him a Politburo seat. These merits, however, could not compensate for the fact that Abakumov had concealed something from the dictator, and this was something Stalin would not forget. Abakumov could no longer be trusted. In December 1950 Stalin announced that the minister of state security would go from having four deputies to seven. A short time later the dictator appointed chaperones to accompany Abakumov, and by this point at the latest Abakumov must have realized that his life was in jeopardy. In July 1951 fate took its course when Mikhail Ryumin, the head of the department for investigation in the Ministry of State Security, denounced Abakumov to Stalin. What had happened? In November 1950 a Jewish doctor by the name of Yakov Etinger was reportedly tortured into confessing that he had intentionally killed the Moscow party boss Andrei Shcherbakov by prescribing harmful medications. Ryumin was convinced that Etinger had been part of a grand conspiracy that had involved other eminent doctors, who were plotting terrorist attacks against the leaders of the Soviet Union. Abakumov, however, had discounted the doctor's statements as being "far-fetched" and had thrown Etinger into the "coldest cell" of the Lefortovo prison to die. The only explanation for Abakumov's behavior then was that he had wanted to cover up his own involvement in the grand conspiracy, so Ryumin naturally considered it his duty to inform Stalin: "Comrade Abakumov, according to my observations, has a tendency to deceive the government organs by concealing the serious deficiencies in the work of the organs of the Ministry of State Security."[177]

In July 1951 Stalin called together a special Politburo commission that included Molotov, Bulganin, Malenkov, and Beria and had the task of questioning Abakumov. The result of the interrogation, of course, had already been determined. Abakumov had left Etinger to die to conceal his involvement in a conspiracy of doctors that had been masterminded by foreign powers. In August 1951 Abakumov was removed from his post, replaced by Semion Ignatiev, and had to suffer everything he had inflicted on others. He was arrested, imprisoned, and abused so severely that soon he was little more than a shadow of his former self. His agony lasted nearly three long years, as it was part of Stalin's strategy to keep him alive long enough to torture him into betraying friends and colleagues. In November 1952 Ignatiev informed Stalin that Abakumov had been bound in chains and placed in complete isolation. He was being interrogated by two Chekists who were "capable of fulfilling special assignments, namely applying physical punishment." As long as Abakumov still lived and spoke, no one in Stalin's vicinity was safe from being "betrayed." Abakumov did, however, outlive his betrayer. Ryumin's career ended abruptly in November 1952 when Stalin had him arrested, and then in July 1953 Stalin's successors had him shot— one year before getting rid of Abakumov.[178]

Not even Beria was safe. In September 1951 Stalin invited the head of Georgian state security, Nikolai Rukhadze, to his holiday retreat in Abkhazia, to receive a report on conditions in Georgia. In passing, the two men discussed the dominance of the Mingrelians in Georgia's state and party leadership, and how they seemed to be enjoying Beria's support and protection. Soon thereafter, in November 1951, Stalin instructed Rukhadze to brief him on patronage relations within the Georgian Communist Party. Rukhadze reported that the second secretary of the Georgian party organization, Baramiya, had taken bribes and was protecting his relatives. In Stalin's name, Rukhadze then condemned the Georgian for doing something that had been always been done and had never before been a problem. But this was beside the point. The point was to smash Beria's Georgian power base by making his Mingrelian supporters into suspects. The Georgian party boss, Kandid Charkviani, was deposed and replaced by Stalin's confidant Akaki Mgeladze. Then, all of Beria's adherents and their vassals were arrested. And finally, in November 1952 over 11,200 people were deported from Georgia to Kazakhstan. In April 1952 Beria himself was forced to travel to Tbilisi to expose his own people as "spies" and "crooks," who were allegedly trying to "liquidate Soviet power in Georgia" and cede the republic to Turkey. Beria now knew that his own life hung in the balance and that a mere nod and wink from the dictator could seal his fate.[179]

On March 1, 1953, while at his dacha in Kuntsevo, Stalin suffered a stroke that left him partially paralyzed. He lay unconscious on the floor for four hours because the guards did not dare set foot in his bedroom. They phoned the Kremlin to find out what they should do next, and Beria, Malenkov, Khrushchev, and Bulganin arrived in Kuntsevo that evening. Beria and Malenkov ordered the guards to open the door, and when they saw Stalin lying there in his drenched pajamas the impossibility of their predicament was clear to them. Should the dictator ever recover, he would never forgive them for having seen him this way. Beria turned to the dictator's head bodyguard and barked at him, "Lozgachev, what kind of panic are you spreading here? Can't you see? Comrade Stalin is fast asleep. You leave him alone and don't bother us." When the bodyguards left the compound, Beria and the others drove back to the Kremlin. They returned the next morning with several doctors in tow, but they were unable to save the dictator's life. He died on March 5.[180] "My father died a difficult and terrible death," recalled Stalin's daughter Svetlana:

> His face altered and became dark. His lips turned black and the features grew unrecognizable. The last hours were nothing but a slow strangulation. The death agony was horrible. He literally choked to death as we watched. At what seemed like the very last moment he suddenly opened his eyes and cast a glance over everyone in the room. It was a terrible glance, insane or perhaps angry and full of the fear of death and the unfamiliar faces of the doctors bent over him. The glance swept over everyone in a second. Then something incomprehensible and awesome happened that to this day I can't forget and don't understand. He suddenly lifted his left hand as though he were pointing to something above and bringing down a curse on us all. The gesture was incomprehensible and full of menace, and no one could say to whom or at what it might be directed. The next moment, after a final effort, the spirit wrenched itself free of the flesh.[181]

On the nights of March 1 and 2, the Politburo met in Stalin's Kremlin office to discuss the rearrangement of power relations, and ultimately they agreed upon a truce. Apparently no one believed that the dictator would recover from his stroke, and for the first time ever the group could openly discuss the new balance of power without fear. Even Molotov and Mikoyan, who had been banished from Stalin's court, came to the Kremlin for these meetings. On March 5, when Stalin was still alive, the members of the Central Committee were summoned to

Moscow. As the writer and committee member Konstantin Simonov recalled, most of the members were already in their seats half an hour before the session was due to begin:

> I arrived long before the meeting was due to begin, about forty minutes early; over half of all participants had already gathered in the room. Ten minutes later no one was missing. Only two or three came half an hour before the beginning. Several hundred people, most of whom knew each other professionally, personally, from many encounters—these hundreds of people sat for forty minutes, those who had arrived before me even longer, in complete silence and waited for it to begin. Sat there huddled together, shoulder to shoulder, looking at each other without speaking a single syllable. No one asked anyone anything. It seemed to me as though none of those present had even the faintest desire to speak. The room was so silent that I would not have considered it possible for three hundred to sit so closely and remain so silent had I not witnessed this silence for forty minutes myself.

Why had the members of the Central Committee been summoned to Moscow? Was the dictator really dead, or was this eerie scene nothing more than a continuation of Stalin's power machinations? The faces in the crowd relaxed visibly when the members of the Politburo entered the room. Everyone could see that Stalin's seat remained vacant, whereas Molotov and Mikoyan, who had been banished from the dictator's inner circle, were occupying their old seats. "It seemed to me as though one could sense a faint feeling of relief among the men who entered the Presidium from the back room, the former members of the Politburo," remembered Simonov. "It was as though these people there in the Presidium had freed themselves from a heavy burden. Indeed, they seemed quite relaxed." Beria and Malenkov had spoken soberly but no longer even mentioned Stalin by name.[182] Khrushchev announced that Stalin was sick and that the leadership thus needed to act and remain united. "Everyone is aware of the tremendous responsibility for the leadership of the country that now lies with us all," he told the members of the Central Committee. "It is clear to everyone that this country cannot allow a single hour of uncertainty in its leadership." Stalin's companions distributed posts and appointed new ministers, established clear boundaries and secured power for the period after the dictator's death. No one opposed Beria and Malenkov when they presented their personnel choices to the Central Committee. The delegates, it seemed, felt a deep relief.[183] Although no one had pronounced it, the horror was over.

Andrei Sakharov, who was in Moscow when Stalin died, bore witness to the mass panic that accompanied the final act: the despot's funeral. "Downtown Moscow was invaded by hundreds of thousands of Soviet citizens who wanted to view Stalin's body laid out in the Hall of Columns. The authorities had not predicted the extent of this flood of people, and in a situation where the usual orders from above were absent, they failed to establish the necessary security precautions in time. Hundreds of people, possibly thousands died."[184] Stalin would have enjoyed this scene. Millions had already fallen victim to the almighty Stalin and his regime of terror. And then, while being carried to the grave, Stalin had been responsible for the deaths of several thousand more. "Such was his incredible talent for death," writes Martin Amis, "he showed that he could kill people violently even from his coffin."[185] And yet, the despot was dead. His evil spirit was extinguished forever. His companions were exhausted, and after so many decades of terror and violence they had grown weary of it all. The end of Stalinism was the end of despotism. A new age had dawned.

7   Stalin's Heirs

A GOD HAD died. How could this have happened? "How could the Leader of Mankind have been sick?" The Polish student Janusz Bardach, who was in Moscow when the dictator died, was not the only one to ponder this question. "How could Stalin be like an ordinary human being? Men and women cried openly in public, but I couldn't tell how much of the sorrow was genuine. Certainly a great deal of it was raw grief, even terror of being abandoned, but much of it was a mask that had to be put on because the occasion called for it. Although the Great Leader was no longer watching, no one knew what would happen next or how his or her behavior would later be interpreted by the Party and secret police."[1] Nothing was as it had been because there was no one who could fill Stalin's role except Stalin. For years the word of the despot had been law. Every decision his associates made had been justified by invoking the great leader and wise teacher. Who was to rule the country now? And how could anyone legitimize the rule of the few now that their sole source of authority was gone?

The feeling of uncertainty was omnipresent. No one knew what would happen. As Bardach recalled of the mood on the streets of Moscow after Stalin's death, "most of the citizens seemed to be waiting for the apocalypse."[2] And this is why Stalin's cronies needed to act immediately. Within weeks of his death, the charges against the "murderer doctors" had been dropped, the use of torture had been outlawed, and the punitive authority of the security apparatus had been limited. Furthermore, the last remaining victims of the "Mingrelian Affair" were released from prison, and Mikhoels, the assassinated chairman of the Jewish Antifascist Committee, was rehabilitated posthumously. As long as Stalin had been alive, Mikhoels's murderers had been safe. Now, though, they would pay for the crime they had carried out for Stalin, and in April 1953 they were arrested.[3] Despotism would disappear from daily life, and fear and dread would no longer be the ruling standard. Stalin's companions, after all, had experienced for themselves what it meant to live in constant fear. They agreed to divide power among themselves and terminate the game of death. Nikita Khrushchev became the new party leader, Georgi Malenkov was made prime minister, Vyacheslav Molotov was allowed to return to his former post as foreign minister, and Stalin's executioner Lavrenty Beria assumed control of the Ministry of Internal Affairs and the state security apparatus. Just weeks earlier, they would have denounced or killed each other without delay in panicked attempts at saving their own lives. Now, however, they were making an agreement to end the violence. There was no longer anyone there, before whom they would have to debase themselves. Just one last time, in June 1953, they resorted to the old Stalinist methods to deal with Lavrenty Beria. After some time in prison, Stalin's most unscrupulous former henchman was shot. All his sadistic helpers and confidants died along with him. On June 26, 1953, Malenkov announced to the Politburo that the party needed to bring the intelligence services and the Ministry of Internal Affairs under its control once and for all. Beria, who was still in prison at this time, wrote to his former companions from his cell, reminding them of the friendship and the loyalty they had once sworn to each other. He pledged that he was prepared to work "with all [his] soul and with complete energy," anywhere they wished, if only his "dear comrades" could forgive him. His comrades, however, elected to get rid of him instead.[4] Just months earlier, Stalin alone had been the master over life and death. Now his successors could decide among themselves to dispose of one of their own. Never again would a single person be allowed absolute power over everyone else, and Stalin's successors committed one final murder to complete the destruction of despotic rule.

"I have no doubt," wrote Georgi Arbatov, who belonged to the fore-runners of perestroika, "that Stalin's cruelty, perfidy, and despotism were repugnant to Khrushchev, who had been personally humiliated by Stalin more than once."[5] Stalin was to disappear from his life for ever. Within weeks of the despot's death, all visible traces of his all-pervading presence were gone, as his former companions had no desire to be reminded of the humiliations they had suffered in the past. Sta-lin's books, his record collection, and his private belongings were dis-posed of. His employees and servants were dismissed, and his dacha in Kuntsevo was bolted shut. Now, not even the dictator's closest relatives would be spared. In April 1953, Stalin's greedy, violent, alcoholic son Vasily was arrested. During his father's life he had abused subordinates as an officer in the Air Force, embezzled foreign currency, and hosted sexual orgies for himself and his friends. Stalin's successors had him put on trial, and he was sentenced to eight years in prison. "Not only did no one come forward in his defense," remembered his sister Svetlana, "but everyone added fuel to the flames. Everybody gave evidence against him: his former adjutants, aides who'd served under him, generals he hadn't gotten along with, even the Minister of Defense himself."[6]

Soon the functionaries too began to feel the effects of the end of ar-bitrary rule. In the final years of Stalin's despotic regime, ministers and higher officials had been required to remain in their offices until the dictator had decided to go to bed. In summer 1953 Khrushchev abol-ished this practice and made it known that from now on functionaries were free to leave work whenever they deemed fit. The fear had van-ished. Never again would officials be taken from their offices or homes by NKVD officers, simply because the dictator had decided that their services were no longer required.[7]

Khrushchev and his supporters in the Politburo had achieved a lot. They could have simply stopped there and let the atrocities of the past remain covered by a shroud of silence—no one was demanding that they speak about them. But Khrushchev was determined to call the dictator's crimes by the right name. There were moral reasons for this, but Khrushchev also apparently believed the time would come when the truth would have to be told. "For three years we were unable to break with the past," he wrote in his memoirs, "unable to muster the courage and the determination to lift the curtain and see what had been hidden from us about the arrests, the trials, the arbitrary rule, the executions, and everything else that had happened during Stalin's reign. It was as though we were enchained by our own activities under Stalin's leadership and couldn't free ourselves from his control even after he was dead."[8]

Ultimately, though, Khrushchev did find the courage to face the past, including his own. "Sooner or later people will be coming out of the prisons and the camps, and they'll return to the cities," he warned the members of the Politburo shortly before the Twentieth Party Congress in February 1956:

> They'll tell their relatives, friends, comrades, and everyone back home what happened. The whole country and the entire Party will find out that people have spent ten to fifteen years in prison—and all for what? For nothing! The accusations against them were trumped up! If they were brought to trial, the prosecution's cases against them were conjured out of thin air! I ask you to think about something else, comrades: We are conducting the first Congress after Stalin's death, and therefore we're obliged to make a clean breast to the delegates about the conduct of the party leadership during the years in question. We're supposed to be giving an account of ourselves for the period after Stalin's death, but as members of the Central Committee while Stalin was still alive, we must tell about this period as well. How can we pretend not to know what happened?[9]

Khrushchev himself had been one of Stalin's enforcers. He too had signed death lists and issued terror orders. He had not contradicted Stalin but had instead diligently followed his every order. But he had done it out of fear—both for himself and for his family—and now he hoped to cast off the moral burden that was weighing down on his shoulders like lead.

Khrushchev's de-Stalinization was a cultural revolution. It was a civilizational accomplishment, and it changed the lives of millions. Immediately after the despot's death the camp gates were opened. No one knew what to do with the hundreds of thousands of criminals and traumatized, uprooted individuals who were now being released. Where would they live and work? What would they eat, and whose apartment could they share? What would happen when the victims encountered perpetrators and denouncers? Although there were no good answers to these questions, the reformers refused to let themselves be dissuaded, especially as more and more information about what had taken place inside the camps came to light. Among the first to speak were the wives and relatives of Stalin's former associates, who had been removed and arrested—Molotov's wife among them. Week after week, Khrushchev and other members of the Politburo received letters from Communists who had been released from the camps and were now prepared to bear witness to the arbitrariness and cruelty they had been forced to endure.

In 1955 Khrushchev gave Pyotr Pospelov, head of the Central Committee Secretariat, the task of collecting material on the crimes of the past. Pospelov and his staff identified perpetrators and victims and presented the Politburo with interrogation protocols, death lists, and letters that the tortured had written to the dictator. "If this is true," exclaimed the first deputy premier, Maxim Saburov, at a Politburo meeting, "then what kind of communism is this? This cannot be forgiven."[10] The dam had burst, and no one could evade the presence of dread any longer. And so the members of the leadership allowed themselves to be carried along by the wave of events. At the Twentieth Party Congress Khrushchev spoke openly and unsparingly about Stalin's crimes, loudly proclaiming all the things that everyone knew but had never dared to speak about. Finally, in 1961 Khrushchev had the dictator's body removed from the mausoleum on Red Square.

It would take decades for the fear and the mistrust to dissipate from the bodies and souls of the people. But even by the late 1950s, everyone seemed to sense that the age of death and arbitrary persecution was over. The mortal fear that had once ruled daily life was gone and would never return. Words were followed by actions, and slowly people saw that this time the leadership was serious. In 1956, after Khrushchev's secret speech, tens of thousands of Chechens who had been deported to Kazakhstan in 1944 were able to return home. Between April 1953 and January 1956 alone over 1.5 million prisoners were released from the camps. Rehabilitation commissions were established by the Public Prosecutor's Office, and by 1960 700,000 victims of Stalinist terror had been rehabilitated, with several million more petitions still being processed.[11] Within years of the dictator's passing, novels and stories describing the sufferings of the past began to appear. Among these were Vladimir Dudintsev's *Not by Bread Alone* and Ilya Ehrenburg's *The Thaw*—which gave an entire era its name. Later came *One Day in the Life of Ivan Denisovich* by Alexander Solzhenitsyn. Solzhenitsyn's account of everyday life in a Stalinist prison camp was cleared for publication in 1962 by Khrushchev himself.[12]

Although Khrushchev and his supporters believed that they had accomplished a great deal, not everyone shared this view. In a society of scarcity every prisoner that was released meant one more person competing for scarce resources. Furthermore, every criminal released meant another security risk. The return of deportees and the release of former convicts were rarely looked on as acts of kindness. In Georgia and Azerbaijan students took to the streets in protest of Khrushchev's defamation of their home-grown hero as a villain.[13] When was the last time that an open debate or a demonstration had ended without the killing of its organizers? By spring 1956 the secret speech had been forwarded to local party committees throughout the Soviet Union, and people everywhere were discussing it. Although the Stalinist perpetrators were not held accountable, this was the first time ever that the horrors experienced by millions could be openly discussed. The regime discovered that it could generate obedience without coercion, and the war against its own people was ended. Even the nationalist Ukrainian partisans, who had fought Soviet power during the Second World War, were allowed to return home, as no one considered them a threat anymore.[14]

The state authorities refrained from the use of excessive violence and restored domestic peace. Never again would people be stigmatized and deported or killed as representatives of imagined collectives. Life in the Soviet Union after Stalin's demise was markedly easier, and conditions were improving in a way that was palpable to everyone. In Stalin's world, peasants and workers were required to make sacrifices for the glory of the authoritarian state. Khrushchev, in contrast, imagined a world of flourishing landscapes and life in abundance. And he tied his own fate to the fulfillment of the promise that nobody in the Soviet Union would ever go hungry again or be made into a slave. For the first time ever kolkhoz farmers began to receive a modest wage for their work and were integrated into the pension scheme to guarantee them support in their old age. They were no longer slaves who could be harassed and robbed at will. Millions of Soviet citizens spent their holidays in union hostels, sanatoriums, and hotels on the Black Sea coast or in the Caucasus. Wages and salaries increased, and the range of items available for purchase also grew, as consumption had become state power's last source of legitimization.[15] Millions of people abandoned their overcrowded communal apartments and derelict houses and moved into modern apartments with indoor plumbing and running water. Only someone familiar with the conditions these people had experienced before can fathom the joy they must have felt. Apartments became spaces of retreat, where everything that was unthinkable beyond one's own four walls was possible. They allowed for a kind of privacy that most Soviet citizens had never before experienced.[16]

Khrushchev also freed the Soviet Union from its isolation. Foreigners were allowed to visit and travel the country, Western artists performed on Soviet stages, and Soviet musicians toured Europe and the United States. Khrushchev had opened a window to the West, from which the crude hatred and xenophobia of the Stalinist years could escape. Scientists, artists, and functionaries could now see how people beyond Soviet borders lived, and the West, which was no longer a threat to anyone, was no longer demonized. The paranoia and xenophobic hysteria of the Stalinist years disappeared from peoples' lives, and it was as if people were awaking from a terrible nightmare.[17] Georgi Arbatov would later recall the spiritual liberation he experienced during these years. In 1964 he went to see a film in a Moscow cinema that began with a newsreel showing Khrushchev at the inauguration ceremony of a canal in central Asia. The portly general secretary could be seen clambering down the muddy slope, making a speech on the canal bed accompanied by wild gesticulations, and then struggling back up the muddy slope again. The audience had roared with laughter at Khrushchev's awkwardness.[18] Who would have ever dared to laugh at Stalin in a public cinema? What cinema director would ever have allowed such an unflattering portrayal of the despot to be shown? The Russian writer Andrei Bitov, who saw the same newsreel when he was a young man, found the proper words for this scene: Khrushchev had given the people back their laughter. The day it became possible for the citizens to publicly laugh at their leaders was the day that Stalinism was truly dead. "Anyone who has not skated on that surrealist rink," wrote the physicist Yuri Orlov in his memoirs, "will never comprehend how enormously liberated people were by Khrushchev's turn to elementary legality. Society remained totalitarian, but at least it had ceased to wallow in blood and vomit."[19]

Stalinism was gone. Four years after the demise of the despot this was certain. Although Chekists still existed, everything that had been a matter of course for them in 1953 had become unthinkable by 1957. Critics and dissidents could still be placed under surveillance and harassed by the KGB, but they could no longer be taken from their homes or shot in the middle of the night. Khrushchev gave the intelligence service a civilian image and stripped it of its punitive authority. Its operatives traded in their leather jackets and uniforms for tailored suits, and they were reinvented as upstanding guardians of order. The Lubianka, it was also decided, would no longer be a house of dread where people were tortured and put to death.[20]

Khrushchev himself had experienced what it meant to live in fear and dread. He had been humiliated by Stalin, and he had known the despot's cruelty. He too understood "the crushing loss of human dignity that comes from constant fear" that Arbatov had spoken of.[21] All this now disappeared from daily life in the inner circle of leadership as well. An unfavorable vote or a disagreement no longer led to people being locked up or murdered. All of Stalin's companions who had signed death orders and been prepared to denounce one another just a few years earlier had now reached a mutual agreement to end their game of death. When Lazar Kaganovich, one of Stalin's most loyal and unscrupulous cronies, was defeated in the power struggle of 1957 he expected the worst. He pleaded with Khrushchev to refrain from having him killed, as undoubtedly would have happened had he opposed Stalin. "Comrade Khrushchev, I have known you for many years, I beg of you not to allow them to deal with me as they would have settled accounts with people under Stalin." But "Iron Lazar" received only a mild punishment. He was removed from the Politburo in 1957 and then sent to the Urals to become the director of an asbestos factory.[22]

Criticism and opposition became calculable. The defeated faced the prospect of losing their posts but not of going to prison. Thus, in summer 1964, when Khrushchev's former supporters decided to depose the general secretary they were taking only a small risk. Khrushchev offered no resistance and did not even attempt to organize support for his political survival. In October 1964 when he was definitively overthrown by his own people he was neither publicly humiliated nor punished. He retired and left the Kremlin a free man. He was glad, he told the Presidium of the Central Committee on October 13, 1964, that the party organs had become adult and could "control any given person."[23] On the evening after his fall from power Khrushchev discussed the significance of the events with Anastas Mikoyan. "Could anyone," Khrushchev asked, "have even dreamed of telling Stalin that he was not to our liking anymore and suggest that he retire? There would have been nothing left of us (*Ot nas by mokrogo mesta ne ostalos*). Now everything is different. The fear has disappeared, and we can speak to each other as equals. That is my contribution."[24]

Khrushchev freed Soviet society from mass terror and ubiquitous violence, but the horrors of the past could not simply vanish from people's minds without a trace. Terror, wrote Hannah Arendt, "substitutes for the boundaries and channels of communication between individual men a band of iron which holds them so tightly together that it is as though their plurality had disappeared into One Man of gigantic dimensions."[25] In a society contaminated by mistrust and violence, there could be no ruthless accounting for the bloody past, as the reformers had been among the perpetrators themselves, and the victims had no other choice but to remain voiceless. Millions had died, millions had lost their freedom, and millions were left traumatized. Victims had become perpetrators, and perpetrators had become victims, and most people never discovered why they had been arrested or why their relatives had been killed. There was probably not one single family in the Soviet Union that could claim that it had not in some way been a victim of the violence. And since the terror seemed to strike at random it eventually consumed the executioners themselves. The survivors were forced to remember what had happened in the Soviet Union in 1937 as a natural catastrophe, an event without an author. Like an incredible force of nature, akin to a tidal wave, the terror had swept the land. No one took offense at the fact that the Donskoe cemetery in Moscow was not only the burial site for the remains of Stalin's murder victims but also the final resting place for Stalin's executioner Vasily Blokhin. Even in death perpetrators and victims remained shoulder to shoulder.[26] How could the past possibly have been dealt with in a manner that would do justice to this human catastrophe? In truth there was no alternative to silence and total absolution, as speaking about their experiences would have cost both the victims and the perpetrators their sanity. For those without the experience of total violence, the practice of total absolution remains incomprehensible.

Throughout the years of de-Stalinization, it remained the great exception for any of the crimes against defenseless individuals to be prosecuted. In Azerbaijan Mir Jafar Baghirov, the "little Stalin," was tried. Some of the Chekists were also confronted with their victims, and the torturers of the past were relieved of their duties. But only a few were actually convicted.[27] Both perpetrators and victims reached a tacit agreement to never again speak of what had occurred. In the Soviet Union, every memory of past suffering was a memory of silence. The victims were unable to speak of their experiences because the strength required for putting their dreadful ordeal into words was too great. It simply could not be done without ravaging the victims' own souls. Forgetting was a means of preserving sanity. Furthermore, nobody knew for certain whether the peace could really be trusted, whether the violence of the regime was really gone forever, or whether it might someday return. When there is no hope that the dictatorship under which one lives will ever end, no one can bear to be excluded completely. Victims and perpetrators alike had to do the best they could with the social order that was available to them. It was the only one they had.[28]

And still no one wanted to believe that the suffering of millions had been for nothing. No one can bear being a mere victim of fate or coincidence. And so the mass murders vanished into the heroic epos of the Great Patriotic War, the second founding myth of the Soviet Union. In the war, everyone had been a victim, and everyone had been a victor. Even those who did not see themselves as victors could at least stop lamenting the losses of the past because nothing in the past had been as horrible as the war. After everything they had been through together, it was easier to forgive the perpetrators and remember the past in a more favorable light. All the suffering of the prewar years now seemed justified. The seemingly pointless deaths were endowed with a higher purpose, and the collective suffering of millions allowed perpetrators and victims to imagine that they were members of the same indissoluble community.[29] For once in their lives, peasants had been allowed to be victors. Why should they have declined the offer of the dictatorship and insisted on always being the victims? Everyone had been a hero, and anyone who had experienced something dreadful was to remain silent about it forever. This was the price that had to be paid for the reestablishment of the Soviet Union. The victims received recognition, and the power holders would refrain from using violence to extort consent. It became possible to mourn one's own fate and also admire Stalin at the same time.[30]

People who know nothing but dictatorship develop different standards of valuation than people who were once free and then lose their freedom. After the reign of terror there were no longer any competing interpretative elites, no church as a moral institution, no emigration with a voice, no reminders of the time before communism, no Western television, no "brothers and sisters" abroad, and no occupiers to blame for the misery and oppression. There was nothing but the dictatorship, either in the present or in the past.[31] The Russian writer Lev Kopelev remembered how, in the 1950s, his mother would speak of the time of peace before the Great War. But this time of peace was a very distant memory to her. The war had broken out in 1914 and had not ended until 1953. Kopelev's mother had experienced Stalin's reign as a time of war. In the memories of survivors, Stalinist mass terror fused with the exterminatory excesses of the National Socialist conquerors into a single great catastrophe that had befallen them through no fault of their own. Everything that had happened before 1941 was eclipsed by the apocalyptic horrors of the Great War. Stalin's successors made peace, and they allowed victims and perpetrators alike to find their places in the grand narrative of the survivors.

The recollections of a former Red Army soldier, who had been in German captivity before being interned in the Stalinist camps, vividly convey the fatalism of those who survived. To people from the West this man's life might look like one long series of misfortunes, but that is because we measure it with the yardstick of life in a democracy, a life that was wholly foreign to Russia at that time. The soldier's account, however, reads like a list of one fortunate circumstance after another. And from the vantage point of someone who survived the excesses of Stalinist terror by chance, while millions of others perished, it was.

> I have always been extremely fortunate, particularly in the difficult periods of my life. I am lucky that my father was not arrested; that the teachers at my school were good; that I did not fight in the Finnish War; that I was never hit by a bullet; that the hardest year of my captivity I spent in Estonia; that I did not die working in the mines in Germany; that I was not shot for desertion when I was arrested by the Soviet authorities; that I was not tortured when I was interrogated; that I did not die on the convoy to the labor camp, though I weighed only 48 kilograms and was 1.8 meters tall; that I was in a Soviet labor camp when the horrors of the Gulag were already in decline. I am not bitter from my experience and have learned to accept life as it really is.[32]

Still, to this day the empire is celebrated, and the authoritarian state is praised. Stalin has been resurrected as a symbol of lost greatness. "Victory is the Stalinist era," wrote the Russian civil rights activist Arseny Roginsky, "but terror is also the Stalinist era. It is impossible to reconcile these two images of the past, except by rejecting one of them, or at least making serious corrections to it. And this is what happened—the memory of the terror receded. It has not disappeared completely, but it has been pushed to the periphery of the collective consciousness."[33] Stalin is not dead. The ax outlives its master. This could be the title of the story of Stalinism that is presented to the post-Soviet public on a daily basis. It is a story of heroes who won wars, erected dams, and created empires, defeated enemies and conquered nations, a dictator with benevolent intentions who made Russia great and its enemies small. In such representations, the dictator cannot be depicted as anything other than a wise statesman—certainly not as a murderer and a tyrant. Stalin continues to be adulated and praised in films, books, and public exhibitions. As long as memory remains chained in the "shackles of victory,"[34] any authoritarian regime will have easy work talking its people into believing that controlled democracy is democracy in its truest form.

Notes

The following archive abbreviations are used in the notes.

FSO   Archive of the Research Centre for East European Studies, University of Bremen
GARF   State Archive of the Russian Federation, Moscow
RGANI   Russian State Archive of Contemporary History, Moscow
RGASPI Russian State Archive of Socio-Political History, Moscow
TsAMO   Central Archive of the [Soviet] Ministry of Defense. Library of Congress, Manuscript Division, Dmitrii Antonovich Volkogonov Papers (followed by container and reel numbers)

PREFACE

1. Martin Walser, "Über das Selbstgespräch: Ein flagranter Versuch," in *Ich vertraue: Querfeldein. Reden und Aufsätze* (Frankfurt am Main: Suhrkamp, 2000), 149.

2. Arthur Koestler, Ignazio Silone, and André Gide, *The God That Failed: Six Studies in Communism* (London: Hamish Hamilton, 1950), 75–76.

CHAPTER ONE. WHAT WAS STALINISM?

1. Aleksandr I. Solzhenitsyn, *Gulag Archipelago 1918–1956: An Experiment in Literary Investigation*, vol. 1 (New York: Harper & Row, 1974), 69–70.

2. Il'ia E. Zelenin, *Stalinskaia "revoliutsiia sverchu" posle "velikogo pereloma," 1930–1939: Politika, osushchestvlenie, rezultaty* (Moscow: Nauka, 2006), 17.

3. Quoted in Orlando Figes, *The Whisperers: Private Life in Stalin's Russia* (London: Penguin, 2007), 242.

4. Such histories have already been written. See, for example, Manfred Hildermeier, *Geschichte der Sowjetunion 1917–1991: Entstehung und Niedergang des ersten sozialistischen Staates* (Munich: Beck, 1998); Dietrich Beyrau, *Petrograd, 25. Oktober 1917: Die russische Revolution und der Aufstieg des Kommunismus* (Munich: Deutscher Taschenbuch Verlag, 2001); Ronald G. Suny, *The Soviet Experiment: Russia, the USSR, and the Successor States* (Oxford: Oxford University Press, 1998). Two exceptions: Martin Malia, *Vollstreckter Wahn: Rußland 1917–1991* (Stuttgart: Klett-Cotta, 1994); and Gerd Koenen, *Utopie der Säuberung: Was war der Kommunismus?* (Berlin: Fest, 1998).

5. Stéphane Courtois, "Die Verbrechen des Kommunismus," in *Das Schwarzbuch des Kommunismus: Unterdrückung, Verbrechen und Terror,* ed. Courtois et al. (Munich: Piper, 1998), 11–43.

6. Summaries of research in Jörg Baberowski, "Wandel und Terror: Die Sowjetunion unter Stalin 1928–1941," *Jahrbücher für Geschichte Osteuropas* 43 (1995): 97–129; Manfred Hildermeier, "Interpretationen des Stalinismus," *Historische Zeitschrift* 264 (1997): 655–74; Sheila Fitzpatrick, ed., *Stalinism: New Directions* (London: Routledge, 2000); Michael Geyer and Sheila Fitzpatrick, "After Totalitarianism: Stalinism and Nazism Compared," in *Beyond Totalitarianism. Stalinism and Nazism Compared,* ed. Geyer and Fitzpatrick (Cambridge: Cambridge University Press, 2009), 1–37.

7. Carl J. Friedrich, *Totalitäre Diktatur* (Stuttgart: W. Kohlhammer, 1957), 17.

8. Ibid., 9.

9. Ibid., 16.

10. Ibid., 18.

11. Hannah Arendt, "Ideologie und Terror: Eine neue Staatsform," in *Wege der Totalitarismusforschung,* ed. Bruno Seidel and Siegfried Jenkner (Darmstadt: Wissenschaftliche Buchgesellschaft, 1974), 163.

12. For this charge, see Wolfgang Wippermann, *Totalitarismustheorien: Die Entwicklung der Diskussion von den Anfängen bis heute* (Darmstadt: Wissenschaftliche Buchgesellschaft, 1997).

13. See, for example, Hans Mommsen, "Leistungen und Grenzen des Totalitarismus-Theorems: Die Anwendung auf die nationalsozialistische Diktatur," in *"Totalitarismus" und "Politische Religionen," Konzepte des Diktaturenvergleichs,* ed. Hans Maier (Paderborn: Schöningh, 1996), 291–300; Ludolf Herbst, "Das nationalsozialistische Herrschaftssystem als Vergleichsgegenstand und der Ansatz der Totalitarismustheorien," in *Totalitarismus: Sechs Vorträge über Gehalt und Reichweite eines klassischen Konzepts der Diktaturforschung,* ed. Klaus-Dietmar Henke (Dresden: Hannah-Arendt-Institut für Totalitarismusforschung, 1999), 19–26.

14. See, for example, Sheila Fitzpatrick, ed., *Cultural Revolution in Russia, 1928–1931* (Bloomington: Indiana University Press, 1978); J. Arch Getty, *The Origins of the Great Purges: The Soviet Communist Party Reconsidered* (Cambridge: Cambridge University Press, 1985); as well as the debates in the *Russian Review* (1986).

15. Ian Kershaw, *Hitler, 1936–1945* (Munich: Deutsche Verlags-Anstalt, 2000).

16. Lynne Viola, *The Best Sons of the Fatherland: Workers in the Vanguard of Soviet Collectivization* (New York: Oxford University Press, 1987); Sheila Fitzpatrick, "Stalin and the Making of a New Elite," in *The Cultural Front: Power and Culture in Revolutionary Russia* (Ithaca: Cornell University Press, 1992), 149–82.

17. Peter Kenez, "Stalinism as Humdrum Politics," *Russian Review* 45 (1986): 395–400.

18. Geoff Eley, "History with the Politics Left Out—Again?" ibid., 385–94.

19. Hannah Arendt, *The Origins of Totalitarianism* (Orlando: Harcourt, 1985), 475. For the idea that human beings are nodes of power, see Michel Foucault, *In Verteidigung der Gesellschaft: Vorlesungen am Collège de France 1975–1976* (Frankfurt am Main: Suhrkamp, 1999), 38. For the Soviet state of mind, see esp. Jochen Hellbeck, *Revolution on My Mind: Writing a Diary under Stalin* (Cambridge, Mass.: Harvard University Press, 2006); Igal Halfin, *Terror in my Soul: Communist Autobiographies on Trial* (Cambridge, Mass.: Harvard University Press, 2003). Critical reactions: Aleksandr Etkind, "Soviet Subjectivity: Torture for the Sake of Salvation?" *Kritika* 6 (2005): 171–86; Jörg Baberowski, "Was war der Stalinismus? Anmerkungen zur Historisierung des Kommunismus," *Deutschland-Archiv* 41 (2008): 1047–56.

20. Arthur Koestler, *The Invisible Writing: The Second Volume of an Autobiography 1932–1940* (London: Hutchinson, 1969), 187–88.

21. Figes, *The Whisperers*.

22. See on this point Simon Sebag Montefiore, *Stalin: The Court of the Red Tsar* (London: Weidenfeld & Nicolson, 2003).

23. Lynne Viola, *Peasant Rebels under Stalin: Collectivization and the Culture of Peasant Resistance* (Oxford: Oxford University Press, 1996); Lynne Viola, *The Unknown Gulag: The Lost World of Stalin's Special Settlements* (Oxford: Oxford University Press, 2007); Jörg Baberowski, "Stalinismus von oben: Kulakendeportationen in der Sowjetunion 1929–1933," *Jahrbücher für Geschichte Osteuropas* 46 (1998): 572–95; Nikolai A. Ivnitskii, *Kollektivizatsiia i raskulachivanie, nachalo 30-kh godov* (Moscow: Magistr, 1996).

24. See Marc Jansen and Nikita Petrov, *Stalin's Loyal Executioner: People's Commissar Nikolai Yezhov 1895–1940* (Stanford: Hoover Institution Press, 2002; also Paul R. Gregory, *Terror by Quota: State Security from Lenin to Stalin* (New Haven: Yale University Press, 2009).

25. David J. Nordlaender, "Origins of a Gulag Capital: Magadan and Stalinist Control in the Early 1930s," *Slavic Review* 57 (1998): 791–812.

26. Lars Lih, ed., *Stalin: Briefe an Molotov 1925–1936* (Berlin: Siedler, 1996); Oleg V. Khlevniuk, *Stalin i Kaganovich: Perepiska* (Moscow: ROSSPEN, 2001).

27. Viola, *Peasant Rebels under Stalin;* Sarah Davies, *Popular Opinion in Stalin's Russia: Terror, Propaganda, and Dissent, 1934–1941* (Cambridge: Cambridge University Press, 1997); Elena Osokina, *Our Daily Bread: Socialist Distribution and the Art of Survival in Stalin's Russia, 1927–1941* (New York: M. E. Sharpe, 2001); Sheila Fitzpatrick, *Everyday Stalinism: Ordinary Life in Extraordinary Times: Soviet Russia in the 1930s* (Oxford: Oxford University Press, 1999.

28. Zygmunt Bauman, *Moderne und Ambivalenz: Das Ende der Eindeutigkeit* (Frankfurt am Main: Fischer-Taschenbuch-Verlag, 1995), 13–71, 320–29.

29. Arthur Koestler, R. H. S. Crossman, et al., eds., *Ein Gott, der keiner war* (Munich: Deutscher Taschenbuch Verlag, 1962), 29. See also Michail Ryklin, *Kommunismus als Religion: Die Intellektuellen und die Oktoberrevolution* (Frankfurt am Main: Verlag der Weltreligionen, 2008), 125–33.

30. Bauman, *Moderne und Ambivalenz*, 45.

31. Joseph Brodsky, *Less Than One: Selected Essays,* 2d ed. (New York: Farrar, Straus and Giroux, 1986), 10.

32. See the arguments by an American sociologist published more than forty years ago: Barrington Moore, *Totalitäre Elemente in vorindustriellen Gesellschaften,* in *Zur Geschichte der politischen Gewalt* (Frankfurt am Main: Suhrkamp, 1966), 68–78; and the brilliant study by Alexander Hinton of the mass terror inflicted by the Khmer Rouge in Cambodia: Alexander L. Hinton, "Why Did You Kill? The Cambodian Genocide and the Dark Side of Face and Honor," *Journal of Asian Studies* 57 (1998): 93–122.

33. Nina Lugovskaia, *The Diary of a Soviet Schoolgirl 1932–1937* (Moscow: Glas, 2003), 140. For criticism of this concept of modernity, see Jörg Baberowski, "Diktaturen der Eindeutigkeit: Ambivalenz und Gewalt im Zarenreich und in der frühen Sowjetunion," in *Moderne Zeiten? Krieg, Revolution und Gewalt im 20. Jahrhundert,* ed. Jörg Baberowski (Göttingen: Vandenhoeck & Ruprecht, 2006), 37–59, esp. 37–41; Michael Riekenberg, *Gewaltsegmente: Über einen Ausschnitt der Gewalt in Lateinamerika* (Leipzig: Leipziger Universitäts-Verlag, 2003), 81–112; Hiroaki Kuromiya, *Freedom and Terror in the Donbass: A Ukrainian-Russian Borderland, 1870s–1990s* (Cambridge: Cambridge University Press, 1998). For criticism of those theories that view mass violence as characteristic of modernity, see also Lawrence H. Keeley, *War Before Civilization: The Myth of the Peaceful Savage* (Oxford: Oxford University Press, 1996).

34. Gerald Easter, *Reconstructing the State: Personal Networks and Elite Identity in Soviet Russia* (Cambridge: Cambridge University Press, 2000)

35. See for example, Vladimir Buldakov, *Krasnaia smuta: Priroda i posledstviia revoliutsionnogo nasiliia* (Moscow: ROSSPEN, 1997); Delano DuGarm, "Local Politics and the Struggle for Grain in Tambov, 1918–21," in *Provincial Landscapes,* ed. Donald J. Raleigh (Pittsburgh: University of Pittsburgh Press, 2001), 59–81.

36. Quote in Sergei Parfenov, "'Zheleznyi Lazar': Konets kar'ery," *Rodina* 2 (1990): 74. See also Feliks Chuev, *Tak govoril Kaganovich: Izpoved' stalinskogo apostola* (Moscow: Otechestvo, 1992); Feliks I. Chuev, *Molotov Remembers: Inside Kremlin Politics. Conversations With Felix Chuev* (Chicago: Ivan D. Ree, 1993); Valerii A. Torchinov and Aleksei M. Leontiuk, eds., *Vokrug Stalina: Istoriko-biograficheskii spravochnik* (Saint Petersburg: Filol. Fak. Sankt-Peterburgskogo Gosudarstvennogo Univ., 2000), 237–39.

37. Martin Amis, *Koba the Dread: Laughter and the Twenty Million* (London: Jonathan Cape, 2002), 178.

38. Oleg V. Khlevniuk, *Master of the House: Stalin and His Inner Circle* (New Haven: Yale University Press, 2009). On Stalin as thug, see especially Montefiore, *Stalin*; and Jörg Baberowski, "Misstrauen und Gewalt: Stalinismus als Despotie," *Geschichte für Heute* 3 (2010): 37–53.

39. See Jörg Baberowski, "Gewalt verstehen," *Zeithistorische Forschungen* 5, no. 1 (2008): 5–17.

40. Chuev, *Molotov Remembers,* 258. Many historians have agreed with this idea, but Norman Naimark has pointed out that the mass terror of the 1930s was stopped when Stalin expected that war was imminent. See Norman Naimark, *Stalin's Genocides* (Princeton: Princeton University Press, 2010).

41. Imre Kertész, *Ich—ein anderer: Roman* (Reinbek bei Hamburg: Rowohlt, 1999), 72.

CHAPTER TWO. IMPERIAL SPACES OF VIOLENCE

1. Jean-Jacques Rousseau, *On the Social Contract,* trans. G. D. H. Cole (New York: Cosimo, 2008), 49.

2. Dietrich Geyer, "Gesellschaft als staatliche Veranstaltung," *Jahrbücher für Geschichte Osteuropas* 14 (1966): 21–50.

3. Manfred Hildermeier, "Der russische Adel von 1700–1917," in *Europäischer Adel 1750–1950,* ed. Hans Ulrich Wehler (Göttingen: Vandenhoeck & Ruprecht, 1990), 166–216; Dominic Lieven, *Abschied von Macht und Würden: Der europäische Adel 1815–1914* (Frankfurt am Main: Fischer, 1995), 281–98; Marc Raeff, "Der wohlgeordnete Polizeistaat und die Entwicklung der Moderne im Europa des 17. und 18. Jahrhunderts: Versuch eines vergleichenden Ansatzes," in *Absolutismus,* ed. Ernst Hinrichs (Frankfurt am Main: Suhrkamp, 1986), 310–43; Robert Edward Jones, *The Emancipation of the Russian Nobility, 1762–1785* (Princeton: Princeton University Press, 1973).

4. See B. W. Lincoln, *In the Vanguard of Reform: Russia's Enlightened Bureaucrats 1825–1861* (DeKalb: Northern Illinois University Press, 1982); Richard Wortman, *The Development of a Russian Legal Consciousness* (Chicago: University of Chicago Press, 1976); Jörg Baberowski, *Autokratie und Justiz: Zum Verhältnis von Rechtsstaatlichkeit und Rückständigkeit im ausgehenden Zarenreich* (Frankfurt am Main: V. Klostermann, 1996).

4a. Richard S. Wortman, *Scenarios of Power: Myth and Ceremony in Russian Monarchy, vol. 2: From Alexander II to the Abdication of Nicholas II* (Princeton: Princeton University Press, 2000), 68.

5. Richard S. Wortman, *Scenarios of Power: Myth and Ceremony in Russian Monarchy,* vol. 2: *From Alexander II to the Abdication of Nicholas II* (Princeton: Princeton University Press, 2000), 68.

6. Laura Engelstein, "Combined Underdevelopment: Discipline and the Law in Imperial and Soviet Russia," *American Historical Review* 98 (1993): 338–53; Jörg Baberowski, "Auf der Suche nach Eindeutigkeit: Kolonialismus und zivilisatorische Mission im Zarenreich und in der Sowjetunion," *Jahrbücher für Geschichte Osteuropas* 47 (1999): 482–504.

7. Amin Maalouf, *In the Name of Identity: Violence and the Need to Belong* (New York: Arcade Publishing, 2001), 43.

8. For the abolition of serfdom and its consequences, see David Moon, *The Russian Peasantry 1600–1930* (London: Longman, 1999), 108–12; Daniel Field,

The End of Serfdom: Nobility and Bureaucracy in Russia, 1855–1861 (Cambridge, Mass.: Harvard University Press, 1976); Terence Emmons, *The Russian Landed Gentry and the Peasant Emancipation of 1861* (Cambridge: Cambridge University Press, 1968); Esther Kingston-Mann and Timothy Mixter, eds., *Peasant Economy, Culture, and Politics of European Russia 1800–1921* (Princeton: Princeton University Press, 1991).

9. Stephen P. Frank, *Crime, Cultural Conflict, and Justice in Rural Russia, 1856–1914* (Berkeley: University of California Press, 1999), 19–50.

10. Christoph Schmidt, *Sozialkontrolle in Moskau: Justiz, Kriminalität und Leibeigenschaft 1649–1785* (Stuttgart: F. Steiner, 1996); Jörg Baberowski, *Autokratie und Justiz.*

11. Frank, *Crime, Cultural Conflict, and Justice,* 209–12; Christine D. Worobec, *Peasant Russia: Family and Community in the Post-Emancipation Period* (DeKalb: Northern Illinois University Press, 1995), 118–50; Barbara Alpern Engel, *Between the Fields and the City: Women, Work, and Family in Russia, 1861–1914* (Cambridge: Cambridge University Press, 1996), 7–33; Barbara Alpern Engel, "Horse Thieves and Peasant Justice in Post-Emancipation Imperial Russia," *Journal of Social History* 21 (1987): 281–93.

12. See the descriptions by the estate owner Aleksandr Nikolaevich Engelgardt of the peasants' violence and their custom of offering economic compensation by way of atonement: Aleksandr Nikolaevich Engelgardt, *Aleksandr Nikolaevich Engelgardt's Letters from the Country, 1872–1887,* ed. Cathy A. Frierson (Oxford: Oxford University Press, 1993), 34–35; Frank, *Crime, Cultural Conflict, and Justice,* 85–114.

13. Abraham Ascher, *The Revolution of 1905: Russia in Disarray* (Stanford: Stanford University Press, 1988), 233.

14. Jörg Baberowski, "Vertrauen durch Anwesenheit: Vormoderne Herrschaft im späten Zarenreich," in *Imperiale Herrschaft in der Provinz: Repräsentationen politischer Macht im späten Zarenreich,* ed. Jörg Baberowski, David Feest, and Christoph Gumb (Frankfurt am Main: Campus, 2008), 17–37; Dominic C. B. Lieven, *Russia's Rulers under the Old Regime* (New Haven: Yale University Press, 1989); Andrew Verner, *The Crisis of Russian Autocracy: Nicholas II and the 1905 Revolution* (Princeton: Princeton University Press, 1990).

15. Robert Johnson, *Peasant and Proletarian: the Working Class of Moscow in the Late Nineteenth Century* (New Brunswick: Rutgers University Press, 1979); Charters Wynn, *Workers, Strikes, and Pogroms: The Donbass-Dnepr Bend in Late Imperial Russia, 1870–1905* (Princeton: Princeton University Press, 1995); Joan Neuberger, *Hooliganism: Crime, Culture and Power in St. Petersburg, 1900–1914* (Berkeley: University of California Press, 1993).

16. Vladimir Naumov and Iurii Sigachev, eds., *Lavrentii Beriia 1953: Stenogramma iiul'skogo plenuma TsK KPSS i drugie dokumenty* (Moscow: Mezhdunarodnyi fond "Demokratiia," 1999), 93–94.

17. Wynn, *Workers, Strikes, and Pogroms*; Theodore H. Friedgut, *Iuzovka and Revolution,* 2 vols. (Princeton: Princeton University Press, 1989–1994); Jörg Baberowski, "Nationalismus aus dem Geiste der Inferiorität: Autokratische Modernisierung und die Anfänge muslimischer Selbstvergewisserung im östlichen

Transkaukasien 1828–1914," *Geschichte und Gesellschaft* 26 (2002): 371–406; Sergei I. Potolov, ed., *Rabochie i intelligentsiia Rossii v epokhu reform i revol'iutsii 1861–1917* (Saint Petersburg: Rossiiskaia Akademiia Nauk, 1997); Semen Kanatchikov, *A Radical Worker in Tsarist Russia: The Autobiography of Semen Ivanovich Kanatchikov,* ed. R. E. Zelnik (Stanford: Stanford University Press, 1986).

18. Ivan I. Petrunkevich, *Iz zapisok obshchestvennogo deiatelia* (Prague: Speer & Schmidt, 1934), 429–33.

19. Mikhail Gershenzon, "Creative Self-Consciousness," in *Vekhi—Landmarks: A Collection of Articles about the Russian Intelligentsia,* ed. Marshall S. Shatz and Judith E. Zimmerman (Armonk: M. E. Sharpe, 1994), 51–71, esp. 64.

20. Maxim Gorki, *Unzeitgemäße Betrachtungen über Kultur und Revolution* (Frankfurt am Main: Suhrkamp, 1974), 149.

21. Orlando Figes, *A People's Tragedy: The Russian Revolution 1891–1924* (London: Pimlico, 1996), 122, 154; Richard Pipes, *Die russische Revolution,* vol. 1: *Der Zerfall des Zarenreiches* (Berlin: Rowohlt, 1992).

22. Vladimir I. Lenin, *The Military Programme of the Proletarian Revolution,* vol. 23 of *Lenin, Collected Works* (Moscow: Progress Publishers, 1964), 78–79.

23. Aleksei Brusilov, *Moi vospominaniia* (Moscow: ROSSPEN, 2001), 213.

24. See, e.g., Viktor L. Mal'kov, ed., *Pervaia mirovaia voina: Prolog XX veka* (Moscow: Nauka, 1998); Igor' V. Narskii and Ol'ga Iu. Nikonova, eds., *Chelovek i voina: Voina kak iavlenie kul'tury* (Moscow: AIRO-XX, 2001); Norman Stone, *The Eastern Front, 1914–1917* (London: Houghton Mifflin, 1978); Brusilov, *Moi vospominaniia.*

25. Ol'ga S. Porshneva, "Rossiiskii krest'ianin v pervoi mirovoi voine, 1914—fevral' 1917," in Narskii and Nikonova, *Chelovek i voina,* 190–215; Joshua A. Sanborn, *Drafting the Russian Nation: Military Conscription, Total War, and Mass Politics 1905–1925* (DeKalb: Northern Illinois University Press, 2003), 96–131; Peter Holquist, *Making War, Forging Revolution: Russia's Continuum of Crisis, 1914–1921* (Cambridge, Mass.: Harvard University Press, 2002), 12–46. On the propaganda of the tsarist regime see Hubertus Jahn, *Patriotic Culture in Russia during World War I* (Ithaca: Cornell University Press, 1995).

26. Victor Dönninghaus, *Die Deutschen in der Moskauer Gesellschaft: Symbiose und Konflikte, 1494–1941* (Munich: R. Oldenbourg, 2002), 373–516.

27. Vladimir V. Lapin et al., eds., *Sovet ministrov Rossiiskoi imperii v gody pervoi mirovoi voiny: Bumagi A. N. Iachontova* (Saint Petersburg: Dmitrii Bulanin, 1999), 147; Eric Lohr, "The Russian Army and the Jews: Mass Deportations, Hostages, and Violence during World War I," *Russian Review* 60 (2001): 404–19; A. B. Tsfasman, "Pervaia mirovaia voina i evrei Rossii, 1914–1917," in Narskii and Nikonova, *Chelovek i voina,* 171–80, esp. 174.

28. Peter Gatrell, "War, Population, Displacement and State Formation in the Russian Borderlands, 1914–1924," in *War, Population and Statehood in Eastern Europe and Russia, 1918–1924,* ed. Nick Baron and Peter Gatrell (London: Anthem Press, 2004), 10–34, esp. 12–15; Ulrike von Hirschhausen, *Die Grenzen der Gemeinsamkeit: Deutsche, Letten, Russen und Juden in Riga 1860–1914* (Göttingen: Vandenhoeck & Ruprecht, 2006).

29. Peter Gatrell, *A Whole Empire Walking: Refugees in Russia during World War I* (Bloomington: Indiana University Press, 1999), 17–19, 23–25, 36, 66; Peter Holquist, "To Count, to Extract, and to Exterminate: Population Statistics and Population Politics in Late Imperial and Soviet Russia," in *A State of Nations: Empire and Nation Making in the Age of Lenin and Stalin,* ed. Roland G. Suny and Terry Martin (Oxford: Oxford University Press, 2001), 115; Lohr, "The Russian Army and the Jews," 404–19; Tsfasman, "Pervaia mirovaia voina," 171–80, esp. 174.

30. Vladimir Nabokov, *Petrograd 1917: Der kurze Sommer der Revolution* (Berlin: Rowohlt, 1992), 136.

31. See Elies Cherikover, *Antisemitizm i pogromy na Ukraine 1917–1918 gg: K istorii ukrainsko-evreiskikh otnoshenii* (Berlin: Ostjüdisches Histor. Archiv Berlin-Charlottenburg, Büchervertrieb "Grani," 1923), 29–31; Nikolaus Katzer, *Die weiße Bewegung in Rußland: Herrschaftsbildung, praktische Politik und politische Programmatik im Bürgerkrieg* (Cologne: Böhlau, 1999), 281.

32. Igor Narskii, *Zhizn' v katastrofe: Budni naseleniia Urala v 1917–1922 gg.* (Moscow: ROSSPEN, 2001), 196–206; Kuromiya, *Freedom and Terror in the Donbass,* 77–79, 82–84.

33. See the striking episodes of violence of soldiers in the revolution recounted by Vladimir Buldakov: Vladimir P. Buldakov, *Krasnaia smuta: Priroda i posledstviia revoliutsionnogo nasiliia* (Moscow: ROSSPEN, 2010), 220–66.

34. Michael C. Hickey, "The Rise and Fall of Smolensk's Moderate Socialists: The Politics of Class and the Rhetoric of Crisis in 1917," in Raleigh, *Provincial Landscapes,* 14–35; R. T. Manning, "Bolsheviks without the Party: Sychevka in 1917," ibid., 40–52; John Channon, "The Peasantry in the Revolutions of 1917," in *Revolution in Russia: Reassessments of 1917,* ed. Edith R. Frankel, Jonathan Frankel, Baruch Knei-Paz, and Israel Getzler (Cambridge: Cambridge University Press, 1992), 106–7; John Keep, *The Russian Revolution: A Study in Mass Mobilization* (New York: Weidenfeld & Nicolson, 1976), 159–61.

35. Orlando Figes and Boris Kolonitskii, *Interpreting the Russian Revolution: The Language and Symbols of 1917* (New Haven: Yale University Press, 1999), 108–24, 127–52.

36. Fedor F. Kokoshkin, *Avtonomiia i federatsiia* (Petrograd: Partiia Nar. Svob, 1917); Hickey, "The Rise and Fall of Smolensk's Moderate Socialists," 14–35; Figes, *A People's Tragedy,* 354–61.

37. Konstantin N. Teploukhov, *Cheliabinskie khroniki: 1899–1924* (Cheliabinsk: Cheliabinsk Tsentr Istoriko-Kultur'nogo Naslediia, 2001), 293.

38. Vladimir I. Lenin, *Polnoe sobranie sochinenii,* 55 vols. (Moscow: Gosudarstvennoe izdatel'stvo politicheskoi literatury, 1958–1965) 35:204; Donald J. Raleigh, *Experiencing Russia's Civil War: Politics, Society and Revolutionary Culture in Saratov, 1917–1922* (Princeton: Princeton University Press, 2002), 34–36, 246–81.

39. Morgan P. Price, *My Reminiscences of the Russian Revolution* (London: G. Allen & Unwin, 1921), 349; Andrea Graziosi, *Bol'sheviki i krest'iane na Ukraine, 1918–1919 gody* (Moscow: AIRO-XX, 1997), 82.

40. Figes, *A People's Tragedy,* 384–405, 474–536; Kuromiya, *Freedom and Terror in the Donbass,* 85–88. On the revolution in Voronezh see Stefan Karsch, *Die*

bolschewistische Machtergreifung im Gouvernement Voronezh (Stuttgart: Steiner, 2006).

41. Carl Schmitt, *Politische Theologie: Vier Kapitel zur Lehre von der Souveränität* (1922; 3d ed., Berlin: Duncker & Humblot, 1979), 54.

42. Mark Meerovich, *Nakazanie zhilishchem: Zhilishchnaia politika v SSSR kak sredstvo upravleniia liud'mi 1917–1937* (Moscow: ROSSPEEN, 2008), 13–17.

43. Sinaida Hippius, *Petersburger Tagebuch* (Berlin: Aufbau-Verlag, 1993), 31–32, 85–86.

44. Gorky, *Untimely Thoughts*, 122–24; Aleksei A. Tatishchev, *Zemli i l'udi: V gushe pereselencheskogo dvizheniia, 1906–1921* (Moscow: Russkii Put', 2001), 275; Narskii, *Zhizn' v katastrofe*, 202–6; Tanja Penter, *Odessa 1917: Revolution an der Peripherie* (Cologne: Böhlau Verlag, 2000), 246–48; Tsuyoshi Hasegawa, "Crime, Police, and Mob Justice in Petrograd during the Russian Revolution of 1917," in *Religious and Secular Forces in Late Tsarist Russia*, ed. Charles E. Timberlake (Seattle: University of Washington Press, 1992), 260; Kuromiya, *Freedom and Terror in the Donbass*, 84–85; Jörg Baberowski, *Der Feind ist überall: Stalinismus im Kaukasus* (Munich: Deutsche Verlags-Anstalt, 2003), 109–41.

45. Gorky, *Untimely Thoughts*, 235.

46. Pavel N. Miliukov, *The Russian Revolution*, vol. 1: *The Revolution Divided* (Gulf Breeze: Academic International Press, 1978), 1. See also Anna Geifman, *Thou Shalt Kill: Revolutionary Terrorism in Russia, 1894–1917* (Princeton: Princeton University Press, 1993), 154–80; Simon Sebag Montefiore, *Young Stalin* (London: Weidenfeld & Nicolson, 2007), 153–59; Arno J. Mayer, *The Furies: Violence and Terror in the French and the Russian Revolutions* (Princeton: Princeton University Press, 2000), 239.

47. Raleigh, *Experiencing Russia's Civil War*, 332–37; Figes, *A People's Tragedy*, 589–603.

48. Katzer, *Die weiße Bewegung*, 399–423; Figes, *A People's Tragedy*, 555–75, 589–603.

49. Vladimir I. Lenin, *The State and Revolution* (Whitefish: Kessinger, 2004), 86. See also Jane Burbank, "Lenin and the Law in Revolutionary Russia," *Slavic Review* 54 (1995): 23–44.

50. See the interpretation by Koenen, *Utopie der Säuberung*, 63–94.

51. Kuromiya, *Freedom and Terror in the Donbass*, 99–105; Narskii, *Zhizn v katastrofe*, 238.

52. Historical documents give differing numbers of victims. See Pipes, *Die russische Revolution*, vol. 3: *Rußland unter dem neuen Regime* (Berlin: Rowohlt, 1993), 188; Iurii Larin, *Evrei i antisemitizm v SSSR* (Moscow: Gosudarstvennoe izdatel'stvo politicheskoi literatury, 1929), 55; Katzer, *Die weiße Bewegung*, 287. For the mentality and motivation of the White officers and warlords, see Leonid Heretz, "The Psychology of the White Movement," in *The Bolsheviks in Russian Society: The Revolution and the Civil Wars*, ed. Vladimir Brovkin (New Haven: Yale University Press, 1997), 105–21; Norman G. O. Pereira, "Siberian Atamanshchina: Warlordism in the Russian Civil War," ibid., 122–38. For the Makhno movement and its handling of violence, see Felix Schnell, *Räume des Schreckens:*

Gewalt und Gruppenmilitanz in der Ukraine 1905–1933 (Hamburg: Hamburger Edition, 2012).

53. Julie A. Cassiday, *The Enemy on Trial: Early Soviet Courts on Stage and Screen* (DeKalb: Northern Illinois University Press, 2000), 28–50; A. Lindenmeyr, "The First Soviet Political Trial: Countess Sofia Panina before the Petrograd Revolutionary Tribunal," *Russian Review* 60 (2001): 505–25.

54. Quoted in George Leggett, *The Cheka: Lenin's Political Police* (Oxford: Clarendon Press, 1981), 114.

55. Robert Service, *Lenin: Eine Biographie* (Munich: Beck, 2000), 421; Figes, *A People's Tragedy*, 536.

56. *Dekrety sovetskoi vlasti*, vol. 3 (Moscow: ROSSPEN, 1961), 291.

57. "Krasnyi terror v gody grazhdanskoi voiny: Po materialam osoboi sledstvennoi komissii," *Voprosy istorii*, no. 9 (2001): 17–18; Leggett, *The Cheka*, 101–20. Additional examples in Sergei P. Mel'gunov, *Krasnyi terror v Rossii* (Berlin, 1923; repr., Moscow: Postskriptum, 1991), 20–32; Sergei A. Pavliuchenkov, *Voennyi kommunizm v Rossii: Vlast' i massy* (Moscow: RKT Istoriia, 1997), 202–26.

58. Graziosi, *Bol'sheviki i krest'iane*, 152.

59. Mel'gunov, *Krasnyi terror*, 24, 43–87; Leggett, *The Cheka*, 103; Anatolii G. Latyshev, *Rassekrechennyi Lenin* (Moscow: Izdat. Mart., 1996), 20, 44–45, 57; Richard Pipes, ed., *The Unknown Lenin: From the Secret Archive* (New Haven: Yale University Press, 1996), 46; Service, *Lenin*, 510–11.

60. Quoted in Koenen, *Utopie der Säuberung*, 22.

61. See Andrei A. Plekhanov, ed., *Feliks E. Dzerzhinskii—predsedatel' VChK-OGPU 1917–1926* (Moscow: Mezhdunarodnyi fond "Demokratiia," 2007), 155–57, 209.

62. Quoted in Mel'gunov, *Krasnyi terror*, 107. Insights into the Bolsheviks' early paranoia and spy mania are provided by the document collection *Krasnaia kniga VChK*, vol. 2 (1922; repr., Moscow: Politizdat, 1989). See also Stephen A. Smith, *Red Petrograd: Revolution in the Factories, 1917–1918* (Cambridge: Cambridge University Press, 1983), 167.

63. Mel'gunov, *Krasnyi terror*, 109–59.

64. Ibid., 10–12, 116–38, 145; Nikolai M. Borodin, *One Man in His Time* (London: Constable, 1955), 19.

65. Sergei A. Pavliuchenkov, *Krest'ianskii Brest ili predistoriia bol'shevisttkogo NEPa* (Moscow: Russkoe Knigoizd., 1996), 34–40.

66. Quotations: Narskii, *Zhizn' v katastrofe*, 273, and Harold H. Fischer, *The Famine in Soviet Russia 1919–1923: The Operations of the American Relief Administration* (New York: Macmillan, 1971), 87–88; Daniel R. Brower, "'The City in Danger': The Civil War and the Russian Urban Population," in *Party, State, and Society in the Russian Civil War: Explorations in Social History*, ed. Diane P. Koenker and William G. Rosenberg (Bloomington: Indiana University Press, 1989), 58–80; Sergei Pavliuchenkov, "Workers' Protest Movement against War Communism," in Brovkin, *The Bolsheviks in Russian Society*, 149; Figes, *A People's Tragedy*, 603–15.

67. Stephen A. Smith, "The Socialist-Revolutionaries and the Dilemma of Civil War," in Brovkin, *The Bolsheviks in Russian Society*, 94–95; Jonathan Aves, *Work-*

ers against Lenin: Labour Protest and the Bolshevik Dictatorship (London: Tauris Academic Studies, 1996), 18–25; Pavliuchenkov, *Voennyi kommunizm,* 148–50; Pavliuchenkov, "Workers' ProtestMovement against War Communism," 146–49; Koenen, *Utopie der Säuberung,* 76–77.

68. *IX s"ezd RKP(b), mart–aprel' 1920 goda: Protokoly* (Moscow: Gospolitizdat, 1972), 406, 415, 554–56; Isaac Deutscher, *Trotzki,* vol. 1: *Der bewaffnete Prophet 1879–1921,* 2d ed. (Stuttgart: Kohlhammer, 1972), 460–78; quotes, 469, 470, 472. See also Baruch Knei-Paz, *The Social and Political Thought of Leon Trotskii* (Oxford: Clarendon Press, 1978), 260–69; Leonard Schapiro, *The Origin of the Communist Autocracy: Political Opposition in the Soviet State: First Phase: 1917–1922* (London: Macmillan, 1977), 211–34; Aves, *Workers against Lenin,* 5–8, 31.

69. Emma Goldman, *Living My Life* (New York: Dover, 1970), 753; Pavliuchenkov, *Voennyi kommunizm,* 154–64; Paul Avrich, *Kronstadt, 1921* (Princeton: Princeton University Press, 1970), 151–54, 202–16; Figes, *A People's Tragedy,* 763–67; Alexander Berkman, *The Bolshevik Myth: Diary 1920–1922* (London: Hutchinson, 1925), 303; Aves, *Workers against Lenin,* 111–57.

70. Orlando Figes, *Peasant Russia, Civil War: The Volga Countryside in Revolution 1917–1921* (Oxford: Oxford University Press, 1989), 188–95; Raleigh, *Experiencing Russia's Civil War,* 312–47; Taisiia V. Osipova, *Rossiiskoe krest'ianstvo v revoliutsii i grazhdanskoi voiny* (Moscow: Strelets, 2001), 173–91.

71. Quotes: Narskii, *Zhizn' v katastrofe,* 281; Latyshev, *Rassekrechennyi Lenin,* 57, 65–66; Mel'gunov, *Krasnyi terror,* 96–100.

72. Pavliuchenkov, *Voennyi kommunizm,* 109–17, 138–40; Osipova, *Rossiiskoe krest'ianstvo,* 322–36; Raleigh, *Experiencing Russia's Civil War,* 382–87; Graziosi, *Bol'sheviki i krest'iane,* 135–56; Delano DuGarm, "Peasant Wars in Tambov Province," in Brovkin, *The Bolsheviks in Russian Society,* 177–98; Oliver H. Radkey, *The Unknown Civil War in Soviet Russia: A Study of the Green Movement in the Tambov Region, 1920–1921* (Stanford: Hoover Institution Press, 1976); Erik C. Landis, *Bandits and Partisans: The Antonov Movement in the Russian Civil War* (Pittsburgh: Pittsburgh University Press, 2008), 122–51.

73. Graziosi, *Bol'sheviki i krest'iane,* 140; Figes, *A People's Tragedy,* 752–57; Figes, *Peasant Russia,* 321–53; John E. Hodgson, *With Denikin's Armies: Being a Description of the Cossack Counter-Revolution in South-Russia, 1918–1920* (London: Lincoln Williams, 1932), 118.

74. Mel'gunov, *Krasnyi terror,* 100–101; Raleigh, *Experiencing Russia's Civil War,* 382–88.

75. Semen R. Esikov and L. Potrassov, "Antonovshchina: Novye podchody," *Voprosy Istorii,* no. 6/7 (1992): 52; Osipova, *Rossiiskoe krest'ianstvo,* 337–41. See also Alexandr Ia. Livshin and Igor' B. Orlov, eds., *Pis'mo vo vlast' 1917–1927: Zaiavleniia, zhaloby, donosy, pis'ma v gosudarstvennye struktury i bol'shevistskim vozhdiam* (Moscow: ROSSPEN, 1998), 294; Landis, *Bandits and Partisans,* 265–69.

76. V. L. Genis, "Raskazachivanie v Sovetskoi Rossii," *Voprosy Istorii* 1 (1994): 42–47, 54; Mel'gunov, *Krasnyi terror,* 30–31; *Izvestiia TsK KPSS: Informatsionnyi ezhemesiachnyi zhurnal* 6 (1989): 177–78; Holquist, *Making War, Forging Revolution,* 166–205.

77. See Baberowski, *Der Feind ist überall,* 163–65; Pipes, *Die russische Revolution,* 3:173–92.

78. Easter, *Reconstructing the State,* 25–63. Quote from Lenin: Service, *Lenin,* 288.

79. Marc Raeff, *Russia Abroad: A Cultural History of the Russian Emigration, 1919–1939* (New York: Oxford University Press, 1990); Karl Schlögel, ed., *Der große Exodus: Die russische Emigration und ihre Zentren, 1917–1941* (Munich: Beck, 1994).

80. Sheila Fitzpatrick, "The Legacy of the Civil War," in Koenker and Rosenberg, *Party, State, and Society in the Russian Civil War,* 385–98; Dietrich Beyrau, "Der Erste Weltkrieg als Bewährungsprobe: Bolschewistische Lernprozesse aus dem 'imperialistischen' Krieg," *Journal of Modern European History* 1 (2003): 96–124.

CHAPTER THREE. PYRRHIC VICTORIES

1. Alan M. Ball, *And Now My Soul Is Hardened: Abandoned Children in Soviet Russia, 1918–1930* (Berkeley: University of California Press, 1994), 5–9; Raleigh, *Experiencing Russia's Civil War,* 395–404; Kuromiya, *Freedom and Terror in the Donbass,* 127. Quotes: Harold H. Fisher, The *Famine in Soviet Russia, 1919–1923: The Operations of the American Relief Administration* (New York: Macmillan, 1927), 89–90, 96; Borodin, *One Man in His Time,* 26–40; Roger Pethybridge, *One Step Backward, Two Steps Forward: Soviet Society and Politics under the New Economic Policy* (Oxford: Clarendon Press, 1990), 95–96.

2. Ball, *And Now My Soul Is Hardened,* 1–9.

3. Sanborn, *Drafting the Russian Nation,* 180–81; Pethybridge, *One Step Backward, Two Steps Forward,* 104–7; Kuromiya, *Freedom and Terror in the Donbass,* 119–20; Beyrau, *Petrograd, 25. October 1917,* 75; Baberowski, *Der Feind ist überall,* 352–58, 413–20, 511.

4. S. A. Krasil'nikov, ed., *Sudebnyi protsess nad sotsialistami-revoliutsionerami (iiun'–avgust 1922 g.): Podgotovka, provedenie, itogi. Sbornik dokumentov* (Moscow: ROSSPEN, 2002), 172.

5. "Iz stenogrammy zasedaniia petrogradskogo soveta," in *"Ochistim Rossiiu nadolgo . . . ": Repressii protiv inakomysliashchikh. Konets 1921–nachalo 1923 g.,* ed. A. N. Artisov (Moscow: Mezhdunarodnyi fond "Demokratiia," 2008), 315.

6. RGASPI, f. 82, op. 2, d. 148, ll. 169, 173–74. Even Stalin criticized shooting the leaders of the uprising. See RGASPI, f. 558, op. 11, d. 133, ll. 34–35. Markus Wehner, *Bauernpolitik im proletarischen Staat: Die Bauernfrage als zentrales Problem der sowjetischen Innenpolitik, 1921–1928* (Cologne: Böhlau, 1998). An overview: Pethybridge, *One Step Backward, Two Steps Forward;* L. H. Siegelbaum, *Soviet State and Society between Revolutions, 1918–1929* (Cambridge: Cambridge University Press, 1992).

7. On the strikes in 1923, see e. g. A. A. Kulakov and Zh.-P. Depretto, eds., *Obshchestvo i vlast': Rossiiskaia provintsiia, 1917–1980-e gody,* vol. 1: *1917–seredina 30-kh godov* (Moscow: Institut Rossiiskoi Istorii, RAN, 2002), 250–59. On Dzerzhinsky see "Dokladnaia zapiska predsedatelia OGPU F. E. Dzerzhinskogo v Po-

litbiuro TsK VKP(b) ob ekonomicheskom polozhenii 9 iiulia 1924 g.," in *Sovetskaia derevnia glazami VChK-OGPU-NKVD 1918–1939: Dokumenty i materialy v 4 tomakh,* ed. Alexis Berelovich and Viktor Danilov, vol. 2 (Moscow: ROSSPEN, 2000), 223–27, esp. 224. For the economic debate, see Robert W. Davies and Mark Harrison, eds., *The Economic Transformation of the Soviet Union, 1913–1945* (Cambridge: Cambridge University Press, 1994), 8–12, 110–13, 135–36; A. Erlich, *Die Industrialisierungsdebatte in der Sowjetunion 1924–1928* (Frankfurt am Main: Europäische Verlagsanstalt, 1971).

8. Wehner, *Bauernpolitik im proletarischen Staat,* 238–286; David R. Shearer, *Industry, State and Society in Stalin's Russia, 1926–1934* (Ithaca: Cornell University Press, 1996), 27–52.

9. Boris N. Mironov, "Peasant Popular Culture and the Origins of Soviet Authoritarianism," in *Cultures in Flux: Lower-Class Values, Practices, and Resistance in Late Imperial Russia,* ed. Stephen P. Frank (Princeton: Princeton University Press, 1994), 54–73.

10. Pethybridge, *One Step Backward, Two Steps Forward,* 121–27, 382–88; Helmut Altrichter, *Die Bauern von Tver: Vom Leben auf dem russischen Dorfe zwischen Revolution und Kollektivierung* (Munich: Oldenbourg, 1984); Baberowski, *Der Feind ist überall,* 413–20; Oleg V. Khlevniuk, *Das Politbüro: Mechanismen der Macht in der Sowjetunion der dreißiger Jahre* (Hamburg: Hamburger Edition, 1998), 30.

11. Iakov Shafir, *Gazeta i derevnia* (Moscow: Krasnaia nov', 1924), 99–104; "Iz obzora informotdela OGPU o politicheskom sostoianii SSSR za dekabr' 1926 g.," in Berelovich and Danilov, *Sovetskaia derevnia,* 2:473–85, esp. 485.

12. Roger Pethybridge, *The Social Prelude to Stalinism* (London: Macmillan, 1974), 132–86; Peter Kenez, *The Birth of the Propaganda State: Soviet Methods of Mass Mobilization, 1917–1929* (Cambridge: Cambridge University Press, 1985); Altrichter, *Die Bauern von Tver,* 47; Baberowski, *Der Feind ist überall,* 609–25.

13. "Zapiska F. E. Dzerzhinskogo v Politbiuro TsK RKP (b) o sel'korakh," in *Lubianka: Stalin i VChK-GPU-OGPU-NKVD, ianvar' 1922–dekabr' 1936,* ed. V. N. Khaustov, V. P. Naumov, and N. S. Plotnikova (Moscow: Mezhdunarodnyi fond "Demokratiia," 2003), 97; "Iz obzora informotdela OGPU o politicheskom sostoianii SSSR za sentiabr' 1926 g.," in Berelovich and Danilov, *Sovetskaia derevnia,* 2:445–53, esp. 448–49; Pethybridge, *The Social Prelude to Stalinism,* 185; Pethybridge, *One Step Backward, Two Steps Forward,* 174–77.

14. William B. Husband, *"Godless Communists": Atheism and Society in Soviet Russia, 1917–1932* (DeKalb: Northern Illinois University Press, 2000), 36ff.; Glennys Young, *Power and the Sacred in Revolutionary Russia: Religious Activists in the Village* (University Park: Pennsylvania State University Press, 1997).

15. "Iz obzora informotdela OGPU o politicheskom sostoianii SSSR za sentiabr' 1926 g.," in Berelovich and Danilov, *Sovetskaia derevnia,* 2:449; Moshe Levin, "Who Was the Soviet Kulak?" in *The Making of the Soviet System: Essays in the Social History of Interwar Russia,* ed. Alexis Berelovich (New York: Pantheon, 1985), 121–41.

16. Wehner, *Bauernpolitik im proletarischen Staat,* 287–308; Altrichter, *Die Bauern von Tver,* 90–100, 134–45.

17. "Postanovlenie III s"ezda sovetov SSSR," in *KPSS v rezoliutsiiakh,* vol. 2 (Moscow: Gospolitizdat, 1960), 79; Golfo Alexopoulos, *Stalin's Outcasts: Aliens, Citizens, and the Soviet State, 1926–1936* (Ithaca: Cornell University Press, 2003), 17–41; Wehner, *Bauernpolitik im proletarischen Staat,* 204, and Wehner, "'Licom k derevne': Sowjetmacht und Bauernfrage 1924–1925," *Jahrbücher für Geschichte Osteuropas* 42 (1994), 20–48; Siegelbaum, *Soviet State and Society between Revolutions,* 138–49.

18. Fedor I. Gurvich, *Dva goda skitanii* (Berlin: H. S. Hermann & Co., 1922), 253; Alexandre Barbine, *One Who Survived: The Life Story of a Russian under the Soviets* (New York: Putnam, 1945), 125; Alan Ball, "Private Trade and Traders during NEP," in *Russia in the Era of NEP: Explorations in Soviet Society and Culture,* ed. Sheila Fitzpatrick and Alexander Rabinowitch (Bloomington: Indiana University Press, 1991), 89–105; Allan Ball, *Russia's Last Capitalists: The Nepmen, 1921–1929* (Berkeley: University of California Press, 1987), 15–37, 98–100.

19. For some instructive documents on the situation in Nizhny Novgorod, see Kulakov and Depretto, *Obshchestvo i vlast',* 1:251–59, 596–601; unemployed worker quote: A. Ia. Livshin and Igor' B. Orlov, eds., *Pis'ma vo vlast': Zaiavleniia, zhaloby, donosy, pis'ma v gosudarstvennye struktury i bol'shevistskim vozhdiam* (Moscow: ROSSPEN, 1998), 609; John B. Hatch, "Labor Conflict in Moscow, 1921–1925," in Fitzpatrick and Rabinowitch, *Russia in the Era of NEP,* 58–59; Baberowski, *Der Feind ist überall,* 369–97, quote 377–78; Pethybridge, *One Step Backward, Two Steps Forward,* 269–88; Kuromiya, *Freedom and Terror in the Donbass,* 140–42.

20. Kuromiya, *Freedom and Terror in the Donbass,* 148; Borodin, *One Man in His Time,* 59.

21. Sheila Fitzpatrick, "The 'Soft' Line on Culture and its Enemies: Soviet Cultural Policy, 1922–1927," in *The Cultural Front: Power and Culture in Revolutionary Russia, ed.* Sheila Fitzpatrick (Ithaca: Cornell University Press, 1992), 91–114; Kuromiya, *Freedom and Terror in the Donbass,* 142–46; Baberowski, *Der Feind ist überall,* 408–9.

22. *Vos'moi s"ezd RKP(b): Mart 1919 goda. Protokoly* (Moscow: Gosudarstvennoe izdatel'stvo politicheskoi literatury, 1959), 53, 92; *Natsional'nyi vopros na perekrestke mnenii, 20-e gody: Dokumenty i materialy* (Moscow: Nauka, 1992), 15–16.

23. *Natsional'nyi vopros na perekrestke mnenii,* 19.

24. *Dvenadtsatyi s"ezd RKP(b), 17–25 aprelia 1923 goda: Stenograficheskii otchet* (Moscow: Gosudarstvennoe izdatel'stvo politicheskoi literatury, 1968), 613. On the policy of indigenization, see Terry Martin, *The Affirmative Action Empire: Nations and Nationalism in the Soviet Union 1923–1939* (Ithaca: Cornell University Press, 2001), 42–44; Baberowski, *Der Feind ist überall,* 184–214, 316–49; Yuri Slezkine, "The USSR as a Communal Apartment, or How a Socialist State Promoted Ethnic Particularism," *Slavic Review* 53 (1994): 414–52.

25. *Vos'moi s"ezd,* 107; *Desiatyi s"ezd RKP(b), Mart 1921 goda: Stenograficheskii otchet* (Moscow: Gosudarstvennoe izdatel'stvo politicheskoi literatury, 1963), 213; Vladimir I. Lenin, "Über das Selbstbestimmungsrecht der Nationen," in *Lenin, Ausgewählte Werke,* vol. 1 (Berlin: Dietz, 1978), 688. For Lenin's conception of the

nation see J. Smith, *The Bolsheviks and the National Question, 1917–23* (London: Macmillan, 1999), 7–28.

26. Sheila Fitzpatrick, "Ascribing Class: The Construction of Social Identity in Soviet Russia," *Journal of Modern History* 65 (1993): 745–70; Terry Martin, "Modernization or Neo-Traditionalism? Ascribed Nationality and Soviet Primordialism," in *Stalinism: New Directions,* ed. Sheila Fitzpatrick (London: Routledge, 2000), 348–67; Slezkine, "The USSR as a Communal Apartment," 414–52; Baberowski, *Der Feind ist überall,* 317–21.

27. Martin, *The Affirmative Action Empire,* 209ff.; Baberowski, *Der Feind ist überall,* 316ff.

28. Wehner, *Bauernpolitik im proletarischen Staat,* 94–122; Kendall E Bailes, *Technology and Society under Lenin and Stalin: Origins of the Soviet Technical Intelligentsia, 1917–1941* (Princeton: Princeton University Press, 1978).

29. Edward Keenan formulated this idea some time ago for the tsarist period. See Edward Keenan, "Muscovite Political Folkways," *Russian Review* 45 (1986): 115–81.

30. RGASPI, f. 17, op. 3, d. 680; Paul Gregory, "The Politburo's Role as Revealed in the Lost Transcripts," in *The Lost Politburo Transcripts: From Collective Rule to Stalin's Dictatorship,* ed. Paul R. Gregory and Norman Naimark (New Haven: Yale University Press, 2008), 16–37.

31. Leo Trotzki, *Mein Leben: Versuch einer Autobiographie* (Berlin: Dietz, 1990), 447–60; Robert Service, *Trotsky: A Biography* (Cambridge, Mass.: Harvard University Press, 2009), 310–12.

32. Alexander Vatlin, "'Class Brothers Unite!': The British General Strike and the Formation of the 'United Opposition,'" in Gregory and Naimark, *The Lost Politburo Transcripts,* 57–77; Service, *Trotsky,* 352–55.

33. Paul Gregory, *The Political Economy of Stalinism: Evidence from the Soviet Secret Archives* (Cambridge: Cambridge University Press, 2004), 29–30.

34. On the intraparty debates, see Robert V. Daniels, *The Conscience of the Revolution: Communist Opposition in Soviet Russia* (Cambridge, Mass.: Harvard University Press, 1960); Khlevniuk, *Das Politbüro,* 34–66; Service, *Trotsky,* 349–57; Viktor P. Danilov et al., eds., *Ob"edinennyj plenum TsK i TsKK VKP (b) 6–11 aprelia 1928,* vol. 1 of *Kak lomali NEP: Stenogrammy plenumov TsK VKP (b) 1928–1929,* 5 vols. (Moscow: Mezhdunarodnyi fond "Demokratiia," 2000); Jan Plamper, *Alkhimiia vlasti: Kult Stalina v izobrazitel'nom iskusstve* (Moscow: Novoe Literaturnoe Obozrenie, 2010).

35. Benno Ennker, "Politische Herrschaft und Stalinkult 1929–1939," in *Stalinismus: Neue Forschungen und Konzepte,* ed. Stefan Plaggenborg (Berlin: Verlag Spitz, 1998), 151–82; Plamper, *Alkhimiia vlasti.*

36. Khlevniuk, *Master of the House,* 21–29.

37. Anastas I. Mikoian, *Tak bylo: Razmyshleniia o minuvshem* (Moscow: Vagrius, 1999), 347–48.

38. Boris Bazhanov, *Vospominaniia byvshego sekretaria Stalina* (Paris, 1930; Moscow: NP "III Tysiacheletie," 2002).

39. Quoted in Service, *Trotsky,* 347.

40. Gregory, "The Politburo's Role as Revealed in the Lost Transcripts," 16–37. See also documentation with comments in Oleg V. Khlevniuk et al., eds., *Stalinskoe politbiuro v 30-e gody: Sbornik dokumentov* (Moscow: AIRO-XX, 1995).

41. James Harris, "Stalin as General Secretary: The Appointments Process and the Nature of Stalin's Power," in *Stalin: A New History*, ed. Sarah Davies and James Harris (Cambridge: Cambridge University Press, 2005), 63–82.

42. Daniels, *The Conscience of the Revolution*, 154–88, 238–41. on the party: Robert Service, *The Bolshevik Party in Revolution: A Study in Organisational Change, 1917–1923* (London: Macmillan, 1979); Thomas H. Rigby, *Communist Party Membership in the USSR 1917–1967* (Princeton: Princeton University Press, 1968). On Stalin's role: Robert C. Tucker, *Stalin as Revolutionary 1879–1929* (New York: Norton, 1973), 292–329; Graeme Gill, *The Origins of the Stalinist Political System* (Cambridge: Cambridge University Press, 1990), 23–198.

43. Golfo Alexopoulos, "Stalin and the Politics of Kinship: Practices of Collective Punishment, 1920s–1940s," *Comparative Studies in Society and History* 50, no. 1 (2008): 91–117; Easter, *Reconstructing the State*, 7–17; Pethybridge, *One Step Backward, Two Steps Forward*, 145–188; Baberowski, *Der Feind ist überall*.

44. Thomas H. Rigby, *Political Elites in the USSR: Central Leaders and Local Cadres from Lenin to Gorbachev* (Aldershot: Elgar, 1990), 12–42.

45. On recruitment issues in the 1920s, see Thomas H. Rigby, *Communist Party Membership in the USSR 1917–1967* (Princeton: Princeton University Press, 1968), 110–64; Baberowski, *Der Feind ist überall*, 322–31.

46. Mikoian, *Tak bylo*, 288. Almost all the leading Bolsheviks wrote in their memoirs of their own experiences with violence; e. g., Kliment I. Voroshilov, *Rasskazy o zhizni: Vospominaniia* (Moscow: Gosudarstvennoe izdatel'stvo politicheskoi literatury, 1971), 6–7.

47. Strobe Talbott, ed., *Khrushchev Remembers*, 2 vols. (Boston: Little, Brown, 1970), 1:26–27, 37, 57, 62–63; Mikoian, *Tak bylo*, 351–56; Montefiore, *Stalin*, 33–37.

48. Quotes: RGASPI, f. 85, op. 1s, d. 110, ll. 1–2; Service, *Trotsky*, 347. See also Oleg V. Khlevniuk, *In Stalin's Shadow: The Career of "Sergo" Ordzhonikidze* (Armonk: M. E. Sharpe, 1995), 16; Fitzpatrick, *Everyday Stalinism*, 15–24.

49. This is how Molotov remembered the debates of the twenties. Chuev, *Molotov Remembers*, 215–16.

50. Mikoian, *Tak bylo*, 272–77, 286–89; Robert Service, *Stalin: A Biography* (London: Macmillan, 2004), 277; J. Arch Getty and Oleg V. Naumov, *Road to Terror: Stalin and the Self-Destruction of the Bolsheviks, 1932–1939* (New Haven: Yale University Press, 1999), 93.

51. Quotes in Daniels, *The Conscience of the Revolution*, 240.

52. Benno Ennker, *Die Anfänge des Leninkults in der Sowjetunion* (Cologne: Böhlau, 1997); Ilya Zbarski, *Lenin und andere Leichen: Mein Leben im Schatten des Mausoleums* (Stuttgart: Klett-Cotta, 1997), 19–35. On the group dynamics of isolated sects, see the sociological study by Heinrich Popitz, "Realitätsverlust in Gruppen," in *Soziale Normen*, ed. Heinrich Popitz, Friedrich Pohlmann, and Wolfgang Eßbach (Frankfurt am Main: Suhrkamp, 2006), 175–86.

53. RGASPI, f. 558, op. 11, d. 735, ll. 7–13, quote: l. 13.

54. Service, *Stalin*, 219–23; J. Arch Getty, "Samokritika Rituals in the Stalinist Central Comitee, 1933–1938," *Russian Review* 58 (1999): 49–70; Tomsky quote in Pravda, 19 November 1927, quoted in Charters Wynn, "The 'Right Opposition' and the 'Smirnov-Tolmachev Affair,'" in Gregory and Naimark, *The Lost Politburo Transcripts*, 112.

CHAPTER FOUR. SUBJUGATION

1. James C. Scott, *Seeing Like a State: How Certain Schemes to Improve the Human Condition Have Failed* (New Haven: Yale University Press, 1998), 2; Barrington Moore, *Zur Geschichte der politischen Gewalt*, 3d ed. (Frankfurt am Main: Suhrkamp, 1969), 34–35.

2. Leo Trotzki, *Denkzettel: Politische Erfahrungen im Zeitalter der permanenten Revolution*, ed. Isaac Deutscher (Frankfurt am Main: Suhrkamp, 1981), 371–373. See also the remarks by Koenen, *Utopie der Säuberung*, 125–34.

3. Katerina Clark, *Petersburg: Crucible of Cultural Revolution* (Cambridge, Mass.: Harvard University Press, 1995), 78–87, 100–134.

4. Torsten Rüting, *Pavlov und der neue Mensch: Diskurse über Disziplinierung in Sowjetrussland* (Munich: Oldenbourg, 2002), 180.

5. Ibid., 192–93.

6. Sanborn, *Drafting the Russian Nation*, 174–80.

7. Stefan Plaggenborg, *Revolutionskultur: Menschenbilder und kulturelle Praxis in Sowjetrußland* (Cologne: Böhlau, 1996), 73–75, 86; N. Nikiforov, *Protiv starogo byta* (Moscow: Moskovskii rabochii, 1929), 86.

8. Fannina W. Halle, *Frauen des Ostens: Vom Matriarchat bis zu den Fliegerinnen von Baku* (Zürich: Europa Verlag, 1938), 142–43; Cassiday, *The Enemy on Trial*, 51–80.

9. Brooks described Stalinist reality as a play in which the rulers and the ruled simulated a nonexistent society in formulaic language. See Jeffrey Brooks, *Thank You, Comrade Stalin: Soviet Public Culture from Revolution to Cold War* (Princeton: Princeton University Press, 2000).

10. Catriona Kelly, "'Thank You for the Wonderful Book': Soviet Child Readers and the Management of Children's Reading, 1950–1975," *Kritika* 6 (2005): 717–53, esp. 724.

11. Stephan Lovell, *The Russian Reading Revolution: Print Cultures in the Soviet and the Post-Soviet Eras* (Basingstoke: Macmillan, 2000); Jane Zavisca, "The Status of Cultural Omnivorism: A Case Study of Reading in Russia," *Social Forces* 84 (2005): 1233–55, esp. 1237.

12. For the Bolshevik civilizing mission, see David L. Hoffmann, *Stalinist Values: The Cultural Norms of Soviet Modernity 1917–1941* (Ithaca: Cornell University Press, 2003), 15–56, 64–67.

13. Maurice Friedberg, "Soviet Russia's Bibliophiles and Their Foes: A Review Article," *Slavic Review* 35 (1976): 699–714, esp. 702.

14. Plaggenborg, *Revolutionskultur*, 125–30.

15. Jeffrey Brooks, "The Breakdown in Production and Distribution of Printed Material, 1917–1927," in *Bolshevik Culture: Experiment and Order in the Russian*

Revolution, ed. Abbott Gleason (Bloomington: Indiana University Press, 1985), 151–74; Plaggenborg, *Revolutionskultur,* 140.

16. Richard Stites, *Revolutionary Dreams: Utopian Vision and Experimental Life in the Russian Revolution* (New York: Oxford University Press, 1989), 111–12.

17. Figes, *The Whisperers,* 14–16; Elena Bonner, *Mothers and Daughters* (New York: Alfred A. Knopf, 1992), 42, 59, 60, 250–53.

18. For the history of Soviet festivals, see Malte Rolf, *Das sowjetische Massenfest* (Hamburg: Hamburger Edition, 2006); Rolf, "Constructing a Soviet Time: Bolshevik Festivals and Their Rivals during the First Five-Year Plan," *Kritika* 1 (2000): 447–73; Rolf, "Feste der Einheit und Schauspiele der Partizipation: Die Inszenierung von Öffentlichkeit in der Sowjetunion während des Ersten Fünfjahrplanes," *Jahrbücher für Geschichte Osteuropas* 50 (2002): 163–71.

19. Monica Rüthers, "Öffentlicher Raum und gesellschaftliche Utopie: Stadtplanung, Kommunikation und Inszenierung von Macht in der Sowjetunion am Beispiel Moskaus zwischen 1917 und 1964," in *Sphären von Öffentlichkeit in Gesellschaften sowjetischen Typs: Zwischen parteistaatlicher Inszenierung und kirchlichen Gegenwelten,* ed. Gabor Rittersporn et al. (Frankfurt am Main: Lang, 2003), 65–96.

20. Karl Schlögel, "Der zentrale Gorkij-Kultur-und Erholungspark in Moskau: Zur Frage des öffentlichen Raumes im Stalinismus," in *Stalinismus vor dem Zweiten Weltkrieg,* ed. Manfred Hildermeier (Munich: Oldenbourg, 1998), 255–74; Brooks, *Thank You, Comrade Stalin,* 83–105.

21. Brodsky, *Less Than One,* 14. On the beginnings of the *kommunalka* see Meerovich, *Nakazanie zhilishchem,* 11–24; Karl Schlögel, "Kommunalka oder Kommunismus als Lebensform: Zu einer historischen Topographie der Sowjetunion," *Historische Anthropologie* 6 (1998): 337–38.

22. Victor Buchli, *An Archaeology of Socialism* (Oxford: Berg, 1999), 77–98; Schlögel, "Kommunalka oder Kommunismus als Lebensform," 332–33; Natal'ia B. Lebina, *Povsednevnaia zhizn' sovetskogo goroda: Normy i anomalii, 1920–1930 gody* (Saint Petersburg: Zhurnal "Neva," Izdatel'sko-torgovyi dom "Letnii sad," 1999), 177–202; Svetlana Boym, *Common Places: Mythologies of Everyday Life in Russia* (Cambridge, Mass.: Harvard University Press, 1994), 121–67; Natalja B. Lebina, "Die Leningrader—Gedanken über die Bewohner einer Stadt," in *Sankt Petersburg: Schauplätze einer Stadtgeschichte,* ed. Karl Schlögel (Frankfurt am Main: Campus, 2007), 401–14, esp. 403; Julia Obertreis, *Tränen des Sozialismus: Wohnen in Leningrad zwischen Alltag und Utopie, 1917–1937* (Cologne: Böhlau, 2004); Obertreis, "Jedes Haus eine 'proletarische Festung'? Wohngenossenschaften in Leningrad zwischen Hausverwaltung, Klassenkampf und Kulturpolitik (1922–1937)," in *St. Petersburg, Leningrad, St. Petersburg: Eine Stadt im Spiegel der Zeit,* ed. Stefan Creuzberger (Stuttgart: DVA, 2000), 162–78.

23. S. Tadzhiev, "Novyi latinizirovannyi alfavit—moshchnoe orudie kulturnoi revoliutsii," in *Revoliutsiia i natsional'nosti* 2 (1930): 64–67; Andreas Frings, "Playing Moscow Off against Kazan: Azerbaijan Maneuvring to Latinization in the Soviet Union," *Ab Imperio* 4 (2009): 249–66; Baberowski, *Der Feind ist überall,* 609–24; Douglas Northrop, *Veiled Empire: Gender and Power in Stalinist Russia* (Ithaca: Cornell University Press, 2004); Ingeborg Baldauf, *Schriftreform und Schriftwechsel bei den muslimischen Rußland- und Sowjettürken (1850–1937):*

Ein Symptom ideengeschichtlicher und kulturpolitischer Entwicklungen (Budapest: Akadémiai Kiado, 1993).

24. GARF, f. 3316, op. 20, d. 201, l. 323.

25. Douglas T. Northrop, "Hujum: Unveiling Campaigns and Local Responses in Uzbekistan, 1927," in Raleigh, *Provincial Landscapes,* 125–45; Northrop, "Nationalizing Backwardness: Gender, Empire, and Uzbek Identity," in Suny and Martin, *A State of Nations,* 191–220; Northrop, *Veiled Empire;* Marianne R. Kamp, *The New Woman in Uzbekistan: Islam, Modernity, and Unveiling under Communism* (Seattle: University of Washington Press, 2006); Baberowski, *Der Feind ist überall,* 617–25, 633–62; Adrianne L. Edgar, *Tribal Nation: The Making of Soviet Turkmenistan* (Princeton: Princeton University Press, 2004).

26. Nikolai N. Pokrovskii, ed., *Politbiuro i tserkov 1922–1925* (Moscow: Rossiiskaia polit. entsiklopediia, 1997), 132. For the persecution of the church after 1922 see Natal'ia A. Krivova, *Vlast' i tserkov' v 1922–1925 gg.* (Moscow: AIRO-XX, 1997); Husband, "'Godless Communists,'" 54–59; Jonathan W. Daly, "'Storming the Last Citadel': The Bolshevik Assault on the Church, 1922," in Brovkin, *The Bolsheviks in Russian Society,* 235–60, Mikhail V. Škarovskij, "Die russische Kirche unter Stalin in den 1920er und 1930er Jahren des 20. Jahrhunderts," in Hildermeier, *Stalinismus vor dem Zweiten Weltkrieg,* 233–39.

27. Quoted in Richard Pipes, ed., *The Unknown Lenin: From the Secret Archive* (New Haven: Yale University Press, 1999), 152–53.

28. Pokrovskii, *Politbiuro i tserkov',* 140–44, 232–45; Krivova, *Vlast' i tserkov',* 53–74; Škarovskij, "Die russische Kirche," 237.

29. Tikhon's declaration of repentance is reprinted in Pokrovskii, *Politbiuro i tserkov',* 285–86. See also Škarovskij, "Die russische Kirche," 238–39. On the church schism, see Gregory L. Freeze, "Counter-Reformation in Russian Orthodoxy: Popular Response to Religious Innovation 1922–1925," in *Slavic Review* 54 (1995): 305–39; Husband, "'Godless Communists,'" 57–58; Ayslu B. Yunusova, *Islam v Bashkirii 1917–1994* (Ufa: VEGU, 1994), 41–47; Baberowski, *Der Feind ist überall,* 436–42.

30. Škarovskij, "Die russische Kirche," 233–54.

31. Michael David-Fox, "What Is Cultural Revolution?" in *Russian Review* 58 (1999): 181–201. For the attribution of collective identities see Fitzpatrick, "Ascribing Class," 745–70.

32. Gregory L. Freeze, "The Stalinist Assault on the Parish, 1929–1941," in Hildermeier, *Stalinismus vor dem Zweiten Weltkrieg,* 209–32, quote 216; Arto Luukanen, *The Religious Policy of the Stalinist State, A Case Study: The Central Standing Commission on Religious Questions, 1929–1938* (Helsinki: Suomen Historiallinen Seura, 1997), 50–53; Viola, *Peasant Rebels under Stalin,* 38–44; Lev Kopelew, *Und schuf mir einen Götzen: Lehrjahre eines Kommunisten* (Munich: Deutscher Taschenbuch Verlag, 1981), 242.

33. Alexopoulos, *Stalin's Outcasts,* 13–43.

34. Figes, *The Whisperers,* 132–36.

35. Ibid., 145; Fitzpatrick, *Everyday Stalinism,* 155–22; Jochen Hellbeck, ed., *Tagebuch aus Moskau 1931–1939* (Munich: Deutscher Taschenbuch Verlag, 1996).

36. Quote in Figes, *The Whisperers,* 139; Hellbeck, *Tagebuch aus Moskau,* 94.

37. Fitzpatrick, *Cultural Revolution in Russia*, 23–27, 32–40; Fitzpatrick, "Stalin and the Making of a New Elite," 149–82.

38. Iurii Druzhnikov, *Informer 001: The Myth of Pavlik Morozov* (New Brunswick: Transaction Publishers, 1997), vii–viii, 13–43, 97.

39. On denunciations see Jörg Baberowski, "'Die Verfasser von Erklärungen jagen den Parteiführern einen Schrecken ein': Denunziation und Terror in der stalinistischen Sowjetunion 1928–1941," in *Denunziation und Justiz: Historische Dimensionen eines sozialen Phänomens*, ed. Friso Ross and Achim Landwehr (Tübingen: Edition Diskord, 2000), 165–98; Sheila Fitzpatrick, "Signals from Below: Soviet Letters of Denunciation of the 1930s," *Journal of Modern History* 68 (1996): 831–66; Fitzpatrick, "Supplicants and Citizens: Public Letter Writing in Soviet Russia in the 1930s," *Slavic Review* 55 (1996): 78–105; Figes, *The Whisperers*, 262–63.

40. Quote in Lewis Siegelbaum and Andrei Sokolov, eds., *Stalinism as a Way of Life: A Narrative in Documents* (New Haven: Yale Univ. Press, 2000), 111.

41. Danilov et al., *Kak lomali NEP*, 1: 234–35.

42. Cassiday, *The Enemy on Trial*, 110–33; Eugene Lyons, *Assignment in Utopia* (New York: Harcourt Brace, 1937), 114–30; Peter H. Solomon, *Soviet Criminal Justice under Stalin* (Cambridge: Cambridge University Press, 1996), 82–104; Andrei Vyshinskii, *Itogi i uroki shakhtinskogo dela* (Moscow: Gosudarstvennoe izdatel'stvo politicheskoi literatury, 1928); Arkadii E. Vaksberg, *Gnadenlos: Andrei Vyshinski, Mörder im Dienste Stalins* (Bergisch-Gladbach: Lübbe, 1991), 60–64.

43. Quotes from Stalin's speeches in RGASPI, f. 558, op. 11, d. 118, ll. 77, 81–84; *Izvestiia TsK KPSS* nos. 5 (1991): 194–96, and 7 (1991): 179, 182; V. G. Kosachev, "Nakanune kollektivizatsii: Poezdka I. V. Stalina v Sibir'," *Voprosy Istorii* 5 (1998): 101–5; James R. Hughes, *Stalin, Siberia and the Crisis of the New Economic Policy* (Cambridge: Cambridge University Press, 1991).

44. Danilov et al., *Kak lomali NEP*, 1:153.

45. Viktor Danilov and Lynne Viola, eds., *Tragediia sovetskoi derevni: Kollektivizatsiia i raskulachivanie. Dokumenty i materialy v 5 tomakh*, 5 vols. (Moscow: Rossiiskaia politicheskaia entsiklopediia, 1999–2006), vol. 2: *noiabr' 1929–dekabr' 1930*, 73; Viola, *Peasant Rebels under Stalin*, 26–27. Ivnitskii, *Kollektivizatsiia i raskulachivanie*, 10–27.

46. RGASPI, f. 82, op. 2, d. 138, ll. 76–77.

47. Quoted in Schnell, *Räume des Schreckens*, 412.

48. See the GPU reports from the Kuban area, representative of many, in RGASPI, f. 85, op. 1s, d. 119, ll. 3–4, 11–14; Danilov and Viola, *Tragediia sovetskoi derevni*, vol. 3: *Konets 1930–1933*, 612–13.

49. "Vypiski informotdela OGPU iz dokladov s mest o terrore po pochve *kollektivizatsii*, oktiabr' 1929," in Berelovich and Danilov, *Sovetskaia derevnia*, 2:960–63, esp. 962. Examples of the band's activity in Danilov and Viola, *Tragediia sovetskoi derevni*, 3:164–65; Schnell, *Räume des Schreckens*, 348–57.

50. RGASPI, f. 81, op. 3, d. 210, l. 48.

51. RGASPI, f. 82, op. 2, d. 140, ll. 48–49.

52. Viola, *Peasant Rebels under Stalin*, 13–66; Baberowski, *Der Feind ist überall*, 669–85; Fitzpatrick, *Stalin's Peasants*, 48–79.

53. Viktor Danilov, ed., *Plenum TsK VKP(b) 4–12 iuliia 1928 g.*, vol. 2 of *Kak lomali NEP*, 241.

54. Viktor Danilov, ed., *Plenum TsK VKP(b) 10–17 noiabria 1929 g.*, vol. 5 of *Kak lomali NEP*, 373.

55. RGASPI, f. 82, op. 2, d. 60, ll. 139–41; Molotov quote in RGASPI, f. 82, op. 2, d. 60, ll. 129–30, 134, 139–41, 152–53; Jörg Baberowski, "Die Kollektivierung der Landwirtschaft und der Terror gegen die Kulaken," in *Europa und die Europäer: Quellen und Essays zur modernen europäischen Geschichte*, ed. Rüdiger Hohls, Iris Schröder, and Hannes Siegrist (Stuttgart: Steiner, 2005), 315–32; Baberowski, "Stalinismus von oben: Kulakendeportationen in der Sowjetunion, 1929–1934," *Jahrbücher für Geschichte Osteuropas* 46 (1998): 572–95; Getty and Naumov, *Road to Terror*, 193.

56. Aleksandr Shapovalov, *Put' molodogo rabochego* (Moscow: Izd. Molodaia gvardiia, 1923), 66; Kopelew, *Und schuf mir einen Götzen*, 289–337, esp. 294, 306; Vasilii S. Grossman, *Alles fließt . . .* (Munich: Knaus, 1985), 135; Yuri Orlov, *Dangerous Thoughts: Memoirs of a Russian Life* (New York: William Morrow, 1991), 23–24; Maxim Gorky, *Childhood* (Chicago: Ivan R. Dee, 2010), 184.

57. RGASPI, f. 85, op. 1a, d. 123, l. 11; Norman N. Naimark, *Stalin's Genocides* (Princeton: Princeton University Press, 2010), 57. See also Schnell, *Räume des Schreckens*, 382–89.

58. RGASPI, f. 82, op. 2, d. 138, l. 87.

59. RGASPI, f. 85, op. 1s, d. 118, ll. 49, 58; RGASPI, f. 17, op. 114, d. 265, l. 232.

60. Lyudmila S. Gatagova and Lyudmila P. Kosheleva, eds., *TsK RKP(b)-VKP(b) i natsional'nyi vopros*, vol. 1 (Moscow: ROSSPEN, 2005), 673.

61. *Obshchestvo i vlast'. 1930-e gody: Povestvovanie v dokumentakh* (Moscow: ROSSPEN, 1998), 25.

62. RGASPI, f. 558, op. 11, d. 827, ll. 1–22.

63. RGASPI, f. 85, op. 1s, d. 118, ll. 49, 58; RGASPI, f. 17, op. 114, d. 265; Kopelew, *Und schuf mir einen Götzen*, 289–337, esp. 294, 306; Fitzpatrick, *Stalin's Peasants*, 50–53; Merle Fainsod, *Smolensk under Soviet Rule* (Cambridge, Mass.: Harvard University Press, 1958), 247–48; on the displacement of moral coordinates in the state of emergency see Harald Welzer, *Täter: Wie aus ganz normalen Menschen Massenmörder werden* (Frankfurt am Main: Fischer, 2005), 257–168.

64. Khlevniuk, *Stalin i Kaganovich*, 285–86.

65. See Nicolas Werth, "Ein Staat gegen sein Volk: Gewalt, Unterdrückung und Terror in der Sowjetunion," in Courtois, *Das Schwarzbuch des Kommunismus*, 181; Il'ia E. Zelenin, "Zakon o pyati koloskakh: Razrabotka i osushchestvlenie," *Voprosy Istorii* 1 (1998): 114–23; Elena Osokina, *Za fasadom "stalinskogo izobiliia": Raspredelenie in rynok v snabzhenii naseleniia v gody industrializatsii 1927–1941* (Moscow: ROSSPEN, 2008), 161; Viola, *Peasant Rebels under Stalin*, 56–57; Fitzpatrick, *Stalin's Peasants*, 70–75; Solomon, *Soviet Criminal Justice under Stalin*, 126; Gabor T. Rittersporn, "Das kollektivierte Dorf in der bäuerlichen Gegenkultur," in Hildermeier, *Stalinismus vor dem Zweiten Weltkrieg*, 151.

66. Molotov: RGASPI, f. 82, op. 11, d. 141, l. 7; Kaganovich: RGASPI, f. 81, op. 3, d. 214, ll. 4, 12. Stalin's order to deport peasants from the Kuban is printed in Danilov and Viola, *Tragediia sovetskoi derevni*, 3:549.

67. RGASPI, f. 558, op. 11, d. 45, l. 82.

68. RGASPI, f. 558, op. 11, d. 45, l. 65.

69. RGASPI, f. 558, op. 11, d. 45, l. 45.

70. RGASPI, f. 81, op. 3, d. 215, ll. 1–3, 23–24. A similar case had already occurred a few months earlier, when Molotov was in Ukraine. See RGASPI, f. 82, op. 2, d. 138, ll. 93–96.

71. Nicolas Werth and Gaël Moullec, eds., *Rapports secrets soviétiques 1921–1991: La société russe dans les documents confidentiels* (Paris: Gallimard, 1994), 112–62; Ivnitskii, *Kollektivizatsiia i raskulachivanie*, 120; Kopelew, *Und schuf mir einen Götzen,* 320; Viktor Kondrashin, *Golod 1932–1933 godov: Tragediia rossiiskoi derevni* (Moscow: Rossiiskaia polit. entsiklopediia, 2008). For the debate on the causes of the famine, see Robert Conquest, *Ernte des Todes: Stalins Holocaust in der Ukraine 1929–1933* (Munich: Langen-Müller, 1988); Stefan Merl, "Wie viele Opfer forderte die 'Liquidierung der Kulaken als Klasse'? Zu einem Buch von Robert Conquest," *Geschichte und Gesellschaft* 14 (1988): 534–40; N. Osokina, "Zhertvy goloda 1933: Skol'ko ikh?" *Otechestvennaia istoriia* 5 (1995): 18–26; Werth, "Ein Staat gegen sein Volk," 182–88; Martha B. Olcott, "The Collectivization Drive in Kazakhstan," *Russian Review* 40 (1981): 122–42, 136; Fitzpatrick, *Stalin's Peasants,* 75.

72. RGASPI, f. 82, op. 2, d. 148, ll. 192–93; Robert Kindler, "Die Starken und die Schwachen: Zur Bedeutung physischer Gewalt während der Hungersnot in Kasachstan (1930–34)," *Jahrbücher für Geschichte Osteuropas* 59 (2011): 51–78.

73. Quoted in Kondrashin, *Golod 1932–1933 godov,* 180.

74. Ivnitskii, *Kollektivizatsiia i raskulachivanie,* 203; Danilov and Viola, *Tragediia sovetskoi derevni,* 3:639.

75. RGASPI, f. 82, op. 2, d. 687, ll. 96–98; RGASPI, f. 82, op. 2, d. 670, ll. 11–14; RGASPI, f. 82, op. 2, d. 148, ll. 192–93.

76. Kondrashin, *Golod 1932–1933 godov,* 250.

77. Talbott, *Khrushchev Remembers,* 1:235.

78. RGASPI, f. 558, op. 11, d. 741, l. 3; Danilov and Viola, *Tragediia sovetskoi derevni,* 3:644–45.

79. GARF, f. 3316, op. 25, d. 938, l. 22; David Shearer, *Policing Stalin's Socialism: Repression and Social Order in the Soviet Union, 1924–1953* (New Haven: Yale University Press, 2009), 243–84; Ivnitskii, *Kollektivizatsiia i raskulachivanie,* 204; Viola, *Peasant Rebels under Stalin,* 45–66; Fitzpatrick, *Stalin's Peasants,* 92–95; Baberowski, "Stalinismus von oben," 584–85; Davies, *Popular Opinion in Stalin's Russia,* 177.

80. Nicolas Werth, *Die Insel der Kannibalen: Stalins vergessener Gulag* (Munich: Siedler, 2006), 30–38, 171–79; quote in N. Vert, S. V. Mironenko, and I. A. Ziuzina, ed., *Istoriia stalinskogo Gulaga,* vol. 1: *Massovye repressii v SSSR: Konets 1920-kh–pervaia polovina 1950-kh godov* (Moscow: ROSSPEN, 2004), 155.

81. The government's order on July 11, 1929 to send prisoners to work camps is reproduced in N. V. Petrov, N. I. Vladimirtsev, and Iu. N. Afanasev, eds., *Istoriia stalinskogo Gulaga,* vol. 2: *Karatel'naia sistema: Struktura i kadry* (Moscow: ROSSPEN, 2004), 58–59; Oleg V. Khlevniuk, "The Economy of the OGPU, NKVD, and MVD of the USSR, 1930–1953: The Scale, Structure, and Trends of

Development," in *The Economics of Forced Labor: The Soviet Gulag,* ed. Paul Gregory and Valery Lazarev (Stanford: Hoover Institution Press, 2003), 43–66; Anne Applebaum, *Der Gulag* (Berlin: Siedler, 2003), 94, 104–5; Christopher Joyce, "The Gulag in Karelia 1929 to 1941," in Gregory and Lazarev, *The Economics of Forced Labor,* 167; Cynthia A. Ruder, *Making History for Stalin: The Story of the Belomor-Canal* (Gainesville: University Press of Florida, 1998), 61–63.

82. Quoted in Applebaum, *Der Gulag,* 61.

83. Wolfgang Sofsky, *The Order of Terror: The Concentration Camp* (Princeton: Princeton University Press, 1999), 23.

84. Jan-Philipp Reemtsma, *Vertrauen und Gewalt: Versuch über eine besondere Konstellation der Moderne* (Hamburg: Hamburger Edition, 2008), 180.

85. Arvo Tuominen, *Stalins Schatten über Finnland: Erinnerungen eines ehemaligen Führers der finnischen Kommunisten* (Freiburg: Herder, 1986), 55–57.

86. The Politburo's order of February 2, 1930, is reproduced in V. P. Danilov and S. A. Krasil'nikov, eds., *Istoriia stalinskogo Gulaga,* vol. 5: *Spetspereselentsy v SSSR* (Moscow: ROSSPEN, 2004), 97–100.

87. Nikolai Teptsov, *V dni velikogo pereloma: Istoriia kollektivizatsii, raskulachivaniia i krest'ianskoi ssylki v Rossii (SSSR) po pis'mam i vospominaniiam 1929–1933 gody* (Moscow: Zvonnica, 2002), 162–64; Lynn Viola, "The Other Archipelago: Kulak Deportations to the North in 1930," *Slavic Review* 60, no. 4 (2001): 730–55, quotes 744–45. See also Viola, *The Unknown Gulag.*

88. Quote in J. V. Stalin, *Works,* vol. 13 (Moscow: Foreign Languages Publishing House, 1954), 40–41; Beyrau, *Petrograd, 25. October 1917,* 136–39.

89. Robert W. Davies, "Industry," in Davies and Harrison, *The Economic Transformation of the Soviet Union,* 136–38; Stephen Kotkin, *Magnetic Mountain: Stalinism as a Civilization* (Berkeley: University of California Press, 1995); Klaus Gestwa, *Die Stalinschen Großbauten des Kommunismus: Sowjetische Technik- und Umweltgeschichte, 1948–1967* (Munich: Oldenbourg, 2010), 48–68.

90. Stalin, *Works,* 13:40. For the mentality of Stalinist engineers, see Susanne Schattenberg, *Stalins Ingenieure: Lebenswelten zwischen Technik und Terror in den 1930er Jahren* (Munich: Oldenbourg, 2002), 209–52.

91. Quoted in Paul Gregory and Andrei Markevich, "Creating Soviet Industry: The House That Stalin built," *Slavic Review* 61 (2002): 798–99.

92. Khlevniuk, *Stalin i Kaganovich,* 109–10.

93. Lih, *Stalin: Briefe an Molotov,* 217–18, 228. In November 1929 Stalin had proposed granting the GPU the right to have arsonists setting fire to factories shot. See RGASPI, f. 558, op. 11, d. 27, l. 27.

94. Schattenberg, *Stalins Ingenieure,* 209, 223; Fitzpatrick, "Stalin and the Making of a New Elite"; Kotkin, *Magnetic Mountain,* 73.

95. Kotkin, *Magnetic Mountain,* 73–93, quote 92. See also the memoirs of the American worker John Scott, who worked in Magnitogorsk in the 1930s: John Scott, *Behind the Urals: An American Worker in Russia's City of Steel* (1942; repr., Bloomington: Indiana University Press, 1989).

96. Quoted in Osokina, *Za fasadom "stalinskogo izobilia,"* 165. For the trend in wages, see John D. Barber and Robert W. Davies, "Employment and Industrial

Labour," in Davies and Harrison, *The Economic Transformation of the Soviet Union* 81–105, esp. 103.

97. Hellbeck, *Tagebuch aus Moskau,* 127–28.

98. David L. Hoffman, *Peasant Metropolis: Social Identities in Moscow, 1929–1941* (Ithaca: Cornell University Press, 1994), 158–89; Tanja Penter, *Kohle für Stalin und Hitler: Arbeiten und Leben im Donbass 1929 bis 1953* (Essen: Klartext, 2010), 44–45.

99. Hellbeck, *Tagebuch aus Moskau,* 118–19, 259, 262–63.

100. Kuromiya, *Freedom and Terror in the Donbass,* 151–200; Penter, *Kohle für Stalin und Hitler,* 44–45; Hoffman, *Peasant Metropolis,* 158–89; Stephen Kotkin, "Coercion and Identity: Workers' Lives in Stalin's Showcase City," in *Making Workers Soviet: Power, Class, and Identity,* ed. L. H. Siegelbaum and Ronald G. Suny (Ithaca: Cornell University Press, 1994), 274–10; Kotkin, *Magnetic Mountain,* 280–354; David Shearer, "Factories within Factories: Changes in the Structure of Work and Management in Soviet Machine-Buildung Factories, 1926–1934," in *Social Dimensions of Soviet Industrialization,* ed. William G. Rosenberg and Lewis H. Siegelbaum (Bloomington: Indiana University Press, 1993), 193–222; Shearer, *Industry, State and Society in Stalin's Russia,* 76–79; Scott, *Behind the Urals,* 137–72.

101. RGASPI, f. 81, op. 3, d. 213, ll. 93–95.

102. RGASPI, f. 82, op. 2, d. 884, ll. 163–85; Galina M. Ivanova, *Der Gulag im totalitären System der Sowjetunion* (Berlin: Schletzer, 2001), 63–67.

103. RGASPI, f. 558, op. 11, d. 730, l. 22.

104. Gustav Herling, *A World Apart* (London: Heinemann, 1951), 235. See also Lev Razgon's memoirs: Lev Razgon, *Nichts als die reine Wahrheit: Erinnerungen* (Berlin: Volk und Welt, 1992), 289.

CHAPTER FIVE. DICTATORSHIP OF DREAD

1. Nina Lugovskaya, *I Want to Live: The Diary of a Young Girl in Stalin's Russia* (New York: Houghton Mifflin, 2006), 20.

2. See on this issue the remarks by Heinrich Popitz, "Realitätsverlust in Gruppen," in Popitz et al., *Soziale Normen,* 175–86. On the Stalin cult see James L. Heizer, *The Cult of Stalin, 1929–1939* (Ph.D. diss., University of Kentucky, 1977); Plamper, *Alkhimiia vlasti,* 55–135; Gerd Koenen, *Die großen Gesänge: Lenin, Stalin, Mao Tse-Tung. Führerkulte und Heldenmythen des 20. Jahrhunderts* (Frankfurt am Main: Eichborn, 1992); Reinhard Löhmann, *Der Stalin-Mythos: Studien zur Sozialgeschichte des Personenkultes in der Sowjetunion, 1929–1935* (Münster: Lit, 1990); Ennker, "Politische Herrschaft und Stalinkult," 151–82; Davies, *Popular Opinion in Stalin's Russia,* 147–82; For the ideology of gift giving and on Socialist Realism, see Brooks, *Thank You, Comrade Stalin,* 54–82; Thomas Lahusen, *How Life Writes the Book: Real Socialism and Socialist Realism in Stalin's Russia* (Ithaca: Cornell University Press, 1997); Hans Günther, ed., *The Culture of the Stalin Period* (New York: St. Martin's Press, 1990).

3. Quote in Figes, *The Whisperers,* 242; see also Alexopoulos, *Stalin's Outcasts,* 1–11, 13–44, 97–128; and the diaries of L. A. Potemkin and S. F. Podlubnyi,

in *Das wahre Leben: Tagebücher aus der Stalin-Zeit,* ed. Véronique Garros, Natalia Korenevskaia, and Thomas Lahusen (Berlin: Rowohlt, 1998), 259–312.

4. Quoted in Figes, *The Whisperers,* 255.

5. Quoted ibid., 251.

6. Heinrich Popitz, *Phänomene der Macht,* 2d ed. (Tübingen: Mohr, 1992), 223; Reemtsma, *Vertrauen und Gewalt,* 158–62; Moore, *Zur Geschichte der politischen Gewalt,* 35.

7. Arendt, *The Origins of Totalitarianism,* 440; Friedrich, *Totalitäre Diktatur*; Robert Conquest, *Der Große Terror: Sowjetunion 1934–1938* (Munich: Langen-Müller, 1992); Robert C. Tucker, *Stalin in Power: The Revolution from Above 1928–1941* (New York: Norton, 1990), 44–65; Getty, *Origins of the Great Purges,* 1–37.

8. Gregory, *Terror by Quota,* 271.

9. Felix Chuev, *Sto sorok besed s Molotovym* (Moscow: Terra, 1991), 392; see also Oleg Khlevniuk, "The Objectives of the Great Terror, 1937–1938," in *Soviet History 1917–1953: Essays in Honour of R. W. Davies* (London: Macmillan, 1995), 165; Kuromiya, *Freedom and Terror in the Donbass,* 204–5; Paul Hagenloh, "'Socially Harmful Elements' and the Great Terror," in Fitzpatrick, *Stalinism: New Directions,* 286–308; Shearer, *Policing Stalin's Socialism,* 299–303; Shearer, "Crime and Social Disorder in Stalin's Russia: A Reassessment of the Great Retreat and the Origins of Mass Repression," *Cahiers du monde russe* 39 (1998): 119–48; Hiroaki Kuromiya, *Stalin's Great Terror and Espionage* (Seattle: National Council for Eurasian and East European Research, 2009), 1–20; Koenen, *Utopie der Säuberung,* 215–70. In the orders to inflict terror, as Rolf Binner and Marc Junge point out, there was no mention of any connection between the liquidation of the kulaks and threats posed by foreign countries. See Rolf Binner and Marc Junge, "'S etoi publikoi tseremonit'sia ne sleduet': Die Zielgruppen des Befehls Nr. 00447 und der Große Terror aus der Sicht des Befehls Nr. 00447," *Cahiers du Monde Russe* 43 (2002): 181–228, esp. 227.

10. As pointed out by Norman Naimark. See Naimark, *Stalin's Genocides,* 136–37.

11. See Hiroaki Kuromiya, "Anti-Russian and Anti-Soviet Subversion: The Caucasian-Japanese Nexus, 1904–1905," *Europe-Asia Studies* 61 (2009): 1415–40; quote from Sigmund Freud, *Why War? The Correspondence between Albert Einstein and Sigmund Freud* (Chicago: Chicago Institute for Psychoanalysis, 1933), 210. For the psychogenesis of mass murderers, see Rolf Pohl, "Normalität und Pathologie: Sozialpsychologische Anmerkungen zur Psychogenese von Massenmördern," in *Massenhaftes Töten: Krieg und Genozide im 20. Jahrhundert,* ed. Peter Gleichmann and Thomas Kühne (Essen: Klartext, 2004), 158–79, esp. 161–63.

12. Wolfgang Sofsky, *Order of Terror: The Concentration Camp* (Princeton: Princeton University Press, 2001), 21; Erving Goffman, *Interaktionsrituale: Über Verhalten in direkter Kommunikation* (Frankfurt am Main: Suhrkamp, 1986), 9; Baberowski, "Gewalt verstehen," 5–17; Reemtsma, *Vertrauen und Gewalt,* 179–80.

13. Reemtsma, *Vertrauen und Gewalt,* 179–80; Gerd Spittler, "Administrative Despotism in Peasant Societies," in *The Foundations of Bureaucracy in Economic*

and Social Thought, ed. Bill Jenkins and Edward C. Page, vol. 1 (Northhampton: Elgar, 2004), 339–50.

14. Georgy Arbatov, *The System: An Insider's Life in Soviet Politics* (New York: Three Rivers Press, 1992), 41.

15. Heinrich Popitz, "Über die Präventivwirkung des Nichtwissens," in Popitz et al., *Soziale Normen,* 158–74, esp. 171.

16. On Tomsky: Anna Larina, *This I Cannot Forget: The Memoirs of Anna Larina, Nikolai Bukharin's Wife* (London: Pandora, 1993), 107; Lorenz Erren, *"Selbstkritik" und Schuldbekenntnis: Kommunikation und Herrschaft unter Stalin, 1917–1953* (Munich: Oldenbourg, 2008), 33–92, esp. 61.

17. Quotes in Figes, *The Whisperers,* 34.

18. Lih, *Stalin: Briefe an Molotov,* 217.

19. On how Stalin expressed his suspicion, see Khlevniuk, *Master of the House,* 17–18.

20. RGASPI, f. 17, op. 17, d. 40, l. 190.

21. Oleg Khlevniuk, "Stalin, Syrtsov, Lominadze: Preparations for the 'Second Great Breakthrough,'" in Gregory and Naimark, *The Lost Politburo Transcripts,* 78–96; Khlevniuk, *Master of the House,* 19–29, quote 19.

22. Larina, *This I Cannot Forget,* 127; Service, *Stalin,* 285.

23. RGASPI, f. 82, op. 2, d. 903, ll. 10–26. Quotes ll. 11, 13, 15, 20, 22.

24. The Ryutin program is reproduced in I. V. Kurilova, M. N. Mikhailov, and V. P. Naumov, eds., *Reabilitatsiia: Politicheskie protsessy 30–50-kh godov* (Moscow: Politizdat, 1991), 334–443; Khlevniuk, *Master of the House,* 57–68. On Ryutin's character, see Martem'ian Riutin, *Na koleni ne vstanu,* ed. Boris A. Starkov (Moscow: Gosudarstvennoe izdatel'stvo politicheskoi literatury, 1992). See also V. A. Kozlov, *Neizvestnaia Rossiia,* vol. 1 (Moscow: Istoricheskoe nasledie, 1992), 56–128; Tucker, *Stalin in Power,* 212. For Nadezhda Alliluyeva's suicide, see Montefiore, *Stalin,* 1–18, 88–90.

25. "Ob"edinennoe zasedanie politbiuro TsK i prezidiuma TsKK VKP(b) po voprosu o gruppe Smirnova A. P., Eismonta i dr.," RGASPI, f. 17, op. 163, d. 1011, ll. 84, 91. On November 18, 1932, the GPU interrogated one Ogarev, who admitted having encountered Stalin on the Kremlin grounds on October 18. He was recorded as having intended to use his revolver to kill him but been unable to do so because Stalin was accompanied by eight bodyguards. The record of interrogation is reproduced in Khaustov et al., *Lubianka* (2003), 286.

26. RGASPI, f. 17, op. 2, d. 514, ll. 41–44. See also Kondrashin, *Golod 1932–1933 godov,* 255.

27. Getty and Naumov, *The Road to Terror,* 76–77.

28. Quote in "Ob"edinennoe zasedanie politbiuro TsK i prezidiuma TsKK VKP(b) po voprosu o gruppe Smirnova A. P., Eismonta i dr.," RGASPI, f. 17, op. 163, d. 1011, l. 35; RGASPI, f. 82, op. 2, d. 903, ll. 10–26. For the debate in the Politburo and the Central Committee, see Wynn, "The 'Right Opposition' and the 'Smirnov-Tolmachev Affair'"; Getty and Naumov, *The Road to Terror,* 76–77. On Kalinin: Larina, *This I Cannot Forget,* 332.

29. Hiroaki Kuromiya, "Stalin in the Light of the Politburo Transcripts," in Gregory and Naimark, *The Lost Politburo Transcripts,* 41–56, esp. 53; Roy F. Baumeister, *Evil: Inside Human Cruelty and Violence* (New York: W. H. Freeman, 1997), 194–96.

30. Quoted in Oleg F. Suvenirov, *Tragediia RKKA 1937–1938* (Moscow: Terra, 1998), 31.

31. Getty and Naumov, *The Road to Terror*, 34–73; Getty, "Samokritika Rituals in the Stalinist Central Comitee.".

32. The testimony on the crime by the NKVD bodyguards, interrogated as early as December 1, 1934, was consistent. See RGASPI, f. 671, op. 1, d. 113, ll. 1–2, 8, 10–13, 43–47, 59–62. The perpetrator said much the same when interrogated on December 3. See Matthew E. Lenoe, *The Kirov Murder and Soviet History* (New Haven: Yale University Press 2010), 157; Iu. N. Zhukov, "Sledstvie i sudebnye protsessy po delu ob ubiistve Kirova," *Voprosy istorii* 2 (2000): 33–51.

33. Alla Kirilina, *Neizvestnyi Kirov* (Saint Petersburg: OLMA-PRESS, 2001), 198–200, 215–16, 236–56; Lenoe, *The Kirov Murder and Soviet History*, 173–75, 182–94, 220–21.

34. Feliks Chuev, ed., *Molotov: Poluderzhavnyi vlastelin* (Moscow: OLMA-PRESS, 1999), 376.

35. Quoted in Kirilina, *Neizvestnyi Kirov*, 232.

36. In Razgon's version, nobody was in the room except Stalin and Nikolaev, but this version was based on rumors. See Razgon, *Nichts als die reine Wahrheit*, 216. According to Kirilina's version, based on archival materials and interviews, Stalin interrogated Nikolaev in the presence of several Politburo members. Kirilina, *Neizvestnyi Kirov*, 264; see also Lenoe, *The Kirov Murder and Soviet History*, 265.

37. J. Arch Getty and Oleg Naumov, *Yezhov: The Rise of Stalin's "Iron Fist"* (New Haven: Yale University Press, 2008), 115–34; Lenoe, *The Kirov Murder and Soviet History*, 253.

38. Khaustov et al., *Lubianka* (2003), 579, 613–16; Getty and Naumov, *Yezhov*, 143; Lenoe, *The Kirov Murder and Soviet History*, 370–71.

39. Shatunovskaya's letter is published in Vladimir Iu. Afiani, ed., *Doklad N. S. Khrushcheva o kul'te lichnosti Stalina na XX s"ezde KPSS: Dokumenty* (Moscow: ROSSPEN, 2002), 170–71. On the political exploitation of the attack see Lenoe, *The Kirov Murder and Soviet History*, 170–48, 389–452.

40. Eugene Huskey, "Vyshinskii, Krylenko, and the Shaping of the Soviet Legal Order," *Slavic Review* 46 (1987): 414–28; Robert W. Thurston, *Life and Terror in Stalin's Russia, 1934–1941* (New Haven: Yale University Press, 1996), 5–9, 10–13; Solomon, *Soviet Criminal Justice under Stalin*, 153–95; Khlevniuk, *Master of the House*, 108–26. On Vyshinsky's character, see Vaksberg, *Gnadenlos;* and the memoirs of the American ambassador in Moscow, Walter B. Smith, *Meine drei Jahre in Moskau* (Hamburg: Hoffmann & Campe, 1950), 15, 53.

41. Arkadii Vaksberg, *The Prosecutor and the Prey: Vyshinsky and the 1930s Moscow Show Trials* (London: Weidenfeld and Nicolson, 1990).

42. Solomon, *Soviet Criminal Justice under Stalin*, 230–66; Getty, *Origins of the Great Purges*, 265; Lesley A. Rimmel, "A Microcosm of Terror, or Class Warfare in Leningrad: The March 1935 Exile of 'Alien Elements,'" *Jahrbücher für Geschichte Osteuropas* 48 (2000): 528–51.

43. RGASPI, f. 671, op. 1, d. 121, ll. 105–17, source for all quotes.

44. Pierre Broué, *Trotskii* (Paris: Fayard, 1988), 703–9.

45. All quotes are from the interrogation records in *Lubianka: Stalin i Glavnoe upravlenie gosbezopasnosti NKVD, 1937–1938,* ed. V. N. Khaustov, V. P. Naumov,

and N. S. Plotnikova (Moscow: Mezhdunarodnyi fond "Demokratiia," 2004), 599–612, 629, 648–50.

46. Ibid., 663–69.

47. On the debates at the Central Committee plenum see also Getty and Naumov, *The Road to Terror,* 161–77.

48. Stalin's letters to Enukidze from 1930 and 1933 and quotes in RGASPI, f. 558, op. 11, d. 728, ll. 29, 40.

49. Quotes in Khaustov et al., *Lubianka* (2004), 658–60; see also Anna Larina, *Nezabyvaemoe* (Moscow: Vagrius, 2002), 147–48. In his memoirs, Razgon claims that Enukidze was a confidant of Stalin's sexual debaucheries and therefore had to step down. See Razgon, *Nichts als die reine Wahrheit,* 22–23; on Enukidze's transfer to the provinces, see Stalin's letters to Kaganovich from September 7 and 8, 1935, in Khlevniuk, *Stalin i Kaganovich,* 557–58, 560, 580, 583.

50. Khaustov et al., *Lubianka* (2003), 686–87, 689–90, 714–16.

51. Volkskommissariat für Justizwesen der UdSSR, *Prozessbericht über die Strafsache des sowjetfeindlichen Trotzkistischen Zentrums* (Moscow: Volkskommissariat fur Justizwesen der UdSSR, 1937), 522–25, 558–63. See also Theo Pirker, ed., *Die Moskauer Schauprozesse 1936–1938* (Munich: Deutscher Taschenbuch-Verlag, 1963), 169, 175.

52. Volkskommissariat für Justizwesen der UdSSR, *Prozessbericht über die Strafsache des antisowjetischen "Blocks der Rechten und Trotzkisten"* (Moscow: Volkskommissariat fur Justizwesen der UdSSR, 1938), 750–54; Pirker, *Die Moskauer Schauprozesse,* 225.

53. Larina, *This I Cannot Forget,* 172–73.

54. Khlevniuk, *Stalin i Kaganovich,* 630–42.

55. RGASPI, f. 558, op. 11, d. 93, l. 34. On the confrontations in Stalin's office, see Getty and Naumov, *The Road to Terror,* 370–72. The letters Stalin wrote on vacation to Kaganovich show how he was directing this "play": Khlevniuk, *Stalin i Kaganovich,* 630–42, quotes 631, 634, 635, 641, 642; Larina, *This I Cannot Forget,* 287.

56. Lion Feuchtwanger, *Moskau 1937: Ein Reisebericht für meine Freunde,* 2d ed. (Berlin: Aufbau-Taschenbuch-Verlag, 1993), 87, 93; Georgi Dimitrov, *The Diary of Georgi Dimitrov, 1933–1943* ed. Ivo Banac, vol. 1 (New Haven: Yale University Press, 2003), 140.

57. Larina, *This I Cannot Forget,* 83; Gregory, *Terror by Quota,* 160; Figes, *The Whisperers,* 248; Roy Medvedev, *Let History Judge: The Origins and Consequences of Stalinism* (New York: Columbia University Press, 1990), 348–83; Conquest, *Der Große Terror,* 396–400.

58. RGASPI, f. 558, op. 11, d. 710, ll. 164–65.

59. Larina, *This I Cannot Forget,* 299; Getty and Naumov, *The Road to Terror,* 310.

60. Larina, *This I Cannot Forget,* 312.

61. RGASPI, f. 558, op. 11, d. 710, ll. 180–81.

62. Quotes in "Materialy fevral'sko-martovskogo plenuma TsK VKP(b) 1937 goda, 26 fevralia 1937 g.: Utrennee zasedanie," *Voprosy istorii,* no. 2 (1992): 13, 17, 18, 20, 26, 27; no. 1 (1994): 12–13; Getty and Naumov, *The Road to Terror,* 412–15; Larina, *This I Cannot Forget,* 339–40.

63. Figes, *The Whisperers*, 230–33, 310–12; Boris Starkov, "Avangardnye boi staroi partinoi gvardii," in *Oni ne molchali*, ed. A. V. Afanas'ev (Moscow: Politizdat, 1991), 215–25.

64. The letter was published in *Istochnik* o (1993): 23–25. See also Getty and Naumov, *The Road to Terror*, 556–60.

65. A. N. Sakharov, et al., eds., *"Sovershenno sekretno": Lubianka. Stalinu o polozhenii v strane, 1922–1934 gg.* (Moscow: Institut rossiiskoi istorii RAN, 2008); Paul Gregory, *Politics, Murder, and Love in Stalin's Kremlin: The Story of Nikolai Bukharin and Anna Larina* (Stanford: Hoover Institution Press, 2010), 142–43; Chuev, *Molotov Remembers*, 263.

66. RGASPI, f. 558, op. 11, d. 710, ll. 135–36. Anna Larina, Bukharin's second wife, later claimed that Lukina had turned in her party card and told Stalin she no longer wished to remain in the party when she had learned of the charges against Bukharin. She did not remember her role as informant. See Larina, *This I Cannot Forget*, 140.

67. RGASPI, f. 558, op. 11, d. 779, l. 106.

68. RGASPI, f. 558, op. 11, d. 93, ll. 61, 76.

69. Georgii A. Kumanev, *Riadom so Stalinym: Otkrovennye svidetel'stva. Vstrechi, besedy, interv'iu, dokumenty* (Moscow: Bylina, 1999), 79; Georgii A. Kumanev, *Govoriat stalinskie narkomy: 60-letiiu Velikoi Pobedy posviashchaetsia* (Smolensk: Rusich, 2005), 104.

70. Chuev, *Molotov Remembers*, 264.

71. Khlevniuk, *Stalin i Kaganovich*, 613–14; Khaustov et al., *Lubianka* (2003), 688–89.

72. Rigby, *Communist Party Membership*, 52; Getty, *Origins of the Great Purges*, 22, 38–48; Gill, *Origins of the Stalinist Political System*, 201–18.

73. RGASPI, f. 17, op. 120, d. 179, ll. 110, 313.

74. Examples and quotes in Fainsod, *Smolensk under Soviet Rule*, 212–16; Baberowski, *Der Feind ist überall*, 786–87; Getty, *Origins of the Great Purges*, 31–34.

75. RGASPI, f. 17, op. 120, d. 179, ll. 110, 313; Getty, *Origins of the Great Purges*, 85–87.

76. RGASPI, f. 17, op. 2, d. 561, ll. 129, 162; Getty, *Origins of the Great Purges*, 87–90.

77. See the investigations by the purge commissions in Smolensk: RGASPI, f. 81, op. 3, d. 227, ll. 91, 159–61.

78. Gill, *Origins of the Stalinist Political System*, 6; Easter, *Reconstructing the State*, 11–17; Sheila Fitzpatrick, "Intelligentsia and Power: Client-Patron Relations in Stalin's Russia," in Hildermeier, *Stalinismus vor dem Zweiten Weltkrieg*, 35–54; James Harris, "The Purging of Local Cliques in the Urals Region, 1936–1937," in Fitzpatrick, *Stalinism: New Directions*, 262–85; Gerd Spittler, "Volkszählung und bürokratische Herrschaft in Bauernstaaten," in *Bauerngesellschaften im Industriezeitalter*, ed. Christian Giordano and Robert Hettlage (Berlin: Reimer, 1989), 97–110.

79. RGASPI, f. 81, op. 3, d. 227, ll. 163–64; RGASPI, f. 81, op. 3, d. 228, ll. 84–87.

80. RGASPI, f. 81, op. 3, d. 227, l. 160.

81. RGASPI, f. 81, op. 3, d. 230, ll. 4–6.

82. RGASPI, f. 81, op. 3, d. 227, l. 163; quote in Khaustov et al., *Lubianka* (2004), 92; James Harris, "Resisting the Plan in the Urals, 1928–1956, or, Why Regional Officials Needed 'Wreckers' and 'Saboteurs,'" in *Contending with Stalinism: Soviet Power and Popular Resistance in the 1930s,* ed. Lynne Viola (Ithaca: Cornell University Press, 2002), 201–28, esp. 203–8; Kotkin, *Magnetic Mountain,* 298–332; Sergei A. Papkov, *Stalinskii terror v Sibiri, 1928–1941* (Novosibirsk: Izdat. Sibirskogo Otd. Rossiiskoi Akad. Nauk, 1997), 184–85.

83. James Harris, "Dual Subordination? The Political Police and the Party in the Urals Region 1918–1953," *Cahiers du monde russe* 42 (2001): 2–4, 423–45.

84. RGASPI, f. 81, op. 3, d. 228, ll. 67, 74. See also Fainsod, *Smolensk under Soviet Rule,* 60.

85. "Materialy fevral'sko-martovskogo plenuma TsK VKP(b) 1937 goda," *Voprosy Istorii,* no. 11/12 (1995): 10–13; Mikhail Shreider, *NKVD iznutri: Zapiski Chekista* (Moscow: Vozvrashchenie, 1995), 110.

86. "Materialy fevral'sko-martovskogo plenuma," *Voprosy Istorii,* no. 2 (1995): 17; Khlevniuk, *Das Politbüro,* 201–2; Thurston, *Life and Terror in Stalin's Russia,* 34; Getty, *Origins of the Great Purges,* 121–22.

87. RGASPI, f. 558, op. 11, d. 94, ll. 123, 131; Khlevniuk, *Stalin i Kaganovich,* 683; Khlevniuk et al., *Stalinskoe politbiuro v 30-e gody,* 149–50; Jansen and Petrov, *Stalin's Loyal Executioner,* 53–54.

88. Jansen and Petrov, *Stalin's Loyal Executioner,* 56; Papkov, *Stalinskii terror,* 184–186; Harris, "Resisting the Plan in the Urals," 207–8. Quotes in Khaustov et al., *Lubianka,* 767; and Larina, *This I Cannot Forget,* 300.

89. Gregory, *Terror by Quota,* 220.

90. Wendy Goldman and Arch Getty defend this interpretation, although they differ in nuances. See Wendy Goldman, "Stalinist Terror and Democracy: The 1937 Union Campaign," *American Historical Review* 110 (2005): 1427–53; Goldman, *Terror and Democracy in the Age of Stalin: The Social Dynamics of Repression* (Cambridge: Cambridge University Press, 2007), 95–130; J. Arch Getty, "'Excesses Are Not Permitted': Mass Terror and Stalinist Governance in the Late 1930s," *Russian Review* 61 (2002), 113–38. Quotes in "Materialy fevral'sko-martovskogo plenuma," *Voprosy Istorii,* no. 5 (1993): 4–5, 14; no. 6 (1993): 22.

91. "Materialy fevral'sko-martovskogo plenuma," *Voprosy Istorii,* no. 5 (1993): 4–5, 14; 6 (1993): 22.

92. "Materialy fevral'sko-martovskogo plenuma," ibid., no. 7 (1993): 10.

93. On Stalin's order, the Politburo had decided on February 5, 1937, that Ordzhonikidze would address the Central Committe on 'lessons to be drawn from the wreckers' activity, and the sabotage and espionage conducted by Japanese-German-Trotskyite agents." See RGASPI, f. 17, op. 3, d. 983, l. 64. See also Mikoian, *Tak bylo,* 328–32, quote 328; Khlevniuk, *In Stalin's Shadow,* 126–49.

94. "Materialy fevral'sko-martovskogo plenuma," *Voprosy Istorii,* no. 8 (1993): 3, 11; "Materialy fevral'sko-martovskogo plenuma," ibid., no. 8 (1994): 15–16.

95. "Materialy fevral'sko-martovskogo plenuma," ibid., no. 9 (1993): 30.

96. "Materialy fevral'sko-martovskogo plenuma," ibid., no. 1 (1994): 24–27.

97. "Materialy fevral'sko-martovskogo plenuma," ibid., no. 2 (1994): 15–18, 22, 28.

98. "Materialy fevral'sko-martovskogo plenuma," ibid., no. 8 (1994): 20.

99. "Materialy fevral'sko-martovskogo plenuma," ibid., no. 10 (1994): 13–27, quotes, 25, 27. Molchanov had already been arrested on February 3. See N. V. Petrov and K. V. Skorkin, eds., *Kto rukovodil NKVD 1934–1941: Spravochnik* (Moscow: Zven'ia, 1999), 307.

100. "Materialy fevral'sko-martovskogo plenuma," *Voprosy Istorii,* no. 12 (1994): 3–39, quotes 5, 7, 9.

101. "Materialy fevral'sko-martovskogo plenuma," ibid., 10–29, quote 15.

102. "Materialy fevral'sko-martovskogo plenuma," ibid., no. 2 (1995): 7, 21. In 1934, Sosnovsky was deputy director of the Special Department of State Security, and he was assigned the investigation of the Kirov murder. On Yevdokimov's role in 1927, see also Stephen Wheatcroft, "Agency and Terror: Evdokimov and Mass Killing in Stalin's Great Terror," *Australian Journal of Politics and History* 53 (2007): 20–43, esp. 30.

103. "Materialy fevral'sko-martovskogo plenuma," *Voprosy Istorii,* no. 3 (1995): 4; no. 11/12, 13.

104. "Materialy fevral'sko-martovskogo plenuma," ibid., no. 11/12 (1995): 17–18.

105. Chuev, *Molotov Remembers,* 272, 274, 276; Kumanev, *Govoriat stalinskie narkomy,* 107; Khaustov et al., *Lubianka* (2004), 136; Vaksberg, *The Prosecutor and the Prey,* 167, 197–98; Montefiore, *Stalin,* 367.

106. I. N. Mel'nikov (Korrespondent "Izvestii" po Azerbaidzhanskoi SSSR), "Zapiska o protsesse M. Bagirova i ego soobshchnikov," FSO, f. 23 (Chingiz Guseinov), 4, 8.

107. Amy W. Knight, *Beria: Stalin's First Lieutenant* (Princeton: Princeton University Press, 1993), 67–86; Donald Rayfield, *Stalin und seine Henker* (Munich: Blessing, 2004), 365; Baberowski, *Der Feind ist überall,* 775–76.

108. On Vyshinsky see RGASPI f. 82, op. 2, d. 884, l. 79; on Khataevich see Khaustov et al., *Lubianka* (2004), 136, 245–46, 252–55, quote 209; see also *Istochnik* 3 (1994): 72–88.

109. RGASPI, f. 82, op. 2, d. 152, ll. 16–18.

110. RGASPI, f. 81, op. 3, d. 227, ll. 1–3; on Mirzoian see Shreider, *NKVD iznutri,* 110.

111. Kumanev, *Govoriat stalinskie narkomy,* 105.

112. RGASPI, f. 558, op. 11, d. 57, l. 103; Mikoian, *Tak bylo,* 583; Khaustov et al., *Lubianka* (2004), 200–201, 383, 516; Shreider, *NKVD iznutri,* 63; Khlevniuk, *Das Politbüro,* 281; Youngok Kang-Bohr, *Stalinismus in der ländlichen Provinz: Das Gebiet Voronezh 1934–1941* (Essen: Klartext, 2006), 142–51.

113. On Andreyev's role see RGASPI, f. 558, op. 11, d. 57, ll. 79, 95, 117–18; Liudmila S. Gatagova, ed., *MCK VKP(B) i natsional'nyi vopros,* vol. 2 (Moscow: ROSSPEN, 2009), 294–96; Montefiore, *Stalin,* 223–25.

114. Shreider, *NKVD iznutri,* 65.

115. Ibid., 64; RGASPI, f. 81, op. 3, d. 226, ll. 22–25, 44–45.

116. RGASPI, f. 81, op. 3, d. 229, ll. 45, 64, 82, 91, 95, 100.

117. Shreider, *NKVD iznutri,* 66.

118. RGASPI, f. 81, op. 3, d. 229, l. 102.

119. RGASPI, f. 81, op. 3, d. 229, ll. 103–5; Shreider, *NKVD iznutri,* 66.

120. RGASPI, f. 81, op. 3, d. 229, l. 109.

121. Shreider, *NKVD iznutri,* 68–69.

122. Ibid., 70, 80. The lists with the names of those arrested are found in RGASPI, f. 81, op. 3, d. 230, ll. 36–74.

123. Suvenirov, *Tragediia RKKA,* 49–55, 58; Roger R. Reese, "Red Army Opposition to Forced Collectivization, 1929–1930: The Army Wavers," *Slavic Review* 55 (1996): 24–45; Reese, *Stalin's Reluctant Soldiers: A Social History of the Red Army* (Lawrence: University Press of Kansas, 1996); Wynn, "'The Right Opposition' and the 'Smirnov-Tolmachev Affair,'" 101–2; Easter, *Reconstructing the State,* 98–99; Tucker, *Stalin in Power,* 382.

124. Boris Viktorov, "Zagovor v Krasnoi armii," in *Istoriia bez "belykh piaten":* *Daidzhest pressy, 1987–1988,* ed. E. B. Nikanorova et al. (Leningrad: Lenizdat, 1990), 254; Thurston, *Life and Terror in Stalin's Russia,* 50–51; Zinaida N. Pasternak, *Vospominaniia* (Moscow: Klassika-XXI, 2004), 76–77.

125. RGASPI, f. 17, op. 165, d. 58, ll. 1–59.

126. RGASPI, f. 17, op. 165, d. 60, ll. 140–56.

127. RGASPI, f. 17, op. 165, d. 61, ll. 66–108.

128. Khaustov et al., *Lubianka* (2004), 202–9.

129. Quoted in Suvenirov, *Tragediia RKKA,* 93.

130. Chuev, *Molotov Remembers,* 254.

131. Suvenirov, *Tragediia RKKA,* 193–95, 202, 209–12.

132. Ibid., 137–38, 309, 338–41.

133. Stalin's orders in RGASPI, f. 558, op. 11, d. 57, l. 71; RGASPI, f. 82, op. 2, d. 152, ll. 20–28, quote l. 27; Gregory, *Terror by Quota,* 75–79; V. S. Zhukovskii, *Lubianskaia imperiia NKVD 1937–1938* (Moscow: Veche, 2001), 42; Harris, "Resisting the Plan in the Urals," 208; Kuromiya, *Freedom and Terror in the Donbass,* 219–20.

134. RGASPI, f. 558, op. 11, d. 713, ll. 122–24.

135. RGASPI, f. 82, op. 2, d. 884, l. 83.

136. On this issue, see the vignettes provided by Karl Schlögel, *Terror und Traum: Moskau 1937* (Munich: Hanser, 2009).

137. Bonner, *Mothers and Daughters,* 276.

138. Yuri Trifonov, *Another Life; and, The House on the Embankment* (Evanston: Northwestern University Press, 1999).

139. Shreider, *NKVD iznutri,* 64; Pasternak, *Vospominaniia,* 72–73; Medvedev, *Let History Judge,* 524–33.

140. Stalin certainly did not invent this ruling technique. Despots have always surrounded themselves with cronies who are at their mercy because they have nowhere else to turn for support. For this technique, see the biography of the Roman emperor Caligula by Aloys Winterling, *Caligula: Eine Biographie* (Munich: Beck, 2003), 152–53. For information on Stalin's Praetorian Guard, see Petrov and Skorkin, *Kto rukovodil NKVD,* 497–99; Nikita Petrov, "Die Kaderpolitik des NKVD während der Massenrepressalien 1936–39," in *Stalinistischer Terror 1934–1941: Eine Forschungsbilanz,* ed. Vladislav Hedeler (Berlin: BasisDruck, 2002), 16–17.

141. RGASPI, f. 558, op. 11, d. 716, ll. 18–19.

142. Anatolii A. Chernobaev, ed., *Na prieme u Stalina: Tetradi (zhurnaly) zapisei lits, priniatych I. V. Stalinym (1924–1953gg.)* (Moscow: Novyi Khronograf, 2010), 197–228.

143. Quote in RGASPI, f. 558, op. 11, d. 57, l. 5; Petrov, "Kaderpolitik," 24; Dmitrii A. Volkogonov, *Triumf i tragediia: Politicheskii portret I. V. Stalina*, vol. 1 (Moscow: Izd-vo Agentstva pechati Novosti, 1998), 576–77; Suvenirov, *Tragediia RKKA*, 240.

144. RGASPI, f. 558, op. 11, d. 1120, ll. 28–44.

145. Chuev, *Molotov Remembers*, 274–75; Khlevniuk, *Das Politbüro*, 305–360.

146. RGASPI, f. 558, op. 11, d. 779, l. 23.

147. Margarete Buber-Neumann, *Von Potsdam nach Moskau: Stationen eines Irrweges* (Munich: Ullstein Taschenbuch, 2002), 274–75.

148. Kumanev, *Govoriat stalinskie narkomy*, 105; Mikoian, *Tak bylo*, 583.

149. Khlevniuk, *Stalin i Kaganovich*, 284. See also Vadim S. Rogovin, *Partiia rasstreliannykh* (Moscow: Moskovskaia Tip, 1997), 34; Kumanev, *Riadom so Stalinym*, 80–82; Razgon, *Nichts als die reine Wahrheit*, 76–82; Mevedev, *Let History Judge*, 547–48; Jansen and Petrov, *Stalin's Loyal Executioner*, 170–71; Thurston, *Life and Terror in Stalin's Russia*, 42.

150. Montefiore, *Stalin*, 185; Valerii A. Torchinov and Aleksei M. Leontiuk, eds., *Vokrug Stalina: Istoriko-biograficheskii spravochnik* (Saint Petersburg: Sankt-Peterburg Filol. Fak. Sankt-Peterburgskogo Gosudarstvennogo University., 2000), 236–37.

151. Tucker, *Stalin in Power*, 539.

152. Georgi Dimitrov, *Diary*, 1:65; Oleg V. Volobuev and Sergei V. Kuleshov, *Ochishchenie: Istoriia i perestroika. Publisticheskie zametki* (Moscow: Izd-vo Agentstva pechati Novosti, 1989), 146; Petrov, "Kaderpolitik," 24.

153. Semen S. Vilenskii, *Deti GULAGa 1918–1956* (Moscow: Mezhdunarodnyi fond "Demokratiia," 2002), 234–38, 242; Khaustov et al., *Lubianka* (2004), 226, 238–39; C. Kuhr, "Kinder von 'Volksfeinden' als Opfer des stalinistischen Terrors 1936–1938," in Plaggenborg, *Stalinismus*, 391–418. Kommunisticheskaia partiia Sovetskogo Soiuza, *XXII s"ezd KPSS, 17–31 oktiabria 1961 goda: Stenograficheskii otchet*, vol. 3 (Moscow: Izd-vo Politicheskoi literatury, 1962), 152; Chuev, *Molotov Remembers*, 277.

154. Kuromiya, *Freedom and Terror in the Donbass*, 213; Penter, *Kohle für Stalin und Hitler*, 136–45.

155. RGASPI, f. 81, op. 3, d. 228, l. 62.

156. *Pravda*, October 27, 1935; Lewis H. Siegelbaum, *Stakhanovism and the Politics of Productivity in the USSR, 1935–1941* (Cambridge: Cambridge University Press, 1988), 66–98; Mary Buckley, *Mobilizing Soviet Peasants: Heroines and Heroes of Stalin's Fields* (Oxford: Berg, 2006), 26–27; Robert Maier, *Die Stachanow-Bewegung 1935–1938: Der Stachanowismus als tragendes und verschärfendes Moment der Stalinisierung der sowjetischen Gesellschaft* (Stuttgart: Steiner, 1990).

157. Khlevniuk, *In Stalin's Shadow*, 78–91; Kevin Klose, *Russia and the Russians: Inside the Closed Society* (New York: Norton, 1984), 60.

158. Scott, *Behind the Urals,* 195–97; Kuromiya, *Freedom and Terror in the Donbass,* 214–215. Quote in Chuev, *Molotov Remembers,* 210.

159. RGASPI, f. 81, op. 3, d. 228, ll. 49–50.

160. Quotes in RGASPI, f. 558, op. 11, d. 57, l. 7, ll. 30, 56, 71, 78; RGASPI, f. 82, op. 2, d. 153, ll. 183–96; RGASPI, f. 17, op. 2, d. 625, l. 40; I. N. Mel'nikov (Korrespondent "Izvestii" po Azerbaidzhanskoi SSSR), "Zapiska o protsesse M. Bagirova i ego soobshchnikov," FSO, f. 23 (Chingiz Guseinov), 4, 8; Fitzpatrick, *Stalin's Peasants,* 296–312.

161. RGASPI, f. 81, op. 3, d. 229, l. 14; RGASPI, f. 558, op. 11, d. 57, ll. 25, 99; RGASPI, f. 81, op. 3, d. 230, ll. 85–86, 94; Andrei Kabackov, "Repressii protiv rabochich Prikam'ia 1937–1938 gg.," in *"Vkliuchen v operaciju:" Massovyi terror v Prikame'e v 1937–1938 gg.,* ed. Oleg Leibovich (Moscow: ROSSPEN, 2009), 134–80; Kuromiya, *Freedom and Terror in the Donbass,* 210–12, 227–30; Penter, *Kohle für Stalin und Hitler,* 145–49; Scott, *Behind the Urals,* 186–87; Papkov, *Stalinskii terror v Sibiri,* 174; Lewis Siegelbaum and Andrei Sokolov, *Stalinism as a Way of Life: A Narrative in Documents* (New Haven: Yale University Press, 2000), 390; Rolf Binner and Marc Junge, "Wie der Terror 'Groß' wurde: Massenmord und Lagerhaft nach Befehl 00447," *Cahiers du Monde Russe* 42 (2001): 557–614, esp. 559.

162. RGASPI, f. 17, op. 120, d. 256, ll. 35–40.

163. RGASPI, f. 81, op. 3, d. 228, l. 51.

164. Catherine Merridale, "The 1937 Census and the Limits of Stalinist Rule," *Historical Journal* 39 (1996): 225–40.

165. RGASPI, f. 82, op. 2, d. 884, ll. 14–15; RGASPI, f. 82, op. 2, d. 537, ll. 96–155; RGASPI, f. 81, op. 3, d. 229, ll. 73–74; RGASPI, f. 81, op. 3, d. 228, ll. 50–52; "Materialy fevral'sko-martovskogo plenuma," *Voprosy Istorii,* no. 5 (1993): 14–15; no. 6 (1993): 5–6, 21–25.

166. Voroshilov quote: Khlevniuk et al., *Stalinskoe politbiuro v 30-e gody,* 144. See also Shearer, *Policing Stalin's Socialism,* 181–218, 231–33; Shearer, "Modernity and Backwardness on the Soviet Frontier: Western Siberia in the 1930s," in Raleigh, *Provincial Landscapes,* 203–6; Shearer, "Crime and Social Disorder in Stalin's Russia: A Reassessment of the Great Retreat and the Origins of Mass Repression," in *Cahiers du Monde Russe* 39 (1998): 119–48. Binner and Junge, "'S etoi publikoi tseremonit'sia ne sleduet,'" 181–228, esp. 185–94.

167. Khaustov et al., *Lubianka* (2004), 234–35.

168. RGASPI, f. 17, op. 162, d. 21, ll. 94–99; Khaustov et al., *Lubianka* (2004), 239–42; Aleksandr I. Kokurin and Nikita V. Petrov, eds., *GULAG 1917–1960* (Moscow: Mezhdunarodnyi fond "Demokratiia," 2000), 96–104; Paul Hagenloh, *Stalin's Police: Public Order and Mass Repression in the USSR, 1926–1941* (Baltimore: Woodrow Wilson Center Press, 2009), 242–51; Getty, "'Excesses Are Not Permitted,'" 127; Jansen and Petrov, *Stalin's Loyal Executioner,* 83. On the preparations for Order 00447 see Rolf Binner and Marc Junge, eds., *Stalinismus in der sowjetischen Provinz 1937–1938: Die Massenaktion aufgrund des operativen Befehls Nr. 00447* (Berlin: Akad.-Verl., 2010).

169. Shreider, *NKVD iznutri,* 40–41; Jansen and Petrov, *Stalin's Loyal Executioner,* 82–87; Shearer, *Policing Stalin's Socialism,* 335; Marc Junge and Rolf Binner consider Shreider's claim that the quotas were criticized to be an invention.

Mark Iunge, Gennadii Bordiugov, and Rol'f Binner, eds., *Vertikal' bol'shogo terrora: Istoriia operatsii po prikazu NKVD Nr. 00447* (Moscow: Novyi Khronograf, 2008), 33.

170. A. G. Tepliakov, *Protsedura: Ispolneniia smertnykh prigovorov v 1920–1930-kh godakh* (Moscow: Vozvrashchenie, 2007), 53; Papkov, *Stalinskii terror v Sibiri*, 209–11; Jansen and Petrov, *Stalin's Loyal Executioner*, 82–87; Shearer, *Policing Stalin's Socialism*, 335.

171. RGASPI, f. 558, op. 11, d. 65, ll. 88, 97, 108; RGASPI, f. 558, op. 11, d. 57, l. 136; Khaustov et al., *Lubianka* (2004), 325, 471, 517; Papkov, *Stalinskii terror v Sibiri*, 207; Binner and Junge, "Wie der Terror 'Groß' wurde," 579–84.

172. E. A. Bakirov et al., *Butovskii Poligon: Kniga pamiati zhertv politicheskikh repressii* vol. 8 (Moscow: Izd-vo "Panorama," 2004), 64–65; Shreider, *NKVD iznutri*, 67; Shearer, *Policing Stalin's Socialism*, 345.

173. Khaustov et al., *Lubianka* (2004), 335; Iunge, Bordiugov, and Binner, *Vertikal' bol'shogo terrora*, 156; Viktor Ivanov, "Die Kriminellen als Zielgruppe im Gebiet Leningrad," in Binner, Bonwetsch, and Junge, *Stalinismus in der sowjetischen Provinz*, 217–234.

174. Oleg Khlevniuk, "Les mécanismes de la 'Grande Terreur' des années 1937–1938 au Turkménistan," *Cahiers du Monde Russe* 39 (1998): 202–5; Shearer, *Policing Stalin's Socialism*, 347–48.

175. Bakirov et al., *Butovskii Poligon*, 4, 64. For the troikas' methods of interrogation, see also Alexander Vatlin, *Tatort Kunzewo: Opfer und Täter des Stalinschen Terrors 1937/38* (Berlin: BasisDruck, 2003), 44–68.

176. Dmitrii Goichenko, *Skvoz' raskulachivanie i golodomor: Svidetel'stvo ochevidtsa* (Moscow: Russkii put', 2006), 59, 65.

177. Bakirov et al., *Butovskii Poligon*, 85–96; Tepliakov, *Protsedura*, 10; Khaustov et al., *Lubianka* (2004), 335, 386.

178. Bakirov et al., *Butovskii Poligon*, 72; Binner and Junge, "Wie der Terror 'Groß' wurde," 567–68, 588–90; Razgon, *Nichts als die reine Wahrheit*, 352–53; Tepliakov, *Protsedura*, 58, 66–67; Barry McLoughlin, "Die Massenoperationen des NKWD: Dynamik des Terrors 1937/38," in Hedeler, *Stalinistischer Terror*, 42–44; Shreider, *NKVD iznutri*, 59, 86–87; Timothy Colton, *Moscow: Governing the Socialist Metropolis* (Cambridge, Mass.: Belknap Press of Harvard University Press, 1995), 286; Rayfield, *Stalin und seine Henker*, 375.

179. Bakirov et al., *Butovskii Poligon*, 70–71; Montefiore, *Stalin*, 369, 379; Tepliakov, *Protsedura*, 58–59, 72, 74.

180. Tepliakov, *Protsedura*, 25, 66.

181. Svetlana Alexievich, "Henker und Beil: Vom Ende des roten Menschen. Sowjetische und russische Lebensläufe," *Lettre International* 82 (2008): 28.

182. Erik van Ree, "Heroes and Merchants: Stalin's Understanding of National Character," *Kritika* 8 (2007): 41–65; Alfred J. Rieber, "Stalin: Man of the Borderlands," *American Historical Review* 106 (2001): 1651–91; Jörg Baberowski, "Stalinismus und Nation: Die Sowjetunion als Vielvölkerreich 1917–1953," *Zeitschrift für Geschichtswissenschaft* 3 (2006): 199–213.

183. RGASPI, f. 558, op. 11, d. 1122, l. 164; RGASPI, f. 558, op. 11, d. 1125, ll. 17–18; Georgi Dimitroff, *Tagebücher 1933–1943*, vol. 1 (Berlin: Aufbau Verlag,

2000), 376; Vladimir Nevezhin, *Zastol'nye rechi Stalina: Dokumenty i materialy* (Moscow: AIRO-XX, 2003), 260–61; Viktor Jerofejew, *Der gute Stalin* (Berlin: Berlin Verlag, 2004), 51.

184. Mary M. Leder, *My Life in Stalinist Russia: An American Woman Looks Back* (Bloomington: Indiana University Press, 2001), 61.

185. RGASPI, f. 81, op. 3, d. 124, ll. 32, 35, quote l. 28.

186. For the discussion of the origins of Bolshevik terror inflicted on ethnic groups, see Eric Weitz, "Racial Politics without the Concept of Race: Reevaluating Soviet Ethnic and National Purges," *Slavic Review* 61 (2002): 1–29; Weitz, *A Century of Genocide: Utopias of Race and Nation* (Princeton: Princeton University Press, 2003), 53–101; Francine Hirsch, "Race without the Practice of Racial Politics," *Slavic Review* 61 (2002): 30–43.

187. Khaustov et al., *Lubianka* (2004), 125; Victor Dönninghaus, *Minderheiten in Bedrängnis: Sowjetische Politik gegenüber Deutschen, Polen und anderen Diaspora-Nationalitäten 1917–1938* (Munich: Oldenbourg, 2009), 407–43; see in general Timothy Snyder, *Bloodlands: Europe between Hitler and Stalin* (New York: Basic Books, 2010), 59–88.

188. Khaustov et al., *Lubianka* (2004), 464.

189. RGASPI, f. 17, op. 162 (osobaia papka), d. 8, l. 99.

190. Gosudarstvennyi Arkhiv Noveishei Istorii Azerbaidzhanskoi Respubliki, f. 27, op. 1, d. 190, ll. 3–6, 42, 82, 99, 119; Martin, *The Affirmative Action Empire*, 322.

191. O. N. Pobol' and P. M. Polian, *Stalinskie deportatsii: 1928–1953* (Moscow: Mezhdunarodnyi fond "Demokratiia," 2005), 41–42; Martin, *The Affirmative Action Empire*, 322–24. See also Michael J. Gelb, "An Early Soviet Ethnic Deportation: The Far-Eastern Koreans," *Russian Review* 54 (1995): 389–411; A. Zakir, "Zemel'naia politika v kolkhoznom dvizhenii sredi koreitsev," *Revoliutsiia i natsional'nosti*, nos. 2/3 (1931): 76–81.

192. RGASPI, f. 558, op. 11, d. 45, l. 106. See also the reports by the Ukrainian GPU boss Balitsky on the alleged threat by nationalistic movements supported by the Nazis and the Polish espionage service: RGASPI, f. 671, op. 1, d. 238, ll. 1–15.

193. Danilov and Viola, *Tragediia sovetskoi derevni*, 3:577, 584, 611.

194. Martin, *The Affirmative Action Empire*, 326–27.

195. RGASPI, f. 671, op. 1, d. 70, ll. 9–20; Danilov and Viola, *Tragediia sovetskoi derevni*, vol. 4: *1934–1936*, 550–51; Viktor N. Zemskov, *Spetsposelentsy v SSSR 1930–1960* (Moscow: Nauka 2003), 78–79.

196. RGASPI, f. 17, op. 162, d. 22, ll. 9–10.

197. RGASPI, f. 558, op. 11, d. 57, l. 72. On Volsky's arrest see Khaustov et al., *Lubianka* (2004), 368–73.

198. RGASPI, f. 17, op. 162, d. 22, l. 105. See also Martin, *The Affirmative Action Empire*, 328–35; N. F. Bugai, "Vyselenie sovetskikh koreitsev s Dal'nego Vostoka," *Voprosy Istorii*, no. 5 (1994): 141–48; Zemskov, *Spetsposelentsy*, 80–82; Khlevniuk, *Das Politbüro*, 277–78; RGASPI, f. 558, op. 11, d. 57, l. 72; RGASPI, f. 82, op. 2, d. 671, l. 53; Gelb, "An Early Soviet Ethnic Deportation," 389–412; Gelb, "Ethnicity during the Yezhovshchina: A Historiography," in *Ethnic and Na-*

tional Issues in Russian and East European History, ed. John Morison (London: Macmillan, 2000), 192–213; Terry Martin, "The Origins of Soviet Ethnic Cleansing," *Journal of Modern History* 70 (1998): 813–61.

199. RGASPI, f. 17, op. 162, d. 22, ll. 16–17, 27, 121–22, 161–62; RGASPI, f. 558, op. 11, d. 57, l. 72.

200. Khaustov et al., *Lubianka* (2004), 251, 301–3, 352–59.

201. RGASPI, f. 82, op. 2, d. 400, l. 30; Kokurin and Petrov, *GULAG 1917–1960,* 104–6; Vladimir I. Piatnitskii, *Zagovor protiv Stalina* (Moscow: Sovremennik, 1998), 72–73; Jansen and Petrov, *Stalin's Loyal Executioner,* 98–99.

202. Quotes in RGASPI, f. 558, op. 11, d. 57, l. 72; Suvenirov, *Tragediia RKKA,* 208; Jansen and Petrov, *Stalin's Loyal Executioner,* 98.

203. RGASPI, f. 558, op. 11, d. 57, ll. 1–3; Michael J. Gelb, "The Western Finnic Minorities and the Origins of the Stalinist Nationalities Deportations," *Nationalities Papers* 24 (1996): 237–86; Papkov, *Stalinskii terror v Sibiri,* 199; Kuromiya, *Freedom and Terror in the Donbass,* 231–34; Hiroaki Kuromiya, *The Voices of the Dead: Stalin's Great Terror in the 1930s* (New Haven: Yale University Press, 2007), 125–40.

204. Alexander Weissberg-Cybulski, *Hexensabbat* (Frankfurt am Main: Suhrkamp, 1977), 276–77, 286–87.

205. RGASPI, f. 558, op. 11, d. 57, l. 72; RGASPI, f. 82, op. 2, d. 671, l. 53; Khlevniuk, *Das Politbüro,* 277–78; Hagenloh, *Stalin's Police,* 267, 279.

206. Khaustov et al., *Lubianka* (2004), 468–69.

207. Khlevniuk, *Master of the House,* 184. Slightly different figures in McLoughlin, "Die Massenoperationen des NKWD," 42; Jansen and Petrov, *Stalin's Loyal Executioner,* 99, 103; Binner and Junge, "'S etoi publikoi tseremonit'sia ne sleduet,'" 207–8.

208. See on this Binner and Junge, "'S etoi publikoi tseremonit'sia ne sleduet,'" 215–18. Getty presents the "revisionist" interpretation. He asserts that the leaders prohibited the local organs from committing atrocities. See Getty, "'Excesses Are Not Permitted.'"

209. Khlevniuk et al., *Stalinskoe politbiuro v 30-e gody,* 159–63. See also Khlevniuk, *Das Politbüro,* 306–22.

210. Arendt, *The Origins of Totalitarianism,* 466.

211. N. Ochotin and A. Roginskij, "Zur Geschichte der 'Deutschen Operation' des NKWD 1937–1938," *Jahrbuch für historische Kommunismusforschung* (2001): 89–125, esp. 116; Hagenloh, *Stalin's Police,* 279–283; Jansen and Petrov, *Stalin's Loyal Executioner,* 137, 165; Tepliakov, *Protsedura,* 20; Papkov, *Stalinskii terror v Sibiri,* 230–31.

212. RGASPI, f. 82, op. 2, d. 897, l. 30.

213. RGASPI, f. 558, op. 11, d. 1121, l. 19; Khlevniuk et al., *Stalinskoe politbiuro v 30-e gody,* 159; Khaustov et al., *Lubianka* (2004), 249, 434, 464.

214. Quotes in Khaustov et al., *Lubianka* (2004), 545, 552–54, 611, 629; Jansen and Petrov, *Stalin's Loyal Executioner,* 133–80; Rayfield, *Stalin und seine Henker,* 369; Chernobaev, *Na prieme u Stalina,* 246.

215. Quotes in RGASPI, f. 558, op. 11, d. 20, l. 53; Nikolai G. Kuznetsov, "Krutye povoroty: Iz zapisok admirala," *Voenno-istoricheskii zhurnal* 7 (1993): 50;

Medvedev, *Let History Judge*, 458–60; Khaustov and Naumov, eds., *Lubianka: Stalin i NKVD-NKGB-GUKR "Smersh" 1939–mart 1946* (Moscow: Mezhduna-rodnyi fond "Demokratiia," 2006), 29, 52–53.

216. Khaustov et al., *Lubianka* (2006), 140–41; Medvedev, *Let History Judge*, 458–60; Getty and Naumov, *Road to Terror*, 561–62; Jansen and Petrov, *Stalin's Loyal Executioner*, 181–93; Aleksei Pavliukov, *Ezhov: Biografiia* (Moscow: Zakharov, 2007), 535–36; Montefiore, *Stalin*, 367–68.

217. Aleksandr S. Iakovlev, *Tsel' zhizni: Zapiski aviakonstruktora* (Moscow: Politizdat, 1974), 249.

218. Quotes in Teresa Torańska, *"Them": Stalin's Polish Puppets* (New York: Harper & Row, 1987), 104.

219. See examples in Service, *Stalin*, 163–74.

220. RGASPI, f. 558, op. 11, d. 1122, l. 162.

221. Roberto Saviano, *Gomorrah: Italy's Other Mafia* (London: Macmillan, 2008), 300; Tucker, *Stalin in Power;* Ronald G. Suny, "Beyond Psychohistory: The Young Stalin in Georgia," *Slavic Review* 50 (1991): 48–58; Mikoian, *Tak bylo,* 354; Alfred E. Rieber, "Stalin: Man of the Borderlands," *American Historical Review* 53 (2001): 1651–91.

222. RGASPI, f. 558, op. 11, d. 1122, l. 162.

223. Alexander Orlow, *Kreml-Geheimnisse* (Würzburg: Marienburg-Verlag, 1956), 410; see Montefiore, *Stalin*, 176.

224. Kirill Stoliarov, *Palachi i zhertvy* (Moscow: Olma-Press, 1997), 264; Iurii V. Trifonov, "Zapiski soseda," *Druzhba narodov* 10 (1989): 39; Tucker, *Stalin in Power*, 373; Andrei Sakharov, *Mein Leben* (Munich: Piper, 1991), 183–86; Torchinov and Leontiuk, *Vokrug Stalina*, 257–58, 384; Dmitrii Shepilov, "Vospominaniia," *Voprosy istorii*, no. 4 (1998): 6; Jansen and Petrov, *Stalin's Loyal Executioner*, 139, 152,186, 199–201; Tepliakov, *Protsedura*, 71, 75; Shearer, *Policing Stalin's Socialism*, 345–49; Rayfield, *Stalin und seine Henker*, 423–30; Petrov and Skorkin, *Kto rukovodil NKVD*, 233–34, 354–55, 400–401; Montefiore, *Stalin*, 325–26, 267.

225. Quotes in Torańska, *"Them,"* 206.

226. Alexievich, *"Henker und Beil,"* 28.

CHAPTER SIX: WARS

1. Popitz, *Phänomene der Macht*, 236–40, quote 239.

2. Quote in Nikita S. Khrushchev, *Vremia, Liudi, Vlast': Vospominaniia* (Moscow: Moskovskie novosti, 1999), 764; Nikita Petrov, *Pervyi predsedatel' KGB Ivan Serov* (Moscow: Materik, 2005), 204. Khrushchev's telegram to Stalin on April 3, 1941 is reproduced in RGASPI, f. 558, op. 11, d. 59, l. 5, also in Khaustov et al., *Lubianka* (2006), 246.

3. RGASPI, f. 82, op. 2, d. 884, ll. 181–85, Botskov quote l. 161; Shearer, *Policing Stalin's Socialism*, 405–36; Hagenloh, *Stalin's Police*, 228–331; Khaustov et al., *Lubianka* (2006), 177; Vert et al., *Istoriia stalinskogo Gulaga*, 1:411–14; Penter, *Kohle für Stalin und Hitler*, 149–54; Davies, *Popular Opinion in Stalin's Russia*, 45.

4. Jan T. Gross, *Revolution from Abroad: The Soviet Conquest of Poland's Western Ukraine and Western Belorussia* (Princeton: Princeton University Press, 2002), 45.

5. Aleksander Wat, *My Century: The Odyssey of a Polish Intellectual* (Berkeley: University of California Press, 1988), 98–99.

6. Gross, *Revolution from Abroad*, 45–50, 230; Sandra Kalniete, *With Dance Shoes in Siberian Snows* (Elmwood Park: Dalkey Archive Press, 2009), 48; Catherine Merridale, *Ivan's War: The Red Army 1939–45* (London: Faber & Faber, 2005), 65–67.

7. Dimitrov, *Diary*, 1:124.

8. Fyodor Vasilevich Mochulsky, *Gulag Boss: A Soviet Memoir*, trans. Deborah Kaple (New York: Oxford University. Press, 2011), 36–37; Khaustov et al., *Lubianka* (2006), 155–59, 181. For the Finnish-Soviet war, see also Catherine Merridale, *Ivan's War*, 44–71; Roger R. Reese, *The Soviet Military Experience. A History of the Soviet Army 1917–1991* (London: Routledge, 2000), 99.

9. RGANI, f. 89, op. 58, d. 1, ll. 2–5. See also Inessa Iazhborovskaia, Anatolii Iablokov, and Valentina Parsadanova, *Katynskii sindrom v sovetsko-pol'skikh otnosheniiakh* (Moscow: ROSSPEN, 2009), 66–67; Gross, *Revolution from Abroad*, 12.

10. TsAMO, f. 5, op. 176702, d. 1, ll. 310–20 (Container 5, Reel 3). See also R. G. Pikhoia and Aleksandr Geishtor, eds., *Katyn'. Plenniki neob''iavlennoi voiny* (Moscow: Mezhdunarodnyi fond "Demokratiia," 1997), 14; Gross, *Revolution from Abroad*, 37; Iazhborovskaia et al., *Katynskii sindrom*, 71; Gross, *Revolution from Abroad*, 35–45; Marek Wierzbicki, "Western Belarus in September 1939: Polish-Jewish Relations in the Kresy," in *Shared History—Divided Memory: Jews and Others in Soviet Occupied Poland, 1939–1941*, ed. Elazar Barkan, Elisabeth A. Cole, and Kai Struve (Leipzig: Leipziger Universitätsverlag, 2007), 135–46.

11. RGANI, f. 89, op. 69, d. 1, ll. 1–2; RGASPI, f. 17, op. 162, d. 26, ll. 20, 71; Pikhoia and Geishtor, *Katyn'*, 16, 121–23, 167–168; George Sanford, *Katyn and the Soviet Massacre of 1940: Truth, Justice and Memory* (London: Routledge, 2005), 43.

12. Chuev, *Molotov: Poluderzhavnyi vlastelin*, 19; Service, *Stalin*, 404.

13. Service, *Stalin*, 404; Kees Boterbloem, *The Life and Times of Andrei Zhdanov, 1896–1948* (Montreal: McGill-Queen's University Press, 2004), 198–208; Elena Zubkova, *Pribaltika i Kreml'* (Moscow: ROSSPEN, 2008), 93–127; Björn M. Felder, *Lettland im zweiten Weltkrieg: Zwischen sowjetischen und deutschen Besatzern 1940–1946* (Paderborn: Schöningh, 2009), 31–54; Kalniete, *With Dance Shoes in Siberian Snows*, 39–52.

14. See on this point Felder, *Lettland im zweiten Weltkrieg*, 75–99; Felder, "Stalinismus als 'russisch-jüdische' Herrschaft: Sowjetische Besatzung und ethnische Mobilisierung im Baltikum 1940–1941," *Zeitschrift für Geschichtswissenschaft* 57, no. 1 (2009): 5–25.

15. Gross, *Revolution from Abroad*, 230; Irena Gross and Jan Tomasz Gross, *War Through Children's Eyes: The Soviet Occupation of Poland and the Deportations, 1939–1941* (Stanford: Hoover Institution Press, 1981), 27.

16. RGASPI, f. 17, op. 162, d. 27, ll. 71–72; Pikhoia and Geishtor, *Katyn'*, 375–78; Gross, *Revolution from Abroad*, 71–91.

17. Khaustov et al., *Lubianka* (2006), 141–42; Pobol' and Polian, *Stalinskie deportatsii*, 122, 126; Gross, *Revolution from Abroad*, 208–9.

18. Stalin's orders and Beria's instructions have been published in Vert et al., *Istoriia stalinskogo Gulaga,* 1:390–93, 400; Anna M. Cienciala and N. Lebedeva, eds., *Katyn: A Crime without Punishment* (Bloomington: Indiana University Press, 2007), 121, 138–39; Bogdan Musial, *"Konterrevolutionäre Elemente sind zu erschießen": Die Brutalisierung des deutsch-sowjetischen Krieges im Sommer 1941* (Berlin: Propyläen, 2000), 31–34. See also Gross, *Revolution from Abroad,* 187–224, figures on p. 194; Sergei G. Filippov, "Deiatel'nost' organov VKP(b) v zapadnykh oblast'iakh Ukrainy i Belorussii v 1939–1941 gg.," in *Repressii protiv poliakov i pol'skikh grazhdan,* ed. Aleksei E. Gur'ianov (Moscow: Zven'ia, 1997), 44–76; Oleg A. Gorlanov and Arsenii B. Roginskii, "Ob arestakh v zapadnykh oblast'iakh Belorussii i Ukrainy v 1939–1941 gg.," ibid., 77–113; A. E. Gur'ianov, "Masshtaby deportatsii naseleniia v glub SSSR v mae-iune 1941 g.," ibid., 137–75; Valentina Parsadanov, "Deportatsiia naselenii iz Zapadnoi Ukrainy i Zapadnoi Belorussii," *Novaia i Noveishaia Istoriia* 2 (1989): 26–44; Wanda K. Roman, "Die sowjetische Okkupation der polnischen Ostgebiete 1939 bis 1941," in *Die polnische Heimatarmee: Geschichte und Mythos der Armia Krajowa seit dem Zweiten Weltkrieg,* ed. Bernhard Chiari (Munich: Oldenbourg, 2003), 104–6; Keith Sword, *Deportation and Exile: Poles in the Soviet Union, 1939–1948* (London: Macmillan, 1994); Werth, "Ein Staat gegen sein Volk," 232–35; Salomon W. Slowes, *The Road to Katyn: A Soldier's Story* (Oxford: Blackwell, 1992).

19. TsAMO, f. 32, op. 11289, d. 5, ll. 163–66, 200, quotes ll. 163–64, 200; TsAMO, f. 32, op. 11309, d. 46, ll. 177–97, quote l. 187; (both Container 5, Reel 3).

20. RGANI, f. 89, op. 18, d. 3, ll. 3–6; RGANI, f. 89, op. 18, d. 6, ll. 1–4; Vert et al., *Istoriia stalinskogo Gulaga,* 1:401, 404–5; Zubkova, *Pribaltika i Kreml',* 126–27; Aldis Purs, "Soviet in Form, Local in Content: Elite Repression and Mass Terror in the Baltic States, 1940–1953," in *Stalinist Terror in Eastern Europe: Elite Purges and Mass Repression,* ed. Kevin McDermott and Matthew Stibbe (Manchester: Manchester University. Press, 2010), 19–38; Igor Casu, "Stalinist Terror in Soviet Moldavia, 1904–1953," ibid., 39–56, esp. 39–40.

21. Kalniete, *With Dance Shoes in Siberian Snows,* 53; Gross, *Revolution from Abroad,* 187–224, quote 214.

22. Quotes: Gross, *Revolution from Abroad,* 217.

23. Pobol' and Polian, *Stalinskie deportatsii,* 128–36; Wat, *My Century,* 111.

24. Pikhoia and Geishtor, *Katyn',* 384–92; George Sanford surmises that the decision was made between February 8 and March 5. See Sanford, *Katyn and the Soviet Massacre of 1940,* 73; Sword, *Deportation and Exile;* Werth, "Ein Staat gegen sein Volk," 232–35. See, for example, the memoirs of Slowes, *The Road to Katyn.*

25. An overview of the possible motives is provided by Pikhoia and Geishtor, *Katyn',* 136–48; and Sanford, *Katyn and the Soviet Massacre of 1940,* 76–86, quote 85.

26. Slowes, *The Road to Katyn,* 70.

27. Pikhoia and Geishtor, *Katyn',* 121–36, quote 125.

28. See ibid.; Sanford, *Katyn and the Soviet Massacre of 1940,* 95, 97–114.

29. Quote: Joseph Goebbels, *The Goebbels Diaries 1939–1941,* trans. and ed. Fred Taylor (New York: Putnam, 1983), 423; Peter Longerich, *Politik der Vernich-*

tung: Eine Gesamtdarstellung der nationalsozialistischen Judenvernichtung (Munich: Piper, 1998), 296; Götz Aly, *"Endlösung": Völkerverschiebung und der Mord an den europäischen Juden* (Frankfurt am Main: Fischer Taschenbuch, 1998), 392–93.

30. Ralf Reuth, ed., Joseph Goebbels, *Tagebücher 1924–1945,* vol. 4: *1940–1942* (Munich: Piper, 1992), 1645.

31. See on this issue in general Jörg Baberowski and Anselm Doering-Manteuffel, *Ordnung durch Terror: Gewaltexzesse und Vernichtung im nationalsozialistischen und im stalinistischen Imperium* (Bonn: Dietz, 2006); Jörg Baberowski, "Totale Herrschaft im staatsfernen Raum: Stalinismus und Nationalsozialismus im Vergleich," *Zeitschrift für Geschichtswissenschaft* 57, no. 12 (2009): 1013–28, esp. 1026–28; Snyder, *Bloodlands.*

32. Quotes in Knight, *Beria,* 107–8; Gabriel Gorodetsky, *The Grand Delusion: Stalin and the German invasion of Russia* (New Haven: Yale University. Press, 1999), 299; Lev Besymenski, *Stalin und Hitler: Das Pokerspiel der Diktatoren,* 2d ed. (Berlin: Aufbau-Verlag, 2003), 444; Dónal O'Sullivan, *Dealing With the Devil: Anglo-Soviet Intelligence Cooperation in the Second World War* (New York: Peter Lang, 2010), 91.

33. On Mikoyan: David E. Murphy, *What Stalin Knew: The Enigma of* Barbarossa (New Haven: Yale University Press, 2005), 213; on Rychagov: ibid., 194, 225, 259.

34. Quote: Mikoian, *Tak bylo,* 390; Hiroaki Kuromiya, *Stalin* (Harlow: Longman, 2005), 151.

35. Bernd Bonwetsch, "The Purge of the Military and the Red Army's Operational Capability during the 'Great Patriotic War,'" in *From Peace to War: Germany, Soviet Russia, and the World, 1939–1941,* ed. Bernd Wegner (Oxford: Berghahn, 1997), 395–415; Goebbels, *Tagebücher,* 4:1627, quote 1628; Michael Burleigh, *Die Zeit des Nationalsozialismus: Eine Gesamtdarstellung* (Frankfurt am Main: Fischer, 2000), 565.

36. Bernhard R. Kroener, "The 'Frozen *Blitzkrieg*': German Strategic Planning against the Soviet Union and the Causes of Its Failure," in Wegner, *From Peace to War,* 135–51; Rüdiger Overmans, *Deutsche militärische Verluste im Zweiten Weltkrieg* (Munich: Oldenbourg, 2000), 277–78.

37. Goebbels, *Tagebücher,* entries for October 30, November 1, and November 30, 1941, 4:1687, 1689, 1715.

38. Quotes in Willy P. Reese, *"Mir selber seltsam fremd": Die Unmenschlichkeit des Krieges. Russland 1941–44,* 2d ed. (Munich: Claassen, 2003), 127, 136–37.

39. Amir Weiner, "Something to Die For, a Lot to Kill For: The Soviet System and the Barbarization of Warfare 1939–1945," in *The Barbarization of Warfare,* ed. George Kassimeris (New York: New York University Press, 2006), 101–25, esp. 107; Kroener, "The 'Frozen *Blitzkrieg*,'" 135–51; Omer Bartov, *Hitlers Wehrmacht: Soldaten, Fanatismus und die Brutalisierung des Krieges* (Reinbek: Rowohlt-Taschenbuch-Verlag, 1999); on the alleged idological commitment of Wehrmacht soldiers, see Bartov, *The Eastern Front 1941–1945: German Troops and the Barbarization of Warfare* (London: Macmillan, 1985); Bartov, "A View from Below: Survival, Cohesion, and Brutality," in Wegner, *From Peace to War,* 325–43. On

brutalization where the state is weak, see Jörg Baberowski, "Kriege in staatsfernen Räumen: Russland und die Sowjetunion 1905–1950," in *Formen des Krieges: Von der Antike bis zur Gegenwart,* ed. Dietrich Beyrau, Michael Hochgeschwender, and Dieter Langewiesche (Paderborn: F. Schöningh, 2007), 291–310, esp. 305–9; Mark Edele and Michael Geyer, "States of Exception: The Nazi-Soviet War as a System of Violence, 1939–1945," in *Beyond Totalitarianism: Stalinism and Nazism Compared,* ed. Michael Geyer and Sheila Fitzpatrick (Cambridge: Cambridge University Press, 2009), 345–95.

40. On the development of the war, see Alexander Werth, *Russland im Krieg, 1941–1945* (Munich: Droemer Knaur, 1965); Gerhard Weinberg, *Eine Welt in Waffen: Die globale Geschichte des Zweiten Weltkriegs* (Stuttgart: Deutsche Verlags-Anstalt, 1995), 294–96; Merridale, *Ivan's War.*

41. Walter Kempowski, *Das Echolot: Barbarossa '41. Ein kollektives Tagebuch* (Munich: Knaus, 2002), 164–65.

42. Musial, *"Konterrevolutionäre Elemente sind zu erschießen,"* 147–56, 172–78. On Latvia: Felder, *Lettland im Zweiten Weltkrieg,* 213–23. See also Leder, *My Life in Stalinist Russia,* 185; Irina Ehrenburg, *So habe ich gelebt: Erinnerungen* (Berlin: Berlin-Verlag, 1995), 75.

43. Vladimir Solonari, "Patterns of Violence: The Local Population and the Mass Murder of Jews in Bessarabia and Northern Bukowina, July–August 1941," *Kritika* 8 (2007): 749–88.

44. Quote in Kempowski, *Das Echolot,* 101–2. More reports on atrocities committed by Lithuanians ibid., 65–66, 129–31.

45. Leder, *My Life in Stalinist Russia,* 193–94; Herling, *A World Apart,* 231; Slowes, *The Road to Katyn,* 120.

46. Karel Berkhoff, *Harvest of Despair: Life and Death in Ukraine under Nazi Rule* (Cambridge, Mass.: Belknap Press of Harvard University Press, 2004), 23–24, 61–62; Leder, *My Life in Stalinist Russia,* 193–94.

47. Quote in Penter, *Kohle für Stalin und Hitler,* 181–182; Kuromiya, *Freedom and Terror in the Donbass,* 263–268.

48. On Kiev, Zhitomir and Kherson, see TsAMO, f. 32, op. 11309, d. 70, ll. 1–2 (Container 8, Reel 5); Berkhoff, *Harvest of Despair,* 23–24, 61–62; Herling, *A World Apart,* 231.

49. Andrei Sakharov, *Memoirs* (New York: Knopf, 1990), 43.

50. Ehrenburg, *So habe ich gelebt,* 130–31; Gennadi Bordiugov, "The Popular Mood in the Unoccupied Soviet Union: Continuity and Change during the War," in *The People's War: Responses to World War II in the Soviet Union,* ed. R. W. Thurston and B. Bonwetsch (Urbana: University of Illinois Press, 2000), 54–70, esp. 59; Richard Bidlack, "Survival Strategies in Leningrad during the First Year of the Soviet-German War," ibid., 84–107, esp. 100; Mikhail M. Gorinov, "Muscovite Moods, 22 June 1941 to May 1942," ibid., 108–34, esp. 119–24; John Barber, "The Moscow Crisis of October 1941."

51. Quotes in Berkhoff, *Harvest of Despair,* 28–29.

52. Kempowski, *Echolot,* 107, 172, 296.

53. Alexander Dallin, *Deutsche Herrschaft in Rußland 1941–1945: Eine Studie über Besatzungspolitik* (Düsseldorf: Droste, 1958), 71.

54. Berkhoff, *Harvest of Despair*, 12–13; Barber, "The Moscow Crisis of October 1941," 206; Dallin, *Deutsche Herrschaft in Rußland*, 624–27; Andrei Angrick, *Besatzungspolitik und Massenmord: Die Einsatzgruppe D in der südlichen Sowjetunion 1941–1943* (Hamburg: Hamburger Edition, 2003), 157, 459–61, 466–85; Catherine Andreyev, *Vlasov and the Russian Liberation Movement* (Cambridge: Cambridge University. Press, 1987); Matthias Schröder, *Deutschbaltische SS-Führer und Andrej Vlasov 1942–1945: 'Rußland kann nur von Russen besiegt werden.' Erhardt Kröger, Friedrich Burchardt und die 'Russische Befreiungsarmee'* (Paderborn: Schöningh, 2001); Joachim Hoffmann, *Die Ostlegionen 1941–1943: Turkotataren, Kaukasier und Wolgafinnen im deutschen Heer* (Freiburg: Rombach, 1976).

55. Dallin, *Deutsche Herrschaft in Rußland*, 42–43; Gerd Ueberschär, "Dokumente zum 'Unternehmen Barbarossa' als Vernichtungskrieg im Osten," in *Der deutsche Überfall auf die Sowjetunion: "Unternehmen Barbarossa" 1941*, ed. Ueberschär and Wolfram Wette (Paderborn: Schöningh, 1984), 249, 251, 260, 285; Theo Schulte, *The German Army and Nazi Policies in Occupied Russia* (Oxford: Berg, 1989), 219; Andrew Nagorski, *The Greatest Battle: Stalin, Hitler and the Desperate Struggle for Moscow that Changed the Course of World War II* (New York: Simon & Schuster, 2007), 92; Marcel Stein, *Field Marshal von Manstein, a Portrait* (London: Helion, 2007), 306–7.

56. Alfred Streim, "International Law and Soviet Prisoners of War," in Wegner, *From Peace to War*, 293–309, esp. 305; Streim, *Sowjetische Gefangene in Hitlers Vernichtungskrieg* (Heidelberg: Juristischer Verlag, 1982); Christian Streit, *Keine Kameraden: Die Wehrmacht und die sowjetischen Kriegsgefangenen, 1941–1945* (Stuttgart: Deutsche Verlags-Anstalt, 1978); Burleigh, *Die Zeit des Nationalsozialismus*, 589–604. See also the memoirs of Gabriel Temkin, who was able to escape from a German prisoner of war camp: Gabriel Temkin, *My Just War: The Memoir of a Jewish Red Army Soldier in World War II* (Novato: Presidio, 1998), 55–65.

57. Quote in Sönke Neitzel and Harald Welzer, *Soldaten: Protokolle vom Kämpfen, Töten und Sterben* (Frankfurt am Main: Fischer, 2011), 140–41.

58. Twelve-year-old boy quote in Swetlana Alexijewitsch, *Die letzten Zeugen: Kinder im Zweiten Weltkrieg* (Berlin: Aufbau-Taschenbuch-Verlag, 2005), 153–154; Dallin, *Deutsche Herrschaft in Rußland*, 40–113; Bernhard Chiari, *Alltag hinter der Front: Besatzung, Kollaboration und Widerstand in Weißrußland 1941–1944* (Düsseldorf: Droste, 1998); Christian Gerlach, *Kalkulierte Morde: Die deutsche Wirtschafts-und Vernichtungspolitik in Weißrußland, 1941–1944* (Hamburg: Hamburger Edition, 1999).

59. Bogdan Musial, *Sowjetische Partisanen: Mythos und Wirklichkeit, 1941–1944* (Paderborn: Schöningh, 2009), 61–83, 176–317; Aleksandr Gogun, "Partizany protiv naroda," in *Pod okkupatsiei v 1941–1944 gg: Stat'i i vospominaniia* (Moscow: Posev, 2004), 4–53; Gogun, *Mezhdu Gitlerom i Stalinym: Ukrainskie povstantsy* (Saint Petersburg: Izdat. Dom "Neva," 2004), 124–65, quote 131; Franziska Bruder, "Kollaboration oder Widerstand? Die ukrainischen Nationalisten während des Zweiten Weltkrieges," *Zeitschrift für Geschichtswissenschaft* 1 (2006): 20–44; Alexander Hill, *The War Behind the Eastern Front: The Soviet*

Partisan Movement in North-West Russia 1941–1944 (London: Cass, 2005), 120–63.

60. Mikoian, *Tak bylo,* 388–91, quotes 390–91; Montefiore, *Stalin,* 375.

61. Chernobaev, *Na prieme u Stalina,* 337–41; See also Dimitrov, *The Diary of Georgi Dimitrov.*

62. Stalin's speech is reproduced in Ueberschär, "Dokumente zum 'Unternehmen Barbarossa,'" 272–75; Werth, *Rußland im Krieg,* 187; Solomon Volkov, ed., *Testimony: The Memoirs of Dmitri Shostakovich* (New York: Limelight Editions, 1984), 104. See also Georgii K. Schukow, *Erinnerungen und Gedanken* (Stuttgart: Deutsche Verlags-Anstalt, 1969), 278–85; Bordiugov, "The Popular Mood in the Unoccupied Soviet Union," 66–67.

63. Metropolitan quote in Steven Merrit Miner, *Stalin's Holy War: Religion, Nationalism, and Alliance Politics, 1941–1945* (Chapel Hill: University of North Carolina Press, 2003), 69, 79–89.

64. Volkov, *Testimony,* 135–36.

65. John Barber, "The Image of Stalin in Soviet Propaganda and Public Opinion during World War 2," in *World War 2 and the Soviet People,* ed. J. Garrard and C. Garrard (London: St. Martin's Press, 1993), 38–49; Brooks, *Thank You, Comrade Stalin,* 159–94; Bernd Bonwetsch, "War as a 'Breathing Space': Soviet Intellectuals and the 'Great Patriotic War,'" in Thurston and Bonwetsch, *The People's War,* 137–53; Werth, *Rußland im Krieg,* 294–310.

66. Mark Harrison, *Accounting for War: Soviet Production, Employment, and the Defence Burden, 1940–1945* (Cambridge: Cambridge University Press, 1996); Harrison, "'Barbarossa': The Soviet Response, 1941," in Wegner, *From Peace to War,* 415–31; Klaus Segbers, *Die Sowjetunion im Zweiten Weltkrieg: Die Mobilisierung von Verwaltung, Wirtschaft und Gesellschaft im 'Großen Vaterländischen Krieg,' 1941–1943* (Munich: Oldenbourg, 1987); Frederick Kagan, "The Evacuation of Soviet Industry in the Wake of 'Barbarossa': A Key to the Soviet Victory," *Journal of Slavic Military Studies* 8 (1995): 337–414; John Barber and Mark Harrison, *The Soviet Home Front 1941–1945: A Social and Economic History of the USSR in World War II* (London: Longman, 1991), 127; Mikoian, *Tak bylo,* 394–414.

67. Quotes in Berkhoff, *Harvest of Despair,* 12–13.

68. On Mekhlis and for the Stalin quote: Montefiore, *Stalin,* 364–65; Iurii. V. Rubtsov, *Iz-za spiny vozhdia: Politicheskaia i voennaia deiatel'nost' L. Z. Mekhlisa* (Moscow: Kompaniia Ritm esteit, 2003), 115–85.

69. A list of the generals arrested can be found in TsAMO, f. 33, op. 11454, d. 179, l. 320 (Container 8, Reel 5); Mikoian, *Tak bylo,* 415–425; Seweryn Bialer, ed., *Stalin and His Generals: Soviet Military Memoirs of World War II* (New York: Pegasus, 1969), 207–12; Konstantin M. Simonov, *Aus der Sicht meiner Generation: Gedanken über Stalin* (Berlin: Verlag Volk und Welt, 1990), 300–397; "'Mne bylo prikazano byt' spokoinym i ne panikovat. Tragediia Zapadnogo fronta i ego komanduiushchego D. G. Pavlova," in *Neizvestnaia Rossiia,* vol. 2, ed. V. Kozlov (Moscow: Istoricheskoe nasledie 1992), 57–111; K. A. Merezkow and Arno Specht, *Im Dienste des Volkes* (Berlin: Deutscher Militärverlag, 1972), 279. On Meretskov: Constantine Pleshakov, *Stalin's Folly: The Tragic First Ten Days of World War II*

on the Eastern Front (Boston: Houghton Mifflin, 2005), 100, 186, 195; Barber and Harrison, *The Soviet Home Front,* 28.

70. TsAMO, f. 127, op. 12915, d. 16, ll. 132–37 (Container 6, Reel 4).

71. TsAMO, f. 3, op. 11556, d. 1, ll. 119–20 (Container 7, Reel 4).

72. Nauchnyi Arkhiv Instituta Rossiiskoi Istorii Akademii Nauk, f. 2. I thank Jochen Hellbeck, now working on a history of the battle of Stalingrad, for drawing my attention to this event. See also Antony Beevor and Luba Vinogradova, eds., *A Writer at War: Vasily Grossman with the Red Army, 1941–1945* (New York: Pantheon, 2005), 146.

73. Sergei Khrushchev, ed., *Memoirs of Nikita Khrushchev,* vol. 1: *Commissar (1918–1945)* (University Park: Pennsylvania State University Press, 2004), 396; Marius Joseph Broekmeyer, *Stalin, the Russians, and Their War: 1941–1945* (Madison: University of Wisconsin Press, 2004), 216.

74. On Vashugin: Pleshakov, *Stalin's Folly,* 186, 195.

75. Chuikov's order in TsAMO, f. 345, op. 5487, d. 5, l. 445(Container 7, Reel 4).

76. Temkin, *My Just War,* 117.

77. Quote in Broekmeyer, *Stalin, the Russians, and Their War,* 97–98.

78. Anthony Beevor, *Stalingrad* (Munich: C. Bertelsmann, 1999), 143, 145, 198–221; Injured sergeant quote in A. M. Beliaev, I. Iu. Bondar', and T. K. Orlova, *Kuban v gody Velikoi otechestvennoi Voiny 1941–1945: Chronika sobytii,* vol. 1 (Krasnodar; Sovetskyi Kuban', 2000), 65; Roger R. Reese, *The Soviet Military Experience: A History of the Soviet Army, 1917–1991* (London: Routledge, 2000), 93–137; Broekmeyer, *Stalin, the Russians, and Their War,* 216; Temkin, *My Just War,* 103; Karl-Heinz Frieser, "Die Schlacht im Kursker Bogen," in *Das Deutsche Reich und der Zweite Weltkrieg,* vol. 8: *Die Ostfront 1943/44: Der Krieg im Osten und an den Nebenfronten,* ed. Militärgeschichtliches Forschungsamt (Munich: Deutsche Verlags-Anstalt, 2007), 132–33.

79. Leonid Rabichev, "Voina vse spishet," *Znamia* 2 (2005): 21:

80. Number of death sentences: RGANI, Fond 89, opis' 18, delo 8, ll. 1–3; TsAMO, f. 32, op. 11309, d. 70, ll. 147, 154 (Container 8, Reel 5); Beevor, *Stalingrad,* 143, 145, 198–221; Beevor and Vinogradova, *A Writer at War,* 141; Reese, *The Soviet Military Experience,* 93–137; Jörg Ganzenmüller, *Das belagerte Leningrad, 1941–1944: Die Stadt in den Strategien von Angreifern und Verteidigern* (Paderborn: Schöningh, 2005), 113–21.

81. Petr Astakhov, *Zigzagy sud'by: Iz zhizni sovetskogo voennoplennogo* (Moscow: ROSSPEN, 2005), 45–46. See also Temkin, *My Just War,* 179. The soldier Vladimir Gelfand had a similar experience in January 1945 near the Oder River front. See Wladimir Gelfand, *Deutschland-Tagebuch 1945–1946: Aufzeichnungen eines Rotarmisten* (Berlin: Aufbau-Verlag, 2005), 37–38. See also the diaries of Vasily Grossman: Beevor and Vinogradova, *A Writer at War,* 103–4.

82. *Iosif Stalin v ob'iatiakh sem'i: Iz lichnogo arkhiva* (Moscow: Edition Q, 1993), 69–100; V. Naumov and L. Reshin, "Repressionen gegen sowjetische Kriegsgefangene und zivile Repatrianten in der UdSSR 1941 bis 1956," in *Die Tragödie der Gefangenschaft in Deutschland und in der Sowjetunion, 1941–1956,* ed. Klaus-Dieter Müller and Konstantin Nikischkin (Cologne: Böhlau, 1998), 339–40.

83. TsAMO, f. 3, op. 11556, d. 6, ll. 23–24 (Container 7, Reel 4).

84. Quote in Vladimir But, "Orel—reshka," *Druzhba narodov* 4 (1995): 23–95, esp. 43. I thank Franziska Exeler for this reference.

85. Quotes in TsAMO, f. 3, op. 11556, d. 6, ll. 112; TsAMO, f. 32, op. 11289, d. 289, l. 252; (both Container 7, Reel 4).

86. Reese, *The Soviet Military Experience,* 115–16.

87. Michail Delagrammatik, "Voennye tribunaly za rabotoi," in *Novyi mir* 6 (1997): 130–39, esp. 138. I am grateful to Franziska Exeler for this reference.

88. Merridale, *Ivan's War,* 56; Broekmeyer, *Stalin, the Russians, and Their War,* 98.

89. Merridale, *Ivan's War,* 114. See also Beevor and Vinogradova, *A Writer at War,* 73.

90. Vasilii Khristoforov, ed., *Lubianka v dni bitvy za Moskvu: Po ressekrechennym dokumentam FSB RF* (Moscow: Zvonnitsa, 2002), 230.

91. Reese, *The Soviet Military Experience,* 93–137; Beevor, *Stalingrad,* 143, 145, 198–221; Arbatov, *The System;* Knight, *Beria,* 114; Temkin, *My Just War,* 85–90; Barber, "The Moscow Crisis of October 1941," 206; Harrison, "'Barbarossa,'" 443.

92. Herling, *A World Apart,* 82–84.

93. Quotes in Kempowski, *Echolot,* 205.

94. Merridale, *Ivan's War,* 137; Beevor and Vinogradova, eds., *A Writer at War,* 100; Vladimir Shnaider, "Neizvestnaia voina," *Voprosy Istorii* 1 (1995): 104–13; L. Rubinshtein, "Izpoved' shchastlivogo al'pinista: Glavy iz trilogii," *Zvezda* 5 (1995): 5–52; Beevor, *Stalingrad,* 143, 145, 198–221; Broekmeyer, *Stalin, the Russians, and Their War,* 169–71; Alexander Jakovlev, *Ein Jahrhundert der Gewalt in Sowjetrussland* (Berlin: Berlin-Verlag, 2004), 259–60; Reese, *The Soviet Military Experience,* 93–137; Bernd Bonwetsch, "Sowjetunion—Triumph im Elend," in *Kriegsende in Europa: Vom Beginn des deutschen Machtzerfalls bis zur Stabilisierung der Nachkriegsordnung 1944–1948,* ed. Ulrich Herbert and Axel Schildt (Essen: Klartext, 1998), 68; Bonwetsch, "Die sowjetischen Kriegsgefangenen zwischen Stalin und Hitler," *Zeitschrift für Geschichtswissenschaft* 41 (1993): 135–42.

95. Krisztian Ungváry, *Battle for Budapest: One Hundred Days in World War II* (London: I. B. Tauris, 2011), 20.

96. Ibid., 20 n. 46.

97. Grigorii F. Krivosheev, "Ob itogakh statisticheskikh issledovanii poter' vooruzhennykh sil SSSR v Velikoi Otechestvennoi voine," in *Liudskie poteri SSSR v period vtoroi mirovoi voiny: Sbornik statei,* ed. Rostislav Evdokimov (St. Petersburg: Izd-vo "Russko-Baltiiskii informatsionnyi tsentr BLITS," 1995), 75; Harrison, "'Barbarossa,'" 443.

98. Swetlana Alexijewitsch, *Der Krieg hat kein weibliches Gesicht* (Berlin: Berliner Taschenbuch-Verlag, 2004), 254; Beevor and Vinogradova, eds., *A Writer at War,* 120–21. See also the image and document collection by Swetlana A. Aleksijewitsch and Peter Jahn, *Mascha + Nina + Katjuscha: Frauen in der Roten Armee 1941–1945* (Berlin: Links, 2003), 160.

99. Astakhov, *Zigzagy sud'by,* 46; On training the soldiers' bodies in war, see Joanna Bourke, "Auge in Auge mit dem Feind: Das Töten von Angesicht zu Angesicht in den Kriegen des 20. Jahrhunderts, 1914–1975," in Gleichmann and Kühne,

Massenhaftes Töten, 286–306; Thomas Kühne, "Gruppenkohäsion und Kameradschaftsmythos in der Wehrmacht," in *Die Wehrmacht: Mythos und Realität*, ed. Rolf-Dieter Müller and Hans Erich Volkmann (Munich: Oldenbourg, 1999), 534–49.

100. Swetlana Aleksijewitsch, "Der Mensch zählt mehr als der Krieg: Aus dem Tagebuch einer Schriftstellerin," in Aleksijewitsch and Jahn, *Mascha + Nina + Katjuscha*, 36–48, esp. 48. For reports on cases of rape in Budapest see Andrea Pető, "Stimmen des Schweigens: Erinnerungen an Vergewaltigungen in den Hauptstädten des "ersten Opfers" (Wien) und des "letzten Verbündeten" Hitlers (Budapest)," *Zeitschrift für Geschichtswissenschaft* 47 (1999): 892–914.

101. Rabichev, "Voina vse spishet," 29. See also Gelfand, *Deutschland-Tagebuch*, 79–80.

102. Ephraim Kishon, *Nichts zu lachen: Erinnerungen* (Munich: Langen Müller, 1993), 114–15.

103. Weiner, "Something to Die For," 107.

104. Broekmeyer, *Stalin, the Russians, and Their War*, 52.

105. Anatoli Rybakov, *Roman der Erinnerung* (Berlin: Aufbau-Verlag, 2001), 112.

106. Stalin's orders in TsAMO, f. 127, op. 12915, d. 16, ll. 50–52 (Container 6, Reel 4); TsAMO, f. 3, op. 11556, d. 1, ll. 41–42 (Container 7, Reel 4); TsAMO, f. 3, op. 11556, d. 6, l. 13 (Container 7, Reel 4); Dmitrii Levinskii, *My iz sorok pervogo . . . Vospominaniia* (Moscow: Novoe Izdatel'stvo, 2005), 129–31; Berkhoff, *Harvest of Despair*, 30–32; Pleshakov, *Stalin's Folly*, 232–33. For the regime's evacuation policy in the Second World War, see Rebecca Manley, *To the Tashkent Station: Evacuation and Survival in the Soviet Union at War* (Ithaca: Cornell University Press, 2009), 32–41.

107. Gross, *Revolution from Abroad*, 178–86; Musial, *"Konterrevolutionäre Elemente sind zu erschießen"*; Felder, *Lettland im zweiten Weltkrieg*, 160–61. See also the letters of German soldiers in Kempowski, *Echolot*, 122, 215–16, 227–28, where the quote from the German officer can also be found.

108. Berkhoff, *Harvest of Despair*, 27; Victor Kravchenko, *I Chose Freedom: The Personal and Political Life of a Soviet Official* (1946; reprint, New York: Scribner's, 1947), 405.

109. The order of November 1941 in RGANI, f. 89, op. 18, d. 9, ll. 3–4; Stalin's orders of 1943 in RGASPI, f. 17, op. 162, d. 37, ll. 72, 79; Bordiugov, "The Popular Mood in the Unoccupied Soviet Union," 60; Barber, "The Moscow Crisis of October 1941," 207, 213; Gorinov, "Muscovite Moods," 115–17; Montefiore, *Stalin*, 348–49; Kuromiya, *Freedom and Terror in the Donbass*, 263–68, Penter, *Kohle für Stalin und Hitler*, 181. At the beginning of the war, the number of politically motivated sentences rose from 8,011 in 1941 to 23,278 in 1942. See V. P. Popov, "Gosudarstvennyi terror v sovetskoi Rossii, 1923–1953 gg: Istochniki i ikh interpretatsiia," *Otechestvennye arkhivy* 2 (1992): 28.

110. Dmitry S. Likhachev, *Reflections on the Russian Soul: A Memoir* (New York: Central European University Press, 2000), 234, 255.

111. Ganzenmüller, *Das belagerte Leningrad*, 106–13 (Stalin quote, 106), 215–29, 255–77, 279–313.

112. Stalin quote in TsAMO, f. 3, op. 11556, d. 5, l. 252 (Container 7, Reel 4). See also *Velikaia Otechestvennaia Voina*, ed. Vladimir A. Zolotar', vol. 1: *Stavka VGK: Dokumenty i materialy 1941 god* (Moscow: Nauka, 1996), 195–96; Anna Reid, *Leningrad: Tragedy of a City under Siege, 1941–1944* (London: Bloomsbury Publishing, 2011), 126.

113. I rely mainly on the dissertation by Ganzenmüller, *Das belagerte Leningrad*, 106–13, 215–29, 255–77, 279–313; John Barber and Andrei Dzenkevich, *Life and Death in Besieged Leningrad, 1941–1944* (Houndmills: Palgrave Macmillan, 2005); Bidlack, "Survival Strategies in Leningrad during the First Year of the Soviet-German War," 96–99; "GULAG v gody Velikoi Otechestvennoi voiny," *Voenno-istoricheskii zhurnal* 4 (1991): 23.

114. Lidiya Ginzburg, *Blockade Diary* (London: The Harvill Press, 1995), 84; Likhachev, *Reflections on the Russian Soul*, 255. See also Reid, *Leningrad*.

115. Pobol' and Polian, *Stalinskie deportatsii*, 287–313, quotes 288, 309. See also Irina L. Shcherbakova, *Nakazannyi narod: Repressii protiv rossiiskikh nemtsev* (Moscow: Zven'ia, 1999); Wolfgang Leonhard, *Die Revolution entläßt ihre Kinder*, 3d ed. (Cologne: Kiepenheuer & Witsch, 1981), 125–30; Benjamin Pinkus, "The Deportation of the German Minority in the Soviet Union, 1941–1945," in Wegner, *From Peace to War*, 449–63; Robert Conquest, *Stalins Völkermord: Wolgadeutsche, Krimtataren, Kaukasier* (Wien: Europaverlag, 1970).

116. Chuev, *Molotov Remembers*, 195. Kaganovich said the same in the 1960s. See Parfenov, "'Zheleznyi Lazar': Konets kar'ery," 74. On the Deportation of about 25,000 Bulgars, Greeks, and Armenians in May 1944 and of 225,000 Crimean Tatars in July 1944, see GARF, f. 9401s, op. 2, d. 65, ll. 161–63, 275.

117. Quotes in GARF, f. 9401, op. 2, d. 65, ll. 311–14; GARF, f. 9479, op. 1, d. 177, ll. 1–6; GARF, f. 9479, op. 1, d. 153, ll. 42–43; "'Pogruzheny v eshelony i otpravleny k mestam poeselenii. . . .' L. Beriia—I. Stalinu," *Istoriia SSSR* 1 (1991): 143–60; Nikolai F. Bugai, *L. Beriia—I. Stalinu: 'Soglasno vashemu ukazaniiu . . .'* (Moscow: AIRO-XX, 1995), 27ff., for the quotes, 104–5, 128; Nikolai F. Bugai, "K voprosu o deportatsii narodov SSSR v 30–40-kh godakh," *Istoriia SSSR* 6 (1989): 135–44; GARF, f. 9401, op. 2, d. 64, l. 161; "Krovavyi pepel Khaibakha," in *Tak eto bylo: Natsional'nye repressii v SSSR 1919–1952 gody*, ed. Svetlana Alieva (Moscow: Rossiiskii Mezhdunarodnyi fond kul'tury Insan, 1993), 170–79; Norman Naimark, *Fires of Hatred: Ethnic Cleansing in Twentieth-Century Europe* (Cambridge, Mass.: Harvard University Press, 2001), 85–107; N. F. Bugai and A. M. Gonov, *Kavkaz: Narody v eshelonakh: 20-e-60-e gody* (Moscow: INSAN, 1998), 118–222; John B. Dunlop, *Russia Confronts Chechnya: Roots of a Separatist Conflict* (Cambridge: Cambridge University Press, 1998), 70–71; Viktor V. Zemskov, "Spetsposelentsy, po dokumentatsii NKVD-MVD SSSR," *Sotsiologicheskie Issledovaniia* 11 (1990): 3–17; Zemskov, "Zakliuchennye, spetsposelentsy, ssyl'noposelentsy, ssyl'nye i vyslannye: Statistiko-geograficheskii aspekt," *Istoriia SSSR* 5 (1991): 151–65; Weitz, *A Century of Genocide*, 79–82; A. M. Nekrich, *Punished Peoples: The Deportation and Fate of Soviet Minorities at the End of the Second World War* (New York: Norton, 1978), 124–26; Vera Tolz, "New Information about the Deportation of Ethnic Groups in the USSR during World War 2," in Garrard and Garrard, *World War and the Soviet People*, 161–79.

118. Herling, *A World Apart*, 229–31.

119. Alexijewitsch, *Der Krieg hat kein weibliches Gesicht*, 325. The war diary of the soldier Vladimir Gelfand contains similar descriptions. See Gelfand, *Deutschland-Tagebuch*, 29.

120. Likhachev, *Reflections on the Russian Soul*, 256.

121. Andrei Sakharov, *Memoirs* (London: Hutchinson, 1990), 41; Bordiugov, "The Popular Mood in the Unoccupied Soviet Union," 65.

122. RGASPI, f. 82, op. 2, d. 897, ll. 127–31. See also Iurii S. Aksenev, "Apogei Stalinizma: poslevoennaia piramida vlasti," *Voprosy Istorii KPSS* 11 (1990): 93; Sheila Fitzpatrick, "Postwar Soviet Society: The 'Return to Normalcy,' 1945–1953," in *The Impact of World War II on the Soviet Union*, ed. Susan J. Linz (Totowa: Rowman & Allanheld, 1985), 129–56; Bonwetsch, "Sowjetunion—Triumph im Elend," 52–88; Julie Hessler, "A Postwar Perestroika? Toward a History of Private Enterprise in the USSR," *Slavic Review* 57 (1998): 516–42; E. Zubkova, "Obshchestvo vyshchedshee iz voiny: Russkie i nemtsy v 1945 godu," *Otechestvennaia istoriia* 3 (1995): 90–100; Zubkova, "Die sowjetische Gesellschaft nach dem Krieg: Lage und Stimmung in der Bevölkerung, 1945/46," *Vierteljahreshefte für Zeitgeschichte* 4) (1999). 303–03.

123. Janusz Bardach, *Surviving Freedom after the Gulag* (Berkeley: University of California Press, 2003), 82.

124. Yuri Orlov, *Dangerous Thoughts*, 96.

125. Brodsky, *Less Than One*, 18–19.

126. RGASPI, f. 558, op. 11, d. 888, l. 108.

127. Lev Kopelev, *No Jail for Thought* (London: Secker & Warburg, 1977), 102–3.

128. Ibid.; Brodsky, *Less Than One*, 27. On the culture shock experienced by Red Army soldiers in Western Europe, see among others: Barbara Stelzl-Marx, "Ideologie, Kontrolle, Repression: Als sowjetischer Besatzungssoldat im Westen," *Jahrbuch für Historische Kommunismusforschung* (2010): 179–191. For the atmosphere after the war, see Zubkova, "Die sowjetische Gesellschaft nach dem Krieg," 373.

129. RGASPI, f. 558, op. 11, d. 888, ll. 51–56. See also Alec Nove, "Soviet Peasantry in World War II," in Linz, *The Impact of World War II on the Soviet Union*, 87–89; Fitzpatrick, "Postwar Soviet Society," 149.

130. The letter from a peasant in the area of Stalingrad and the report of the Moldavian minister for state security are in RGANI, f. 89, op. 57, d. 20, ll. 113–16, 124. See also Beria's reports to Stalin on the December 1946 famine in V. N. Khaustov, V. P. Naumov, and N. S. Plotnikova, *Lubianka: Stalin i MGB SSSR mart 1946–mart 1953* (Moscow: Mezhdunarodnyi fond "Demokratiia," 2007), 37–40, peasant quote 39. For the famine, see Michael Ellman, "The 1947 Famine and the Entitlement Approach to Famines," *Cambridge Journal of Economics* 24 (2000): 603–30; Veniamin F. Zima, "Poslevoennoe obshchestvo: Golod i prestupnost'," *Otechestvennaia istoriia* 5 (1995): 45–59.

131. RGASPI, f. 17, op. 121, d. 673, ll. 2–9, 21, 29, 47–50.

132. On the deportation of the Kalmyks from the area of Rostov-on-the-Don, see the report by the party secretary of Rostov, Dvinsky, in RGASPI, f. 84, op. 1,

d. 134, l. 69; Mark R. Elliot, *Pawns of Yalta: Soviet Refugees and America's Role in their Repatriation* (Urbana: University of Illinois Press, 1982), 104, 194; Ulrike Goeken-Haidl, *Der Weg zurück: Die Repatriierung sowjetischer Zwangsarbeiter und Kriegsgefangener während und nach dem Zweiten Weltkrieg* (Essen: Klartext, 2006), 85, 165, 340–41, 388–89; Nikolai Tolstoi, *Die Verratenen von Jalta: Englands Schuld vor der Geschichte* (Munich: Langen, 1978); Nicholaus Bethell, *The Last Secret: Forcible Repatriation to Russia, 1944–1947* (London: Deutsch, 1974), 80ff.; Naumov and Reshin, "Repressionen gegen sowjetische Kriegsgefangene und zivile Repatrianten in der UdSSR," 339–64.

133. Naumov and Reshin, "Repressionen gegen sowjetische Kriegsgefangene und zivile Repatrianten in der UdSSR," 339–64; Viktor N. Zemskov, "K voprosu o repatriatsii sovetskikh grazhdan 1944–1951 gody," *Istoriia SSSR* 4 (1999): 26–41; Pavel Poljan, *Deportiert nach Hause: Sowjetische Kriegsgefangene im "Dritten Reich" und ihre Repatriierung* (Munich: Oldenbourg, 2001), 165–187.

134. Goeken-Haidl, *Der Weg zurück*, 85, 165, 340–41, 388–89, female forced laborer quote, 390.

135. See ibid.; Naumov and Reshin, "Repressionen gegen sowjetische Kriegsgefangene und zivile Repatrianten in der UdSSR," 339–64; Zemskov, "K voprosu o repatriatsii sovetskikh grazhdan"; Poljan, *Deportiert nach Hause*, 165–87; Temkin, *My Just War*, 85–90; Bonwetsch, "Sowjetunion—Triumph im Elend," 68–70; Razgon, *Nichts als die reine Wahrheit*, 329; Fitzpatrick, "Postwar Soviet Society," 134–37.

136. Quotes in Penter, *Kohle für Stalin und Hitler*, 334; Ehrenburg, *So habe ich gelebt*, 174–77.

137. RGASPI, f. 82, op. 2, d. 897, ll. 106–23, 135–39, 143–45. See also Gogun, *Mezhdu Gitlerom i Stalinym*, 212–52; Bruder, "Kollaboration oder Widerstand?" 28–29; Frank Golszewski, "Ukraine: Bürgerkrieg und Resowjetisierung," in Herbert and Schildt, *Kriegsende in Europa*, 89–99; Fitzpatrick, "Postwar Soviet Society," 134.

138. RGASPI, f. 82, op. 2, d. 897, ll. 106–23, 135–39, 143–45; Elena Zubkova, "'Lesnye brat'ia' v Pribaltike: Voina posle voiny," *Otechestvennaia Istoriia* 3 (2007): 14–30, esp. 16, 28; Kalniete, *With Dance Shoes in Siberian Snows*, 131; Purs, "Soviet in Form, Local in Content," 31–32; Vanda Kasauskiene, "Deportations from Lithuania under Stalin, 1940–1953," *Lithuanian Historical Studies* 3 (1998): 79–80; Toivo U. Raun, *Estonia and the Estonians*, 2d ed. (Stanford: Hoover Institution Press, 1991), 181–83; E. Laasi, "Der Untergrundkrieg in Estland, 1945–1953," in *Auch wir sind Europa*, ed. Ruth Kibelka (Berlin: Aufbau-Taschenbuch-Verlag, 1991), 70–82; Igor Casu, "Stalinist Terror in Soviet Moldavia, 1904–1953," in McDermott and Stibbe, *Stalinist Terror in Eastern Europe*, 49; David Feest, *Zwangskollektivierung im Baltikum: Die Sowjetisierung des estnischen Dorfes 1944–1953* (Cologne: Böhlau, 2007), 408–27.

139. Bardach, *Surviving Freedom after the Gulag*, 116–17.

140. See also Sheila Fitzpatrick, "Cultural Orthodoxies under Stalin," in Fitzpatrick, *The Cultural Front*, 246; Dietrich Beyrau, *Intelligenz und Dissens: Die russischen Bildungsschichten in der Sowjetunion, 1917–1985* (Göttingen: Vandenhoeck & Ruprecht, 1993), 80–101; Vera S. Dunham, *In Stalin's Time: Middle Class Val-*

ues in Soviet Fiction (Cambridge: Cambridge University Press, 1976); S. Frederick Starr, *Red and Hot: Jazz in Rußland von 1917–1990* (Vienna: Hannibal-Verlag, 1990); Elena Zubkova, "Stalin i obshchestvennoe mnenie v SSSR, 1945–153 gg.," in *Stalin i kholodnaia voina*, ed. I. V. Gaiduk, N. I. Egorova, and A. O. Chubar'ian (Moscow: Institut vseobshchei istorii RAN, 1998), 281–85.

141. Bardach, *Surviving Freedom*, 93–94.

142. Khaustov et al., *Lubianka* (2007), 60–65, 77–79, quote 62.

143. Frank Grüner, *Patrioten und Kosmopoliten: Juden im Sowjetstaat 1941–1953* (Cologne: Böhlau, 2008), 55–128, 416–51; Shimon Redlich, *War, Holocaust and Stalinism: A Documented History of the Jewish Anti-Fascist Commitee in the USSR* (Luxembourg: Harwood Academic Publishers, 1995); Vladimir P. Naumov, "Die Vernichtung des jüdischen Antifaschistischen Komitees," in *Der Spätstalinismus und die 'jüdische Frage': Zur antisemitischen Wende des Kommunismus*, ed. Leonid Luks (Cologne: Böhlau, 1998), 123–26; Naumov, ed., *Nepravednyi sud: Poslednyi stalinskii rasstrel. Stenogramma sudebnogo protsessa nad chlenami Evreiskogo Antifashistskogo Komiteta* (Moscow: Nauka, 1994); Gennadii Kostyrchenko, *Out of the Red Shadows: Anti-Semitism in Stalin's Russia* (Amherst: Prometheus Books, 1995); Arno Lustiger, *Rotbuch: Stalin und die Juden* (Berlin: Aufbau-Verlag, 1998), 108–22; Alexander Borschtschagowski, *Orden für einen Mord: Die Judenverfolgung unter Stalin* (Berlin: Propyläen, 1997); Sakharov, *Mein Leben*, 177–78.

144. RGASPI, f. 558, op. 11, d. 183, l. 51; Khaustov et al., *Lubianka* (2007), 239–44.

145. Court record in Library of Congress, Manuscript Division, The Papers of Dmitrii Antonovich Volkogonov, Container 3, Reel 2; Naumov, *Nepravednyi sud*, 375–82, quotes 373, 378. Overview in Grüner, *Patrioten und Kosmopoliten*, 452–88.

146. RGASPI, f. 82, op. 2, d. 148, ll. 126–31; RGASPI, f. 558, op. 11, d. 904, ll. 27–35, 39.

147. D. G. Nedzhafov and Z. S. Belousova, eds., *Stalin i kosmopolitizm: Dokumenty Agitpropa TsK KPSS 1945–1953* (Moscow: Moiak, 2005), 265.

148. Ibid., 651–52. On the doctors' plot see Yakov Etinger, "The Doctors' Plot: Stalin's Solution to the Jewish Question," in *Jews and Jewish Life in Russia and the Soviet Union*, ed. Yaacov Ro'i (Ilford: Frank Cass, 1995), 103–24; Alexander Lokshin, "The Doctors' Plot: The Non-Jewish Response," ibid., 157–67; Zhores A. Medvedev, "Stalin i 'delo vrachei': Novye materaly," *Voprosy istorii*, no. 1 (2003): 78–103; Yakov Rapoport, *The Doctors' Plot of 1953* (London: Fourth Estate, 1991); Jonathan Brent and Vladimir Naumov, *Stalin's Last Crime: The Plot against the Jewish Doctors, 1948–1953* (New York: HarperCollins, 2003), 283–311; Grüner, *Patrioten und Kosmopoliten*, 489–507.

149. Talbott, *Khrushchev Remembers*, 1:286–87.

150. Quoted in Torańska, *"Them,"* 314. Bardach tells of a similar experience: *Surviving Freedom*, 187.

151. RGASPI, f. 558, op. 11, d. 904, ll. 27–35, 38–39; RGASPI, f. 82, op. 2, d. 148, ll. 126–31.

152. Dmitrii Shepilov, *The Kremlin's Scholar: A Memoir of Soviet Politics under Stalin and Krushchev* (New Haven: Yale University Press, 2007), 5.

153. RGASPI, f. 558, op. 11, d. 765, l. 107; Oleg Khlevniuk and I. Gorlitskii, eds., *Politbiuro TsK VKP(b) i Sovet Ministrov SSSR 1945–1953* (Moscow: ROSSPEN, 2002), 191.

154. Ibid., 238.

155. Pavel A. Sudoplatov, *Razvedka i kreml': Zapiski nezhelatel'nogo sveidetelia* (Moscow: TOO Geia, 1996), 383. On Stalin's vacations, see Yoram Gorlitzki and Oleg Khlevniuk, *Cold Peace: Stalin and the Soviet Ruling Circle, 1945–1953* (Oxford: Oxford University Press, 2003), 105.

156. Khaustov et al., *Lubianka* (2007), 135–136.

157. GARF, f. 9401, op. 2, d. 99, l. 386; RGANI, f. 89, op. 18, d. 27, ll. 1–2. See also Khaustov et al., *Lubianka* (2006), 539–40.

158. Quoted in N. Kovaleva and A. Korotkov, eds., *Molotov, Malenkov, Kaganovich, 1957: Stenogramma iiun'skogo plenuma TsK KPSS i drugie dokumenty* (Moscow: Mezhdunarodnyi fond "Demokratiia," 1998), 47.

159. Nami Mikoian, *S liubov'iu i pechal'iu: Vospominaniia* (Moscow: Terra, 1998), 106–109.

160. Talbott, *Khrushchev Remembers,* 1:297.

161. Ibid., 298–302. Berman: Torańska, *"Them."* Stalin's visitors' book, kept by his secretary, Aleksandr Poskrebyshev, is also informative about Stalin's work schedule. See Chernobaev, *Na prieme u Stalina.*

162. Talbott, *Khrushchev Remembers,* 1:303.

163. Ibid., 257–58, 296–306; Gorlitzki and Khlevniuk, *Cold Peace,* 45–65.

164. For the medical diagnosis, see RGASPI, f. 558, op. 11, d. 1483, ll. 9–10; Sudoplatov, *Razvedka i kreml',* 383; Zhores A. Medvedev and Roy A. Medvedev, *The Unknown Stalin* (London: I. B. Tauris, 2006), 8.

165. Stalin's telegram and the replies of Malenkov, Beria, and Mikoyan are in RGASPI, f. 558, op. 11, d. 99, ll. 86, 95, 103–5; Gorlitzki and Khlevniuk, *Cold Peace,* 19–25.

166. RGASPI, f. 558, op. 11, d. 99, ll. 120.

167. Mikoian, *Tak bylo,* 534–36, 559–80, quote 559; Abakumov and the court of honor: RGASPI, f. 17, op. 3, d. 1069, l. 28; Michael Parrish, *The Lesser Terror: Soviet State Security, 1939–1953* (Westport: Praeger, 1996), 215–21, 236–40; Aksenev, "Apogei Stalinizma," 100–104; Werth, "Ein Staat gegen sein Volk," 272–73; Jonathan Harris, "The Origins of the Conflict between Malenkov and Zhdanov: 1939–1941," *Slavic Review* 35 (1976): 287–303; Bernd Bonwetsch, "Die 'Leningrad-Affäre' 1949–1951: Politik und Verbrechen im Spätstalinismus," *Deutsche Studien* 28 (1990): 306–22; Chernobaev, *Na prieme u Stalina,* 520; Voznesensky quote in Khlevniuk and Gorlitskii, *Politbiuro TsK VKP(b) i Sovet Ministrov SSSR,* 298. See also Gorlitzki and Khlevniuk, *Cold Peace,* 87.

168. Khlevniuk and Gorlitskii, *Politbiuro TsK VKP(b) i Sovet Ministrov SSSR,* 307–10.

169. Court record in Library of Congress, Manuscript Division, The Papers of Dmitrii Antonovich Volkogonov, Container 3, Reel 2. On the wave of persecution in Leningrad see RGASPI, f. 558, op. 11, d. 66, l. 125; Khaustov et al., *Lubianka* (2007), 303–4; Vladimir Denisov, ed., *TsK VKP(b) i regional'nye partiinye komitety 1945–1953* (Moscow: ROSSPEN, 2004), 185–97.

170. Raissa Orlowa-Kopelew, *Eine Vergangenheit, die nicht vergeht: Rückblicke aus fünf Jahrzehnten* (Munich: Knaus, 1985), 217.

171. Denisov, *CK VKP(b) i regional'nye partiinye komitety,* 210–21, quotes 210, 212–15.

172. Molotov's letter: RGASPI, f. 17, op. 163, d. 1518, l. 164; Chuev, *Molotov Remembers,* 323.

173. Mikoian, *Tak bylo,* 534–36, 559–80, quotes 535–36, 572–76.

174. Khlevniuk and Gorlitskii, *Politbiuro TsK VKP(b) i Sovet Ministrov SSSR,* 334.

175. Khaustov et al., *Lubianka* (2007), 151–55.

176. Ibid., 169.

177. Ibid., 336–38, quote 337.

178. Ibid., 519–23.

179. Denisov, *TsK VKP(b) i regional'nye partiinye komitety,* 252–59; Gorlitzki and Khlevniuk, *Cold Peace,* 109–19; Elena Subkowa, "Kaderpolitik und Säuberungen in der KPdSU, 1945–1953," in *Terror: Stalinistische Parteisäuberungen 1936–1953,* ed. Hermann Weber and Ulrich Mählert (Paderborn: Schöningh, 1998), 187–206.

180. Zhores A. Medvedev, "Zagadki smerti Stalina," *Voprosy Istorii,* no. 1 (2000): 83–91; quote in A. T. Rybin, *Kto otravil Stalina? Zapiski telochranitelia* (Moscow: Izdatel'stvo Veteran, 1995), 13. For the medical care given Stalin between March 2 and March 5, see RGASPI, f. 558, op. 11, d. 1486, ll. 81–202; RGASPI, f. 82, op. 2, d. 897, ll. 145–50.

181. Svetlana Alliluyeva, *Twenty Letters to a Friend* (New York: Harper & Row, 1967), 10.

182. Konstantin Simonow, *Aus der Sicht meiner Generation: Gedanken über Stalin* (Berlin; Verlag Volk und Welt, 1990), 248–49, 250–51; Zhores Medvedev and Roi Medvedev, *Neizvestnyi Stalin* (Moscow: Vremia, 2002), 40–41.

183. Quote: Khlevniuk and Gorlitskii, *Politbiuro TsK VKP(b) i Sovet Ministrov SSSR,* 101.

184. Sakharov, *Memoirs,* 164.

185. Amis, *Koba the Dread,* 231.

CHAPTER SEVEN. STALIN'S HEIRS

1. Bardach, *Surviving Freedom,* 241.

2. Ibid.

3. Naumov and Sigachev, *Lavrentii Beriia,* 19–66.

4. Ibid., 69, 78.

5. Arbatov, *The System,* 51.

6. Svetlana Alliluyeva, *Twenty Letters to a Friend,* 216.

7. For the ending of Stalin's work schedule in the ministries in September 1953 see Khlevniuk and Gorlitskii., *Politbiuro TsK VKP(b) i Sovet Ministrov SSSR,* 409. For the arrest of Vasily Stalin, see the interrogation record of May 9, 1953 in RGANI, f. 89, op. 68, d. 3, ll. 151–66.

8. Talbott, *Khrushchev Remembers,* 1:343.

9. Ibid., 348.

10. Afiani, *Doklad N. S. Khrushcheva o kul'te lichnosti Stalina,* 175.

11. Miriam Dobson, *Khrushchev's Cold Summer: Gulag Returnees, Crime, and the Fate of Reform after Stalin* (Ithaca: Cornell University Press., 2009), 5, 51. On the prehistory and results of the secret speech see Vladimir Naumov, "Zur Geschichte der Geheimrede N. S. Khrushchevs auf dem XX. Parteitag der KPdSU," *Forum für Osteuropäische Ideen- und Zeitgeschichte* 1 (1997): 137–77.

12. See Denis Kozlov, "Naming the Social Evil: The Readers of *Novyi mir* and Vladimir Dudintsev's *Not By Bread Alone,* 1956–59 and Beyond," in *The Dilemmas of De-Stalinization: Negotiating Cultural and Social Change in the Khrushchev Era,* ed. Polly A. Jones (London: Routledge, 2006), 80–98.

13. Polly Jones, "From the Secret Speech to the Burial of Stalin: Real and Ideal Responses to De-Stalinization" in Jones, *The Dilemmas of De-Stalinization,* 41–63. For the life story of a returneee, see Friedrich Gorenstein's novel *Der Platz* (Berlin: Aufbau Verlag, 1995), Russian: *Mesto* (Moscow: Slovo, 1991).

14. Amir Weiner, "The Empire Pays a Visit: Gulag Returnees, East European Rebellions, and Soviet Frontier Politics," *Journal of Modern History* 78 (2006): 333–76.

15. Alastair McAuley, *Economic Welfare in the Soviet Union: Poverty, Living Standards, and Inequality* (Madison: University of Wisconsin Press, 1979); Stefan Plaggenborg, "'Entwickelter Sozialismus' und Supermacht 1964–1985," in *Handbuch der Geschichte Russlands,* vol. 5: *1945–1991: Vom Ende des Zweiten Weltkrieges bis zum Zusammenbruch der Sowjetunion,* ed. Stefan Plaggenborg (Stuttgart: Hiersemann, 2002), 419–29.

16. Mark Smith, *Property of Communists: The Urban Housing Program from Stalin to Khrushchev* (DeKalb: Northern Illinois University Press, 2010); Hans-Henning Schröder, "'Lebendige Verbindung mit den Massen': Sowjetische Gesellschaftspolitik in der Ära Chruščev," *Vierteljahrshefte für Zeitgeschichte* 34 (1986): 532–60.

17. Vladislav Zubok, *Zhivago's Children: The Last Russian Intelligentsia* (Cambridge, Mass.: Belknap Press of Harvard University Press, 2009), 88–120.

18. Arbatov, *The System,* 108–9.

19. Orlov, *Dangerous Thoughts,* 139.

20. Julie Elkner, "The Changing Face of Repression under Khrushchev," in *Soviet State and Society under Nikita Khrushchev,* ed. Melanie Ilic and Jeremy Smith (London: Routledge, 2009), 142–61.

21. Arbatov, *The System,* 49.

22. Parfenov, "'Zheleznyi Lazar': Konets kar'ery"; see also Chuev, *Tak govoril Kaganovich*; Chuev, *Molotov Remembers*; Torchinov and Leontiuk, *Vokrug Stalina,* 237–39.

23. Aleksandr A. Fursenko, *Prezidium TsK KPSS 1954–1964,* vol. 1: *Chernovye protokol'nye zapiski sazedanii. Stenogrammy* (Moscow: ROSSPEN, 2003), 872; William J. Tompson, "The Fall of Nikita Khrushchev," *Soviet Studies* 43, no. 2 (1991): 1101–21.

24. Andrej Artizov, ed., *Nikita Khrushchev 1964: Stenogrammy plenuma TsK KPSS i drugie dokumenty* (Moscow: Mezhdunarodnyi Fond "Demokratiia," 2007);

Mikojan, *Tak bylo*, 614–16; Iurii Aksiutin, *Khrushchevskaia "ottepel'" i obshches-tvennye nastroeniia v SSSR v 1953–1964 gg.* (Moscow: ROSSPEN, 2004), 459.

25. Arendt, *The Origins of Totalitarianism*, 465–66.

26. Arsenij Roginskij, "Nach der Verurteilung: Der Donskoe-Friedhof und seine österreichischen Opfer," in *Stalins letzte Opfer: Verschleppte und erschossene Österreicher in Moskau 1950–1953* (Wien: Böhlau, 2009), 97–139, esp. 135.

27. I. N. Mel'nikov (Korrespondent "Izvestii" po Azerbaidzhanskoi SSSR), "Zapiska o protsesse M. Bagirova i ego soobshchnikov," FSO, f. 23 (Chingiz Guseinov); Kuromiya, *The Voices of the Dead*, 248–49.

28. Figes, *The Whisperers*, 793–824.

29. Bernd Bonwetsch, "Der 'Große Vaterländische Krieg' und seine Geschichte," in *Die Umwertung der sowjetschen Geschichte*, ed. Dietrich Geyer (Göttingen: Vandenhoeck & Ruprecht, 1991), 167–87; Nina Tumarkin, *The Living and the Dead: The Rise and Fall of the Cult of World War II in Russia* (New York: Basic Books, 1994); Martin Hoffmann, "Der Zweite Weltkrieg in der offiziellen sowjetischen Erinnerungskultur," in *Krieg und Erinnerung: Fallstudien zum 19. und 20. Jahrhundert*, ed. Helmut Berding, Klaus Heller, and Winfried Speitkamp (Göttingen: Vandenhoeck & Ruprecht, 2000), 129–43; Corinna Kuhr-Korolev, "Erinnerungspolitik in Russland: Die vaterländische Geschichte und der Kampf um historisches Hoheitsgebiet," *Neue Politische Literatur* 3 (2009): 369–84.

30. Lev Gudkov, "Die Fesseln des Sieges: Russlands Identität aus der Erinnerung an den Krieg," in *Osteuropa* 55, nos. 4–6 (2005): 56–73; Boris Dubin, "Erinnern als staatliche Veranstaltung: Geschichte und Herrschaft in Russland," *Osteuropa* 58, no. 6 (2008): 57–65.

31. The Baltic republics and western Ukraine were exceptions. See Katja Wezel, "'Okkupanten' oder 'Befreier'? Geteilte Erinnerung und getrennte Geschichtsbilder in Lettland," *Osteuropa* 58, no. 6 (2008): 147–57; Karsten Brüggemann, "Denkmäler des Grolls: Estland und die Kriege des 20. Jahrhunderts," ibid., 129–46; Gerhard Simon, "Holodomor als Waffe: Stalinismus, Hunger und der ukrainische Nationalismus," ibid., 54, no. 12 (2004): 37–56.

32. Quote: Figes, *The Whisperers*, 607–8.

33. Arsenij Roginskij, "Fragmentierte Erinnerung: Stalin und der Stalinismus im heutigen Russland," *Osteuropa* 59, no. 12 (2009): 37–56.

34. Gudkov, "Die Fesseln des Sieges," 64; Maria Feretti, "Unversöhnliche Erinnerung: Krieg, Stalinismus und die Schatten des Patriotismus," *Osteuropa* 55, nos. 4–6 (2005): 45–55, esp. 54; Michail Ryklin, *Mit dem Recht des Stärkeren: Russische Kultur in Zeiten der "gelenkten Demokratie"* (Frankfurt am Main: Suhrkamp, 2006).

Index

The Man
Who Lost
China

Books by Brian Crozier

THE REBELS
THE MORNING AFTER
NEO-COLONIALISM
SOUTH-EAST ASIA IN TURMOIL
THE STRUGGLE FOR THE THIRD WORLD
FRANCO
THE MASTERS OF POWER
SINCE STALIN
DE GAULLE
A THEORY OF CONFLICT

The Man Who Lost China

THE FIRST FULL

BIOGRAPHY OF

CHIANG KAI-SHEK

BY

BRIAN CROZIER

WITH THE

COLLABORATION OF

ERIC CHOU

CHARLES SCRIBNER'S SONS

NEW YORK

Library of Congress Cataloging in Publication Data

Crozier, Brian.
  The man who lost China.

  Bibliography: p.
  Includes index.
  1. Chiang, Kai-shek, 1887–1975.   I. Chou, Eric,
1915–   joint author.   II. Title.
DS778.C55C7   951.04′2′0924   76–10246
ISBN 0–684–14686–X

1 3 5 7 9 11 13 15 17 19 C/C 20 18 16 14 12 10 8 6 4 2

PRINTED IN THE UNITED STATES OF AMERICA

Contents

ILLUSTRATIONS

Author's Note

Chiang Kai-shek was a hero of my boyhood and adolescence. I knew nothing about him except through the conversation of my elders and the headlines in the newspapers. My sympathies were naturally on China's side, for it was evident that the Chinese were peaceful folk who were being abused and whose territory was being invaded by the hateful and aggressive Japanese. Later, in my Left Book Club days, my hitherto uncritical admiration was shaken by allegations that Chiang had on occasion massacred many people. There were writers unkind enough to call him "fascist" and "a militarist". I didn't like people who were those things, and wondered whether after all the hero really was one.

Then came the Second World War, and suddenly Chiang Kai-shek was a hero again, even to those on the Left who had been denouncing him. For my part, in any case, I had lost the childish readiness to admire distant heroes. The eye-opening year for me was 1943, when I was working on the Central Desk of Reuters' news agency in London. I noticed almost simultaneously that two popular heroes of the early years of the war had ceased to be heroic, for reasons I didn't immediately grasp. One was Chiang Kai-shek; the other was Drazha Mihailovic, the leader of the legendary Yugoslav Chetniks. Mihailovic, as the senior men on the desk explained to me, was now "discredited", because he had stopped fighting the Nazis and instead was fighting his political rival, Josip Broz, better known as Tito. Indeed, Tito was now the new, generally approved "hero". Poor Mihailovic: the dustbin of history, as Khrushchev would have put it many years later, was about to claim him.

And what of Generalissimo Chiang Kai-shek? Now he was the head of a brutal and inefficient regime and had long since stopped fighting the Japanese. The men who were doing the fighting—those well-informed seniors of mine explained in all their patience to a junior foreign sub-editor—were Mao Tse-tung and his Communist guerrillas. I was not that ignorant, even then: the Left Book Club choice for a particular month had been Edgar Snow's *Red Star Over China*. From him I had learned that Mao and his men were really just "agrarian reformers", hardly Communists at all in the orthodox sense. I had even read as much (though to be accurate, this could have been later)—an identical assessment of the Chinese Communists—in the austere editorial columns of *The Times*.

Then came my years on the foreign desk of the London *News Chronicle* and the evidence—too strong by far to be ignored or dismissed—of the Kuomintang's corruption, brutality, and inefficiency. During the Chinese Civil War, the NC's China correspondent, Stuart Gelder, regaled his readers and ourselves with unbelievable tales (but true) of Nationalists transporting the same pile of captured Japanese equipment from place to place to impress foreign visitors to the "front". Was it he, or some other war correspondent (it does not matter) who claimed he had marked a Japanese helmet with a scratch and found it again in another pile in another place? What price then, my boyhood hero?

Even great men are flawed, of course, and the flaws may be in proportion to their greatness in other respects. Was Stalin a great man? He built "socialism in one country"—and sent millions to their deaths. And Hitler? He rescued a demoralised Germany from the slough of six million unemployed, and the consequences of a short-sighted and manifestly unjust peace treaty—and he exterminated millions of Jews. A Churchill, a Roosevelt, a de Gaulle—these men were not monsters as Stalin and Hitler were, but they had gigantic faults along with their extraordinary qualities. The case of Chiang Kai-shek was clearly no less complex than theirs, and the riddle of his fluctuating reputation was puzzling. Why was he a hero in some years, a scoundrel in others, again a hero, then forever a failure, a loser, and a reactionary fascist into the bargain?

The "McCarthy era" in the 1950s presented an unedifying spectacle of Americans in the grip of a witch-hunt, with its attendant fear and hysteria. But for all the distaste and indeed the revulsion at the Senator's demagogic antics, his investigations did throw a lurid light on some of the secret byways of the International Communist Movement, and in particular on the use made of writers and journalists—not necessarily Communists or even far to the Left—in the dissemination of falsehood, half-truths, calumnies, or subtle praise. In all conscience, there was enough to criticise in the Kuomintang regime and in Chiang Kai-shek's conduct of public affairs.

But the image-builders were not necessarily concerned with the facts as such. To give an extreme example, Hitler automatically and instantly ceased to be a blood-stained tyrant and murderer of the Jews and workers when Ribbentrop and Molotov signed their treaty in 1939; that is, he ceased to be so described in the columns of the Soviet press, on the bandwaves of the Soviet radio, and in the Communist press throughout the world. In Britain, the then leader of the Communist Party, the late Harry Pollitt, had his own moment of brief and public outrage, but he soon came to heel. It was too much for Stalin to expect of progressive and liberal writers in the West that they should suddenly find Hitler not to be such a bad chap after all. But they were far more responsive to the needs of Soviet-directed propaganda in the distant and less emotive case of Chiang Kai-shek.

I had thought about these problems from time to time over the years, before deciding that the time had come for a more searching inquiry into the life of the Generalissimo. This book is the outcome. As in the case of my previous biographies, *Franco* and *De Gaulle*, this is in no sense an approved, and still less an authorised, biography. I met and interviewed Chiang Kai-shek in January 1957, when on a tour of countries "in China's shadow" as special correspondent of *The Economist*. Since Chiang didn't speak English, the interview had to be interpreted from his language into mine and vice versa—which halved its material duration and diminished its interest. The physical description with which the book begins was, however, based on this meeting, and in other respects our conversathon threw an interesting light on the Generalissimo's thought processes. I discovered, somewhat to my surprise, that much progress was being made on Taiwan and that in particular a successful land-reform programme had been accomplished. On my return, I said as much in print and on the air, and was greeted with much scepticism, although specialists much better qualified than I to pronounce on the success or otherwise of a land-reform programme later confirmed my findings. The regime, then, was not as bad as it had been generally painted.

I returned to Taiwan in September 1974, to give some lectures by invitation of the Institute of International Relations in Taipei; but of course to take advantage of this opportunity to meet as many well-informed people as possible, not only in Taiwan itself but also in Hong Kong on my way, and probe their memories of Chiang at different times of his long career. For by then, I had begun my research for this biographical study. Among the personalities of the Kuomintang establishment who were kind enough to give me their very clear reminiscences were Ch'en Li-fu, who had been Chiang's private secretary at the time of the Nationalist entry into Shanghai in 1927, and Wang Shih-chieh, who as Foreign Minister had signed the Sino-Soviet treaty of 1945. There were many others besides, both in 1957 and in 1974; nor was my time spent exclusively with supporters of the regime, although I cannot reveal the names of opponents who gave me their views. I wish to record my grateful thanks to Dr. Han Lih-wu, then Director of the Institute of International Relations, and Dr. Ch'ien Fu, at that time Director-General of the Government Information Office, for the friendly efficiency with which they organised my appointments; Mr. G. M. ("Jimmy") Wei, Director of China Central News, for kindly making available to me most of the pictures that appear in this book; and others, too numerous to mention, who helped me with various kindnesses. In Hong Kong, too, I found people with long memories and a willingness to share them.

Among the informants who were not concerned to preserve their anonymity was a distinguished "old China hand", Mr. Kenneth Cantlie, who contributed some interesting anecdotes out of a store of ancient memories. I record my grateful thanks to him.

For the rest, as with my other biographical works, I have used the tools of the historian and academic researcher, as well as of the journalist. (By profession, I am the latter, not the former.) But by far my most important "live" source was Eric Chou, the well-known journalist and scholar, who lived through the years of war and civil war in China, in Chungking, Nanking, Peiping, and other places. Mr. Chou contributed liberally from his great fund of personal memories, retained by a remarkably photographic memory, and in addition translated copious extracts of Chinese books. Moreover, he read and commented on my text in detail, as a guarantee of its accuracy and "Chinese" authenticity. The writing, of course, is mine, as are the conclusions, and any undetected errors are my responsibility.

Since my own knowledge of the Chinese language is limited, and since I am not myself an academic, I lay no claims to having written a work of scholarship. What I do claim is that this was—at the time of writing—the first attempt of which I have knowledge to tell the story of Chiang Kai-shek's life from cradle to grave and to place it in the context of the history of his time. I can also say that the book includes a great deal of Chinese source material not previously published in English; and a considerable infusion of entirely new material, mainly from Eric Chou but also from my own conversations with qualified informants. It is perhaps relevant to add that for ten years—from 1954 to 1964—I was *The Economist*'s specialist on Chinese and Far Eastern affairs.

Apart from my own interest in the subject, the need for a serious study and reappraisal of Chiang has long been evident. When I finished this book in the late summer of 1975, only two biographies had appeared in English. Both were by Chinese writers: Hollington K. Tong (whose authorised biography first appeared in 1938, and was later brought up to date in a revised edition in 1953), and the other by S. I. Hsiung, better known in Western capitals for his successful play, *Lady Precious Stream*. In the first edition of Tong's biography, he was able to write without any sense of incongruity:

> Recent events in China have proved Generalissimo Chiang Kai-shek to be the greatest soldier-statesman of our time on the Continent of Asia. (Preface)

In a supplementary Preface some months later, he commented on "the disappearance of the Red menace". For when the Japanese had invaded China, the Communists had proved that they, too, were "Chinese". Few Western readers would have raised an eyebrow on reading these passages. Yet how distant and out of perspective these judgments seem today!

I have tried to take a more objective view of my erstwhile hero.

London, September 1975.